Scale of Miles

0   20   40   60   80

R. Clyde

R. Tweed

CHEVIOT HILLS

GALLOWAY

Widdybank
Fell

LAKE
DISTRICT
Helvellyn
Esthwaite L.
Mickle
Fell
Teesdale

W. Windermere

R. Ure

ISLE
OF
MAN

Walney I.
Ingleborough
Humphrey Hd.
Malham

Flamborough Hd.

IRISH

SEA

CRAVEN

R. Aire

Harrogate

Humber

Gt. Ormes Hd.
Llandudno

Holyhead

Wirral

PEAK
DISTRICT

Sheffield

SNOWDONIA

Boston

THE
WASH

Holt

Aberystwyth

Stokesay
Ludlow

R. Severn

WELSH MARCHES

Burton

Cannock
Chase

R. Trent

Kings
Lynn

THE
BROADS

Lowestoft

R. Ouse

EAST

BRECKLAND

ANGLIA

Cambridge

St. Davids
Hd.

Brecon
Beacons

R. Wye

Droitwich

R. Avon

Tewkesbury

Hitchin

Dunstable

Walton
on-the-Naze

Tintern

COTSWOLDS

R. Thames

CHILTERNS

Epping
Forest

Fyfield

Ongar

Gower

Cardiff

Bristol
Bath

R. Avon

Burnham
Beeches

LONDON

R. Lea

Greenhithe

Sheppey

BRISTOL CHANNEL

Steep Holm

Weston
s/Mare

Cheddar

Guildford

Mickleham

Medway

Faversham

Ashford

Lundy I.

Braunton

Burnham

WESSEX

THE WEALD

Heathfield

S. Molton

NEW
FOREST

Southampton

R. Arun

Exeter

R. Tamar

DARTMOOR

Dawlish

Purbeck

Solent

Selsey
Bill

Shoreham-on-Sea

Beachy Hd.

Phyllack
Towans

Plymouth

Torquay

Berry Hd.

Chesil
Beach

ISLE OF WIGHT

Slapton Ley

Lizard
Peninsula

ENGLISH

Alderney

CHANNEL
Guernsey
ISLANDS
St. Ouens Jersey
Bay

THE POCKET
GUIDE TO WILD FLOWERS

The

Pocket Guide to

WILD FLOWERS

By

DAVID McCLINTOCK, T.D., M.A., F.L.S.

and

R. S. R. FITTER

assisted by

FRANCIS ROSE, PH.D., F.L.S.

Illustrated by Dorothy Fitchew, Pamela Freeman, Heather Child, Cynthia Newsome-Taylor, Evangeline Dickson, Francis Rose, Ceres Esplan

COLLINS
ST JAMES'S PLACE, LONDON

ACKNOWLEDGMENTS

A BOOK so full of facts cannot be wholly free of errors (of which we should be glad to be told). Their number has been reduced by the help of numerous expert friends, who saw and commented on various parts of the manuscript, though they are of course in no way responsible for any shortcomings. Over eighty sent us flowers, with such success that fewer than 50 of the 1306 plants illustrated were not painted from live specimens. We much regret that extreme pressure on space prevents our detailing the names of the 120 people who helped with information or specimens. We are deeply grateful to them all, but at the risk of invidiousness must mention especially the following, who have read substantial parts of the text: F. M. Day, J. E. Lousley, D. Swinscow, Mrs. B. Welch and, most of all, Dr Francis Rose, Lecturer in Botany at Bedford College, who came to our rescue in the later stages. Maisie Fitter retyped almost the whole of the manuscript, and was largely responsible for the index, in which she was also helped by Jenny, Julian and Alastair Fitter. Miss C. M. Rob guided us skilfully through the pitfalls of the English names and J. E. Dandy advised us on the Latin names. To all these we owe a special degree of thanks, as we do also to our indefatigable team of artists.

Of the degree of neglect this book has caused our families, the less said the better.

R.S.R.F.
Chinnor, Oxon

D.McC.
Platt, Kent
August 1955

First Impression,	1956
Fifth Impression,	1965
Sixth Impression,	1967
Seventh Impression,	1969
Eighth Impression,	1971
Ninth Impression,	1972
Tenth Impression,	1974

ISBN 0 00 212188 3

HOW TO FIND
THE FLOWER YOU WANT

THE BOOK offers three main ways of naming a plant.

1. If you have a rough idea of its name, or at any rate of its affinities, e.g. if it looks like a Buttercup or an Orchid, look it up in the index. This will direct you to the main text, which is a directory of plants arranged by families.

2. If you have no idea what it is, search the plates, which are arranged broadly by colour. See p. 319 for a note on the plates.

3. If you are still defeated, the General Keys (pp. 308–316) are designed to help you to run it down by a process of elimination. Trees, shrubs and waterweeds are fully analysed, and for the much more numerous non-woody land plants, you can check against certain conspicuous or easily found features, such as prickles, aromatic leaves, fragrant flowers or red berries.

 For 4-petalled flowers, see p. 10

 For peaflowers, see p. 55

 For flowers in umbels, see p. 91

 For 2-lipped flowers, see p. 150

 For daisy-like flowers, see p. 170

 For thistle-like flowers, see p. 181

 For dandelion-like flowers, see p. 186

CONTENTS

ILLUSTRATIONS

In Colour (between pages 52 and 53)

In Black and White (between pages 148 and 149)

Line Drawings

Plates 1–32 are by Pamela Freeman: Plates 33–68 by Dorothy Fitchew: Plates 69–93 by Heather Child: Plates 94–112 by Cynthia Newsome-Taylor: Plates 113–115 by Francis Rose and Ceres Esplan: Plates 116–120 and the individual drawings in the text by Francis Rose: Plates 121–140 by Evangeline Dickson: and the drawing of the Iris on p. 215 by Mary Benbow

INTRODUCTION

THIS BOOK is designed to enable anybody to name any wild flower, grass, sedge, tree or shrub that he or she is reasonably likely to see in the British Isles. The study of wild flowers has two great advantages as a hobby over some other branches of natural history: flowers stay put and do not run or fly away, and the great majority of the common ones can easily be named without the aid of any equipment at all.

The book demands no special knowledge from the reader, for the plants are arranged on the plates primarily by the colour of their flowers. When wanting to identify a plant that is in flower, always look first at the plates, but never rely on the plates alone; check back to the text with the aid of the reference number attached to each flower on the plate. If the plant is not in flower, a search through the general keys (pp. 308–16) may help. If you have some idea what the plant is to start with, you can look it up in the index and go straight to the main text.

The most experienced botanist cannot expect to name straightaway every plant he finds. Upwards of 5,000 different kinds of plant have been recorded growing wild in the British Isles, though the majority are so uncommon that it is good work to find 800 or 900 in a year. In the average country parish 400 or 500 is nearer the mark.

If you are a beginner, it is wise to concentrate on the easier plants, and leave the more complicated groups until you have a good grounding in the others. But you will soon want to go on to those that frightened you at first, such as umbellifers (cow parsley, hemlock, etc.), docks, rushes and grasses. If you can tell the difference between the three common kinds of Buttercup (11–13), there is no reason at all why you should not be able to name the common docks, sedges and grasses after a little practice.

Once you get past the lowest rungs on the ladder, there is one small piece of equipment that you will find useful, a small wide-field pocket lens—× 10 is best. Not only will it enable you to detect more certainly such important points as whether a plant is hairy or hairless, but it will often reveal fresh and unsuspected beauties.

THE SEQUENCE OF PLANTS IN THE TEXT

The main text basically follows the order of Clapham, Tutin & Warburg's *Flora of the British Isles* (Cambridge, 1952), except that it begins with the flowering plants and ends with the Ferns and their allies. To the beginner the scientific systematic order used here may seem complicated and arbitrary, but in fact it shows the main branches of the plant kingdom in the approximate order in which they are supposed to have evolved over the ages, those assumed to be most primitive coming first. For many years British botanists have used the order of Bentham and Hooker's *British Flora*, but the order we have adopted is closer to the current practice of Continental and American botanists, though we have put the primitive and flowerless ferns last.

The scientific classification arranges plants in groups called Families, which are broken down into smaller groups of closely related individual species called Genera. Where groups have some fairly obvious common character—e.g. the two-lipped flowers of the Labiates or the jointed stems of the Pinks—we have given a short note at the beginning of the family (e.g., Cabbage Family, p. 9) or genus (e.g., Buttercups, p. 2), and this often contains basic information for the identification of the species that follow, which is not repeated. Thus it would be tedious to repeat under each member of the Cabbage Family the essential information that the flower has four petals arranged crosswise. So look to the beginning of the family and genus to see if any common characters are described there. There are also keys to certain families and genera, for a note on which, see p. xii.

NAMES

The names of plants present a difficult problem. There is no accepted standard list of English names; and these vary enormously, from book to book and from county to county. Some names, such as Bluebell, Lady's Slipper and Mother of Thousands, are used for different plants in different parts of the country. We have normally given the commonest English names in general use, but where these are misleading, as with Mountain St. John's Wort (137), which in Britain never grows on mountains, we have used some other name. We are immensely indebted to Miss C. M. Rob, the official referee of the Botanical Society of the British Isles on this subject, for making out a full list of English names of the plants in this book, which we have followed in all but a handful of cases. She had to find, and in a few cases actually to coin, new English names for quite a number of scarce and introduced plants.

The English names are used as the standard reference throughout the book; but at the head of the account of each species the 'Latin' name is also given, based on the new *British Plant List*, published by the Botanical Society of the British Isles. Where these scientific names differ from those in Clapham, Tutin and Warburg's *Flora of the British Isles*, Bentham and Hooker's *British Flora* or Butcher and Strudwick's *Further Illustrations of British Plants*, we have given the synonyms used in these books either on the line below or at the end of the account, together with any particularly well known alternative English names. It is true that, in the past, the scientific names of plants have changed more often than have their common names; and we cannot promise that they will not change again, though all naturalists would welcome stability. 'Latin' names preceded by ' incl.' are not synonyms but very similar or rare species covered by the descriptions of the numbered plant in question.

The scientific name of a plant is part of the international language of science, enabling botanists in one country to know what those in another are talking about. For instance, 'Daisy' might mean nothing to a foreign botanist, but *Bellis perennis* would. The scientific or specific name of a plant consists of two words, a generic name, which has a capital initial, followed by a trivial name, which here, following modern trends, always has a small initial. Generic names are abbreviated to their initial after their first mention. The trivial name is followed by the name of the 'author', that is the person who first gave the plant this name, and his name may be placed in brackets and in turn followed by the name of the author who gave the plant its present full name. Thus the scientific name of the Bulbous Buttercup (12) is *Ranunculus bulbosus* L., which indicates that it belongs to the genus of Buttercups (*Ranunculus*), from other species of which it was distinguished by the great Swedish naturalist Linnaeus, who gave it the trivial name of *bulbosus*. The Yellow Water-lily (33), on the other hand, named *Nymphaea lutea* by Linnaeus, was removed by Sir J. E. Smith to the genus *Nuphar*, so that it is now called *Nuphar lutea* (L.) Smith.

There is no need, in general use, to cite the names of authors, i.e. *Ranunculus bulbosus* is enough. We give the names of authors in full, instead of the usual baffling abbreviations, such as Rchb. for Reichenbach, except for Linnaeus and de Candolle, whom we accord their time-honoured 'L.' and 'DC.', and for certain European botanists with long double-barrelled names, such as Marschall von Bieberstein, who becomes just Bieberstein. Names of authors repeated in synonyms may, however, be abbreviated. We also omit the initials of authors where, as with Brown, there may be more than one of the same name. Where any 'Latin' names have in the past been applied in error, or are otherwise uncertain, we place them in inverted commas, e.g. '*Cyclamen europaeum*'.

A hybrid plant—that is, a cross between two distinct species—is indicated by an ' × ' in front of the trivial name, e.g. *Equisetum × litorale* (1270 × 1273). We have been able to mention only very few of the commonest hybrids by name, owing to pressure on space, but have indicated in the text any genera or families in which hybrids are especially frequent. If a very puzzling plant is found, combining the characters of two described plants, suspect a hybrid—especially if its fruits are not formed properly.

NUMBERS

Every plant in the book has a number. Plants which are illustrated run from 1 to 1306, and those which are not illustrated have a letter after the number, and are referred to as *abc* plants. This number is quoted wherever the plant is mentioned in the text, or figured on the plates, and gives you an immediate reference to its description without going through the index.

The *abc* plants resemble the illustrated plant whose number they bear, and which immediately precedes them, so that they may be recognised from its picture. They are usually less common than their illustrated partner, but they may be equally common, as with White Willow (569a) and Crack Willow (569). *Unless definitely stated otherwise the descriptions of the* abc *plants only show where they differ from their illustrated partner, and details of description which are not repeated are the same.* Thus the description of Adderstongue Spearwort (19b) refers back to Lesser Spearwort (19), not to Creeping Spearwort (19a).

Some numbered species also are described by reference to other numbered species, e.g. Hoary mustard (53) by reference to Black mustard (48), and here again details of description which are not repeated or contradicted are the same.

STARS

We have devised a star system to show how common or rare a plant is, to add to the pleasure of finding something uncommon, and to discourage rash identification of unlikely rarities. Stars are prefixed to the English names at the head of each description, and indicate the degree of rarity *as a wild plant in Britain*. Common and widely distributed plants, e.g. Marsh Marigold (1) have no stars. One star is for a plant which is only locally common, e.g. *Grass of Parnassus (411). Two stars are for scarce plants, which usually grow only in limited areas, e.g. **Crested Cow-wheat (724), but may be thinly scattered over a wide area, e.g. **Narrow Helleborine (1059). Three stars are for real rarities, growing in only a few places, and usually rare even there, e.g. ***Cheddar Pink (160). Before claiming any starred plant always consider the possibility that it is really something else commoner.

ABBREVIATIONS

At the head of each description, after the plate reference, is given a page reference to the first edition of Clapham, Tutin and Warburg's *Flora of the British Isles* (*CTW*), for those who wish for more details than can be included in a Pocket Guide. Plants not in *CTW* are indicated as CTW†. CTW references are given for *abc* plants only when they are a page or two away from their illustrated partner. We are grateful to the three authors of the *Flora* for allowing us to give these references.

The symbol 𝔓 denotes a plant poisonous in greater or less degree to man in one or more of its parts at one or more seasons.

For the significance of 'L.' and 'DC.' in plant names see under 'Names' above, and for the meaning of ' *abc* plants ' see under ' Numbers ' above. ' Incl.' means including.

THE DESCRIPTIONS

We have tried to avoid technical botanical terms. Those we have had to use, such as 'sepal', 'calyx' and 'bract', are defined in the Glossary on pp. 317-9. We have given heights, except for trees, but so often the size of a plant is 'the length of a piece of string', and may range from 1 in. to 3 ft. Thus plants may be dwarfed on lawns or cliffs, or coarse and luxuriant on manure-heaps and in rich soil. A daisy head on each plate indicates scale.

Plants are assumed to be both erect and branched unless otherwise stated. The terms 'annual' and 'perennial' may both include biennial. Roots we rarely mention, so as to discourage people from uprooting plants to examine them. Leaves may often be fleshier by the sea. The terms 'large' and 'small' are relative to the size of the plant.

Our descriptions are of mature plants, e.g. with fully open flowers or ripe fruits, as found growing wild in the British Isles. It is easy to misname quite common plants from immature specimens; and abroad some plants may look different and have different habitats.

We have not found it easy to describe either scents or colours, for what is fragrant to some is foetid to others, what is pink to some is purple to others. Moreover the strength of a scent varies from plant to plant and according to weather, warmth and time of day. For consistency we have matched many flowers with the R.H.S. Horticultural Colour Chart.

HABITAT AND RANGE

We give only typical habitats in the British Isles, for almost any plant may appear as a casual or garden escape outside its normal habitat and range. By 'widespread' we mean 'throughout the British Isles'. 'British' and 'British Isles' include both Ireland and the Channel Isles, and all groups of offshore islands. The Channel Isles are generally included in the general phrase 'S England' or 'S W England', for they have many plants in common with Devon and Cornwall. A general reference to 'the N' or 'the S' means Great Britain roughly north or south of a line drawn from the Trent to the Dovey estuary; and ' the W ' means Wales and the W side of England and Scotland.

No brief description of range can be really comprehensive, for every district has its own surprising scarcities and abundances, even among plants generally common. Thus the Red Campion (155) is virtually absent from Cambridgeshire. Nothing can be taken for granted in plant distribution.

FLOWERING PERIOD

Flowering periods can be a useful guide to identification. Those we have given are for average seasons—in south central England for southerly or generally distributed plants. The term 'onwards' signifies that the plant goes on blooming till winter sets in. Most plants may occasionally be found in bloom earlier or later than we state. In the extreme south-west dates may be a month or more ahead, and summer flowers may overwinter and be still in bloom in spring.

THE PLANTS IN THE BOOK

WE HAVE INCLUDED all the commoner flowering plants likely to be found wild or looking wild in the British Isles, including the Channel Isles, together with all the rarer natives and as many rare naturalised plants as space would permit. By botanical tradition we also include Ferns, Horsetails and Clubmosses. The remaining non-flowering plants, true mosses, liverworts, stoneworts, lichens, seaweeds, algae, and fungi are omitted. We have included plants irrespective of whether they are native, long-established aliens, garden escapes, casuals or recent arrivals. The criterion is, do they look wild or not? It would have been quite impracticable to deal with every plant that has ever been found growing wild in the British Isles, for this would have quadrupled the number of plants in the book; many have been found once only. We have therefore left out a great many ephemerals found only in rubbish dumps and other waste and industrial sites, though queer-looking plants found in such places, and on fields that have been manured with shoddy, may be of special interest.

The aliens we have included are the really widespread ones, like Himalayan Balsam (260), and others which people send in for identification, or which are often overlooked or confused with other plants. People who are unaware of the other frequent, spreading and similar species of *Sisymbrium* often claim to have found the rare London Rocket (108a). Many aliens are far more often seen than some of our rare natives, recognised, respectable and found in all the books. A comprehensive, up-to-date alien flora of Britain is badly needed.

We have found it especially hard to draw the line between blatant garden escapes or relics of cultivation, and plants on the way to becoming thoroughly naturalised, but we have stuck firmly to our rule that they must be found looking really wild somewhere in Britain. We have also omitted most shrubs, notably the common Rhododendron (*R. ponticum* L.), for they usually look so obviously planted, even though the Rhododendron seeds itself and forms thickets in many parts of the country.

We have omitted a few plants because they are probably or certainly extinct in the British Isles, among them the Summer Lady's Tresses orchid (*Spiranthes aestivalis* (Poiret) Richard). A few other plants are omitted because they were wrongly identified in the first place, or were never proved to grow where they were reported, or are not true species but just part of a swarm of hybrids. Nor have we attempted to describe the microspecies into which certain groups have been split by experts, though except for the over 500 Brambles (346) and over 300 Hawkweeds (946–947) we have given the 'Latin' names of these microspecies in footnotes, since they are often quoted.

Drastic cutting in order that the book might retain its 'pocket' status has to some extent upset the original balance in our choice of species. Many rare plants now illustrated were intended to have been balanced by other rare *abc* plants which have had to be left out. Lists and identification details of many of the plants, and other matter deleted for this reason, will be produced as a small supplement available from Miss C. M. Rob, Catton Hall, Thirsk, Yorks.

DICOTYLEDONS AND MONOCOTYLEDONS

These are the two main divisions of the Flowering Plants, having respectively two and one seed-leaves, but are not here used as a basis of identification. The Dicotyledons (Buttercup Family to Daisy Family, 1–956) are woody or non-woody plants, with usually broad, often stalked and almost always net-veined leaves; and their flower-parts in multiples of 4 or 5 (very rarely 3). Our Monocotyledons (Water-plantain Family to Grass Family, 957–1256) are all non-woody (except Butchers Broom 994), and have usually narrow and unstalked, often parallel-sided and almost always parallel-veined leaves; and their flower-parts in multiples of 3, though in Sedges, Grasses and to a less extent Orchids, reduced as a result of evolution.

The Conifers (species 1257–1259) are Gymnosperms, whose seeds are not contained in a fruit but borne naked on the scales of cones.

A NOTE ON THE KEYS

Neither the General Keys (pp. 308–316) nor the keys to families and genera scattered through the text are exhaustive. They are intended to help by suggesting which plants have certain prominent features, such as spiny stems, an aromatic scent or berry-like fruits. They are therefore arranged in the form of lists of these characters. Often only one plant may have any particular combination of characters, but even if you are left with two or three possibilities you can check with the text and plates and decide for yourself. The *abc* plants (see p. ix) are normally covered by the reference to their illustrated partner.

As an example, you find a lilac-coloured flower growing in a damp meadow with the characteristic four crosswise petals of the cabbage family shown on p. v. Turn to the Key on p. 10, and check under Purple or Lilac Flowers. Your plant is hairless and has pinnate (see Glossary) leaves, and only nos. 86 and 87 combine these characters. A glance at the text (p. 18) will show that you are much more likely to have found the common Lady's Smock (86), which grows in damp meadows, than the rarer Large Bittercress (87), which prefers shady places. A final look at the colour of the anthers will in this case make the identification decisive.

The Keys, both in the text and on pp. 308–316, are primarily the work of R. S. R. Fitter.

DESCRIPTIONS OF PLANTS

BUTTERCUP FAMILY Ranunculaceae

MOSTLY NON-WOODY PLANTS, the flowers with many stamens; fruiting heads with many *separate* nutlets or tiny pods.

1. MARSH MARIGOLD *Caltha palustris* L. Plate 38. *CTW, p. 71*
   Looks like a thick-set Buttercup, making a brilliant splash of gold in the wet spring meadows: a hairless tufted perennial, with fat hollow stems up to 18 in. high, and glossy, dark green, kidney-shaped leaves, the lowest well stalked. Flowers glossy yellow, an inch or more across, with no green sepals. Especially on mountains, it may be slenderer, and prostrate, and have narrower petals (actually sepals). Fruit a head of many-seeded pods. *Habitat:* Widespread, common in marshy places. March–June. Kingcup.

2. **GLOBE FLOWER *Trollius europaeus* L. Plate 38. *CTW, p. 72*
   Our only wild plant with flowers that look like 'orbed moons of pale yellow', an inch across; a hairless perennial, 1–2 ft. high, with palmate leaves deeply cut and very like those of Meadow Buttercup (11) or Meadow Cranesbill (233), but not downy. *Habitat:* Locally frequent in gullies and damp pastures in and below hill districts from Wales northwards, and in N W Ireland. May–August.

3. **STINKING HELLEBORE *Helleborus foetidus* L. Plate 65. *CTW, p. 73* 𝔇
   A stout foetid perennial, 2–3 ft. high, with terminal clusters of numerous, bell-shaped, bright yellow-green, purple-edged flowers rising well above the contrasting mass of dark evergreen palmate leaves, with lanceolate toothed leaflets. *Habitat:* Very local in woods and scrub on chalk and limestone in S England; rare elsewhere; not wild in Ireland. March–May.

4. **GREEN HELLEBORE *H. viridis* L. Plate 65. *CTW, p. 73* 𝔇
   Much shorter than the last species, with Christmas-rose-like flowers which are nearly the same mid-green colour as the leaves and only 2–4 in a cluster, wider and more toothed leaflets and no foetid scent. A low perennial, 6–12 in. high, the leaves appearing with the flowers and growing steadily larger till summer. *Habitat:* Local in colonies in woods, usually among Dog's Mercury (541) on chalk or limestone, in S England; rare elsewhere; not in Ireland. March–May.

5. ***WINTER ACONITE *Eranthis hyemalis* (L.) Salisbury Pl. 38. *CTW, p. 75*
   The only yellow spring flower with a sepal-like green frill or ruff, often carpeting the ground: an unbranched hairless perennial, 2–4 in. high, with palmate glossy leaves appearing after the chalice-shaped flowers and dying back by June. *Habitat:* Naturalised in a few parks and woodlands. January–March.

6. **MONKSHOOD *Aconitum anglicum* Stapf Plate 12. *CTW, p. 76* 𝔇
   A fine, dark green, hairless perennial, 4–6 ft. high, with spikes of helmeted, bluish-violet flowers, very like the later-flowering Garden Monkshood (*A. napellus*

L.), which occasionally escapes, but with its palmate leaves much more deeply cut. *Habitat:* Local by shady stream-sides in S W England and in Wales; rare elsewhere in England. May–June. ' *A. napellus* '

7. **BANEBERRY   *Actaea spicata* L.   Plate 80.   *CTW, p. 79*   ⑫

A stocky perennial, 1–2 ft. high, with 2-pinnate leaves, well-toothed leaflets, and a spike of feathery white flowers, followed by berries, green at first, then shining black. *Habitat:* Local in ashwoods and rock crevices on limestone in N England. May–June.

8. WOOD ANEMONE   *Anemone nemorosa* L.   Plate 84.   *CTW, p. 80*

A low perennial, 3–6 in. high, carpeting many woodlands in spring with its graceful nodding solitary white flowers, an inch or so across, with numerous yellow anthers, sometimes with a pink or purple tinge beneath, very occasionally ice-blue. Leaves trifoliate, much divided; fruits downy, in a rounded cluster. *Habitat:* Widespread and common in and near woods, and hedge-banks, also on mountains. March–May.

9. **PASQUE FLOWER   *Pulsatilla vulgaris* Miller   Plate 4.   *CTW, p. 81*
A. pulsatilla L.

One of our most gorgeous wild flowers, with its rich violet sepals, boss of golden anthers and silky hairs on the back; low perennial, 3–9 in. high, with silky 2-pinnate leaves. The long silky plumes attached to the seeds may persist on the lengthened dead flower-heads well into the summer. *Habitat:* Very local in short turf on chalk and limestone from the Thames to the Humber. April–May.

10. *TRAVELLER'S JOY   *Clematis vitalba* L.   Plate 76.   *CTW, p. 82*

A woody climber with trusses of faintly fragrant, greenish-white flowers, the stamens prominent, better known with its autumnal 'old man's beard' formed by the woolly greyish-white plumes on the hairy fruits and reminiscent at a distance of wisps of dirty lambswool; bark shredding. Our only climber with opposite pinnate leaves, the stalks often twining and leaflets often toothed. *Habitat:* Characteristic of woods and hedgerows on chalk and limestone, often reaching high into trees and hanging down like lianas; also running along the ground; frequent in the S; very rare in the N; scattered over Ireland. July–September.

BUTTERCUPS   *Ranunculus*   ⑫

MOST Buttercups (11–22) have glossy yellow flowers, but the Water Crowfoots (21) have white flowers. Fruit a close head of 1-seeded nutlets. The following key includes also Marsh Marigold (1) and Globe Flower (2), but not such yellow, more or less buttercup-like flowers, as the St John's Worts (130–138), Rock-roses (139–142), Potentillas (348–357) and Yellow Saxifrages (400, 408).

KEY (Nos. 1, 2, 11–20, 22)

PLANT *annual* 14, 15, 16, 19*b*; *creeping* 12, 19; *tall* 2, 11, 18; *prostrate* 1, 12, 16, 19, 22; *hairless* 1, 18, 19, 20, 22; *with stem swollen at base* 13.
LEAVES UNDIVIDED: *long* 18, 19; *roundish*, 1, 16, 17, 19, 22; *with bulbils* 22.

FLOWERS *over 1 in. across* 1, 2, 18; *imperfect* 17; *with furrowed stalks* 12, 13, 15, 19, 20; *with narrow petals* 1, 16, 22; *with sepals turned down* 13, 15, 20; *sepals three*, 22; *no green sepals* 1, 2, *globular* 2.

FRUITS *in elongated heads* 11a, 20; *spiny* 14, 20a; *downy* 17; *several-seeded* 1, 2.

HABITAT: *wetter places* 1, 12, 18, 19, 20; *woods* 12, 16, 17, 22; *arable*, 12, 14, 16.

11. MEADOW BUTTERCUP *Ranunculus acris* L.   Plate 39.   *CTW, p. 85*

The tallest and most graceful of our common yellow Buttercups, a hairy perennial, 1–3 ft. high, with deeply cut palmate leaves, the topmost unstalked, and fruits in a roundish head. A variable plant, which differs from the still hairier Bulbous Buttercup (13) in its erect or spreading sepals; from Creeping Buttercup (12) in having no runners; and from both in its more numerous flower-heads and unfurrowed flower-stalks. *Habitat:* Widespread and common in damper grassland. May onwards.

11a. ***Jersey Buttercup, *R. flabellatus* Desfontaines, is shorter and rarely branched, and has even narrower leaflets, larger and usually solitary flowers, and fruits in an elongated head. Very rare, on hot dry banks in Jersey. May.

12. CREEPING BUTTERCUP   *R. repens* L.   Plate 39.   *CTW, p. 86*

Rather like a low-growing Bulbous Buttercup (13), but may be 2 ft. high or more, and can readily be told by its erect or spreading sepals and prolific rooting runners, which may be hidden in the herbage. *Habitat:* Widespread and common on roadsides and disturbed ground, and in woods, preferring moister places. May onwards.

13. BULBOUS BUTTERCUP   *R. bulbosus* L.   Plate 39.   *CTW, p. 87*

The commonest yellow Buttercup that has down-turned sepals when the flowers are fully open; with a markedly swollen base to the stem; smaller, hairier and less branched than Meadow Buttercup (11), and with furrowed flower-stalks. Fruits smooth. *Habitat:* Widespread and common in drier grassland. March–June, both starting and finishing earlier than the two previous species.

14. **CORN BUTTERCUP   *R. arvensis* L.   Plate 39.   *CTW, p. 88*

A slender, pale green, slightly hairy annual, 6–18 in. high, with smallish pale yellow flowers and very distinctive bur-like heads of spreading spiny fruits (Fig.). Upper leaves much forked with narrow leaflets, lower ones with broader leaflets toothed at the tip. *Habitat:* A widespread but now scarce weed of cornfields and waste places. June–July.

Figs. all × 2.

14   15   18   19   19a   20   34   34a

15. *HAIRY BUTTERCUP   *R. sardous* Crantz   Plate 39.   *CTW, p. 89*

Not unlike a small hairier Bulbous Buttercup (13), having down-turned sepals, but annual, with paler flowers, no swollen stem-base, and pale green, often shining, 3-lobed root-leaves. Fruits with a green border and a ring of warts within it (Fig.). *Habitat:* Local in grassy places, especially near the coast, becoming rarer northwards; not in Ireland. May–July.

16. **SMALL-FLOWERED BUTTERCUP *R. parviflorus* L. Pl. 46. *CTW, p. 89*
A pale green hairy annual, weedy, sprawling up to a foot long, and not immediately obvious as a Buttercup; root-leaves small, rounded in outline, lobed and deeply toothed. Flowers with tiny pale yellow petals, on furrowed stalks. Fruits very rough. *Habitat:* Widespread but local on bare dry ground, mostly on chalk or limestone; rare in Ireland; not in Scotland. May–July.

17. *WOOD GOLDILOCKS *R. auricomus* L.   Plate 39.   *CTW, p. 90*
Our only non-acrid yellow Buttercup, smaller and usually less hairy than Meadow Buttercup (11), and with fewer flowers, the petals having no scale at their base, and often imperfect or absent; sepals purple-tipped. Root-leaves deeply-lobed, but kidney-shaped. Fruits downy. *Habitat:* Widespread but rather local in woods, occasionally on rocks. April–May.

18. *GREATER SPEARWORT *R. lingua* L.   Plate 39.   *CTW, p. 90*
A tall stately Buttercup, 2–3 ft. high, with yellow flowers twice as large as Meadow Buttercup (11), narrow, lanceolate, toothed, hairless leaves, unfurrowed flower-stalks, and roughish winged fruits with a curved beak (Fig.). *Habitat:* Local but nowhere common in fens, marshes and ditches. June–August.

19. LESSER SPEARWORT *R. flammula* L.   Plate 39.   *CTW, p. 91*
A variable common yellow Buttercup of wet places, 6 in. to 2 ft. high, with lanceolate, often toothed hairless leaves, the upper narrow, the lower more oval. Usually much shorter and slenderer than the last species, but large specimens differ from small Great Spearworts in having flowers generally less than half the size, slightly furrowed flower-stalks, more oval lower leaves and a short blunt beak to the smooth unwinged fruits (Fig., p. 3). *Habitat:* Widespread, frequent in ditches and marshes, and by ponds and lakes, especially in the N and W. June onwards.
19*a.* *****Creeping Spearwort**, *R. reptans* L., is smaller, extremely slender and dainty, and prostrate, and has arching, rooting runners, and fruits almost hooked (Fig.). A not uncommon prostrate form of Lesser Spearwort is larger and coarser, and does not root at all the leaf-junctions. Confined to one or two gravelly loch-sides in the N. June–July.
19*b.* *****Adderstongue Spearwort**, *R. ophioglossifolius* Villars, is an annual, with broader spoon-shaped root-leaves, warty fruits, and smaller flowers, intermediate between Lesser Spearwort and the next species. Now confined to two marshes in Glos. June–August.

20. CELERY-LEAVED BUTTERCUP *R. sceleratus* L.   Plate 39.   *CTW, p. 92*
The smallest-flowered Buttercup of wet places, with pale yellow petals no bigger than the turned-down sepals. A pale green, usually hairless, upright, often bushy annual, 6–18 in. high, with stout hollow stems; shiny, deeply lobed, toothed root-leaves; and narrower, less divided stem-leaves. Fruits numerous, small, hairless, in an elongated head. *Habitat:* Widespread and fairly common in muddy places. May–September.
20*a.* *****Scilly Buttercup**, *R. muricatus* L. (*CTW, p. 88*), is lower, darker green and bushier, with larger flowers and fruits like Corn Buttercup (14), but with shorter, erect spines mostly towards the edges (Fig. as 20). A pest in bulb fields in the Scilly Is.; also recorded in Cornwall. February–May.

21. **WATER CROWFOOT** *R. aquatilis* L. Plate 80. *CTW, p. 93*

Very variable aquatic perennials, with floating white buttercup flowers, often in glorious masses, with stems numerous and trailing or short and creeping. Floating leaves, when present, rather small, hairless, kidney-shaped or variously lobed; submerged leaves, when present, are more numerous, in long tresses or short stiffly curled bunches. The stems and leaves may vary in one place as the water recedes, or in the same species from fast currents to still water. *Habitat:* Widespread and common in and by fresh and brackish water. March–August, but at their best in May–June.

Beginning with those usually found on mud and ending with those of deeper and faster rivers, the 13 British species generally recognised may be divided into four groups, as follows: in each a typical species is taken as an example:

21*a*. **Ivy-leaved Crowfoot**, *R. hederaceus* L. (*CTW, p. 93*), has shiny fleshy ivy-shaped floating leaves, nearly always no submerged ones, flowers only ¼-in. across, and hairless fruits. Common and usually on mud, rooting at intervals. The group includes (i) **R. lenormandii* Schultz, more local with larger flowers and leaves and beak of fruit more terminal, less lateral ; and (ii) ***R. lutarius* (Rével) Bouvet, uncommon, with leaves rather deeply lobed and the base of the fruit hairy.

21*b*. **Various-leaved Crowfoot**, *R. heterophyllus* Weber (*CTW, p. 98*), has both floating leaves cut to half-way and finely cut submerged leaves collapsing when out of the water; flowers ½-in. across, and hairy fruits on stalks shorter than the leaves. Common in ponds and ditches. The group includes (i) *R. peltatus* Schrank, with floating leaves kidney-shaped and not deeply cut, submerged leaves not collapsing, flowers twice as large and fruit-stalks longer than the leaves; and (ii) *R. baudotii* Godron with floating leaves 3-lobed to their stalk, like a Clover, submerged leaves not collapsing and hairless fruits on long stalks ; near sea.

21*c*. **Thread-leaved Crowfoot**, *R. trichophyllus* Chaix (*CTW, p. 97*), with submerged leaves only, not longer than broad, and forming a stiff tassel-like spray; flowers ½-in. across, and hairy fruits. Common in still waters. The group includes (i) *R. drouetii* Godron, with leaves collapsing, smaller flowers and hairless fruits; (ii)* *R. circinatus* Sibthorp, with the stiff segments of the leaves forming a rimless wheel 1 in. across; and (iii)** *R. sphaerospermus* Boissier & Blanche, with rigid leaves forming dense globular masses, larger flowers an inch across and fruits nearly spherical.

21*d*. **River Crowfoot**, *R. fluitans* Lamarck (*CTW, p. 96*), has only submerged leaves, all much longer than broad, 6–12 in. long, and flowers an inch across. Locally common in fast running rivers and streams. The group includes *R. pseudofluitans* (Syme) Baker & Foggitt, with much shorter leaves, 2–3 in. long, and occasional floating leaves.

22. **LESSER CELANDINE** *R. ficaria* L. Plate 38. *CTW, p. 101*

One of the first heralds of spring, a low hairless perennial 2–6 in. high, with long-stalked heart-shaped dark green leaves, sometimes with dark or light patches; and occasionally longer stems with bulbils at base of leaf-stalks. Flowers usually solitary, with narrow, very glossy yellow petals, which may fade white, and close in dull weather; sepals 3. Fruits in a small rounded head. *Habitat:* Widespread and common, usually in dampish shady places, sometimes a tiresome garden weed. March–May.

23. ****PHEASANT'S EYE** *Adonis annua* L. Plate 14. *CTW, p. 102*

A hairless annual, 6–15 in. high, not unlike a very small-flowered de Caen Anemone, with a black base to the 5–8 deep scarlet petals, and spreading sepals.

Foliage feathery and very bushy, rather concealing the flowers. Fruits in a compact, long-stalked, elongated head. *Habitat:* Scarce and decreasing in chalky cornfields in S England. June onwards.

24. **MOUSETAIL *Myosurus minimus* L.   Plate 106.   *CTW, p. 102*

A low tufted, unbranched annual, 2–4 in. high, with grass-like but rather fleshy leaves in a basal tuft. Its minute green flowers are solitary on long leafless stalks and produce each an elongated cylindrical plantain-like fruiting head of tiny nutlets, 1–2½ in. long, fancifully resembling a mouse's tail; petals tubular; sepals spurred. *Habitat:* Very local in usually sandy ploughed or bare grass fields and by sea-walls in the lowlands of England and Wales. April–July.

25. **COLUMBINE *Aquilegia vulgaris* L.   Plate 12.   *CTW, p. 103*

A popular garden perennial, easily recognised by its dark violet, blue, rose-pink or white flowers having 5 tubular petals, whose spurs in the wild are short and curved back, with sepals of the same colour; usually hairless, 2–3 ft. high, with slightly greyish, 2-trifoliate root-leaves. *Habitat:* Widespread but local in open woods and fens, usually as an escape except on chalk and limestone. May–July.

26. *COMMON MEADOW-RUE *Thalictrum flavum* L.   Plate 50.   *CTW, p. 105*

A tall perennial, 2–4 ft. high, whose flowers have very small whitish petals but appear yellowish and feathery from the numerous stamens long after the petals have fallen. Slightly resembling Meadow-sweet (342), but yellower and with a narrower flower-cluster and very different 2–3 pinnate leaves, the wedge-shaped leaflets longer than broad. *Habitat:* Widespread and fairly frequent in wet meadows and fens and by ditches and streams. June–August.

27. **ALPINE MEADOW-RUE *T. alpinum* L.   Plate 50.   *CTW, p. 105*

A slender little perennial, merging easily into the surrounding grass, with delicate, dark green, often 2-trifoliate leaves, mostly from the root, and a single 3-in. spike of tiny flowers with prominent feathery yellow and purplish-brown anthers. *Habitat:* Frequent on moist ledges and turf, especially on mountains, northwards from N Wales and N Yorks; local in W Ireland. May–July.

28. **LESSER MEADOW-RUE *T. minus* L.   Plate 50.   *CTW, p. 106*

A very variable, almost hairless, perennial, 9 in. to 4 ft. high, with a usually broad open cluster of delicate, often purple-tinged, greenish-yellow flowers with very prominent dangling stamens. Stems slender, wiry, often somewhat zigzag; leaves 3–4 pinnate with most leaflets about as broad as long. *Habitat:* Widespread and locally frequent in very diverse places, from dunes and limestone grassland to rocky places, mountains and shingle by fresh water; very local in Midlands; absent in SE England. June–August.

PEONY FAMILY Paeoniaceae

29. ***WILD PEONY *Paeonia mascula* (L.) Miller   Plate 15 *CTW, 108*

A single Peony, occasionally to be seen in gardens, with a glorious deep red flower, 3–5 in. across; perennial, 1–2 ft. high, with large, dark green, shiny leaves, and normally fewer petals than on Plate 15. *Habitat:* Long naturalised on Steep Holm in the Bristol Channel. May. '*P. officinalis*'

BARBERRY FAMILY Berberidaceae

30. **BARBERRY *Berberis vulgaris* L. Plate 64. *CTW, p. 110*
A deciduous shrub, 6–10 ft. high, with usually 3-forked spines on the grooved twigs, neat, sharply toothed, oval leaves, and small yellow flowers in hanging clusters. Fruit an oblong red berry, edible. *Habitat:* Widespread but now very scarce in hedgerows and bushy places. May–June.

31. OREGON GRAPE *Mahonia aquifolium* (Pursh) Nuttall Pl. 64. *CTW, 111*
Now the most frequent Barberry growing wild, resembling the native plant (30) in its scented yellow flowers, which are in larger upright clusters. An evergreen undershrub, 1–4 ft. high, spineless on the stem; leaves alternate, pinnate, holly-like, bronzed in winter. Berries round, blue-black, with a whitish bloom. *Habitat:* Widespread and frequently naturalised in shrubberies, shelter-belts and game-coverts. March–May.

WATER-LILY FAMILY Nymphaeaceae

32. WHITE WATER-LILY *Nymphaea alba* L. Plate 69. *CTW, p. 112*
The largest floating white flower, 4–8 in. across, with conspicuous yellow stamens; flowers fragrant, fully open only in sunshine; a perennial, with all leaves floating, rather smaller and rounder than in the next species. Fruits green, roundish, warty. *Habitat:* Widespread and frequent in sheltered fresh water. June–August. (Incl. *N. occidentalis* (Ostenfeld) Moss.)

33. YELLOW WATER-LILY *Nuphar lutea* (L.) Smith Plate 59. *CTW, p. 113*
The largest and commonest floating yellow flower, usually projecting a few inches out of the water; a perennial, with oval leaves 5–15 in. across, leathery when floating, cabbagy when submerged. Flowers 2–3 in. across, with petals usually shorter than sepals; smelling faintly of brandy, whence the name 'Brandy-bottle'. Fruits green, smooth, carafe-shaped. *Habitat:* Widespread and frequent in still and slow fresh water. June–September.
    33a. *****Least Yellow Water-lily**, *N. pumila* (Timm) DC. is smaller, with leaves 2–6 in., flowers ½–1½ in., and wider gaps between the petals and the lobes at the base of the leaves. Hybridises with the last species. Rare in lakes in hill districts in Scotland, also in Salop and Merioneth. July–August.

HORNWORT FAMILY Ceratophyllaceae

34. HORNWORT *Ceratophyllum demersum* L. Plate 68. *CTW, p. 115*
A completely submerged waterweed, not unlike a diminutive, bushy, aquatic fir-tree, differing from Water Milfoils (441–442) and Marestail (443) in its stiff, forked, toothed leaves. A brittle rootless perennial, having, at the base of the leaves, minute unstalked solitary green flowers, male and female separate; a shy flowerer. Ripe fruits warty, beaked, with two spines at base (Fig., p. 3, × 2). *Habitat:* Locally common in still water in England; rare elsewhere. July–September.
    34a. ****Spineless Hornwort**, *C. submersum* L., has greener and laxer leaves, but the only certain distinction is the fruit, spineless when ripe (Fig., p. 3, × 2). Less common inland, commoner near the sea, perhaps only in S and E England.

POPPY FAMILY Papaveraceae

Non-woody plants, normally with white or yellow juice, the solitary flowers having four, generally rather large and floppy, opposite petals, crumpled in bud, with numerous stamens and 2 sepals which soon fall.

35. CORN POPPY *Papaver rhoeas* L.   Plate 14. *CTW, p. 117*

The commonest Poppy in the S, with spreading hairs on the flower-stem and a hairless flat-topped globular seed-pod. Flowers 2–3 in. across, deep scarlet, petals often with a dark patch at the base; stamens blue-black. A hairy annual, usually 9 in. to 2 ft. high, with white juice and 1–2-pinnate leaves. The origin of garden Shirley Poppies, which sometimes escape in various colours, often with yellow stamens. Hybridises with the next species. *Habitat:* Widespread and often abundant on arable and roadsides, but scarce in the N. June onwards.

36. LONG-HEADED POPPY *P. dubium* L.   Plate 14.   *CTW, p. 119*
(incl. *P. lecoqii* Lamotte)

The commonest Poppy in the N, and the only one with long hairless seed-pods. Flowers 1½–2 in. across, pale scarlet petals with no dark patch at the base; hairs on the flower-stalk closely appressed. A hairy annual, usually 9–18 in. high, with juice usually white but occasionally yellow or colourless; leaves 1–2-pinnate. *Habitat:* Widespread and frequent in arable fields and on roadsides. June–August.

37. **BRISTLY POPPY *P. hybridum* L.   Plate 14.   *CTW, p. 119*

Our only Poppy with egg-shaped seed-pods thickly covered with long, spreading straw-coloured bristles. Flowers 1–1½ in. across, the small, deep crimson petals, with a purplish-black patch at the base, strikingly different in colour from our other Poppies. A hairy annual, 6–15 in. high, usually with white juice, spreading or appressed hairs on flower-stalks, and neat, rather stiff, 1–2-pinnate leaves. *Habitat:* Widespread but local in arable fields, usually on chalk or limestone; rare in the N. June–August.

38. *PALE POPPY *P. argemone* L.   Plate 14.   *CTW, p. 120*

Our only Poppy with sparsely bristled, long narrow seed-pods; a weak hairy annual, 4–12 in. high, normally with whitish juice, hairs on flower-stalks appressed, 1–2-pinnate leaves, flowers ½–1½ in. across and pale scarlet, narrow, spaced-out petals, with a dark patch at the base. *Habitat:* Widespread and locally frequent in arable fields. May–July.

39. **OPIUM POPPY *P. somniferum* L.   Plate 14.   *CTW, p. 120*

A frequent variable annual, 18 in. to 4 ft. high, greyish, waxy, often hairless, with wavy, coarsely toothed leaves clasping the stem. Flowers often large, lilac-coloured, with a purple patch at the base of the petals. *Habitat:* A widespread but uncommon escape, very occasionally in cornfields. June–August.

40. **WELSH POPPY *Meconopsis cambrica* (L.) Viguier Pl. 38. *CTW, p. 122*

A dainty and attractive yellow Poppy; a tufted, slightly hairy perennial, about a foot high, with pinnate, pale green leaves and yellow juice, fruit long and narrow, beaked. *Habitat:* Fairly frequent in rocky places in hill districts in Wales and NW England, rare in SW England and W Ireland; elsewhere an occasional garden weed or escape. June–August.

41. *YELLOW HORNED POPPY *Glaucium flavum* Crantz Pl. 38. *CTW, 123*
A conspicuous seaside perennial, 1–2 ft. high, with yellow juice and clumps of silvery grey leaves, the root ones pinnately lobed and wavy, the upper ones deeply lobed and clasping the stem. Flowers orange-yellow, rarely pale yellow, 2–3 in. across. Seed-pods 6–12 in. long, sickle-shaped. *Habitat:* Widespread and locally frequent on the coast, usually on shingle; very rare inland. June–September.

42. GREATER CELANDINE *Chelidonium majus* L. Plate 38. *CTW, p. 124*
Resembles Lesser Celandine (22) only in name, being a rather greyish, sparsely hairy, bushy perennial, 12–18 in. high, with orange juice and thin, fleshy irregularly pinnate leaves, the leaflets coarsely toothed. Flowers rich yellow, ½-in. across. Seed-pod thin, cylindrical. *Habitat:* Widespread and frequent on walls and hedge-banks, usually near buildings. May–September.

 FUMITORY FAMILY Fumariaceae

NON-WOODY PLANTS with much-divided leaves, characterised by the curious shape of the flowers, tubular with a short spur (Fig.), the stamens joined in two bundles of three.

43. **CLIMBING CORYDALIS *Corydalis claviculata* (L.) DC.
Plate 102. *CTW, p. 126*
A delicate climber, with clusters of small, pale creamy-yellow flowers, and short seed-pods; a hairless annual, 6 in. to 3 ft. long, with pinnate leaves ending in tendrils, unlike the white-flowered clambering forms of Fumitory (45). *Habitat:* Widespread but distinctly local in bushy and rocky places, mostly on acid soils, or on shingle. June onwards.

44. *YELLOW CORYDALIS *C. lutea* (L.) DC. Plate 43. *CTW, p. 127*
A hairless tufted perennial, 6–9 in. high, with 2-pinnate leaves greyish beneath, and opposite the upper ones long stalks bearing short spikes of rich yellow flowers. *Habitat:* Widespread and frequent on walls near gardens. May onwards.

45. FUMITORY *Fumaria officinalis* L.[1] Plate 26. *CTW, p. 133*
A very variable, hairless annual, either low and bushy or long—to 3 ft.—and clambering; leaves 1–3-pinnate with no tendrils. Flowers in spikes, elongating in fruit, of various shades of pinkish-purple or creamy white, often tipped with maroon. Fruits small, globular, 1-seeded. Seen in quantity at a distance the greyish foliage has the faint smoky appearance that gives the plant its name. *Habitat:* A widespread and often plentiful weed of cultivated ground, waste places and hedge-banks. May onwards.

CRUCIFER OR CABBAGE FAMILY Cruciferae

MOSTLY NON-WOODY PLANTS, with flowers in erect spikes or heads, the 4 (occasionally no) petals arranged crosswise, 4 sepals, and usually 6 stamens. The seeds are contained in a usually beaked pod, developing above the petals.

---

[1] Including *F. occidentalis* Pugsley, *F. capreolata* L., *F. purpurea* Pugsley, *F. bastardii* Boreau, *F. martinii* Clavaud, *F. muralis* Koch, *F. boraei* Jordan, *F. neglecta* Pugsley, *F. micrantha* Lagasca, *F. vaillantii* Loiseleur and *F. parviflora* Lamarck.

Four-petalled flowers that might be mistaken for Crucifers, but are not included in the Key, include Greater Celandine (42), Tormentil (356), Willow herbs (425–434), and Bedstraws (808–818).

KEY TO CRUCIFERS (Nos. 46–112)

I. Purple or Lilac Flowers

PLANT *all hairy* 56, 79, 102, 103; *all hairless* 59, 70, 74, 75, 86, 87.

LEAVES *clasping stem* 70, 74; *fleshy* 59; *hoary grey* 102; *lanceolate* 67, 79, 102, 103; *pinnate* 56, 86, 87, 91, 93; *rosette* 86, 93; *rounded* 74, 75; *with bulbils at base* 86, 91.

FLOWERS *fragrant* 102, 103; *with petals of unequal size* 67.

SEED-PODS *beaded* 56; *globular* 67, 74, 75, 79; *notched* 67, 70; *oval* 70; *roundish* 79; *winged* 67, 70; *waisted* 59; *cylindrical* 56, 86, 87, 93, 102, 103.

HABITAT: *maritime only* 56, 59, 74, 75, 102.

II. Yellow Flowers

PLANT *all hairy* 49, 51, 52, 53, 56, 58, 77, 78, 97, 104, 105, 106, 107, 108; *all hairless* 46, 47a, 50, 55, 66, 92, 99, 100, 101, 111; *foetid* 54, 55; *greyish* 46, 47, 48, 53, 66, 78, 97; *with stem woody below* 46, 50a, 54, 55, 56a, 105.

LEAVES *clasping stem* 47, 66, 92, 97, 100, 111; *all fleshy* 46; *hoary* 66, 78, 97; *all lanceolate* 78, 81, 97, 101, 104, 105, 111; *all pinnate* 49, 50, 52, 54, 55, 56, 77, 92cd, 99, 100, 107, 109, 112; *rosette* 46, 47, 50, 53, 54, 81, 97.

FLOWERS *fragrant* 105; *1 in. across* 105; *with notched petals* 78.

SEPALS *erect* 46, 49, 50, 53, 56, 78, 81, 92, 97, 99, 104, 107, 108, 111; *spreading* 47, 48, 51, 52, 54, 55, 58, 77, 100, 101, 108, 109, 112.

SEED-PODS *appressed* 48, 53, 58, 92, 97, 107; *beaded* 49, 56, 112; *disc-shaped* 78; *elliptical* 79, 81, 100, 111; *4-angled* 92, 104; *globular* 58, 77, 79, 101, 111; *hanging* 66; *downy* 51, 52, 56, 78, 107; *jointed* 56, 58; *notched* 78; *warty* 77; *cylindrical* 46, 56, 92, 97, 99, 104–5, 107–9, 112.

HABITAT: *maritime only* 48, 50, 56a.

III. White or Greenish Flowers

PLANT *all hairy* 56, 60, 65, 78, 79, 80, 82, 83, 89, 90, 95, 96, 102, 103, 110; *all hairless* 57, 59, 61, 62, 63, 65, 68, 71, 74, 75, 76, 85, 86, 87, 88, 91, 98, 106; *foetid* 61, 68; *garlicky* 106; *greyish* 57, 62, 69, 70, 94, 102; *fleshy* 57, 59, 74, 75.

STEM *wavy* 89; *woody below* 57, 102.

LEAVES *clasping stem* 60, 65, 69, 70, 72, 74, 83, 88, 95, 97; *heart-shaped* 75, 106; *hoary* 94, 102; *pinnate* 63, 64, 71, 73, 86, 87, 88, 89, 90, 91, 98; *rosette* 71, 72, 82, 83, 84, 86, 89, 90, 94, 95, 96, 110; *rounded* 74; *with bulbils at base* 86, 91.

FLOWERS *fragrant* 79, 102, 103; *with spreading sepals* 57.

PETALS *cleft or notched* 78, 80, 82, 84; *of unequal size* 67, 71; *shorter than sepals* 61, 73; *none* 61.

SEED-PODS *appressed* 95, 97; *globular* 57, 62, 65, 67, 74, 75, 79, 80; *jointed* 56; *notched* 60, 64, 67, 68, 69, 70, 72; *oblong* 60; *oval* 62, 68, 71, 73, 76, 82, 83, 84; *roundish* 68, 69, 78, 84; *triangular* 72; *twisted* 82; *winged* 60, 61, 67, 68, 69, 70; *wrinkled* 63; *waisted* 59; *cylindrical* 56–7, 86–90, 93–8, 102–3, 106, 110.

HABITAT: *maritime only* 56a, 57, 59, 62, 64, 74, 75, 78, 79, 102; *fresh water* 76, 98.

46. **WILD CABBAGE** *Brassica oleracea* L.   Plate 45.   *CTW, p. 151*

A stout hairless perennial, 1–2 ft. high, the origin of numerous 'greens'; mature plants have a stout woody stem covered with leaf-scars. Can be told from the next species by all leaves being fleshy and greyish, the upper no broader at the base and not or hardly clasping the stem, the lower cabbagy and persisting; buds always well above the pale yellow open flowers; erect sepals; and shorter beak to pods. *Habitat:* A scarce native on sea-cliffs in Wales, S. England and Yorks; elsewhere, on waste ground, a result of neglect in gardens. May–August.

47. BARGEMAN'S CABBAGE *B. campestris* L. Plate 45. *CTW, p. 153*

An annual, 1–3 ft. high, with pinnately lobed leaves, the upper greyish, un-stalked, broad at the base, the lower green, bristly and sometimes withering early; buds well below the bright yellow opened flowers, spreading sepals, long thin beak to cylindrical pods, and grey or blackish seeds. The Turnip (*B. rapa* L.) is a biennial form with a swollen white-fleshed root, not constricted at the top. *Habitat:* Widespread and locally frequent on bare ground, especially by rivers and as a relic of cultivation. April onwards.

47a. Rape, *B. napus* L. (incl. *B. oleifera* Moench, *B. napobrassica* (L.) Miller), is another biennial, with the buds slightly overtopping the paler yellow flowers; sepals rather less spreading; root-leaves sparsely bristly or hairless, greyish, usually withering and dropping off before flowering; pods often longer; and seeds blue-black with a whitish bloom. The Swede is very similar, but has flowers sometimes buff, and a tuberous root with the neck narrowed at the top. Both are frequent relics of cultivation.

48. BLACK MUSTARD *B. nigra* (L.) Koch Plate 45. *CTW, p. 155*

An upright perennial, with somewhat slender stems 2–3 ft. high, differing from the last three species in its leaves being all stalked and its pods appressed to the stem. Lower leaves coarsely pinnate and bristly, upper lanceolate and hairless. Flowers yellow, with stalks not longer than the half-spreading sepals. Pods about $\frac{1}{2}$-in. long, with a short thin beak. *Habitat:* Locally common in disturbed ground on sea-cliffs, stream-banks and waste places; sometimes also a relic of cultivation. May onwards.

49. ***HAIRY ROCKET *Erucastrum gallicum* (Willdenow) Schulz

Brassica gallica (Willdenow) Druce Plate 45. *CTW, p. 156*

Slender, bristly annual, 9–18 in. high, with yellow flowers; the only yellow crucifer with both hairy, pinnately lobed leaves and erect sepals. Pods hairless, cylindrical, with a short thin beak. *Habitat:* A casual, established in one or two places in the S and E. May–August.

50. **DUNE CABBAGE *Rhynchosinapis monensis* (L.) Dandy Pl. 45. *CTW, 157*

A maritime biennial, 6–12 in. high, with yellow flowers, hairless and almost leafless stems, and a rosette of neat hairless pinnate root-leaves, with small, dark green, shiny leaflets; sepals erect, hairy, never shorter than flower-stalks. Seed-pods short-stalked, cylindrical, with seeds in one row and a long, seeded beak. *Habitat:* Very local by the sea in NW England, rarer in Wales and SW Scotland. June–August. *Brassica monensis* (L.) Hudson.

50a. ***Lundy Cabbage, *R. wrightii* (Schulz) Dandy, is a much larger, cabbagy, hairy perennial, with stem woody below; more stem-leaves; and larger, deeper yellow flowers, on stalks usually longer than the sepals. Lundy Is. only.

50b. **Wallflower Cabbage, *R. erucastrum* (L.) Dandy (*B. cheiranthos* Villars), is somewhat hairy, taller and much more branched, and has several stem-leaves. Occurs with varying persistence in waste places in the S.

51. CHARLOCK   *Sinapis arvensis* L.   Plate 45.   *CTW, p. 159*
Wild Mustard, Runch; *Brassica sinapis* Visiani

A very common coarse annual yellow crucifer, 6–18 in. high, known to country-men under a variety of names; usually bristly at least below. Differs from White Mustard (52) in its less divided leaves, and long conical beak shorter than seed-pod. Lower leaves lobed and stalked, upper toothed and unstalked; sepals spreading or turned down. Seed-pods short-stalked, cylindrical, beaked, usually hairless but may be covered with short stiff hairs. *Habitat:* A widespread and abundant pest of waste and cultivated ground where selective weed-killers are not used. May onwards.

52. WHITE MUSTARD   *S. alba* L.   Plate 45.   *CTW, p. 159*
The mustard of 'mustard and cress', often grown as a crop; differs from Charlock (51) in its paler, more divided leaves, which are all stalked and pinnately lobed; and the flattened beak, usually hairless at the top, being at least as long as the well-stalked, stubbier pod, which is thickly covered with spreading white hairs. *Habitat:* A widespread and common arable weed or relic of cultivation, especially on chalky soils. May onwards. *Brassica alba* (L.) Rabenhorst.

53. **HOARY MUSTARD   *Hirschfeldia incana* (L.) Lagrèze-Fossat
Brassica adpressa Boissier   Plate 45 (a young plant).   *CTW, p. 160*
Rather like Black Mustard (48), but annual, paler green and rough with coarse whitish hairs all over the lower stems and leaves; flowers paler yellow, sepals more erect, and a 1-seeded beak to the stouter seed-pod (Fig.). Lower leaves pinnately lobed and stalked, upper ones lanceolate, unstalked and often quite hairless. *Habitat:* A casual, becoming established in a few waste places in S England; plentiful in the Channel Is. May–September.   Fig. × 1½.

54. *STINKWEED   *Diplotaxis muralis* (L.) DC.   Plate 43.   *CTW, p. 161*
Apart from Wall Rocket (55) our only pale yellow crucifer with a disagreeable smell when bruised; usually an annual, 6–12 in. high, with stems slightly hairy and unbranched, occasionally woody below; leaves pinnately lobed, mostly in a rosette at base; sepals half-spreading. Seed-pods cylindrical, with seeds in two rows and a short seedless beak, spreading on stalks and at an angle with the stem (Fig.). *Habitat:* Widespread but local in waste and disturbed ground, especially on sandy soils, thinning out northwards. May–Sept. *Brassica muralis* (L.) Hudson.

55. *WALL ROCKET   *D. tenuifolia* (L.) DC.   Plate 43.   *CTW, p. 162*
A perennial, usually much larger, bushier and much more branched than Stinkweed (54); differs also in the hairless and almost woody stem, no basal rosette, but a bushy bunch of leaves low down, larger flowers on longer stalks, and the constriction between the end of the flower-stalk and the beginning of the seed-pods, which are held well away from but roughly parallel to the stem (Fig.). Sometimes confused with the uncommon biennial form of Stinkweed, which has lost its basal rosette and may be branched, but can usually be told by the pods. *Habitat:* Locally plentiful on walls, chalk railway cuttings and banks and waste sites, and occasionally a weed of cultivation, in S England; casual elsewhere. May onwards. *Brassica tenuifolia* (L.) Boissier.

56. WILD RADISH *Raphanus raphanistrum* L. Plate 45. *CTW, p. 165*
Like a straggly Charlock (51), with lilac-veined white petals, less often pale yellow; longer flower-stalks; erect sepals; pods more markedly beaded and with a slender beak and pinnately lobed leaves with a large rounded lobe at the end. *Habitat:* A widespread and often common farm and garden weed. May onwards.

56a. **Sea Radish,** *R. maritimus* Smith, a coarse, stout, bushy perennial, 2–3 ft. high, with flowers usually yellow and less veined, and pods of 1–3 globular, 1-seeded joints, much constricted and beaded (Fig.); is abundant by the sea in the Channel Is., frequent in SW England, rare elsewhere. June–August.

56b. **Garden Radish,** *R. sativus* L., the familiar salad plant, 3–9 in. high, with a tuberous root, flowers usually white or lilac, and inflated elliptical pods hardly beaded and with a stout beak (Fig.), is an occasional outcast or casual.

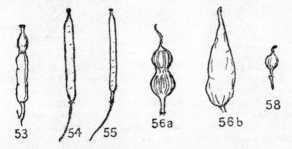

53 54 55 56a 56b 58

57. **SEA KALE *Crambe maritima* L. Plate 93. *CTW, p. 167*
The only white crucifer with large cabbagy leaves, the origin of the vegetable; a squat thick-set hairless perennial, 1–2 ft. high, growing in large clumps, with stem woody at base; leaves greyish, waxy, very thick and fleshy, with crinkly lobes. Flowers in a very broad cluster, not unlike a bolted cauliflower; sepals spreading. Seed-pods small, globular, not splitting open. *Habitat:* Widespread but local on sand and shingle by the sea. June–August.

58. **BASTARD CABBAGE *Rapistrum orientale* (L.) Crantz. Plate 45.
(Incl. *R. rugosum* (L.) Allioni; *R. hispanicum* (L.) Crantz). *CTW, p. 169*
An often bushy, mustard-like annual, 2–3 ft. high, hairy at least below, with pale yellow flowers, and erect or half-spreading sepals, its small, globular, ridged seed-pods, shaped like Chianti bottles, with a long slender beak, on longish stalks closely appressed to the stem (Fig.). Leaves rather like those of Charlock (51). *Habitat:* Increasing in waste places, chiefly near London. May onwards.

59. *SEA ROCKET *Cakile maritima* Scopoli Plate 93. *CTW, p. 170*
The only lilac-coloured flower of the sea-shore that has pinnately lobed, shiny, sometimes linear, fleshy leaves. Floppy, rather bushy, hairless annual, 4–12 in. high, with stubby, waisted seed-pods, the upper part larger. *Habitat:* Widespread and typical of the drift line and above on sandy shores. June–August.

60. COMMON PEPPERWORT *Lepidium campestre*(L.) Brown Pl. 92. *CTW,174*
An annual rather like a tall, stiff, hoary, dense, often unbranched Shepherd's Purse (72), with upper leaves toothed and clasping the stem and lower ones

lanceolate, untoothed and soon withering. Flowers very small, white, with yellow-ish anthers; petals little longer than the sepals. Seed-pods shovel-shaped, oblong, flattened, winged above, rough, slightly notched, the tiny beak hardly projecting; held parallel to the stem on spreading stalks. *Habitat:* Widespread and fairly common in coppiced woods or open ground, decreasing northwards; local in Ireland. May–August.

60a. *Smith's Cress, *L. smithii* Hooker, is perennial, sometimes prostrate, and more branched, and has petals longer than sepals, anthers violet, and more oval seed-pods, usually rather smooth and with a longer beak (Fig.). Much less common, but sometimes replacing Pepperwort, especially in Ireland.

Figs. × 2, except 68 × 1.

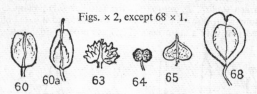

60   60a   63   64   65   68

61. *NARROW-LEAVED PEPPERWORT *L. ruderale* L. Pl. 92. *CTW, 176*

A very weedy, often bushy, slender hairless annual, 6–12 in. high, smelling of cress and with minute greenish flowers, 2–4 stamens and usually no petals. Lower leaves pinnate, soon withering, the upper linear, not clasping the stem. Seed-pods small, flattened, notched, longer than broad but shorter than their stalks. *Habitat:* Locally frequent on waste ground, chiefly in the S and on banks near the sea; not in Ireland. June–August.

61a. **Garden Cress, *L. sativum* L., the cress of 'mustard and cress', is greyer and less bushy, and always has larger white petals and 6 stamens; pods longer than their stalks. An occasional escape.

62. **DITTANDER   *L. latifolium* L.   Plate 93.   *CTW, p. 178*

A greyish hairless perennial, 2–4 ft. high, with a creeping rootstock; whitish stems; broad lanceolate toothed root-leaves, somewhat like Horseradish (85) but smaller and more abruptly narrowed into the stalk; and fine clusters of small white flowers, the sepals edged white. Seed-pods small, rounded, with a very short beak. *Habitat:* Rather local in damp places on coasts of E and S England, Wales and S Ireland; occasionally spreading inland. July–August.

63. COMMON WART CRESS   *Coronopus squamatus* (Forskal) Ascherson
Swine's Cress; *C. ruellii* Allioni   Plate 89.   *CTW, p. 179*

A coarse stiff prostrate greyish hairless annual, with pinnate leaves and small white flowers tightly bunched at the base of the leaves. Seed-pods gnarled, broader than long, flattened, with a very short beak, and longer than their very short stalk (Fig.). *Habitat:* A weed of well-trodden places, frequent in S England and S Ireland, thinning out northwards. May onwards.

64. *SLENDER WART CRESS   *C. didymus* (L.) Smith   Pl. 89.   *CTW, p. 180*

A low lax pale green annual, often prostrate, usually hairy on the stem, smelling rather like Garden Cress (61a) when rubbed; leaves pinnate. Flowers with tiny white or no petals, in spikes up the stems; stamens usually 2. Seed-pods scarcely wrinkled, flattened, notched at top and bottom, broader than long but shorter than their long stalk (Fig.). *Habitat:* Widespread and frequent on disturbed and waste ground, especially near the sea in S, thinning out northwards. June–September. Lesser Swine's Cress.

65. HOARY CRESS *Cardaria draba* (L.) Desvaux   Plate 94. *CTW, p. 180*
Hoary Pepperwort, Thanet Weed; *Lepidium draba* L.
An untidy, often hairless perennial, a foot or so tall, with creeping rootstock, broad lanceolate toothed grey-green leaves, the upper clasping the stem, and a loose terminal cluster of small white flowers. Seed-pods small, kidney-shaped, broader than long, with a prominent beak, on long spreading slender stalks (Fig.). *Habitat:* A locally common weed of roadsides and disturbed or waste ground, still spreading W and N from SE England into Scotland and Ireland. May–July.

66. ***WOAD *Isatis tinctoria* L.   Plate 50. *CTW, p. 181*
Our only crucifer with seed-pods hanging like earrings; a biennial, 18 in. to 3 ft. high, with lower leaves greyish downy and lanceolate, the upper less or not hairy and clasping the stem with an arrow-shaped base; and fine trusses of small yellow flowers. Pods flattened, dark shining brown. *Habitat:* Long established on cliffs near Tewkesbury and Guildford; a rare casual elsewhere. June–August.

67. **WILD CANDYTUFT *Iberis amara* L.   Plate 92. *CTW, p. 182*
The wild original of some garden Candytufts, distinctive for its large outer petals twice as long as the inner ones; a slightly downy annual, 2–9 in. high, with pinnately lobed leaves, no rosette, and flowers, usually white but sometimes going mauve, in flat heads, lengthening in fruit. Seed-pod a winged, notched disc. The usual annual garden Candytuft (*I. umbellata* L.), which may escape, normally has flower-heads coloured and not tending to lengthen in fruit. *Habitat:* Very local on bare patches on chalky soils in the S; frequent in the Chilterns, rare elsewhere. May–August.

68. COMMON PENNY-CRESS *Thlaspi arvense* L.   Plate 92. *CTW, p. 184*
A rather stout, hairless foetid annual, 6–18 in. high, differing from all other shepherds-purse-like crucifers in its disc-like, broadly winged, deeply notched seed-pods, $\frac{1}{2}$-in. across (Fig.); also from Shepherd's Purse (72) itself in its yellower-green, shinier lanceolate leaves being toothed but undivided, the lower unstalked and not in a rosette. Flowers white. *Habitat:* A widespread and locally common weed of arable and waste ground. May onwards.

69. ***COTSWOLD PENNY-CRESS *T. perfoliatum* L.   Pl. 92. *CTW, p. 184*
Like a small neat greyish hairless Shepherd's Purse (72), with leaf-bases almost encircling the stem; a low annual, 2–6 in. high, with rather broad undivided, sometimes slightly toothed leaves. Flowers white, with yellow anthers. Seed-pods oval, flattened, winged, notched. *Habitat:* Very local on bare ground in the Cotswolds, especially in old quarries. April–May.

70. **ALPINE PENNY-CRESS *T. alpestre* L.   Plate 92. *CTW, p. 184*
A low hairless perennial, 3–12 in. high, varying between each of its widely separated localities; leaves similar to the last species, but the upper only slightly clasping the stem. Flowers small, white or sometimes lilac; anthers usually violet, rarely yellow. Seed-pods flattened, narrowly heart-shaped, winged, with varying depth of notch and length of beak. *Habitat:* Very local on rocks and old lead

workings on limestone hills in the Mendips and from Derbyshire northwards. April–July. (Incl. '*T. calaminare*').

71. *SHEPHERD'S CRESS *Teesdalia nudicaulis* (L.) Brown Pl. 91. *CTW, 186*

A low tufted, often hairless, shepherd's-purse-like annual, but with the tiny white outer petals longer than the inner; stamens sometimes 4. Leaves pinnate, mostly in a neat rosette, from which several almost leafless, often incurving flowering stems arise. Seed-pods small, oblong, concave above, slightly notched. *Habitat:* Widespread but very local on bare sandy heaths and on gravel or shingle. April–June.

72. SHEPHERD'S PURSE *Capsella bursa-pastoris* (L.) Medicus Pl. 92. *CTW,187*

The commonest small white crucifer, with distinctive triangular seed-pods, flattened and notched; a dull green, usually downy annual, 3–18 in. high, with narrow, very variable root-leaves, ranging from very slightly toothed to deeply pinnate, the upper less toothed, clasping the stem. *Habitat:* A widespread and abundant weed of cultivated and waste places. Throughout the year.

73. **HUTCHINSIA *Hornungia petraea* (L.) Reichenbach Pl. 90. *CTW, 188*

A delicate, often bushy, early-flowering annual, 1–4 in. high, with minute whitish flowers, and neat pinnate root- and stem-leaves. Seed-pods flattened, unwinged, elliptical. *Habitat:* Very local in bare places on limestone, and on walls and sand-dunes, in the W, from the Mendips and Gower to the Craven Pennines, and in Jersey. March–May. *Hutchinsia petraea* (L.) Brown.

74. COMMON SCURVY-GRASS *Cochlearia officinalis* L. Pl. 93. *CTW, p. 189*

A hairless perennial, 4–9 in. high, with long-stalked, dark green, fleshy, heart- or kidney-shaped, untoothed root-leaves, the upper bluntly pointed, with 1–2 broad teeth, clasping the stem. Flowers white, sometimes lilac. Seed-pods globular. All Scurvy-grasses can be variable and perplexing, appearing to merge into each other and produce presumable hybrids. *Habitat:* Widespread and common on cliffs and banks by the sea; rare inland. April–August.

74*a*. **Upland Scurvy-grass, *C. alpina* Watson (incl. *C. micacea* Marshall), is very similar, but is less rigid and varies greatly in size; leaves less fleshy; pods more egg-shaped. Local in wet places on mountains. June–August.

74*b*. *Long-leaved Scurvy-grass, *C. anglica* L., has larger flowers and longer, narrower leaves, the root ones narrowed gradually into the stalk. Muddy shores, chiefly in the S; rare in Ireland. April–May.

75. EARLY SCURVY-GRASS *C. danica* L. Plate 90. *CTW, p. 191*

Smaller than the previous Scurvy-grasses (74), but annual and usually prostrate, and with flowers more often lilac, appearing earlier; leaves usually all stalked, the lower more heart-shaped, the upper ivy-shaped. Seed-pods egg-shaped. Dwarf forms somewhat recalling Whitlow-grass (84) may star the ground in spring. *Habitat:* Widespread and frequent on sandy and shingly shores, walls and rocks by the sea, especially in the SW; rarely inland on railway tracks. February–September. (Incl. *C. scotica* Druce).

76. **AWLWORT *Subularia aquatica* L. Plate 66. *CTW, p. 192*

A tiny 1–3 in. aquatic annual, nearly always submerged. Its pale green, cylindrical, finely pointed leaves look like those of Shore-weed (794), and similar plants, which often grow with it, but are slenderer, shorter and narrower. Its tiny, narrow-petalled white flowers and swollen egg-shaped seed-pods, on leafless stems, are however very distinctive. *Habitat:* Rather rare on the gravelly or stony bottoms of shallow lakes in hill districts in the N and W, especially in the W and C Highlands and in W Ireland. June–September.

77. ****WARTY CABBAGE** *Bunias orientalis* L. Plate 44. *CTW, p. 195*
A stout, hairy, mustard-like perennial, with warty stems 2–3 ft. high, notable for its shining, warty, pointed, asymmetrically globular seed-pods. Leaves dark green, pinnately lobed, pointed, the lower long, stalked, toothed, and lobed, the topmost unstalked and lanceolate. Flowers sulphur-yellow, long-stalked, with petals twice as long as the spreading sepals. *Habitat:* Casual or locally established on waste ground, railway banks, etc., chiefly around London and especially on chalk. May–August.

78. *****SMALL ALISON** *Alyssum alyssoides* (L.) L. Plate 44. *CTW, p. 196*
A low modest annual, 2–6 in. high, often branched, covered with grey hairs; leaves narrow lanceolate. Flowers small, opening yellow but soon fading, with narrow notched petals. Seed-pods disc-shaped, downy, slightly notched, persisting on the dried-up plant. *Habitat:* Now only in a very few sandy fields in the Breckland. April–June.

79. ****SWEET ALISON** *Lobularia maritima* (L.) Desvaux Pl. 92. *CTW, p. 197*
A familiar fragrant garden edging plant, usually less compact when growing wild; a 3–8 in. annual with appressed grey hairs and narrow lanceolate leaves. Flowers white, occasionally mauve, with broad rounded petals. Seed-pods globular, flattened, not notched. *Habitat:* Widespread but local in sandy places, walls and waste ground, especially near the sea or close to gardens. June–September. *Alyssum maritimum* (L.) Lamarck.

80. *****HOARY ALISON** *Berteroa incana* (L.) DC. Pl. 92. *CTW, p. 197*
A greyish annual, 6–18 in. high, with spreading hairs; lanceolate leaves often somewhat toothed; white petals deeply cleft; and erect seed-pods elliptical, beaked, flattened. *Habitat:* A rare casual, sometimes persisting. June–August.

81. *****YELLOW WHITLOW-GRASS** *Draba aizoides* L. Pl. 43. *CTW, 198*
A low, neat, early-flowering perennial, 2–3 in. high, with bright yellow flowers on hairless, leafless stems over a cushion of stiff lanceolate leaves fringed with white bristles; petals broad, hardly notched; sepals hairless. Seed-pods elliptical. *Habitat:* Limestone cliffs and walls in the Gower peninsula; very rarely established elsewhere. March–April.

82. ****TWISTED WHITLOW-GRASS** *D. incana* L. Plate 90. *CTW, p. 199*
A rigid hoary biennial, 3–12 in. high, not unlike Hairy Rock-cress (95), with much shorter, broader seed-pods, twisted when ripe, and a slight notch in the white petals. Leaves short, lanceolate, toothed, in a rosette and up the stem. *Habitat:* Local on hill and mountain ledges and sandy turf northwards from Snowdonia and Peak District, and in Ireland. May–July.

82a. *****Rock Whitlow-grass,** *D. norvegica* Gunnerus, a perennial, is easily confounded with dwarfed plants of the last, but is only 1–2 in. high, and has more notched petals, untwisted elliptical pods and usually completely leafless stems.

Very high on a very few Scottish mountains. May–June, going over much earlier.
D. rupestris Brown.

83. **WALL WHITLOW-GRASS   *D. muralis* L.   Plate 90.   *CTW, p. 200*

Similar to Hoary Whitlow-grass (82), but annual and slenderer; petals not
notched; pods elliptical and not twisted, spreading when ripe; leaves broader,
the upper fewer and clasping the stem. *Habitat:* Uncommon on walls and rocks
in limestone districts in W England, from Mendips to Pennines; rare elsewhere,
and especially in nurseries. April–June.

84. COMMON WHITLOW-GRASS   *Erophila verna* (L.) Chevallier   Plate 90.

(Incl. *E. spathulata* Lang, *E. praecox* (Steven) DC.); *Draba verna* L. *CTW, 201*
A slender hairy, very variable ephemeral annual, 1–3 in. high, with very deeply
cleft white petals, leafless unbranched flower-stems, a rosette of lanceolate,
sometimes toothed, leaves, and flattened, roundish or elliptical seed-pods on long
stalks. *Habitat:* Widespread and frequent on bare sandy ground, walls, and
rocks; sometimes on mountains. March–June.

85. HORSE-RADISH   *Armoracia rusticana* Gaertner, Meyer & Scherbius
Cochlearia armoracia L.   Plate 93.   *CTW, p. 202*

The well-known kitchen-garden plant, whose roots provide the sauce; a hairless
perennial, 1–3 ft. high, with large shiny dock-like root-leaves, usually wavy and
slightly toothed, but sometimes very deeply cut. Flowers numerous, white, in
long, leafy spikes. Seed-pods small, globular, but rarely if ever ripened in Britain.
Habitat: Widely naturalised on waste ground; rare in Ireland. May–August.

86. LADY'S SMOCK   *Cardamine pratensis* L.   Plate 25.   *CTW, p. 204*

A graceful plant, one of the first to bloom in moist meadows, arriving with the
cuckoo, and so called Cuckoo Flower; an unbranched hairless variable perennial,
9–15 in. high, with pinnate leaves, the root ones in a rosette, the leaflets of the
lowest leaf oval, the terminal leaflet much larger, rounded, of the upper usually
very narrow. Flowers large, from deep lilac to white; anthers yellow. Seed-pods
with a short thick beak, not always ripened. *Habitat:* Widespread and common
in damp meadows and woods, also on mountain ledges. April–June.

87. *LARGE BITTERCRESS   *C. amara* L.   Plate 91.   *CTW, p. 204*

Somewhat like a broad, open, leafy Lady's Smock (86), but with watercress-like
leaves, the leaflets all rather similar, oval, pale green; petals not quite so large
and nearly always white, anthers conspicuously violet, and slender beak to
pod. *Habitat:* Widespread but local in damp shady places; Ireland, only in N.
May–June.

88. **NARROW-LEAVED BITTERCRESS   *C. impatiens* L.
Plate 91.   *CTW, p. 205*

Not unlike a large bushy, untidy-looking, hairless Wavy Bittercress (89), but
has leaf-stalks clasping the straight stem with down-pointed bases, leaflets very
deeply toothed, and often no petals; anthers greenish-yellow. *Habitat:* Very
local in damp shady and rocky places in limestone districts, mainly in W England;
in Kent only on the banks of the R. Medway; not in Ireland. June–July.

89. WAVY BITTERCRESS   *C. flexuosa* Withering   Plate 91.   *CTW, p. 205*

Not always easy to separate from Hairy Bittercress (90), but is usually biennial,
hairier, thicker and taller, with stems leafier, often slightly zigzag and more

often branched, and ripe pods not or hardly overtopping the normally 6-stamened flowers. *Habitat:* Widespread and frequent in damp shady places and on mountain ledges. April–August.

90. HAIRY BITTERCRESS *C. hirsuta* L. Plate 91. *CTW, p. 206*

A common weed, a low, hairy annual, with straight, sometimes hairless stems, and slender hairy pinnate leaves, the root ones in a rosette, the lowest having rounded, the topmost narrower leaflets. Flowers small, white, usually 4-stamened; seed-pods cylindrical, erect, always overtopping the flowers and exploding with some violence when ripe. Often confused with Shepherd's Purse (72), which is usually larger and has heart-shaped seed-pods; with Thale Cress (110), which is very slender and has undivided leaves and spreading seed-pods; and with the stouter Wavy Bittercress (89). *Habitat:* Widespread on rocks, walls, dunes and other bare places; often a pest in gardens. March onwards.

91. **CORALROOT *Dentaria bulbifera* L. Plate 25. *CTW, p. 207*
Cardamine bulbifera (L.) Crantz

Like a taller stiffer woodland Lady's Smock (86), with no rosette and fewer, larger, dark green leaves; leaflets 3–7, narrow lanceolate, 1–1½ in. long, toothed; and dark purple bulbils at the base of the upper stem-leaves. (Lady's Smock may have bulbils at the base of the lower leaves.) Flowers rose-pink; seed-pods rarely ripened in Britain. *Habitat:* Local in damp loamy or sandy woods in the Chilterns and the Weald; occasionally established elsewhere. May.

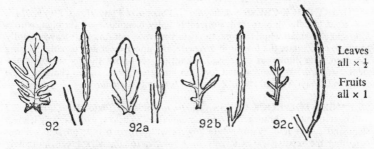

92   92a   92b   92c

Leaves all × ½

Fruits all × 1

92. COMMON WINTER-CRESS *Barbarea vulgaris* Brown Pl. 43. *CTW, 208*

A stocky hairless bitter-tasting mustard-like perennial, a foot or so high, with shining dark green leaves, the lowest pinnate with a large terminal lobe, the topmost (Fig.) broad, toothed, clasping the stem. Flowers yellow with petals twice as long as the hairless sepals. Seed-pods long, narrow, 4-sided, short-beaked, erect (Fig.). The Winter Cress of commerce is 98 × 98a. *Habitat:* Widespread, frequent by streams and roads, thinning out in Scotland. May–July.

92a. ***Small-flowered Land-cress, *B. stricta* Andrzcjewski, is a slenderer biennial with the topmost leaves much less deeply toothed (Fig.), the lowest with the terminal lobe broader than the leaflets. Petals smaller, little longer than the sepals, whose tips are hairy in bud. Pods stiffly appressed (Fig.). Rare.

92b. **Early Winter-cress, *B. intermedia* Boreau, flowers earlier, and has pinnately lobed upper leaves (Fig.); lowest leaves with the terminal lobe smaller; smaller flowers; and slightly longer pods (Fig.). Uncommon in waste places and seed-fields. April–May.

92c. **American Land-cress,** *B. verna* (Miller) Ascherson, a salad plant, has larger flowers, the petals much longer than the sepals, paler green leaves, more open growth, and longer, more spreading pods (Fig.); stem-leaves narrowly pinnate with only a small terminal lobe (Fig.). Not infrequent in SW England; rare elsewhere. April–June.

93. **NORTHERN ROCK-CRESS   *Cardaminopsis petraea* (L.) Hiitonen
Arabis petraea (L.) Lamarck   Plate 91.   *CTW, p. 211*
An attractive ' alpine ', not unlike a Bittercress (90), 4–8 in. high, but with lower leaves long-stalked and pinnately lobed, the topmost lanceolate and toothed, and rounded white or lilac petals.   *Habitat:* Widespread but local on mountains in N. Wales, Scotland and Ireland; also washed down on river shingle. June–August.

94. **GARDEN ARABIS   *Arabis caucasica* Willdenow   Pl. 90.   *CTW, p. 213*
A hoary mat-forming rockery perennial, 3–6 in. high, with large white fragrant flowers, the petals broad and suddenly narrowed at the base; leaves oblong, toothed, the upper clasping the stem. Seed-pods cylindrical, spreading.   *Habitat:* Established on limestone cliffs in Derbyshire; occasional elsewhere. April–May.
94a. ***Alpine Rock-cress,** *A. alpina* L., has smaller, unscented flowers, with less suddenly narrowed petals, and broader, greener leaves, their teeth usually deeper and extending further down the less narrowed base. Pods more erect. Found virtually only under one rock on the Coolins in Skye. May–June.

95. HAIRY ROCK-CRESS   *A. hirsuta* (L.) Scopoli   Plate 91.   *CTW, p. 214*
A rigid, usually unbranched, noticeably hairy biennial, 6–18 in. high, with a long spike of small white flowers, the petals narrow, not notched; leaves slightly toothed, lanceolate, the lowest in a rosette, the upper erect and usually clasping the stem. The numerous appressed cylindrical seed-pods thickly surround the stem.   *Habitat:* Widespread but local on limestone rocks and in chalk or dune grassland. May–August. (Incl. *A. brownii* Jordan ('*A. ciliata* ').)

96. ***BRISTOL ROCK-CRESS   *A. stricta* Hudson   Plate 91.   *CTW, p. 215*
A neat, usually unbranched 3–6-in. perennial, hairy below, with a nearly leafless stem and rather few creamy white flowers with broad petals, on stalks about equalling the sepals; leaves largely in a rosette, rough, dark green, pinnately lobed but less so above. Pods cylindrical, erect on short stalks.   *Habitat:* On limestone in the Avon Gorge at Bristol; very rare elsewhere. March–May.

97. **TOWER MUSTARD   *Turritis glabra* L.   Plate 43.   *CTW, p. 216*
A greyish narrow unbranched, stiffly erect biennial, 1–3 ft. high, with creamy yellow flowers, and a rosette of broadly toothed, lanceolate, yellowish hairy leaves often withering as the flowers appear; upper leaves narrowly arrow-shaped, untoothed, grey-waxy hairless, clasping the stem. Seed-pods cylindrical, closely and bushily appressed, much as in Hairy Rock-cress (95); seeds in 2 rows. *Habitat:* Very local on dry, sandy banks and in sandy freshly coppiced woods; not in Wales or Ireland. May–July. *Arabis glabra* (L.) Bernhardi.

98. WATERCRESS   *Rorippa nasturtium-aquaticum* (L.) Hayek   Pl. 93.   *CTW, 217*
The well known salad plant, the green or summer cress of commerce; a hairless creeping aquatic perennial, variable in size but usually 4–12 in. high, often

gregarious; stems hollow.   Leaves pinnate, green throughout the year, sometimes confused with Fool's Watercress (475). Flowers white with petals gradually narrowed to their base. Seed-pods cylindrical, with netted seeds in two rows. *Habitat:* Widespread and common in shallow fresh water and on mud. June onwards. *Nasturtium officinale* Brown.

98 × 98a. *R.* × *sterilis* Airy-Shaw, the brown or winter cress of commerce but totally different from Common Winter-cress (92), has leaves turning purple-brown in cold weather, and rarely sets seed, so that its pods are usually short and deformed. In some areas the commonest Watercress, often away from both parents.

98a. **Brown-leaved Watercress,** *R. microphylla* (Boenninghausen) Hylander (*N. microphyllum* (B.) Reichenbach), has stems more prostrate, leaves turning purple-brown in cold weather, larger petals abruptly narrowed to their base, and smaller, much more netted seeds in a single row in each pod, which is also usually longer, narrower and longer-stalked. Also widespread and common.

99. *CREEPING YELLOW CRESS   *R. sylvestris* (L.) Besser   Pl. 44.   *CTW, 219*

A hairless, often rather sprawling perennial, 6–18 in. high, with creeping stems, and leaves pinnately lobed, looking tattered from the well toothed leaflets. Flowers yellow, with petals longer than the half-spreading sepals. Seed-pods short, slender, cylindrical, beaked, pointing slightly upwards on short stalks. *Habitat:* Widespread and fairly frequent on river banks, damp or waste ground and as a garden weed. June onwards. *Nasturtium sylvestre* (L.) Brown.

100. MARSH YELLOW CRESS   *R. islandica* (Oeder) Borbás
Nasturtium palustre (L.) DC.   Plate 44.   *CTW, p. 220*

An annual, stiffer and more erect than the last species, with darker leaves, smaller flowers, the petals no longer than the spreading sepals, and much dumpier milk-bottle-shaped pods.   *Habitat:* Widespread and frequent by pond-sides and river banks; also in dry spots, especially railway tracks. June onwards.

101. *GREATER YELLOW CRESS   *R. amphibia* (L.) Besser   Pl. 44.   *CTW, 220*

Much larger than the two previous species, a hairless perennial 2–4 ft. high, with hollow stems and variable toothed or lobed lanceolate leaves, the upper often half-clasping the stem. Flowers large, yellow, with petals twice as long as sepals. Seed-pods very small, egg-shaped, many-seeded, shortly beaked, on long stalks. *Habitat:* Widespread and fairly frequent in vegetation by fresh water; rare in Scotland. June–September. *Nasturtium amphibium* (L.) Brown.

101a. ***Austrian Yellow Cress, *R. austriaca* (Crantz) Besser, has solid stems 1–2 ft. high, with much smaller flowers and long-beaked globular pods half the size. Rare but increasing on waste ground.

102. **SEA STOCK   *Matthiola incana* (L.) Brown   Plate 93.   *CTW, p. 222*

Very like its garden variety, the Brompton Stock, hoary grey, usually perennial, 9–15 in. high, with stem woody below, and stiff untoothed narrow lanceolate leaves. Flowers an inch or so across, from white to purple, fragrant, on stalks about equalling the sepals. Seed-pods cylindrical, downy.   *Habitat:* Very local and decreasing on sea-cliffs in the S; elsewhere a garden escape. May–July.

102a. ***Great Sea Stock, *M. sinuata* (L.) Brown, is stouter, much woollier, and bushier, and has black dots mixed with its down, toothed or lobed basal leaves and usually smaller darker flowers on shorter stalks. Cliffs and dunes in N Devon, S Ireland and Jersey, occasionally elsewhere. June–August.

103. *DAME'S VIOLET *Hesperis matronalis* L.   Plate 93.   *CTW, p. 224*

A stout green hairy perennial, 2–3 ft. high, with short-stalked toothed lanceolate leaves, very fragrant white or violet flowers ¾-in. across, and long cylindrical seed-pods curving upwards. *Habitat:* Widely naturalised; usually near gardens except in the extreme N. May–August.

104. TREACLE MUSTARD *Erysimum cheiranthoides* L.   Pl. 44.   *CTW, p. 226*

A slender yellow-flowered annual, 6 in. to 2 ft. high, with markedly long 4-angled seed-pods; downy with appressed hairs; leaves lanceolate, entire or only slightly toothed; petals twice as long as the erect sepals. *Habitat:* Widespread and fairly frequent on stream-banks and as a weed of stubble and waste ground; rare in Ireland. June onwards.

105. WALLFLOWER *Cheiranthus cheiri* L.   Plate 41.   *CTW, p. 227*

Well known, grown as a biennial, as the gardener's mainstay for spring bedding; a bushy perennial, 9–18 in. high, with stiff untoothed narrow lanceolate leaves covered with branched appressed hairs. Flowers nearly an inch across, fragrant, usually yellow, orange or brick-red. Pods cylindrical. *Habitat:* Widespread and frequent on cliffs, walls, and railway cuttings. March–June.

106. GARLIC MUSTARD *Alliaria petiolata* (Bieberstein) Cavara & Grande

Jack by the Hedge, Hedge Garlic; *A. officinalis* Bieb   Plate 93.   *CTW, p. 228*

A common spring hedgerow biennial, 1–3 ft. high, smelling of garlic when bruised, hairy only below, the fresh green leaves stalked, heart-shaped and toothed. Flowers white. Seed-pods ribbed, cylindrical, 2 in. long, on short stout stalks. *Habitat:* Widespread and usually plentiful in light shade in woods and on hedge-banks. April–June.

107. HEDGE MUSTARD *Sisymbrium officinale* (L.) Scopoli Pl. 44. *CTW, 229*

A common rigid, usually hairy mustard-like annual, 1–2 ft. high, usually with wide-angled branches; lower leaves pinnate with 3 or more broad, toothed lobes, the end one the largest; upper leaves smaller and with fewer lobes. Flowers tiny, yellow, with petals less than twice as long as the erect sepals. Seed-pods cylindrical, ½–¾-in. long, well below the flowers and closely appressed to the stem; usually downy, but occasionally hairless, when the whole plant is a paler green. *Habitat:* Widespread and common on bare and waste ground. May onwards.

108. *EASTERN ROCKET *S. orientale* L.   Plate 44.   *CTW, p. 231*

A loose weedy variable hairy annual; leaves pinnate with narrow lobes, the end one long; uppermost leaves often narrow lanceolate. Flowers yellow with petals twice as long as the erect or half-spreading sepals. Seed-pods cylindrical, 2–3 in. long, hairy below at first, spreading on very short thick stalks, not or little over-topping the flowers. *Habitat:* Spreading on waste ground in S England. May–August.

108*a*. ***London Rocket, *S. irio* L., is equally untidy, often shorter and hairless, and has all leaves pinnately lobed, the end lobe shorter; petals half the size and scarcely longer than the half-spreading sepals; pods half the size, slenderer, always hairless, narrowed at both ends, on longer thinner stalks, the younger ones freely overtopping the flowers. Much confused with the last and the next two species. A rare casual, chiefly near London and Dublin.

108*b*. ***False London Rocket, *S. loeselii* L., differs from London Rocket in having long bristly spreading hairs on at least the lower part of the stem; petals brighter yellow, twice as long as the finally spreading sepals; and shorter pods, somewhat recalling Treacle Mustard (104), never overtopping the flowers. An increasing casual of waste places, especially around London. July onwards.

109. *TUMBLING MUSTARD *S. altissimum* L. Plate 44. *CTW, p. 232*
A mustard-like annual, rather like Eastern Rocket (108), but hairy only below, usually taller, and much branched. Leaves all pinnate, with very much narrower lobes, especially the topmost. Flowers paler, often larger, with spreading sepals. Seed-pods 2–3 in. long, stiff, spreading, always hairless, on short thick stalks, not or scarcely overtopping the flowers. *Habitat:* Widespread and locally frequent in waste places. June–August.

110. THALE CRESS *Arabidopsis thaliana* (L.) Heynhold
Arabis thaliana L. Plate 91. *CTW, p. 233*
A hairy annual, 3–12 in. high, somewhat like a slender Shepherd's Purse (72), but with totally different cylindrical seed-pods; leaves lanceolate, sometimes slightly toothed, the lowest in a rosette, the upper not clasping the stem. Flowers small, white, on stalks longer than the sepals. *Habitat:* Widespread and frequent on walls and bare ground, especially on sandy soils. April–July.

111. ***GOLD OF PLEASURE *Camelina sativa* (L.) Crantz Pl. 44. *CTW, 234*
An almost hairless annual, 6 in. to 2 ft. high, with narrowly arrow-shaped leaves, whose basal points half-clasp the stem. Flowers small, yellow. Seed-pods egg-shaped, several-seeded, with a short tapering beak. *Habitat:* A constituent of bird-seed mixtures, occasional on rubbish-dumps. June onwards.
111a. ***Ball Mustard, *Neslia paniculata* (L.) Desvaux (*CTW, p. 194*), is minutely downy, with darker yellow flowers and small spreading 1-seeded globular pods, with a ridge from top to bottom and a very long beak. A rare casual.

112. FLIXWEED *Descurainia sophia* (L.) Prantl Plate 43. *CTW, p. 236*
An often very bushy annual, 1–3 ft. high, hairy below, with extremely finely divided 2–3-pinnate leaves, and tiny pale yellow flowers, the narrow petals no longer than the half-spreading sepals. Seed-pods slender, cylindrical, up to an inch long. *Habitat:* Widespread but rather uncommon in bare places. June–August. *Sisymbrium sophia* L.

MIGNONETTE FAMILY Resedaceae

113. WELD *Reseda luteola* L. Plate 50. *CTW, p. 237*
A hairless biennial, 2–4 ft. tall, stiffer and less bushy than Wild Mignonette (114), with narrow lanceolate, untoothed darker green, wavy-edged leaves. Flowers in long, narrow spikes, yellowish-green. Seed-pods globular, open at the top, with three distinct points. *Habitat:* Widespread and locally common on disturbed ground, especially on chalk and limestone. June–Sept. Dyer's Rocket.

114. WILD MIGNONETTE *R. lutea* L. Plate 50. *CTW, p. 238*
A pale green, floppy biennial, 6–12 in. high, differing from the sweetly fragrant Garden Mignonette (*R. odorata* L.), which has orange anthers, in its greenish-yellow, hardly fragrant flowers with yellow anthers, and its pinnate wavy-edged leaves. Pods erect oblong, with three short points. *Habitat:* Locally common in

open grassy places, typically on chalk and limestone in England and Wales, thinning out northwards. June onwards.

114*a*. ****White Mignonette**, *R. alba* L., is stouter, darker green, usually much taller and often perennial; and has long spikes of white flowers with peach-coloured anthers and pods almost always with four points. A widespread but uncommon casual.

114*b*. *****Corn Mignonette**, *R. phyteuma* L., a low floppy annual, differs from Wild Mignonette in its white flowers and fatter drooping pods with more prominent sepals, and from the stout White Mignonette in its pods having three sharp points. A rare weed of loose chalky soils in the S, occasionally persisting.

VIOLET FAMILY   Violaceae

SMALL NON-WOODY plants with long-stalked solitary flowers, similar to the garden Violets, Violas and Pansies, with 5 irregular petals, the lower ones spurred, blue-violet, yellow or white; sepals 5, unequal, with persistent appendages. Fruits roughly egg-shaped. Hybrids are frequent.

The Violets (115–122) are all perennials, mostly with toothed heart-shaped leaves. As well as their showy spring flowers they have inconspicuous petalless later ones which are the main seed-bearers. The Pansies (123–125) are sometimes annuals, their leaves toothed and generally broad lanceolate, with very prominent leaf-like stipules at the base of their stalks; flowers flatter. The Water-Violet (616) is quite different, and belongs to the Primrose Family.

KEY TO VIOLETS AND PANSIES   (Nos. 115–125)

PLANT *annual* 124, 125; *creeping* 115, 121, 122, 123; *with central non-flowering rosette* 117, 118.

LEAVES *broad lanceolate* 120, 121, 123, 124, 125; *heart-shaped* 115, 116, 117, 118, 119, 121; *kidney-shaped* 117*a*, 122; *all from stem-base* 115, 116, 122.

FLOWERS *blue* 119; *blue-violet* 115, 116, 117, 118, 123, 124; *lilac* 115, 118, 120, 121, 122; *pink* 115; *apricot* 115; *yellow* 115, 121, 123, 124; *cream* 121, 125; *white* 115, others occasionally; *fragrant* 115; *with rounded petals* 121, 122; *with blunt sepals* 115, 116, 122.

SPUR *same colour as flower* 115, 116, 122, 123, 124, 125; *violet* 118; *yellowish* 117, 119; *whitish* 117; *greenish* 120, 121; *notched* 117.

FRUITS *downy* 115, 116, 117*a*.

115. SWEET VIOLET   *Viola odorata* L.   Plate 1.   *CTW, p. 241*

Our only fragrant Violet, with long runners and short down-turned or no hairs on the 2–4-in. leaf- and flower-stalks, which arise in tufts directly from the stem base; leaves heart-shaped, downy, enlarging in summer. Flowers usually violet, often white, occasionally lilac, pink, yellow or apricot; sepals blunt. Hybridises with the next species. *Habitat:* Widespread and common in hedge-banks and shady places. March–May, sometimes again in autumn.

116. HAIRY VIOLET   *V. hirta* L.   Plate 1.   *CTW, p. 242*

Can resemble Sweet Violet (115), but is unscented and has no runners; leaves longer, narrower and hairier, especially when young, their stalks with long spreading hairs. Flowers nearly always pale blue-violet; late-flowering forms have narrower petals and a very short spur. Can be separated from the Dog Violets (117–120) by its blunt sepals. *Habitat:* Widespread and locally common in dry turf, especially on chalk and limestone; rare in Ireland. March–May, sometimes again in autumn. (Incl. *V. calcarea* (Babington) Gregory).

117. COMMON DOG VIOLET *V. riviniana* Reichenbach Pl. 1. *CTW, p. 244*
Generally much the commonest wild Violet, easily separated from the last two species by its pointed sepals and hairless or only slightly downy leaves and stalks, not arising from stem-base; leaves heart-shaped, as broad as long, mostly in a central non-flowering rosette. Flowers blue-violet, the petals usually overlapping, with a stout curved pale, often creamy spur, notched at the tip; appendages of sepals enlarging in fruit. Hybridises with the next four species (117a–120). *Habitat:* Widespread and plentiful in many kinds of wooded and grassy places, and on mountains. April–June, and sometimes again in autumn.
117a. ***Teesdale Violet, *V. rupestris* Schmidt, the only Dog Violet with a downy fruit, is smaller and more downy all over, and has rounder leaves, the stipules at their base broader and with fewer, shorter teeth. Confined to the sugar limestone on Widdybank Fell, Teesdale. May.

118. WOOD DOG VIOLET *V. reichenbachiana* Jordan Plate 1. *CTW, p. 245*
Very like the Common Dog Violet (117), but rather less robust, with somewhat smaller, narrower, paler, more upright-looking flowers, their narrower petals not overlapping, and the straight spur dark violet and not notched; appendages to sepals smaller and less prominent in fruit. Leaves paler, more pointed, longer than broad. *Habitat:* Widespread but less plentiful in woods and hedge-banks; most frequent in S England, and in woods on chalk. Starts flowering a fortnight earlier, at the end of March. ' *V. sylvestris*'.

119. HEATH DOG VIOLET *V. canina* L. Plate 1. *CTW, p. 245*
Can be separated from Common Dog Violet (117) by its bluer flowers, often with a yellow spur, by the appendages to the sepals not enlarging in fruit, and by having no central non-flowering rosette of leaves, which are heart-shaped, but are thicker, darker and distinctly longer than broad. Hybridises with the next two species. *Habitat:* Widespread and often common in dry turf, especially on sandy heaths; rarely in fens. April–June, later than Common Dog Violet.

120. **PALE HEATH VIOLET *V. lactea* Smith Plate 1. *CTW, p. 246*
Like a tall, pale-flowered Heath Dog Violet (119), with broad lanceolate leaves wedge-shaped below, and petals pale milky blue, sometimes almost white, the spur short and greenish. *Habitat:* More restricted, only on heaths; very local in the S, chiefly in the SW, and in SW Ireland. May–June, our latest Violet.

121. ***FEN VIOLET *V. stagnina* Kitaibel Plate 1. *CTW, p. 247*
An almost hairless Violet, 4–12 in. high, with a creeping rootstock and narrowly triangular leaves, much longer than broad; rounded bluish-white or yellowish petals; and a short greenish spur hardly longer than the large appendages of the pointed sepals. *Habitat:* Very local in long herbage in fens in E and N England and in damp places on limestone (turloughs) in W Ireland. May–June.

122. MARSH VIOLET *V. palustris* L. Plate 1. *CTW, p. 248*
A neat short, hairless Violet, 2–4 in. high, with a creeping rootstock; conspicuously rounded almost kidney-shaped, leaves; and small pale lilac flowers veined dark purple, their spur hardly longer than the appendages to the blunt sepals.

Leaf- and flower-stalks arising direct from stem-base. *Habitat:* Widespread but local in acid marshes, bogs, and boggy woods, at various altitudes; common in the N, much more local in SE England. April–July.

123. *MOUNTAIN PANSY *V. lutea* Hudson   Plate 42.   *CTW, p. 249*
    One of our prettiest wild flowers, like a small Garden Pansy, with flowers yellow, violet or both; an almost hairless perennial, with a creeping root stock; can be told from the annual Heartsease (124) by its larger flowers, often an inch or more long, with the spur usually 2–3 times as long as the appendages of the sepals. The Garden Viola (*V. cornuta* L.) and its hybrids have much broader, more deeply divided stipules at the base of the leaves. *Habitat:* Widespread and locally plentiful in short turf in N England, Wales and Scotland, especially in hilly districts; rare in Ireland. May-August. (Incl. *V. saxatilis* Schmidt).
    123*a*. ****Seaside Pansy,** *V. curtisii* Forster, is tufted and half-prostrate, and has smaller, more numerous and always yellow flowers. Plentiful on some coastal dunes in the N and W, and in Ireland; and on E Anglian heaths. April onwards.

124. HEARTSEASE *V. tricolor* L.   Plate 1.   *CTW, p. 249*
    A variable annual, sometimes like Mountain Pansy (123), but is taller and leafier, and has no runners and smaller flowers, usually less than an inch across, their spur rather longer than the appendages; petals purple, yellow or both, longer than the sepals. Self-sown degenerate forms of the numerous Garden Pansies (usually *V.* × *wittrockiana* Gams) have all petals overlapping and are usually more richly and variously coloured. Hybridises with the next species. *Habitat:* Widespread and locally common in cultivated and grassy places. April onwards. Wild Pansy.

125. FIELD PANSY *V. arvensis* Murray   Plate 87.   *CTW, p. 251*
    An extremely variable annual, differing from Heartsease (124) in its insignificant flowers, less than ½-in. long, with the sepals longer than the small cream-coloured petals, which often have patches of orange and streaks of pale violet; spur about equalling appendages. *Habitat:* Widespread and common in arable fields. April onwards. (Incl. *V. nana* (DC.) Godron).

 MILKWORT FAMILY Polygalaceae

Low, OFTEN PROSTRATE, slender, hairless, variable perennials, with leafy stems, the leaves unstalked, lanceolate, usually alternate. Flowers in short spikes, oblong, about ¼-in. long, of various shades of blue, pink or white; sepals 5, the two inner large and petal-like on either side of the smaller 3–5 true petals (Fig.); stamens prominent, petal-like, in two bundles of four, joined in a Y. Fruits flat, inversely heart-shaped, slightly winged.

126. COMMON MILKWORT *Polygala vulgaris* L.   Plate 5.   *CTW, p. 253*
    (incl. *P. oxyptera* Reichenbach)
    The commonest Milkwort, with scattered, alternate pointed leaves, broadest at or below the middle, the lower shorter and broader than the upper and not forming a rosette. Flowers usually blue, but often mauve, pink, white, or white tipped magenta or blue. Fruits shorter than the inner sepals. *Habitat:* Widespread and common in drier grassland. May onwards.

127. HEATH MILKWORT *P. serpyllifolia* Hose   Plate 5.   *CTW, p. 255*
   P. serpyllacea Weihe
   Like a small Common Milkwort (126), but with at least the lower leaves opposite and more crowded, and flowers in shorter spikes, most often dark blue, or dark pink. Northern plants often look different from southern ones.   *Habitat:* Widespread and common on heaths and in dry acid grassland. May–September.

128. *CHALK MILKWORT *P. calcarea* Schultz   Plate 5.   *CTW, p. 255*
   A lovely Milkwort, with flowers usually gentian blue but sometimes pale blue, pink or white. Leaves all rather thick, and blunt, alternate, the lower stalked, broadest at the tip, grouped in an irregular false rosette from the loss of the leaves on the stem below; upper leaves smaller, shorter, and broadest above the middle. Fruits broader than the inner sepals.   *Habitat:* Locally common in chalk and limestone turf in the S half of England, differing somewhat at the extremes of its range near Dover and in S Lincs. April to June.

129. ***KENTISH MILKWORT *P. austriaca* Crantz   Plate 5.   *CTW, p. 256*
   A small, dingy, slender Milkwort, with a few inconspicuous, slaty-mauve flowers, stem-leaves rather broad, the lower ones larger, in a rosette. Fruits broader than the inner sepals.   *Habitat:* Extremely local in open chalk grassland, recently seen only in Kent. May–June.
   129a. ***Yorkshire Milkwort**, *P. amara* L., is very similar but more erect and compact, with larger pink or blue flowers and rather more pointed stem-leaves. Confined to damp limestone grassland in Upper Teesdale and the Craven Pennines. May–July.

ST. JOHN'S WORT FAMILY   Hypericaceae

PERENNIALS or undershrubs, whose untoothed opposite leaves have translucent veins and sometimes also dots. Flowers usually in clusters, yellow, with a rather furry appearance due to the many stamens, which are united at the base into 3 or 5 bundles; petals and sepals 5, often black-dotted. Fruits usually dry.

130. *TUTSAN *Hypericum androsaemum* L.   Plate 41.   *CTW, p. 258*
   A bushy hairless undershrub, with 2-winged, often reddish stems 1–3 ft. high, and large broad oval half-evergreen leaves, faintly aromatic if crushed. Flowers yellow, nearly an inch across; sepals unequal. Fruit a succulent berry, green, then red, finally purplish-black.   *Habitat:* Widespread but rather local in shady places and on cliff ledges. June–August.

131. ROSE OF SHARON *H. calycinum* L.   Plate 41.   *CTW, p. 259*
   Much the largest-flowered St John's Wort, a creeping, carpeting, evergreen undershrub up to a foot high, unmistakable with its usually solitary yellow flowers about 3 in. across, and very numerous stamens with red anthers; styles 5. Leaves elliptical. Fruits rarely ripening.   *Habitat:* Not infrequently naturalised in shrubberies and on banks. June onwards.

132. COMMON ST JOHN'S WORT *H. perforatum* L.   Pl. 41.   *CTW, p. 259*
   Generally the commonest St John's Wort, a hairless perennial, 1–2 ft. high, with golden-yellow flowers. Best separated from the two other common erect hairless St John's Worts (133, 135) by its combination of stems with only two raised lines, small oblong leaves with many transparent dots, and black dots

usually on the petals and sometimes on the pointed sepals. *Habitat:* Widespread and common in hedge-banks and scrub, but local in N. July onwards.

133. SQUARE ST JOHN'S WORT   *H. tetrapterum* Fries   Pl. 41.   *CTW, p. 260*
A thick-set hairless St John's Wort, with square 4-winged stems 1–2 ft. high, transparent-dotted leaves almost clasping the stem, and smallish pale yellow flowers with narrow undotted pointed sepals. Hybridises with 132.   *Habitat:* Widespread and common in damp places. July–Sept. '*H. quadrangulum*'.

133a. **Wavy St John's Wort,** *H. undulatum* Schousboe, is slenderer and more open, with slight wings on the stem, wavy edges to the leaves, and fewer, brighter flowers with largish petals red beneath and the broader sepals dotted. Rare in boggy places in SW England and W Wales.

133b. *Imperforate St John's Wort,** *H. maculatum* Crantz (*H. dubium* Leers), has the stems square but not winged and hardly clasped by the usually undotted leaves; and larger darker flowers with broader blunt sepals. Local and prefers shadier places on heavier soils.

134. TRAILING ST JOHN'S WORT   *H. humifusum* L.   Pl. 41.   *CTW, p. 260*
A prostrate hairless perennial with thin wiry stems, and small, pale green elliptical leaves, often with black dots on the edges beneath, the upper also usually with a few transparent dots. Flowers small, along the stem, the yellow petals with a few black dots and rarely much longer than the sometimes black-dotted unequal sepals.   *Habitat:* Widespread and locally common in heathy places and open woodland. June onwards.

134a. ***Flax-leaved St John's Wort,** *H. linarifolium* Vahl, can look very similar, but is stouter, stiffer and often more erect, with narrower leaves, the margins often inrolled, and less or not dotted, and terminal heads of larger flowers, the petals often red beneath and 2–3 times as long as the equal sepals. Hybridises with the last species. Rare on dry rocky slopes in SW England, Wales and the Channel Is.

135. ELEGANT ST JOHN'S WORT   *H. pulchrum* L.   Plate 41.   *CTW, p. 261*
A dainty perennial, 9–18 in. high, or rarely prostrate, with short erect branches, and a few pairs of small oblong to heart-shaped leaves. Differs from the other two common hairless, erect St John's Worts (132, 133) in its combination of stem not ridged or winged and half-clasped by the leaves, which are heart-shaped below, transparent-dotted and often with inrolled margins, with rich yellow flowers, the petals red beneath and edged with red and black dots, and small broad, blunt sepals also edged with black dots.   *Habitat:* Widespread and locally common in heathy places. July–August.

136. HAIRY ST JOHN'S WORT   *H. hirsutum* L.   Plate 41.   *CTW, p. 261*
The only common downy St John's Wort of dry places, yellow-green and 1–3 ft. high, with elliptical, transparent-dotted leaves, and large clusters of pale yellow flowers, with stalked black dots on the margins of the pointed sepals, and sometimes also on the petals.   *Habitat:* Widespread and locally common in shady places, especially on chalk, limestone, and clay. July–September.

137. *PALE ST JOHN'S WORT   *H. montanum* L.   Plate 41.   *CTW, p. 262*
Stiffer than the last species, with fewer and shorter, or no branches, and less hairy stems; leaves broader, smoother, almost hairless above, and with no trans-

parent dots but a row of black dots on the margin beneath, and shorter fewer-flowered clusters of pale flowers. *Habitat:* Local in shady places, usually on chalk or limestone, in England and Wales; very rare in Scotland. July–September.

138. *MARSH ST JOHN'S WORT *H. elodes* L. Plate 46. *CTW, p. 262*
A weak low greyish mat-forming perennial, not obviously like a St John's Wort, with lower stems creeping and rooting, very downy roundish leaves, and sepals of resinous scented yellow flowers joined below and fringed with red dots. *Habitat:* Widespread but local in acid bog pools, and ponds, commonest in the N and W. June-September.

ROCK-ROSE FAMILY Cistaceae

139. ***ANNUAL ROCK-ROSE *Tuberaria guttata* (L.) Fourreau
Helianthemum guttatum (L.) Miller Plate 46. *CTW, p. 263*
A low downy annual, not obviously like a Rock-rose, with narrow lanceolate 3-veined unstalked leaves, and yellow flowers, whose small petals, often with a red spot at the base, drop early in the day; sepals 5, unequal, black-dotted. Fruits egg-shaped, on down-turned stalks. *Habitat:* Rare in dry places near the sea in N Wales, W Ireland and the Channel Is. May–August.

140. COMMON ROCK-ROSE *H. chamaecistus* Miller Plate 38. *CTW, p. 264*
Well-known, like the next species, in gardens in several forms and colour varieties; the inch-wide 5-petalled flowers of the wild plant are almost always a good yellow, but sometimes smaller and paler. A low, open, often prostrate, under-shrub, with narrow lanceolate 1-veined leaves green above and downy white beneath, on stalks shorter than the very narrow stipules at their base. Hybridises with the next two species. *Habitat:* Widespread and common in grassy places on chalk and limestone; also on acid soils in Scotland; in Ireland confined to one tiny patch in Donegal. May–September.

141. ***WHITE ROCK-ROSE *H. apenninum* (L.) Miller Pl. 84. *CTW, p. 265*
Very like a white Common Rock-rose (140), but is larger and its leaves are downy grey on both sides, with inrolled margins, the lower on stalks equalling the stipules. *Habitat:* Confined to limestone turf near Weston-super-Mare and Torquay, but there plentiful. May–July. *H. polifolium* Miller.

142. **HOARY ROCK-ROSE *H. canum* (L.) Baumgartner Pl. 38. *CTW, 265*
A compact, closely prostrate mat-forming undershrub, with small narrow silvery leaves that vary in size and hairiness from one locality to another, and erect stems bearing small yellow flowers. Unlike the last two species has no stipules. *Habitat:* Very rare on limestone rocks in Wales and N England; abundant round Galway Bay. May–June.

TAMARISK FAMILY Tamaricaceae

143. *TAMARISK *Tamarix gallica* L. Plate 17. *CTW, p. 266*
A graceful evergreen shrub, 6–10 ft. high, with reddish twigs and feathery, pale green foliage, the minute leaves overlapping and, unlike the resinous Cypresses which they somewhat resemble, alternate. Flowers small, in spikes, the pink petals persisting in fruit. *Habitat:* A frequent hedge-plant by the sea in the S. July onwards. (Incl. *T. anglica* Webb).

SEA-HEATH FAMILY Frankeniaceae

144. **SEA-HEATH *Frankenia laevis* L.   Plate 27. *CTW, p. 267*
    A dark green, prostrate, often matted, woody perennial, with short fleshy, whorled linear leaves with inrolled margins, not unlike those of the true Heaths (591–595), but its small, solitary crinkly pink-petalled flowers open flat. *Habitat:* Local in the drier parts of salt-marshes from the Wash to the Solent. July–August.

WATERWORT FAMILY Elatinaceae

145. **WATERWORT *Elatine hexandra* (Lapierre) DC.   Pl. 27. *CTW, p. 268*
    A very small, very charming, but elusive, creeping, freely rooting aquatic annual, often completely submerged. Frequently all that can be seen of it is a serried row of short, narrow, fresh green opposite leaves above the mud, its delightful stalked, 6-stamened pink flowers not visible at all; sometimes in a thick mat, often turning red. Stipules at base of leaves tiny. Seeds nearly straight. *Habitat:* Widespread but scarce in or by peaty pools and lakes. July–August.
    145*a*. ***Eight-stamened Waterwort**, *E. hydropiper* L., is not always easy to distinguish, but has longer leaves narrowed at the base, 8 stamens and hooked seeds, and may have shorter or no flower-stalks. Rarer, least so in Co. Down.

PINK FAMILY Caryophyllaceae

NON-WOODY PLANTS with stems characteristically swollen at their junctions with the opposite pairs of usually untoothed and unstalked leaves. Flowering shoots repeatedly forked, with a flower in the centre of each fork. Flowers with 4–5 separate petals, or none, and 4–5 sepals which are often joined at the base, sometimes forming a tube or a more or less inflated bladder. Fruits dry, many-seeded.

146. BLADDER CAMPION *Silene vulgaris* (Moench) Garcke
    S. cucubalus Wibel   Plate 85. *CTW, p. 275*
    A shiny greyish-green, usually hairless perennial, 9 in. to 2 ft. high, shorter and bushier than White Campion (156), with pointed oval, often wavy-edged leaves and no non-flowering shoots. Flowers white, very rarely pink, with 5 very deeply cleft petals and the calyx inflated into a purplish or yellowish net-veined bladder; styles 3. *Habitat:* Widespread and common in thinly grassy ground. June–August.

147. SEA CAMPION *S. maritima* Withering   Plate 85. *CTW, p. 276*
    Much shorter than Bladder Campion (146), 6 in. or so high, but unbranched and with a mat of non-flowering shoots; smaller and thicker waxier leaves; and larger flowers, usually solitary and with broader petals. *Habitat:* Widespread and common on cliffs and shingle by the sea; inland rare and chiefly on mountains. June–August.

148. **SAND CATCHFLY *S. conica* L.   Plate 22. *CTW, p. 277*
    A neat grey, stickily downy annual, 2–9 in. high, with narrow leaves, a strongly veined inflated calyx concealing the fruit, and flowers which may be rich or washy pink, with small, notched petals; styles 3. *Habitat:* Local in sandy places, chiefly near the coast in the S. May–July.

149. *SMALL-FLOWERED CATCHFLY *S. anglica* L.
(incl. *S. gallica* L. and *S. quinquevulnera* L.) Plate 85. *CTW, p. 278*
A hairy annual about a foot high, with sticky stems and narrow upper and broader lower leaves. Flowers small, with calyx sticky (inflated in fruit) and narrow, shallowly notched petals, which are oftenest dirty white, but sometimes larger and pink, or crimson with a white edge. *Habitat:* Widespread but scarce in fields and waste places; frequent in the Channel Is. June onwards.

150. **MOSS CAMPION *S. acaulis* (L.) Jacquin Plate 23. *CTW, p. 279*
One of our most attractive perennial alpines, its rose-pink flowers often starring the cushions of tiny pointed leaves, which end in a more prominent tooth than Cyphal (185), male and female flowers sometimes on different plants. *Habitat:* Plentiful on some mountains in Scotland, descending to sea-level in the N; also in Snowdonia, the Lake District and NW Ireland. June–July.

151. **BRECKLAND CATCHFLY *S. otites* (L.) Wibel Plate 78. *CTW, p. 280*
An unbranched, stickily hairy perennial, 9–18 in. high, looking very unlike other Catchflies, with dark green leaves, broadest towards the tip, in rosettes with a few up the stem. Flowers in whorls in broad spikes, small, yellowish-green, with 5 narrow petals; 10 prominent stamens on male plants; 3 styles on female ones. *Habitat:* Local on grass heaths in the Breckland. June–July.

152. **NOTTINGHAM CATCHFLY *S. nutans* L. Plate 85. *CTW, p. 280*
(incl. *S. dubia* Herbich)
A variable, often stickily hairy perennial, 9 in. to 2 ft. high, with long-stalked basal leaves broadest near the tip. Flowers often drooping, in very open clusters, night-scented and night-opening, whitish or pinkish, with narrow, deeply cleft, rolled back petals, each with a pair of small scales towards the base; styles 3. Variable. *Habitat:* Widespread but very local on rocks, sea cliffs, and in other dry places, including shingle, chiefly in the S; not in Ireland. May–July.

153. **RED CATCHFLY *Viscaria vulgaris* Bernhardi Plate 14. *CTW, p. 283*
Lychnis viscaria L.
A tufted perennial, a foot or so high, with hairless, often purplish, sticky stems, almost hairless lanceolate leaves, and broad spikes of red flowers, the notched petals each with a pair of prominent scales towards the base; calyx hairless, 5-veined. *Habitat:* Rare in rocky places in Wales and Scotland. May–June.
153a. ***Alpine Catchfly, *V. alpina* (L.) Don, is not sticky and has much shorter stems, most of the leaves at the base, and flowers in a terminal cluster. their petals deeply cleft. Known only high in the Lake District and Angus, June–July. *L. alpina* L.

154. *NIGHT-SCENTED CATCHFLY *Melandrium noctiflorum* (L.) Fries
Silene noctiflora L. Plate 85. *CTW, p. 284*
Like a smallish, rather starved, stickily hairy, less branched White Campion (156), but with pinkish petals often rolled up during the day and showing only their yellowish undersides; at night the flowers are fragrant. 3 styles and 10 stamens together. Fruits with 6 recurved teeth. *Habitat:* Widespread but local in cornfields; rare in Ireland. July–September.

155. RED CAMPION *M. dioicum* (L.) Cosson & Germain
Lychnis dioica L. ; *M. rubrum* (Weigand) Garcke   Plate 14.   *CTW, p. 284*
A hairy or shaggy perennial, 1–2 ft. high, with pointed oval leaves, the lower narrowed to a wing on the stalk. Flowers in clusters, large, bright rosy-pink, unscented, the cleft petals each with a pair of white scales towards the base; calyx with short teeth, often red; the 10 stamens and 5 styles on different plants. Fruits with 10 teeth rolled back when ripe. Hybridises with the next species. *Habitat:* Widespread and often common in woods and hedge-banks, also on sea-cliffs and mountains; rarer and decreasing in E Anglia. April onwards.

156. WHITE CAMPION *M. album* (Miller) Garcke   Plate 85.   *CTW, p. 285*
Differs from the occasional pure white Red Campion (155) in being usually larger and more branched, with larger flowers on longer stalks, lower leaf-stalks unwinged, the teeth of the greener calyx slenderer and twice as long, flowers slightly fragrant at night, and larger fruits with more or less erect teeth. Confusable with the smaller Bladder Campion (146). *Habitat:* Widespread and locally common on disturbed ground; spreading, especially in the S and E. May onwards. *Lychnis alba* Mill. (Incl. *M. macrocarpum* (Willkomm) Boissier & Reuter.)

157. RAGGED ROBIN *Lychnis flos-cuculi* L.   Plate 14.   *CTW, p. 286*
Somewhat like a slenderer, much less hairy Red Campion (155), but with 'ragged' red petals, much more deeply cleft into 4 narrow and unequal lobes, the styles and stamens together, lanceolate leaves, and fruits with 5 teeth. *Habitat:* Widespread and common in marshes, fens and wet woods. May–July.

158. **CORN-COCKLE *Agrostemma githago* L.   Plate 14.   *CTW, p. 287*
A softly hairy annual, 2–4 ft. high, with narrow lanceolate leaves and solitary campion-like reddish-purple flowers, an inch or two across, the calyx-tube slightly inflated and with long narrow teeth, which protrude well beyond the unnotched petals, giving a rather starfish effect. *Habitat:* Increasingly scarce in arable fields. June–August. *Lychnis githago* (L.) Scopoli.

159. *DEPTFORD PINK *Dianthus armeria* L.   Plate 22.   *CTW, p. 290*
A slightly downy, dark green annual, with stiff stems 4–18 in. high, narrow lanceolate leaves, and small crowded heads of small, unscented, bright pink flowers, the toothed petals often with darker or paler spots, and hidden in bud among the long narrow sepal-like bracts. The hairless garden Sweet William (*D. barbatus* L.), which sometimes escapes, has similarly crowded but broader flat heads of much larger flowers of various colours, and very much broader leaves. *Habitat:* Widespread but scarce in dry open grassy places; not in Ireland. June–August.

160. ***CHEDDAR PINK *D. gratianopolitanus* Villars Plate 22. *CTW, p. 292*
An attractive rarity, often grown in gardens; a low hairless greyish mat-forming perennial, with short linear leaves minutely rough at the edge, and solitary pink flowers smelling of cloves, the toothed petals hairy towards the base; styles 2. *Habitat:* On sunny cliffs and rocks in Cheddar Gorge; rarely naturalised elsewhere. June–July. *D. caesius* Smith.
  160a. ***Common Pink**, *D. plumarius* L., is often larger and branched, with pale mauve or white, almost hairless petals, much more deeply cut; calyx with longer teeth. A denizen on a very few ancient walls. July.

160*b*. ***Clove Pink, *D. caryophyllus* L., is still stouter and more branched, and has hairless petals toothed like Cheddar Pink, a longer calyx and leaves smooth at the edges. Very rarely naturalised on walls. July.

161. **MAIDEN PINK   *D. deltoides* L.   Plate 22.   *CTW, p. 292*
A sprawling tenuous, shortly hairy, often greyish perennial, 6–12 in. high, with a few short non-flowering shoots and rough-edged linear leaves. Flowers pink, freckled with darker or paler spots, with petals toothed, not fragrant; they close in dull weather when the plant merges into the surrounding grass; styles 2. *Habitat:* Widespread but very local in dry grassy places. June–August.

162. SOAPWORT   *Saponaria officinalis* L.   Plate 25.   *CTW, p. 293*
A pale green, hairless sprawling creeping perennial, with thick brittle stems 1–2 ft. long, and lanceolate leaves. Flowers pink, an inch across, with a long, scarcely inflated calyx; double flowers are not uncommon; styles 2. Fruits with 4 teeth.   *Habitat:* Widespread and fairly frequent, especially on roadsides and by streams. July–September.

163. ***CHILDLING PINK   *Kohlrauschia prolifera* (L.) Kunth Pl. 22.   *CTW, 294*
Differs from all other Pinks by the large brownish chaffy bracts enfolding the close cluster of small pale pink flowers, which usually emerge one or two at a time; petals notched. A thin, hairless, little branched, greyish annual, 4–12 in. high, with short, rough-edged, linear leaves.   *Habitat:* Rare, mainly on shingle and dunes near the sea, in S England and Jersey. July–September. *Dianthus prolifer* L.

KEY TO CHICKWEED-LIKE FLOWERS

This key covers Nos. 164–197, the smaller, mostly white-flowered members of the Pink Family (see p. 30), with a greater or less resemblance to Common Chickweed (169). All have the opposite leaves and somewhat jointed stems typical of the family. Somewhat chickweed-like plants in other families include Fairy Flax (231), All-seed (232) and Knotgrass (527).

PLANT *over 1 ft. high* 168, 169*bc*, 170, 171, 172, 173, 187, 190; *cushioned* 177, 179, 181, 182, 185; *conspicuously hairy or downy* 165, 166, 167, 170, 171, 174, 175, 188, 194, 195; *with sticky hairs* 167*a–e*, 190; *with lines of hairs on stem* 164, 169; *with reddish stems* 167*d*, 192*b*, 194, 196; *creeping*, 165, 186.
LEAVES *broad* 166, 167, 168, 169, 173, 179*a*, 186, 187, 188, 189, 193, 196; *fleshy* 176, 186, 192; *purplish* 166*b*, 167*d*, 176; *stalked* 168, 169, 187, 193; *whorled* 190, 191, 192, 193; *with short bristle at tip* 175, 177, 178, 179, 191; *with stipules at base* 190, 191, 192, 193, 194, 195, 196; *topmost all whitish* 172, 190, 193; *topmost with whitish edges* 166, 167, 171, 173.
FLOWERS *conspicuous* 164, 165, 166, 168, 169*b*, 170, 171, 180, 181, 189; *greenish* 169*b*, 175, 176, 177, 182, 185, 193, 195, 196, 197; *pinkish* 191, 192.
PETALS *cleft to base* 168, 169, 170, 171, 172, 173; *cleft to half-way* 164, 165, 166, 167; *notched* 167*e*, 193; *none* 169, 173, 175, 176, 177, 185, 194, 195, 197.
SEPALS *all green* 173, 175, 176, 177, 178, 179, 180; *all white* 196.

164. **STARWORT MOUSE-EAR   *Cerastium cerastoides* (L.) Britton
C. trigynum Villars   Plate 85.   *CTW, p. 297*
A mountain counterpart of the Field Mouse-ear (165), with smaller flowers and narrower petals; hairless except for two lines of hairs on alternate sides of the

stem; styles usually 3. *Habitat:* Local, high in the Lake District and Scotland, especially the Cairngorms. July–August.

165. *FIELD MOUSE-EAR   *C. arvense* L.   Plate 85.   *CTW, p. 297*

A low spreading perennial, often forming broad patches, downy all over, with the large white flowers of the Greater Stitchwort (170), but with less deeply cleft petals, combined with the stems and short narrow leaves of a Mouse-ear; styles 5. *Habitat:* Widespread but local in dry grassy or bare places on chalk, limestone or gravel. April–August.

165*a*. *Snow-in-Summer, *C. tomentosum* L., is almost white with short woolly hairs, and has a mat of longer leaves, longer and erecter flower-stalks, and larger flowers with narrower petals. A familiar far-spreading rockery plant, often naturalised. May–August.

166. **ALPINE MOUSE-EAR *C. alpinum* L.   Plate 85.   *CTW, p. 298*

Has the large white flowers of the Field Mouse-ear (167), but its white hairs are even shaggier than Snow-in-Summer (165*a*). A low, often tufted perennial, with oval leaves, the upper having whitish margins; styles 5. *Habitat:* Not uncommon on mountains from Snowdonia northwards. June–August.

166*a*. ***Arctic Mouse-ear, *C. nigrescens* Watson (*C. edmondstonii* (Wats.) Murbeck & Ostenfeld; incl. *C. arcticum* Lange), is intermediate between Starwort (164) and Alpine Mouse-ears, and greener and less shaggy than the latter, with narrower leaves, the upper all green. Rare in Snowdonia, on some Scottish mountains, and near the sea in Unst.

167. COMMON MOUSE-EAR   *C. holosteoides* Fries   Plate 86.   *CTW, p. 300*

A ubiquitous hairy, but not sticky, variable chickweed-like perennial, often flowering when very young, with leafy non-flowering shoots, and unstalked darker green leaves thicker than Common Chickweed (169), the upper usually having whitish margins; stems also thicker and stiffer than Common Chickweed. Flowers small, tending to be larger on mountains, in a cluster, with deeply cleft white petals often longer than the white-edged sepals; stamens usually 10, styles 5. Fruits twice as long as sepals, which are shorter than the fruit-stalks. *Habitat:* Widespread and often abundant in grassy places and disturbed ground. April onwards. Mouse-ear Chickweed; '*C. vulgatum*'.

167*a*. Sticky Mouse-ear, *C. glomeratum* Thuillier ('*C. viscosum*'), is an erect, rather stickily hairy, often yellowish-green annual, with almost oval leaves, the upper without transparent margins. Flowers smaller, sometimes petalless, in more compact clusters, the narrow petals about equalling the sepals, which in turn about equal the fruit-stalks, which are never turned down. Common in dry bare places.

167*b*. ***Grey Mouse-ear, *C. brachypetalum* Persoon, is a small, erect, very hairy, almost shaggy greyish annual, with the upper leaves not white-edged, and small flowers with petals much shorter than the sepals, which in turn are much shorter than their fruit-stalks; fruits also scarcely longer than sepals. So far detected only in one railway cutting in Bedfordshire. May–June.

167*c*. *Dark Green Mouse-ear, *C. atrovirens* Babington, is a variable, often prostrate, stickily hairy annual, with thin stems; spreading branches; upper leaves rather dark green with no transparent margin; petals slightly shorter than sepals, which are much shorter than the fruit-stalks, which droop at first but are finally erect; fruits sometimes scarcely longer than sepals; and styles and stamens usually 4. Locally common on sandy ground near the sea, but rare inland and chiefly by railways. April–July. *C. tetrandrum* Curtis.

167*d*. **Curtis's Mouse-ear**, *C. pumilum* Curtis, is a small upright sticky grey-green annual, usually reddish-purple below, with very narrow transparent margins to the upper leaves, and fruit-stalks drooping at first but becoming erect; stamens and styles 5. Uncommon in bare places on chalk and limestone in the S. April–June.

167*e*. **Little Mouse-ear**, *C. semidecandrum* L., is a small, pale green annual, noticeable for its upper leaves whose whole upper half is transparent and colourless, its slightly notched petals being shorter than the sepals, and its fruit-stalks drooping at first but finally becoming erect; stamens and styles 5. Widespread and frequent in bare sandy ground. April–May.

168. WATER CHICKWEED *Myosoton aquaticum* (L.) Moench

Water Stitchwort; *Stellaria aquatica* (L.) Scopoli   Plate 86.   *CTW, p. 304*

An outsize fleshier Common Chickweed (169), with large white flowers and very deeply cleft petals normally nearly half as long again as the sepals; stamens 10, styles 5. A straggling perennial, hairless below but downy above; leaves pointed oval often wavy-edged, the lower stalked. *Habitat:* Frequent by fresh water in England and Wales; local in Scotland. July onwards.

169. COMMON CHICKWEED *Stellaria media* (L.) Villars   Pl. 86.   *CTW, 306*

One of our really common weeds, a weak, usually prostrate, pale green annual, with hairs in lines along the rounded stems, on alternate sides between the leaf-junctions; leaves pointed oval, the lower stalked. Flowers small, very occasionally petalless, but normally with white petals no longer than the sepals and so deeply cleft that the 5 petals appear to be 10; stamens usually about 5, styles 3; sepals hairy with a narrow whitish margin. Fruit-stalks elongating, drooping; seeds reddish-brown. *Habitat:* Widespread and abundant in disturbed ground. Throughout the year.

169*a*. **Lesser Chickweed**, *S. pallida* (Dumortier) Piré ('*S. apetala*'), is brittle and slenderer, and has smaller pale yellowish-green leaves, all usually stalked, petals minute or none, sepals small, 1–3 stamens, fruit-stalks usually not drooping and small paler seeds. Locally common on sandy soils. April–June.

169*b*. **Greater Chickweed,** *S. neglecta* Weihe (*S. umbrosa* Opiz), is often perennial and more robust and luxuriant, 1–2 ft. high, but usually has 10 stamens and fruit-stalks finally erect. Differs from Wood Chickweed in its lines of hairs on the stem and smaller flowers; and from Water Chickweed (168) in its thinner leaves, lines of hairs, and 3 styles. Widespread but local among shady herbage, commonest in the W. April–July.

169*c*. **Wood Chickweed**, *S. nemorum* L., is paler green and less fleshy than Greater Chickweed, and always perennial, and has stems either hairless or rather hairy all round at the top, shorter flower-stalks and petals larger and much longer than the sepals. Local in damp shady places in the N and W. May–August.

170. GREATER STITCHWORT   *S. holostea* L.   Plate 86.   *CTW, p. 307*

A conspicuous spring hedgerow flower, often forming patches, the fine large white flowers with deeply cleft petals; a straggly perennial, with 4-angled stems 1–2 ft. high, and greyish, minutely rough-edged, unstalked, narrow lanceolate leaves ending in a long point; sepals faintly 3-veined. *Habitat:* Widespread and common in open woods and on hedgebanks. April–May.

171. **MARSH STITCHWORT** *S. palustris* Retzius   Plate 86.   *CTW, p. 308*
A straggling hairless perennial, 1–2 ft. long, with flowers intermediate in size between the Greater (170) and Lesser Stitchworts (172). It is more like the Greater, but has narrower, usually more waxy and greyer, smooth-edged leaves, the topmost being whitish at the margins, petals cleft to the base and a broader whitish margin to the distinctly 3-veined sepals. From the Lesser it can be told by its larger flowers and the green centres to the topmost leaves. *Habitat:* Widespread but local in fens and other wet places. June–August. *S. dilleniana* Moench.

172. **LESSER STITCHWORT** *S. graminea* L.   Plate 86.   *CTW, p. 309*
Weaker and slenderer than Greater Stitchwort (170), with shorter smooth-edged leaves, the topmost all whitish with hairy edges, and much smaller petals cleft to the base and often scarcely exceeding the narrower green-veined sepals. *Habitat:* Widespread, common in dry heathy herbage on acid soils. June–Aug.

173. **BOG STITCHWORT** *S. alsine* Grimm   Plate 86.   *CTW, p. 309*
A weak straggling, virtually hairless perennial, whose unstalked pointed oval leaves, tapered below, are shaped more like the broad-leaved Chickweeds than the narrow-leaved Stitchworts. Differs from Common Chickweed (169) in its unstalked leaves, with whitish edges to the topmost, the complete lack of hairs on the angled stems, and the star-like appearance of the small flowers, whose deeply cleft white petals are always much shorter than the green-veined sepals. *Habitat:* Widespread and fairly common in wet places, including mountain flushes and boggy woodlands. May–September. *S. uliginosa* Murray.

174. *DWARF CHICKWEED   *Moenchia erecta* (L.) Gaertner, Meyer &
                                Scherbius   Plate 86.   *CTW, p. 310*
A tiny erect stitchwort-like annual, 1–3 in. high, which can be very hard to detect in the turf, especially when its comparatively large white flowers are closed, as they are except briefly in sunshine, but to the practised eye its grey waxy hue gives it away; leaves rigid, linear. Petals not notched, shorter than the 4-pointed, white-edged sepals; stamens and styles 4. *Habitat:* Widespread but local in sandy and gravelly turf in England and Wales. April–June.

175. **ANNUAL PEARLWORT** *Sagina apetala* Arduino   Plate 89.   *CTW, p. 312*
A small diffuse weedy wiry, often minutely hairy, pale green annual, 2–4 in. high or half-prostrate, with no marked central rosette; leaves linear, ending in a short bristle. Flowers long-stalked, with minute unnotched greenish petals, or often none; sepals 4, with no noticeable veins, blunt, hairless, spreading crosswise horizontally from the ripe fruit (Fig.); stamens and styles 4. *Habitat:* Widespread and frequent in dry bare and cultivated places. April–August. Fig. p. 39, × 3.

175a. *Fringed Pearlwort*, *S. ciliata* Fries (incl. '*S. reuteri*' and *S. filicaulis* Jordan), is very similar, but has hairless sepals appressed to the ripe seed-capsule, the two inner rather blunt, the two outer pointed (Fig.). Less common, always in drier places. Fig. × 3.

176. *SEA PEARLWORT   *S. maritima* Smith   Plate 89.   *CTW, p. 313*
A dark green or purplish, fleshy, annual, 1–3 in. high, with the main stem flowering, differing from both Annual (175) and Mossy Pearlworts (177) in having thick blunt leaves with no bristle, and sepals not or only half-spreading from the ripe fruit. *Habitat:* Widespread but local in bare places near the sea. June–September.

177. MOSSY PEARLWORT *S. procumbens* L. Plate 89. *CTW, p. 313*

A prostrate, hairless little perennial, often looking like a tuft of moss, with stems 1–6 in. long and rooting as they spread, and a central non-flowering rosette; leaves linear, ending in a minute bristle. Flowers on long slender stalks, with 4 (or no) minute greenish petals, much shorter than the 4 blunt sepals, which spread outwards crosswise after the fruit is ripe; stamens and styles 4. *Habitat:* Widespread and abundant in bare places, even high on mountains; a tiresome weed in gardens and between stone flags. April onwards.

178. **ALPINE PEARLWORT *S. saginoides* (L.) Karsten Pl. 89. *CTW, 314*

A low hairless perennial, 1–3 in. long, sprawling with slender stems among the herbage, with a central rosette that always flowers; leaves linear, ending in a minute bristle. Flowers long-stalked, with 5 white petals, almost equalling the blunt sepals, which remain erect when the longer fruit is ripe; stamens 10, styles 5; fruit-stalks nodding at first. Hybridises with the last species. *Habitat:* Rare in turf and wet places on Scottish mountains. June–August.

178a. *****Lesser Alpine Pearlwort**, *S. intermedia* Fenzl (*S. nivalis* Fries), is a tiny compact tufted plant, usually about an inch across, very easily overlooked, with flowering stems scarcely above the blunter leaves, petals no longer than the sepals which equal the ripe fruit, and fruit-stalks always erect. Very rare, very high on mountains in the C Highlands.

179. *HEATH PEARLWORT *S. subulata* (Swartz) Presl Plate 90. *CTW, p. 316*

An attractive, slightly hairy perennial with relatively large white flowers on long slender stalks 1–3 in. high, arising from a mat of linear leaves ending in a short bristle, and with a central non-flowering rosette. Petals 5, about as long as the sepals, which are erect in fruit; stamens 10, styles 5. *Habitat:* Widespread but local in dry sandy and gravelly places. June–August.

180. *KNOTTED PEARLWORT *S. nodosa* (L.) Fenzl Plate 90. *CTW, p. 316*

Another attractive perennial Pearlwort, with wiry stems 2–8 in. long and hard 'knots' at the leaf-junctions on the stem, formed by clusters of the short blunt linear leaves, rarely with tiny bulbils at their base. Flowers rather large, with usually 5 white petals twice as long as the sepals, which remain erect in fruit. The 'knots', the short non-flowering central rosette, and the 5 styles distinguish it from Spring Sandwort (181). *Habitat:* Widespread but local in bare, dry or wet places on sand or gravel near the sea. July–September.

181. **SPRING SANDWORT *Minuartia verna* (L.) Hiern Pl. 90. *CTW, 317*

A dainty, low, often downy, perennial, not unreminiscent of Knotted Pearlwort (180), with a mat of 3-veined linear leaves, and attractive white flowers with petals longer than the veined, white-edged sepals; styles 3. *Habitat:* Scattered locally over the W side of Great Britain and in N and W Ireland in dry grassy and rocky places, especially on limestone and among old lead workings. May onwards. *Arenaria verna* L.

182. ***RED SANDWORT *M. rubella* (Wahlenberg) Hiern

Arenaria rubella (Wahl.) Smith Plate 87. *CTW, p. 318*

An insignificant tufted perennial, 1–2 in. high, with short linear leaves, and usually solitary whitish flowers, the pointed veined sepals much longer than the 5 inconspicuous petals. Differs from Lesser Alpine Pearlwort (178a) in bearing is usually 3-styled flowers on hairy stalks well above the mat of 3-veined leaves. *Habitat:* A rarity high up on a very few Scottish mountains, and extremely elusively by the sea in Unst. July–August.

183. ***TEESDALE SANDWORT   *M. stricta* (Swartz) Hiern
Arenaria uliginosa DC.   Plate 87.   *CTW, p. 318*

Not unlike a starved, hairless specimen of Spring Sandwort (181), but it never forms any mats, and its leaves are unveined and flowers less prominent, the narrower petals no longer than the unveined sepals.   *Habitat:* Confined to bare wet stony limestone ground on Widdybank Fell, Upper Teesdale. June–July.

184. **FINE-LEAVED SANDWORT   *M. tenuifolia* (L.) Hiern Pl. 87. *CTW, 319*

A delicate, usually hairless annual, 2–4 in. high, slightly like Thyme-leaved Sandwort (188), but more upright and with the narrow leaves of a Pearlwort, but 3-veined. Petals white, shorter than the narrow, pointed, white-edged, veined sepals.   *Habitat:* Rather local in dry stony places, including railway tracks, especially on chalk and limestone in the S. May–July. *Arenaria tenuifolia* L.

185. **CYPHAL   *Cherleria sedoides* L.   Plate 89.   *CTW, p. 319*

A low, often humped, pale green cushion-like plant, similar to Moss Campion (150), but with yellow-green, often petalless, flowers scarcely emerging above it. The cushion gets sadly tattered with age; when growing in turf the stiff, pointed stumpy leaves are distinctive.   *Habitat:* Local on mountains in the Scottish Highlands and Islands. June–August. *Arenaria sedoides* (L.) Hanbury.

186. SEA SANDWORT   *Honkenya peploides* (L.) Ehrhart Pl. 89. *CTW, 320*

A distinctive prostrate creeping hairless fleshy perennial, with numerous thick tough broad pointed yellow-green leaves in angular rows up the stem. Flowers small, whitish, the narrow petals about equalling the sepals on the male flowers, but much shorter on the female ones, which are often on different plants. Fruits yellow-green, like small peas.   *Habitat:* Widespread and frequent on coastal sand and shingle. May–July. Sea Purslane; *Arenaria peploides* L.

187. THREE-VEINED SANDWORT   *Moehringia trinervia* (L.) Clairville
Arenaria trinervia L.   Plate 86.   *CTW, p. 321*

A weak, straggly, downy annual, 6–12 in. high, with inconspicuous flowers on long slender stalks, the white petals half the length of the narrow pointed sepals, which have a broad white edge; stamens 10, styles 3. It differs from Common Chickweed (169) in its stem being hairy all round, its leaves having 3–5 conspicuous veins beneath, and its shorter petals being undivided.   *Habitat:* Widespread and frequent in woods and hedge-banks. April–July.

188. THYME-LEAVED SANDWORT *Arenaria serpyllifolia* L. Pl. 86. *CTW, 322*

Slightly like a small rather downy greyish-green Common Chickweed (169), but with undivided petals and no leaves stalked; a low, weedy, usually prostrate annual, with stubby leaves, white petals shorter than pointed oval sepals, and fruits carafe-shaped (Fig.).   *Habitat:* Widespread and frequent in bare and cultivated places. April onwards. Fig. × 2.

188*a*. **Small Thyme-leaved Sandwort,** *A. leptoclados* (Reichenbach) Gussone, is much slenderer and more straggly, with leaves generally narrower; longer, more open clusters of even smaller flowers, with petals half the length of the lanceolate sepals; and narrower, more cylindrical fruits (Fig.). Generally on lighter soils. Fig. × 2.

175   175a   188   188a   192   192a

189. ***SCOTTISH SANDWORT** *A. norvegica* Gunnerus Pl. 85.   *CTW, 324*
A low, loosely tufted, almost hairless perennial, 2–3 in. high with oval leaves and large white flowers, the petals undivided and longer than the sepals; styles usually 3.   *Habitat:* Very rare in bare stony places not far from the sea in Argyll, Rhum, W Sutherland and Unst. June–August.

189a. ***Yorkshire Sandwort**, *A. gothica* Fries, is often an annual with narrower leaves and larger flowers. Confined to the limestone on and near Ingleborough. May–September.

189b. ***Irish Sandwort**, *A. ciliata* L., with hairs on the margins of the leaves and on the veins of the sepals, is restricted to limestone cliffs by Ben Bulben.

190. **CORN SPURREY** *Spergula arvensis* L.   Plate 87.   *CTW, p. 325*
A weak weedy annual, 9–15 in. high, often stickily hairy, with conspicuous whorls of greyish linear leaves, furrowed beneath and blunt at the tip. Flowers small, white, with petals about as long as the sepals. Fruits longer than sepals, on long stalks, drooping at first; seeds with a very narrow winged edge. A very distinct variety, flowering from February to April, and only 1–3 in. high, is frequent in sandy turf near the sea in the Channel Is.   *Habitat:* A widespread and common arable weed, avoiding chalk and limestone. May onwards.

191. **SAND SPURREY** *Spergularia rubra* (L.) Presl   Plate 27.   *CTW, p. 327*
A prostrate, often matted, stickily downy annual, with whorls of short grey-green linear leaves ending in a tiny bristle, and two silvery lanceolate stipules beneath each whorl. Flowers small, pale pink, with undivided petals shorter than the lanceolate sepals, on longer stalks; styles 3. Seeds unwinged.   *Habitat:* Widespread and frequent in bare sandy and gravelly places. May–September.

191a. ***Greek Sand Spurrey**, *S. bocconi* (Scheele) Foucaud ('*S. campestris*'), is often biennial, and has smaller flowers on shorter stalks, in bigger, stickier, one-sided spikes, lengthening in fruit; stipules triangular and not silvery. Very rare in SW England and S Wales, less so in the Channel Is.

192. **SEA SPURREY** *S. marina* (L.) Grisebach   Plate 27.   *CTW, p. 329*
Larger and fleshier than Sand Spurrey (191), with longer trailing stems, thick bright yellowish-green leaves, stipules triangular and not silvery, larger, often white-centred flowers; stalks longer than fruit, and pale brown seeds, the upper unwinged and with only a thickened border (Fig.).   *Habitat:* Widespread and common in the drier parts of salt- and brackish marshes. June–September. *S. salina* Presl. Fig. × 2.

192a. **Greater Sea Spurrey**, *S. media* (L.) Presl, is a robuster, wider-spreading perennial, generally hairless except above, with larger flowers, the pale violet-pink, usually white-centred petals rather longer than the sepals, stalk shorter than or equalling fruit, and winged seeds (Fig.). Nearly as frequent, and also in muddier marshes. *S. marginata* Kittel.

192*b*. *Cliff Spurrey, *S. rupicola* Le Jolis, is a stocky perennial, stickily hairy, with stems often purplish, stipules somewhat silvery, all-pink flowers with petals equalling sepals, and seeds dark brown, all unwinged. Local on cliffs, walls and rocks by the sea, mainly in the S and W.

193. ***FOUR-LEAVED ALL-SEED *Polycarpon tetraphyllum* (L.) L.
Plate 105. *CTW, p. 331*

A low weedy hairless, much branched annual, the stalked oval leaves grouped in twos and fours with small chaffy stipules at their base. Flowers in forked heads, with tiny chaffy bracts at their base, the 5 insignificant white petals, which fall soon after opening, shorter than the keeled hooded white-edged sepals. Fruits rounded, with numerous seeds. *Habitat:* Common in cultivated and waste ground in the Channel Is.; very rare in bare places in SW England. May onwards.

194. ***STRAPWORT *Corrigiola littoralis* L. Plate 104. *CTW, p. 331*

An attractive small prostrate greyish hairless annual, 2–8 in. long, with stems sometimes red and alternate blunt linear leaves that have minute chaffy stipules at their base. Flowers in leafy clusters, very small, but conspicuous when in quantity; the 5 white-edged sepals often maroon in the centre, rather longer than the white petals. Fruit a tiny nutlet. *Habitat:* Now regularly seen only on the damp sandy margins of Slapton Ley, where it varies in quantity from month to month and year to year. July–September.

195. ***RUPTURE-WORT *Herniaria ciliata* Babington
Pl. 105. *CTW, p. 333*

A prostrate, often matted, pale green perennial, woody at the base, with tiny hairs on the stems, margins of the very small oval leaves, and sepals; leaves with tiny silvery stipules at their base, the upper normally alternate. Flowers in small clusters along the leafy stems, with minute green petals shorter than the blunt sepals. *Habitat:* Plentiful in sandy turf by the sea in the Channel Is., also in the Lizard Peninsula. July–August.

195*a*. ***Smooth Rupture-wort, *H. glabra* L., is less matted and often only annual, with stems and leaves usually and sepals always hairless, stipules often green and flower clusters shorter in less leafy branches off the stems. Rare in bare places in the Breckland; occasionally elsewhere.

196. ***CORAL NECKLACE *Illecebrum verticillatum* L. Pl. 104. *CTW, p. 334*

A charming slender prostrate hairless little annual, 2–6 in. long, with pink stems and tiny apple-green oval opposite leaves, having at their base both minute chaffy stipules and conspicuous opposite clusters of shorter white flowers; sepals also whitish, corky, persistent, hooded, with a very long point, and longer than the petals. Fruits containing a single brown seed. *Habitat:* Rare in damp sandy places S of the Thames. June onwards.

197. KNAWEL *Scleranthus annuus* L. Plate 89. *CTW, p. 335*

A small, easily overlooked, wiry, rather bushy, greyish annual or biennial, prostrate or 1–4 in. high, with pointed linear leaves, and heads of minute petalless flowers, the pointed green sepals narrowly bordered whitish and somewhat spreading in fruit. *Habitat:* Widespread and locally frequent in dry sandy and gravelly places and in cornfields. June–August.

197a. ***Perennial Knawel**, *S. perennis* L., has a woody base to its less branched, stiffer stems; somewhat greyish leaves; and broader whitish margins to the slightly blunter sepals, which curve in over the ripe fruit. Often mistaken for the biennial form of Knawel, which tends to be a bit woody at the base. A rare plant of sandy fields in the Breckland, and one dry rocky hill in Radnorshire.

PURSLANE FAMILY Portulacaceae

198. BLINKS *Montia fontana* L. Plate 105. *CTW, p. 337*

A small, normally prostrate, pale green waterweed, often developing into a thick cushion, with stems sometimes reddish, and small, narrow or oval, opposite leaves. Flowers tiny, white, in clusters towards the end of the stems, on short stalks which lengthen in fruit and are finally erect; styles usually 3. Fruits roundish, longer than the 2 sepals; seeds 3, black. *Habitat:* Widespread and frequent in open wet (or even dry) places, from springs to sand-pits, especially in the N and W, avoiding lime. April onwards.

199. *SPRING BEAUTY *Claytonia perfoliata* Willdenow Pl. 80. *CTW, p. 339*

A hairless, pale green annual, 3–12 in. high, with very long-stalked broad or lanceolate root-leaves, and a pair of fused leaves encircling the stem immediately beneath the stalked cluster of small white flowers. Petals slightly longer than the 2 sepals, and not or only slightly notched. *Habitat:* Widespread and locally established in open sandy soils, occasionally in cultivated ground; not yet in Ireland. April–July.

200. *PINK PURSLANE *C. alsinoides* Sims Plate 23. *CTW, p. 339*

A rather fleshy annual, 6–15 in. high, with an opposite pair of oval stem-leaves, unstalked but not joined together, very long-stalked root-leaves and pink or white flowers with notched, often veined, oblong petals much longer than the 2 sepals. *Habitat:* Widespread but very local in damp, shady places, chiefly in the N. April–July. *C. sibirica* L.

MESEMBRYANTHEMUM FAMILY Ficoidaceae

201. **KAFFIR FIG *Carpobrotus edulis* (L.) Brown Plate 15. *CTW, p. 341*
Mesembryanthemum, Hottentot Fig.

A thick fleshy prostrate perennial, whose densely matted stems may drape whole cliffs; leaves numerous, dark green, succulent, 3-angled, about 3 in. long, reddening at the tip in autumn. Flowers 3–4 in. across, many-petalled, pink or yellow, with a yellow centre. *Habitat:* A prominent feature of many cliffs and sandy banks by the sea in Devon, Cornwall and the Channel Is. May–August.

AMARANTH FAMILY Amaranthaceae

KEY TO AMARANTH AND GOOSEFOOT FAMILIES

Nos. 202–220; cf. also Dog's and Annual Mercuries (514).

PLANT *perennial* 204, 212, 216, 217a, 220a; *a small bush* 203, 216, 217a, 219; *prostrate* 203, 205, 206, 210, 211, 212, 214, 215, 217, 218, 220c; *hairy or downy* 202, 218; *spiny* 218, 219; *mealy* 204, 206, 207, 208, 211, 213, 214, 215, 216; *foetid* 206; *grey* 202, 206, 207, 215, 216, 218; *reddish* 204, 205, 211, 214c, 220.

LEAVES *cylindrical* 217, 218, 219, 220; *diamond-shaped* 207, 208, 210, 215; *elliptical or oval* 205, 206, 216; *lanceolate* 207, 211, 213, 214; *triangular* 204, 209, 212, 214; *shiny* 212, 217; *unstalked* 215, 217, 218, 219, 220; *toothed* 204, 207, 208, 209, 210, 211, 212, 215, *linear* 213, 219.

202. **PIGWEED   *Amaranthus retroflexus* L.   Plate 106.   *CTW, p. 342*

A weedy downy grey-green annual, 6 in. to 2 ft. high, with stalked, pointed oval leaves. Flowers small, dry, chaffy, greenish, in dense spikes, mixed with shining bristle-like bracts with a green midrib and twice as long as the broad-tipped 5 sepals (Fig.). *Habitat:* A not infrequent casual, rarely persisting. August till the frosts.

202a. *****Green Pigweed,** *A. chlorostachys* Willdenow (*CTW*†), is yellowish-green and nearly or quite hairless, with stubby branches in its laxer, sometimes nodding flower-spike, and pointed sepals (Fig.). An ephemeral but sometimes plentiful weed of waste places, and fields manured with shoddy.

203. ***WHITE PIGWEED, *A. albus* L.   Plate 104.   *CTW, p. 342*

A hairless annual, with thin stiff white stems, prostrate or forming a bush a foot or so high, and rather few stalked, oblong, small, pale green rounded leaves. Flowers small, greenish, in clusters along the stem; sepals 3. Seeds small and wrinkled. *Habitat:* A scarce casual. August till the frosts.

GOOSEFOOT FAMILY   Chenopodiaceae

GOOSEFOOTS   *Chenopodium,* AND ORACHES   *Atriplex*

THESE ARE mostly unattractive mealy annual weeds, prostrate or growing to 6–18 in. or in rich soils a good deal taller still. Their leaves are usually stalked, thick, toothed and alternate, and their small greenish petalless flowers are in spikes. They are often hard to tell apart, except by the rather technical botanical character that the Goosefoots have their stamens and styles in the same flower, while the Oraches have them in separate male and female flowers on the same plant (Fig.). Another distinction is that the fruits of Goosefoots (Fig.) are surrounded by 3–5 small sepals in a ring, while those of Oraches (Fig.), are enclosed in 2 triangular bracts, which swell as the fruits ripen, become much larger and more obvious than in the Goosefoots, and give the spike an interrupted appearance as the male flowers wither.

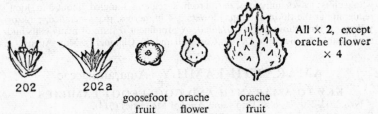

All × 2, except
orache flower
× 4

202   202a   goosefoot   orache   orache
fruit   flower   fruit

204. *GOOD KING HENRY *Chenopodium bonus-henricus* L. Pl. 110. *CTW, 346*

Our only perennial Goosefoot, a foot or so high, often mealy when young, the whole plant sometimes reddish, with many largish broadly triangular leaves.

Flowers in rather long, narrow, tapering, almost leafless spikes; sepals not enlarging in fruit; stigmas long. *Habitat:* Widespread but rather local and normally near houses, especially by roadsides and in farmyards. May–August.

205. *MANY-SEEDED GOOSEFOOT   *C. polyspermum* L.   Pl. 110.   *CTW, 346*

An often half-prostrate annual, 6 in. to 2 ft. high, sometimes well branched, usually hairless and often red, with usually 4-angled stems and untoothed pointed oval leaves that decrease in size into the branched flower-spike. *Habitat:* Widespread and locally frequent in disturbed, especially light, soils, chiefly in the S. July onwards.

206. **STINKING GOOSEFOOT   *C. vulvaria* L.   Plate 110.   *CTW, p.* 348

A grey, mealy, usually prostrate annual, 3–12 in. long, which gives off a cloying stench of rotting fish when handled. Flowers yellowish, in small clusters at the base of the oval leaves, which are untoothed or occasionally have a single angle towards the base on each side. *Habitat:* Very local, mostly near the sea in the S. June–September.

207. FAT HEN   *C. album* L.   Plate 110.   *CTW, p.* 348

(incl. *C. reticulatum* Aellen, *C. suecicum* Murr, and *C. berlandieri* Moquin)

Much the commonest and most variable Goosefoot, well branched, upright and with tough, stiff 1–3 ft. stems that may be streaked red, and a whitish meal on the young shoots; leaves lanceolate to diamond-shaped, the lower almost always toothed. Flower-spike varying from narrow to broad and branched, usually leafy; sepals 5. Seeds black, flat, smooth. *Habitat:* Widespread and often excessively abundant in cultivated and waste ground. June onwards.

207a. **Grey Goosefoot, *C. opulifolium* Schrader (*CTW, p. 350*), is similar, but never has red stems, and has grey-green, usually smaller leaves, the lower and middle ones as broad or broader than long (Fig.). Flowers in strongly grey mealy, branched, dense, interrupted spikes. An uncommon casual, very occasionally plentiful, chiefly in the S. August–September. Figs. all × ½.

207b. **Fig-leaved Goosefoot, *C. ficifolium* Smith (*CTW, p. 351*), has leaves narrowly but distinctly 3-lobed, the middle lobe oblong, with a broad lobe at the bottom (Fig.); upper leaves linear. Flower-spike rather loose and small-flowered. Seeds dotted. An occasional casual, chiefly in the S. August–September.

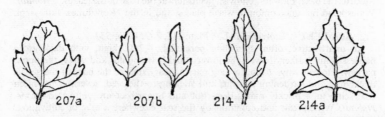

207a   207b   214   214a

208. *NETTLE-LEAVED GOOSEFOOT   *C. murale* L.   Pl. 110.   *CTW, p. 351*

Sometimes mistaken for an upright Red Goosefoot (210), but has slightly mealy diamond-shaped leaves, which rarely go red, coarsely and unequally toothed with the teeth pointing upwards and inwards, and narrowed at the base. The flower-spike is much laxer and spreading, with short branches and leafy almost to the top; sepals 5. Seeds flat, black, their skin-like covering not easily rubbed off. *Habitat:* Local in waste and cultivated places, mainly in the S. July-September.

209. *SOWBANE *C. hybridum* L. Plate 110. *CTW, p. 352*

A hairless green annual, 9 in. to 2 ft. high, with large thin triangular, or often heart-shaped leaves, with a few large teeth, the upper narrower and less toothed. Flowers in loose branched leafless clusters, resembling some forms of Fat Hen (207). Seeds black, pitted, larger than in our other Goosefoots, and not covered by the sepals. *Habitat:* An uncommon weed in the S. July–September.

210. RED GOOSEFOOT *C. rubrum* L. Plate 110. *CTW, p. 353*

A fleshy annual, not mealy, 3 in. to 2 ft. high, but often prostrate and sometimes red; leaves thick, diamond-shaped, usually coarsely and deeply toothed, shiny and either red or green on both sides. Flowering spikes leafy, compact and upright; all flowers, except the terminal, with 2–3 stamens, and 2–4 sepals which persist and cover the fruit, joined to the middle or near the base. Seeds tiny, red-brown, mostly upright, their skin-like covering easily rubbed off. *Habitat:* Widespread and common in waste and cultivated ground, especially by the sea and on manure heaps; rare in Ireland. July–September.

210*a*. ***Upright Goosefoot, *C. urbicum* L., is duller green with triangular not diamond-shaped leaves, never red and always erect, and has a narrower, less leafy or leafless flower-spike, 5 sepals, 5 stamens, and larger, rougher black seeds, all horizontal and rather longer than the sepals, their covering not easily rubbed off. Very rare, now only seen regularly on one farm in Dorset.

210*b*. **Small Red Goosefoot, *C. botryodes* Smith, is usually smaller, though it can be a bushy plant, most commonly prostrate or with long horizontal branches from the base, and has smaller, much less toothed leaves, finally crimson below, a proportionately larger, less leafy flower-spike with smaller very numerous flowers in rather dense clusters, rich crimson in fruit and the keeled sepals joined almost to the top. Very local, on mud in marsh ditches near the SE coast of England. August onwards.

211. **OAK-LEAVED GOOSEFOOT *C. glaucum* L. Plate 110. *CTW, p. 353*

A normally prostrate annual, 3–15 in. long, with neat, rather narrow leaves, green and hairless above, mealy white below, all evenly toothed and narrowed towards the base. Flowers yellowish in clusters at the base of the leaves. *Habitat:* Widespread but uncommon in waste places, and in the N on dunes. June–Sept.

212. SEA BEET *Beta vulgaris* L. Plate 111. *CTW, p. 354*

An unattractive, often sprawling perennial, 1–2 ft. high, with dark green hairless shiny leathery leaves, the lower roughly triangular and wavy, the upper narrow. Flowers tiny, green, in long narrow leafy spikes; the base of the sepals thickening and hardening in fruit, and sticking to the seed, several fruits often coalescing in a prickly mass. Beet-root and Sugar-beet are cultivated forms. *Habitat:* Widespread and common by the sea; elsewhere a relic of cultivation. June–September. *B. maritima* L.

213. GRASS-LEAVED ORACHE *Atriplex littoralis* L. Pl. 111. *CTW, p. 356*

An upright, often fleshy, leafy annual, 1–2 ft. high, with erect branches and all leaves broad linear, sometimes a little toothed and with very faint side-veins. Flower-spikes similar to Common Orache (214), but less leafy. Fruits also similar, but more toothed and covered with numerous small warts. Confusable with the narrow-leaved forms of Common Orache, which have more spreading branches. *Habitat:* Widespread and frequent on bare ground near the sea. July–Sept.

214. COMMON ORACHE *A. patula* L. Plate 111. *CTW, p. 356*

A very variable, usually mealy, often prostrate, sometimes reddish, weedy annual, 9 in. to 2 ft. high, with many widely spreading lower branches; lanceolate, more or less toothed upper leaves; and usually broadly triangular, sometimes opposite lower ones, the basal teeth pointing forwards and narrowing into the stalk (Fig., p. 43), but sometimes like the upper ones. Flowers small, greenish, unstalked, male and female, in slender open leafy spikes. Fruits triangular, with few or no warts and hardly toothed, the two sides joined less than half-way up. *Habitat:* A widespread and abundant weed of bare ground, both inland and by the sea. July–September.

214a. Halberd-leaved Orache, *A. hastata* L., is more often erect and has the lowest and largest teeth of the lower leaves pointing outwards at right angles to the stalk (Fig., p. 43); tends to have shorter branches to the flower-spike and leaves less often mealy. Frequent, mostly near the sea.

214b. *Babington's Orache, *A. glabriuscula* Edmondston (*A. babingtonii* Woods), is more compact, shorter-branched, generally prostrate, and mealy, and has thicker smaller neater leaves like the last species, with shorter basal teeth. Flower-spikes leafy almost to the tip. Fruits diamond-shaped, hard at the base, the two sides joined at least half-way up. Local on shingly sea-shores.

215. **FROSTED ORACHE *A. laciniata* L. Plate 111. *CTW, p. 357*

A more or less prostrate annual, much more silvery-white in appearance than our other Oraches, the buff or rose-coloured stems and the neat, silvery, fleshy, alternate, short-stalked, diamond-shaped, toothed leaves being both frosted with meal. Flowers like Common Orache (214), in short spikes at the base of the unstalked upper leaves. Fruits much as in Babington's Orache (214b), but with more prominent teeth. *Habitat:* Widespread but local on sea-shores. August–September. *A. sabulosa* Rouy.

216. SEA PURSLANE *Halimione portulacoides* (L.) Aellen Pl. 111. *CTW, 358*

A gregarious, mealy grey, straggly, much branched orache-like undershrub, with brown stems 8–18 in. high, and untoothed elliptical leaves, the lower opposite. Flowers small, yellowish-green, in short slender interrupted spikes, the stamens and styles in different flowers on the same plant. Fruits unstalked, with the two 3-lobed sides joined nearly to the top. *Habitat:* Common in saltmarshes, often fringing creeks and pools, in E and SE England and Wales; rare in Scotland and Ireland. July onwards. *Atriplex portulacoides* L.

217. COMMON SEABLITE *Suaeda maritima* (L.) Dumortier Pl. 111. *CTW, 359*

A hairless, often prostrate annual, 3–9 in. long, often dark bluish-green or reddish, with many short narrow pointed cylindrical fleshy alternate leaves, and inconspicuous unstalked greenish flowers at their base; stamens 5, styles 2. Seeds broad, flat, horizontal, purplish-black. *Habitat:* Widespread and common by the sea, especially on salt-marshes, often between high and low tide-marks. July onwards.

217a. **Shrubby Seablite, *S. fruticosa* Forskal, is an evergreen bush, with stout woody stems 1–4 ft. high, denser shorter leaves, rounded at the tip, 3 styles and upright nearly globular jet-black seeds. Locally abundant on a few shingle beaches above the highest tides, Wash to Chesil Beach; very rare in S Wales.

218. SALTWORT *Salsola kali* L. Plate 111. *CTW, p. 360*
A stiff prickly leafy, sometimes rather hairy, usually prostrate, grey-green annual, with thick, often pink-striped stems and a spine at the tip of its short fat fleshy leaves. Flowers inconspicuous, greenish, usually solitary in a tuft of leaf-like bracts at the base of the leaves. Fruits flower-like, with winged edges. *Habitat:* Widespread and fairly frequent on sandy coasts; a typical plant of the drift-line. July–September.

219. ***RUSSIAN THISTLE *S. pestifera* Nelson Plate 111. *CTW, p. 361*
A rather wiry, stiff, very bushy, erect annual, 6–18 in. high, with flowers like Saltwort (218), but the plant not fleshy and looking different, with longer, darker green, almost thread-like, less spiny leaves. *Habitat:* An increasing casual. August–September. '*S. tragus*'.

GLASSWORTS *Salicornia*

THESE ARE curious succulent salt-loving plants, with no obvious beauty except when they go red. They are mostly annuals and vary from prostrate to 9 in. high, from slender unbranched stems to thick lush little bushes. The fat shining jointed cylindrical stems bear pairs of branches and opposite leaves, which are fused in pairs and reduced to fleshy sheaths. Their flowers, minute, petalless and visible chiefly as 1–2 stamens, are sunk in the stems at these junctions, 1–3 together, in spikes at the end of the branches; seeds minute, hairy. The various forms of Glasswort are not clearly demarcated, and hybrids are probably frequent, but those summarised below may be reasonably distinct.

220. GLASSWORT *Salicornia europaea* L. Plate 111. *CTW, p. 363*
    Marsh Samphire; *S. herbacea* (L.) L., *S. stricta* Dumortier
Erect and yellow-green, with pairs of sometimes branched branches, the flowers in threes in long blunt cylindrical, not beaded, spikes with 6–12 segments. *Habitat:* Widespread and plentiful in saltmarshes. August-September.
    220a. ***Bushy Glasswort,** *S. dolichostachya* Moss, grows often in large and rounded green bushes up to 9 in. across, with floppy cylindrical obese branches often 3–4 together, and more numerous segments in the long, more pointed flower-spikes. Local in soft mud.
    220b. **Twiggy Glasswort,** *S. ramosissima* Woods (incl. *S. gracillima* (Townsend) Moss), is green, yellow, red or purple, more branched, and the short, few-flowered, rather pointed spikes have much swollen segments, giving the stems a beaded appearance. Widespread and common in firmer mud.
    220c. ***Seablite Glasswort,** *S. prostrata* Pallas, is prostrate, usually red and slightly like Seablite (217), with branches rather long and more or less at right angles, the spikes rather few-flowered with much smaller segments. Frequent on firmer mud in the S. (incl. *S. appressa* (Dum.) Dumortier and *S. smithiana* Moss).
    220d. ****Fragile Glasswort,** *S. pusilla* Woods, differs in having its flowers nearly all solitary, in spikes with short blunt branches with very few segments breaking into 2-seeded joints as the seeds ripen. Local on firmer mud in the S. *S. disarticulata* Moss.
    220e. ***Perennial Glasswort,** *S. perennis* (Gouan) Miller, our only perennial

species, is often orange-green or crimson, creeping, forming patches with flexuous stems, the lower woody and thin, long and floppy and often unbranched above, with rather few segments. Not uncommon on firm muddy and gravelly salt marshes in S England; very rare in Wales.

LIME FAMILY Tiliaceae

221. **SMALL-LEAVED LIME *Tilia cordata* Miller Plate 70. *CTW, p. 366*
Differs from Common Lime (222) in having smaller leaves, greyish below with faint side-veins and small tufts of reddish hairs, flower clusters more or less erect, and fruits hardly ribbed. *Habitat:* Widespread but local in woods and on inland cliffs, especially on limestone; not infrequently planted. July. Red Lime.

222. COMMON LIME *T. europaea* L. Plate 71. *CTW, p. 367*
A frequent street and park tree, a fertile hybrid between the last and next species, very much more commonly seen than either; a tall tree with bosses on trunk, smooth dark brown bark, and young twigs usually hairless; leaves heart-shaped, dark green and hairless above, paler below with a few tufts of whitish hairs, often covered with honey-dew from aphides. Flowers yellowish, heavily scented, hanging in umbel-like clusters, usually of about 6, on stalks half joined to a large oblong leaf-like bract. Fruits globular, downy, ribbed. *Habitat:* Almost always planted, occasionally in hedges and copses away from houses. No limes are native in Ireland. July. Linden; *T. vulgaris* Hayne.
  222a. **Large-leaved Lime**, *T. platyphyllos* Scopoli, has no bosses on the trunk, young twigs usually downy, larger and more abruptly pointed leaves that are uniformly downy beneath with all veins prominent, and only about 3 larger flowers in each cluster. Fruits very downy, strongly ribbed. Widespread but scarce in woods and on inland cliffs, especially in the S Welsh Marches; occasionally planted. June–July.

MALLOW FAMILY Malvaceae

MOSTLY NON-WOODY plants, usually downy or softly hairy, the usually large stalked flowers characterised by having a double calyx, the inner ring larger and often appearing rather inflated; also 5 notched petals and a prominent bunch of stamens. Leaves palmately lobed or cut, stalked and toothed. Fruits disc-shaped, 'rounde and flat, made lyke little cheeses', whence the name 'Cheesecakes'.

223. MUSK MALLOW *Malva moschata* L. Plate 15. *CTW, p. 369*
A graceful, hairy, usually unbranched perennial, 1–2 ft. high, with stem-hairs often purple-based and leaves deeply and narrowly cut, the lowest less so and rarely undivided. Flowers a handsome rose-pink, up to 2 in. across, in loose spikes; petals broad. *Habitat:* Widespread and fairly frequent in dry grassy and bushy places. July-August.

224. COMMON MALLOW *M. sylvestris* L. Plate 15. *CTW, p. 369*
A coarse, hairy, often sprawling perennial, 1–3 ft. high, with crinkly ivy-like leaves, often with a small dark spot at the base. Flowers an inch or more across, the rather narrow pinkish-purple petals with darker veins, much longer than the calyx, whose outer ring is joined right at the base or not at all. *Habitat:* Widespread and frequent in waste places, especially near houses and by the sea, thinning out northwards. June onwards.

224*a*. ***Cornish Mallow**, *Lavatera cretica* L. (*L. sylvestris* Brotero) (*CTW*, *p. 372*), is a softer, paler green annual, with rounded, much less lobed leaves and pink flowers with no trace of purple, the outer ring of the calyx being joined some way from the base into a lobed cup. Rare near the sea in W Cornwall, Pembrokeshire and the Scilly and Channel Is.; casual elsewhere.

225. DWARF MALLOW *M. neglecta* Wallroth   Plate 15.   *CTW, p. 370*

A normally prostrate, or at least, broadly spreading, coarse hairy annual, with stems a foot or so long; leaves rounded, crinkled, lobed. Flowers rather small, pale rose-purple, the petals about twice as long as the calyx, the lower part bearded. Fruits smooth, with round edges.   *Habitat:* Widespread and frequent in waste places, farmyards and the like. June onwards. '*M. rotundifolia*'.

226. **TREE MALLOW *Lavatera arborea* L.   Plate 15.   *CTW, p. 372*

A fine substantial tall well branched biennial, which may exceed 8 ft., woody below and softly downy all over; leaves ivy-shaped, crinkled. Flowers 1½–2 in. across, with broad pinkish-purple petals, darker at the base, and the outer ring of the calyx conspicuously cup-shaped, with 3 broad lobes.   *Habitat:* Locally frequent in rocky and waste places on the coast, commonest in the SW, rare elsewhere. July–September.

227. *MARSH MALLOW *Althaea officinalis* L.   Plate 15.   *CTW, p. 373*

A velvety grey, little branched perennial, remarkably soft to the touch, growing in clumps 3–4 ft. high, with broad, shallowly lobed leaves, and soft pink flowers an inch or so across, the outer ring of the calyx with 6–9 lobes.   *Habitat:* Widespread and local in dykes near the sea, and in the drier parts of salt-marshes; Scotland, only in the SW. August–September.

228. ***ROUGH MALLOW *A. hirsuta* L.   Plate 15.   *CTW, p. 373*

Rather like a small Musk Mallow (223), but annual, half the size, often prostrate and with bristly hairs, small flowers and scarcely notched petals, the outer ring of the calyx joined at the base into a lobed cup.   *Habitat:* Rare in bare and cultivated dry places, permanent only in two or three localities S of the Thames. June–July.

FLAX FAMILY Linaceae

229. *PALE FLAX *Linum bienne* Miller   Plate 6.   *CTW, p. 375*

A slender grey-green perennial, with wiry, often unbranched stems up to a foot high, and a few small alternate linear leaves. Flowers pale bluish-lilac, ½–¾ in. across, with 5 petals that drop early, and 5 very pointed sepals nearly as long as the pointed globular fruit.   *Habitat:* Widespread but local in dry grassy places, especially near the sea. May–September.

230. *CULTIVATED FLAX *L. usitatissimum* L.   Plate 6.   *CTW, p. 375*

A slender hairless greyish-green annual, 9–18 in. high, with narrow lanceolate 3-veined leaves and bright blue flowers an inch or so across, the sepals pointed and shorter than the globular fruit.   *Habitat:* Widespread and frequent in waste ground, usually as a relic of cultivation. June–July. Linseed.

230*a*. **Perennial Flax, *L. anglicum* Miller ('*L. perenne*'), is a greyer tufted perennial, with a wirier stem, narrower shorter stiffer 1-veined leaves, and blunt sepals much shorter than the fruit. Very local in chalk and limestone turf in E and N England.

231. FAIRY FLAX *L. catharticum* L. Plate 87. *CTW, p. 376*

A low graceful slender annual, 2–6 in. high, with small 1-veined untoothed oblong opposite leaves, and loose branched heads of small white flowers on thread-like stalks rather like a Sandwort (188), but the plant is hairless and its 5 petals are much longer than the all-green lanceolate sepals. Fruit globular. *Habitat:* Widespread and common in short turf, especially on chalk and limestone and in fens. May onwards.

232. *FLAX-SEED *Radiola linoides* Roth Plate 105. *CTW, p. 377*

A tiny delicate, often bushy annual, rarely over 2 in. high, with stiff thread-like stems, repeatedly forked, and tiny pointed oval opposite leaves. Flowers in terminal clusters, with 5 minute white petals no longer than the toothed sepals. Fruits globular. *Habitat:* Widespread but local on bare moist patches on sand or peat, on heaths or woodland rides, often with Chaffweed (625). July–August.

GERANIUM FAMILY Geraniaceae

CRANESBILLS *Geranium*

NON-WOODY PLANTS whose deeply palmately lobed or cut leaves have stipules at their base. Their flowers are some shade of pink, red, mauve or purple, with 5 petals, 5 sepals often ending in a bristle, and prominent stamens. Their fruits have 5 segments curling upwards from the base when ripe, and end in a long pointed beak, whence the name 'crane's bill'. The garden 'Geraniums' mostly belong to the closely related tender genus *Pelargonium*.

233. *MEADOW CRANESBILL *Geranium pratense* L. Pl. 12. *CTW, p. 379*

A fine, handsome plant, with its bright blue flowers, slightly tinged violet and over an inch across, on long stalks. A hairy perennial, 1–2 ft. high, sticky above, with stems often reddish, long-stalked leaves very deeply lobed and cut, petals not notched and fruit-stalks bent down when ripe. *Habitat:* Widespread and locally frequent in grassy places, rare in the SE, N Scotland and Ireland. June onwards.

234. *WOOD CRANESBILL *G. sylvaticum* L. Plate 12. *CTW, p. 381*

The northern counterpart of the Meadow Cranesbill (233), but has less jagged leaves, rather smaller and mauver, less blue flowers, and the fruit-stalks erect when ripe. *Habitat:* Widespread and locally common in open woods and grassy and heathery places; rare in Wales and Ireland, not in S England. June–July.

235. ***FRENCH CRANESBILL *G. endressi* Gay Plate 16. *CTW, p. 382*

Rather taller than the next species, with more sharply toothed leaves and flowers of a pure unstreaked pink, their veins darkening as they fade. A hybrid with 236 is probably more frequent than pure 235. *Habitat:* An uncommon garden escape, usually in patches on hedge-banks, mainly in the S. June–August.

236. **PENCILLED CRANESBILL *G. versicolor* L. Plate 16. *CTW, p. 383*

A hairy perennial, 9–15 in. high, growing in large tufts, with the general look of a small Wood Cranesbill (234), but not sticky above, and with less sharply toothed leaves, less widely open pale pink flowers and petals distinctly notched and exquisitely pencilled with violet veins. *Habitat:* A garden escape, usually in isolated clumps on hedge-banks, mainly in the SW. May–July.

237. ***KNOTTED CRANESBILL* *G. nodosum* L. Plate 16. *CTW, p. 383*

Differs from the last species in its smaller shorter-stalked purple-veined mauve flowers; much less hairy, rather stiff stems swollen at the leaf-junctions; and darker green, less deeply toothed leaves. *Habitat:* A rare escape. May–August.

238. **DUSKY CRANESBILL* *G. phaeum* L. Plate 35. *CTW, p. 384*

Our only Cranesbill with maroon flowers which open flat and are relatively small and numerous for the size of the plant; petals wavy-edged. A hairy perennial, 1–2 ft. high, the leaves lobed to at least half-way, often with a darker blotch. *Habitat:* A widespread but uncommon escape, especially in hedge-banks. May–June.

239. *BLOODY CRANESBILL* *G. sanguineum* L. Plate 16. *CTW, p. 384*

A hairy spreading perennial, 4–12 in. high, with strikingly bright purplish-crimson solitary flowers, an inch or so across; petals shallowly notched. Leaves rather small, very deeply cut. A prostrate pale pink form (*G. lancastriense* Withering) is found on dunes on Walney Is. (Lancs.). *Habitat:* Widespread but local in dry grassy places, especially among limestone rocks and on dunes; also an occasional garden escape; not in the SE. June–August.

240. ***ITALIAN CRANESBILL* *G. macrorrhizum* L. Plate 16. *CTW, p. 385*

An aromatic, often reddish, perennial, 6–9 in. high, with very deeply lobed leaves and clusters of pinkish-red flowers up to an inch across, the petals with a very long basal part, and the stamens especially prominent. *Habitat:* A very rare garden escape in the SW. June–July.

241. *PYRENEAN CRANESBILL* *G. pyrenaicum* Burman Pl. 16. *CTW, 385*

A downy perennial, 9–18 in. high, with roundish leaves, lobed to about half-way. Flowers numerous, about ½ in. across, usually mauvish-pink, with well notched petals and pointed sepals. Fruits downy, smooth. *Habitat:* Widespread, locally common and increasing, chiefly on railway banks and roadsides. May onwards.

242. *LONG-STALKED CRANESBILL* *G. columbinum* L. Pl. 16. *CTW, 386*

A graceful, often reddish downy annual, 4–12 in. high, often hard to detect in the herbage, with rose-coloured flowers ½-in. across, on thin stalks 1–5 in. long, the petals not notched, the sepals ending in a long bristle. Leaves cut almost to the base, like the next species, but much slenderer. Fruits hairless, smooth. *Habitat:* Widespread but rather local in dry open turf, chiefly on chalk and limestone. May–August.

243. *CUT-LEAVED CRANESBILL* *G. dissectum* L. Plate 16. *CTW, p. 387*

A rather coarse, untidy hairy annual, 6–18 in. high, with leaves lobed almost to the base, the lobes narrow and jaggedly cut. Flowers small, pinkish-purple, ¼-in. across, with notched petals and sepals ending in a bristle. Fruits downy; seeds pitted. *Habitat:* Widespread and common in grassy places and disturbed ground. May onwards.

244. DOVESFOOT CRANESBILL   *G. molle* L.   Plate 16.   *CTW, p. 388*

The commonest of the small-flowered Cranesbills, with all leaves rounded and lobed, the stem ones to half-way or below; a low often prostrate, loosely hairy annual, 3–8 in. high, with flowers of varying shades of pinkish-purple; petals notched, sepals pointed. Fruits hairless, normally wrinkled; seeds smooth. *Habitat:* Widespread, common in fields, waste and sandy places. April–Sept.

244a. ****Round-leaved Cranesbill,** *G. rotundifolium* L., is robuster and bushier, with leaves wavy at the edge, less deeply lobed and looking rounder. Flowers pinker, with petals not notched, recalling Shining Cranesbill (246), but with much more spreading sepals. Fruits hairy, not wrinkled; seeds dotted. Distinctly local, not in Scotland. June–August.

245. SMALL-FLOWERED CRANESBILL   *G. pusillum* L.   Pl. 16.   *CTW, p. 388*

Closely downy, with stem-leaves usually smaller than Dovesfoot Cranesbill (244), more narrowly cut to over half-way, and approaching those of Cut-leaved Cranesbill (243). Flowers usually smaller and pale bluish-lilac, but sometimes rather similar in colour, with petals less notched and half the stamens without anthers. Fruits unwrinkled, downy. *Habitat:* Similar to Dovesfoot but less common. May onwards.

246. *SHINING CRANESBILL   *G. lucidum* L.   Plate 16.   *CTW, p. 389*

Our only Cranesbill with smallish glossy rounded leaves, lobed to about half-way. An attractive, almost hairless annual, 4–12 in. high, often going red, with neat pink flowers, less than ½-in. across; petals narrow and not notched; sepals inflated at the base and ending in a bristle. *Habitat:* Widespread but rather local in hedge-banks and on walls. May–August.

247. HERB ROBERT   *G. robertianum* L.   Plate 16.   *CTW, p. 390*

A hairy, rather strong-smelling annual, 6–15 in. high, often reddish, especially on the stems, with triangular, fern-like leaves divided into 3–5 pinnately lobed segments; and pink ½-in. flowers with petals not notched; pollen orange. Fruits slightly wrinkled. Very variable, and sometimes prostrate and hairless with smaller flowers, when it is often taken for Little Robin (248). *Habitat:* Widespread and abundant in light shade, also on walls, rocks and shingle. April onwards.

248. **LITTLE ROBIN   *G. purpureum* Villars   Plate 16.   *CTW, p. 391*

Closely related to Herb Robert (247), but often taller and always with small narrow-petalled flowers rather like Shining Cranesbill (246) and yellow pollen. Leaves stiffer and more narrowly cut; fruits with more and thicker wrinkles. *Habitat:* Very local on dry banks and in stony places near the sea in SW England, S Wales and S Ireland.

STORKSBILLS   *Erodium*

ANNUALS differing from Cranesbills in their pinnate or toothed leaves, and the long spiral twist to the beak of their fruits. Flowers usually pinkish-purple, with unnotched petals, only half the 10 stamens with anthers.

249. **SEA STORKSBILL   *Erodium maritimum* (L.) L'Héritier
                                       Plate 89.   *CTW, p. 392*

A small prostrate downy annual, usually very compact or only a tiny rosette, but sometimes extending to 4–6 in.; leaves small, oval, toothed, not pinnate. Few people ever see flowers with petals, which are pale pink. *Habitat:* Scattered on sand-dunes, bare ground and dry turf near the sea, often plentiful on the SW and W coasts of England and Wales; rare elsewhere and inland. May–August.

250. **MUSK STORKSBILL *E. moschatum* (L.) L'Héritier
Plate 22. *CTW, p. 392*
Usually larger and rougher than Common Storksbill (251), and sometimes smells of musk when handled; leaves larger, usually only 1-pinnate; stipules broader. Flowers often of a mauver pink, crowded in a close cluster, their short stalks covered with sticky hairs. *Habitat:* Widespread but scarce on bare open ground, mainly near the coast in the S and W or in fields manured with shoddy; not in Scotland. May onwards.

251. COMMON STORKSBILL *E. cicutarium* (L.) L'Héritier Pl. 22. *CTW, 393*
Much the commonest Storksbill, often prostrate, rarely in a cushion, and sometimes a foot or more high; varies also in hairiness, and may be stickily hairy by the sea, so that sand adheres. Leaves 2-pinnate with lanceolate stipules at their base. Flowers in small loose heads, varying in size, and in colour from white to deep pink, occasionally with a blackish spot at the base of the two upper petals. *Habitat:* Widespread and generally common in dry grassy and sandy places, especially near the sea. May–September. (Incl. *E. glutinosum* Dumortier.)

WOOD-SORREL FAMILY Oxalidaceae

RATHER WEAK, NON-WOODY plants, mostly perennials, up to about a foot high, with long-stalked trefoil leaves, the leaflets often closing up at night. Flowers open cup-shaped, white, pink or yellow, with 5 petals, sepals and styles, and 10 stamens, 5 long and 5 short. Fruits exploding when ripe.

252. WOOD-SORREL *Oxalis acetosella* L. Plate 84. *CTW, p. 395*
A delicate, pale green, creeping perennial, with tufts of root-leaves, sometimes purple beneath, and solitary flowers, $\frac{1}{2}$-in. across, white usually veined mauve, on taller leafless stalks 2–4 in. high. *Habitat:* Widespread and common in shady places, often in patches; also on mountains. April–May.
252a. ****Pale Oxalis,** *O. incarnata* L. (*CTW†*), is taller and bushier, with tufts of smaller leaves up the branched stems, and little veined pearly-pink flowers on branched stalks. A garden escape, chiefly in the SW. June–August.

253. *SLEEPING BEAUTY *O. corniculata* L. Plate 43. *CTW, p. 396*
A normally prostrate, downy perennial with runners, the leaves quite often purplish with inconspicuous oblong stipules at their base. Flowers yellow, singly or in pairs along the leafy stems. Fruits pointed cylindrical, ridged, their immediate stalks normally bent right back. *Habitat:* A not uncommon weed in and near gardens, often between stone flags. May–September.

254. **UPRIGHT OXALIS *O. europaea* Jordan Plate 43. *CTW, p. 396*
Is usually erect and also differs from Sleeping Beauty (253) in being often hairless and having leaves rarely purplish and then paler, no visible stipules, flowers often more than two together and fruit-stalks not bent back. *Habitat:* Widespread but much less common. May–September. '*O. stricta*'.

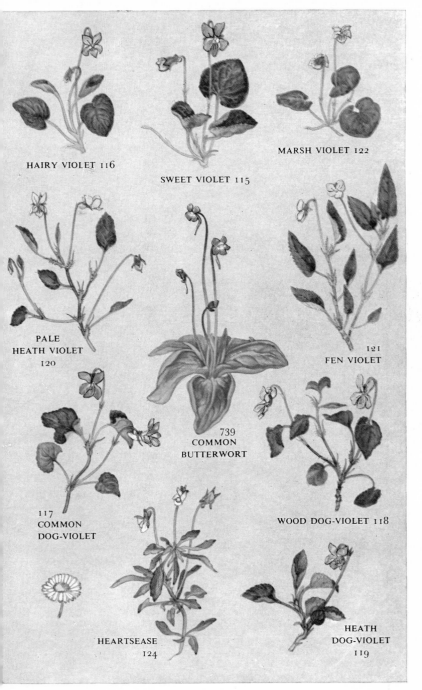

HAIRY VIOLET 116

SWEET VIOLET 115

MARSH VIOLET 122

PALE
HEATH VIOLET
120

739
COMMON
BUTTERWORT

121
FEN VIOLET

117
COMMON
DOG-VIOLET

WOOD DOG-VIOLET 118

HEARTSEASE
124

HEATH
DOG-VIOLET
119

1

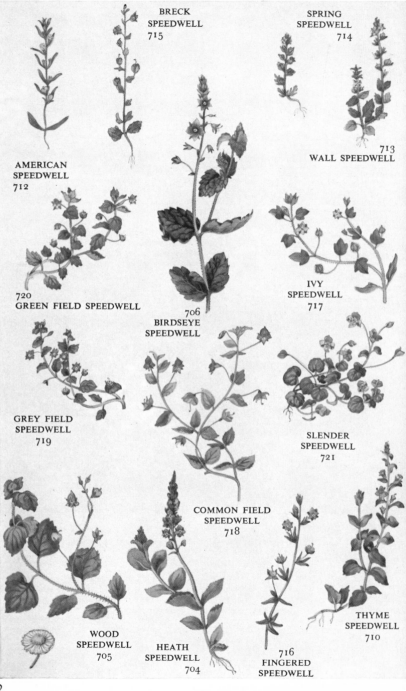

BRECK
SPEEDWELL
7¹⁵

SPRING
SPEEDWELL
7¹⁴

7¹³
WALL SPEEDWELL

AMERICAN
SPEEDWELL
7¹²

720
GREEN FIELD SPEEDWELL

7⁰6
BIRDSEYE
SPEEDWELL

IVY
SPEEDWELL
7¹⁷

GREY FIELD
SPEEDWELL
7¹⁹

SLENDER
SPEEDWELL
721

COMMON FIELD
SPEEDWELL
7¹⁸

WOOD
SPEEDWELL
7⁰⁵

HEATH
SPEEDWELL
7⁰⁴

7¹⁶
FINGERED
SPEEDWELL

THYME
SPEEDWELL
7¹⁰

2

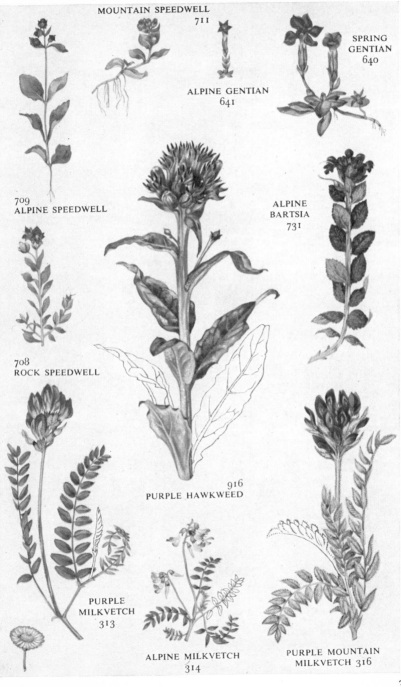

MOUNTAIN SPEEDWELL
711

ALPINE GENTIAN
641

SPRING
GENTIAN
640

709
ALPINE SPEEDWELL

ALPINE
BARTSIA
731

708
ROCK SPEEDWELL

916
PURPLE HAWKWEED

PURPLE
MILKVETCH
313

ALPINE MILKVETCH
314

PURPLE MOUNTAIN
MILKVETCH 316

3

HAREBELL 799

PASQUE FLOWER 9

FIELD
GENTIAN
642

798
CLUSTERED
BELLFLOWER

643
FELWORT

800
SPREADING
BELLFLOWER

CANTERBURY
BELL
801

797
CREEPING
BELLFLOWER

GIANT
BELLFLOWER
796

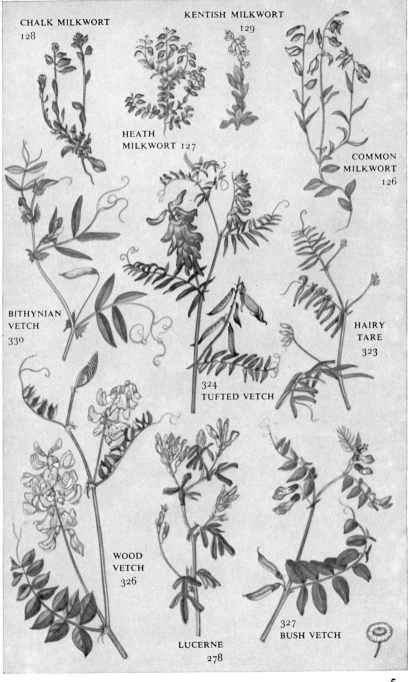

CHALK MILKWORT
128

KENTISH MILKWORT
129

HEATH
MILKWORT 127

COMMON
MILKWORT
126

BITHYNIAN
VETCH
330

HAIRY
TARE
323

324
TUFTED VETCH

WOOD
VETCH
326

327
BUSH VETCH

LUCERNE
278

5

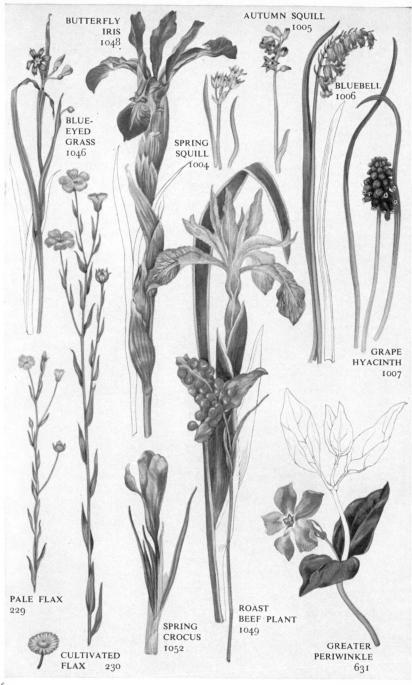

BUTTERFLY
IRIS
1048

AUTUMN SQUILL
1005

BLUEBELL
1006

BLUE-
EYED
GRASS
1046

SPRING
SQUILL
1004

GRAPE
HYACINTH
1007

PALE FLAX
229

ROAST
BEEF PLANT
1049

CULTIVATED
FLAX   230

SPRING
CROCUS
1052

GREATER
PERIWINKLE
631

6

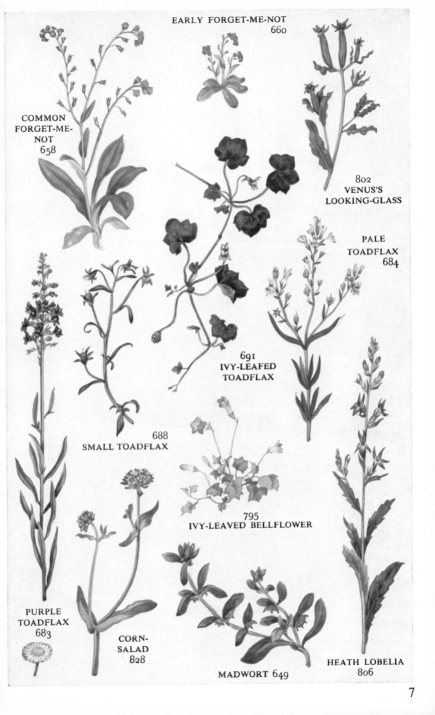

EARLY FORGET-ME-NOT
660

COMMON
FORGET-ME-
NOT
658

802
VENUS'S
LOOKING-GLASS

PALE
TOADFLAX
684

691
IVY-LEAFED
TOADFLAX

688
SMALL TOADFLAX

795
IVY-LEAVED BELLFLOWER

PURPLE
TOADFLAX
683

CORN-
SALAD
828

MADWORT 649

HEATH LOBELIA
806

7

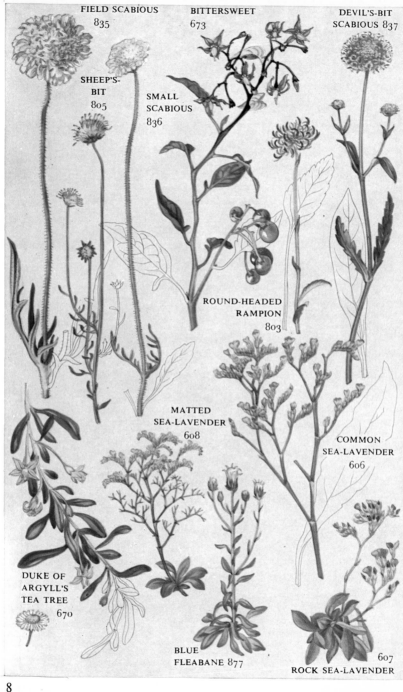

FIELD SCABIOUS
835

BITTERSWEET
673

DEVIL'S-BIT
SCABIOUS 837

SHEEP'S-
BIT
805

SMALL
SCABIOUS
836

ROUND-HEADED
RAMPION
803

MATTED
SEA-LAVENDER
608

COMMON
SEA-LAVENDER
606

DUKE OF
ARGYLL'S
TEA TREE
670

BLUE
FLEABANE 877

607
ROCK SEA-LAVENDER

8

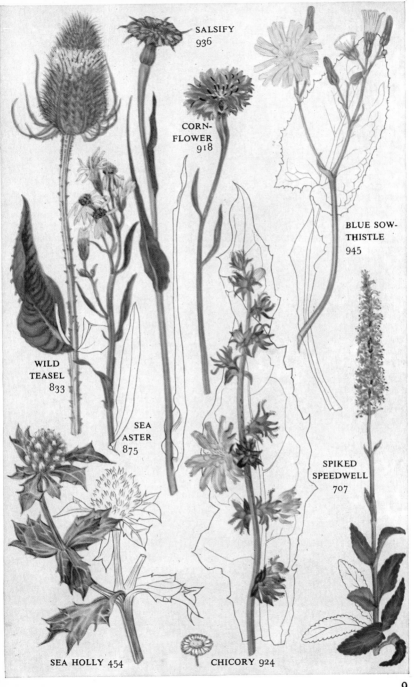

SALSIFY
936

CORN-
FLOWER
918

BLUE SOW-
THISTLE
945

WILD
TEASEL
833

SEA
ASTER
875

SPIKED
SPEEDWELL
707

SEA HOLLY 454

CHICORY 924

9

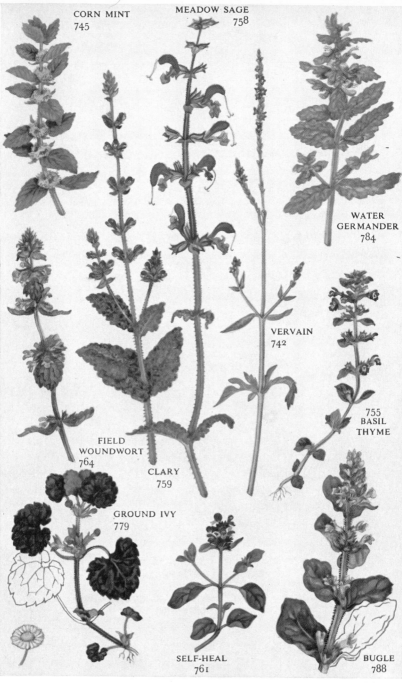

CORN MINT
745

MEADOW SAGE
758

WATER
GERMANDER
784

VERVAIN
742

FIELD
WOUNDWORT
764

CLARY
759

755
BASIL
THYME

GROUND IVY
779

SELF-HEAL
761

BUGLE
788

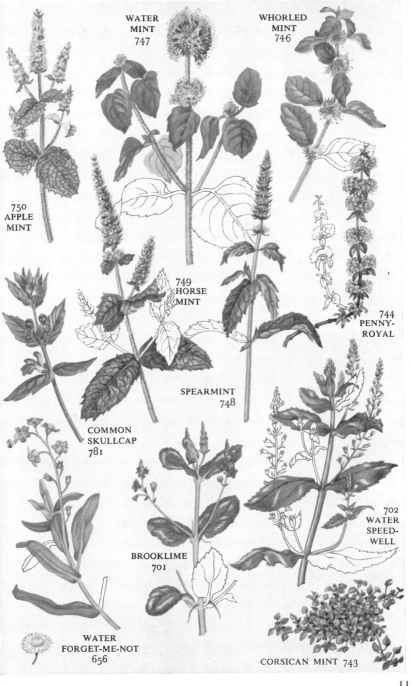

WATER MINT 747

WHORLED MINT 746

750 APPLE MINT

749 HORSE MINT

744 PENNY-ROYAL

SPEARMINT 748

COMMON SKULLCAP 781

702 WATER SPEED-WELL

BROOKLIME 701

WATER FORGET-ME-NOT 656

CORSICAN MINT 743

11

WOOD
CRANES-
BILL
234

COLUMBINE
25

JACOB'S
LADDER
646

MONKSHOOD
6

MEADOW
CRANESBILL
233

BUDDLEIA
628

SCOTTISH
LUPIN
268

MARSH GENTIAN 639

12

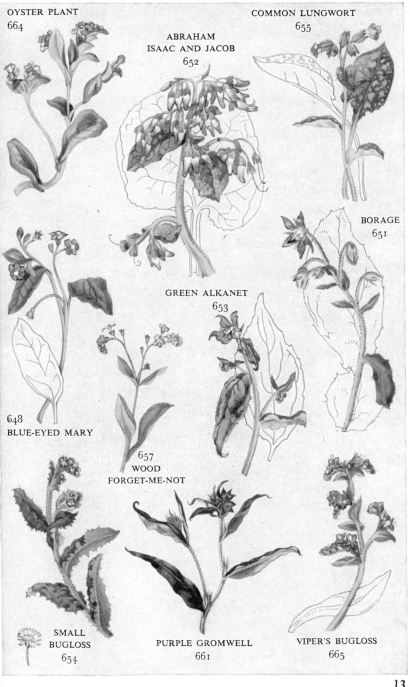

OYSTER PLANT
664

ABRAHAM
ISAAC AND JACOB
652

COMMON LUNGWORT
655

BORAGE
651

GREEN ALKANET
653

648
BLUE-EYED MARY

657
WOOD
FORGET-ME-NOT

SMALL
BUGLOSS
654

PURPLE GROMWELL
661

VIPER'S BUGLOSS
665

13

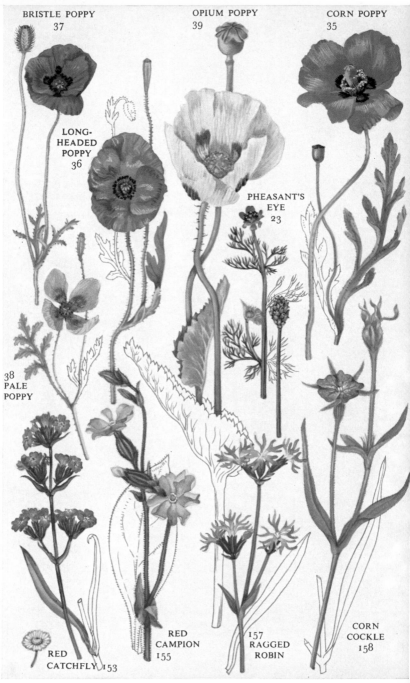

BRISTLE POPPY
37

OPIUM POPPY
39

CORN POPPY
35

LONG-
HEADED
POPPY
36

PHEASANT'S
EYE
23

38
PALE
POPPY

RED
CATCHFLY 153

RED
CAMPION
155

157
RAGGED
ROBIN

CORN
COCKLE
158

14

ROUGH MALLOW
228

KAFFIR FIG
201

MARSH
MALLOW
227

MUSK
MALLOW
223

TREE
MALLOW
226

225
DWARF MALLOW

29
WILD PEONY

COMMON
MALLOW 224

15

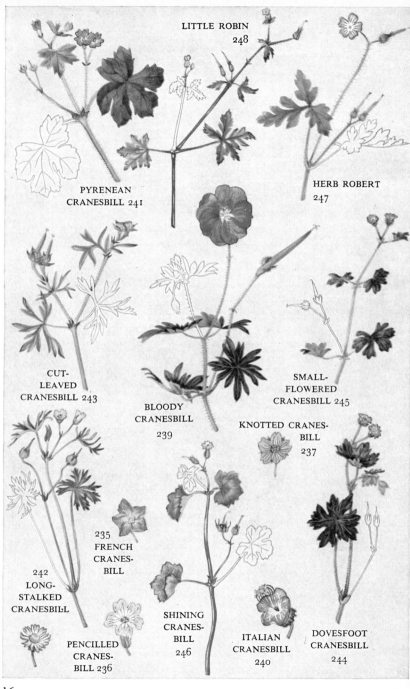

LITTLE ROBIN
248

PYRENEAN
CRANESBILL 241

HERB ROBERT
247

CUT-
LEAVED
CRANESBILL 243

BLOODY
CRANESBILL
239

SMALL-
FLOWERED
CRANESBILL 245

KNOTTED CRANES-
BILL
237

242
LONG-
STALKED
CRANESBILL

235
FRENCH
CRANES-
BILL

PENCILLED
CRANES-
BILL 236

SHINING
CRANES-
BILL
246

ITALIAN
CRANESBILL
240

DOVESFOOT
CRANESBILL
244

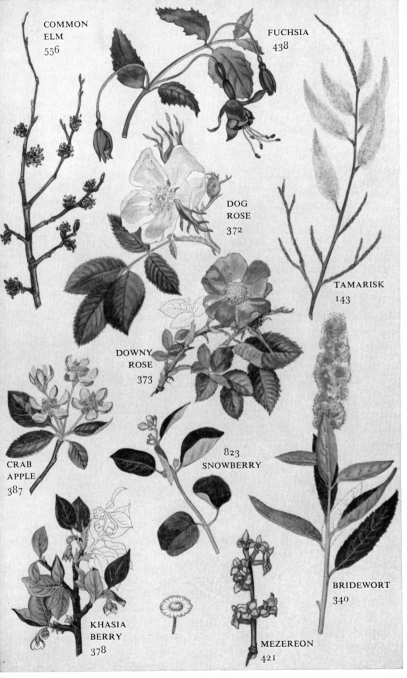

COMMON
ELM
556

FUCHSIA
438

DOG
ROSE
372

TAMARISK
143

DOWNY
ROSE
373

CRAB
APPLE
387

823
SNOWBERRY

BRIDEWORT
340

KHASIA
BERRY
378

MEZEREON
421

EVERLASTING PEA
336

MARSH
PEA
337

335
FYFIELD
PEA

HAIRY PEA
333

332
GRASS
VETCH-
LING

339
BITTER
VETCH

275
REST-HARROW

325
UPRIGHT
VETCH

329
COMMON
VETCH

SEA PEA
338

18

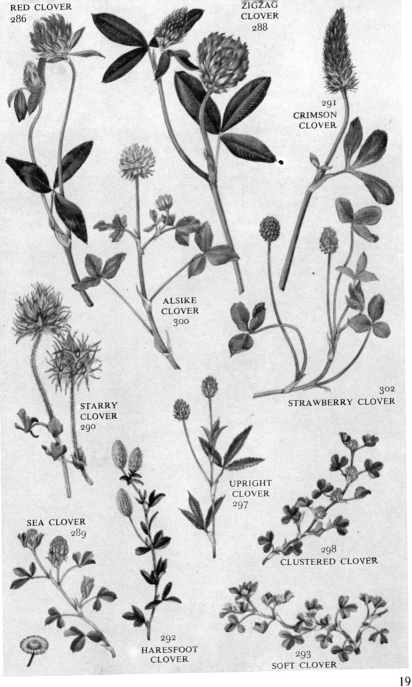

RED CLOVER
286

ZIGZAG
CLOVER
288

291
CRIMSON
CLOVER

ALSIKE
CLOVER
300

STARRY
CLOVER
290

302
STRAWBERRY CLOVER

SEA CLOVER
289

UPRIGHT
CLOVER
297

298
CLUSTERED CLOVER

292
HARESFOOT
CLOVER

293
SOFT CLOVER

19

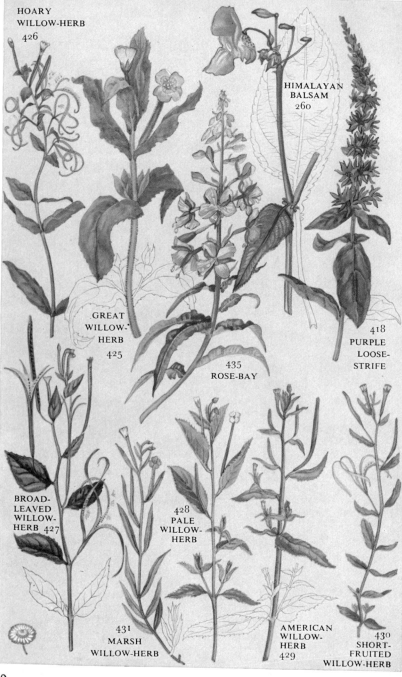

HOARY
WILLOW-HERB
426

HIMALAYAN
BALSAM
260

GREAT
WILLOW-
HERB
425

435
ROSE-BAY

418
PURPLE
LOOSE-
STRIFE

BROAD-
LEAVED
WILLOW-
HERB 427

428
PALE
WILLOW-
HERB

431
MARSH
WILLOW-HERB

AMERICAN
WILLOW-
HERB
429

430
SHORT-
FRUITED
WILLOW-HERB

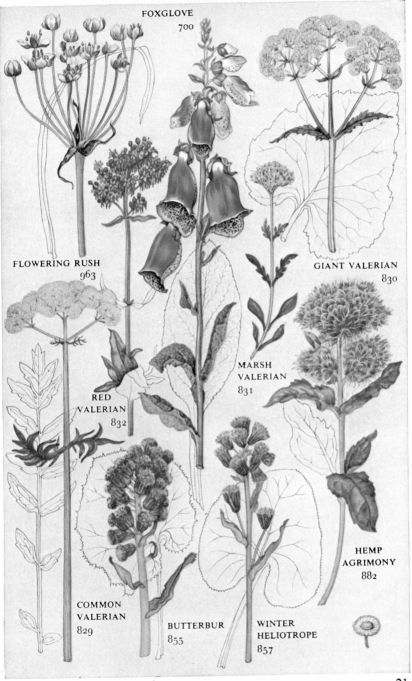

FOXGLOVE
700

FLOWERING RUSH
963

GIANT VALERIAN
830

RED
VALERIAN
832

MARSH
VALERIAN
831

HEMP
AGRIMONY
882

COMMON
VALERIAN
829

BUTTERBUR
855

WINTER
HELIOTROPE
857

21

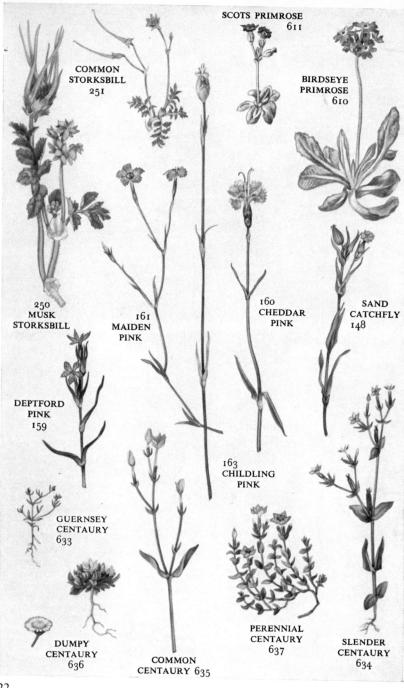

SCOTS PRIMROSE
611

COMMON
STORKSBILL
251

BIRDSEYE
PRIMROSE
610

250
MUSK
STORKSBILL

161
MAIDEN
PINK

160
CHEDDAR
PINK

SAND
CATCHFLY
148

DEPTFORD
PINK
159

163
CHILDLING
PINK

GUERNSEY
CENTAURY
633

DUMPY
CENTAURY
636

COMMON
CENTAURY 635

PERENNIAL
CENTAURY
637

SLENDER
CENTAURY
634

22

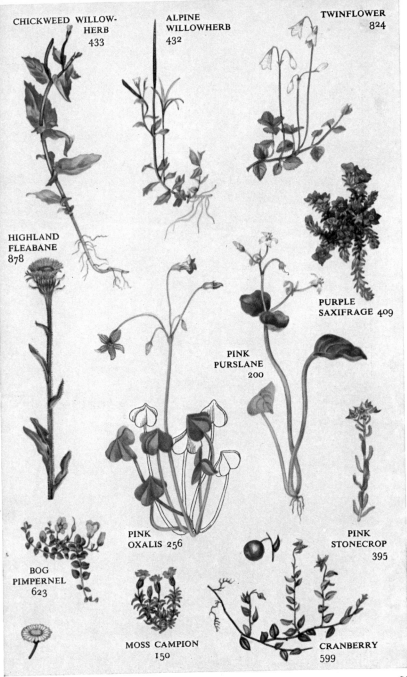

CHICKWEED WILLOW-
HERB
433

ALPINE
WILLOWHERB
432

TWINFLOWER
824

HIGHLAND
FLEABANE
878

PURPLE
SAXIFRAGE 409

PINK
PURSLANE
200

PINK
OXALIS 256

BOG
PIMPERNEL
623

PINK
STONECROP
395

MOSS CAMPION
150

CRANBERRY
599

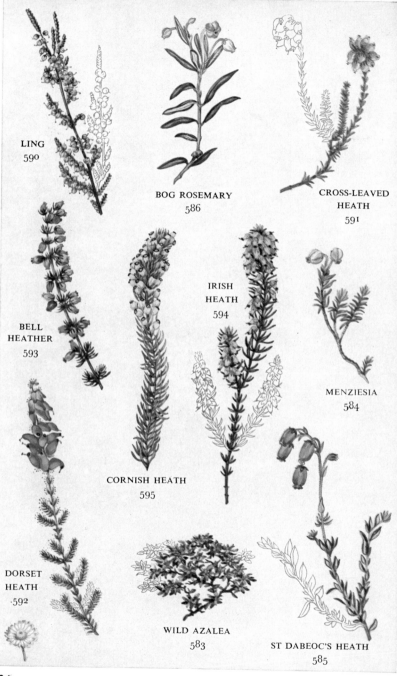

LING
590

BOG ROSEMARY
586

CROSS-LEAVED
HEATH
591

BELL
HEATHER
593

IRISH
HEATH
594

MENZIESIA
584

CORNISH HEATH
595

DORSET
HEATH
·592

WILD AZALEA
583

ST DABEOC'S HEATH
585

PINK
MASTERWORT
453

349
MARSH
CINQUEFOIL

CORALROOT
91

LADY'S SMOCK
86

WATER
AVENS
361

SOAPWORT
162

SAINFOIN
322

PITCHER PLANT
417

CROWN
VETCH
320

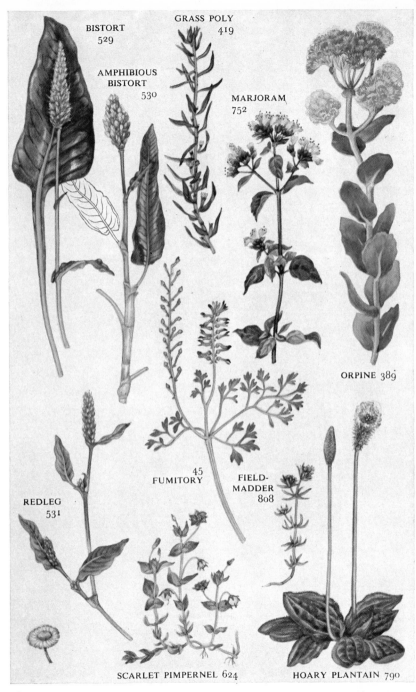

BISTORT
529

GRASS POLY
419

AMPHIBIOUS
BISTORT
530

MARJORAM
752

ORPINE 389

45
FUMITORY

FIELD-
MADDER
808

REDLEG
531

SCARLET PIMPERNEL 624

HOARY PLANTAIN 790

26

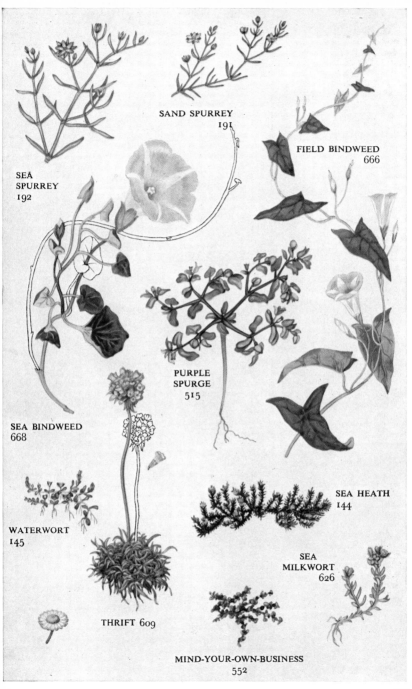

SAND SPURREY
191

FIELD BINDWEED
666

SEA
SPURREY
192

PURPLE
SPURGE
515

SEA BINDWEED
668

WATERWORT
145

SEA HEATH
144

SEA
MILKWORT
626

THRIFT 609

MIND-YOUR-OWN-BUSINESS
552

27

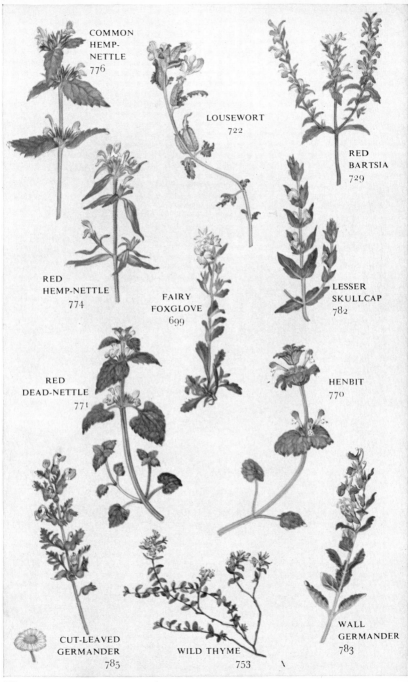

COMMON
HEMP-
NETTLE
776

LOUSEWORT
722

RED
BARTSIA
729

RED
HEMP-NETTLE
774

FAIRY
FOXGLOVE
699

LESSER
SKULLCAP
782

RED
DEAD-NETTLE
771

HENBIT
770

CUT-LEAVED
GERMANDER
785

WILD THYME
753

WALL
GERMANDER
783

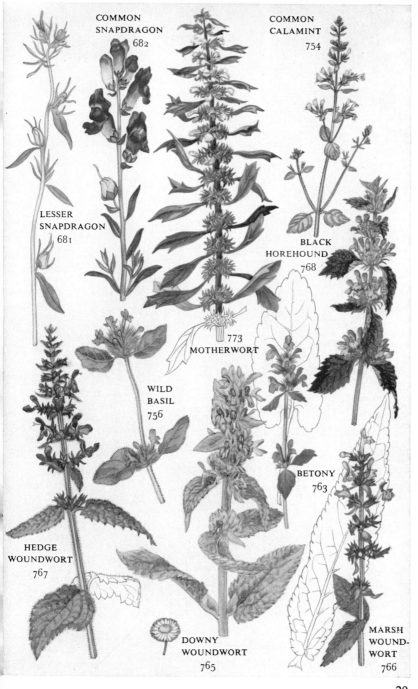

COMMON
SNAPDRAGON
68²

COMMON
CALAMINT
754

LESSER
SNAPDRAGON
68₁

BLACK
HOREHOUND
768

773
MOTHERWORT

WILD
BASIL
75⁶

BETONY
76³

HEDGE
WOUNDWORT
76⁷

DOWNY
WOUNDWORT
76⁵

MARSH
WOUND-
WORT
766

29

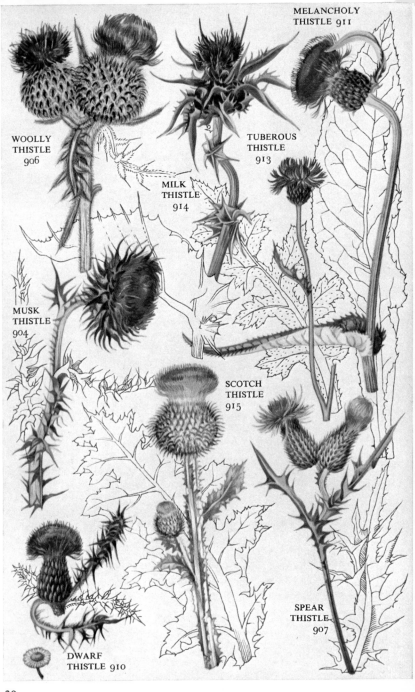

WOOLLY
THISTLE
906

MELANCHOLY
THISTLE 911

TUBEROUS
THISTLE
913

MILK
THISTLE
914

MUSK
THISTLE
904

SCOTCH
THISTLE
915

SPEAR
THISTLE
907

DWARF
THISTLE 910

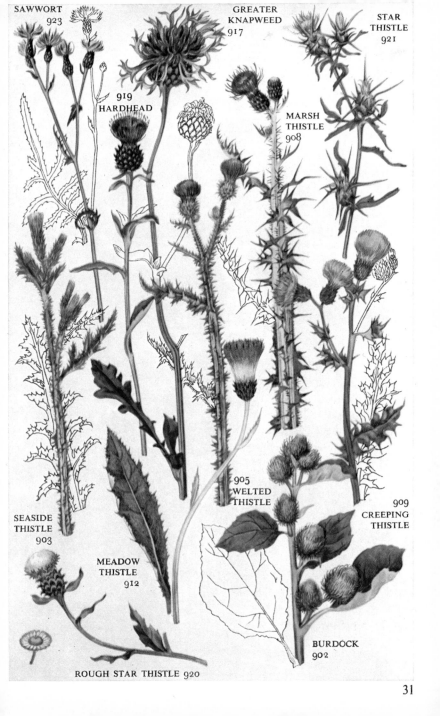

SAWWORT
923

GREATER
KNAPWEED
917

STAR
THISTLE
921

919
HARDHEAD

MARSH
THISTLE
908

905
WELTED
THISTLE

909
CREEPING
THISTLE

SEASIDE
THISTLE
903

MEADOW
THISTLE
912

BURDOCK
902

ROUGH STAR THISTLE 920

31

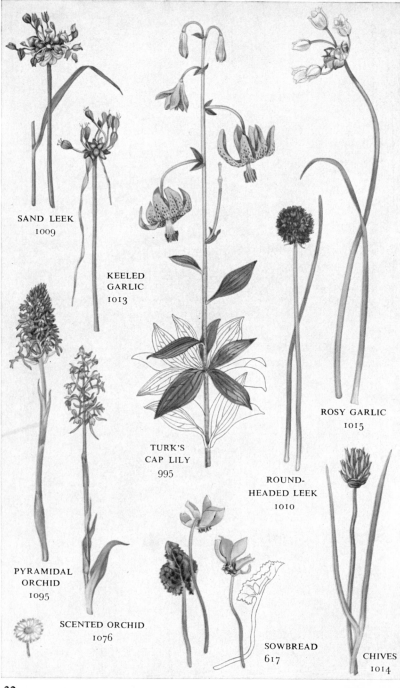

SAND LEEK
1009

KEELED
GARLIC
1013

PYRAMIDAL
ORCHID
1095

SCENTED ORCHID
1076

TURK'S
CAP LILY
995

ROUND-
HEADED LEEK
1010

SOWBREAD
617

ROSY GARLIC
1015

CHIVES
1014

32

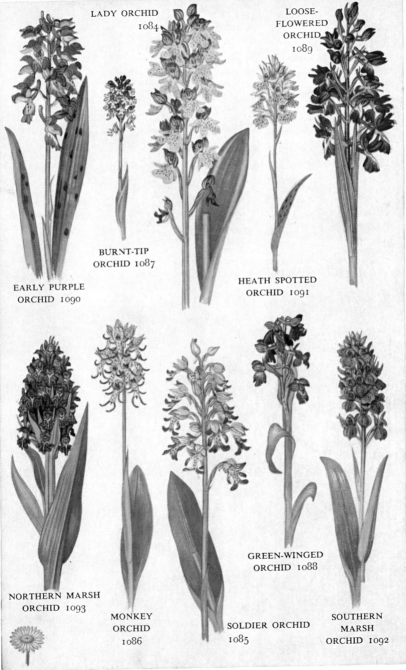

LADY ORCHID
1084

LOOSE-
FLOWERED
ORCHID
1089

BURNT-TIP
ORCHID 1087

EARLY PURPLE
ORCHID 1090

HEATH SPOTTED
ORCHID 1091

NORTHERN MARSH
ORCHID 1093

MONKEY
ORCHID
1086

GREEN-WINGED
ORCHID 1088

SOLDIER ORCHID
1085

SOUTHERN
MARSH
ORCHID 1092

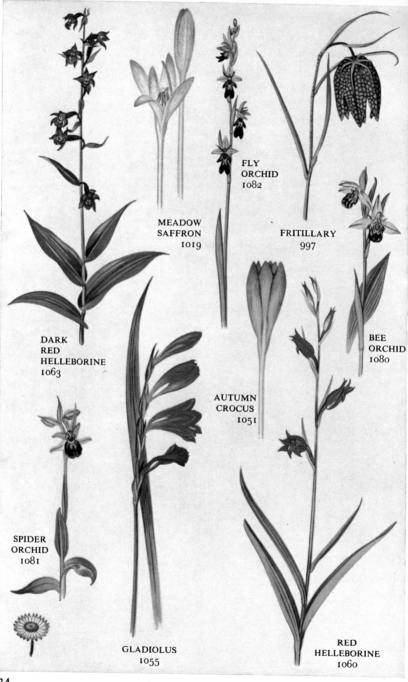

DARK
RED
HELLEBORINE
1063

SPIDER
ORCHID
1081

MEADOW
SAFFRON
1019

FLY
ORCHID
1082

GLADIOLUS
1055

AUTUMN
CROCUS
1051

FRITILLARY
997

BEE
ORCHID
1080

RED
HELLEBORINE
1060

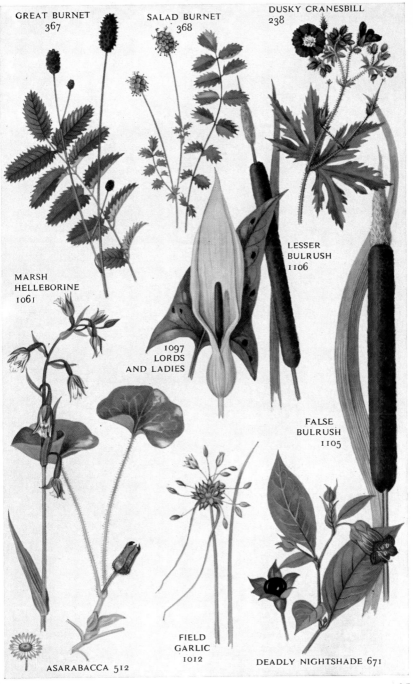

GREAT BURNET
367

SALAD BURNET
368

DUSKY CRANESBILL
238

MARSH
HELLEBORINE
1061

LESSER
BULRUSH
1106

1097
LORDS
AND LADIES

FALSE
BULRUSH
1105

ASARABACCA 512

FIELD
GARLIC
1012

DEADLY NIGHTSHADE 671

35

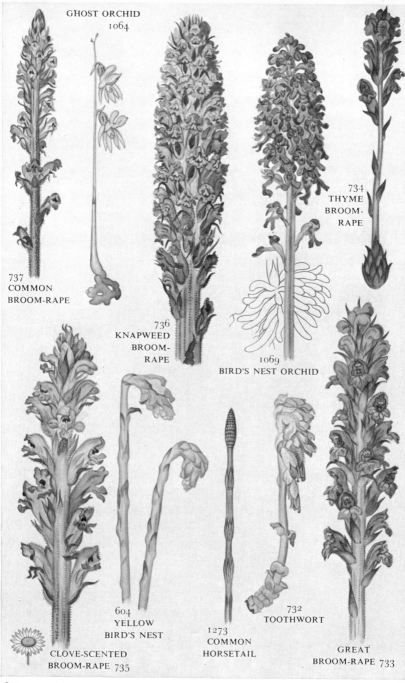

GHOST ORCHID
1064

737
COMMON
BROOM-RAPE

736
KNAPWEED
BROOM-
RAPE

734
THYME
BROOM-
RAPE

1069
BIRD'S NEST ORCHID

604
YELLOW
BIRD'S NEST

1273
COMMON
HORSETAIL

732
TOOTHWORT

CLOVE-SCENTED
BROOM-RAPE 735

GREAT
BROOM-RAPE 733

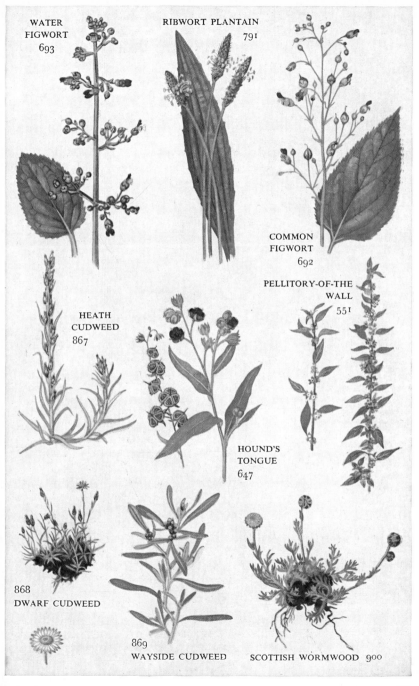

WATER
FIGWORT
693

RIBWORT PLANTAIN
791

COMMON
FIGWORT
692

PELLITORY-OF-THE
WALL
551

HEATH
CUDWEED
867

HOUND'S
TONGUE
647

868
DWARF CUDWEED

869
WAYSIDE CUDWEED

SCOTTISH WORMWOOD 900

37

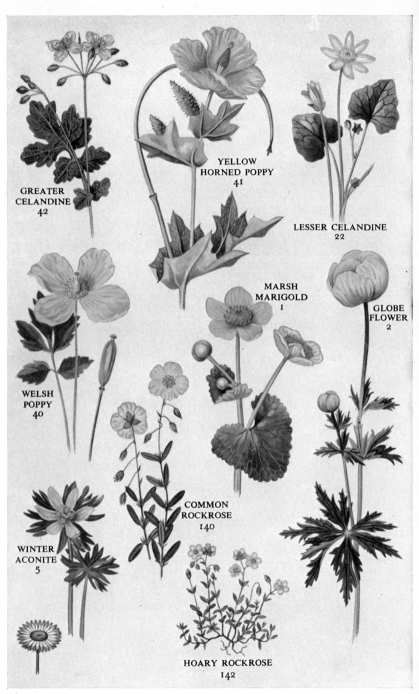

GREATER
CELANDINE
42

YELLOW
HORNED POPPY
41

LESSER CELANDINE
22

WELSH
POPPY
40

MARSH
MARIGOLD
1

GLOBE
FLOWER
2

COMMON
ROCKROSE
140

WINTER
ACONITE
5

HOARY ROCKROSE
142

38

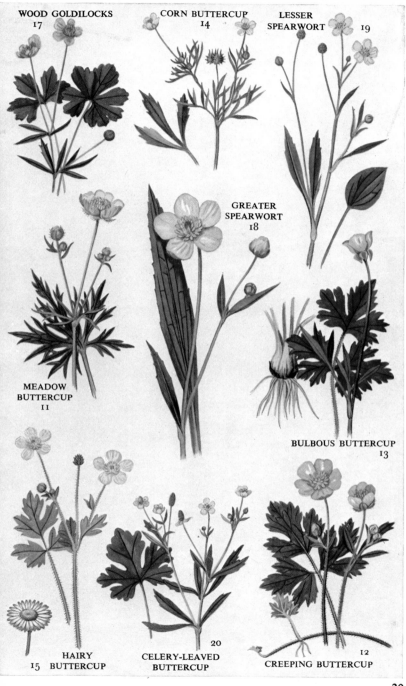

WOOD GOLDILOCKS
17

CORN BUTTERCUP
14

LESSER
SPEARWORT   19

GREATER
SPEARWORT
18

MEADOW
BUTTERCUP
11

BULBOUS BUTTERCUP
13

HAIRY
15   BUTTERCUP

CELERY-LEAVED
BUTTERCUP
20

CREEPING BUTTERCUP
12

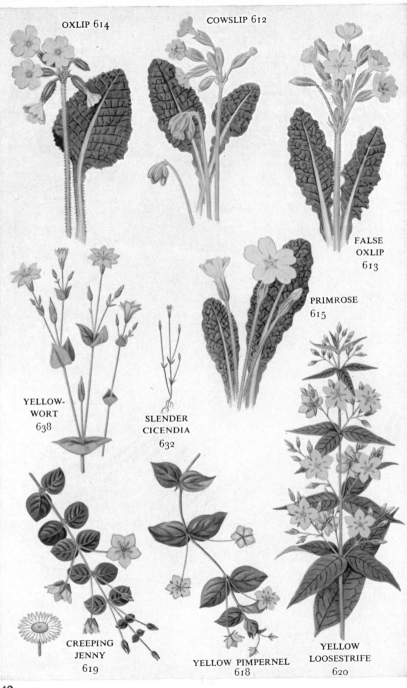

OXLIP 614

COWSLIP 612

FALSE OXLIP 613

PRIMROSE 615

YELLOW-WORT 638

SLENDER CICENDIA 632

CREEPING JENNY 619

YELLOW PIMPERNEL 618

YELLOW LOOSESTRIFE 620

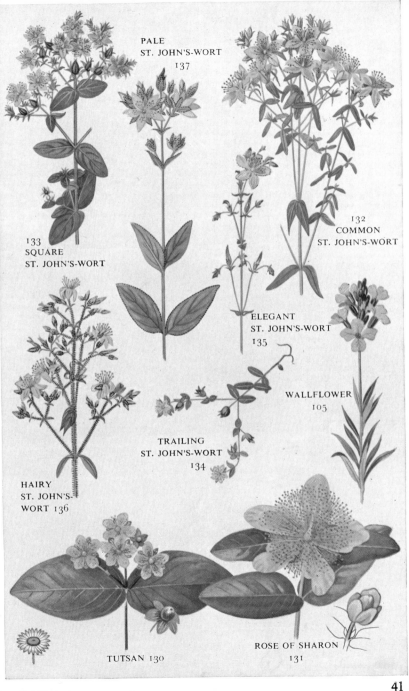

PALE
ST. JOHN'S-WORT
137

133
SQUARE
ST. JOHN'S-WORT

132
COMMON
ST. JOHN'S-WORT

ELEGANT
ST. JOHN'S-WORT
135

WALLFLOWER
105

TRAILING
ST. JOHN'S-WORT
134

HAIRY
ST. JOHN'S-
WORT 136

TUTSAN 130

ROSE OF SHARON
131

41

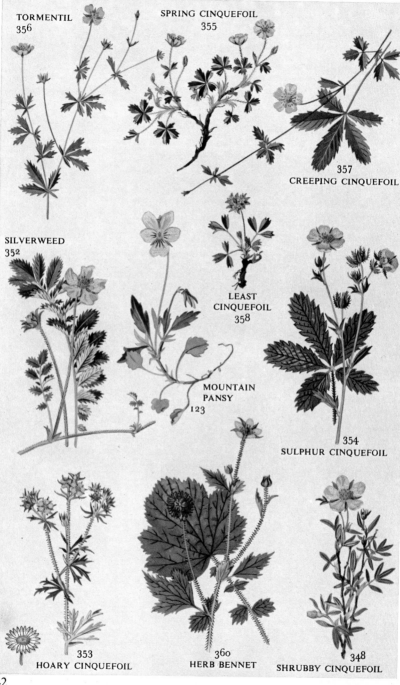

TORMENTIL
356

SPRING CINQUEFOIL
355

357
CREEPING CINQUEFOIL

SILVERWEED
352

LEAST
CINQUEFOIL
358

MOUNTAIN
PANSY
123

354
SULPHUR CINQUEFOIL

353
HOARY CINQUEFOIL

360
HERB BENNET

348
SHRUBBY CINQUEFOIL

42

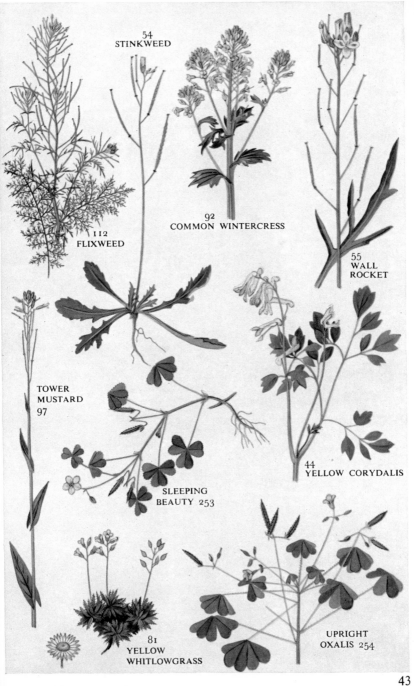

54
STINKWEED

112
FLIXWEED

92
COMMON WINTERCRESS

55
WALL
ROCKET

TOWER
MUSTARD
97

44
YELLOW CORYDALIS

SLEEPING
BEAUTY 253

81
YELLOW
WHITLOWGRASS

UPRIGHT
OXALIS 254

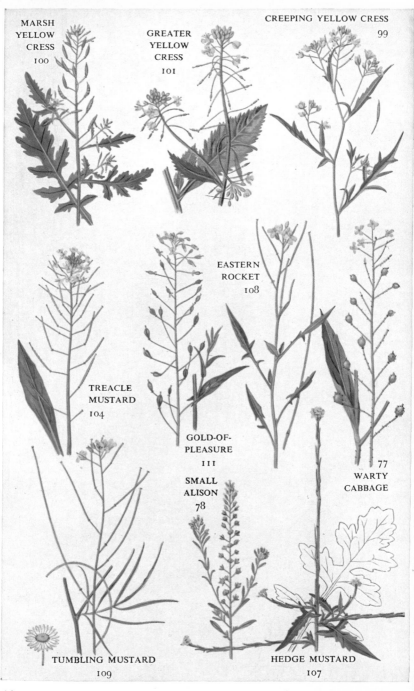

MARSH
YELLOW
CRESS
100

GREATER
YELLOW
CRESS
101

CREEPING YELLOW CRESS
99

TREACLE
MUSTARD
104

EASTERN
ROCKET
108

GOLD-OF-
PLEASURE
111

SMALL
ALISON
78

77
WARTY
CABBAGE

TUMBLING MUSTARD
109

HEDGE MUSTARD
107

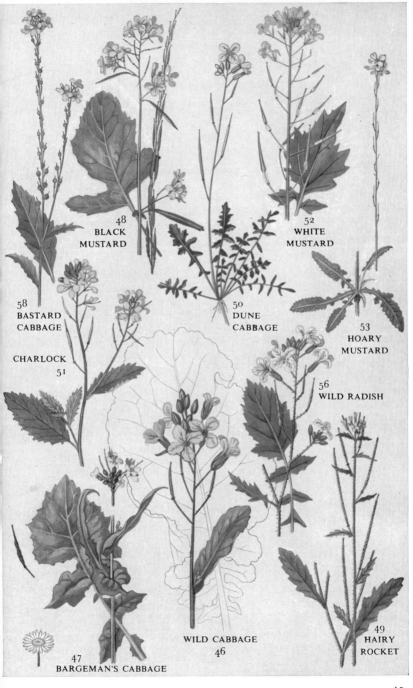

48
BLACK
MUSTARD

52
WHITE
MUSTARD

58
BASTARD
CABBAGE

50
DUNE
CABBAGE

53
HOARY
MUSTARD

CHARLOCK
51

56
WILD RADISH

47
BARGEMAN'S CABBAGE

WILD CABBAGE
46

49
HAIRY
ROCKET

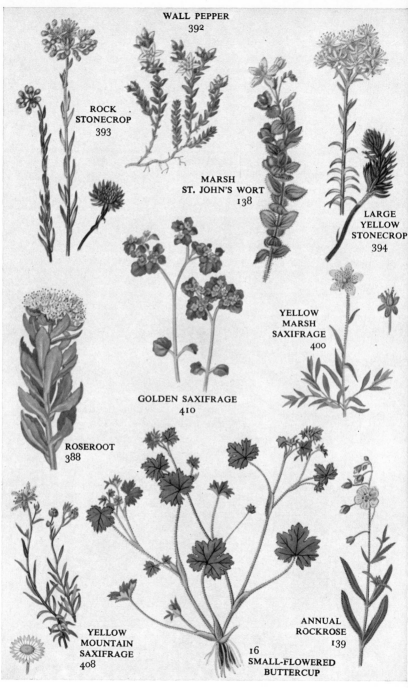

WALL PEPPER
392

ROCK
STONECROP
393

MARSH
ST. JOHN'S WORT
138

LARGE
YELLOW
STONECROP
394

YELLOW
MARSH
SAXIFRAGE
400

GOLDEN SAXIFRAGE
410

ROSEROOT
388

YELLOW
MOUNTAIN
SAXIFRAGE
408

16
SMALL-FLOWERED
BUTTERCUP

ANNUAL
ROCKROSE
139

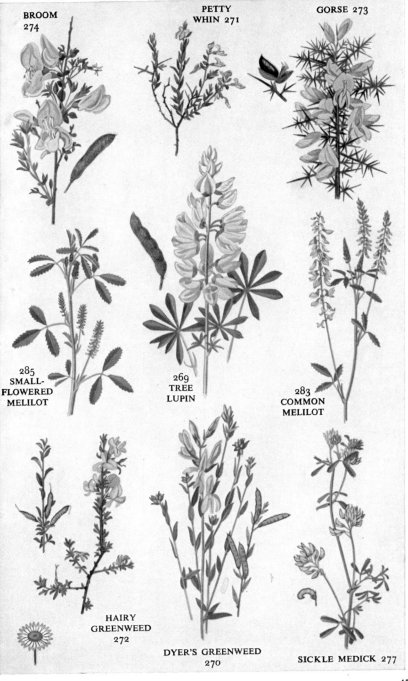

BROOM
274

PETTY
WHIN 271

GORSE 273

285
SMALL-
FLOWERED
MELILOT

269
TREE
LUPIN

283
COMMON
MELILOT

HAIRY
GREENWEED
272

DYER'S GREENWEED
270

SICKLE MEDICK 277

47

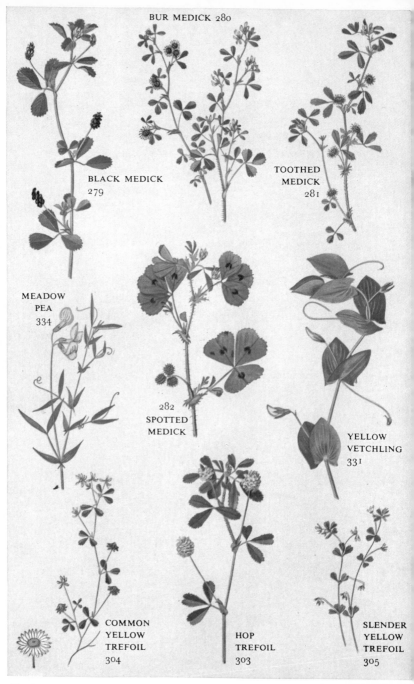

BUR MEDICK 280

BLACK MEDICK
279

TOOTHED
MEDICK
281

MEADOW
PEA
334

282
SPOTTED
MEDICK

YELLOW
VETCHLING
331

COMMON
YELLOW
TREFOIL
304

HOP
TREFOIL
303

SLENDER
YELLOW
TREFOIL
305

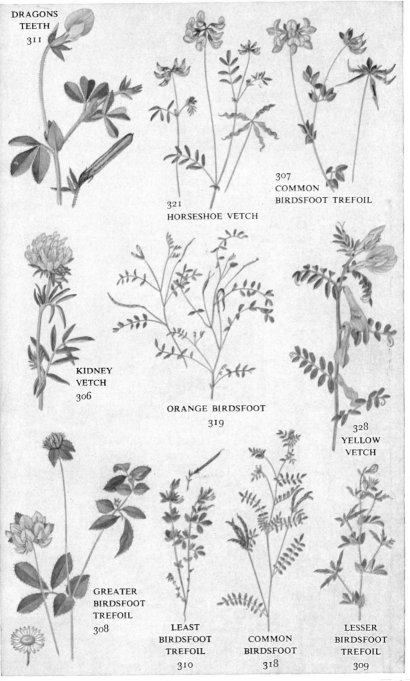

DRAGONS
TEETH
311

321
HORSESHOE VETCH

307
COMMON
BIRDSFOOT TREFOIL

KIDNEY
VETCH
306

ORANGE BIRDSFOOT
319

328
YELLOW
VETCH

GREATER
BIRDSFOOT
TREFOIL
308

LEAST
BIRDSFOOT
TREFOIL
310

COMMON
BIRDSFOOT
318

LESSER
BIRDSFOOT
TREFOIL
309

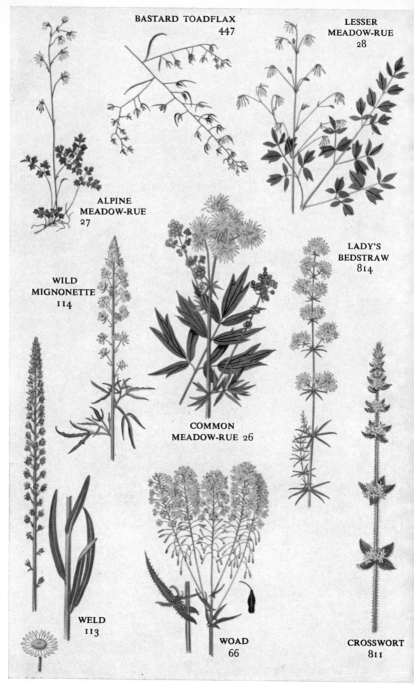

BASTARD TOADFLAX
447

LESSER
MEADOW-RUE
28

ALPINE
MEADOW-RUE
27

LADY'S
BEDSTRAW
814

WILD
MIGNONETTE
114

COMMON
MEADOW-RUE 26

WELD
113

WOAD
66

CROSSWORT
811

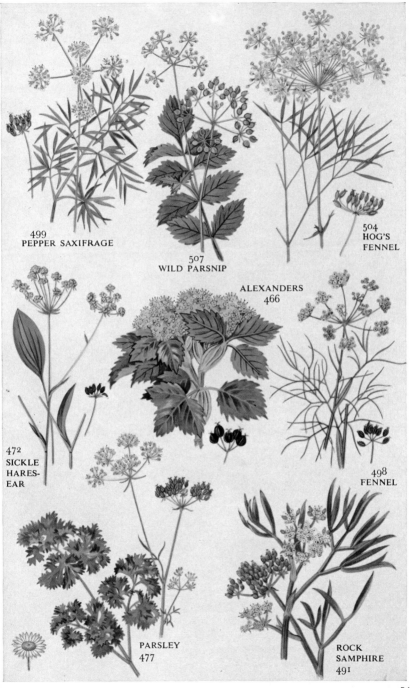

499
PEPPER SAXIFRAGE

507
WILD PARSNIP

504
HOG'S
FENNEL

ALEXANDERS
466

472
SICKLE
HARES-
EAR

498
FENNEL

PARSLEY
477

ROCK
SAMPHIRE
491

51

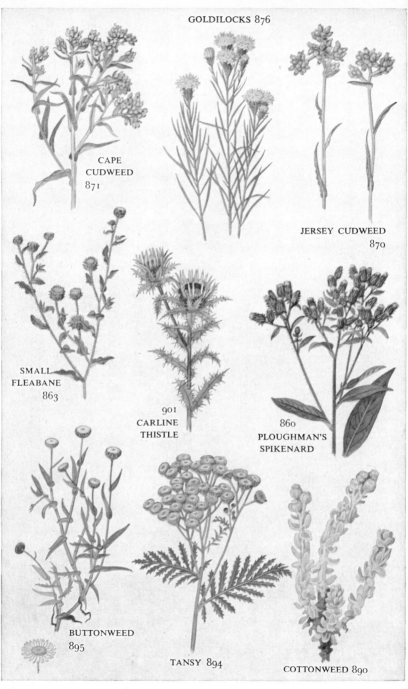

GOLDILOCKS 876

CAPE
CUDWEED
871

JERSEY CUDWEED
870

SMALL
FLEABANE
863

901
CARLINE
THISTLE

860
PLOUGHMAN'S
SPIKENARD

BUTTONWEED
895

TANSY 894

COTTONWEED 890

52

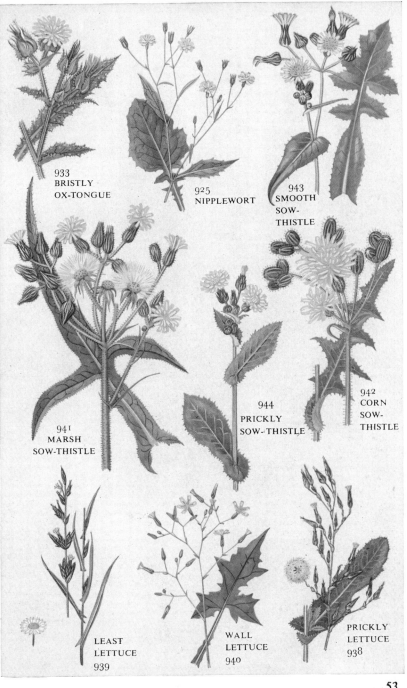

933
BRISTLY
OX-TONGUE

925
NIPPLEWORT

943
SMOOTH
SOW-
THISTLE

941
MARSH
SOW-THISTLE

944
PRICKLY
SOW-THISTLE

942
CORN
SOW-
THISTLE

LEAST
LETTUCE
939

WALL
LETTUCE
940

PRICKLY
LETTUCE
938

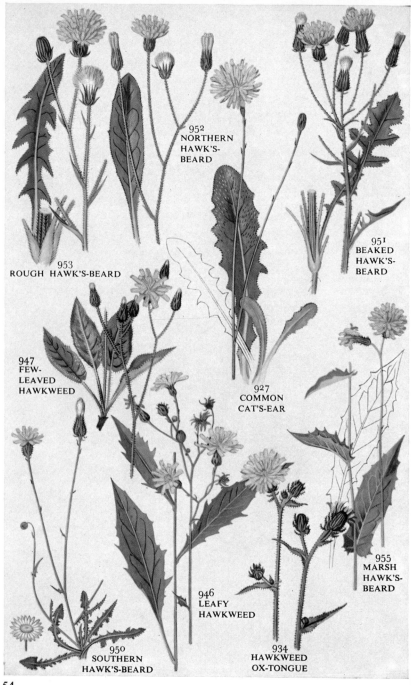

952 NORTHERN HAWK'S-BEARD

953 ROUGH HAWK'S-BEARD

951 BEAKED HAWK'S-BEARD

947 FEW-LEAVED HAWKWEED

927 COMMON CAT'S-EAR

955 MARSH HAWK'S-BEARD

946 LEAFY HAWKWEED

950 SOUTHERN HAWK'S-BEARD

934 HAWKWEED OX-TONGUE

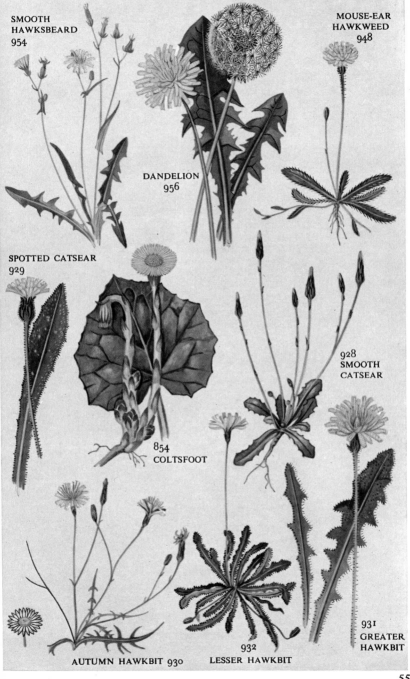

SMOOTH
HAWKSBEARD
954

MOUSE-EAR
HAWKWEED
948

DANDELION
956

SPOTTED CATSEAR
929

928
SMOOTH
CATSEAR

854
COLTSFOOT

931
GREATER
HAWKBIT

AUTUMN HAWKBIT 930

932
LESSER HAWKBIT

55

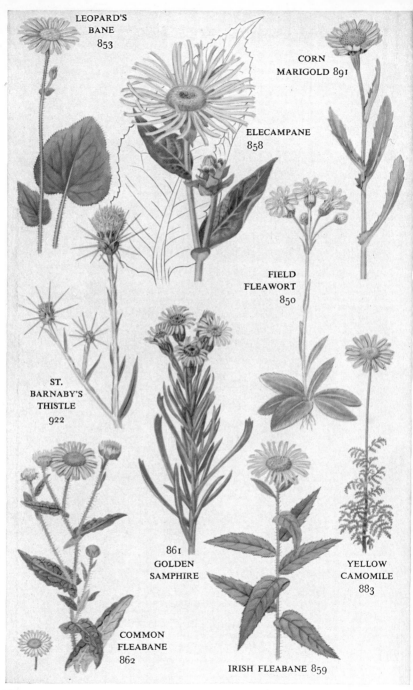

LEOPARD'S
BANE
853

ELECAMPANE
858

CORN
MARIGOLD 891

FIELD
FLEAWORT
850

ST.
BARNABY'S
THISTLE
922

861
GOLDEN
SAMPHIRE

YELLOW
CAMOMILE
883

COMMON
FLEABANE
862

IRISH FLEABANE 859

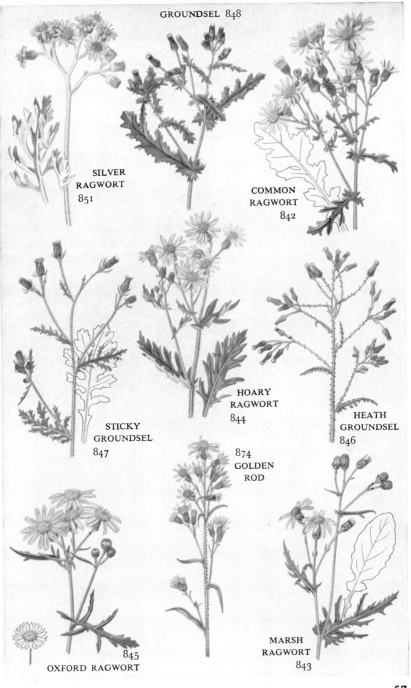

GROUNDSEL 848

SILVER
RAGWORT
851

COMMON
RAGWORT
842

STICKY
GROUNDSEL
847

HOARY
RAGWORT
844

HEATH
GROUNDSEL
846

874
GOLDEN
ROD

OXFORD RAGWORT
845

MARSH
RAGWORT
843

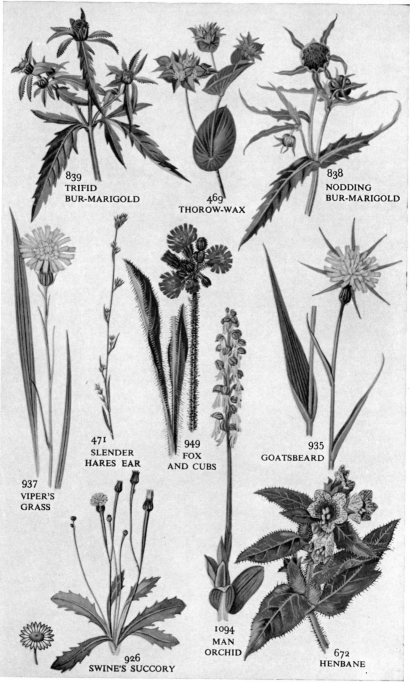

839
TRIFID
BUR-MARIGOLD

469
THOROW-WAX

838
NODDING
BUR-MARIGOLD

471
SLENDER
HARES EAR

949
FOX
AND CUBS

935
GOATSBEARD

937
VIPER'S
GRASS

926
SWINE'S SUCCORY

1094
MAN
ORCHID

672
HENBANE

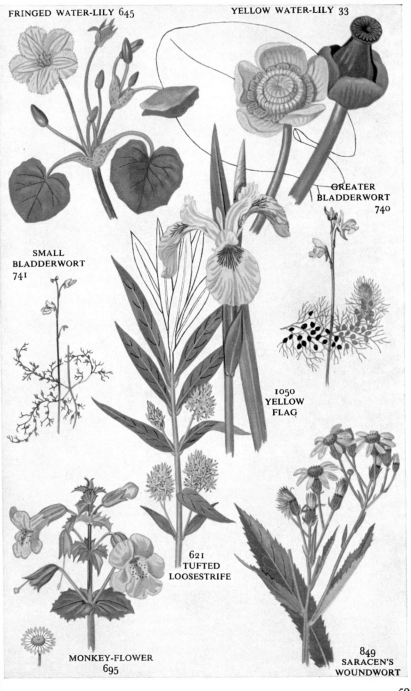

FRINGED WATER-LILY 645

YELLOW WATER-LILY 33

GREATER
BLADDERWORT
740

SMALL
BLADDERWORT
741

1050
YELLOW
FLAG

621
TUFTED
LOOSESTRIFE

MONKEY-FLOWER
695

849
SARACEN'S
WOUNDWORT

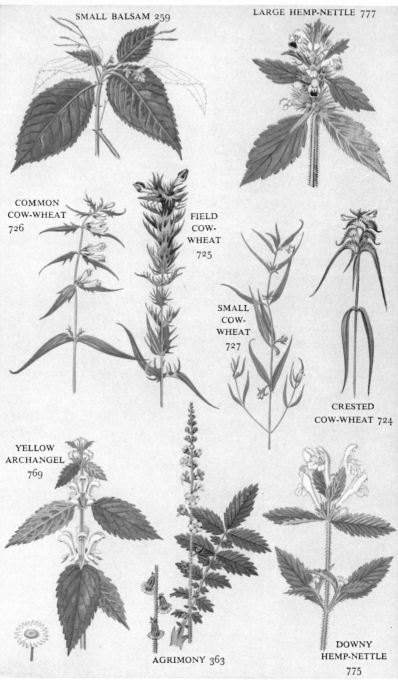

SMALL BALSAM 259

LARGE HEMP-NETTLE 777

COMMON COW-WHEAT 726

FIELD COW-WHEAT 725

SMALL COW-WHEAT 727

CRESTED COW-WHEAT 724

YELLOW ARCHANGEL 769

AGRIMONY 363

DOWNY HEMP-NETTLE 775

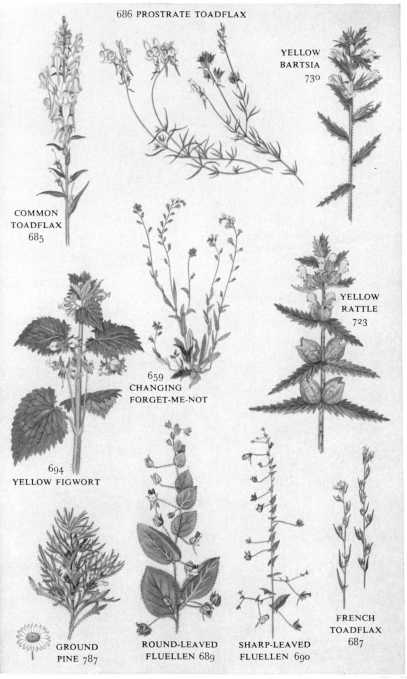

686 PROSTRATE TOADFLAX

YELLOW
BARTSIA
730

COMMON
TOADFLAX
685

YELLOW
RATTLE
723

659
CHANGING
FORGET-ME-NOT

694
YELLOW FIGWORT

GROUND
PINE 787

ROUND-LEAVED
FLUELLEN 689

SHARP-LEAVED
FLUELLEN 690

FRENCH
TOADFLAX
687

HOARY
MULLEIN
678

FRAGRANT
EVENING
PRIMROSE
437

LARGE-FLOWERED
MULLEIN
680

DARK MULLEIN
679

COMMON
MULLEIN
676

436
LARGE EVENING
PRIMROSE

257
TOUCH-ME-NOT

258
JEWEL-WEED

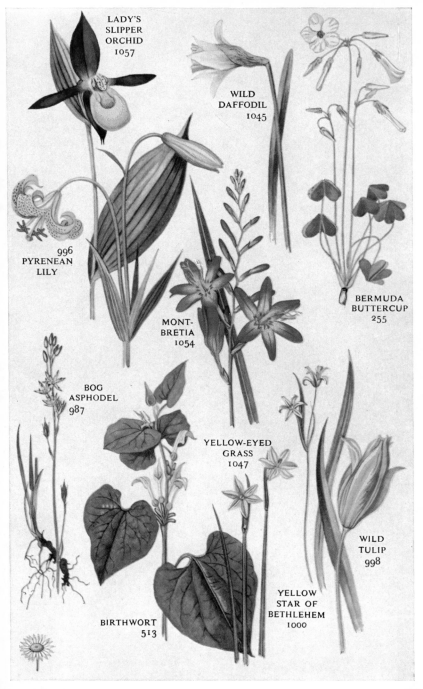

LADY'S
SLIPPER
ORCHID
1057

WILD
DAFFODIL
1045

996
PYRENEAN
LILY

MONT-
BRETIA
1054

BERMUDA
BUTTERCUP
255

BOG
ASPHODEL
987

YELLOW-EYED
GRASS
1047

WILD
TULIP
998

BIRTHWORT
513

YELLOW
STAR OF
BETHLEHEM
1000

63

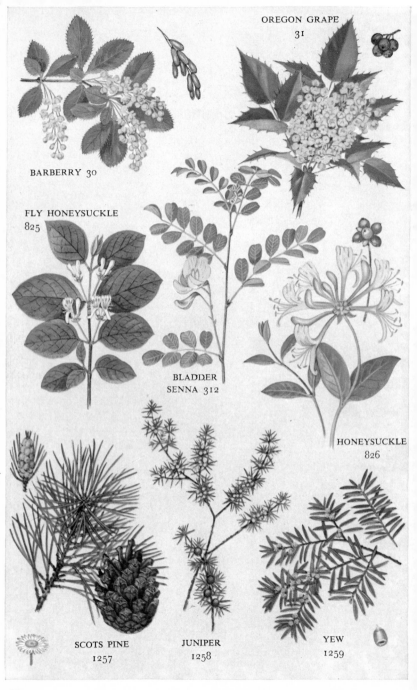

OREGON GRAPE
31

BARBERRY 30

FLY HONEYSUCKLE
825

BLADDER
SENNA 312

HONEYSUCKLE
826

SCOTS PINE
1257

JUNIPER
1258

YEW
1259

255. ***BERMUDA BUTTERCUP *O. pes-caprae* L.   Plate 63.   *CTW*†
An attractive hairless perennial, 6–12 in. high, with large butter-yellow flowers, not unreminiscent of miniature daffodils, in umbels on unbranched leafless stems. Leaves in a tuft at the base, sometimes with pale brown blotch. *Habitat:* Too plentiful in some bulb-fields in the Scilly Is. March–June.

256. **PINK OXALIS *O. floribunda* Lehmann   Plate 23.   *CTW, p. 397*
A favourite cottage plant with large tufts of leaves all from the woody root, the leaflets hairy with numerous pale orange spots beneath. Flowers large, bright rose-pink, in umbels on 6–12-in. stems. *Habitat:* Occasional in bushy and waste places, sometimes well away from gardens. May–September.

BALSAM FAMILY Balsaminaceae

BRITTLE HAIRLESS ANNUALS, with fleshy stems and oval stalked, slightly toothed leaves. Their highly characteristic flowers have a broad lower lip, a small upper hood and a spur behind, often curved. The flower-stalks are usually fairly long, giving the whole blossom a Chinese-lantern effect. The seeds explode from the ripe cylindrical fruits.

257. **TOUCH-ME-NOT *Impatiens noli-tangere* L.   Plate 62.   *CTW, p. 398*
Differs from Jewel-weed (258) in having larger hanging yellow flowers, sometimes speckled red, and with the spur curved downwards. *Habitat:* Very local in damp woods in NW England and N Wales; very rare elsewhere. July–September.

258. *JEWEL-WEED *I. capensis* Meerburgh   Plate 62.   *CTW, p. 398*
Orange Balsam; *I. biflora* Walter
A gay Balsam often forming fine bushes 3–4 ft. high, the orange flowers with numerous blood-red spots, their long slender spur bent right round into a crook; leaves alternate. *Habitat:* Locally common and increasing by river- and stream-sides in the S. July–September.

259. *SMALL BALSAM *I. parviflora* DC.   Plate 60.   *CTW, p. 398*
Our smallest and weediest Balsam, 6 in. to 2 ft. high, with large leaves, and very small pale yellow unspotted flowers with a short straight spur. *Habitat:* Widespread and increasing, but still local, in dry shady and waste places and on river banks, especially in the S. June–September.

260. *HIMALAYAN BALSAM *I. glandulifera* Royle   Plate 20.   *CTW, p. 399*
A tall imposing handsome Balsam, with thick-ribbed, often reddish stems, leaves in twos or threes, with small red teeth, and large flowers varying from palest to darkest pinkish-purple, with a short thin bent spur. *Habitat:* Widespread and local, but increasingly common and often in dense masses, by rivers and streams, also in dry waste places. July onwards.

MAPLE FAMILY Aceraceae

261. SYCAMORE *Acer pseudoplatanus* L.   Plate 70.   *CTW, p. 400*
A familiar wayside tree, whose leaves are ivy-shaped like the smaller Maple (262), but are much larger and almost completely hairless below, attacked in

C

autumn by a fungus which makes large unsightly black blotches. A large deciduous tree, with smooth grey bark, scaling in oblong flakes in old age, and hairless twigs. Flowers, separately male and female, yellowish-green in long, hanging clusters. Fruits hairless, with a long wing on one side, the pairs of keys spreading nearly at right angles. Not to be confused with the London Plane (*Platanus acerifolia* Willdenow), often planted in streets and parks, which has somewhat similar leaves but bark peeling off in irregular patches at all ages and fruits like tiny rolled hedgehogs hanging on long slender stalks. *Habitat:* Widespread and common in woods, parks and hedgerows. May–June.

262. MAPLE *A. campestre* L.   Plate 70.   *CTW, p. 401*
A small deciduous tree or hedgerow shrub, with light grey rough bark, and more or less downy twigs, which later become corky; leaves 5-lobed and ivy-like, downy beneath, often with the inner stalk of a pair shorter, turning bright red and yellow in autumn. Flowers separately male and female, in clusters of rather few, yellowish-green, more or less erect. Fruits like Sycamore (261), usually downy, the keys spreading horizontally. *Habitat:* Widespread and common in woods, thickets and hedgerows, especially on chalk and limestone; rare in Scotland and Ireland. May–June.

HOLLY FAMILY Aquifoliaceae

263. HOLLY *Ilex aquifolium* L.   Plate 76.   *CTW, p.* 404
The familiar Xmas decoration, with its glossy, wavy, usually prickly, thick dark green leaves, and red berries; a small evergreen tree or shrub with grey bark, smooth except in old trees; twigs green. Flowers small, 4-petalled, white, often tinged purple, in close clusters, the male and female on different trees, so that berries only appear on female ones where there is a male nearby. *Habitat:* Widespread and common in woods, hedgerows and thickets. May–August.

SPINDLE-TREE FAMILY Celastraceae

264. SPINDLE-TREE *Euonymus europaeus* L.   Plate 71.   *CTW, p. 405*
Very distinctive in autumn, with its peculiar bright coral-pink berries; much less noticeable in summer. A tall slender deciduous shrub, 6–12 ft. high, with smooth grey bark and green twigs; leaves opposite, lanceolate, slightly toothed, turning pinkish-red in autumn, with the small stalked clusters of insignificant, 4-petalled, greenish-white flowers at their base. The 4 stamens alternate with the petals. The white seeds are covered by an orange coat, and lie in fours within the 4-lobed coral-pink fruit. *Habitat:* Widespread and locally common in and by woods, thickets and hedgerows, especially on chalk and limestone; local in Scotland. May–June.

BOX FAMILY Buxaceae

265. **BOX *Buxus sempervirens* L.   Plate 73.   *CTW, p. 406*
An evergreen shrub, sometimes a small tree, with smooth greyish bark and downy green twigs. Leaves small, oval, shiny, rather leathery, with tiny tufts of petalless greenish-white flowers at the base of the upper ones; male and female flowers separate. *Habitat:* Native only in a few localities on the N and S Downs, Chilterns and Cotswolds; often planted in woods and shrubberies elsewhere. March–May.

BUCKTHORN FAMILY Rhamnaceae

266. COMMON BUCKTHORN *Rhamnus cathartica* L. Pl. 71. *CTW, p. 407* ♓
A tall dense deciduous, often thorny shrub, 8–15 ft. high, with widely spreading branches, the hairless, pointed oval, finely toothed leaves, turning yellow and brown in autumn, with short dense unstalked clusters of tiny 4-petalled green flowers at their base on the old wood; stamens opposite the petals, male and female flowers usually on different plants. Berries black. *Habitat:* Widespread and frequent in thickets, especially on chalk and limestone, and fens, but rare and local in the N and in Ireland. May–June.

267. ALDER BUCKTHORN *Frangula alnus* Miller Plate 71. *CTW, p. 408* ♓
Rhamnus frangula L.
Slenderer than Common Buckthorn (266), and with erect thornless branches; alternate untoothed leaves, turning yellow or red in autumn; 5-petalled flowers, male and female not separate; and berries red when unripe. Rarely it is quite prostrate. *Habitat:* Locally common in damp woods and thickets in England and Wales, preferring acid soils but also in fens; rare in Ireland. May-June.

PEAFLOWER FAMILY Papilionaceae

A LARGE FAMILY with highly distinctive individual flowers; of the 5 petals, the broad and often erect upper one is known as the 'standard', the two narrower side ones as the 'wings', and the two central lower ones, which enfold the 10 bundled stamens, as the 'keel' (Fig.). The seeds are in a pod (legume) of varying size but usually in the general pattern of a garden pea or bean. Leaves mostly alternate, but the top pair sometimes almost opposite; usually stalked and trifoliate (trefoil) or pinnate, with stipules at their base.

× ⅔

KEY TO PEAFLOWERS (Nos. 268–339)
I. Blue, Violet, Lilac and Bluish-Purple Flowers
PLANT *hairless* 278, 323, 326–27, 328; *shaggy* 316; *bushy* 268; *shrub* 269; *with angled stems* 330; *prostrate* 313–4, 316, 328; *over 3 ft.* 268–9, 278, 324, 326–7, 330.
LEAVES *pinnate, ending in a leaflet* 313, 314, 316, 326a; *pinnate, ending in a tendril* 323, 324, 326, 327, 328, 329b; 330; *trefoil* 278; *palmate* 268, 269.
FLOWERS *blue* 268; *lilac* 314, 323, 326, 329b; *partly white* 269, 314, 324a, 326, 330.
PODS *hairless* 278, 323ab, 324, 326, 327, 329b; *spiral* 278; *very short* 323.
II. Red, Pink and Pinkish-Purple Flowers
PLANT *hairless* 276, 297, 298, 300, 301, 302, 307, 308, 320, 329, 332, 333, 335, 336, 337, 338, 339; *prostrate* 275, 276, 289, 293, 300, 301, 302, 306, 307, 320, 322, 329; *fleshy bluish-green* 338; *with angled stems* 332, 333, 335, 338; *with winged stems* 336, 337, 339; *with spiny stems* 275; *sticky* 275.
LEAVES *undivided* 275, 332; *pinnate, ending in a leaflet* 320, 322; *pinnate, ending in a tendril* 329, 332, 333, 335, 336, 337, 338, *pinnate, ending in a point* 325,

339; *trefoil* 286, 288, 297, 298; *with 2 leaflets* 335, 336; *with whitish blotch* 286, 288, 301; *with 5 leaflets* 306–310.

FLOWERS *red* 291, 306, 307, 332; *pale and dark* 333; *markedly turned down* 275b; *solitary or paired* 276, 332; *in spikes* 275, 291, 292, 322; *in unstalked clusters* 293, 295.

PODS *downy* 275, 322, 329, 333, 335; *covered by calyx* 286, 288–293, 295–298, 300–302; *with inflated calyx* 302; *with calyx-teeth spreading* 289, 290, 291, 293, 298.

III. Yellow Flowers

PLANT *a shrub* 269, 273, 274, 312; *an undershrub* 270, 271, 272, 273b, 274; *hairless* 270, 271, 274, 277, 281, 282, 283, 285, 307, 308, 319, 321, 327, 328, 331, 334; *shaggy* 308, 309; *spiny* 271, 273; *prostrate* 270, 272, 273b, 274, 279, 280, 281, 282, 303, 304, 305, 306, 307, 309, 310, 311, 318, 319, 328; *with stems angled* 274, 334; *with stems tendrilled* 331.

LEAVES *undivided* 270, 271, 272, 273, 274, 331; *pinnate, ending in a leaflet* 306, 307, 308, 309, 310, 311, 123, 317, 318, 319, 321; *pinnate, ending in a tendril* 327, 328, 334; *palmate* 269; *trefoil* 274, 277, 279, 280, 281, 282, 283, 285, 287, 303, 304, 305, 311; *with 2 leaflets* 334; *with leaflets blotched darker* 282; *joined at the base* 331; *with 5 leaflets* 306–310.

FLOWERS *veined or tipped red* 307, 311, 312, 318, 319; *solitary or paired* 305, 310, 311, 319, 328, 331; *in a spike* 269, 270, 271, 272, 273, 274, 283, 285, 312.

PODS *downy or hairy* 269, 272, 273, 274, 277, 283a, 317, 328, 334; *spiny* 280, 281, 282; *inflated* 271, 312; *covered by calyx* 287, 303, 304, 305; *curved* 277; *twisted* 279, 280, 281, 282.

IV. White or Creamy Flowers

PLANT *hairless* 276, 284, 299, 300, 301, 315, 320, 326, 330; *prostrate* 276, 295, 306, 315.

LEAVES *pinnate, ending in a leaflet* 306, 315, 317, 318, 320, 326a; *pinnate, ending in a tendril* 326, 330; *trefoil* 276, 284, 287, 291, 292, 294, 295, 296, 299, 300, 301.

FLOWERS *veined red or purple* 318, 326; *partly purple* 330; *solitary or paired* 276; *in spikes* 291, 292; *in unstalked clusters* 294, 295, 299.

PODS *covered by calyx* 287, 291, 292, 294, 296, 299, 300, 301; *with calyx-teeth spreading* 294, 299.

268. **SCOTTISH LUPIN *Lupinus nootkatensis* Sims Plate 12. *CTW, p. 411*

A gregarious downy perennial, 2–3 ft. high, less showy and shorter-spiked than Garden Lupin (*L. polyphyllus* Lindley), an occasional escape, and with fewer (about 7) and shorter lanceolate leaflets on each palmate leaf. Flowers in a stubby spike, of varying shades of blue or purple. Pods hairy. *Habitat:* Locally plentiful on river shingle in the C Highlands and on moorland in Orkney. May–July.

269. **TREE LUPIN *L. arboreus* Sims Plate 47. *CTW, p. 411*

An evergreen bush, 2–4 ft. high, with spikes of sulphur-yellow flowers, sometimes tinged mauve. Leaves palmate, hairless above, silky beneath, with 7–11 lanceolate leaflets. Pods slightly downy. *Habitat:* Widespread but local in waste places, especially on sandy soil. May–August.

270. *DYER'S GREENWEED *Genista tinctoria* L. Plate 47. *CTW, p. 413*

A deciduous bushy undershrub, with erect branches about a foot high, thornless and not unlike a small leafy Broom (274), with a few hairs on the twigs and down along the margins of the lanceolate leaves. Flowers in showy spikes, deep yellow, with standard equalling keel. Pods long, flat, hairless. In a very few bare places by the sea in the SW the plant is prostrate and the pods slightly hairy. *Habitat:* Widespread but local in grassland on clay and chalk; not in Ireland. June–August.

271. *PETTY WHIN *G. anglica* L. Plate 47. *CTW, p. 413*

An open, wide-branching, almost hairless, spiny undershrub, with thin wiry stems 6–12 in. high, and small pointed oval leaves. Flowers small, yellow, in few-flowered spikes, the keel longer than the standard. Pods short, inflated. A spineless form is very rare in Scotland. *Habitat:* Widespread but uncommon on heaths and moors, especially among heather; not in Ireland. May–July.

272. ***HAIRY GREENWEED *G. pilosa* L. Plate 47. *CTW, p. 414*

A prostrate spineless half-evergreen undershrub, differing from the rare prostrate form of Dyer's Greenweed (270) in its small dark green oval leaves, hairy below, its smaller spikes of yellow flowers, and its pods being downy all round. *Habitat:* Rare in dry heathy grassland, now rarely seen outside W Wales, Ashdown Forest, and the Lizard Peninsula. May–June.

273. GORSE *Ulex europaeus* L. Plate 47. *CTW, p. 414*

A familiar, often thick-set, spiny evergreen bush or shrub, up to 8 ft. high, with richly almond-scented deep golden-yellow flowers. Stems furrowed, downy when young; leaves in the form of rigid furrowed spines. Flowers with wings rather longer than keel and standard exceeding both; calyx yellow, with spreading hairs, rather more than half as long as the petals; bracts at the base $\frac{1}{4}$-in. Pods hairy, exploding loudly when ripe. *Habitat:* Widespread and often in masses in rough grassy places, especially heaths and downs. Throughout the year, but finest April–June; 'kissing's out of season when gorse is out of bloom'. Furze, Whin.

273a. *Western Gorse, *U. gallii* Planchon, is generally lower and compacter, in many ways intermediate between the two other Gorses, with spines less or not furrowed. Flowers smaller, less fragrant, looking narrower, of a harder, less rich yellow, the calyx with few appressed hairs, and much tinier bracts. Only on acid soils; commoner in the W, but in Scotland only in the S. July onwards.

273b. *Lesser Gorse, *U. minor* Roth, is often prostrate, differing from Western Gorse also in its shorter, less stout spines; rather fewer, smaller and paler flowers, with wings shorter than keel; and calyx less downy, nearly as long as the petals. Rather local on heaths and moors; rare in the W; not in Ireland. July onwards.

274. BROOM *Sarothamnus scoparius* (L.) Koch Plate 47. *CTW, p. 416*
Cytisus scoparius (L.) Link

An almost hairless deciduous shrub, like a luxuriant willowy spineless Gorse (273), but with markedly angled stems, and leaves either small, short-stalked and lanceolate, or longer-stalked and trefoil, often dropping early in the year. Flowers large, bright golden-yellow, sometimes tinged red, in ones and twos up the stem; calyx 2-lipped. Pods hairy at the edges. In a very few places by the sea in the S it is entirely prostrate, but still bushy and stout. The taller stouter Spanish Broom (*Spartium junceum* L.) has twigs not angled, leaves never trefoil, short leafless terminal flower-spikes, the calyx not 2-lipped but split at the top and closely sheathing the petals, and pods hairy all round. It flowers much later, from July onwards, and is frequently planted by roads and railways. *Habitat:* Widespread and often abundant on dry acid soils, especially on heaths. May–June.

275. REST-HARROW *Ononis repens* L.   Plate 18.   *CTW, p. 417*

A downy woody perennial, up to a foot high, with stems tough—'arresting the harrow'—hairy all round, and often creeping and rooting; occasionally, especially by the sea, with a few weak spines. Leaves small, well-toothed, oval or trefoil, with prominent toothed leaf-like stipules half-clasping the stem at their base. Flowers pink, with wings more or less equalling the hooked keel; calyx longer than pod. *Habitat:* Widespread and common in dry grassland, especially on chalk or limestone and on dunes. July–September. '*O. arvensis*'.

275*a*. *Spiny Rest-Harrow, *O. spinosa* L., is bushier, darker green and not creeping, having erect stems up to 18 in. high, almost always sharply spiny, and rather less evenly hairy. Flowers appearing a sharper red, with wings distinctly shorter than keel, and calyx usually shorter than pod. More local, typically on clays and heavier soils; not in Ireland.

275*b*. ***Small Rest-Harrow, *O. reclinata* L., is an erect 2–4 in. pale grey-green, stickily hairy, annual, with small flowers, the petals scarcely longer than the calyx. As the pods ripen, they hang straight down, giving the plant a Christmas-tree effect. Recently seen only on Berry Head and in the Gower and the Channel Is. May–June, and occasionally later.

276. **FENUGREEK *Trigonella ornithopodioides* (L.) DC.
T. purpurascens Lamarck   Plate 79.   *CTW, p. 418*

A small, hairless, prostrate, unobtrusive, clover-like annual, with heads of 1–3 small spreading white or pale pink flowers, which can look like rows of teeth upright in the turf, on stalks shorter than the trefoil leaves. Can be separated from the clovers by the small pods being much longer than the calyx; rather like Burrowing Clover (296) but not hairy. *Habitat:* Widespread but very local in dry, sandy and gravelly places, usually near the sea. June–July.

277. **SICKLE MEDICK *Medicago falcata* L.   Plate 47.   *CTW, p. 419*

Often resembles a less erect Lucerne (278) but its flowers are smaller and bright or pale yellow, their stalks longer than the calyx-tube, stems thinner, leaflets usually smaller and narrower, and pods more or less sickle-shaped with few seeds. *Habitat:* Fairly common in dry grassy places in the Breckland; occasional elsewhere. June onwards.

277 × 278. **M. × varia* Martin (*M. silvestris* Fries) is fertile, with a wide range of extraordinary flower-colours, including greens and almost black.

278. LUCERNE *M. sativa* L.   Plate 5.   *CTW, p. 419*

A well-known fodder plant; a hairless perennial, 1–2 ft. high, with trefoil leaves, short spikes of flowers of varying shades of violet, whose stalks are shorter than the calyx-tube, and many-seeded pods twisted into a spiral. *Habitat:* Widespread and fairly frequent in grassy and waste places, especially as a relic of cultivation. June onwards.

279. BLACK MEDICK *M. lupulina* L.   Plate 48.   *CTW, p. 420*

A low, often prostrate, usually downy annual, with trefoil leaves, the broad leaflets often minutely pointed, and long-stalked roundish heads of small bright yellow flowers. Often confused with Hop (303) and Common Yellow Trefoils (304), but is downy, stouter and its stalked flowers drop when dead, uncovering the twisted, netted and finally black pods; the stipules at the base of the leaves are long pointed and slightly toothed. Rarely in waste places the pods may be greenish and incurved on longish stalks in looser heads. *Habitat:* Widespread and common in bare and grassy places; also frequently sown by farmers. April onwards. Nonsuch.

280. **BUR MEDICK *M. minima* (L.) Bartalini Plate 48. *CTW, p. 420*

A modest downy, often prostrate annual, with trefoil leaves, heads of small yellow flowers, and a double row of numerous hooked spines on the rounded, several times spirally twisted pods. Differs from our other Medicks in its normally untoothed pointed stipules at the base of the leaves. *Habitat:* Scarce in sandy and gravelly places, mostly near the sea, in E and SE England; also in fields manured with shoddy, where it less rapidly dries up. May–July.

281. **TOOTHED MEDICK *M. hispida* Gaertner Plate 48. *CTW, p. 420*
(incl. *M. denticulata* Willdenow).

Is often taken for Spotted Medick (282), but is usually sparsely hairy, smaller, with leaves never blotched; stipules very deeply toothed; and much flatter, shortly spiral, almost always spined pods, which are more strongly marked with a network of raised lines and have stalks about as long as the leaf-stalks. *Habitat:* Uncommon in bare sandy and gravelly places, chiefly near the sea and in S and E England; also in fields manured with shoddy. May–September.

282. *SPOTTED MEDICK *M. arabica* (L.) Hudson Plate 48. *CTW, p. 421*
Calvary Clover

A prostrate, almost hairless, clover-like annual, often with a small dark blotch on the rather large trefoil leaflets, and with toothed stipules at the base of the leaves. Flowers small, bright yellow, in small heads. Pods spiny, several times spirally coiled, with broad edges and only faintly netted, on stalks rather shorter than the leaf-stalks. *Habitat:* Widespread but local in sandy and waste places, especially near the sea, and in fields manured with shoddy. April–September.

283   283a   307   308

283. COMMON MELILOT *Melilotus officinalis* (L.) Pallas
M. arvensis Wallroth   Plate 47. *CTW, p. 422*

A hairless biennial, 2–4 ft. high, with trefoil leaves, the leaflets rather narrow, and long spikes of small canary-yellow flowers, the keel slightly shorter than the wings and standard. Pod brown, hairless, blunt, wrinkled. (Fig.). *Habitat:* Widespread and fairly common in waste ground. June onwards. Figs. × 2.

283a. *Golden Melilot, *M. altissima* Thuillier ('*M. officinalis*'), is extremely similar but compacter, with darker stems; often broader and darker leaflets; more congested spikes of larger, rather deeper golden-yellow flowers, with wings, keel and standard all more or less equal; and pods larger, black, downy, more pointed and only faintly wrinkled (Fig.). More often in woods and on heavier soils.

284. *WHITE MELILOT *M. alba* Medicus Plate 107 *CTW, p. 422*

Generally resembles Common Melilot (283), which rarely may also have white flowers, but is usually taller, with longer leaflets, and smaller white flowers, with keel and wings equal and shorter than standard. Sown as Bokhara Clover. *Habitat:* Widespread and increasing by roadsides and on waste ground. July onwards.

285. *SMALL-FLOWERED MELILOT *M. indica* (L.) Allioni Pl. 47. *CTW, 422*
A hairless annual, 6–12 in. high, with the leaflets of the trefoil leaves broadest at the tip, the stipules at their base normally untoothed. Flowers tiny, deep yellow, spreading, the wings and keel equal and shorter than the standard, in spikes that elongate in fruit. Pods drooping, net-veined. *Habitat:* Widespread but local in disturbed ground, mainly in the S. June–September.

CLOVERS   *Trifolium*

NON-WOODY PLANTS, rarely over a foot high, with trefoil leaves. The small individual flowers are usually clustered in a dense head; the petals (wings always longer than keel) generally remain after flowering and conceal the tiny pod; calyx 5-toothed.

286. RED CLOVER *Trifolium pratense* L.   Plate 19.   *CTW, p. 424*
The commonest red or purple clover; a slightly downy perennial, 4–18 in. high, whose oval leaflets often have a whitish crescent; upper leaves more or less unstalked; stipules triangular, bristle-pointed. Flowers in dense globular heads, which are normally not or little stalked, of varying shades of pink-purple; calyx often downy. A more luxuriant variety is often cultivated. *Habitat:* Widespread and abundant in grassy and waste places. May onwards.

287. **SULPHUR CLOVER *T. ochroleucon* L.   Plate 79.   *CTW, p. 425*
Rather like a pale lemony-yellow Red Clover (286), differing from occasional whitish specimens of it in the somewhat narrower leaflets never being marked whitish and the generally smaller flower-heads; also grows in wider patches. *Habitat:* Frequent in grassy places in parts of E England, especially on clay. June–July.

288. *ZIGZAG CLOVER *T. medium* Hudson   Plate 19.   *CTW, p. 425*
Can be separated from Red Clover (286) even at a distance by the harder reddish-purple tinge of its flatter, longer-stalked flower-heads, above wider mats of darker green leaves with longer narrower leaflets; upper leaves usually well stalked; stipules very narrow, not bristle-pointed; calyx-tube hairless. The stems often grow in a gentle zigzag. *Habitat:* Widespread but somewhat local in grassy places. June–August.

289. **SEA CLOVER *T. squamosum* L.   Plate 19.   *CTW, p. 426*
A downy 3–6 in. annual, with stalked oval terminal heads of small pale pink flowers, the petals rather longer than the calyx, whose teeth are spreading and prominent in fruit; top pair of leaves almost opposite; the stipules narrow. *Habitat:* Very local in dry ditches and meadows near the sea in the S. June–July.

290. ***STARRY CLOVER *T. stellatum* L.   Plate 19.   *CTW, p. 426*
A low annual, softly hairy all over, with large stalked rounded heads of pink flowers, fading to white; calyx-teeth long and whiskery, spreading in fruit to give the characteristic starry appearance. Leaves all alternate, the stipules broad. *Habitat:* Known for 150 years on shingle at Shoreham-by-Sea. May–June.

291. *CRIMSON CLOVER *T. incarnatum* L.   Plate 19.   *CTW, p. 426*

A vivid crimson Clover, with dense oblong stalked flower-spikes; an annual, 6–12 in. high, downy with spreading hairs; calyx-teeth spreading in fruit. *Habitat:* Widespread and not infrequent as a relic of cultivation, but rarely persisting long. A smaller, bushier form with creamy or pale pink flowers is native at the Lizard and in Jersey. June–July. (Incl. *T. molinerii* Balbis.)

292. HARESFOOT CLOVER, *T. arvense* L.   Plate 19.   *CTW, p. 427*

A softly hairy annual, 3–12 in. high, distinctive with its oblong stalked flower-heads, the small pale pink or white flowers often shorter than the very long fine soft fawn-coloured calyx-teeth. Leaflets narrow, hardly toothed. *Habitat:* Widespread and common in dry grassy places, especially on sandy soils and near the sea; less so in Ireland. Jeun–August.

293. SOFT CLOVER *T. striatum* L.   Plate 19.   *CTW, p. 427*

Differs from Rough Clover (294) in having pale pink flowers, and the calyx-tube swollen in fruit, with short, erect, less stiff teeth. The only small pink annual clover with leaves downy on both sides. *Habitat:* Widespread but rather local in dry grassy places. June–July, a fortnight later.

294. *ROUGH CLOVER *T. scabrum* L.   Plate 79.   *CTW, p. 427*

A small, usually prostrate annual, with leaflets downy on both sides. Flower-heads small, unstalked, along the stems, with tiny white flowers, the stiff calyx-teeth curving outwards in fruit, unlike Soft Clover (293). *Habitat:* Widespread but rather local in dry grassy places, nearly always by the sea; in Ireland only on SE coast. May–June.

295. ***TWIN-FLOWERED CLOVER *T. bocconei* Savi Pl. 79.   *CTW, p. 428*

A low, little-branched, erect annual, with leaflets downy only beneath, and small unstalked egg-shaped flower-heads, nearly always in unequal pairs, the small pinkish-white petals longer than all except the lowest calyx-tooth. *Habitat:* Confined to a few dry grassy places on the Lizard Peninsula and probably still in Jersey. June–July.

296. *BURROWING CLOVER *T. subterraneum* L.   Plate 79.   *CTW, p. 428*

A rather coarse, prostrate hairy annual, with broad leaflets and stalked heads of a few unstalked largish creamy flowers, spreading like fingers, the calyx-tube hairless, and pods with the singular habit of clawing into the ground. *Habitat:* Local in grassy places on sand and gravel in the S; and in Co. Wicklow. May–June.

297. ***UPRIGHT CLOVER *T. strictum* L.   Plate 19.   *CTW, p. 429*

A low neat slender erect hairless annual, the narrow, strongly veined leaflets with small sharp teeth and large broad white-centred toothed stipules. Flowers small, pinkish-purple, in long-stalked rounded heads; calyx hairless, markedly ribbed, with long narrow teeth. *Habitat:* Confined to a few grassy places in the Lizard Peninsula, and the Channel Is. June.

298. **CLUSTERED CLOVER *T. glomeratum* L.   Plate 19.   *CTW, p. 429*

A low, usually prostrate hairless annual, with broadish leaflets, strongly veined and often with a pale patch at the base. Flowers small, pinkish-purple, in dense round unstalked heads along the stems, the short teeth of the hairless calyx turned back in fruit. *Habitat:* Very local in dry, bare and grassy places on light soils, mainly near the sea, in the S, and in SE Ireland. June–July.

299. **SUFFOCATED CLOVER. *T. suffocatum* L. Plate 79. *CTW. p, 429*

A distinctive tufted hairless annual, which can often be spotted by the way its leaves are held aloft over the congested unstalked heads, which lie on the ground several together, of very small whitish flowers. These are largely hidden by the green calyx-teeth, which turn back in fruit. *Habitat:* Very local in turf or on bare sandy or gravelly ground, usually near the sea in the S and E; very rare inland. August.

300. ALSIKE CLOVER *T. hybridum* L. Plate 19. *CTW, p. 429*

Rather like a more upright White Clover (301), but not creeping, and with stems often hollow, leaflets narrower and never with white markings, the stalked flower-heads often pink, especially as they go over, the calyx white with green teeth. *Habitat:* Widespread and common on waste ground, especially as a relic of cultivation. June onwards.

301. WHITE CLOVER *T. repens* L. Plate 79. *CTW, p. 430*

The 'wild white' or Kentish clover of agriculture; a low, creeping and rooting, hairless perennial, the toothed leaflets usually with a whitish mark at the base. Flowers white, sometimes pinkish, rarely rich purple, in roundish heads on stalks much longer than Alsike Clover (300). Calyx white, with teeth and sometimes veins green. *Habitat:* Widespread, abundant in grassy places. June onwards. Dutch Clover.

302. *STRAWBERRY CLOVER *T. fragiferum* L. Plate 19. *CTW, p. 430*

Like a modest White Clover (301), which is our only other creeping Clover, but with smaller neater unstalked pink flowers, the denser heads having prominent green sepal-like bracts; leaflets without whitish marks. In fruit it is distinctive, with pods enclosed in the inflated hairy calyces so that the whole head looks like a small fawn-pink berry. *Habitat:* Widespread but local in meadows on clay, especially near the sea. June onwards.

303. HOP TREFOIL *T. campestre* Schreber Plate 48. *CTW, p. 431*

Larger than Common Yellow Trefoil (304), its globular heads containing about 40 larger pale yellow flowers, pale brown in fruit, when the broad standard folds forward (Fig.). *Habitat:* Widespread and often common in grassy places. May onwards.

303   304

304. COMMON YELLOW TREFOIL *T. dubium* Sibthorp Pl. 48. *CTW, 432*

A low almost hairless annual, sometimes going purplish, with loose, long-stalked roundish heads of some 10–20 small yellow flowers on short stalks; the middle leaflet with the longest stalk. Very like the downy Black Medick (279), but has very slightly notched leaflets with no minute point, and the dead flowers turn brown, the standard folding sideways and downwards (Fig.) to cover the straight drooping egg-shaped pods, which have a short hooked beak. *Habitat:* Widespread and common in dry grassy places. May onwards.

305. *SLENDER YELLOW TREFOIL *T. micranthum* Viviani Pl. 48. *CTW*, *432*
Like a small, slender Common Yellow Trefoil (304), but with darker yellow
flowers, about 2–6 on each lax, long-stalked head, each on thread-like stalks as
long as or longer than the calyx-tube; leaves and leaflets with very short or no
stalks. *Habitat:* Widespread and frequent but easily overlooked in turf on
lighter soils, thinning out northwards. May–August. '*T. filiforme*'.

306. KIDNEY VETCH *Anthyllis vulneraria* L. Plate 49. *CTW*, *p. 433*
A silky, often greyish perennial, prostrate or up to a foot high, with undivided
elliptical root-leaves, pinnate stem-leaves, and yellow flowers in crowded heads,
which are sometimes in pairs; calyx swollen, cotton-woolly below, with prominent
palmate green sepal-like bracts. Near the sea flower colour varies widely, from
pale yellow through orange to a glowing fiery red, and the leaves are thick and
fleshy. *Habitat:* Widespread and common in dry grassy places, especially on
chalk and limestone and near the sea; also on mountains. May onwards.

307. COMMON BIRDSFOOT TREFOIL *Lotus corniculatus* L. Pl. 49. *CTW*, *434*
One of our commonest and gayest yellow peaflowers, a usually prostrate,
mostly hairless perennial, with unstalked apparently trifoliate leaves, with a
lower pair of small oval leaflets looking like stipules. Flowers up to 8 in a head,
on a longish stalk, with 3 sepal-like bracts often veined or suffused reddish or
orange; calyx-teeth erect in bud, the 2 upper with an obtuse angle between
them (Fig., p. 59). Pods about an inch long, in a head resembling a bird's foot.
Habitat: Widespread and abundant in dry grassland. May onwards. Figs. × 3.

307*a*. ***Slender Birdsfoot Trefoil**, *L. tenuis* Willdenow, is rather slenderer,
wirier, erecter and more branched and forms larger tufts, with usually longer
stems, much narrower lanceolate leaflets, and smaller and narrower yellow
flowers, fewer to a head, the rear calyx-teeth converging. Much more local,
especially near the sea and on heavier soils.

308. GREATER BIRDSFOOT TREFOIL *L. uliginosus* Schkuhr Pl. 49. *CTW*, *435*
More luxuriant, darker green and larger than Common Birdsfoot Trefoil (307),
and with runners, stouter hollow stems, broader leaflets, and more flowers in a
head, the calyx-teeth spreading in bud and the 2 upper at an acute angle (Fig.,
p. 59). It is usually very hairy but may be almost entirely hairless. *Habitat·* Widespread and common in moist grassland and marshes. June–August. '*L. major*'.

309. **LESSER BIRDSFOOT TREFOIL *L. hispidus* DC. Pl. 49. *CTW*, *p. 435*
A small prostrate annual, usually 3–4 in. long, but sometimes forming wide
mats, shaggier than Common Birdsfoot Trefoil (307) with much smaller deep
orange flowers, 2–4 in a head, on stalks much longer than the leaves. Pods ¼-in.
long. *Habitat:* Very local in dry grassy places near the coast in SW England,
W Wales and Co. Cork. June–September.

310. **LEAST BIRDSFOOT TREFOIL *L. angustissimus* L. Pl. 49. *CTW*, *435*
Less shaggy than the last species, with which it may grow, and with yellower
flowers only 1–2 in a head, on stalks usually shorter than the leaves, and slender
pods about 1 in. long. *Habitat:* Scarcer and only S of the Thames, E to Kent.
May–August.

311. **DRAGON'S TEETH *Tetragonolobus maritimus* (L.) Roth
Lotus siliquosus L. Plate 49. *CTW, p. 435*
A sprawling hairy grey-green perennial, forming large patches, with large broad leaves like those of Common Birdsfoot Trefoil (307), the 2 stipule-like leaflets erect up the stem. Flowers solitary, an inch long, pale yellow, the standard and calyx-tube red-veined, and the hard hooked tip of the keel green. Pods 2 in. long, dark brown, prominently 4-angled. *Habitat:* Well naturalised in a few grassy places in the SE. June–September.

312. **BLADDER SENNA *Colutea arborescens* L. Plate 64. *CTW, p. 437*
A deciduous shrub, 5–10 ft. high, with alternate pinnate leaves, the oval leaflets hairy beneath. Flowers deep yellow, rarely orange, with red markings, $\frac{1}{2}$-in. long in spikes of 2–6 on stalks shorter than the leaves. Pods inflated, papery. 2–3 in. long. *Habitat:* Occasionally naturalised in waste places, especially on railway banks near London. June–August.

313. **PURPLE MILK-VETCH *Astragalus danicus* Retzius Pl. 3. *CTW, 437*
A prostrate downy perennial, with neat short-stalked pinnate leaves ending in a leaflet, and rich violet flowers in erect, crowded heads on leafless stalks usually much longer than the leaves. Pods covered with white hairs. *Habitat:* Local in chalk and limestone turf, mainly from the Cotswolds and Chilterns to N Yorkshire, and thence also on dunes to NE Scotland; absent in the SE and SW; Ireland, only in the Aran Is. May–July.

314. ***ALPINE MILK-VETCH *A. alpinus* L. Plate 3. *CTW, p. 438*
Slenderer than the last species, with hanging lilac-white purple-tipped flowers on looser heads on stalks about as long as the leaves, and brown hairs on the pods. *Habitat:* Very rare on 3 mountain ledges in the E Highlands. June–July.

315. *WILD LIQUORICE *A. glycyphyllos* L. Plate 79. *CTW, p. 438*
A stout, straggling hairless perennial, with zigzag branched stems about 3 ft. long. Differs from all our vetches and peas in the oval heads of large dirty greenish-cream flowers which are on stalks shorter than the large pinnate leaves which end in a leaflet, with leaf-like stipules at their base. Pods large (1–1$\frac{1}{2}$ in.) stout, curved. *Habitat:* Widespread but local, rare in the N, on warm banks on chalk and limestone; not in Ireland. June–August. Milk-Vetch.

316 ***PURPLE MOUNTAIN MILK-VETCH *Oxytropis halleri* Bunge
'*O. uralensis*'. Plate 3. *CTW, p. 438*
Differs from the Purple Milk-vetch (313) in having very silky leaves and a sharply pointed, not blunt, tip to the keel of the glowing rosy-purple flowers, which fade all too soon. On cliffs and rocks it grows in tufts. *Habitat:* Very rare, on mountain rocks in Perthshire; on sea-cliffs in E. Ross; locally plentiful on dunes on the N coast of Scotland. May-June.

317. ***YELLOW MILK-VETCH *O. campestris* (L.) DC. Pl. 79. *CTW, p. 439*
Larger and more tufted than the last species, and with longer, greyer-green, rather less silky leaves and pale creamy flower-heads held stiffly erect on stalks shorter than the leaves. *Habitat:* Very rare on mountain rocks in Glen Clova and near L. Loch. June–July.

318. COMMON BIRDSFOOT *Ornithopus perpusillus* L. Plate 49. *CTW, p. 439*
A prostrate slender downy annual, 2–12 in. long, with long, short-stalked pinnate leaves, with a terminal leaflet, and few-flowered heads of tiny red-veined, very pale yellow flowers with a pinnate leaf-like bract at their base. Pods beaded, hairless and curved so that two or three together look like a bird's foot. *Habitat:* Widespread and frequent in dry, sandy and gravelly places. May–August.

319. ***ORANGE BIRDSFOOT *O. pinnatus* (Miller) Druce Pl. 49. *CTW, 440*
A delicate prostrate, almost hairless annual, with long-stalked pinnate leaves, and fewer leaflets than the last species, but more than any of the Birdsfoot Trefoils (307–310). Flowers small, orange, in heads of 1–3, with no leaf-like bract at their base. *Habitat:* Rare on dry ground near the sea in the Scilly Is. and Guernsey. May onwards.

320. **CROWN VETCH *Coronilla varia* L. Plate 25. *CTW, p. 440*
A straggling hairless perennial, 2–3 ft. long, with handsome rounded heads, 1½ in. across, of pale pink, purple-tipped peaflowers, on stalks longer than the pinnate leaves, which differ from all true vetches and peas by ending in a leaflet. Pods beaded, slender, ending in a whisker. *Habitat:* Uncommon on waste ground. June–August.

321. *HORSESHOE VETCH *Hippocrepis comosa* L. Plate 49. *CTW, p. 441*
Differs from Common Birdsfoot Trefoil (307) most obviously in having larger, thicker mats of pinnate leaves with narrower and very numerous leaflets, but also in having smaller, more numerous flowers of a harder yellow, often veined but never suffused red; calyx blackish-green. The slender wavy pods with curved joints are supposed to resemble horseshoes joined together. *Habitat:* Widespread and locally common N to mid Scotland, in chalk and limestone turf of which it is highly characteristic; not in Ireland. May–July.

322. *SAINFOIN *Onobrychis viciifolia* Scopoli Plate 25. *CTW, p. 441*
A distinctive fodder plant, with conspicuous spikes of bright pink flowers, a bushy or straggly, rarely prostrate, downy perennial, up to 15 in. high, with narrow leaflets on the pinnate leaves. Pods oval, warted, heavily net-veined, not bursting. *Habitat:* Locally frequent in grassland, especially as a relic of cultivation on chalk and limestone in the S. June onwards.

VETCHES AND PEAS *Vicia and Lathyrus*

CLIMBING or clambering non-woody plants, their leaves normally pinnate with no terminal leaflet but often a single or branched tendril. Flowers solitary or in heads on stalks from the base of the leaves. Pods long and more or less flattened. The Vetches (except 330) are best separated from the Peas by not having winged or angled stems and usually having more leaflets.

323. HAIRY TARE *Vicia hirsuta* (L.) Gray Plate 5. *CTW, p. 443*
A slender, often hairless annual, 6 in. to 2 ft. long with 6–8 pairs of usually alternate leaflets and a tendril at the end. Flowers insignificant, pale lilac, in a long-stalked spike of 1–6, with long slender calyx-teeth, all more or less equal. Pods two-seeded, downy. *Habitat:* Widespread and common in rough grassy places. May onwards.

323*a*. **Smooth Tare**, *V. tetrasperma* (L.) Schreber, has 3–6 pairs of leaflets, usually only 1–2 larger rich lilac flowers, the 2 upper calyx-teeth shorter than the rest, and usually 4 seeds in a hairless pod. Rather less common.

323*b*. ****Slender Tare**, *V. tenuissima* (Bieberstein) Schinz & Thellung (*V. gracilis* Loiseleur), is like Smooth Tare, but has 3–4 pairs of leaflets, usually 3–4 still larger flowers on longer stalks, and 5 or more seeds in each pod. Very local in fields and by roadsides in S and E England.

324. TUFTED VETCH   *V. cracca* L.   Plate 5.   *CTW, p. 444*

A slightly downy perennial, often festooning the hedges with its showy, long-stalked, one-sided spikes of numerous bright blue-violet flowers. Leaves with 8–12 pairs of leaflets ending in a tendril, with narrow untoothed stipules at their base. Pods hairless.   *Habitat:* Widespread and common in hedgerows and bushy places. June–August.

324*a*. *****Lesser Tufted Vetch**, *V. villosa* Roth (incl. *V. dasycarpa* Tenore) (*CTW*†), is smaller and usually annual, with 6–8 pairs of leaflets; looser clusters of fewer, longer and narrower flowers which may have a white standard and all open much at the same time (not the lower ones first); and broader pods. An uncommon casual of arable and waste places. June–August.

325. **UPRIGHT VETCH   *V. orobus* DC.   Plate 18.   *CTW, p. 444*

The only true Vetch with no tendrils but a tiny point at the end of the leaves. A slightly downy, erect tufted perennial, 9–18 in. high, with short spikes of pinkish-purple flowers. Pods hairless. Sometimes confused with the other Bitter Vetch (339), which has winged stems, the sprawling Crown Vetch (320) and the larger Goat's Rue (326*a*).   *Habitat:* Extremely local on rocky ground in the N and in heathy meadows in the W and SW. May–June. Bitter Vetch.

326 **WOOD VETCH   *V. sylvatica* L.   Plate 5.   *CTW, p. 445*

A far-scrambling bushy hairless perennial, with large long-stalked 1-sided showy spikes of white flowers beautifully veined with purple, and long hairless pods. Leaves with numerous rather small leaflets, branched tendrils and much-toothed stipules at their base.   *Habitat:* Widespread but very local at the edges of woods, also on mountains and sea-cliffs; commoner in the N and W. June–August.

326*a*. ****Goat's Rue**, *Galega officinalis* L. (*CTW, p. 436*), has somewhat similar white or pinkish-lilac flowers, but looks quite different as it grows in erect clumps about 3 ft. high and has leaves rather like 315, with broader leaflets and a terminal one instead of a tendril. An occasional garden escape. July–September.

327. BUSH VETCH   *V. sepium* L.   Plate 5.   *CTW, p. 445*

A climbing perennial, the downy leaves with 5–8 pairs of bluntly heart-shaped leaflets and branched tendrils. Flowers in short-stalked spikes of 2–6, rather dingy purple, fading bluer, rarely yellow, tending to be bluer in the N. Pods hairless.   *Habitat:* Widespread and common in hedgerows and bushy places. April onwards, flowering late into the autumn.

328. **YELLOW VETCH   *V. lutea* L.   Plate 49.   *CTW, p. 445*

The only peaflower with both tendrils on the pinnate leaves and solitary yellow-white flowers. A usually prostrate and hairless, greyish-green annual, with thick stems 6–12 in. long; large, usually solitary pinkish-white, turning dirty yellow, flowers; and hairy pods. *Habitat:* Very local near the sea, mostly in grass and on shingle, and inland in waste places. June–September.

329. COMMON VETCH *V. sativa* L. Plate 18. *CTW, p. 446*

A slightly hairy, very variable fodder annual, the leaves with 4–7 pairs of oval leaflets and usually branched tendrils. Flowers solitary or paired, purple, on very short stalks up the stem. Pods slightly hairy, 2 in. or more long, with smooth seeds. *Habitat:* Widespread and common in grassy and waste places, often as a relic of cultivation. June–September.

329a. **Narrow-leaved Vetch,** *V. angustifolia* L., is also very variable, but is slenderer, with narrower, often linear leaflets, especially on the upper leaves; smaller and more often solitary, crimson-purple, flowers; and less beaded hairy pods an inch or so long. Often commoner in dry grassy places. May–July.

329b. ****Spring Vetch,** *V. lathyroides* L., is much smaller and prostrate, with 1–3 pairs of leaflets, an unbranched or no tendril, much smaller flowers, bluer especially as they fade, and hairless pods with rough dotted seeds. Frequently confused with Narrow-leaved Vetch, with which it often grows. Local in short turf, especially near the sea. April–May.

330. **BITHYNIAN VETCH *V. bithynica* (L.) L. Plate 5. *CTW, p. 447*

A scrambling perennial, with 4-angled stems and leaves with 1–2 pairs of broad lanceolate leaflets 1–2 in. long, the stipules at their base very large, usually broad and jaggedly toothed. Flowers large, long-stalked, solitary or paired, the mauve standard often hiding the mostly creamy wings and keel. Pods hairy. *Habitat:* Local in bushy or grassy places in the S, mainly near the coast. May–June.

331. **YELLOW VETCHLING *Lathyrus aphaca* L. Plate 48. *CTW, p. 448*

A very distinctive, grey-green, hairless annual, with unbranched tendrils (the true leaves) direct from the 4-angled stems, pairs of conspicuous broad triangular apparent leaves joined at the base (stipules), and yellow flowers, stalked and usually solitary. *Habitat:* Scarce in dry bushy and grassy places in the S. June–August.

332. *GRASS VETCHLING *L. nissolia* L. Plate 18. *CTW, 2. 449*

The only peaflower with long, narrow apparent leaves, so grass-like that among tall herbage it can be hard to find its solitary or paired crimson flowers on their long hair-like stalks. An erect hairless annual, a foot or two high, with no tendrils, tiny stipules and naturally no ligule; stems angled. Pod long, narrow, hairless. *Habitat:* Local on roadsides and other grassy places in the S. May–July.

333. ***HAIRY PEA *L. hirsutus* L. Plate 18. *CTW, p. 449*

A robust, nearly hairless, grey-green annual, 1–3 ft. high, with winged stems, each leaf of a single pair of narrow leaflets with branched tendrils, stipules narrow, half-arrow shaped, and long-stalked solitary or paired flowers with a purple standard, paler wings fading blue and a small creamy keel. Pods very hairy. *Habitat:* Rare in dry waste and grassy places, occasionally permanent in the SE. June–August.

334. MEADOW PEA *L. pratensis* L. Plate 48. *CTW, p. 449*

The commonest tendrilled yellow peaflower, a scrambling, often bushy perennial, 1–3 ft. long, with angled stems, a single pair of narrow lanceolate leaflets ending in a tendril, and large arrow-shaped stipules at their base, and a long-stalked cluster of flowers. Pods usually hairless. *Habitat:* Widespread and common in hedge-banks and grassy places. June onwards. Meadow Vetchling.

335. ***FYFIELD PEA *L. tuberosus* L. Plate 18. *CTW, p. 450*

A bushy or climbing, hairless perennial, 2–3 ft. high, with an angled stem, each leaf with a single pair of rather short broad leaflets, a tendril and long narrow stipules at their base, and a long-stalked short spike of bright crimson, slightly fragrant flowers ½-in. across. Pods hairless. It has small tubers on the roots. *Habitat:* Long established in grassy and bushy places near Fyfield (Essex); not often persisting elsewhere. June–July.

336. **EVERLASTING PEA *L. sylvestris* L. Plate 18. *CTW, p. 450*

A hairless, often far-scrambling perennial, with markedly winged stems 4–6 ft. long, each leaf with a single pair of long narrow lanceolate leaflets 3–4 in. long, and a branched tendril. Flowers in a long-stalked short spike, yellowish- or greenish-pink, the wings tipped violet, the keel whitish, each ¾-in. across. Pods 2–3 in. long, hairless. *Habitat:* Widespread but local by woods, thickets and hedges, especially near the sea in the W; not in Ireland. June–August.

336*a*. **Garden Everlasting Pea, *L. latifolius* L., has flowers of a more garish magenta-pink and twice as large, shorter broader leaflets and fatter pods. Not uncommon on waste ground, especially by roads and railways. July–Sept.

337. **MARSH PEA *L. palustris* L. Plate 18. *CTW, p. 451*

A slender hairless perennial, 18 in. to 3 ft. high, with winged stems, 2–3 pairs of upright narrow lanceolate leaflets, ending in a branched tendril, and a long-stalked short spike of bluish-purple flowers. Pods hairless. *Habitat:* Widespread but very local in fen herbage; not in Scotland or the SE. June–July.

338. **SEA PEA *L. japonicus* Willdenow Plate 18. *CTW, p. 451*

A prostrate mat-forming hairless fleshy bluish-green perennial, with angled stems, tendrilled leaves with several pairs of oval leaflets, and short-stalked clusters of large, bluish-purple flowers. Pods turgid and very pea-like. *Habitat:* Local and uncommon on shingle beaches, mainly in E and S England. June–August. *L. maritimus* Bigelow.

339. BITTER VETCH *L. montanus* (L.) Bernhardi Plate 18. *CTW, p. 451*

A weak hairless perennial, with winged stems about a foot long, the leaves with 2–4 leaflets and a small green point at the end instead of a tendril. Flowers veined, reddish-purple, fading blue or green, in few-flowered spikes on stalks longer than the leaves; calyx dark blue-green. Pods hairless. *Habitat:* Widespread and often common on heaths and in woods on acid soil. April–July.

ROSE FAMILY Rosaceae

340. **BRIDEWORT *Spiraea salicifolia* L. Plate 17. *CTW, p. 455*
Willow Spiraea

A little-branched deciduous bush, 4–6 ft. high, spreading widely and densely by suckers; leaves short-stalked, thin, lanceolate. Flowers small, pinkish-purple to white, with numerous prominent stamens, in dense spikes. *S.* × *billiardii* Hérincq, *S. alba* Du Roi and *S. douglasii* Hooker are very similar garden shrubs also sometimes escaping. *Habitat:* Occasionally naturalised in hedgerows and on heathland, chiefly in Wales and the N. June–August.

341. *DROPWORT *Filipendula vulgaris* Moench Plate 94. *CTW, p. 456*
Spiraea filipendula L.

The downland Meadowsweet (342), 6–18 in. high, differing from its larger counterpart of the waterside in its darker green pinnate leaves which have many small crowded crisp, finely cut leaflets and which are largely in a basal rosette, and in its fewer larger unscented flowers, the usually 6 petals with a pink tinge on the back. Fruit a group of downy nutlets. *Habitat:* Widespread but rather local in dry sunny turf on chalk and limestone. May–August.

342. MEADOWSWEET *F. ulmaria* (L.) Maximowicz Plate 94. *CTW, p. 457*
Spiraea ulmaria L.

A beautiful and common wild flower, with its foamy upright clusters of small fragrant cream-coloured flowers; stamens numerous, prominent; petals usually 5. A hairless perennial, with stiff stems 2–4 ft. high, and pinnate leaves green above and usually silvery-green below, the larger toothed leaflets interspersed with small ones. Fruits hairless, fused in a spiral. *Habitat:* Widespread and often abundant by fresh water, and in fens and damp woods. June–September.

343. *CLOUDBERRY *Rubus chamaemorus* L. Plate 84. *CTW, p. 460*
A low downy creeping perennial, forming open patches, with often isolated, rounded, palmately lobed mulberry-like leaves and solitary white flowers like a large Bramble (346); a shy flowerer. Fruit like a large hard raspberry, red becoming orange. *Habitat:* Locally common on damp mountain heather-moors in the N. June–July.

344. *STONE BRAMBLE *R. saxatilis* L. Plate 76. *CTW, p. 461*
Rather like a small prostrate slender Bramble (346), but with no or weak prickles; thin stems which die back each winter, and small dirty white flowers with narrow petals, surrounded by conspicuous green sepals, in twos and threes. Leaves long-stalked, trifoliate, pale and downy beneath, with small stipules. Fruit red when ripe, with fewer segments. *Habitat:* Widespread but local on rocks and ledges in the N and W, especially in hilly limestone districts. June–August.

345. RASPBERRY *R. idaeus* L. Plate 78. *CTW, p. 462*
The familiar fruit; a little branched perennial, suckering freely, with woody biennial stems, 3–6 ft. high, usually armed with small weak prickles; pinnate leaves with 3–7 broad toothed leaflets, often whitish below. Flowers in loose clusters, smallish, drooping, white. Fruits red, like Blackberries (346), but easily coming off their base when ripe. *Habitat:* Widespread and frequent in woods and on heaths. June–August.

346. BRAMBLE *R. fruticosus* L. Plate 76. *CTW, p. 463*
A very familiar, very variable, prickly, prostrate or clambering, half-evergreen perennial, with woody stems 2–12 ft. long, frequently rooting at the tips in autumn, Leaves prickly, pinnate with 3–5 broad toothed leaflets (very deeply and narrowly cut and toothed in an escaped cultivated form); turning reddish-purple in autumn. Flowers with 5 white or pink petals; sepals usually turned down in fruit. Fruits —blackberries—composed of several fleshy segments, which turn from green to

red and then to purplish-black, and do not come easily off their base till quite ripe and sweet to the taste. Some 300 widely distributed microspecies have been described in the British Isles. *Habitat:* Widespread and abundant in woods, hedges, and bushy and waste places and on heaths and cliffs. June onwards.

347. DEWBERRY   *R. caesius* L.   Plate 76.   *CTW, p. 484*
Less robust and prickly, and more often prostrate than Bramble (346), with stems greyish when young; leaves always trifoliate, wrinkled, often paler green; flowers looking larger and always white; and insipid blue-black fruits with fewer and larger segments, covered with a plum-like bloom, the sepals never turned down. *Habitat:* Widespread and frequent in bushy and grassy places, also in fens and dune slacks; local in Scotland and Ireland. June onwards, starting earlier.

348. ***SHRUBBY CINQUEFOIL   *Potentilla fruticosa* L.   Pl. 42.   *CTW, p. 485*
A deciduous bush, 18 in. to 3 ft. high, the small hairy stalked pinnate greyish-green leaves with 3 or 5 untoothed leaflets. Flowers yellow, 5-petalled, in loose clusters, male and female usually on separate plants. A rather variable shrub, many varieties and similar species being grown in gardens. *Habitat:* Rare on limestone rock near water on Helvellyn and in Upper Teesdale and W Ireland. May onwards.

349. MARSH CINQUEFOIL   *P. palustris* (L.) Scopoli   Plate 25.   *CTW, p. 486*
A hairless perennial, 9–15 in. high, whose rather large, striking dull dark purple, erect flowers, with pointed petals shorter than the spreading purplish sepals, are unlikely to be confused with anything except conceivably Water Avens (361), which has paler nodding flowers and quite different hairy leaves. Leaves greyish-green, pinnate, with 3–7 toothed leaflets. *Habitat:* Widespread and locally frequent in swamps; uncommon in the S. May–July.

350. BARREN STRAWBERRY   *P. sterilis* (L.) Garcke   Plate 78.   *CTW, p. 487*
A low hairy perennial with white flowers, often confused with the true Strawberry (359), but smaller, with shorter and less erect stems; spreading hairs beneath the rather bluish-green, unshiny, less sharply veined leaves, which have the terminal tooth of the terminal leaflet shorter than its neighbours; gaps between the 5 slightly notched petals; and dry, quite unstrawberry-like fruits. *Habitat:* Widespread and common in dry grassland and woods. February–May, both starting and finishing much earlier than Wild Strawberry.

351. ***WHITE CINQUEFOIL   *P. rupestris* L.   Plate 80.   *CTW, p. 487*
A downy perennial, 6–12 in. high, with pinnate lower leaves and trifoliate stem-leaves, all with toothed leaflets, and loose clusters of 5-petalled white flowers ½-in. or so across. *Habitat:* Rare on limestone rocks on two hills and one river-bank on the Welsh Border. May–June.

352. SILVERWEED   *P. anserina* L.   Plate 42.   *CTW, p. 488*
The only common yellow flower with silvery pinnate leaves; a silky prostrate perennial, with creeping stems, well-toothed leaflets alternately large and small, silvery on both sides, the underside only, or on neither side, apparently never on the upper side only. Flowers largish, solitary, yellow, on long stalks, like Creeping Cinquefoil (357). *Habitat:* Widespread and common in damp grassy and waste places. May–August.

353. **HOARY CINQUEFOIL *P. argentea* L. Plate 42. *CTW, p. 488*

A neat, usually half-prostrate perennial, with wiry stems 4–9 in. long, covered with thick silvery down, the 3–5-lobed palmate leaves with coarsely toothed narrowly wedge-shaped leaflets, the margins slightly inrolled, dark green above, hoary white beneath. Flowers small, yellow, 5-petalled, equalling the sepals. *Habitat:* Widespread but local in dry places usually on sandy or gravelly soils; not in Ireland. June–September.

354. **SULPHUR CINQUEFOIL *P. recta* L. Plate 42. *CTW, p. 490*

A stiff erect hairy perennial, 1–2 ft. high, with hairy, well toothed, 5–7-fingered palmate leaves green on both sides. Flowers in open clusters on branched stems, most commonly pale primrose, but sometimes yellow, nearly an inch across, with 5 notched petals longer than the narrow sepals. *Habitat:* Uncommon but apparently increasing in hot, dry, grassy and waste places. June–August.

354*a*. **Norwegian Cinquefoil, *P. norvegica* L., is much smaller and often biennial, with all leaves 3-fingered, and yellower petals shorter than the sepals, which enlarge in fruit. Also uncommon in waste places.

355. **SPRING CINQUEFOIL *P. tabernaemontani* Ascherson
  '*P. verna*' Plate 42. *CTW, p. 491*

A mat-forming perennial with dark green leaves, rather like Trailing Tormentil (357*a*), but it flowers earlier, is hairier, and has upper leaves trifoliate and unstalked, lower leaves palmate with 5–7 leaflets, and yellow flowers in small clusters on stalks little longer than the root-leaves and with 5 petals longer than the sepals. Is much less slender than the 4-petalled Tormentil (356), and differs from Creeping Cinquefoil (357) in its unstalked upper leaves. *Habitat:* Very local on chalk and limestone in England and Wales; perhaps also still at Montrose. March–June.

355*a* **Alpine Cinquefoil, *P. crantzii* (Crantz) Beck, can be very similar, but flowers later and is slenderer and more tufted and has larger, often orange-spotted flowers. Very local on mountain ledges in the N. June–July.

356. TORMENTIL *P. erecta* (L.) Räuschel Plate 42. *CTW, p. 493*

A very slender, often prostrate, downy perennial, with thread-like stems never rooting, and leaves nearly always all with three toothed leaflets, the stem ones unstalked or nearly so, and looking 5-fingered on account of the two conspicuous leaf-like, usually toothed stipules at their base. Flowers yellow, on long, slender stalks nearly always with 4 petals. Hybridises with the next two species. *Habitat:* Widespread and abundant on moors and in heathy and grassy places, especially characteristic of acid soils. May onwards.

357. CREEPING CINQUEFOIL *P. reptans* L. Plate 42. *CTW, p. 494*

A low downy perennial, far-creeping and rooting, the palmate leaves all on long stalks, with 3–5 large toothed lanceolate leaflets. Flowers solitary, ¾-in. across, twice as large as Tormentil (356), on long slender stalks, with 5 yellow petals longer than the sepals. Hybridises with the next species. *Habitat:* Widespread and common by waysides and in waste places. June onwards.

357*a*. *Trailing Tormentil, *P. anglica* Laicharding (*P. procumbens* Sibthorp), is half-way between Tormentil (356) and Creeping Cinquefoil, with leaflets broader than either. Differs from 356 in having all leaves shortly stalked, some with 4–5 leaflets; stipules usually untoothed, not leaf-like; prostrate stems rooting only in late summer; and larger flowers sometimes 5-petalled. Differs from Creeping

Cinquefoil in being more branched and having frequent leaves with only 3–4 leaflets, stems not rooting early, and flowers often only 4-petalled. Habitat nearer Tormentil; less common than either.

358. **LEAST CINQUEFOIL *Sibbaldia procumbens* L. Pl. 42. *CTW, p. 495*
A prostrate 2–4-in. tufted hairy perennial, with grey trefoil leaves, each leaflet ending in 3 teeth, and leafy clusters of a few small flowers, sometimes lacking the narrow pale yellow petals, which are shorter than the sepals. *Habitat:* Local, high on bare hills and mountains, commonest in the Highlands. July–August. *Potentilla sibbaldi* Haller.

359. WILD STRAWBERRY *Fragaria vesca* L. Plate 78. *CTW, p. 496*
Easily recognisable in fruit as a diminutive Garden Strawberry; a low hairy perennial, with rooting runners, and trefoil leaves, the pointed leaflets with rather deeply etched veins, shiny green above, paler beneath and silky with appressed hairs. Flowers white, on upright stalks, with no gaps between the 5 unnotched petals. The drooping reddish strawberries have the pips (seeds) protruding and sepals turned down. Often confused with the earlier Barren Strawberry (350) *Habitat:* Widespread, common in open woods and grassy places. April onwards.
359a. ****Garden Strawberry** *F.* × *ananassa* Duchesne ('*F. chiloensis*'), is more tufted and much larger in all its parts, with flower- and fruit-stalks less erect, sepals erect, and the pips sunk in the flesh of the fruit. Occasional in waste places, especially railway banks. May–July.

360. HERB BENNET *Geum urbanum* L. Plate 42. *CTW, p. 498*
A hairy perennial, 1–2 ft. high, with toothed pinnate root-leaves, the end lobe round and much the largest, 3-fingered stem-leaves, and roundish leaf-like stipules at their base. Flowers small, yellow, with gaps between the 5 spreading petals which are no longer than the soon down-turned sepals, and with a bunch of kinked red styles and numerous stamens. Fruits hooked, in a bur-like head. Hybridises with the next species. *Habitat:* Widespread and common on hedgebanks and by woods. June onwards.

361. WATER AVENS *G. rivale* L. Plate 25. *CTW, p. 499*
An unbranched downy perennial a foot or so high, which might be taken for a nodding, dull purple garden Geum; root-leaves pinnate, the end lobe very large, the toothed leaflets interspersed with smaller ones. Flowers twice the size of Herb Bennet (360), with notched, orange-pink, very rarely pale yellow, petals, and large purple sepals. Fruits hooked, like Herb Bennet but with a lengthening stalk above the erect sepals. Smaller and hairier than Marsh Cinquefoil (349). *Habitat:* Widespread and common in ditches and other wet and often shady places, also on mountains; absent in SE England. April–June.

362. **MOUNTAIN AVENS *Dryas octopetala* L. Plate 77. *CTW, p. 500*
A beautiful 'alpine' quite often seen in rockeries, its somewhat anemone-like inch-wide white flowers with a mass of golden stamens and usually 8 narrow petals. A creeping undershrub, with flowers borne singly on stalks above the mat of neat small evergreen-oak-like leaves, downy white beneath. Fruit ahead of nutlets with long feathery plumes. *Habitat:* On limestone, local in turf and on rocky ledges on mountains in Snowdonia, from the Craven Pennines northwards,

and in N Ireland; plentiful near sea-level in N Scotland, and the Burren. At its best in May–June.

363. AGRIMONY *Agrimonia eupatoria* L. Plate 60. *CTW, p. 50f*

A softly hairy, little branched perennial, 1–2 ft. high, which may have a faint sweet smell; leaves pinnate, sometimes brown-suffused, the larger toothed and interspersed with smaller ones. Flowers small, yellow, in tall narrow tapering spikes. The fruits are small oval burs, hooked, straight-sided, deeply furrowed, the outer spines spreading, not turned back (Fig.). *Habitat:* Widespread and common in grassy places. June onwards.

363a. *Fragrant Agrimony, *A. odorata* (Gouan) Miller, is usually larger, stouter and more branched, and is often confused with a robust variety of common Agrimony, but its leaves are more fragrant, always green, its larger flowers more often pale yellow, and its usually 2-seeded fruits much wider, bell-shaped and with no or faint furrows at the top only, and bushier because the outer spines are turned back (Fig.). More local and more characteristic of wood-borders on acid soil.

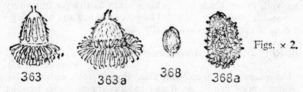

363   363a   368   368a   Figs. × 2.

364. *ALPINE LADY'S MANTLE *Alchemilla alpina* L. Pl. 88. *CTW, p. 504*

Like a small Lady's Mantle (365), but with darker, greyer leaves, almost always divided to the base into 5–9 narrow toothed segments, and exquisitely covered beneath with appressed silvery-silky hairs. Flowers tiny, pale green, in clusters on a floppy stalk. *Habitat:* Common in grassy and rocky places on mountains in the N; very rare in Cos. Kerry and Wicklow. June onwards. (Incl. *A. conjuncta* Babington.)

365. COMMON LADY'S MANTLE *A. vulgaris* L.[1] Plate 88. *CTW, p. 505*

Low, pale green perennial, very variable in size, hairiness and leaf-shape; leaves stalked, roundish, palmate, pleated, with 7–11 toothed lobes, green on both sides. Flowers tiny, yellowish-green, petalless, with the calyx in two rings, in large, lax, leafy clusters. *Habitat:* Widespread and frequent in grassy places, but rare in S and E England. May–September.

366. PARSLEY PIERT *Aphanes arvensis* L. Plate 89. *CTW, p. 512*

An inconspicuous, usually prostrate, greyish downy little annual, with short-stalked 3-lobed leaves, the lobes deeply toothed, and prominent toothed leaf-like stipules at their base. Flowers minute, green, petalless, with the calyx in two rings, in unstalked clusters along the stem. *Habitat:* Widespread and common on arable and dry ground. April onwards. *Alchemilla arvensis* (L.) Scopoli; (incl. *Aphanes microcarpa* (Boissier & Reuter) Rothmaler).

---

[1] Incl. the following microspecies: *A. minor* Hudson, *A. vestita* (Buser) Raunkiaer, *A. filicaulis* Buser, *A. minima* Walters, *A. monticola* Opiz, *A. acutiloba* Opiz, *A. xanthochlora* Rothmaler, *A. glomerulans* Buser, *A. glabra* Neygenfind, *A. obtusa* Buser, *A. wichurae* (Buser) Stefansson.

367. *GREAT BURNET *Sanguisorba officinalis* L. Plate 35. *CTW, p. 513*

A handsome hairless perennial, 18 in. to 3 ft. high, taller and larger in all its parts than Salad Burnet (368), and with distinctive, oblong heads of tiny reddish-purple flowers, all with both style and stamens, on leafy branched stems; leaflets less deeply toothed. *Habitat:* Local in damp grassy places in England and Wales; scarce elsewhere, not in SE England. June–September.

368. SALAD BURNET *Poterium sanguisorba* L. Plate 35. *CTW, p. 514*

An unassuming perennial, hairy only below, about a foot high and smelling of cucumber when crushed; leaves pinnate, with small, well toothed leaflets Flowers tiny, green, petalless male below, female above, in globular heads which are coloured below by the yellow stamens, and above and sometimes also below by the dark red styles. Fruits small with four sides divided by practically straight ridges (Fig., p. 73). *Habitat:* Widespread, locally abundant in grassy places, avoiding acid soils; more local in Scotland and Ireland. May–August.

368a. **Fodder Burnet,** *P. polygamum* Waldstein & Kitaibel, is taller, stouter and leafier, with flower-heads half as large again and larger fruits very deeply pitted on the surfaces which are divided by wider toothed and wavy ridges (Fig.). Usually a relic of cultivation, occasionally persisting.

369. **PIRRI-PIRRI BUR *Acaena anserinifolia* (Forster) Druce
Plate 88. *CTW, p. 515*

Rather like a small downy creeping Salad Burnet (368), with numerous prostrate branches woody below, small soft reddish spines on its bur-like fruits; 4–5 pairs of neat, dark green, less toothed leaflets; and globular whitish flower-heads on erect 3-in. stems, the flowers all with both styles and stamens. *Habitat:* Increasingly naturalised in grassy and heathy places from the Tweed southwards, and in Ireland. June–July.

370. FIELD ROSE *Rosa arvensis* Hudson Plate 75. *CTW, p. 518*

One of the easier to identify of the wild Roses, with the styles making a stout column longer than the numerous yellow stamens in the middle of the cup-shaped flowers, which are always creamy white, and smaller and flowering later than Dog Rose (372). An almost hairless clambering deciduous shrub, with hooked prickles on the long green or purplish trailing stems, which often form matted brakes; leaves pinnate. Hips smaller than Dog Rose, always hairless, sometimes roundish. *Habitat:* Widespread and common in open woods, thickets and hedgerows, but local in the N and in Ireland. July–August.

371. *BURNET ROSE *R. pimpinellifolia* L. Plate 75. *CTW, p. 519*

A distinctive Rose, suckering to form extensive bushy patches, with upright stems 6 in. to 2 ft. high, a dense covering of long and short straight spines, solitary fragrant creamy-white, rarely pale pink flowers and undivided sepals persisting on the purplish-black hips. Leaves deciduous, pinnate, with 7–9 small roundish toothed leaflets. Hybridises with several other Roses. *Habitat:* Widespread and locally common on dunes, heaths, and downs, especially near the sea; also on mountain ledges; uncommon in the SE. May–July. '*R. spinosissima*'.

372. DOG ROSE *R. canina* L. Plate 17. *CTW, p. 522*

The 'English unofficial Rose,' the commonest and most variable wild Rose in the S, with the largest flowers, which are pale pink or white, and fragrant, with numerous yellow stamens. A tall stout deciduous shrub, 4–10 ft. high, with arching stems and stout hooked or curved prickles, the pinnate leaves with toothed leaflets, sometimes downy beneath. Fruits—hips—red, egg-shaped and nearly always hairless, losing the more or less pinnate sepals before they redden. *R. stylosa* has the styles united in a column shorter than the stamens. *Habitat:* Widespread and common in hedgerows and thickets, but rare in Scotland. June–July. (Incl. *R. coriifolia* Fries; *R. stylosa* Desvaux; *R. obtusifolia* Desv.)

373. DOWNY ROSE *R. villosa* L. Plate 17. *CTW, p. 524*

Commoner in the N than Dog Rose (372), from which it differs in its nearly straight prickles; greyer leaflets always doubly toothed and softly downy on both sides; usually deep pink flowers; and globular hips normally covered with bristles and longer-crowned with the erect sepals. *Habitat:* Widespread, locally common in hedges and bushy places. June–July. (Incl. *R. tomentosa* Smith, *R. sherardii* Davies.)

373a. *Sweetbriar, *R. rubiginosa* L. (incl. *R. micrantha* Smith; *R. elliptica* Tausdi; *R. agrestis* Savi), is smaller in all its parts, and is usually readily told by its sweet-smelling leaves, usually stickly hairy below. A smaller shrub, with curved or hooked prickles, smaller and fewer towards the top. Hips egg-shaped, with few or no bristles. Frequent on chalk and limestone in the S; local in Scotland and Ireland.

374. BLACKTHORN *Prunus spinosa* L. Plate 75. *CTW, p. 528*

A common, rigidly thorny, stiff wide-branching deciduous suckering shrub, 4–12 ft. high; young twigs downy, becoming blackish-brown or grey. Flowers small, pure white, in numerous short spikes, appearing before the dull oval undivided leaves, and so contrasting strongly with the dark stems and twigs. Fruit a diminutive blackish plum—sloe—with a bluish bloom and an exceedingly sharp taste. *Habitat:* Widespread and abundant in woods, scrub and hedgerows, often forming impenetrable thickets, especially on sea-cliffs. April–May, a fortnight after Cherry-Plum (375) and a month before Hawthorn (380).

375. *CHERRY-PLUM *P. cerasifera* Ehrhart Plate 75. *CTW, p. 530*

Differs from Blackthorn (374) in its looser spikes of larger flowers appearing much earlier and at the same time as the larger, pale glossy green leaves; also in the normally thornless twigs being hairless from the first and glossy, green or reddish later on. Fruits quite different, yellow or reddish, and globular, but not formed every year. Sometimes a small tree (a variety with purplish leaves is frequent in gardens); never so thick-set; branches erect, pliant. *Habitat:* Frequent in hedgerows in many parts of England. March.

375a. *Wild Plum, *P. domestica* L. is variable (being plums, greengages, bullaces, damsons, and so forth gone wild), but differs in its dull, sometimes thorny, twigs, downy when young, becoming grey or brown later; larger dull leaves; larger flowers appearing later; and often egg-shaped fruits of various colours. April.

376. WILD CHERRY *P. avium* (L.) L. Plate 75. *CTW, p. 531*

A lofty deciduous tree, with smooth, shining, reddish-brown bark peeling horizontally, and drooping, toothed, pointed oval leaves slightly downy beneath, often coppery when young, turning red or pink in autumn. Flowers white, in loose clusters, with calyx-tube narrowed at top, and petals often slightly notched. Fruits red, like pinched cultivated cherries, sweet or bitter. *Habitat:* Widespread and locally common in hedgerows and woods, especially beech-woods, decreasing northwards. April–May, with the leaves.

376a. **Morello Cherry, *P. cerasus* L., a suckering shrub, 3–10 ft. high, has thicker leaves, dark green above, nearly hairless beneath and not drooping; smaller petals not or scarcely notched, calyx-tube not narrowed at top; fruit always bitter. Rare, usually in hedges and woods on acid soils, and often confounded with Wild Cherry (376). May.

377. *BIRD CHERRY *P. padus* L. Plate 75. *CTW, p. 532*

Readily told from the last two species by its long loose spikes of smaller fragrant flowers, and its black pea-sized tart fruits. A deciduous shrub or small tree, with leaves hairy only along the midrib beneath. *Habitat:* Frequent in woods and hedgerows, commonest in Wales and N England, thinning out northwards; usually planted in the S; scattered over Ireland. May.

378. **KHASIA BERRY *Cotoneaster simonsii* Baker Plate 17. *CTW, p. 535*

A half-evergreen shrub, 2–10 ft. high, with erect branches and twigs covered with short, stiff down; leaves pointed oval, an inch long, dark green above, paler and sparsely downy beneath. Flowers small, 2–4 together, with erect, pale pink petals. Berries egg-shaped, orange-red. *Habitat:* Not infrequently bird-sown and naturalised in all sorts of places. May–July.

378a. ***Great Orme Berry, *C. integerrimus* Medicus, is a compact deciduous bush, 1–2 ft. high, with twigs soon becoming hairless, rounder leaves downy grey beneath, and roundish crimson berries. Now extremely rare on Great Ormes Head near Llandudno, where grow also much more of both 378 and 379.

379. **ROCKSPRAY *C. microphyllus* Lindley Plate 71. *CTW, p. 535*

A prostrate evergreen undershrub, with stiff spreading branches, twigs downy when young, and small neat blunt or slightly notched oval leaves, ½-in. long, dark glossy green above and downy grey beneath. Flowers, usually solitary, white, with purple anthers and spreading petals. Berry round, crimson. *Habitat:* Rarely seen in gardens, yet not infrequently bird-sown, especially on chalk and limestone banks. May–June.

379a. ***Wallspray, *C. horizontalis* Decaisne, is deciduous but leafing early, and has branches spreading stiffly and herringbone-wise in a horizontal plane; twigs covered with brownish wool; leaves numerous and thick on the stems, glossy above, almost hairless below, and turning orange and red in autumn; petals pink, erect; and berry red. Often grown in gardens but much less often bird-sown.

380. HAWTHORN *Crataegus monogyna* Jacquin Plate 75. *CTW, p. 537*

A very common, thick-set, thorny deciduous shrub or small tree, with leaves deeply 3–5-lobed, not very shiny above. Flowers white, sometimes becoming pink, on downy stalks, in broad umbel-like clusters, strong-scented, with numerous stamens, pink or purple anthers and usually only 1 style and so only 1 stone in the roundish, dull red berry or 'haw'. Several somewhat similar Hawthorns are often planted on roadsides. *Habitat:* Widespread and abundant in open woods, hedges and thickets, and on downs. May–June. White-thorn, Quick.

380a. *Woodland Hawthorn, *C. oxyacanthoides* Thuillier, is a looser, less thorny shrub, with less deeply lobed, shinier leaves; and fewer flowers on hairless stalks with rather larger petals, and usually 2–3 styles, so 2–3 stones in each haw. Often hybridises with Hawthorn. More a clay-soil and woodland plant, less common in the N. May–June, starting a week or two earlier.

381. ***MEDLAR *Mespilus germanica* L. Plate 75. *CTW, p. 538*

The true wild Medlar is a thorny deciduous shrub, but most Medlars found wild are thornless small trees, probably bird-sown from gardens. Leaves lanceolate, downy, usually untoothed, turning yellow in autumn. Flowers solitary, short-stalked, nearly an inch across, white with brick-red anthers, with long-pointed, rather leaf-like sepals, which persist around the hollow on the top of the brown, rounded fruit, which stays on the tree in winter. *Habitat:* Isolated trees occur very locally in hedgerows in S England. May–June.

382. **JUNE BERRY *Amelanchier intermedia* Spach Plate 74. *CTW, p. 538*

A deciduous shrub or small tree, with finely toothed, pointed oval leaves, turning red or yellow in autumn. Flowers appearing with the leaves but rather sparingly, in loose clusters, with narrow untoothed upright white petals. Fruit a small roundish berry, crowned by the erect sepals, green, red and finally purplish-black. *Habitat:* Naturalised in scrub and woodland in a few areas in S England. April. (Incl. '*A. laevis*' and *A. canadensis* (L.) Medicus.)

383. ROWAN *Sorbus aucuparia* L. Plate 74. *CTW, p. 542*

A graceful small deciduous tree or tall shrub, with smooth grey bark, large alternate pinnate leaves with toothed lanceolate leaflets, flattish heads of small foetid white flowers, followed by small, roundish bright red or orange berries. True Ash-trees (629) have superficially similar opposite leaves but inconspicuous flowers and no berries. *Habitat:* Widespread and common in the N and W, more local elsewhere, in dry woods and rocky places ascending very high in the mountains. May–June. Mountain Ash; *Pyrus aucuparia* (L.) Ehrhart.

384. *WHITE BEAM *S. aria* (L.) Crantz[1] Plate 74. *CTW, p. 549*

A beautiful deciduous tree or shrub, with silvery undersides to its oval toothed leaves, and heads of white flowers and red berries similar to Rowan (383). It varies in height from a scraggy bush to a tall tree, in shape, size and toothing of the leaves, in size of petals, in colour of anthers from pink to cream, and in the shape, markings and size of the berries. Hybridises with 383 and 385. *Habitat:* Widespread and locally frequent at the edge of woods, in scrub and on crags, usually on chalk or limestone. May–June. *Pyrus aria* (L.) Ehrhart.

384a. **Cut-leaved White Beam, *S. intermedia* (Ehrhart) Persoon,[2] is intermediate between White Beam and Rowan, with leaves therefore much more deeply dissected or lobed than White Beam, the lowest pair of lobes in one microspecies actually leaflets, and only greyish downy beneath. Uncommon on rocks, usually limestone, in the W; planted or bird-sown elsewhere.

384b. **French Hales, *S. latifolia* Persoon,[3] is a tree intermediate between White Beam and Wild Service Tree (385), the leaves downy grey below and having larger, but still small, and more triangular lobes than White Beam. Berries

---

[1] Including *S. leptophylla* Warburg, *S. eminens* War., *S. hibernica* War., *S. porrigentiformis* War., *S. lancastriensis* War., *S. rupicola* (Syme) Hedlund, and *S. vexans* War.

[2] Including *S. arranensis* Hedlund, *S. leyana* Wilmott, *S. minima* (Ley) Hedl., *S. anglica* Hedl. and *S. pseudofennica* Warburg.

[3] Including *S. bristoliensis* Wilmott, *S. subcuneata* Wilm., and *S. devoniensis* Warburg.

orange to brownish. Very local in woods and hedges in SW England and SE Ireland; very rarely planted or bird-sown elsewhere.

385. **WILD SERVICE TREE   *S. torminalis* (L.) Crantz
Pyrus torminalis (L.) Ehrhart   Plate 74.   *CTW, p. 556*
A deciduous tree, with flowers and berries like Rowan (383) and White Beam (384), but with rather maple-like leaves green and hairless on both sides when mature, with sharply cut toothed lobes, and twigs and undersides of leaves both somewhat downy when young. Berries brown, egg-shaped. *Habitat:* Thinly scattered in woods on clay or limestone in England and Wales. May–June.

386. *PEAR   *Pyrus communis* L.   Plate 75.   *CTW, p. 557*
A deciduous tree, with blackish-yellow twigs and pointed oval leaves, usually hairless at least above, on longish stalks. Flowers in clusters, white with purple anthers. Fruit a small greenish or brownish pear, crowned by the dead sepals. *Habitat:* Widespread but thinly scattered in woods and hedgerows; rare in Scotland and Ireland. April.
386*a.* ***Plymouth Pear, see p. 307.

387. CRAB APPLE   *Malus sylvestris* Miller (*Pyrus malus* L.)   Pl. 17.   *CTW, 558*
A small deciduous tree, variable since it includes the produce of discarded cultivated apple-cores, the true wild plant spiny, with reddish-brown twigs, and leaves pointed oval, toothed, short-stalked and usually more or less downy. Flowers in umbel-like clusters, pinkish-white, darker on the back, with yellow anthers. Fruit a small tart yellowish-green apple, often turning scarlet. *Habitat:* Widespread and frequent in woods and hedgerows; local in Scotland. May.

STONECROP FAMILY   Crassulaceae

NON-WOODY PLANTS, more or less fleshy or succulent, the undivided leaves with very short or no stalks and no stipules at their base. All except Pink Stonecrop (395) are hairless, and all except Mossy Stonecrop (396) perennials.

388. *ROSE-ROOT   *Sedum rosea* (L.) Scopoli   Plate 46.   *CTW, p. 561*
A tufted greyish succulent, 6–12 in. high, with short broad stiff toothed over-lapping leaves, all up the stem and sometimes tinged purplish. Flowers numerous, small, in broad dense heads, greenish-yellow, or sometimes purple-tinged with purple anthers, male and female on different plants. Fruits orange, often taken for flowers. *Habitat:* Frequent on mountain ledges in Wales and N England, and on sea-cliffs as well in Scotland and Ireland. May–June.

389. *ORPINE   *S. telephium* L.   Plate 26.   *CTW, p. 562*
The only pink succulent to be found in woods, unbranched, a foot or so high, sometimes tinged purple, with all leaves toothed, broad oblong and alternate, and broad heads of numerous small purplish-pink flowers with spreading petals. The similar garden *S. maximum* Suter and *S. spectabile* Boreau are larger and have opposite leaves. *Habitat:* Widespread but local in woods and on hedge-banks. July–September.

390. *ENGLISH STONECROP   *S. anglicum* Hudson   Plate 88   *CTW, p. 563*
The commonest of the white Stonecrops, rarely over 2 in. high, often grey and turning pink, with stubby little, usually alternate leaves. Flowers star-like, white, often tinged pink, very short-stalked, in a short cluster. Fruits red. *Habitat:*

Widespread on acid rocks, dunes and shingle; common in the N and W, scarce elsewhere. June–August.

390a. **Thick-leaved Stonecrop,** *S. dasyphyllum* L., has almost globular, always grey, slightly downy, usually opposite leaves, with minute green or red spots, much longer flower-stalks and broader petals. Occasionally on walls in S England and on limestone in Co. Cork. June–July.

391. **WHITE STONECROP** *S. album* L. Plate 88. *CTW, p. 564*

Larger and twice as tall as English Stonecrop (390), with longer dull green or reddish cylindrical leaves, and broad, flat-topped white flower-heads on thicker stems but drooping in bud. *Habitat:* Widespread but local on rocks and walls, usually near houses. July.

392. **WALL-PEPPER** *S. acre* L. Plate 46. *CTW, p. 564*

The commonest yellow Stonecrop, 2–4 in. high, often in mats, with numerous tiny fat yellow-green leaves, often broadest at the bottom, with a peppery taste, and conspicuous bright yellow star-like flowers, with broad-based petals. *Habitat:* Widespread and common on walls, roofs, dunes, shingle, and other bare places. June–July.

393. **ROCK STONECROP** *S. forsteranum* Smith Plate 46. *CTW, p. 565*

Usually smaller and slenderer than the next species, with the barren shoots shorter and dead leaves often persisting below, the lower leaves on the flowering stems usually erect; flowers unstalked; sepals blunter. *Habitat:* Rather rare in rocky places in Wales and W England, occasionally established elsewhere on banks or shingle. June–July. '*S. rupestre*'.

394. *LARGE YELLOW STONECROP* *S. reflexum* L. Pl. 46. *CTW, p. 566*

A somewhat stout greyish-green perennial, 6–10 in. high, with large, somewhat elongated barren rosettes of fat linear leaves, apparently running down the stem but actually with a spur at the base, with no dead leaves persisting below; the lower leaves on the flowering stems often turned down. Flowers yellow, in heads, stalked, nodding in bud; sepals pointed. *Habitat:* Infrequent on walls and banks usually as a garden escape. July–August.

395. **PINK STONECROP** *S. villosum* L. Plate 23. *CTW, p. 566*

A small downy unbranched, sometimes reddish, succulent biennial, 2–4 in. high, with short, alternate leaves, and small clusters of pink flowers; no barren shoots. *Habitat:* Scarce in wet places on hills from the Pennines to the Central Highlands. July–August.

396. **MOSSY STONECROP** *Crassula tillaea* Lester-Garland Pl. 105. *CTW, 567*

A tiny prostrate annual, often no more than an inch long, with minute oval leaves and solitary whitish flowers. It starts greyish and inconspicuous, but soon turns a brilliant red in the sun; even then its tiny thread-like stems are so slender that it may be overlooked. *Habitat:* Very local on bare patches on sand and gravel in S and E England and Channel Is. May. *Tillaea muscosa* L.

397. *WALL PENNYWORT* *Umbilicus rupestris* (Salisbury) Dandy

Navelwort; '*Cotyledon umbilicus*'. Plate 88. *CTW, p. 568*

A curious fleshy perennial with disc-like, bluntly toothed leaves having a dimple in the centre above the stalk, and spikes of greenish tubular flowers. It varies greatly in size, from low simple plants, 2–3 in. high, on dry walls, to lush branched ones, a foot or more high, with leaves 2 in. across in moist shade. *Habitat:* Locally common on rocks, walls and hedge-banks in the W, especially near the sea; very local elsewhere. June–August.

SAXIFRAGE FAMILY   Saxifragaceae

398. **ARCTIC SAXIFRAGE   *Saxifraga nivalis* L.   Plate 82.   *CTW, p. 571*
Differs from Starry Saxifrage (399) above all in its congested flower-head at the top of a stiff stem which is often black with hairs; also in its leaves being usually purple beneath, the root ones stalked, and its whitish petals with no yellow spots, and erect or spreading sepals.   *Habitat:* Rare on mountain ledges in Snowdonia, the Lake District, Scotland and Co. Sligo. July–August.

399. *STARRY SAXIFRAGE   *S. stellaris* L.   Plate 82.   *CTW, p. 572*
A low, graceful, slightly hairy perennial, with a rosette of unstalked root-leaves; no stem-leaves; and a loose cluster of star-like white flowers, with two yellow spots near the base of each petal and sepals turned down.   *Habitat:* Frequent in wet places in hill and mountainous districts in the N and in Ireland. June–August.

400. ***YELLOW MARSH SAXIFRAGE   *S. hirculus* L.   Pl. 46.   *CTW, p. 572*
A low downy perennial, with beautiful buttercup-like flowers twice the size of Yellow Mountain Saxifrage (408), usually solitary, often with orange spots at the base of the petals, and with the hairy sepals turned down after flowering. Leaves short, thin, narrow lanceolate, stalked, mostly in a creeping mat, often lost in the herbage. It flowers shyly and never in massed abundance, and may therefore seem even rarer than it is.   *Habitat:* Rare in open marshy spots on a very few moors in the N and in Ireland. August.

401. **ST. PATRICK'S CABBAGE   *S. spathularis* Brotero
'*S. umbrosa*'   Plate 82.   *CTW, p. 574*
A graceful perennial, 6–12 in. high, very like the garden London Pride, with leaves in a rosette, thick, hairless, sharp-toothed, broadest at the tip, tapering to the base, ascending, often reddish beneath, on slightly hairy stalks. Flowers small, white, in loose clusters on reddish hairy leafless stalks; each petal spotted red with 3 yellow spots at the base.   *Habitat:* Locally frequent on rocks in W Ireland and Co. Wicklow. June–July.

    401 × 401*a*. *London Pride, *S.* × *cuneifolia* L., is a widespread escape.
    401 × 402. ***S.* × *polita* (Haworth) Link, is fertile and often commoner than 402, and grows also in Connemara where the latter no longer does.
    401*a*. ***Pyrenean Saxifrage, *S. umbrosa* L., is best distinguished by its neater rosette of spreading leaves with blunter teeth and shorter hairier stalks, and by the single yellow spot on the smaller petals. In two Yorkshire ghylls.

402. ***KIDNEY SAXIFRAGE   *S. hirsuta* L.   Plate 82.   *CTW, p. 574*
Rather like St Patrick's Cabbage (401), but has circular leaves with a heart-shaped base, hairy on both sides; long hairy leaf-stalks; and white petals with only one yellow spot and not always red spots.   *Habitat:* Local and decreasing in rocky and shady places in SW Ireland; rarely elsewhere. May–July. '*S. geum*'.

403. FINGERED SAXIFRAGE   *S. tridactylites* L.   Plate 87.   *CTW, p. 575*
A dainty, often reddish, stickily hairy annual, with somewhat zigzag stems

2–4 in. high, and 1–5-fingered leaves, narrowed at the base, with short or no stalks. Flowers small, white, 5-petalled, on slender stalks. Fruits egg-shaped. *Habitat:* Widespread but somewhat local in bare, dry places and on walls. April–May. Rue-leaved Saxifrage.

404. *MEADOW SAXIFRAGE *S. granulata* L. Plate 84. *CTW, p. 576*

A downy, little branched perennial, 4–9 in. high, with bulbils at the base of the stem; long-stalked, gently lobed rounded leaves, few on the stems; and loose clusters of fine white flowers nearly an inch across, with gaps between the petals. *Habitat:* Widespread but rather local in dry meadows and woods and sandy ground. April–June.

405. ***DROOPING SAXIFRAGE *S. cernua* L. Plate 87. *CTW, p. 576*

A low, very slender, almost hairless, unbranched perennial, 2–6 in. high, with a solitary white flower, often large for the size of the plant, and numerous tiny crimson bulbils up the stem at the base of the 3–5-lobed leaves. *Habitat:* Known only on high rocks in Glencoe, and on Ben Lawers, where it is a shy flowerer and grows much smaller. July.

406. ***HIGHLAND SAXIFRAGE *S. rivularis* L. Plate 87. *CTW, p. 577*

A small hairless, almost prostrate perennial, with well stalked, shallowly palmately lobed leaves, the base heart-shaped, and few unpretentious stalked white flowers, the petals little longer than the sepals. *Habitat:* Rare in wet rocky places high in the Highlands, chiefly in the Cairngorms. July–August.

407. *MOSSY SAXIFRAGE *S. hypnoides* L. Plate 84. *CTW, p. 578*

A frequent edging and rockery plant in numerous forms; a very variable, low perennial, with barren shoots forming moss-like mats of shortly palmately lobed leaves, ending in a fine bristle, with a few long hairs on their stalks and sometimes with small bulbils at their base. Flowers white, with usually nodding, often pink-tipped buds, on leafless branched stems, 3–6 in. high. *Habitat:* Locally common on rocks, screes and open grassy places in hill districts, at Cheddar, from Wales northwards, and in Ireland. May–July. (Incl. *S. rosacea* Moench; *S. hartii* Webb.)

407a. ***Tufted Saxifrage, *S. cespitosa* L., is hairier and 1–2 in. high, and never creeps or has bulbils, but has densely tufted rosettes of leaves with usually 3 blunt, broader and less spreading lobes. Flowers smaller, fewer, dirty white, often petalless, on less branched stems. Very rare on sheltered mountain ledges, now probably only high in the Cairngorms and the Ben Nevis range. June–July.

408. *YELLOW MOUNTAIN SAXIFRAGE *S. aizoides* L. Pl. 46. *CTW, 579*

The only at all common yellow Saxifrage, a short mat-forming, sparsely hairy perennial, with thickish unstalked narrow lanceolate leaves and bright yellow, very rarely orange, flowers, often spotted red, with gaps between the petals; anthers red. Biting Stonecrop (392) has stubbier, fleshier leaves. *Habitat:* Locally common in wet lime-rich places on and by mountains in the N, and in N Ireland; also by the sea in N Scotland. June–August.

409. **PURPLE SAXIFRAGE *S. oppositifolia* L. Plate 23. *CTW, p. 580*

One of the earliest mountain plants to flower, and our only purple Saxifrage; a prostrate perennial, with often long trailing thyme-like stems, hairy only on the numerous, very small, hard unstalked opposite oval leaves. Flowers, rather large, solitary, pink-purple, on very short stalks. *Habitat:* Locally frequent in wettish places on lime-rich mountains in the Highlands; more local further S to Yorkshire and S Wales; rare in N and W Ireland; by the sea in N Scotland and Donegal. April–May.

410. *GOLDEN SAXIFRAGE   *Chrysosplenium oppositifolium* L.

Plate 46.   *CTW, p. 581*

A low creeping perennial with mossy mats of thin, bluntly toothed, roundish, sparsely hairy, stalked, pale green leaves, the root ones tapering to the base,

and flat leafy heads of tiny 4-sepalled petalless yellowish flowers on stems with opposite leaves (Fig.). *Habitat:* Widespread and locally common in wet shady places, especially by springs; also on mountains. March–May.

410*a*. **Alternate Golden Saxifrage, *C. alternifolium* L., is a stouter plant, not mat-forming, with kidney-shaped, deeper-toothed root-leaves on stalks twice as long, and larger flower-heads on taller stems with alternate, one or no leaves (Fig.) and glossier golden-green bracts. Grows with Golden Saxifrage, but much less common, usually on lime-rich soils, and flowers earlier in the S; on mountains it grows further in under overhanging rocks.

PARNASSUS-GRASS FAMILY   Parnassiaceae

411. *GRASS OF PARNASSUS   *Parnassia palustris* L.   Plate 84.   *CTW, p. 582*

A pale green hairless tufted perennial, 4–8 in. high, its solitary flowers somewhat like a delicate short white Buttercup or Saxifrage, but with the 5 stamens alternating with beautifully fingered scales. Root-leaves long-stalked, oval, pointed, with usually one unstalked leaf clasping the erect unbranched stem. *Habitat:* Widespread but local in marshes, fens and dune slacks, chiefly in the N and W; not in the SE. July onwards.

GOOSEBERRY FAMILY   Grossulariaceae

412. *RED CURRANT   *Ribes rubrum* L.   Plate 78.   *CTW, p. 585*

A deciduous bush, 2–4 ft. high, familiar in the fruit garden, with often drooping clusters of small green, purple-edged flowers on short stalks of equal length, all becoming roundish acid red, or rarely white, fruits. Leaves not aromatic, 3–5-lobed, blunt-toothed. *Habitat:* Widespread but scattered in woods and hedgerows, especially by streams and in fens. April–May.

412*a*. *Black Currant, *R. nigrum* L., another familiar kitchen-garden bush, is readily told by its slightly larger and sticky, aromatic leaves, the lowest flowers on the longest stalks, and black fruits.

413. *MOUNTAIN CURRANT   *R. alpinum* L.   Plate 78.   *CTW, p. 587*

A much taller, larger, thicker, more branched shrub than Red Currant (412), and with smaller, more deeply toothed leaves; flowers in small erect clusters, the male and female on different bushes; and prominent green bracts at their base, longer than the flower-stalks. Fruits red, tasteless. *Habitat:* Rather local, usually in rocky woods on limestone, chiefly in Wales and N England. April–June.

414. GOOSEBERRY *R. uva-crispa* L. (*R. grossularia* L.) Pl. 78. *CTW, 588*
Another familiar garden fruit; a small, spiny, deciduous bush, 1–3 ft. high, with many branches, small 3–5-lobed blunt-toothed leaves, and small drooping red-tinged green flowers, the petals turning back, 1–2 together on short stalks. Fruits green, egg-shaped, often hairy, and sometimes tinged yellow or red. *Habitat:* Widespread and not infrequent in woods and hedgerows. March–May.

SUNDEW FAMILY Droseraceae

415. *COMMON SUNDEW *Drosera rotundifolia* L. Plate 88. *CTW, p. 589*
A remarkable little plant, slender yet perennial, our only plant with a flat basal rosette of stalked round yellowish-green leaves covered with sticky red hairs, which can curve inwards to trap and digest flies. Flowers white, in small heads on leafless stems, 2–5 in. high, much longer than the leaves and arising from the centre of the rosette. *Habitat:* Widespread and locally frequent in bogs and on wet heaths and moors, often in sphagnum moss. June–August.

416. *GREAT SUNDEW *D. anglica* Hudson Plate 88. *CTW, p. 590*
Stouter and taller than Common Sundew (415), with narrow leaves gradually tapering into the long, usually erect stalk. Hybridises with the last species. *Habitat:* Widespread and frequent in wetter bogs and on gravelly loch-shores in Scotland; very local elsewhere; not in the SE or Midlands. July–August.

416a. *Long-leaved Sundew, *D. intermedia* Heyne ('*D. longifolia*'), is slenderer and less than half the size, and has shorter, relatively broader leaves, little shorter than the short, stouter flower-stalks, which arise from below the rosette and curve upwards. *Habitat:* Similar to Common Sundew; generally scarce, but much commoner in the S than Great Sundew. June–August.

PITCHER-PLANT FAMILY Sarraceniaceae

417. ***PITCHER PLANT *Sarracenia purpurea* L. Plate 25. *CTW, p. 591*
A singular plant, totally unlike any other to be seen wild in the British Isles; a perennial, with fat upright clusters of 4–6-in. root-leaves, luridly marked with green and purple; they are tube-shaped with a flap at the top and usually full of water, in which insects drown. Flowers an inch or more across, solitary, purple, nodding, on leafless 9–12-in. stalks, with a remarkable central umbrella-like style. *Habitat:* Naturalised in bogs in N Central Ireland. June–July.

LOOSESTRIFE FAMILY Lythraceae

418. PURPLE LOOSESTRIFE *Lythrum salicaria* L. Plate 20. *CTW, p. 592*
A striking waterside flower, with long spikes of narrow-petalled, bright red-purple, 6-petalled flowers, arranged in whorls; a slightly downy perennial, with stout 4-sided stems 2–4 ft. high and opposite unstalked untoothed lanceolate leaves, the upper much shorter. Has been confused with Rose-Bay (435) which grows in drier places, such as bombed sites. *Habitat:* Widespread and common by all kinds of fresh water and in fens and marshes. June–August.

419. ***GRASS POLY *L. hyssopifolia* L. Plate 26. *CTW, p. 592*
A low hairless annual, sometimes branched at the base, with small pinkish flowers at the base of the small narrow alternate leaves all up the stems; calyx

long. *Habitat:* Very rare in moist hollows, and on fields manured with shoddy, persisting only in Jersey. July–September.

420. WATER PURSLANE *Peplis portula* L.   Plate 104. *CTW, p. 593*
    A prostrate hairless annual, branching and rooting as it creeps, with stems often reddish, the tinge spreading to the leaves, especially in drier places. Flowers minute, unstalked, green, with 6-pointed calyx-teeth and 6 or often no petals, solitary at the base of the normally opposite, short narrowish bluntly rounded leaves, which taper to the base. *Habitat:* Widespread and locally frequent by ponds and on bare damp paths in woods, not on chalk or limestone. July–August.

DAPHNE FAMILY Thymelaeaceae

421. ***MEZEREON *Daphne mezereum* L.   Plate 17. *CTW, p. 594* ⅌
    A deciduous undershrub, 1–3 ft. high, frequent in cottage gardens, with short spikes of small, fragrant, pinkish-purple flowers appearing before the rather thin, pale green, lanceolate leaves. Fruit a red berry. *Habitat:* Now extremely local and sparse in woods on chalk and limestone in England. February–April.

422. *SPURGE-LAUREL *D. laureola* L.   Plate 73. *CTW, p. 594* ⅌
    An evergreen undershrub, 1–2 ft. high, neither a Spurge nor a Laurel, with dark green, glossy, leathery, broad lanceolate, laurel-like leaves, and numerous bunches of small fragrant green flowers. Fruit a black berry. *Habitat:* Widespread and frequent in woods, especially on chalk and limestone; rare in Wales and the N; not in Ireland. March–April.

OLEASTER FAMILY Elaeagnaceae

423. *SEA-BUCKTHORN *Hippophaë rhamnoides* L.   Plate 73. *CTW, p. 596*
    A thorny deciduous shrub, 5–10 ft. high, often forming thickets, with pale brown stems; narrow lanceolate, silvery mealy leaves, brown below; and minute green flowers. Fruit a conspicuous orange berry, on female plants only, sometimes lasting through the winter. *Habitat:* Local by the sea, especially on sand-dunes and cliffs, chiefly on the E coast of England; frequently planted. April–May, before the leaves.

WILLOW-HERB FAMILY Onagraceae

424. ***HAMPSHIRE PURSLANE *Ludwigia palustris* (L.) Elliott
                                            Plate 104. *CTW, p. 597*
    A prostrate hairless perennial, with stout reddish stems, rather like a large Water Purslane (420), with which it grows, but with much more pointed, glossy, and longer red-veined leaves, and flowers three times as large, with 4 or no petals and 4 sepals free to the base. *Habitat:* Very rare in wet ground, now only in the New Forest. June–July.

WILLOW-HERBS *Epilobium*

THE WILLOW-HERBS are a difficult genus and hybridise readily, so that plants will often be found combining the characters of two of the following species. All are more or less hairy perennials, often with reddish stems, spreading by short off-shoots from the base of the main stem, except the New Zealand Willow-herbs (434), which spread by runners. All, with the same exception, are branched, with mostly toothed lanceolate leaves, the lower opposite, the upper usually alternate; and loose terminal clusters of pinkish flowers with 4 more or less deeply notched petals, 8 stamens and the stigma either club-shaped, or divided into 4 lobes, or in some hybrids intermediate. All have long narrow 4-sided seed-pods that split when ripe to show the plumes of long silky hairs attached to the tiny seeds. The quality and not the quantity of the hairs on the stems, flowers and pods, i.e. whether they are spreading, curled or appressed, is important. The flower is above the ovary.

KEY TO WILLOW-HERBS (Nos. 425–435)

PLANT *tall* 425, 429, 435; *small* 432, 433; *prostrate and rooting* 434.

STEMS *with 4 raised lines* 427a, 428, 429, 430; *with 2 raised lines* 429, 430, 432, 433; *with no raised lines* 425, 426, 427, 431, 434, 435.

LEAVES *unstalked* 425, 426, 430, 431, 434; *half-clasping stem* 425; *running down on to stem* 430; *broad lanceolate* 427, 428, 429, 430, 433; *round* 434; *untoothed* 431, 432, 434, 435; *shiny* 433.

FLOWERS *nodding in bud* 427, 428, 431, 432, 433; *with petals deeply notched* 426, 427, 428, 429; *not notched* 435; *unequal* 435; *with 4-lobed stigma* 425–7, 435.

425. GREAT WILLOW-HERB *Epilobium hirsutum* L. Plate 20. *CTW, p. 599*

Our tallest and largest-flowered Willow-herb, 3–6 ft. high, usually very hairy with soft spreading hairs; leaves long, largely opposite, unstalked, the upper half-clasping the stem. Flowers ¾-in. across, erect in bud, with broad, deep purplish-pink petals; stigma with 4 curved lobes longer than the stamens. *Habitat:* Widespread and often abundant in damp places, especially by streams and ditches, except in NW Scotland. July–September. Codlins and Cream.

426. HOARY WILLOW-HERB *E. parviflorum* Schreber Pl. 20. *CTW, p. 600*

Smaller than the last species, with the lower part of the stem usually covered with woolly hairs, the upper leaves alternate and not clasping the stem, and the flowers smaller and often paler, with deeply notched petals and flat stigma-lobes no longer than the stamens. *Habitat:* Widespread but less common in similar places. July–September.

427. BROAD-LEAVED WILLOW-HERB *E. montanum* L. Pl. 20. *CTW, p. 601*

A common Willow-herb 1–2 ft. high, with broad lanceolate leaves and a 4-lobed stigma; stems round; leaves short-stalked, opposite except among the flowers, rounded at the base. Flowers drooping in bud, with deeply notched, purplish-pink petals. Hairs both short and spreading, and curly and appressed, sparse except on the seed-pods. *Habitat:* Widespread and common in woods and waste places, on hedge-banks and as a garden weed. June onwards.

427a. *Spear-leaved Willow-herb, E. lanceolatum* Sebastiani & Mauri, is much daintier and greyer-green, and has stems slightly 4-angled with short curly hairs; leaves smaller, wavy-edged, narrow lanceolate, with a tapering untoothed base, long-stalked mostly alternate; and flower-spike nodding in bud, the flowers white turning shell-pink later. Local on banks and in waste places, commonest in the SW, spreading E and N. July onwards.

D

428. *PALE WILLOW-HERB   *E. roseum* Schreber   Plate 20.   *CTW, p. 602*

One of our smaller-flowered Willow-herbs, with deeply notched petals, white at first, becoming a characteristic pale rose; and even longer stalks than Spear-leaved Willow-herb (427a) to its mostly alternate, broad elliptical, well toothed greyish leaves; upper part of stem with both spreading and appressed hairs and usually two marked and two faint raised lines. Buds drooping; stigma club-shaped. *Habitat:* Widespread but local in damp and waste places and on river banks; very local in Ireland. July–September.

429. *AMERICAN WILLOW-HERB   *E. adenocaulon* Haussknecht

Plate 20.   *CTW, p. 602*

A recent immigrant, 4 in. to 6 ft. high, with both spreading sticky and appressed hairs; red stems with two faint raised lines at the base, four near the top. Leaves short-stalked, lanceolate with a rounded base, much toothed, often reddish. Flowers small and numerous, erect in bud, with deeply notched purplish-pink petals, both calyx and ovary sticky-hairy, and a club-shaped stigma much shorter than the style. Seed-pods often red, with short hairs, especially at the top; ripe seeds with a very small round pale chestnut or pellucid appendage below the plume of hairs. *Habitat:* Frequent in woods and waste places and by streams in the Midlands and S, spreading N and W. June–August.

430. SHORT-FRUITED WILLOW-HERB   *E. obscurum* Schreber

Plate 20.   *CTW, p. 605*

A frequent Willow-herb, 1–2 ft. high, with hairs almost all appressed, and unstalked lanceolate leaves tapering from a broad rounded base and continuing with usually four raised lines on the stem, which is often widely branching near the base, with elongated creeping offshoots in summer. Flowers erect in bud, with shallowly notched purplish-pink petals, and a club-shaped stigma nearly equalling the style. Seed-pods nearly straight, shorter than in other Willow-herbs. *Habitat:* Widespread and locally common in woods and damp places. July–August.

430a. *Square-stemmed Willow-herb, *E. adnatum* Grisebach ('*E. tetragonum*') (*CTW, p. 603*), has the basal offshoots short, produced in autumn; long, narrower, more parallel-sided leaves; paler flowers, and longer curved seed-pods. Not uncommon in damp clearings and by streams in the S; rare elsewhere.

430b. **Southern Willow-herb, *E. lamyi* Schultz, also produces offshoots in autumn, is greyer and has shorter matt leaves, intermediate between the last two species in breadth, the upper shortly stalked and never continuing down the stem. Flowers larger, of a paler pink; seed-pods long. Rather local in the S.

431. MARSH WILLOW-HERB   *E. palustre* L.   Plate 20.   *CTW, p. 605*

A slender Willow-herb with a round stem 6–15 in. high, and both spreading and appressed hairs; leaves unstalked, narrow lanceolate, tapering at both ends, not or scarcely toothed. Flowers erect in bud, drooping when open, with notched pale violet-pink petals; stigma club-shaped. Seeds with an oblong pellucid appendage below the plume. *Habitat:* Widespread and locally common in wet places on acid soils. June–August.

432. **ALPINE WILLOW-HERB   *E. anagallidifolium* Lamarck

'*E. alpinum*'   Plate 23.   *CTW, p. 606*

A low, very slender, rarely branched, almost hairless, reddish Willow-herb, 2–4 in. high, with small short-stalked, narrowly elliptical, little toothed, often yellowish-green leaves. Flowers drooping in bud, with pinkish-red petals and crimson sepals, on short stalks which expand rapidly for the erect dark red ripe seed-pods. *Habitat:* Locally frequent in wet spots on mountains from the Craven Pennines northwards; not in Ireland. June–August.

433. **CHICKWEED WILLOW-HERB   *E. alsinifolium* Villars
Plate 23.   *CTW, p. 606*

Thicker, lusher and taller than the last species, sometimes branched and with much larger, shortly stalked, broader, more pointed and more toothed leaves. *Habitat:* Locally frequent by mountain rills from Snowdonia and the Craven Pennines northwards; very rare in Co. Leitrim. July–August.

434. **NEW ZEALAND WILLOW-HERB   *E. pedunculare* Cunningham
Plate 105.   *CTW, p. 607*

Quite unlike the other Willow-herbs, with its closely prostrate, mat-forming stems, rooting as they creep; small, toothed, almost circular, stalked hairless coppery-green leaves, all opposite; solitary long-stalked nodding pinkish-white flowers with deeply notched petals along the stem; and erect seed-pods. *Habitat:* Increasing on moist and not-so-moist walls and banks and stony or gravelly ground in the N and W and in Ireland. June–July.

435. ROSE-BAY   *Chamaenerion angustifolium* (L.) Scopoli
Fireweed; *Epilobium angustifolium* L.   Plate 20.   *CTW, p. 608*

A vigorous, showy perennial, untidy when seeding, almost hairless, 2–5 ft. high, with narrow lanceolate alternate leaves, and loose tapering spikes of large bright pinkish-purple flowers, with unequal petals and prominent long narrow reddish sepals. Seed-pods like those of Willow-herbs. *Habitat:* Now widespread and abundant on waste ground, railway banks, heaths and clearing in woods, also on mountains; local in Ireland. June–September.

436. *LARGE EVENING PRIMROSE   *Oenothera erythrosepala* Borbás
'*Oe. lamarkiana*'   Plate 62.   *CTW, p. 610*

Evening Primroses are very variable and produce numerous hybrids and sports frequent in gardens. This is a robust, leafy, somewhat downy annual or biennial, with rigid stems 2–4 ft. high; hairs with red bulbous bases on the stems and fruits; leaves broad lanceolate, crinkly, slightly toothed, in a rosette and almost unstalked spirally up the stems; and erect spikes of 3-in., faintly scented yellow flowers, the petals about equalling the calyx-tube, the 4 narrow and often reddish sepals turned down; stigma 4-lobed, longer than the 8 anthers. Fruits unstalked, stout, erect, cylindrical, often broad-based; seeds reddish-brown, angled. *Habitat:* Widespread but local in waste places and on dunes. June onwards.

436*a*. **Lesser Evening Primrose, *Oe. biennis* L., has no red-based hairs and smaller flowers, 2 in. across, the petals rather shorter than the calyx-tube, green sepals and stigmas equalling anthers. Not common.

436*b*. *Least Evening Primrose, *Oe. parviflora* L. (incl. *Oe. muricata* L.), resembles the last species, but has red-based hairs, and still smaller flowers, about 1½ in. across, the petals less than half the size of the calyx-tube and no longer than the anthers or the slightly longer stigmas; seeds pale brown. Frequent.

437. **FRAGRANT EVENING PRIMROSE   *Oe. stricta* Link
'*Oe. odorata*'   Plate 62.   *CTW, p. 611*

Shorter and slenderer than Large Evening Primrose (437), and less or not branched, with willowy stems, much narrower, toothed leaves, no red-based hairs, and fragrant flowers which turn orange when they go over; seeds not angled. Occasional colonies have leaves purplish-grey and very hairy. *Habitat:* Very locally plentiful in sandy places, especially in SW England. June onwards.

438. **FUCHSIA** *Fuchsia magellanica* Lamarck   Plate 17.   *CTW, p. 612*
(incl. *F. gracilis* Lindley)
A deciduous shrub, of a type well known in gardens, 3–6 ft. high, with opposite toothed pointed oval leaves and highly distinctive solitary hanging flowers with turkey-red sepals, plum-purple red-based petals and prominent stigma and stamens. *Habitat:* Much used for hedging in the W of Ireland and well naturalised there, less so in SW England; on moors in Orkney. June onwards.

439. **COMMON ENCHANTER'S NIGHTSHADE**   *Circaea lutetiana* L.
Plate 78.   *CTW, p. 613*
A slightly downy perennial, 6–12 in. high, nothing like the true Nightshades (671–674), with pointed oval or heart-shaped, gently toothed, stalked opposite leaves. Flowers in leafless spikes, tiny, white, with 2 petals slightly notched and sometimes tinged pink; stigma 2-lobed; no tiny bracts at their base. Fruits club-shaped, clinging to clothes with their thick covering of tiny white hooked bristles; seeds 2. *Habitat:* Widespread and often abundant in shady places, especially woods, which it may carpet; can be a troublesome garden weed. June–August.

440. *UPLAND ENCHANTER'S NIGHTSHADE*   *C. intermedia* Ehrhart
Plate 78.   *CTW, p. 613*
Intermediate between the two other Enchanter's Nightshades, and differing from the last in having crinkly, shiny, well-toothed, more heart-shaped leaves; petals deeply notched; stigma notched; and tiny bracts at base of the flowers. *Habitat:* Frequent in woods and shady places in hill districts in the N and W; very local in Ireland. July–August.

440a. ***Alpine Enchanter's Nightshade**, *C. alpina* L., is much smaller and slenderer, with stubbier, thinner leaves on winged stalks, smaller flowers; and fruits with softer, less hooked hairs and 1 seed. Rare, often confused with and hard to tell from the last species.

WATER-MILFOIL FAMILY   Haloragaceae

441. *WHORLED WATER-MILFOIL*   *Myriophyllum verticillatum* L.
Plate 68.   *CTW, p. 615*
A long, bushy or trailing submerged waterweed, with feathery pinnate leaves, usually in whorls of 5, reaching to the top of the stem and each much longer than the length of stem between each whorl. In shallow places the upper leaves may be a little longer than the inconspicuous unstalked greenish flowers at their base, which usually project from the water in leafy spikes, the upper with stamens, the lowest with styles. *Habitat:* Widespread but local in slow-moving or still fresh water; not in Scotland. July–August.

442. **SPIKED WATER-MILFOIL**   *M. spicatum* L.   Plate 68.   *CTW, p. 616*
A long, trailing or bushy, submerged waterweed, with feathery pinnate leaves, in whorls of 4 or 5, equalling or exceeding the length of stem between each whorl, the topmost undivided. Flowers small, in whorls on an almost leafless erect spike, and projecting above the surface of the water, the lowest with styles,

the topmost with yellow anthers and ruby red petals, and a whorl or two in between with both. Fruits globular. *Habitat:* Widespread and common in slow-moving and still fresh or brackish water. June–September.

442a. *Alternate Water-Milfoil, *M. alterniflorum* DC., is slenderer and has shorter leaves with fewer segments, the upper ones pinnate; shorter, slenderer, yellower, few-flowered spikes drooping in bud, the upper flowers often alternate; fruits smaller, longer than broad. Mainly in the N and W, preferring acid water.

MARESTAIL FAMILY Hippuridaceae

443. *MARESTAIL *Hippuris vulgaris* L. Plate 137. *CTW, p. 617*
An erect unbranched perennial waterweed, with conspicuous tapering spikes above the surface, but largely submerged in fairly fast water. Often taken for a Horsetail (1268–1273), but has tiny pink petalless flowers at the base of the soft blunt strap-like, dark green (not hard and thread-like) leaves in whorls of 6–12; and no terminal 'cones'. Fruit a greenish nut. *Habitat:* Widespread but rather local in streams and lakes. June–July.

WATER-STARWORT FAMILY Callitrichaceae

444. COMMON WATER STARWORT *Callitriche palustris* L.[1]
Plate 66. *CTW, p. 619*
A very variable, slender, pale green waterweed, swaying in tufts in the water or sprawling on mud with weak stems, leaves more or less oval in the dense floating rosettes; usually narrower on the submerged stems. Flowers minute, green, petalless, the male showing as yellow stamens in the floating rosettes or at the base of the leaves. Fruits tiny, with 4 close segments, often not formed, especially in deeper water. *Habitat:* Widespread and common in still and slow-moving fresh water, also on mud and in damp woodland rides. April–September.

445. *NARROW WATER STARWORT *C. hermaphroditica* L.
(*C. autumnalis* L.; incl. *C. truncata* Gussone) Plate 66. *CTW, p. 622*
Differs from Water Starwort (444) in having all leaves submerged and narrow, and the larger fruit-segments readily separating; stems often yellowish or reddish. One of the forms included under Water Starwort may have all its leaves linear, but can be told by its very small fruit. *Habitat:* Much more local, and chiefly in the N. May–September.

MISTLETOE FAMILY Loranthaceae

446. *MISTLETOE *Viscum album* L. Plate 73. *CTW, p. 624*
A familiar plant with its sticky white berries at Christmas when, according to the Rev. C. A. Johns, it is 'the symbol of a strange spirit of superstitious frivolity too well known to need description'. A rather woody, yellow-green evergreen semi-parasite, 1–2 ft. high, with pairs (rarely threes) of narrow leathery leaves usually growing so high on trees (where its bunches may be mistaken for birds' nests or witches' brooms) that its inconspicuous greenish flowers (male and female on different plants) are rarely seen. There are three races, of which the

[1] Includes the following: *C. stagnalis* Scopoli, *C. polymorpha* Lönnroth, *C. verna* L., *C. obtusangula* Hegelmaier, and *C. intermedia* Hoffmann.

commonest grows on many broad-leaved trees, mostly Apple and Poplar, very rarely nowadays on Oak; the others, very rare in Britain, grow respectively on Pines and Larches, and on Firs. *Habitat:* Widespread and locally common, especially in parks and orchards, in England and Wales, chiefly in the S and W. March–May.

SANDALWOOD FAMILY Santalaceae

447. **BASTARD TOADFLAX *Thesium humifusum* DC. Pl. 50. *CTW, p. 625*
A slender prostrate, often mat-forming, hairless yellow or olive-green semi-parasitic perennial, with many wiry branches, not at all resembling the true Toadflaxes; leaves linear, always alternate. Flowers in loose spikes, tiny, star-like, white within, with long narrow leaf-like bracts at their base. *Habitat:* Local in chalk and limestone turf in the S, and on dunes in the Channel Is. June–August.

CORNEL FAMILY Cornaceae

448. DOGWOOD *Thelycrania sanguinea* (L.) Fourreau Pl. 74. *CTW, p. 626*
A deciduous shrub, 4–8 ft. high, easily picked out in winter by its dark crimson twigs; leaves stalked, opposite, pointed oval, not toothed, downy at first, turning red in autumn, with the main veins parallel to the outer edges. Flowers in erect clusters, with 4 narrow creamy white petals, faintly foetid; stamens alternate with petals; style club-shaped. Fruit a black berry. *Habitat:* Widespread and common in woods, thickets and hedges, especially on chalk and limestone; more local in the N and in Ireland. June–July. *Cornus sanguinea* L.

449. **DWARF CORNEL *Chamaepericlymenum suecicum* (L.) Ascherson &
Cornus suecica L. Graebner. Plate 84. *CTW, p. 627*
A modest slender rarely branched low perennial, 4–8 in. high but often hidden under the Heather or Bilberry, with creeping roots and small, pointed oval, unstalked, pale green leaves. A shy flowerer, but when it does so has striking purplish-black flower-heads, surrounded by 4 creamy petal-like bracts, turning to a small cluster of red berries. *Habitat:* Locally frequent on hills in the N, rare except in the Highlands. June.

IVY FAMILY Araliaceae

450. IVY *Hedera helix* L. Plate 76. *CTW, p. 628*
A familiar evergreen woody climber, trailing on the ground or climbing by tiny roots; leaves very variable, dark green or especially in winter, purplish, shiny, leathery; those on non-flowering shoots of the well-known 5-lobed ivy-shape; those on bushy, flowering branches, often larger, pointed but not lobed. Flowers small, green, with yellow anthers, in erect clusters. Fruit a black berry. *Habitat:* Widespread and abundant in woods, often carpeting the ground, in hedgerows and on walls and rocks. September onwards.

MARSH PENNYWORT FAMILY Hydrocotylaceae

451. MARSH PENNYWORT *Hydrocotyle vulgaris* L. Pl. 105. *CTW, p. 629*
A prostrate, creeping and rooting perennial, with inconspicuous heads or whorls of minute pinkish-white flowers, hard to see at the base of the round

disc-like; very shallowly lobed leaves, which usually are held aloft umbrella-like, with the stalk in the middle. *Habitat:* Widespread and locally common in damp and wet places, preferring acid soils. June–August.

UMBELLIFER FAMILY   Umbelliferae

MOST UMBELLIFERS are easily known by their flowers being arranged in an umbrella-shaped umbel. In a few, such as Sea Holly (454), the spokes of the umbrella are so short as to conceal the basic design, but in a typical species, such as Cow Parsley (458), the spokes ('rays') of the umbel terminate in secondary umbels, which consist of a number of small 5-petalled flowers arranged in a similar umbrella-shape, usually with a flattish top. The tops of the secondary umbels make up the top of the whole umbrella. Unless otherwise stated there are small green bracts at the base of both the main umbels (lower bracts) and the secondary umbels (upper bracts).

Many white-flowered umbellifers can also be found tinged pink. Many species vary in the hollowness of their stems, from top to bottom and between young and old plants. Many have finely divided, twice or thrice pinnate leaves that can be mistaken for ferns. The shape of the fruits is always a great help in identifying these apparently tediously similar plants; these are below the petals and consist of 2 more or less closely joined 1-seeded portions, which separate suspended when ripe (Fig.).

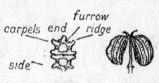

KEY TO UMBELLIFERS   (Nos. 452–510)

I. Pink Flowers
PLANT *small* 462, 463, 465; *markedly hairy* 461, 462, 463, 508; *more or less hairless* 452, 465, 487, 500, 503; *aromatic* 500; *foetid* 465.
STEMS *solid* 461, 462, 463, 465; *hollow* 487, 500, 503, 508.
LEAVES *palmate* 452; *shiny* 452, 465, 487; *bushily whorled* 500.
BRACTS *no lower* 462, 463, 465, 487, 503, 508; *no upper* 487.
UMBELS *opposite leaves* 463; *unstalked* 463; *with no secondary umbels* 463.
FRUITS *aromatic* 465; *bristly* 462, 463; *bur-like* 452, 461; *globular* 465.

II. Yellowish Flowers
PLANT *very tall* 498, 507; *markedly hairy* 507; *fleshy* 466, 491, 498; *aromatic* 477, 498, 500.
STEMS *solid* 466, 477, 491, 498, 499, 504, 507; *hollow* 472, 498, 500, 507.
LEAVES *undivided* 472; *with long narrow leaflets* 491; *1-pinnate* 507; *whorled* 500; *with hairless segments* 498, 500, 504; *shiny* 466, 477.
BRACTS *no lower* 466, 498, 499, 503, 507; *no upper* 466, 498, 507.
FRUITS *egg-shaped* 472, 498, 499; *globular* 466, 477; *corky* 491.

III. White Flowers
PLANT *prostrate* 463, 475, 476; *under 6 in.* 459, 462, 473, 497; *over 5 ft.* 468, 489, 503, 508a; *markedly hairy* 456, 461, 462, 463, 486, 508, 509, 510; *greyish* 478, 481, 493; *aromatic* 460, 474, 478, 494–5, 500–2; *foetid* 465, 468, 479.
STEMS *spotted or suffused purple* 456, 468, 502, 503; *markedly swollen at leaf-junctions* 456.
LEAVES *palmate* 452; *shiny* 487; *with long narrow leaflets* 480, 481; *bushily whorled* 482, 500.

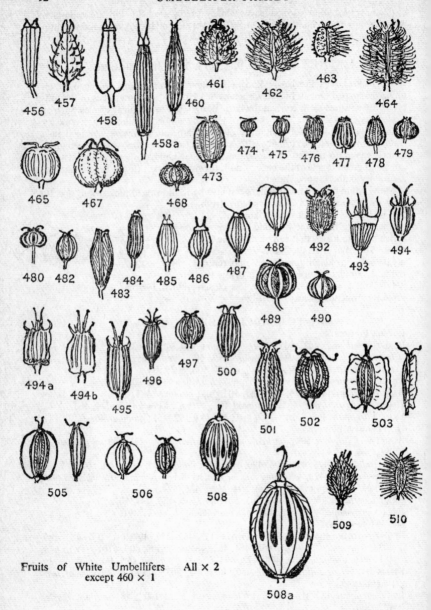

Fruits of White Umbellifers   All × 2
except 460 × 1

BRACTS *lower pinnate* 510; *lower large and toothed* 489, 490; *upper none* 474, 483, 485, 486, 487, 498; *upper broad* 459; *upper toothed* 489, 490; *upper only on outer side of umbel* 468, 497.

UMBELS *opposite leaf-stalks* 457, 459, 463, 474, 475, 476, 490, 496; *with no secondary umbels* 459, 463; *unstalked or almost so* 463, 475.

FLOWERS *red or purple in centre of umbel* 510; *with unequal petals* 508.

FRUITS *aromatic* 465, 478, 483; *bristly* 457, 462, 463; *bur-like* 452, 461, 464, 510; *downy* 492; *very long* 459, 460; *shiny* 460; *globular* 465, 467, 468, 474, 479, 480, 490.

452. SANICLE   *Sanicula europaea* L.   Plate 97.   *CTW, p. 638*

A hairless perennial, about a foot high, with long-stalked shiny, deeply palmately 3–5-lobed, toothed leaves, and small, bobbly secondary umbels of white or pinkish flowers. Fruits roundish, with hooked spines.   *Habitat:* Widespread and common in woods, especially beechwoods on chalk, where it may carpet the ground. May–July.

453. ***PINK MASTERWORT   *Astrantia major* L.   Plate 25.   *CTW, p. 638*

A hairless perennial, 1–2 ft. high, with large long-stalked, deeply palmately lobed, toothed leaves, and close head-like umbels of small pinkish or whitish flowers cupped in longer purple-tinged white sepal-like bracts, giving the effect of a Scabious rather than of an umbellifer. Flowers with a sickly smell.   *Habitat:* Long known in Stokesay Wood near Ludlow; a rare outcast in shady places elsewhere, chiefly in the N. June–August.

454. *SEA HOLLY   *Eryngium maritimum* L.   Plate 9.   *CTW, p. 639*

An unmistakable plant, its spiny bluish-green leaves with white edges and veins, and its globular, spiny flower heads of a lovely and striking powder-blue and mauve, with broad spiny bracts. A stiff hairless perennial, 6–12 in. high, creeping widely,   *Habitat:* Widespread but now rather local by the sea, especially on sand. July–August.

455. ***WATLING STREET THISTLE   *E. campestre* L.   Pl. 106.   *CTW, p. 639*

Taller, paler, not bluish-green and less thick-set than Sea Holly (454), and with thinner stems, longer branches, much smaller white flower-heads, and longer narrow bracts.   *Habitat:* Very rare in dry grassland in S England. July–August.

456. ROUGH CHERVIL   *Chaerophyllum temulentum* L.   Plate 99.   *CTW, p. 640*

A common white umbellifer of the hedge-banks in summer, flowering between Cow Parsley (458) and Hedge Parsley (461), and differing from both in its solid, more or less purple-spotted stems, markedly swollen beneath the leaf-stalks. The much taller, hairless Hemlock (468) is the only other common white umbellifer with noticeably spotted stems. A coarsely hairy biennial, 2–3 ft. high, with 2–3-pinnate, blunt-lobed leaves, later turning purple. Normally no lower bracts, the upper lanceolate. Fruits long, narrow, ridged, broader above (Fig.).   *Habitat:* Widespread and common in light shade, but thinning out in Scotland. June–July.

457. *BUR CHERVIL   *Anthriscus caucalis* Bieberstein   Plate 99.   *CTW, p. 641*
   A. neglecta Boissier & Reuter; *Chaerophyllum anthriscus* (L.) Crantz

A distinctive delicate annual, less stout and tall than Cow Parsley (458), with hairless, hollow stems. Flowers white in small umbels on stalks opposite the very finely cut leaves, hairy beneath; usually no lower bracts, the upper tiny, pointed oval. Fruits beaked, egg-shaped, covered with very short hooked bristles (Fig.). *Habitat:* Widespread but local on sandy banks, at the foot of walls and in waste places, especially near the sea; rarer in the N. May–June.

458. COW PARSLEY *A. sylvestris* (L.) Bernhardi Plate 99. *CTW, p. 642*
Wild Chervil; *Chaerophyllum sylvestre* L.
Generally the commonest white umbellifer of the later spring hedgerows, often whitening roadsides; a perennial, 2–4 ft. high, with large fresh green 2–3-pinnate leaves, which may appear before Christmas. No lower bracts, the upper pointed oval. Fruits long, smooth, broad towards tne base (Fig.). Differs from the later-flowering Rough Chervil (456) in its much less hairy grass-green leaves, its unspotted, usually hollow stems, only slightly swollen at the joints, and from the still later Hedge Parsley (461) in its broader more dissected leaves and its hollow stem being much less or not downy above. *Habitat:* Widespread and often abundant in shady places. April–June.
458a. ***Golden Chervil**, *Chaerophyllum aureum* L. (*CTW, p. 641*), is slightly larger, with a solid, sometimes purple-spotted stem, leaves smelling like liquorice, twice as many rays in the umbel, narrower upper bracts, and longer, ribbed and yellow-brown fruits twice as long, with long styles (Fig.). Rare, chiefly by the R. Teith in C Scotland. July.

459. SHEPHERD'S NEEDLE *Scandix pecten-veneris* L. Pl. 96. *CTW, p. 643*
The needle-like fruits make this one of the easiest white umbellifers to identify in fruit; a fresh green, almost hairless annual, 4–8 in. high, with delicate, rather bushy, 2–3-pinnate leaves opposite the small umbels, which sometimes have 2 secondary umbels; no lower bracts, upper ones broad, deeply toothed. Fruits with a 1–2-in. beak. *Habitat:* A widespread arable weed, quite frequent in England; less so elsewhere. April onwards

460. *SWEET CICELY *Myrrhis odorata* (L.) Scopoli Plate 99. *CTW, p. 644*
A pleasantly aromatic white umbellifer, frequent in the N; rather like a large stout Cow Parsley (458), often with small white flecks on the large leaves which smell of aniseed when crushed; upper bracts narrower. Fruits upright, ribbed, nearly an inch long, dark shiny brown (Fig.). *Habitat:* Grassy places, often near houses, in hilly districts in N England, S and C Scotland and NE Ireland, thinning out northwards and southwards; very rare in S England. May–June.

461. HEDGE PARSLEY *Torilis japonica* (Houttuyn) DC. Pl. 99. *CTW, p. 644*
The latest to flower of the common medium-sized white hedgerow umbellifers; a stiffer wirier greyer-green annual than the other two, with thinner solid unspotted, roughly hairy stems, not swollen at the joints, and narrowly triangular-oblong, less divided, more roughly hairy leaves. Flowers in long-stalked umbels, often pink, with both upper and lower bracts. Fruits egg-shaped, with purple hooked bristles (Fig.). *Habitat:* Widespread and often common in hedge-banks and at the edge of woods. July–September. *Caucalis anthriscus* (L.) Hudson.

462. **SPREADING BUR PARSLEY *T. arvensis* (Hudson) Link
Caucalis arvensis Hudson Plate 96. *CTW, p. 645*
A squat bushy wiry roughish, dull green annual, usually 3–8 in. high, with sharply pointed, 1–2-pinnate leaves. Flowers fewer than in 461, usually white;

lower bracts one, or more often none, the upper long and narrow. Fruits egg-shaped, larger than in 461, with spines not hooked (Fig.). *Habitat:* A local and uncommon weed, especially in arable fields on chalk and limestone; not in Scotland or Ireland. July onwards.

463. *KNOTTED BUR PARSLEY *T. nodosa* (L.) Gaertner Pl. 96. *CTW, 645*
A lanky, roughly hairy annual, 4–12 in. long or prostrate, with 1–2-pinnate leaves opposite the small, usually very short-stalked, compact few-flowered white or pinkish umbels; no lower bracts, the upper ones longer than the flowers. Fruits warty on the inside, with straight bristles on the outside. (Fig.). *Habitat:* Widespread and not infrequent on dry sunny banks especially near the sea, mainly in the S. May–July. *Caucalis nodosa* (L.) Scopoli.

464. ***HEDGEHOG PARSLEY *Caucalis royeni* (L.) Crantz
' *C. lappula*', ' *C. daucoides*'   Plate 96. *CTW, p. 646*
A pale green annual, 4–9 in. high, with solid stems roughly hairy at the base, and 2–3-pinnate leaves. Flowers white, in 3–5-rayed umbels, with usually no lower bracts and conspicuous upper ones. Fruits largish, oblong, with long stout hooked spines (Fig.). *Habitat:* A decreasing weed of chalky soils. June–July.

465. ***CORIANDER *Coriandrum sativum* L. Plate 96. *CTW, p. 647*
A hairless annual, 4–9 in. high, with a nauseous smell; solid stems; and lower leaves 1–2-pinnate with broad segments, the upper 2-pinnate with narrow segments. Flowers usually pinkish, the outer petals longer, with no lower bracts. Fruits globular, gently ridged, reddish-brown, pleasantly aromatic when ripe. (Fig.). *Habitat:* An uncommon casual. June–August.

466. *ALEXANDERS *Smyrnium olusatrum* L. Plate 51. *CTW, p. 647*
A stout bushy hairless biennial, with solid stems 2–4 ft. high; our only yellow umbellifer with large glossy, dark green 3-trifoliate leaves, the leaflets broad and toothed; usually no upper or lower bracts; and black globular, rather compressed, sharply ridged fruits. *Habitat:* Widespread and locally common in hedge-banks and waste places near the sea; uncommon inland, most often in chalky districts. April–June.

467. ***BLADDER-SEED *Physospermum cornubiense* (L.) DC.
Danaa cornubiensis (L.) Burnat   Plate 99. *CTW, p. 648*
An almost hairless perennial, rather like Cow Parsley (458), but with stems always solid; far broader and darker green leaflets; lower bracts present; and distinctive swollen ridged fruits, like a pair of small bladders (Fig.). *Habitat:* Rare in woods in Cornwall, S Devon and near Burnham Beeches (Bucks.). July–August.

468. HEMLOCK *Conium maculatum* L. Plate 97. *CTW, p. 648* ⊅
The only white umbellifer with both hollow purple-spotted stems and an unpleasant smell when bruised; a tall hairless biennial, 3–7 ft. high, with elegant, finely cut, 2–5-pinnate leaves: upper bracts only round the outer edge of the secondary umbels. Fruits globular with wavy ridges (Fig.). Many other umbellifers are loosely referred to as 'hemlock'. *Habitat:* Widespread and locally frequent by roads and streams and on waste ground. June–July.

469. *****THOROW-WAX**   *Bupleurum rotundifolium* L.   Plate 58.   *CTW*, *p. 649*
  A singular greyish annual, hairless and 4–12 in. high, scarcely recognisable as
an umbellifer by the uninitiated, with its 'branches which passe or goe thorow the
leaves as though they had been drawne or thrust thorow', as Gerard wrote.
Flowers tiny, straw-yellow, in 4–8-rayed umbels, the secondary umbels cupped
in conspicuous greenish-yellow petal-like upper bracts, which are erect in fruit;
no lower bracts. Fruits small, oblong, smooth, very slightly ridged.   *Habitat:*
A weed of cornfields in the S, mainly on chalk; now rare. July–August.

470. *****NARROW HARE'S-EAR**   *B. opacum* (Cesati) Lange   Pl. 105.   *CTW*, 650
  An inconspicuous grey-green hairless annual, looking even less like an umbellifer than Thorow-wax (469); 1–3 in. high and often extremely hard to detect
in the turf, many other plants being hopefully mistaken for it. Leaves linear,
soon withering. Flowers yellowish, in tiny heads, enshrouded by the sharp brown
leaf-like upper bracts; lower bracts narrower. Fruits egg-shaped.   *Habitat:*
Very rare in turf on Beachy and Berry Heads, and the Channel Is. June–July.

471. ****SLENDER HARE'S-EAR**   *B. tenuissimum* L.   Plate 58.   *CTW*, *p. 650*
  Another unumbelliferlike umbellifer, also hard to detect in the long grass; an
upright hairless perennial, with thin wiry stems 4–12 in. high, linear leaves up
the stems and tiny clusters of yellowish flowers shorter than but not concealed
by the linear upper bracts. Fruits globular, dotted.   *Habitat:* Local at the back
of saltmarshes, sea walls, and in other dry grassy places close to the sea in England
and Wales; very rare inland. August–September.

472. *****SICKLE HARE'S-EAR**   *B. falcatum* L.   Plate 51.   *CTW*, *p. 650*
  The only umbellifer-like Hare's-ear; a graceful hairless perennial, with hollow
stems 1–3 ft. high, curved lanceolate leaves, the upper narrower, and umbels of
rich yellow flowers. Fruits egg-shaped, ridged.   *Habitat:* Now confined to a
single grassy road-verge near Ongar, Essex. July–September.

473. *****HONEWORT**   *Trinia glauca* (L.) Dumortier   Plate 99.   *CTW*, *p. 651*
  A rather squat-looking, much branched hairless perennial, 2–6 in. high, the
base of its solid stem covered with fibrous remains of leaf-stalks; the 2–3-pinnate
leaves with narrow lobes. Flowers white, male and female on different plants.
Fruits ridged, egg-shaped (Fig.).   *Habitat:* Very local in dry limestone turf on
Berry Head, the Mendips and the Avon Gorge. May–June.

474. **WILD CELERY**   *Apium graveolens* L.   Plate 98.   *CTW*, *p. 652*
  Readily identifiable by its pungent smell of celery; a hairless yellow-green
biennial, 1–3 ft. high, with shiny pinnate leaves like Garden Celery, having large
toothed leaflets, the upper trifoliate and unstalked. Flowers white, in shortly
or not stalked umbels, often opposite the leaves; no upper or lower bracts. Fruits
tiny, globular (Fig.).   *Habitat:* Widespread but local in wet places near the sea;
unusual elsewhere. June–August.

475. **FOOL'S WATERCRESS**   *A. nodiflorum* (L.) Reichenbach
  (incl. *A. repens* (Jacquin) Reichenbach)   Plate 97.   *CTW*, *p. 652*
  A weak, sometimes prostrate, hairless perennial, 1–2 ft. long, whose leaves
bear a certain resemblance to Watercress (98), with which it may grow, but it
has its white flowers in umbels, and finely toothed and somewhat pointed leaflets.

Confused too with Lesser Water Parsnip (490) which has many lower bracts. Umbels short- or unstalked, opposite and overtopped by the leaves at whose base they arise; usually no lower bracts. Fruits ridged, egg-shaped (Fig.). *Habitat:* Widespread and common in wet places. June onwards.

476. *MARSHWORT *A. inundatum* (L.) Reichenbach Pl. 104. *CTW, p. 653*
A small, easily overlooked, prostrate hairless aquatic perennial, rather like a Water Crowfoot in foliage, rooting as it creeps, the pinnate leaves with narrow leaflets, hairlike when submerged; very small, 2–4-rayed, stalked umbels of white flowers; no lower bracts; and narrow fruits (Fig.). *Habitat:* Widespread but local in and by ponds and marshes. June–July.

477. **PARSLEY *Petroselinum crispum* (Miller) Turrill
Carum petroselinum (L.) Bentham Plate 51, *CTW, p. 654*
A familiar kitchen-garden herb, with a pleasant fresh clean smell; a hairless, bright green biennial, fading to yellow-green; with solid stems 9–18 in. high; shiny 3-pinnate leaves, the lower ones triangular, much crisped in cultivated forms; and umbels of greenish-yellow flowers. Fruits globular (Fig.). *Habitat:* Local on rocks, especially by the sea; impermanent elsewhere. June–August.

478. *CORN PARSLEY *P. segetum* (L.) Koch Plate 95. *CTW, p. 654*
A grey-green hairless biennial, 1–2 ft. high, with a solid wiry stem, smelling somewhat of parsley; leaves pinnate, with toothed leaflets, the basal ones withering early. Umbels with rather few white flowers on unequal rays, not unlike Stone Parsley (479); petals shallowly notched. Fruits egg-shaped (Fig.). *Habitat:* Occasional in hedge-banks and dry grassy places in the S, nearly always near the sea. August–September. Corn Caraway; *Carum segetum* (L.) Hooker.

479. STONE PARSLEY *Sison amomum* L. Plate 99. *CTW, p. 655*
A hairless bushy biennial, with a disagreeable pungent smell when crushed, very pale green, often turning vinaceous as it goes over, with solid wiry stems 18 in. to 3 ft. high, and pinnate leaves, the upper with very narrow leaflets, the lower larger and coarsely toothed, withering early. Umbels lax, with very long unequal rays and few white flowers with deeply notched petals, giving a Gypsophila-like appearance. Fruits more globular than the last species (Fig.). *Habitat:* Locally frequent in hedge-banks and on waysides, especially on clay soils in the S. July–August.

480. **COWBANE *Cicuta virosa* L. Plate 98. *CTW, p. 656* ⚘
A stout hairless aquatic perennial, 2–4 ft. high, sometimes half-floating, with hollow stems, 2–3-pinnate leaves with well toothed leaflets. Flowers white, in rather large umbels; no lower bracts. Leaf-segments narrower than Water Parsnip (489), which has simply pinnate leaves. Fruits globular ridged, with long styles and prominent calyx-teeth (Fig.). *Habitat:* Very local in and by fresh water in E Anglia, N Ireland and E Scotland; very rare elsewhere. July–August.

481. ***LONGLEAF *Falcaria vulgaris* Bernhardi Plate 95. *CTW, p. 657*
A hairless greyish perennial, 1–3 ft. tall, growing in patches from a creeping rootstock, rather laxly branched; leaves 3 or more lobed into long, strap-like, waxy finely toothed segments, and with a general air of garden Gypsophila (*G. paniculata* L.). Flowers white, in open umbels, the primary rays long, erect.

Fruits oblong, very rarely ripening. *Habitat:* Rare in grassy places in S and E England, preferring chalk and limestone. July–August,

482. **WHORLED CARAWAY *Carum verticillatum* (L.) Koch Pl. 98. *CTW, 657*
A rather slender hairless perennial, readily known from our other white umbellifers by the somewhat yarrow-like, long narrow leaves with whorls of thread-like leaflets. Apart from these the flowers of the plant look much like those of any other small umbellifer with both upper and lower bracts. Fruits egg-shaped, ridged (Fig.). *Habitat:* Local in wet grass in the W, chiefly in Scotland; very rare elsewhere. July–August.

483. **CARAWAY *C. carvi* L. Plate 96. *CTW, p. 658*
A hairless biennial, with hollow stems a foot or so high, 2-pinnate leaves, and umbels of white flowers, erect in fruit; usually no upper or lower bracts. The oblong ridged aromatic fruits (Fig.) are much appreciated in 'seed cakes'. *Habitat:* Locally established in meadows in Scotland, especially the extreme N; usually a casual elsewhere. June–July.

484. **GREAT EARTH-NUT *Bunium bulbocastanum* L. Pl. 96. *CTW, p. 658*
Somewhat larger and stouter than Pignut (485), and has solid stems, rather larger leaves, several unequal upper and lower bracts, and longer, more ribbed fruits with a down-turned style (Fig.). Leaves ending in a minute point, hairless on the margins. *Habitat:* Locally plentiful on and at the foot of the chalk ridge from near Cambridge to near Tring, in chalk turf or on ploughland that is reverting to grass. June–July. *Carum bulbocastanum* (L.) Koch.

485. PIGNUT *Conopodium majus* (Gouan) Loret Plate 96. *CTW, p. 659*
A slender, often little-branched, hairless perennial white umbellifer, with a hollow stem 9–18 in. high arising from a rounded brown edible tuber; and delicate 2–3-pinnate leaves, the root ones soon withering, ending in a distinct point, the margins hairy; often no lower bracts, sometimes no upper ones. Fruits oblong, with erect styles (Fig.). *Habitat:* Widespread and common in woods and meadows on light dry soils. May–July. Earth-nut; *C. denudatum* Koch.

486. BURNET-SAXIFRAGE *Pimpinella saxifraga* L. Plate 99. *CTW, p. 660*
Neither a Burnet nor a Saxifrage; a usually downy, branched perennial white umbellifer, 1–2 ft. high, with tough, almost solid, slightly ridged stems and root-stock usually topped with fibrous remains of dead leaf-stalks; leaves variable, those from the root 1-pinnate with broad, rather coarsely toothed, unstalked leaflets, not unlike Salad Burnet (368); the stem ones few, 2-pinnate finely cut, differing markedly; leaf-stalks sheath-like; no upper or lower bracts. Fruits shiny, globular (Fig.). *Habitat:* Widespread and often common in drier grassy places, preferring chalk and limestone. July onwards.

487. *GREATER BURNET-SAXIFRAGE *P. major* (L.) Hudson
Plate 99. *CTW, p. 660*
Much taller, stouter and more branched, and brighter darker green than the last species, with a leafier, conspicuously grooved, hairless, hollow stem; leaves varying less from root to stem, all 1-pinnate, the larger broader-based, stalked shiny leaflets with coarser teeth, the terminal ones 3-lobed. Flowers purer white, locally pinkish. Fruits larger, rougher, with longer styles (Fig.). *Habitat:*

Locally frequent in shady and grassy places in England, S Scotland and S and W Ireland. July–September.

488. GROUND ELDER *Aegopodium podagraria* L.   Plate 97.   *CTW, p. 661*
A hairless creeping perennial, often forming extensive patches, with hollow grooved stems 1–2 ft. high; 1–2 trifoliate leaves with irregularly toothed, broad lanceolate leaflets; and dense umbels of white flowers, usually with no upper or lower bracts. Fruits egg-shaped, ribbed (Fig.). *Habitat:* Widespread and common in shady places; a pernicious weed in gardens. June–August.

489. *GREAT WATER PARSNIP *Sium latifolium* L.   Plate 97.   *CTW, p. 662*
A tall hairless perennial, with ridged hollow stems 3–6 ft. high, 1-pinnate upper leaves, unlike Cowbane (480), with about 5 pairs of toothed leaflets, finely dissected submerged leaves, and large dense long-stalked terminal umbels of white flowers; bracts often large. Fruits egg-shaped, with prominent ridges and inconspicuous styles (Fig.). *Habitat:* Widespread but distinctly local in fen dykes and by fresh water. June–September.

490. LESSER WATER PARSNIP *Berula erecta* (Hudson) Coville
Sium erectum Hudson   Plate 97.   *CTW, p. 662*
Much smaller, commoner and weaker-stemmed than the last species, with 7–10 pairs of irregularly jagged and toothed leaflets; umbels of white flowers on stalks opposite the leaves; and broader, leafy, often 3-cleft bracts. Fruits globular, nearly divided in two with faint ridges and long styles (Fig.). Leaves not unlike Fool's Watercress (475), but coarsely and sharply toothed. Lower bracts many (none in 475). *Habitat:* Widespread and frequent in wet places; local in Scotland and Ireland. July–September.

491. *ROCK SAMPHIRE *Crithmum maritimum* L.   Plate 51.   *CTW, p. 663*
A distinctive yellowish maritime umbellifer, the only one with thick fleshy leaves cut into narrow untoothed leaflets; a squat bushy grey hairless perennial, with solid stems up to a foot high. Fruits egg-shaped, ridged, corky. Used for pickling, like the totally different Marsh Samphire (220). *Habitat:* Frequent by the sea in the S and W, especially on rocky coasts; local in Ireland. July–September.

492. ***MOON CARROT *Seseli libanotis* (L.) Koch   Plate 95.   *CTW, p. 663*
A downy perennial, often taller than the rougher Wild Carrot (510), and with many-grooved stem and narrow undivided lower bracts; the rootstock crowned with the fibrous remains of dead leaf-stalks; leaves 2-pinnate, leaflets much cut and often looking crisped; umbels very many (15–30) rayed; flowers pure white; and downy egg-shaped fruits with prominent calyx-teeth (Fig.). *Habitat:* Rare in dry turf on the chalk near Cambridge, Baldock, Hitchin and Beachy Head. July–September.

493. *TUBULAR WATER DROPWORT *Oenanthe fistulosa* L. Pl. 98. *CTW, 664* 🔲
A greyish hairless aquatic perennial, with rather inflated hollow stems 1–2 ft. high; erect branches; 2-pinnate root-leaves with lanceolate leaflets; 1-pinnate stem-leaves, shorter than the soft hollow leaf-stalks, with linear leaflets; and smallish umbels with 2–3 stout rays bearing well-separated dome-shaped heads of pinkish-white flowers, which become globular in fruit; usually no lower bracts.

Fruits angular, with long styles, and like all Water Dropworts with persistent calyx-teeth (Fig.). *Habitat:* Widespread but local in wet places and shallow fresh water. July–September.

494. *PARSLEY WATER DROPWORT *Oe. lachenalii* Gmelin Pl. 98. *CTW, 665*
A greyish hairless perennial, with stiff, usually solid stems 1–3 ft. high, and 2-pinnate leaves with short blunt leaflets below and longer, narrower, pointed ones above. Umbels with slender spreading rays, white flowers and sometimes no lower bracts. Fruits egg-shaped, ribbed, with short erect styles. (Fig.). *Habitat:* Widespread but local, in brackish marshes and in fens. July–September.

494a. **Callous-fruited Water Dropwort, *Oe. pimpinelloides* L., is stiffer, with globular tubers on the roots, lower leaves with broader wedge-shaped toothed leaflets, very compact flat-topped umbels, fruit stalks thickened, and larger cylindrical fruits with a corky base and long styles and calyx-teeth (Fig.). Very local in often damp grassy places in S England and Co. Cork. July–August.

494b. **Sulphurwort, *Oe. silaifolia* Bieberstein, is larger and often sprawling, with hollow stems; all leaflets narrow, sharply pointed like Pepper Saxifrage (499); and fruits like the last species but with shorter styles and narrowed stalks (Fig.). Local in riverside meadows inland in the S half of England. June–July.

495. *HEMLOCK WATER DROPWORT *Oe. crocata* L. ⚘
Plate 98. *CTW, p. 666*
A stout hairless perennial, smelling of parsley, often forming broad clumps 2–4 ft. high, with usually hollow stems and glossy 3-pinnate leaves with broad leaflets, with wedge-shaped bases and 2–3 toothed. Umbels large, white, with numerous rays and sometimes no lower bracts. Fruits cylindrical, with long styles (Fig.). *Habitat:* Widespread and locally common in or by fresh water, rare on the E side of Britain N of the Thames. June–August.

496. *FINE-LEAVED WATER DROPWORT *Oe. aquatica* (L.) Poiret ⚘
Oe. phellandrium Lamarck Plate 98. *CTW, p. 666*
A hairless, pale green, aquatic biennial, 1–4 ft. high, with fat shiny hollow stems and upper leaves much more graceful and more finely divided than the last species. Umbels on short stout stalks opposite the leaf-stalks; flowers white; usually no lower bracts. Fruits narrow oval, styles and calyx-teeth very short (Fig.). *Habitat:* Widespread but local in slow or still water; Scotland, only in the SE. June–September.

496a. **River Water Dropwort, *Oe. fluviatilis* (Babington) Coleman, grows largely floating on the water with a few erect shoots; leaves 2-pinnate, floating ones with short, blunt leaflets, submerged ones with narrow wedge-shaped leaflets. A shy flowerer. Fruits large, with styles and calyx-teeth proportionately even shorter (Fig.). Very local in streams in the S and in Ireland.

497. FOOL'S PARSLEY *Aethusa cynapium* L. Plate 96. *CTW, p. 667* ⚘
Readily known from other small white umbellifers by the 3–4 long upper bracts on the outer side of each secondary umbel, giving the plant a rather bearded effect; no lower bracts. A hairless, dark green annual, 3–18 in. high, with ribbed stems and 2–3-pinnate very smooth, flat leaves, slightly resembling Parsley when young. Fruits smooth, globular, with tiny styles (Fig.). *Habitat:* A widespread and frequent garden and arable weed, thinning out northwards. June onwards.

498. FENNEL *Foeniculum vulgare* Miller   Plate 51. *CTW, p. 668*

A tall hairless strong-smelling, rather bluish-green perennial, 3–5 ft. high, with very finely and bushily divided 3–4-pinnate leaves with hair-like segments, and large sheathing bases; stems shiny, solid, becoming hollow when old. Flowers yellow, in large umbels, usually with no upper or lower bracts. Fruits narrow egg-shaped, ribbed. *Habitat:* Widespread and locally frequent by the sea and on waste places inland. July onwards.

499. *PEPPER SAXIFRAGE   *Silaum silaus* (L.) Schinz & Thellung
   Silaus flavescens Bernhardi   Plate 51. *CTW, p. 668*

Neither peppery nor a Saxifrage, but a stiff hairless perennial, with solid stems 1–2 ft. high; 2–3-pinnate leaves with pointed, almost linear leaflets; and umbels of dull sulphur-yellow flowers with no lower bracts. Fruits egg-shaped, ridged, with short styles. *Habitat:* Widespread but local in meadows and on roadsides, preferring damp, heavy soils, thinning out northwards; not in Ireland. June–Sept.

500. **SPIGNEL-MEU *Meum athamanticum* Jacquin   Plate 98. *CTW, p. 669*

A tufted hairless aromatic perennial, with hollow stems 9–18 in. high; root-stock crowned by fibrous remains of old leaf-stalks; leaves 2–pinnate, with bushy whorls of numerous short thread-like leaflets much denser than Whorled Caraway (482), whose leaves are not pinnate; and umbels of frothy-looking white flowers, sometimes tinged yellow or pink; sometimes no lower bracts. Fruits egg-shaped, ridged (Fig.). *Habitat:* Local in hill pastures from N Wales to the C Highlands. May–June.

501. ***CAMBRIDGE PARSLEY *Selinum carvifolia* (L.) L.   Pl. 98. *CTW, 669*

A rare white perennial umbellifer, smelling of Parsley, usually less tall than Milk Parsley (505), and with solid well ridged stems; leaflets with very pointed tips somewhat like Pepper Saxifrage (499); no lower bracts; and fruits half the size, with 10 wings and longer styles (Fig., as 502). *Habitat:* Very rare, now apparently only in two fens in Cambridgeshire. August onwards.

502. **LOVAGE *Ligusticum scoticum* L.   Plate 97. *CTW, p. 670*

A hairless tufted stocky perennial, 9–18 in. high, with stiff, ribbed, usually purple stems hollow below; and leathery glossy, bright green, 2–trifoliate leaves, with broad, toothed leaflets and inflated sheathing stalks, smelling of Celery or Parsley when crushed. Flowers white. Fruits flattened oval, ridged (Fig., as 501). Grows in much larger lower clumps than 503, which may also be found on cliffs. *Habitat:* Local on rocky sea cliffs in Scotland, mostly in the N, and in Northumberland and N Ireland. June–July.

503. WILD ANGELICA *Angelica sylvestris* L.   Plate 97. *CTW, p. 671*

A tall stout perennial, often suffused purple, with hollow stems 2–5 ft. high and downy below; 2–3-pinnate leaves with broad, toothed leaflets and inflated sheathing stalks; large umbels of white flowers often tinged pink; usually no lower bracts; and flattened oval fruits with 4 broad wings and no calyx-teeth (Fig.). The larger and coarser Hogweed (508) is roughly hairy all over. *Habitat:* Widespread and common in wet woods, fens and damp grassy places; also on cliffs. July–September.

504. ***HOG'S FENNEL *Peucedanum officinale* L.   Plate 51. *CTW, p. 672*

A hairless, dark green perennial, with solid stems 2–4 ft. high; rootstock crowned with remains of old leaf-stalks; numerous very large leaves repeatedly

3-cleft into linear segments; large broad many-rayed umbels of dark yellow flowers; often no lower bracts; and flattened shiny oval fruits with short turned-down styles. A bushier, darker green plant than Fennel (498), with distinctly flattened, less hair-like leaf-segments and larger, flatter umbels of darker yellow flowers. *Habitat:* In rough grassy places by the sea, still only in the same two areas around Faversham and Walton-on-the-Naze, where Gerard knew it in 1597 'in a medow neere to the seaside'. July–September.

505. **MILK PARSLEY   *Peucedanum palustre* (L.) Moench
Plate 98.   *CTW, p. 672*

A hairless biennial, 3–4 ft. high, with hollow stems yielding a milky juice when young; leaves 2–4-pinnate, with deeply cut, very blunt-tipped leaflets; and umbels of white flowers, with upper and lower bracts turned down. Fruits much flattened, oval, with short styles and two pairs of wings (Fig.). *Habitat:* Very local in fens and marshy places from Yorks southwards, mainly in the E. July–Sept.

506. **MASTERWORT   *P. ostruthium* (L.) Koch   Plate 97.   *CTW, p. 672*

A stocky, usually downy perennial, more tufted than Wild Angelica (503), with hollow stems 1–2 ft. high, numerous 2-trifoliate root-leaves with broad toothed leaflets and inflated sheathing stalks, large umbels of white flowers with no lower bracts; and globular winged fruits with down-turned styles (Fig.). *Habitat:* Thinly scattered in damp grassy places near cowsheds and houses, from Wales northwards and in NE Ireland. June–July.

507. WILD PARSNIP   *Pastinaca sativa* L.   Plate 51.   *CTW, p. 673*

A roughly hairy biennial, 2–4 ft. high, pungent when crushed; our only yellow umbellifer with 1-pinnate leaves, the leaflets broad, toothed and sometimes lobed; no upper or lower bracts. Fruits flat, oval, narrowly winged, with short spreading styles. *Habitat:* Widespread and locally common in rather dry grassy and waste places, especially on chalk and limestone in the S. July–September.

508. HOGWEED   *Heracleum sphondylium* L.   Plate 95.   *CTW, p. 673*

The commonest large wayside white umbellifer of the summer and autumn; a stout coarse, roughly hairy biennial, with hollow stems 2–4 ft. high; 1–3-pinnate leaves with usually very broad, toothed leaflets on stalks ending in a wide sheath; substantial white, pink or even purple umbels, 4–6 in. across, the petals of the outer flowers extremely unequal; usually no lower bracts; and flattened oval, winged fruits with dark streaks (Fig.). *Habitat:* Widespread and abundant on roadsides and in grassy places. June onwards. Cow Parsnip.

508a. **Giant Hogweed**, *H. mantegazzianum* Sommier & Levier (incl. *H. persicum* Desfontaines, etc.), is a confused group of plants, immense in all their parts, with often reddish stems 2–4 in. wide and attaining over 10 ft. in height; leaves 3 ft. long, equalling their stout stalks; umbels 1–4 ft. across; and fruits narrower. Naturalised very locally in shady, moist and waste places. June–July.

509. ***HARTWORT   *Tordylium maximum* L.   Plate 95.   *CTW, p. 675*

A roughly hairy annual, 6–18 in. high, with pinnate toothed leaves, the leaflets of the upper narrow, of the lower broader; and smallish umbels of white flowers, the outermost petals the largest; Fruits rather like Hedge Parsley (461) but much larger; flattened oval, bristly, with a thickened border and prominent calyx-teeth. *Habitat:* Now confined to two or three grassy places on clay soil on the Essex side of the Thames estuary. June–July.

510. WILD CARROT *Daucus carota* L. Plate 95. *CTW, p. 95. CTW, p. 675* (incl. '*D. gingidium*' (*D. gummifer* Lamarck))

The only common white umbellifer with conspicuous 3-forked or pinnate lower bracts fringing the flat dense umbels of dirty white flowers, the centre flower usually deep red; petals often unequal. A roughly hairy biennial, with stiff solid stems 1–2 ft. high, and feathery 3-pinnate leaves. Fruiting umbels become more erect, hollowly concave, and congested; fruits flattened oval, with short styles and spines often hooked (Fig.). *Habitat:* Widespread and common in grassy places, especially on chalk and limestone and near the coast. June onwards.

MELON FAMILY Cucurbitaceae

511. WHITE BRYONY *Bryonia dioica* Jacquin Plate 76. *CTW, p. 677* ℗

A perennial hairy climber, with long tendrils opposite the leaf-stalks; differing from Black Bryony (1056) also in its paler green, ivy-shaped matt leaves, and open clusters of much larger greenish flowers, with 5 dark-veined petals; male and female on different plants. Fruit a red berry. *Habitat:* Frequent in hedges and bushy places in the S, thinning out northwards and westwards. May–September.

BIRTHWORT FAMILY Aristolochiaceae

512. ***ASARABACCA *Asarum europaeum* L. Plate 35. *CTW, p. 678*

A creeping patch-forming perennial, with long-stalked untoothed shiny kidney-shaped leaves, 2–3 in. across, on 1–2 in. downy stalks, and hidden below them the solitary bell-shaped purplish-green flowers. *Habitat:* Rare in a few widely scattered shady places; not in Ireland. March-May.

513. ***BIRTHWORT *Aristolochia clematitis* L. Plate 63. *CTW, p. 679*

A hairless foetid perennial, 1–2 ft. high, forming patches, with small clusters of long tubular, pale yellow flowers at the base of the large, stalked, pale green, heart-shaped leaves. *Habitat:* A herb, formerly used by midwives, surviving in a few places, mainly near habitations; not in Ireland. June–September.

SPURGE FAMILY Euphorbiaceae

514. DOG'S MERCURY *Mercurialis perennis* L. Plate 110. *CTW, p. 680* ℗

A hairy creeping foetid perennial, 4–12 in. high, with stems unbranched and rather leafless below; dark green, broad lanceolate, toothed opposite leaves; and small greenish petalless flowers at their base, the male in long prominent spikes, the female on separate plants 1–3 together on stalks which lengthen as the hairy fruits ripen. *Habitat:* Widespread and common in woods and shady places, often carpeting the ground; also on mountains; local in Ireland. February–May.

514a. ***Annual Mercury,** *M. annua* L., is a nearly hairless, pale green, often branched and so bushy annual, leafier at the base, and with male and female flowers sometimes on the same plant, the female spikes scarcely stalked. A widespread but local weed, chiefly in the S and near the sea. Throughout the year, but mostly from May onwards.

SPURGES *Euphorbia* ℗

All our Spurges are non-woody plants of no great height, with an acrid milky juice and undivided leaves, which in the great majority are also alternate and untoothed. Their flowers are yellowish-green in umbel-like clusters which broaden as they develop. They are a fantastic surrealist jumble of strange miniature shapes, 1-stalked female with three often forked styles among many minute 1-stamened male flowers. This group is based in a fleshy cup with 4 conspicuous oval or crescent-shaped lobes. From this lolls on an elongated stalk the round 3-celled fruit. What appear to be petals are actually outer bracts.

KEY TO SPURGES (Nos. 515–526)

PLANT *prostrate* 515; *under 6 in.* 519, 520, 521, 522, 525; *over 2 ft.* 516; *greyish* 515, 516, 521, 522, 523, 525; *reddish or purplish* 515, 518a, 522, 525, 526; *partly downy* 517, 518, 526.

LEAVES *opposite* 515, 516; *long and narrow* 516, 521, 524, 525, 526; *toothed* 518, 519; *fleshy* 522, 523.

FLOWER-LOBES *roundish* 515, 517, 518, 519; *horned* 516, 520–526.

FRUITS *smooth* 515, 516, 519, 521, 526.

HABITAT: *garden weed* 516, 519, 520, 521; *woods* 516, 517, 518a, 526; *maritime only* 515, 522, 523.

515. ***PURPLE SPURGE** *Euphorbia peplis* L. Plate 27. *CTW, p. 683*
Our only prostrate Spurge, a fleshy annual, with crimson stems 1–3 in. long; small greyish opposite oblong, mostly asymmetrical leaves; and at their base tiny linear stipules and solitary stalked inconspicuous flowers with roundish lobes. Fruits smooth. *Habitat:* Extremely rare on sandy shores; now seen regularly only in the Channel Is., but also appearing very spasmodically in the SW. July–September.

516. ***CAPER SPURGE** *E. lathyrus* L. Plate 109. *CTW, p. 683*
The only non-maritime Spurge with opposite leaves; a greyish waxy, hairless biennial, 1–3 ft. high, with a highly distinctive, 'architectural' appearance; lower leaves lanceolate, upper ones broader at the base. Flowers with bluntly horned lobes. Fruits large, 3-sided resembling green capers. *Habitat:* Extremely local in woods on chalk or limestone in England and Wales; an occasional weed of gardens and waste places. June–August.

517. ***IRISH SPURGE** *E. hyberna* L. Plate 109. *CTW, p. 685*
A little-branched perennial, 1–2 ft. high, often growing in broad clumps, with soft oval leaves, usually slightly downy beneath; bright yellow flowers with rounded lobes which later become brown; and largish warty fruits. *Habitat:* Locally common in rough pastures, hedge-banks and woods in W Ireland; also very local in SW England. April–July.

518. ***BROAD SPURGE** *E. platyphyllos* L. Plate 109. *CTW, p. 685*
An open loose, sometimes downy, often well branched annual, 6–18 in. high, with thin, broad lanceolate leaves, very finely toothed in the outer half and half-clasping the stem. Flowers with rounded lobes. Fruits small, roundish, slightly grooved, with rounded warts, and olive-brown seeds. *Habitat:* A very local and decreasing weed in the S. June onwards.

518a. ****Tintern Spurge**, *E. stricta* L., is rather daintier and bushier, often with red stems, and has smaller fruits covered with tall cylindrical warts and more deeply divided into three, and red-brown seeds. Confined to clearings in limestone woods in the lower Wye valley and a hedge-bank near Bath.

519. SUN SPURGE *E. helioscopia* L. Plate 109. *CTW, p. 686*
Our only common Spurge with toothed leaves; a hairless yellow-green annual, 4–12 in. high, rarely branched, with oval leaves. Flowers yellow, in a wide umbrella-like cluster, with roundish green lobes. Fruits smooth. *Habitat:* Widespread and common as a weed in gardens and elsewhere. April onwards.

520. PETTY SPURGE *E. peplus* L. Plate 109. *CTW, p. 686*
Usually smaller and weedier than Sun Spurge (520), with which it often grows, and with rounder untoothed mid-green leaves; less flat-topped clusters of green flowers, with slender, crescent-shaped horns on the lobes and fruits with wavy ridges. *Habitat:* A widespread and abundant weed of disturbed ground. Throughout the year.

521. DWARF SPURGE *E. exigua* L. Plate 109. *CTW, p. 687*
A low slender hairless greyish annual, differing from Petty Spurge (520) in its short linear leaves and yellower flowers with very slender crescentic horns on the lobes. Fruits smooth. *Habitat:* Widespread and locally common in cultivated ground. May onwards.

522. *PORTLAND SPURGE *E. portlandica* L. Plate 109. *CTW, p. 687*
A hairless greyish biennial, 3–9 in. high, branched only at the base, often tinged red, with numerous small, somewhat leathery, minutely pointed, lanceolate or oval leaves, the midrib prominent below. Flowers with long crescentic horns on lobes. Fruits slightly rough, with grey pitted seeds. *Habitat:* Locally common on dunes, sandy shores and cliffs on the coast from Chichester Harbour to Galloway, and in Ireland. April–September. '*E. segetalis*'.

523. *SEA SPURGE *E. paralias* L. Plate 109. *CTW, p. 687*
A perennial, taller and robuster than the last species, not reddening and with larger, somewhat broader, greyer leaves, not minutely pointed, more numerous, overlapping up the stem and with the midrib less prominent; lobes with short horns. Fruits wrinkled, with smooth seeds. *Habitat:* Local on sand by the sea from Norfolk S and W to Galloway, and in Ireland. June onwards.

524. *HUNGARIAN SPURGE *E. esula* L. Plate 109. *CTW, p. 688*
A hairless, somewhat variable perennial, 9 in. to 2 ft. high, often growing in large patches, with linear leaves; lobes of flowers with crescentic horns and fruits rough. *Habitat:* Uncommon but increasing on roadsides and waste places; not yet in Ireland. June onwards. (Incl. *E. virgata* Waldstein & Kitaibel.)

525. **CYPRESS SPURGE *E. cyparissias* L. Plate 109. *CTW, p. 689*
A hairless, rather bushy perennial, 4–10 in. high, often forming patches and eventually turning a glorious red, with many very narrow linear leaves, the lobes of the flowers with very short crescentic horns. Fruits warty. *Habitat:* Extremely local in turf, usually on chalk or limestone in the SE; occasionally as a garden weed or outcast. May–August.

526. *WOOD SPURGE *E. amygdaloides* L. Plate 65. *CTW, p. 689*
The common spring Spurge of southern woodlands, a downy unbranched perennial, about a foot high, with narrow lanceolate leaves, often tinged red, and flowers with converging crescentic horns on the lobes. Fruits almost smooth.

Habitat: Often plentiful in and by woods in the S, and among heather in the Scilly Is., but thinning out northwards, and not in Scotland; rare in Ireland. March–May.

DOCK FAMILY Polygonaceae

BISTORTS, PERSICARIAS, ETC. *Polygonum*

AN UNDISTINGUISHED genus of generally hairless plants, with stems more or less swollen at the junctions of the alternate undivided leaves, at the base of which are whitish or papery sheaths. Flowers small, pink or whitish, mostly in terminal heads. Fruit a nut.

KEY TO BISTORTS AND BUCKWHEAT (Nos. 527–537)

PLANT *climbing* 533; *creeping* 528, 529, 535, 536; *prostrate* 527, 533; *very tall* 535, 536; *prickly* 534.

LEAVES *very broad* 535, 536; *with dark blotches* 531; *with winged stalks* 529; *floating* 530; *with margins inrolled* 527b.

FLOWERS *pink* 527, 528, 529, 530, 531, 532a, 532b, 533b, 535, 537; *white or green* 527, 528, 531a, 532, 533, 534, 535, 536, 537; *at base of leaves* 527; *in loose spikes* 533, 535–37; *in dense spikes* 528–30, 532,; *in round heads* 534.

527. KNOTGRASS *Polygonum aviculare* L. Plate 104. *CTW, p. 692*

A low variable, often prostrate, hairless annual, 2–12 in. long, with tattered silvery sheaths at the base of the short lanceolate alternate leaves and tiny pink or white flowers all up the stems, giving the so-called knotted effect. The sheaths have unbranched veins and later become brownish. Fruit a 3-sided nut completely covered by the dead flower. *Habitat:* A widespread and abundant weed of cultivated and waste ground, also on the sea-shore. June onwards.

527a. **Slender Sea Knotgrass**, *P. raii* Babington, is compacter and more thick-set, with its larger, glossy chestnut-brown fruit protruding well beyond the dead flower. Very local on sandy and shingly shores; much scarcer than the slenderer maritime form of Knotgrass. August–September.

527b. ***Sea Knotgrass**, *P. maritimum* L., is often confused with the last species, having a similar fruit, but it is a still compacter perennial with a woody base, the margins of its leathery greyish leaves are turned down, and its large silvery sheaths have many branched veins. Now very rarely seen on sandy beaches in the SW. August–September.

528. **ALPINE BISTORT *P. viviparum* L. Plate 103. *CTW, p. 694*

A hairless unbranched perennial, 4–8 in. high, with dark green, narrow lanceolate leaves, tapering at the base, their margins turned down and their midrib prominent, the root ones broader with unwinged stalks and withering early. Flowers in slender spikes, white or very pale pink, the lower ones usually replaced by purplish bulbils. *Habitat:* Locally frequent in damp turf in hill districts in the N; very rare in Ireland. June–August.

529. *BISTORT *P. bistorta* L. Plate 26. *CTW, p. 695*

A hairless, unbranched perennial, 1–2 ft. high, often in conspicuous patches; with narrowly triangular leaves, abruptly contracted at the base into a wing on the upper part of the very long stalk; stem-leaves narrower, sometimes arrow-shaped, short-stalked. Flowers small, pink in fat, compact spikes, like the next two species. *Habitat:* Widespread and fairly frequent in wet pastures, especially in the hills, but rare in the S. June–August.

530. AMPHIBIOUS BISTORT   *P. amphibium* L.   Plate 26.   *CTW, p. 695*

An unbranched far-creeping rooting perennial, 2–3 ft. long, whose thickish, broad lanceolate leaves vary widely, being hairless, floating, long-stalked and abruptly contracted at the base in aquatic plants, and often downy, shorter-stalked and rounded at the base in land plants. Flowers small, pink, in compact spikes, stubbier than Redleg (531), on leafy stalks 6–12 in. high   *Habitat:* Widespread and frequent by and in still and slow fresh water; also an occasional arable weed. July–September.

531. REDLEG   *P. persicaria* L.   Plate 26.   *CTW, p. 696*

An often sprawling, almost hairless annual, 6–18 in. high, usually with red stems: oblong spikes of pink flowers both terminal and up the stems; thin lanceolate leaves, sometimes silky white beneath, and often with a darker blotch in the middle; sheaths all fringed; and nuts 3-sided   *Habitat:* A widespread and common weed of bare damp ground, and in ditches. June onwards. Persicaria.

531*a*. **Pale Persicaria**, *P. lapathifolium* L., has stems usually green: small shiny spots on the usually greenish-white flowers and their stalks; and only the uppermost sheaths fringed. Fruits usually roundish. Almost as common.

531*b*. *Knotted Persicaria**, *P. nodosum* Persoon (*P. petecticale* (Stokes) Druce), is usually bushier than the last species, with dull brick-red flowers, their stalks and the undersides of the leaves thickly dotted with shiny spots: still looser sheaths; and smaller brown roundish nuts. More local than the other two.

532. WATER-PEPPER   *P. hydropiper* L.   Plate 103.   *CTW, p. 697*

A slender half-erect, little branched, almost hairless annual, 9 in. to 2 ft. high, with a peppery taste; narrow lanceolate leaves, the lower gradually tapering to the short stalk; and sheaths not or only shortly fringed   Flowers small, greenish-white, in a slender spike, interrupted especially at the base, more or less nodding at the tip, and covered with yellow dots   Nuts matt, rough.   *Habitat*   Widespread and frequent in wet places, including damp rides in woods. July onwards.

532*a*. **Tasteless Water-pepper**, *P. mite* Schrank, sometimes passed over for a slender Redleg (531), is not peppery, and has leaves abruptly narrowed at the base, sheaths with long fringes, flower-spike hardly nodding and usually undotted, flowers reddish and nuts rather large and shining. Very local, mainly in the S.

532*b*. **Least Water-pepper**, *P. minus* Hudson, is smaller than the last species, not peppery, and is more prostrate, with narrower leaves, a very slender, erect soft pink flower-spike, and nuts half the size. Rather more widespread.

533. BLACK BINDWEED   *P. convolvulus* L.   Plate 102.   *CTW, p. 698*

A hairless, prostrate or climbing annual, 6 in. to 3 ft. long, whose twining well-stalked heart-shaped leaves resemble true Bindweeds (666–667), but it twines clockwise and has angled stems. Flowers small, greenish-pink, short-stalked at, or in long loose spikes from, the base of the leaves, which have greenish silvery sheaths. Nuts triangular, dull black.   *Habitat:* A widespread and common weed of waste and cultivated ground. July onwards.

533*a*. **Copse Bindweed**, *P. dumetorum* L., is much larger, climbing bushily over hedges. It has rounded stems; longer flower-stalks; sepals broadly winged in fruit, the wings running down on to the stalk; and smaller shiny nuts. Often

confused in the absence of fruits with a variety of Black Bindweed which also
has winged sepals in fruit, but not running down on to the stalk. Very local in
hedges and by woods in the S, not always reappearing each year.

533b. ***Russian Vine, *P. baldschuanicum* Regel (incl. Lace Vine, *P. aubertii*
Henry) (*CTW*†), is a larger rampant deciduous woody climber, with wavy-edged
leaves, often bronzy when young; and many large showy clusters of white or
pinkish flowers. Fruits rarely set. Common in gardens and occasionally away from
them.

534. ***TEAR-THUMB   *P. sagittatum* L.   Plate 101.   *CTW, p. 698*
A hairless, little branched, sprawling or clambering annual, with numerous
small, very sharp down-turned prickles on the weak 4-angled stems 1–2 ft. long;
a few short-stalked, narrowly arrow-shaped leaves; and small round heads of
greenish or pinkish flowers.   *Habitat:* Scattered over several acres of wet ground
near Derrynane, Co. Kerry. June–September.

535. *JAPANESE KNOTWEED   *P. cuspidatum* Siebold & Zuccarini
                                              Plate 107.   *CTW, p. 699*
A stout hairless perennial, 3–6 ft. high, often forming small thickets, with
arching, rather zigzag red-brown stems; thick broad pointed leaves abruptly
truncated at the base; short sheaths; and loose, often branched spikes of numerous
small, greenish-white, occasionally pink, flowers along the stem.   *Habitat:*
Increasingly frequent on waste sites and by roads and railways. Sept.–Oct.

536. **GIANT KNOTWEED   *P. sachalinense* Maximowicz   Pl. 107.   *CTW, 699*
Much taller than Japanese Knotweed (535), reaching 10 ft. or so, and hardly
branched, with much larger broad pointed leaves, more or less heart-shaped at
the base, paler beneath and reminiscent of Broad-leaved Dock (545). Flowers in
a longer denser spike.   *Habitat:* An uncommon escape near gardens and by
roadsides. August–September.

537. **BUCKWHEAT   *Fagopyrum esculentum* Moench   Pl. 103.   *CTW, p. 699*
A hairless annual, about a foot high, hardly branched, with stems often red,
differing from all *Polygonums* in its broad branched clusters of pinkish-white
flowers; leaves broad, arrow-shaped, the upper half-clasping the stem, the lower
stalked; the sheaths at their base not fringed. Nuts smooth, sharply 3-angled,
with straight edges.   *Habitat:* Fairly frequent on waste ground or as a relic of
cultivation.   July–September.

DOCKS AND SORRELS   *Rumex* and *Oxyria*

THE GREAT majority of our Docks—Dockens in the north—and Sorrels are both
hairless and perennial. All have alternate leaves, narrowing up the stem, with thin
papery sheaths at their base, and more or less branched terminal spikes of
numerous small stalked greenish flowers, often tinged reddish, with their parts in
twos (*Oxyria*) or threes (*Rumex*). Their fruits are 3-sided nuts, on which in some
Docks are 1 or 3 small warts. Fully ripe fruits are essential for accurate identification of certain Docks; the lower leaves are also useful, but have often withered
by the time the fruit is ripe. The dead brown flowering stems of many Docks
persist conspicuously into the winter.

Our three Sorrels are generally slenderer than our score of Docks, and have
acid-tasting arrow- or halberd-shaped leaves. The two abundant species, Sheep's

(539) and Common Sorrels (540), both have the male and female flowers on separate plants, and often turn a brilliant red as they go over, especially in dry places. Docks, on the other hand, are generally taller, stouter and greener, and unlike the Sorrels, readily hybridise. The most frequent hybrid is between Curled and Broad-leaved Docks; the others are too many to enumerate here.

Goosefoots (204–211) are similar-looking green weedy plants, but have no papery sheaths, and rounded, not 3-angled fruits, and all but one are annuals.

KEY TO DOCKS AND SORRELS (Nos. 538–549)

PLANT *reddish* 539, 540, 544, 547, 548; *creeping* 539, 542, 549; *very tall* 541, 544a; *golden-yellow* 548; *with slightly wavy stem* 547.

LEAVES *rounded* 538; *broad* 541, 542, 544a, 545; *waisted* 546, 547; *arrow-shaped* 539, 540; *wavy-edged* 538, 543, 544, 549; *leathery* 541, 549; *clasping stem* 540.

FLOWERS *in loose leafless spike* 538, 539, 540.

FRUITS *with no warts* 538, 539, 541a, 542, 543; *with 1 wart* 540, 544, 545, 547a; *with 3 warts* 541, 544, 546, 547, 548, 549; *toothed* 541, 544b, 545, 546, 548.

538. *MOUNTAIN SORREL *Oxyria digyna* (L.) Hill Pl. 107. *CTW, p. 700*

A pale green hairless tufted perennial, 4–10 in. high, somewhat like Common Sorrel (540), but with kidney-shaped wavy-edged acid-tasting leaves, very few on the stems, and leafless spikes of red-edged green flowers. *Habitat:* Locally frequent in damp grassy and rocky places on mountains in the N and in W Ireland. June–August.

539. SHEEP'S SORREL *Rumex acetosella* L. Plate 107. *CTW, p. 703*

A low slender perennial, 3–10 in. high, with a creeping rootstock and small narrow halberd-shaped leaves, the lower lobes spreading. Flower-spike leafless, open, with whorls of flowers well spaced out. Fruits small, with no warts. *Habitat:* Widespread and common in heathy and grassy places, preferring thin acid soils. May–August.

540. COMMON SORREL *R. acetosa* L. Plate 107. *CTW, p. 704*

An unbranched tufted perennial, 6 in. to 2 ft. high, with long-stalked, arrow-shaped leaves, the topmost unstalked and clasping the stem; flower-spikes longer, compacter and stouter than Sheep's Sorrel (539), and fruits roundish with a tiny wart. *Habitat:* Widespread and often abundant in grassy places, also on mountains. May–August.

541. GREAT WATER DOCK *R. hydrolapathum* Hudson Pl. 108. *CTW, 705*

A stately plant, sometimes topping 6 feet, with upright branches; dull green, leathery, lanceolate root-leaves, up to 3 ft. long; conspicuous flower-spikes, leafy below; and large triangular fruits, with only a few tiny teeth at the base, and three elongated warts. *Habitat:* Widespread and frequent in wet places, especially by rivers; uncommon in Scotland and Ireland. July–September.

541a. ***Trossachs Dock, *R. aquaticus* L., is also tall, but slenderer and shorter-branched, and has triangular root-leaves with a broad, flat base, and no warts on the pointed fruits. At present known only among the vegetation on the gravelly eastern shore of L. Lomond.

542. **MONK'S RHUBARB *R. alpinus* L. Plate 108. *CTW, p. 705*

A stout perennial, 9–18 in. high, whose wide patches of broad heart-shaped blunt leaves often exclude all other vegetation. Flower-spikes dense, rather leafy below the very erect branches. Fruits thin, triangular, on long slender stalks, with no warts. *Habitat:* By roadsides and streams, usually not far from buildings; not a mountain plant, but most frequent in the C Highlands; also elsewhere in Scotland and N England; very rarely further S. June–July.

543. *BUTTER DOCK   *R. longifolius* DC.   Plate 108.   *CTW, p. 706*

Differs from Curled Dock (544) in its larger and broader leaves; dense, rather narrow, often pale green flower-spikes; and larger fruits with no warts. *Habitat:* By roadsides and streams, most frequent in C Scotland, thinning out N, and S to N England. June–July. '*R. aquaticus*'.

544. CURLED DOCK   *R. crispus* L.   Plate 108.   *CTW, p. 707*

Our most ubiquitous and variable Dock, a weedy perennial 1–3 ft. high, with wavy lanceolate leaves, the root ones narrowed or rounded at the base; rather leafy flower-spikes; and thick untoothed oval fruits with normally only 1 developed wart, but often 3 by the sea. *Habitat:* A widespread and abundant weed of fields and waste places, and by fresh and salt water. June onwards.

544a. **Patience Dock, *R. patientia* L. (incl. *R. cristatus* DC.), easily reaches 6 ft., and looks from a distance like a thick Rhubarb gone to seed. It might also be taken for an outsize Curled Dock, but both starts and finishes flowering earlier, and has denser thick spikes, and broader, hardly wavy root-leaves, with a broad base. Naturalised on waste ground in the S, abundantly in a few places. May–June.

544b. ***Shore Dock, *R. rupestris* Le Gall, looks like a slender, erect-branched Curled Dock with strap-shaped, hardly wavy grey-green leaves and much denser flower-spikes, but the fruits of Clustered Dock (547) with the 3 warts much larger. Rare on rocky coasts and dune-slacks in SW England and S Wales.

545. BROAD DOCK   *R. obtusifolius* L.   Plate 108.   *CTW, p 707*

The sturdier of our two commonest Docks, 1–3 ft. high, with large broad, fresh green root-leaves, heart-shaped at the base and hairy on the veins beneath; lanceolate upper leaves; flower-spikes leafy; and fruits with prominent teeth and only 1 wart. *Habitat:* A widespread and plentiful weed of farms and waste ground. June onwards.

546. *FIDDLE DOCK   *R. pulcher* L.   Plate 108.   *CTW, p. 708*

A smallish Dock, rarely over a foot high, with the lower leaves, especially the early ones, small and often waisted or fiddle-shaped. Flowers in distant leafy whorls on long stiff branches, spreading at right angles and giving a squat appearance recognisable yards away, the spikes often get untidy and flop over, and may even break off. Fruits on short thick stalks, about as broad as long, much veined, with short teeth on each edge, and 3 warts. *Habitat.* Local in dry and sunny places, often on sandy soil, in S England, Wales and Ireland, becoming rare as it leaves the coast. June–August.

547. CLUSTERED DOCK   *R. conglomeratus* Murray   Plate 108.   *CTW, p. 708*

A stiff, rather slender perennial, 1–2 ft. high, with often slightly wavy stems and spreading branches; root-leaves narrow oval, rounded or heart-shaped at the base, sometimes waisted. Flower-spikes leafy nearly to the top and on the branches. Fruits small, much longer than broad, untoothed with 3 elongated warts. *Habitat:* Widespread, mainly on dampish ground; common in lowland districts, but rare in Scotland. June onwards.

547a. **Wood or Red-veined Dock,** *R. sanguineus* L. (*R. nemorosus* Willdenow)
usually has a straight stem with erecter branches; root-leaves never waisted, their
veins occasionally rusty-red; flower-spikes leafy only near the bottom; and fruits
with only one fully formed, round wart. Rarely and never far from houses, its
stems and leaf-veins are purple. Preferring woods, and thinning out northwards.

548. ****GOLDEN DOCK**   *R. maritimus* L.   Plate 108.   *CTW, p. 710*
A distinctive Dock, 3–15 in. high, often annual, and turning golden-yellow in
fruit, when the flower-spikes have a most delicate appearance; with lanceolate
lower leaves, and several long narrow leaves in the densely whorled flower-spikes.
Fruits small, long-stalked, 3-warted, with 2–3 long fine teeth at each edge.
Habitat: Widespread but uncommon by ponds and in marshes, by no means
always near the sea, fluctuating from year to year; not in Scotland. June onwards.
548a. ****Marsh Dock,** *R. palustris* Smith, is often somewhat larger and taller,
and goes greenish-yellow or brown with age. It has more spreading branches with
rather more widely spaced whorls of flowers, and larger shorter-toothed fruits
on shorter thicker stalks. More local, and apparently only in England.

549. *****ARGENTINE DOCK**   *R. cuneifolius* Campdera   Pl. 108.   *CTW, p. 711*
A stout floppy perennial, rarely over a foot high, with a creeping woody
rootstock; coarse, leathery, oval root-leaves with wavy margins and narrowed
at the base; and rather small, thick stout flower-spikes arising from the base
of the lower stem-leaves. Fruits with 3 elongated warts. *Habitat:* Naturalised
in dune slacks in SW England and S Wales; a very rare casual elsewhere. July–
August.

550. *****ICELAND PURSLANE**   *Koenigia islandica* L.   Plate 105.   **(CTW†)**
Perhaps our tiniest land plant, a prostrate, sometimes shortly branched annual,
½–2 in. long, much smaller than Water Purslane (420), with oval leaves and minute
white flowers; petals 3, stamens 3. Fruit a 3-sided nut. It can also be confused with
small plants of Blinks (198), which, however, has 5 petals, and narrower, paler
green leaves. *Habitat:* Recently detected on bare damp ground on hills in
N Skye. June–September.

NETTLE FAMILY Urticaceae

551. **PELLITORY OF THE WALL**   *Parietaria diffusa* Mertens & Koch
'*P. officinalis*'   Plate 37.   *CTW, p. 712*
A spreading, hairy perennial, 6–15 in. long, with reddish-brown stems, stalked,
alternate lanceolate, slightly glossy leaves; and clusters of tiny greenish-brown
flowers with pale yellow anthers, forming leafy spikes. *Habitat:* Widespread
and frequent on and by walls and banks; rare in Scotland. June onwards.

552. ****MIND YOUR OWN BUSINESS**   *Helxine soleirolii* Requien
Mother of Thousands, Baby's Tears   Plate 27.   *CTW, p. 713*
A prostrate mat-forming, slightly downy perennial, with thread-like stems;
tiny roundish untoothed evergreen, scarcely stalked, alternate leaves; and minute
solitary, hardly stalked, bright pink flowers, male and female separate. *Habitat:*
A greenhouse plant now widespread on walls and moist banks, especially in the
SW. May–August.

553. SMALL NETTLE *Urtica urens* L. Plate 102. *CTW, p. 713*

Smaller, greener and less hairy than Stinging Nettle (554), also annual, and often branched, with rounder leaves, the lower shorter than their stalks; male and female flowers in much shorter catkins, both on the same plant. *Habitat:* A widespread and locally common weed of light soils. May onwards.

554. STINGING NETTLE *U. dioica* L. Plate 102. *CTW, p. 713*

A tenacious weed, avoided for its coarse stinging hairs, which very rarely in fens do not sting; an unbranched perennial, 2–4 ft. high, often forming extensive patches, with toothed heart-shaped leaves, all longer than their stalks, and thin branched catkins of tiny greenish, rarely purple, flowers, the male and female on different plants. *Habitat:* Widespread and often abundant, even on mountains, but preferring soils rich in nitrogen. June onwards.

HEMP FAMILY Cannabinaceae

555. *HOP *Humulus lupulus* L. Plate 76. *CTW, p. 714*

A roughly hairy perennial climber, with 4-angled annual stems twining clockwise and reaching 15 ft.; and coarsely toothed, usually ivy-like, pale green leaves. Male and female flowers on different plants; both are small and greenish-yellow, the male in branched catkins, the female in short globular heads, which enlarge in fruit to become the cones which are used to bitter beer and so are commoner. *Habitat:* Widespread and locally frequent in hedges and damp thickets but rare in Scotland and Ireland. July–August.

556

ELM FAMILY Ulmaceae

ELMS *Ulmus*

LOFTY DECIDUOUS TREES with rough bark and stalked, roughly downy toothed alternate leaves, varying from pointed oval to lanceolate, often asymmetrical, and turning yellow in autumn; for identification leaves must be taken from typical shoots on the tree, not from suckers. Flowers showing as a thick tuft of reddish stamens on the bare twigs, well before the leaves. Fruit a pale green, notched disc, about ½-in. wide, round the seed; shed in May.

Our Elms vary widely, especially in the Midlands and E England. Seven species or microspecies are recognised, all of which freely produce fertile hybrids, thus making certain identification beyond the Common and Wych Elms often extremely difficult. The others are: *U. stricta* (Aiton) Lindley, *U. coritana* Melville, *U. carpinifolia* Gleditsch (*U. nitens* Moench), *U. plotii* Druce, *U. diversifolia* Melville.

556. COMMON ELM *Ulmus procera* Salisbury Plate 17. *CTW, p. 721*

The commonest Elm in the S, suckering freely, the lower part of the trunk often bushily covered with side shoots; twigs slender, always downy, sometimes with corky wings; leaves broad, pointed oval (Fig.). Fruits deeply notched just above seed, often infertile. *Habitat:* A familiar hedgerow tree, occasionally in copses, thinning out northwards to S Scotland. February–March. '*U. campestris.*'

556a. **Wych Elm,** *U. glabra* Hudson (*U. montana* Stokes) (*CTW, p. 717,*) is a woodland tree with a dome-shaped crown, very rarely suckering; twigs thicker, never corky above; leaves much larger, broad lanceolate narrowed to the shorter stalk, which is often hidden by the overlapping base of one side of the leaf. Fruits shallowly notched, with the seed in the centre; freely fertile. Widespread, but commoner in the N and W, often in rocky limestone woods and by streams, less frequent in hedgerows.

BOG-MYRTLE FAMILY   Myricaceae

557. *BOG MYRTLE   *Myrica gale* L.   Plate 72.   *CTW, p. 725*

A deciduous bush or shrub, 2–4 ft. high, notable for its delightfully fragrant resinous smell, whence the name 'Sweet Gale'; twigs reddish-brown, shiny; leaves grey-green, narrow oval, broader and toothed above, with resinous dots. Flowers in catkins, long orange male and short red female on separate plants. *Habitat:* Widespread and locally common in bogs, fens and wet heathy places, often forming extensive patches. April–May, before the leaves.

BIRCH FAMILY   Betulaceae

558. SILVER BIRCH   *Betula verrucosa* Ehrhart ('*B. alba*')   Pl. 71.   *CTW, 727*

A graceful and elegant tree, rarely very large, easily recognised by its papery peeling black and white bark, the trunk rugged at the base; twigs shining brown, hairless, often with tiny warts; leaves alternate, very pointed oval, toothed, with some teeth larger than others, turning yellow in autumn. Catkins yellowish, the male longer and looser than the female. Fruits with two wings twice as broad as the seed and longer than the style. Often hybridises with the next species. *Habitat:* Widespread and common in woods and on heaths and hills, preferring sandy and gravelly soils, especially in the S. April–May, with the leaves.

558a. **Downy Birch,** *B. pubescens* Ehrhart, has grey or brown bark; trunk not rugged at base; twigs darker, downy and scarcely shining; leaves duller green, less narrowly pointed, downy at least on the veins beneath, with teeth more or less equal, and sometimes with a resinous smell when young. Fruits with wings as broad as the seed and shorter than the style. Prefers wetter conditions, but very often grows with Silver Birch; the common Birch in Scotland, where it may be only a shrub.

559. **DWARF BIRCH   *B. nana* L.   Plate 73.   *CTW, p. 729*

A low spreading undershrub, with downy twigs and very short-stalked, deeply toothed roundish leaves, downy when young. Catkins small, yellowish, erect. Differs from all the smaller mountain Willows (578–581) in having 3-lobed scales, typical of Birches, at the base of each flower in the catkin, and narrow-winged fruits.   *Habitat:* Very local in high moorland bogs in Scotland. June–July.

560. ALDER   *Alnus glutinosa* (L.) Gaertner   Plate 71.   *CTW, p. 729*

A deciduous waterside tree, often quite small and bushy, with purplish leaf and catkin buds that give it a dull purplish appearance in winter; twigs hairless; and leaves alternate, dark green, toothed, roundish, with a blunt or indented tip, rather variable. Male catkins long, hanging, yellowish; female purplish, short, egg-shaped, erect, and finally cone-like, persisting for months. Fruits with two narrow wings.   *Habitat:* Widespread and common by streams and in swampy places, sometimes forming small woods. March–April, before the leaves.

HAZEL FAMILY Corylaceae

561. *HORNBEAM *Carpinus betulus* L. Plate 71. *CTW, p. 731*
A neat, often smallish, deciduous tree, frequently coppiced, with smooth, grey, fluted bark and slightly downy twigs; leaves toothed and pointed oval, rather like Hazel (562), but narrower and hairy only on the main veins below, turning yellow in autumn. Catkins loose, greenish, hanging, the female smaller, with large leafy 3-lobed bracts hiding the small nut-like fruit. *Habitat.* Widespread, but frequent only in SE England, especially in oak-woods; elsewhere in parks and hedgerows. April–May, with the leaves.

562. HAZEL *Corylus avellana* L. Plate 71. *CTW, p. 732*
A tall deciduous shrub, often coppiced, 4–12 ft. high, sometimes suckering, with smooth peeling red-brown bark; beloved for its early 'lambs' tails', the pale lemon-yellow hanging male catkins, which are visible in bud from October onwards. The erect budlike female catkins have bright red styles, twigs, and yield the nuts, or cobs, encased when unripe in a thick green, jaggedly toothed and lobed husk. Leaves pointed oval, toothed, at first downy on both sides; turning yellow in autumn. *Habitat:* Widespread and common in woods, hedgerows and bushy places. January–March, before the leaves.

BEECH FAMILY Fagaceae

563. BEECH *Fagus sylvatica* L. Plate 70. *CTW, p. 733*
A lofty tree, with a massive round trunk and smooth grey bark; leaves pointed oval, wavy edged, silky and tender green when young, later hairy only on the veins below; in autumn turning a brilliant tawny flame-colour and finally coppery brown. Male flowers in a short, stalked greenish tassel, soon falling; female similar but unstalked. Fruit—or mast—a copper-brown 3-sided nut encased in a tough bristly husk; scarce in many years. *Habitat:* Widespread, but only really common as a woodland tree in S England, especially on the chalk; elsewhere mostly planted and in parks or shelter-belts. April–May, with the leaves.

564. OAK *Quercus robur* L. Plate 70. *CTW, p. 736*
Perhaps the best known British tree, with its broad crown, massive trunk and rugged grey-brown bark; leaves oblong, commonly broad at the base, lobed, paler beneath, hairless when mature, the lobes at the base sometimes overlapping the usually very short stalk (Fig.), turning golden-brown in autumn. Catkins greenish-yellow, slender, often numerous, male and female separate. Fruits—acorns—in a scaly cup, on common stalks an inch or more long. Often hybridises with the next species. *Habitat:* Widespread and common in woods and hedgerows, especially on better soils and in the S. April–May, with the leaves.
564*a*. **Durmast Oak or Sessile Oak,** *Q. petraea* (Mattuschka) Lieblein (*Q. sessiliflora* Salisbury), has leaves tapering to the unlobed base (Fig.) on usually longer stalks, and still downy beneath when mature, at least at the base of the veins; and little or no stalk to the acorn. Also widespread, but especially on the acid soils of the N and W, and S and W Ireland, and on light sandy soils in the S and E.
564*b*. ****Turkey Oak,** *Q. cerris* L., has twigs downy when young, and very distinctive longer narrower, more pointed and more deeply jagged, darker green

leaves (Fig.), slightly downy below; and short-stalked bristly acorn-cups. Naturalised on light soils in parts of S England; less commonly elsewhere.

564c. **Sweet Chestnut or Spanish Chestnut, *Castanea sativa* Miller (*CTW*, *p. 734*), has stiffer, much longer catkins, with a most sickly smell; and leaves large, shining, broad lanceolate and sharply toothed (Fig.). The well-known edible nuts

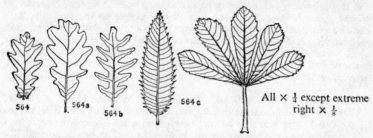

564   564a   564b   564c   All × ¼ except extreme
                                    right × ⅛

are in open green cases covered with long thin spines. Frequently planted and coppiced, and sometimes naturalised, especially on hot, dry, sandy soils in SE England. July. (Not to be confused with the totally different Horse-Chestnut (*Aesculus hippocastanum* L.) (*CTW, p. 403*), which has smooth bark, sticky buds, larger palmate leaves (Fig.), striking 'candles' of white flowers, and chestnut brown nuts, the much prized 'conkers', in a thick fleshy closed case covered with fewer and stouter spines. Common in parks and gardens, the frequent seedling rarely maturing. May–June.)

WILLOW FAMILY   Salicaceae

POPLARS   *Populus*

DECIDUOUS TREES, with broad long-stalked alternate leaves, and small flowers in hanging catkins, which appear before the leaves, the reddish male ones and the greenish female ones on separate trees. The fruiting catkins are woolly from the hairs on the minute seeds, littering the ground when they fall in early summer. Most Poplars sucker freely, and the leaves on these suckers, and sometimes also those produced on the tree in summer, differ from the spring leaves.

565. WHITE POPLAR *Populus alba* L.   Plate 70.   *CTW, p. 740*
A not very tall tree, with numerous black gashes on the smooth pale grey bark, suckering abundantly; young twigs and buds densely covered with cottony white down. Spring leaves on the tree roundish, very coarsely toothed, not lobed, broadest below the middle, soon dark green above, cottony white beneath, becoming greyer and less downy in summer; young summer leaves, and all sucker leaves, deeply palmately lobed, rather maple-like, and more or less persistently cottony white beneath; leaf-stalks scarcely flattened. Scales at the base of each flower in the catkin more or less evenly toothed. *Habitat:* Widespread, frequently planted, sometimes naturalised, especially near the sea. March.

565a. *Grey Poplar, *P. canescens* (Aiton) Smith, is intermediate between White Poplar and Aspen (566), but is usually larger than the former and has greyer down; twigs never so thickly coated; spring leaves broadest above the middle and almost devoid of down in summer; summer and sucker leaves more or less evenly and coarsely toothed, not maple-like; leaf-stalks more flattened; scales deeply and irregularly divided. Scarce in damp woods in the S and E, also not infrequently planted.

566. ASPEN *Populus tremula* L. Plate 70. *CTW, p. 741*

A smallish tree with grey-brown bark, suckering freely; twigs and buds devoid of down, except sometimes when very young. Leaves on the tree thin, dark greyish green, paler beneath, roundish, broadest about the middle, bluntly toothed, soon hairless; leaf-stalks thin and flattened, so that leaves tremble easily in the wind. Sucker leaves deeply palmately lobed, with greyish down beneath. Scales at the base of each flower in the catkin deeply divided. *Habitat:* Widespread, frequent in damp woods and on heaths, especially in the N and W. March.

567. BLACK ITALIAN POPLAR *P.* × *canadensis* Moench Pl. 70. *CTW, 742*

Generally the commonest Black Poplar, a lofty tree, with a long bole, rugged blackish bark, and branches curving upwards to a fan-like crown; sometimes suckering; young twigs slightly angled; buds sticky. Leaves broad, pointed, like a spade at cards, with a clear translucent border, on flattened stalks; appearing after those of other Poplars; turning yellow in autumn. Only male trees are known. *Habitat:* The commonest of several similar Poplars widely planted in parks and hedgerows. April–May. *P. serotina* Hartig.

567a. ****Black Poplar,** *P. nigra* L., is less tall, squatter and more spreading, with branches arching downwards, and large bosses on the shorter mature bole; rarely suckering; young twigs rounded; and leaves smaller with longer, much narrower points. Female trees also occur. Local on rich wet soils, especially by rivers, in the Midlands and E England. March–April.

567b. ****Balsam Poplar,** *P.* × *gileadensis* Rouleau, has smoother bark; numerous suckers; buds and young leaves strongly smelling of balsam; and leaves often much larger, whitish beneath, with no translucent border, their stalks not or hardly flattened. Female trees also occur. One of several similar species sometimes naturalised. March.

WILLOWS, SALLOWS AND OSIERS *Salix*

A GENUS varying from prostrate creeping undershrubs to tall trees, all deciduous, mostly with alternate leaves; nearly always growing at least within reach of moisture. Some of the shrubby, broad-leaved ones are called Sallows or Pussy Willows; Osiers are shrubs with long pliant branches used for basket-work, often with very long narrow leaves. All have their small flowers in catkins, usually short and erect, the male and female on different plants. Male catkins are generally yellow, often white and silky at first, the female grey-green and less noticeable, going silky in fruit. The two kinds of catkin can look so different, especially when there are no leaves and the bushes are far apart, that many people do not realise that they belong to the same species. Many, especially the Pussy Willows, expand their flowers on bare branches well before the leaves, and the male catkins, are then extremely attractive, and known as 'Palm'. Most species have 2 stamens; to count them, and later to see the fruits on the female plants, the individual flowers must be separated in the catkin. A roundish scale will also be found at the base of each flower.

All the Willows hybridise very readily, and indeed some hybrids are more frequent than some species. Nearly 50 hybrids are listed on p. 744 of *CTW*.

KEY TO WILLOWS AND SALLOWS (Nos. 557, 559, 568–581)

TALL OR POLLARDED *tree:* 569; *small tree or large shrub* 568, 570, 571, 572, 573, 574, 575, 576; *bush* 557, 575, 576, 577; *creeping* 577, 580, 581; *undershrub* 559, 577, 578, 579, 580, 581; *with peeling bark* 570.

TWIGS *ridged under bark* 574, 575, 576, 577, 579a; *hairless when young* 557, 568, 569, 571, 576; *downy when mature* 559, 574, 576a; *shining* 568, 571, 576, 578, 579; *with sticky buds* 568.

LEAVES *opposite* 568; *narrow* 569, 570, 571, 572; *very long* 572; *roundish* 559, 580, 581; *downy above when mature* 569a, 575, 577, 578; *hairless above when young* 568, 570, 571, 576, 579, 580; *paler beneath* 568, 569, 570, 571, 576, 579, 580; *shining above* 568, 570, 574, 576, 579, 580; *with a few rusty hairs beneath* 574; *wrinkled* 575, 581; *aromatic* 557, 568.

CATKINS *with reddish or purplish anthers* 557, 571, 574, 578, 579, 580, 581; *with 3-lobed scales* 559; *appearing before leaves* 557, 571, 572, 573, 574, 575, 576a, 577, 578; *appearing with leaves* 568, 569, 570, 576, 578, 579; *appearing after leaves* 559, 579, 580, 581.

HABITAT *mountains only* 559, 578, 579, 580, 581.

568. *BAY WILLOW *Salix pentandra* L. Plate 72. *CTW, p. 752*
A shrub or small tree, with hairless shiny twigs, and fine thick glossy dark green, broad elliptical, toothed leaves, paler beneath, sticky and fragrant when young. Catkins slender, on short leafy stalks. Our only Willow with 5, or rarely more, stamens. Fruits short-stalked, hairless, with short styles. *Habitat:* Frequent, especially by fresh water, in the N, and in N Ireland; occasionally planted elsewhere. May–June, with the leaves.

569. CRACK WILLOW *S. fragilis* L. Plate 72. *CTW, p. 754*
A commonly pollarded riverside Willow, which if left alone becomes a tall tree with branches at a wide angle, grey fissured bark, and hairless twigs that break off easily; leaves long, narrow, toothed, asymmetrical at tip, bright green above, paler beneath, hairless when mature. Catkins slender, on short leafy stalks. Fruits stalked. *Habitat:* Widespread and common by fresh water, thinning out northwards. April, with the leaves.

569a. **White Willow,** *S. alba* L., can be told at a distance by its more upright branches and so narrower crown, when not pollarded, and by its silvery white foliage; rather smoother bark; twigs silky when young, not fragile, orange in a much planted variety; leaves shorter, more finely toothed, often symmetrical at tip, and covered, especially beneath, with silky white hairs; fruits unstalked. Almost as common. April–May.

570. *ALMOND WILLOW *S. triandra* L. Plate 72. *CTW, p. 755*
A tall shrub, 6–15 ft. high, with smooth flaking cinnamon bark, and a smell of almonds; twigs hairless; buds not sticky; leaves lanceolate, rather broad at the base, dark green, hairless, shiny, paler beneath, with persistent stipules at their base. Catkins slender, on short leafy stalks, the male bright yellow. Our only Willow with 3 stamens. Fruits long-stalked, hairless. *Habitat:* Widespread and often frequent by fresh water. April–May, with the leaves.

571. *PURPLE WILLOW *S. purpurea* L. Plate 72. *CTW, p. 757*
A large osier, 6–10 ft. high, beautiful when its neat male catkins are out, with their golden pollen, reddish anthers and dark purple-tipped scales; bark bitter.

E

Leaves almost opposite, at least at the top of the twig, usually lanceolate, broad and toothed at the tip; hairless, dull and slightly bluish above, paler and greyish beneath. Catkins also very often opposite, on short leafy stalks. Our only Willow with 2 stamens which are united to appear as one. Fruits unstalked, silky. *Habitat:* Widespread and locally frequent near fresh water, especially in fens. March–April, before the leaves.

572. OSIER *S. viminalis* L. Plate 72. *CTW, p. 759*

A shrub, 6–15 ft. high, frequently grown for basket-work, with long flexible branches, twigs downy only at first, and very long narrow alternate leaves, sometimes 8–9 in., dark green and hairless above, covered with glistening silky white hairs beneath. Catkins scarcely stalked. Fruits short-stalked, downy, with very long styles. *Habitat:* Widespread and common in moist places. March–April, rather before the leaves. Withy.

573. PUSSY WILLOW *S. caprea* L. Plate 72. *CTW, p. 761*

A tall Sallow, 6–15 ft. high, whose male catkins are the earliest common source of 'palm' in spring; twigs thick, downy only at first, smooth under the bark. Leaves broad, oval, hairless above when mature, but always prominently veined, grey-downy beneath, and soft to the touch. Catkins stout, virtually unstalked; fruits long-stalked, silky, with very short style. *Habitat:* Widespread and frequent in woods and bushy places, often in drier situations than most other Willows. March–April, before the leaves.

574. COMMON SALLOW *S. atrocinerea* Brotero Plate 72. *CTW, p. 762*

The other common source of 'palm' at Easter, differing in its twigs often remaining downy, in having ridges under the bark (best seen if the bark is peeled off a 2–5-year-old twig), and the leaves smaller and narrowed towards the base, rolled at the edges, and usually with at least some minute rust-coloured hairs among the much sparser down beneath, never soft to the touch. *Habitat:* Widespread, common, usually in damp places. March–April, before the leaves.

574a. **Grey Sallow, *S. cinerea* L., is very similar, but has leaves soft to the touch, with no rusty hairs, and mature twigs more thickly covered with down. Sometimes abundant in fens in E England; rare or misrecorded elsewhere.

575. EARED SALLOW *S. aurita* L. Plate 72. *CTW, p. 764*

Smaller in all its parts and more of a bush than the other Sallows, with branches almost at right angles, pale silvery-green, usually downy, rounded, markedly wrinkled leaves, wavy and rolled at the edges, with large and persistent leaf-like stipules at their base. Twigs rather slender, hairless when mature, with ridges under the bark. *Habitat:* Widespread and frequent in damp woods and by water on heaths and moors, especially in the N and W. April–May, before the leaves.

576. *TEA-LEAVED WILLOW *S. phylicifolia* L. Plate 72. *CTW, p. 765*

A tall erect bush or shrub, 3–12 ft. high, the mature twigs reddish and shiny, with ridges under the bark, not downy or sticky; leaves pointed oval to lanceolate, toothed, hairless, not wavy, shiny above, veined and paler beneath. Catkins slender, on short leafy stalks. Fruits long-stalked, downy, with long styles. *Habitat:* Widespread and frequent in hill and mountain districts from the Pennines northwards; in Ireland only in the NW. May–June, usually with the leaves.

576a. *Dark Willow, *S. myrsinifolia* Salisbury, is variable, with more or less downy twigs, thinner darker green leaves, dull above, paler and shiny beneath, and blackening when dried. Fruits hairless. More local in Great Britain, less so in Ireland. *S. nigricans* Smith.

577. CREEPING WILLOW   *S. repens* L.   Plate 73.   *CTW, p. 766*
A very variable bush or undershrub, often under a foot high on dry heaths, but occasionally reaching 6 ft. in fens; our only lowland Willow with a creeping root stock. Stems slender; twigs silky when young, with fine ridges under the bark. Leaves variable, often small, usually untoothed, pointed oval, silky on both sides, sometimes hairless green above. Catkins neat and fat on short leafy stalks. Fruits stalked, with short style.   *Habitat:* Widespread and locally common in damp heaths, fens and dune slacks. April–May, before the leaves.

578. **DOWNY WILLOW   *S. lapponum* L.   Plate 73.   *CTW, p. 767*
A compact grey bush, 1–2 ft. high, differing from 577 also in having no creeping root stock, leaves elliptical, rather large, untoothed and silky, and larger and whiter catkins. Fruits unstalked, downy, with long style.   *Habitat:* Local on moist rock-ledges on mountains in the Lake District and the Highlands. May–June, with the leaves.

578a. ***Woolly Willow, *S. lanata* L., is handsome, with its conspicuous broader woolly silky leaves and large golden male catkins; twigs and buds both stouter; fruits larger, short-stalked, hairless. Very rare in the E Highlands.

579. **WHORTLE-LEAVED WILLOW   *S. myrsinites* L.   Pl. 73.   *CTW, p. 769*
A broad, well branched undershrub, up to a foot high, with twigs downy at first, becoming shiny, smooth under the bark; leaves variable, pointed oval, soon bright green on both sides, with prominent veins, the dead ones often persisting till the following year. Catkins on long leafy stalks, the male purplish; fruits unstalked, downy.   *Habitat:* Very local on wet mountain rocks in Scotland. May–June, with the leaves.

579a. ***Plum-leaved Willow, *S. arbuscula* L., may be more erect, but differs mainly in having its leaves greyish and sometimes slightly downy below, ridges under the bark, and much shorter stalks to the reddish-yellow male catkins. Rare in the Highlands.

580. *LEAST WILLOW   *S. herbacea* L.   Plate 73.   *CTW, p. 769*
A tiny, prostrate undershrub, rarely as much as 2 in. high, whose thin spreading branches normally creep just under the ground and form large open patches. Leaves thin, rounded, hairless, toothed, shining green, slightly paler beneath, with prominent veins. Catkins opposite the last leaf on the shoots on short stalks, with untoothed scales at the base of each flower. Fruits short-stalked, hairless.   *Habitat:* Widespread and frequent on high bare ground and mountain ledges, from the Brecon Beacons northwards, but nearly at sea-level in N Scotland. June, after the leaves.

581. ***NETTED WILLOW, *S. reticulata* L.   Plate 73.   *CTW, p. 770*
An exquisite mat-forming, prostrate undershrub, larger than the last species. Leaves larger, long-stalked, untoothed, dark green and wrinkled, white and beautifully net-veined below. Male catkins bright yellow, on longer stalks. Fruits unstalked, downy.   *Habitat:* Rare on mountain ledges in the Highlands. June, after the leaves.

HEATH FAMILY Ericaceae

582. ***LABRADOR TEA *Ledum groenlandicum* Oeder Pl. 77. *CTW, p. 773*
A broad thick-set evergreen bush, 1–3 ft. high, with rust-coloured down on the twigs and beneath the alternate short-stalked oblong untoothed leaves, which are wrinkled above, with their edges rolled downwards. Flowers in terminal clusters, creamy white. *Habitat:* A very few bushes in a very few mosses in NW England and the S half of Scotland. May–June.

583. **WILD AZALEA *Loiseleuria procumbens* (L.) Desvaux Pl. 24. *CTW, 774*
A prostrate mat-forming hairless evergreen undershrub, with many tiny opposite thick oblong leaves, the margins rolled downwards; young shoots red. Flowers small, with both corolla and calyx pink. *Habitat:* Local on high bare summits and plateaux in the Highlands. May–June.

584. ***MENZIESIA *Phyllodoce caerulea* (L.) Babington
Menziesia caerulea (L.) Swartz Plate 24. *CTW, p. 774*
A heath-like evergreen undershrub, 3–8 in. high, with many alternate short linear rough-edged leaves, which are green below and rather like Crowberry (605), with which it grows. Flowers in small terminal clusters, on slender hairy stalks, nodding, globular, purplish, larger and paler than Bell Heather (593), not persisting in fruit; calyx hairy, with 5 teeth. *Habitat:* Known for 150 years from one small area of heather moor on the Sow of Atholl, Perthshire. June.

585. **ST. DABEOC'S HEATH *Daboecia cantabrica* (Hudson) Koch
Menziesia polyfolia Jussieu Plate 24. *CTW, p. 775*
A hairy, rather straggling, heath-like evergreen undershrub, 1–2 ft. high, with alternate, narrow lanceolate leaves, whitish beneath, the margins rolled downwards. Flowers in short spikes, egg-shaped, nodding, on curving stalks but erect in fruit, pinkish-purple; calyx-teeth 4. *Habitat:* Locally common on heaths and moors in Connemara; rarely established elsewhere. May onwards.

586. **BOG ROSEMARY *Andromeda polifolia* L. Plate 24. *CTW, p. 775*
A hairless evergreen undershrub, usually well under a foot high and straggling in sphagnum moss; leaves linear elliptical, shiny grey-green above, white below, the margins rolled downwards. Flowers few, small, ($\frac{1}{4}$-in. long) stalked, nodding, globular, the corolla and calyx both pink or white, bell-like. *Habitat:* Now very local, owing to draining, in bogs in Wales, the N half of England, S Scotland and Ireland. May–June.

587. ***STRAWBERRY-TREE *Arbutus unedo* L. Plate 77. *CTW, p. 777*
A small evergreen tree, or tall shrub, not infrequently planted, with reddish-brown roughish bark; leaves alternate, thick, lanceolate, slightly toothed, dark green and shiny above. Flowers in drooping clusters, creamy white. Fruit a berry, $\frac{3}{4}$-in. across, warty, turning red as the next year's flowers open. *Habitat:* Very local in rocky woods in Cos. Cork and Kerry and at the W end of L. Gill (Sligo); rarely naturalised elsewhere. August onwards.

588. *BEARBERRY *Arctostaphylos uva-ursi* (L.) Sprengel Pl. 77. *CTW, p. 777*
A prostrate far-trailing mat-forming, almost hairless, evergreen undershrub, with small flat thick untoothed, dark green leaves, paler and more netted beneath,

tapering towards the base. Flowers in clusters, small, globular, white or pinkish. Fruit a shining red berry. Can be told from Cowberry (596) by the leaves being broadest at the tip and by the persistent calyx at the base of the fruits. *Habitat:* Local on rather dry and often bare slopes on moors and mountains from the Peak northwards, and in N and W Ireland. May–June.

589. **BLACK BEARBERRY *Arctous alpinus* (L.) Drude Pl. 77. *CTW, 778***
A prostrate far-spreading deciduous undershrub, often forming wide mats; stems rough with the remains of dead leaves: leaves thin, wrinkled, toothed, tapering to the base, turning a glorious crimson in autumn. Flowers small, globular, white, 2–4 together. Fruit, a black berry. *Habitat:* Very local on hilltops in the N half of Scotland. May–August. *Arctostaphylos alpinus* (L.) Sprengel.

590. LING *Calluna vulgaris* (L.) Hull Plate 24. *CTW, p. 778*
A well-known evergreen undershrub, usually 6–18 in. high, turning huge areas of moorland purple in late summer; leaves numerous, in two opposite rows, rigid, minute, overlapping, linear, sometimes grey with down. Flowers in spikes on numerous branches, small, both corolla and calyx pale purple, rarely white. *Habitat:* Widespread and abundant on heaths, moors and bogs, also in open woods and on old dunes. August–September. Heather.

591. CROSS-LEAVED HEATH *Erica tetralix* L. Plate 24. *CTW, p. 780*
A greyish downy evergreen undershrub, up to a foot high; leaves in whorls of 4, short, linear, fringed with hairs, paler beneath, the margins rolled downwards, sparser under the compact heads of small, drooping, globular, rose-pink flowers. Fruits downy. *Habitat:* Widespread and characteristic of bogs and the wetter parts of heaths. June onwards.
591a. ***Mackay's Heath,** E. *mackaiana* Babington, has the mature twigs hairless; leaves shorter, broader since the hairy margins are less rolled, dark green, hairless above and on the midrib beneath, and growing equally thickly all up the stem; flowers smaller, deeper pink and in a compacter head; calyx-teeth hairy only on the margins; and fruits less downy. Hybridises with Cross-leaved Heath. Confined to wet moors near Roundstone (Galway) and Upper L Nacung (Donegal). July–August.

592. **DORSET HEATH *E. ciliaris* L. Plate 24. *CTW, p. 781***
Sometimes taller and more straggly than Cross-leaved Heath (591), with leaves usually in whorls of 3, broader, greener, hairless above, fringed with longer hairs; flowers in terminal spikes, much larger, curved and narrowed at the tip, rosy-red, with style projecting; and fruits hairless. *Habitat:* Very local on a few damp heaths in Dorset and Cornwall, and on one hillside on Dartmoor. July onwards.

593. BELL HEATHER *E. cinerea* L. Plate 24. *CTW, p. 781*
An evergreen undershrub, up to 18 in. high, with short linear, dark green, often bronzy leaves, the margins rolled down to hide the underside, in whorls of 3 with clusters of smaller leaves at their base. Flowers in heads, or often long spikes, egg-shaped, crimson-purple; calyx hairless, green. Fruits hairless. *Habitat:* Widespread, often abundant on drier heaths and moors. June onwards.

594. **IRISH HEATH *E. mediterranea* L. Plate 24. *CTW, p. 782***
A hairless evergreen undershrub, 2–6 ft. high, with erect branches, and narrow linear spreading leaves, their margins rolled downwards, usually in whorls of 4.

Flowers in a leafy 1-sided spike, oblong, pale purple, with the red-brown anthers slightly protruding. *Habitat:* Very local on wet moors in Mayo and Galway. March–May, and sporadically in winter. '*E. carnea*'.

595. **CORNISH HEATH *E. vagans* L. Plate 24. *CTW, p. 782*

A hairless evergreen undershrub, 1–3 ft. high, with short linear leaves, paler beneath, their margins rolled downwards in whorls of 4–5. Flowers in fat dense leafy spikes, long-stalked, globular, of varying shades of pink or lilac, the chocolate anthers protruding prominently from the open mouth. *Habitat:* Abundant on heaths near the Lizard; one patch at Belcoo, Co. Fermanagh; very rarely naturalised elsewhere. July–September.

596. *COWBERRY *Vaccinium vitis-idaea* L. Plate 77. *CTW, p. 783*

A creeping evergreen undershrub, 6 in. or so high, with twigs round, downy when young; sometimes confused with the more prostrate Bearberry (588). Leaves rather like Box (265), alternate, oval, broadest in the middle, hairless, untoothed, the margins slightly rolled downwards, somewhat leathery, glossy above, paler and dotted beneath. Flowers in small drooping terminal clusters, open-mouthed, white or pinkish; calyx soon falling. Fruit an acid red berry. Hybridises with the next species. *Habitat:* Locally common on moors in the N and W, and in Ireland. May–June.

597. BILBERRY *V. myrtillus* L. Plate 77. *CTW, p. 784*

An erect hairless deciduous undershrub, 9–18 in. high, with angled green twigs; leaves pointed oval, slightly toothed, not leathery, bright green. Flowers solitary or in pairs, globular, drooping, dull, greenish-pink; fruit a small black edible berry, also known as hurt or whort. *Habitat:* Widespread and locally abundant on heaths and moors, and in woods, on acid soils; very local on the E side of England. April–June. Whortleberry, Blaeberry, Huckleberry, Whinberry.

598. **NORTHERN BILBERRY *V. uliginosum* L. Plate 77. *CTW, p. 784*

Grows either as a low, broad bush on ledges, or as straggling stems arising from creeping underground roots. Differs from the last species in having round brownish twigs; smaller, rounder, bluish, waxy, untoothed flat leaves, netted and paler beneath; and pinker flowers, in small clusters; a shy flowerer on moors; berries waxy grey-blue. *Habitat:* Local on high wet moors and rock-ledges in the N. May–June.

599. **CRANBERRY *V. oxycoccus* L. Plate 23. *CTW, p. 785*

Oxycoccus palustris Persoon (incl. *O. microcarpus* Ruprecht)

A prostrate evergreen undershrub, with far creeping, thread-like stems; leaves sparse, alternate, tiny, pointed oval, dark green above, whitish beneath, the margins rolled downwards. Flowers bright pink, with the 4 petals bent back to reveal 8 prominent stamens; 1–4 at the end of a branch, on long stalks, with 2 tiny pink bracts at or below the middle. Fruit a much esteemed round or pear-shaped whitish berry, heavily spotted red or brown; ¼-in. across. *Habitat:* Widespread but local in bogs, especially among sphagnum moss. June–July.

WINTERGREEN FAMILY Pyrolaceae

600. *COMMON WINTERGREEN *Pyrola minor* L. Plate 80. *CTW, p. 787*

A hairless perennial about 6 in. high, with a short spike of bell-shaped, waxy white or pinkish flowers, sometimes taken for a large-flowered Lily of the Valley (989), but with a rosette of much smaller roundish, gently toothed leaves, an inch or so across, and 5-petalled flowers. Style short, straight, often shorter than the stamens (Fig.). *Habitat:* Widespread but local in coniferous woods and on moors and mountain-ledges; rare in the S. June–August.

600*a*. **Greater Wintergreen,** *P. media* Swartz, is generally stouter, with the style very slightly curved, much longer than the stamens, and protruding from the larger flowers (Fig.). Very local in the N, chiefly in pinewoods in E Scotland.

600a 600b
600

600*b*. **Round-leaved Wintergreen,** *P. rotundifolia* L., has still larger, more open and pure white flowers, with a long, much curved style longer than the stamens and petals (Fig.), and rounder leaves. Local in chalk turf, limestone rock ledges, woodland, dune slacks, and fens; very rare in Ireland.

601. **YAVERING BELLS** *Orthilia secunda* (L.) House Pl. 80. *CTW, 789*
Serrated Wintergreen; *Pyrola secunda* L., *Ramischia secunda* (L.) Garcke
Smaller than Common Wintergreen (600), usually 2–4 in. high, with more oval, pointed, toothed, paler green leaves; and smaller bell-shaped greenish-white flowers, all close together on one side of the spike, with the long straight style protruding. *Habitat:* Very scarce in pinewoods and on mountain ledges in the N and W, and very rare on lower ground in N Ireland. July–August.

602. ***ST. OLAF'S CANDLESTICK** *Moneses uniflora* (L.) Gray
One-flowered Wintergreen; *Pyrola uniflora* L. Plate 84. *CTW, p. 789*
A graceful little perennial, with thread-like stems 3–6 in. high, and pale green, toothed, opposite leaves tapering on to the slender stalk. Flowers over ½-in. across, solitary, drooping, open, fragrant, waxy white, with a prominent straight style. *Habitat:* Now very rare in open mossy Scottish pinewoods. June–July.

DIAPENSIA FAMILY Diapensiaceae

603. ***DIAPENSIA** *Diapensia lapponica* L. Plate 77. *CTW†*
A charming low evergreen hairless perennial, growing in dense cushions of untoothed narrow shiny leathery leaves. Flowers solitary, short-stalked, white, rather like a Saxifrage, but with a corolla ½-in. across, 5 petal-like lobes, only 1 style, a 3-lobed stigma, and 3 sepal-like bracts close under the 5 leathery sepals; stalks lengthening and sepals reddening in fruit. *Habitat:* Known only on one bare rocky hill-top in the parish of Arisaig, Inverness-shire. May.

BIRDSNEST FAMILY Monotropaceae

604. **YELLOW BIRDSNEST** *Monotropa hypopitys* L. Plate 36. *CTW, p. 790*
A curious, waxy-looking, pale yellow perennial, later turning brown, with unbranched stems 3–8 in. high, sparsely clad with scale-like leaves. Flowers yellow, tubular, with separate petals, in drooping spikes, erect in fruit. Birds-nest Orchid (1069), near which it may grow, is always brown, with broader erect flower-spikes and lipped flowers. *Habitat:* Local in small patches in woods, especially of beech, and dune slacks in England; rare elsewhere. July–August.

CROWBERRY FAMILY Empetraceae

605. **CROWBERRY* *Empetrum nigrum* L. Plate 77. *CTW, p. 792*
A prostrate trailing, often mat-forming, evergreen undershrub, heath-like but
with flatter shinier leaves spirally up the stem. Flowers minute, pale pinkish, at
the base of the leaves; male and female usually on different plants, except in a
compacter form high on mountains. Fruit a berry, green at first, turning pink,
purple and finally black. *Habitat:* Locally common on moors in the N and W,
and in Ireland. April–May. (Incl. *E. hermaphroditum* (Lange) Hagerup.)

SEA-LAVENDER FAMILY Plumbaginaceae

606. **COMMON SEA-LAVENDER* *Limonium vulgare* Miller
   Statice limonium L.   Plate 8. *CTW, p. 795*
A hairless perennial, 4–12 in. high, that turns some salt-marshes deep lilac in
August, resembling true Lavender (*Lavandula*) only in the colour of its flowers;
with round stems and a rosette of long-stalked, broad lanceolate leaves with
pinnate veins. Flowers small, very closely crowded and overlapping in much
branched, rather flat-topped heads, only at the end of spreading leafless branches,
which usually start well above the middle. *Habitat:* Locally common in many
salt-marshes in England and Wales; rare in Scotland. July onwards.
   606a. ***Lax Sea-Lavender*, *L. humile* Miller, can closely resemble one variety
of the common species, but has stems often angled, and always branched below
the middle; narrower leaves; and flowers well apart, along the whole length of
the longer erecter laxer branches. More local in salt-marshes in Great Britain;
frequent in Ireland.
   606b. ****Alderney Sea-Lavender*, '*L. lychnidifolium*', has leaves broadest at the
tips, with 5–9 unbranched veins, on short stalks; flowering stems branched from
near base, and rather larger flowers. By the sea in Alderney and Jersey.

607. **ROCK SEA-LAVENDER* *L. binervosum* (Smith) Salmon Pl. 8. *CTW, 796*
Very variable, but usually slenderer than Common Sea-Lavender (606), the
normally much smaller neater narrow leaves with 1–3 unbranched veins and
winged stalks; flower-heads smaller; stems branched often well below the middle,
the lowest branches sometimes flowerless. *Habitat:* Widespread and locally
frequent on cliffs and rocks by the sea, occasionally on sand or shingle; Scotland,
only in Galloway. July–September. *Statice binervosa* Smith.

608. ****MATTED SEA-LAVENDER* *L. bellidifolium* (Gouan) Dumortier
   Statice bellidifolia (Gouan) DC.   Plate 8. *CTW, p. 796*
A perennial, 4–6 in. high, much smaller and pinker than Common Sea-
Lavender (606), with the less erect flowering stems branched almost from the
base into numerous zigzag branches, the lower ones always without flowers.
Habitat: Confined to the drier parts of salt-marshes in N Norfolk. July–August.

609. *THRIFT* *Armeria maritima* (Miller) Willdenow Plate 27. *CTW, p. 799*
A tufted perennial, with cushions of rather fleshy, usually 1-veined, linear leaves.
Flowers of every shade of pink, in roundish heads above small broad brown
papery bracts, on leafless usually downy stalks, 2–9 in. high; calyx-teeth with

short bristles. *Habitat:* Widespread and common by the sea; also on mountains. May onwards. Sea Pink.

609a. *****Broad-leaved Thrift,** *A. arenaria* (Persoon) Schultes, is robuster, taller and darker green, with much broader, 3–5-veined leaves, and calyx-teeth ending in very long bristles. Stalks always hairless; bracts large, broad, tapering to a fine point, and forming a prominent hood over the buds. Plentiful in sandy turf in SW Jersey. June–September. *A. plantaginea* Willdenow.

PRIMROSE FAMILY Primulaceae

610. ***BIRDSEYE PRIMROSE** *Primula farinosa* L. Plate 22 *CTW, p. 802*
A charming small perennial, with a rosette of small, pale green, blunt-toothed, narrow lanceolate leaves, broadest near the tip, and white beneath. Flowers lilac-pink with a yellow eye, in an umbel on a leafless stalk 2–6 in. high, with 5 rather narrow petal-like corolla-lobes and pointed calyx-teeth. Fruits cylindrical, stiffly erect. *Habitat:* Locally frequent in damp bare places, mainly on limestone, in N England and S Scotland. May–June. Bonny Birdseye.

611. ****SCOTS PRIMROSE** *P. scotica* Hooker Plate 22. *CTW, p. 802*
Even more of a gem than the last species, a biennial with deeper purple flowers with a rich yellow eye and broader corolla-lobes, on a 1–3-in. stalk which is white with meal, like the smaller, broader, usually untoothed leaves, which are broadest in the middle; calyx swollen, with blunter teeth. *Habitat:* Local in short open coastal turf and dunes, very rarely inland, in N Scotland and Orkney. May–June; July–August.

612. **COWSLIP** *P. veris* L. Plate 40. *CTW, p. 802*
Gay and beloved with its fragrant, deep yellow flowers, orange at the base; a downy perennial, with leaves like Primrose (615) but smaller and abruptly narrowed at the base. Flowers in umbels, drooping usually to one side, on leafless stalks 3–8 in. high; calyx pale green, inflated. *Habitat:* Widespread and locally abundant in grassland, mostly on chalk, limestone, or clay, thinning out northwards. April–May.

613. ***FALSE OXLIP** *P. veris × vulgaris* Plate 40. *CTW, p. 803*
The hybrid between the Cowslip (612) and the Primrose (615), very often confused with the true Oxlip (614), from which it differs in never growing in masses, and in having a shorter stem, leaves more gradually tapered to the base, umbels not 1-sided, and flowers deeper yellow, especially in the centre, with a more ridged calyx, and folds in the throat of the corolla tube. From the Cowslip it can be known by its larger, flatter, paler yellow flowers, and leaves tapered to the base; and from the occasional umbelled Primrose by its smaller, deeper yellow flowers on shorter stalks, and more stalked leaves. *Habitat:* A few plants are sometimes found where Primroses and Cowslips grow together. April–May.

614. ****OXLIP** *P. elatior* (L.) Hill Plate 40. *CTW, p. 803*
Has flowers in a 1-sided, drooping umbel like Cowslip (612), but larger and pale yellow like small Primroses (615), on a common stalk up to a foot high, corolla tube without folds in the throat. Leaves abruptly narrowed at the base like Cowslip, but larger. Hybridises with both Cowslip and Primrose. Often confused with the False Oxlip (613), and the occasional umbelled Primrose.

Habitat: Common in dampish woods on clay on the borders of Suffolk, Essex, Cambs. and Beds., where it largely replaces Primrose. April–May.

615. PRIMROSE *P. vulgaris* Hudson   Plate 40.   *CTW, p. 804*
A universal favourite, a low perennial, with crinkly lanceolate leaves, softly downy beneath. Flowers solitary, pale yellow, rarely pink, with a deep yellow eye and honey-guides, over an inch across, on long shaggy stalks. Occasionally the flower-stalks form a spreading umbel on a single extended fatter common stalk. *Habitat:* Widespread and sometimes abundant in woods and scrub, and on banks, sea cliffs and mountains; rare near large towns. March–May, and sporadically in winter.

616. **WATER VIOLET *Hottonia palustris* L.   Plate 94.   *CTW, p. 804*
A graceful floating, almost hairless, pale green perennial, with whorls of submerged narrowly pinnate leaves. The leafless spikes of pale lilac-white flowers with 5 petal-like corolla-lobes and a yellow throat project above the surface. *Habitat:* Widespread but local in ditches and ponds; rare in Scotland and Ireland. May–June.

617. ***SOWBREAD *Cyclamen hederifolium* Aiton   Plate 32.   *CTW, p. 805*
A low, almost hairless perennial, whose tuft of thick toothed, heart-shaped root-leaves, dark green with whitish markings and often purple beneath, appear after the first of the nodding scentless pink or white flowers on leafless 3-in. stems; corolla with 5 petal-like lobes, an inch long, distinctively bent right back and up like the fat indoor hybrid Cyclamens. Fruits on spiral stalks eventually burying themselves. *Habitat:* In a very few woods and hedge-banks, chiefly in the S. August–September. *C. neapolitanum* Tenore, '*C. europaeum*'.

618. YELLOW PIMPERNEL *Lysimachia nemorum* L.   Pl. 40.   *CTW, p. 806*
A slender creeping hairless perennial, with solitary, pimpernel-like yellow flowers, open in fine weather, on thin stalks usually longer than the opposite, pointed oval leaves; calyx-teeth very narrow. Fruits shorter than calyx. *Habitat:* Widespread and frequent in dampish woods. May onwards.

619. CREEPING JENNY *L. nummularia* L.   Plate 40.   *CTW, p. 806*
A frequent plant of cottage gardens, differing from the last species in having blunter leaves closer together, and larger, paler yellow, more bell-like flowers with broader calyx-teeth on usually shorter, stouter stalks. Fruit never observed in Britain. *Habitat:* Widespread and frequent in moist woods and wet grassy places, rarer in the N and Ireland. June–August. Herb Tuppence, Pennywort.

620. YELLOW LOOSESTRIFE *L. vulgaris* L.   Plate 40.   *CTW, p. 806*
A downy perennial, 2–4 ft. high, with broad lanceolate, sometimes black-dotted leaves 2–4 together, on very short stalks. Flowers yellow, in conspicuous leafy branched terminal clusters, the 5 pointed petal-like corolla-lobes hairless at the edge; calyx-teeth hairy at the reddish edges, no longer than the fruit; stamens 5, red. *Habitat:* Widespread and locally frequent in wet herbage, especially by rivers and ponds and in fens, thinning out northwards. July–August.

620a. *****Dotted Loosestrife**, *L. punctata* L., is shorter, downier and less or not branched, the leaves rather longer-stalked, with hairy margins, never black-dotted; flowers larger, paler, hairy at the edge, on longer stalks, with very narrow, all-green hairy calyx-teeth, longer than the fruit. Rarely naturalised.

621. **TUFTED LOOSESTRIFE *Naumburgia thyrsiflora* (L.) Reichenbach
Lysimachia thyrsiflora L. Plate 59. *CTW, p. 808*
An almost hairless creeping perennial, with unbranched stems 1–2 ft. high and pairs of short dense stalked spikes of small feathery yellow flowers with prominent stamens, at the base of the longer unstalked lanceolate leaves, two-thirds of the way up the stem, with more leaves at the top. *Habitat:* Local in fens and by lakes in the N; rare elsewhere. June–July.

622. **CHICKWEED WINTERGREEN *Trientalis europaea* L. Pl. 80. *CTW, 808*
Neither a Chickweed nor a Wintergreen, a delicate little perennial, about one-third of a foot high (hence *Trientalis*), with a whorl of thin broad lanceolate pale green leaves towards the top of the single slender unbranched stem, surmounted by a loose umbel of a few long-stalked white or pale pink 5–9 petalled, flowers, slightly reminiscent of small Wood Anemones (8). Fruit globular, dry. *Habitat:* Locally common in pinewoods and on moors in Scotland; rare in N England. June–July.

623. *BOG PIMPERNEL *Anagallis tenella* (L.) L. Plate 23. *CTW, p. 809*
A charming slender hairless prostrate, often mat-forming perennial, with short-stalked opposite, ¼-in. oval leaves much shorter than the long thin stalks of the larger bell-shaped veined pink flowers, which open in the sun. *Habitat:* Widespread, local in damp short turf and in fens, often among moss. June–Aug.

624. SCARLET PIMPERNEL *A. arvensis* L. Plate 26. *CTW, p. 809*
A favourite little annual known as the Poor Man's Weatherglass because its flowers close when the sun goes in; low, usually prostrate, almost hairless, with square stems and pointed oval unstalked leaves, usually in pairs but sometimes, especially later in the year, in whorls. Flowers vermilion, with a purple eye, but sometimes pink, flesh, maroon, lilac or blue, the petals fringed with hairs, on turned-down stalks longer than the leaves. Fruits 5-veined. *Habitat:* Widespread and common on bare and disturbed ground and on dunes. June onwards.
624*a*. **Blue Pimpernel**, *A. foemina* Miller, is often confused with the blue variety of the Scarlet Pimpernel, but has its petal-like corolla-lobes narrower, hairless and always blue, concealed by the calyx-teeth in bud, and flower- and fruit-stalks never longer than the leaves; and fruits 5–8-veined. Uncommon.

625. **CHAFFWEED *Centunculus minimus* L. Plate 105. *CTW, p. 810*
A tiny hairless annual, often unbranched and under an inch high, rarely over 2 in.; looking rather like a very dwarf erect Scarlet Pimpernel (624), with minute white or pink flowers on very short stalks, solitary at the base of the mostly alternate stem-leaves, and hidden by the long narrow calyx-teeth. Fruits pinkish, like a miniature apple. Our only plant with a thin black line round all or most of the under edge of the leaf. *Habitat:* Widespread but local on bare sandy ground on heaths or in woodland rides. June–August.

626. SEA MILKWORT *Glaux maritima* L. Plate 27. *CTW, p. 811*
A small usually prostrate, hairless, pale green perennial, with solitary small pale pink petalless flowers at the base of the fleshy, elliptic or oval, opposite leaves along the stem. Petal-like calyx-lobes and stamens 5. Fruits dark brown. *Habitat:* Widespread, frequent in and by drier salt-marshes. June–July.

627. *BROOKWEED   *Samolus valerandi* L.   Plate 87.   *CTW, p. 811*

A little or unbranched, hairless, pale green perennial, 2–10 in. high, with spikes of small white flowers superficially rather like a Crucifer, but with 5 petals joined halfway; flower-stalks long, with a tiny bract about the middle. Stems leafy, arising out of a basal rosette of oval leaves. Fruits globular, shorter than the 5-toothed calyx. *Habitat:* Widespread but local in marshy meadows and ditches, usually near the sea. June–August.

BUDDLEIA FAMILY   Loganiaceae

628. **BUDDLEIA   *Buddleja davidii* Franchet   Plate 12.   *CTW, p. 812*

A deciduous shrub, 3–10 ft. high, well known in gardens and for its attractiveness to butterflies, with long dense spikes of heavily scented mauve flowers at the end of long branches. Leaves up to 10 in. long, opposite, toothed, and variable but usually lanceolate, downy white beneath. *Habitat:* Now frequent on walls, railway banks and waste sites, and in quarries, mainly in the S. July onwards.

OLIVE FAMILY   Oleaceae

629. ASH   *Fraxinus excelsior* L.   Plate 70.   *CTW, p. 813*

A lofty deciduous tree, with smooth grey bark gradually becoming rugged; apart from Elder (820), our only native tree with opposite pinnate leaves. Buds black; leaves 6–10 in. long, with toothed lanceolate dark green leaflets. Flowers appearing as tufts of purplish-black stamens, soon turning greenish. Fruits an inch or so long, with a long narrow wing on one side of the seed, hanging like a bunch of keys. *Habitat:* Widespread and common in woods and hedgerows, especially on limestone. April–May, before the leaves.

630. PRIVET   *Ligustrum vulgare* L.   Plate 74.   *CTW, p. 814*   )

A half-evergreen shrub, 4–8 ft. high, with young twigs faintly downy and opposite untoothed thick hairless lanceolate leaves, often bronzing in winter. Flowers in short fat spikes, strong-smelling, white or very rarely yellow, with the tube of the corolla equalling the petal-like lobes. Fruit a shiny black berry. The Privet commonly planted in gardens and hedges is the usually more completely evergreen Japanese Privet (*L. ovalifolium* Hasskarl), with larger and much broader leaves, young twigs not downy, and the corolla-tube much longer than the lobes. *Habitat:* Frequent in thickets and similar places in England and Wales, especially on chalk or limestone; uncommon elsewhere. June–July.

PERIWINKLE FAMILY   Apocynaceae

631. **GREATER PERIWINKLE   *Vinca major* L.   Plate 6.   *CTW, p. 815*

An almost hairless, evergreen undershrub, common in gardens, with its old stems trailing and rooting at the tip, and broad lanceolate, stalked, rather leathery, dark green, opposite leaves. Flowers up to 2 in. across, stalked, usually solitary, violet, towards the top of shorter erect young stems; calyx-teeth narrow, hairy on the margins. *Habitat:* Usually on grass verges outside gardens. March–July.

631*a.* **Lesser Periwinkle, *V. minor* L., is smaller and prostrate, with thinner, wirier stems rooting at intervals; leaves much narrower, shorter stalked; and flowers half the size, the calyx-teeth broader and hairless. More often on shady banks and in woods away from houses. April–July.

GENTIAN FAMILY   Gentianaceae

632. **SLENDER CICENDIA *Cicendia filiformis* (L.) Delarbre Pl. 40. *CTW, 817*

A tiny, very slender, upright annual, 1–3 in. high, with few or no erect branches and small linear leaves. Flowers solitary, on very long stalks, with 4 broad yellow petal-like corolla-lobes open only in the sun, 4 short broad calyx-teeth and 4 stamens.   *Habitat:* Very local in damp sandy places S of the Thames, and in W Wales and SW Ireland. July–August.

633. ***GUERNSEY CENTAURY   *Exaculum pusillum* (Lamarck) Caruel
Cicendia pusilla (Lam.) Grisebach   Plate 22.   *CTW, p. 817*

Usually even smaller than the last species, with branches nearly at right angles, grey leaves, fawn-pink flowers and long narrow calyx-teeth, not keeled as in the pinker dwarf form of the next species.   *Habitat:* Very rare in damp seaside turf in N Guernsey. August.

634. *SLENDER CENTAURY   *Centaurium pulchelium* (Swartz) Druce
                                 Plate 22.   *CTW, p. 818*

Generally slenderer and more open than Common Centaury (635), often well branched from the base, with no basal rosette at flowering time, but sometimes reduced to a single tiny 1-flowered stem. Flowers smaller, darker red, stalked, wide apart, usually with 5 narrow petal-like corolla-lobes; calyx about equalling the fruit.   *Habitat:* Widespread but local in dampish grassy places, clayey woodland rides and the drier parts of salt-marshes. Rare in Scotland and Ireland. June–September.

    634a. *****Channel Centaury**, *C. tenuiflorum* (Hoffmansegg & Link) Fritsch, is stouter, with broader leaves. Its flowers grow much closer together, with all the branches erect, not spreading, and starting above the middle of the stem, making a flat-topped cluster. Known only from a clayey cliff in Dorset and a salt-marsh in the Isle of Wight.

635. COMMON CENTAURY   *C. erythraea* Rafn   Plate 22.   *CTW, p. 819*

A variable hairless annual, 2–12 in. high, occasionally reduced to a cushion, having at flowering time a basal rosette of pointed oval, prominently 3–7-veined leaves, and a few pairs up the stem. Flowers unstalked, pink, in terminal clusters on short branches; stamens joined to the top of the corolla-tube; calyx with 5 long narrow keeled teeth, shorter than the corolla tube or fruit.   *Habitat:* Widespread and locally common in poor, dry grassy places, and on dunes, thinning out northwards. June onwards. '*C. minus*', '*Erythraea centaurium*'.

    635a. ****Seaside Centaury**, *C. littorale* (Turner) Gilmour (incl. *C. turneri* (Wheldon & Salmon) Butcher)) is usually smaller and has thicker, more leathery, narrow strap-shaped, indistinctly 3-veined leaves, and larger, intenser bluish-pink flowers. Local in sandy places by the sea in NW England, SW Scotland, Holy Island (Northumberland) and Co. Londonderry. July–August.

636. **DUMPY CENTAURY *C. capitatum* (Willdenow) Borbás Pl. 22. *CTW, 819*

Only certainly distinguishable from stunted forms of Common Centaury (635) by the position of the stamens, for it is our only Centaury in which they are separate to the base of the corolla-tube, which is usually shorter than the calyx. It usually grows in a compact cushion, sometimes low and thick-set, with the flowers always in a dense cluster. *Habitat:* Very local on dry cliffs or chalk turf, usually near the sea, in England and Wales. July–August.

637. ***PERENNIAL CENTAURY** *C. scilloides* (L.) Sampaio Pl. 22. *CTW, 820*
   C. portense (Brotero) Butcher, *Erythraea portensis* (B.) Hoffmansegg & Link
   Our only perennial Centaury, with numerous more or less prostrate slender stems, some not flowering, and short roundish leaves, the lower stalked. Flowers large, stalked, pink, in few-flowered heads on erecter stems. *Habitat:* Very rare in maritime turf in N Cornwall and N Pembrokeshire. July–August.

638. **YELLOW-WORT** *Blackstonia perfoliata* (L.) Hudson Pl. 40. *CTW, 821*
   In some ways the yellow counterpart of Common Centaury (635), but the whole plant is waxy-grey, with erect branches at the top of the stem, and its leaves are broader and, except for the lowest, united at the base. Flowers larger, usually fewer, with their parts usually each about 8. *Habitat:* Widespread and fairly frequent in England, Wales and S Ireland in chalk and limestone turf and on dunes. June onwards.

639. **MARSH GENTIAN** *Gentiana pneumonanthe* L. Pl. 12. *CTW, p. 822*
   A striking flower, whose 1–2-in. azure trumpets, streaked with green outside, resemble those of the well known alpine and rockery *G. acaulis* L.; a weak hairless perennial, with opposite linear leaves, and flowers usually solitary on leafy stems 3–9 in. high. *Habitat:* Widespread but very local and decreasing on damp acid heaths (not in marshes) in England and Wales. July–September.

640. ***SPRING GENTIAN** *G. verna* L. Plate 3. *CTW, p. 822*
   A favourite 'alpine', well known for its intense blue flowers, nearly an inch across, solitary on short erect stems an inch or two high; a hairless perennial with a rosette of small oval leaves. *Habitat:* Very rare in limestone turf in N Pennines; more plentiful in the Burren. April–June.

641. ***ALPINE GENTIAN** *G. nivalis* L. Plate 3. *CTW, p. 822*
   A small slender annual, 1–4 in. high, often unbranched, and with flowers of the same intense blue as the last species but much smaller. *Habitat:* Very rare, high up on a very few mountains in the Highlands. July–August.

642. *FIELD GENTIAN** *Gentianella campestris* (L.) Smith Plate 4. *CTW, p. 823*
   Gentiana campestris L. (incl. *Gentianella baltica* (Murbeck) Smith)
   Often confused with the next species, but is generally taller and bushier, with larger, paler, lilac flowers their parts nearly always in fours, the two outer calyx-teeth much larger and broader and overlapping the two inner ones. *Habitat:* Widespread and locally frequent in grassland, especially in hills and among dunes, but very scarce in the S. July onwards.

643. **FELWORT** *G. amarella* (L.) Smith Plate 4. *CTW, p. 825*
   Gentiana amarella L.
   A low hairless, often purplish, biennial, or occasionally annual Gentian, 2–9 in. high, with lanceolate leaves. Flowers in spikes, dull purple, bell-shaped, their parts usually in fives, the narrow and more or less equal calyx-teeth shorter than the corolla tube, which has a fringe of hairs inside. *Habitat:* Widespread, locally frequent, mostly in chalk and limestone turf and on dunes. August–September.
   643a. **Chiltern Gentian**, *G. germanica* (Willdenow) Börner (*Gentiana*

germanica Willd.), is stouter and has broader leaves and much larger, showier, more oblong and openly bell-shaped flowers, of a somewhat clearer purple; calyx not more than half the length of the corolla-tube, 2 teeth broader than the other 3. Very locally frequent on chalk downs, rare except in the Chilterns.

643*b*. **Scottish Gentian, *G. septentrionalis* (Druce) Warburg, is smaller, with flowers usually whitish within and reddish or brownish outside, and 5 unequal calyx-teeth nearly as long as the corolla-tube. Sandy turf and dune slacks near the sea in N Scotland. July–August.

643*c*. **Early Gentian, *G. anglica* (Pugsley) Warburg, differs chiefly in being over before any other Gentian has started to flower, but is also generally much smaller than Felwort, with the lower leaves narrower; the flowers mostly long-stalked and the often 4 calyx-teeth unequal. Very local on chalk downs S of the Thames. May–June.

643*d*. ***Welsh Gentian, *G. uliginosa* (Willdenow) Smith, is rarely over 3 in., and always annual, so that the seed-leaves are still the lowest pair of green leaves when the dull purple flowers are out; branches slender, erect, with long gaps between the leaves; calyx-teeth unequal, some being broader, thus mimicking Field Gentian (642). Very rare on dunes in S Wales.

BOGBEAN FAMILY   Menyanthaceae

644. *BOGBEAN   *Menyanthes trifoliata* L.   Plate 69.   *CTW, p. 827*
A distinctive, far creeping aquatic perennial, with large hairless trifoliate leaves and conspicuous spikes of white flowers, pink outside, with 5 petals fringed inside with white hairs like Turkish towelling; both projecting above the water. *Habitat:* Widespread, local in fens, swamps, and shallow water. May–June. Buckbean.

645. **FRINGED WATER-LILY   *Nymphoides peltata* (Gmelin) Kuntze
Limnanthemum nymphaeoides (L.) Link   Plate 59.   *CTW, p. 827*
With its floating leaves and flowers looks superficially like a Yellow Water-Lily (33), but has small rounded, shallowly toothed leaves, purple below and sometimes purple-spotted above; and flowers with 5 yellow fringed petal-like corolla-lobes.   *Habitat:* Local but spreading in quiet water in the S. July–August.

JACOB'S LADDER FAMILY   Polemoniaceae

646. **JACOB'S LADDER   *Polemonium caeruleum* L.   Plate 12.   *CTW, p. 828*
A beautiful perennial, 1–2 ft. high, with spikes of wide open, inch-wide bright blue flowers, brown at the base; 5 petal-like corolla-lobes; and alternate pinnate leaves, the leaflets narrow.   *Habitat:* Very local in stony places on limestone in N England and N Wales; elsewhere a rare escape. June–July.

BORAGE FAMILY   Boraginaceae

ALL OUR MEMBERS of this family have alternate, undivided leaves, and all but one are roughly hairy. Flowers usually in 1-sided spikes, which are tightly curled at first, like a scorpion's tail, and gradually unroll; buds opening blue; corolla and calyx with parts in 5's. Fruits consisting of 4 nutlets surrounded by the calyx.

647. HOUNDSTONGUE   *Cynoglossum officinale* L.   Plate 37.   *CTW, p. 830*
A softly downy grey perennial, 1–2 ft. high, with a normally strong mousy smell when handled; leaves broad lanceolate. Flowers rather small, maroon, with

velvety scales closing the mouth. Fruits rather flattened, covered with short hooked spines and so readily adhering to clothing, and with a thickened flange *Habitat:* Widespread but rather local in bare dry chalky or sandy turf and on dunes. June–August.

647*a*. ***Green Houndstongue, *C. germanicum* Jacquin ('*C. montanum*') does not smell, is less stiff, and has broader thinner shiny green leaves, nearly hairless above, and smaller paler shorter-stalked flowers. It can look very like shade forms of the last species, which may be much less downy, but its fruits have no thickened flange. Now rare, except near Mickleham, Surrey. May–July.

648. ***BLUE-EYED MARY *Omphalodes verna* Moench Pl. 13. *CTW, p. 831*

A low, rather slender, slightly downy, creeping perennial, 3–6 in. high, often growing in wide patches, with long-stalked thin, pointed oval, fresh green leaves. Flowers in loose spikes, like large bright blue Forgetmenots (657), but the scales closing the throat are not notched. *Habitat:* A rare escape. March–May.

649. ***MADWORT *Asperugo procumbens* L. Plate 7. *CTW, p. 832*

A prostrate hairy, almost prickly annual, with angled stems, lanceolate leaves, and clusters of 1–3 tiny blue flowers on short down-turned stalks. The calyx enlarges into a prominent leaf-like covering for the fruit. *Habitat:* A casual, very rarely naturalised in arable fields. May–June; August–September.

650. COMMON COMFREY *Symphytum officinale* L. Plate 94. *CTW, p. 833*

A bushy, roughly hairy perennial, 2–3 ft. high, with broad lanceolate leaves running down on to the winged stem, the root ones often large. Flowers bell-like, perhaps most often white, but frequently cream, blue, mauve, purple, pink or crimson; calyx-teeth pointed, at least equalling the tube. Nutlets shining. *Habitat:* Widespread and frequent in ditches and on river banks. May onwards.

650 × 650*a*. *Russian Comfrey, *S.* × *uplandicum* Nyman (incl. '*S. peregrinum*') a fodder plant, is not infrequent by dry roadsides.

650*a*. ***Prickly Comfrey, *S. asperum* Lepechin, the tallest and prickliest of our Comfreys, with upper leaves short-stalked and not running down on to the stem; flowers smaller, usually blue; calyx-teeth blunt, enlarging in fruit, which is rare in Britain; and nutlets rough. An escape, occasionally established in drier places. June onwards.

650*b*. **Soft Comfrey, *S. orientale* L., is smaller, paler green and earlier-flowering, with less rough hairs, rounder upper leaves, always white flowers, calyx with blunt teeth only half the length of the tube, and rough nutlets. Another uncommon escape in dry places. April–May.

650*c*. **Tuberous Comfrey, *S. tuberosum* L., is smaller and rougher than Soft Comfrey, with the stem sometimes unbranched; the middle leaves the longest. Flowers always cream; and calyx with pointed teeth three times as long as the tube. Local in shady places, commoner in the N. June–July.

651. *BORAGE *Borago officinalis* L. Plate 13. *CTW, p. 835*

A stout, roughly hairy annual, 1–2 ft. high, with oval leaves and loose spikes of wide open, bright blue flowers, nearly an inch across, with narrow petal-like corolla-lobes alternating with the narrower calyx-teeth, and a prominent column of dark maroon anthers, slightly recalling Bittersweet (673). The juice tastes and smells of cucumber, whence its use in flavouring cups. *Habitat:* Occasional, usually near houses. June onwards.

652. **ABRAHAM, ISAAC AND JACOB   *Trachystemon orientalis* (L.) Don
                                                    Plate 13.   *CTW, p. 835.*
A roughly hairy perennial, with a thick stem up to a foot high, growing in patches, and with long-stalked broad heart-shaped root-leaves. Flowers in broad, branched, leafy clusters, the bluish-violet petals flush back like a jester's cap and twisted, leaving a central pillar of dark-tipped mauve stamens, like Borage (651); if picked, they come forward again and then appear as in Plate 13. *Habitat*: A rare escape in England. March–April, before the leaves.

653. *GREEN ALKANET   *Pentaglottis sempervirens* (L.) Tausch
     Anchusa sempervirens L.   Plate 13.   *CTW, p. 836*
A tufted, roughly hairy perennial, 1–2 ft. high, with small stalked clusters of flat white-eyed, bright blue flowers, rather like a large Forgetmenot or Speedwell, at the base of the broad, pointed oval, net-veined leaves, the lower stalked. Calyx bluntly toothed to half-way. *Habitat:* Not infrequent near gardens, sometimes in hedge-banks. April onwards.

654. SMALL BUGLOSS   *Lycopsis arvensis* L.   Plate 13.   *CTW, p. 836*
An erect bristly annual, up to a foot high, with wavy lanceolate leaves and small blue flowers which are the only ones of the family to have their corolla-tube kinked at the base; calyx with lanceolate teeth, hardly enlarging but much exceeding the fruit. *Habitat:* Widespread and locally frequent in open places on light soils. April onwards.

655. **COMMON LUNGWORT   *Pulmonaria officinalis* L.   Pl. 13.   *CTW, 837*
A roughly downy perennial, with unbranched stems 6–12 in. high, and long-stalked broad, pointed oval, usually pale-spotted root-leaves, abruptly narrowed at the base; stem-leaves unstalked. Flowers in small terminal clusters, pink, often turning bluer; calyx with short broad teeth. Nutlets egg-shaped, pointed. *Habitat:* Naturalised in woods and hedge-banks, mainly in the S. March–May.

655a. **Joseph and Mary, *P. longifolia* (Bastard) Boreau, has softer and weaker hairs; root-leaves narrower, tapering gradually to the base and enlarging greatly after flowering; upper leaves sometimes slightly clasping; flowers rather smaller, the calyx-teeth longer and narrower; and nutlets narrower. Local in bushy places, Hants, Dorset and Isle of Wight, April–May. '*P. angustifolia*'.

656. WATER FORGETMENOT   *Myosotis scorpioides* L.   Pl. 11.   *CTW, 839*
A pale green creeping perennial, a foot or so high, with appressed hairs on the angular stems and unstalked oblong leaves. Flowers ¼-in., cobalt blue, occasionally remaining pink, with white honey-guides and a yellow eye, like garden Forgetmenots; petal-like corolla-lobes flat; calyx short-toothed, with appressed hairs, shorter than the fruit-stalks. Spikes elongating in fruit. *Habitat:* Widespread, common in wet places. June onwards. *M. palustris* (L.) Hill.

656a. Creeping Water Forgetmenot, *M. secunda* Murray (*M. repens* Hooker), has numerous leafy runners, stems with hairs spreading below but appressed above; flowers ⅕-in., in spikes leafy below; calyx toothed to at least half-way; and very much longer fruit-stalks, the lowest more or less turned down. Prefers peaty acid soils and hilly districts.

656b. **Northern Water Forgetmenot, *M. brevifolia* Salmon, is smaller, with all hairs appressed; short stubby dark green leaves; very pale flowers, ⅕-in.; and calyx toothed to half-way or more with broad blunt teeth. Local in the N Pennines and S Lowlands.

656c. **Tufted Forgetmenot,** *M. caespitosa* Schultz, is tufted, sometimes annual, branched from lower down, hairless or with all hairs appressed, and with nearly rounded stems; flowers ⅛-in.; and calyx toothed to less than half-way with pointed teeth, and much shorter than the fruit-stalks. Quite common.

656d. *****Jersey Forgetmenot,** *M. sicula* Gussone, is a much smaller, often half-prostrate hairless annual, with slender spreading branches; ⅛-in., pale blue, saucer-shaped flowers in leafless spikes; calyx toothed to half-way, the teeth markedly oblong and blunt; and short fruit-stalks. By one or two ponds in Jersey. April–June.

657. ***WOOD FORGETMENOT** *M. sylvatica* Hoffmann Pl. 13. *CTW, 841*

A hairy perennial, up to a foot high, often grown, with deeper sky-blue flowers, as a biennial in gardens; leaves oblong. Flowers pale blue, far larger and usually flatter than Common Forgetmenot (658), the petal-like corolla-lobes usually twice as long as the tube, which is at least as long as the more deeply toothed calyx, which has spreading hooked hairs; can be told from luxuriant shade forms of Common Forgetmenot by the style being longer than the calyx-tube. Fruit-stalks spreading, longer than calyx. Nutlets dark brown. *Habitat:* Widespread; very local, though often plentiful, in woods; also frequent as a garden escape. April–June.

657a. *****Alpine Forgetmenot,** *M. alpestris* Schmidt, is smaller and stiffer, with delicately scented, richer blue flowers; spikes hardly elongating in fruit; fruit-stalks erect, thicker and no longer than the calyx, which has only very few hooked hairs; and nutlets black. Very rare but locally abundant in limestone turf in Teesdale and on ledges on and by Ben Lawers. July–August.

658. **COMMON FORGETMENOT** *M. arvensis* (L.) Hill Pl. 7. *CTW, p. 842*

Much the commonest wild Forgetmenot, softly hairy, normally annual, 3–10 in. high, with oblong leaves. Flowers in forked spikes, ⅛–⅛-in., grey-blue or pinkish, usually saucer-shaped, the petal-like corolla-lobes shorter than the tube; style shorter than calyx-tube. Fruit-stalks longer than the calyx which has numerous spreading hooked hairs. *Habitat:* Widespread and common in dry bare or disturbed ground, in woods and on dunes. April onwards.

659. **CHANGING FORGETMENOT** *M. discolor* Persoon Pl. 61. *CTW, 842*

Smaller and slenderer than 658, with its scarcely stalked flowers 1/10-in. and yellow or creamy when they first open, normally turning grey-blue; mature corolla-tube twice as long as calyx. Fruit-stalks shorter than the calyx, whose teeth are incurved in fruit. *Habitat:* Widespread and locally frequent in rather bare places, especially on light soils. May onwards. *M. versicolor* Smith.

660. **EARLY FORGETMENOT** *M. hispida* Schlechtendahl Pl. 7. *CTW, 843*

Usually smaller than the last species and only 1–2 in. high, with its tiny flowers always sky-blue, the corolla-tube shorter than the longer-stalked calyx, whose longer teeth are spreading in fruit. *Habitat:* Widespread and locally frequent in bare dry places on light soils. April–June '*M. collina*'.

661. ****PURPLE GROMWELL** *Buglossoides purpurocaerulea* (L.) Johnston
Lithospermum purpurocaeruleum L. Plate 13. *CTW, p. 844*

An unbranched downy perennial, 9–15 in. high, with non-flowering stems rooting at the tip; and numerous narrow lanceolate, dark green leaves, paler beneath. Flowers in leafy terminal clusters, reddish-purple at first, becoming deep blue, ½ in. *Habitat:* Very local on cliffs and limestone scrub and hedgebanks in SW England and Wales; a rockery relic elsewhere. May–June.

662. *COMMON GROMWELL *Lithospermum officinale* L. Pl. 112. *CTW, 844*
A rather leafy, roughly hairy perennial, 18–30 in. high, the unstalked, pointed, lanceolate leaves with prominent veins. Flowers small, cream-coloured, in a cluster of spikes. Fruits smooth, hard, white, shining like glazed china. *Habitat:* Fairly frequent in bushy places in England and Wales, usually on chalk or limestone; rare elsewhere. June–July.

663. *CORN GROMWELL *Buglossoides arvensis* (L.) Johnston Pl. 112. *CTW, 844*
An annual, usually only half as tall as the last species, its strap-shaped leaves with no prominent side veins, the lower blunter and short-stalked. Flowers white. Fruits warty, hard, brown. *Habitat:* Locally frequent in arable fields and on waste ground in England; rare elsewhere. May–July. *L. arvense* L.

664. **OYSTER PLANT *Mertensia maritima* (L.) Gray Pl. 13. *CTW, 845*
A prostrate mat-forming hairless grey fleshy perennial, with thick oval leaves tasting of oysters and setting off the clusters of attractive purplish-blue flowers. *Habitat:* Very scarce and decreasing on coastal shingle in Scotland; very rare elsewhere in the N. June–August.

665. VIPER'S BUGLOSS *Echium vulgare* L. Plate 13. *CTW, p. 846*
A very roughly hairy biennial, 1–2 ft. high, often making a glorious display of vivid blue; leaves lanceolate, with only the midrib prominent. Flowers at first in a drooping grape-like cluster of pink buds, then normally turning blue; curved, trumpet-shaped with 4–5 pinkish-purple stamens protruding. The persistent hairy calyxes give the fruiting spike a mossy appearance. *Habitat:* Widespread and locally common in dry bare places on chalk and other light soils, especially near the sea; rare in Scotland. June–September.

665a. *****Purple Viper's Bugloss,** *E. plantagineum* L., is generally smaller and more spreading, with rather softer hairs, prominent side-veins on the leaves, and upper leaves broader at the base; flowers rather larger, normally a rich reddish-purple, with only 2 or no stamens protruding. Rare near the sea in the SW; casual elsewhere.

BINDWEED FAMILY Convolvulaceae

666. FIELD BINDWEED *Convolvulus arvensis* L. Plate 27. *CTW, p. 847*
An attractive but pernicious perennial, prostrate or twining anti-clockwise, up to 2 ft. long, with arrow- or halberd-shaped leaves. Flowers funnel-shaped, about an inch across, faintly scented, pink or white or both, 1–3 together with a pair of tiny bracts well below on their stalks. *Habitat:* A widespread, common and tenacious weed of cultivated and waste places. June–September.

667. GREAT BINDWEED *Calystegia sepium* (L.) Brown Pl. 102. *CTW, 848*
Much larger than the last species, and 3–8 ft. long, with unscented flowers 2 in. or more across, pure white or occasionally pink, and with two large broad pointed

sepal-like bracts close under the flower and enfolding the 5 narrower true sepal-like calyx-lobes (Fig. × ½).   *Habitat:* Widespread and locally frequent in bushy places, fens, hedges, and on fences and waste ground, thinning out northwards. July–September.   *Convolvulus sepium* L.

667a. **American Bellbine,** *C. sylvestris* (Willdenow) Roemer & Schultes, is larger still, with 3-in. flowers, and bracts very broad, much inflated at the base, often overlapping and completely enveloping the calyx (Fig.). Often commoner especially in and near towns.

668. ****SEA BINDWEED**   *C. soldanella* (L.) Brown   Plate 27.   *CTW, p. 849*
A hairless prostrate creeping perennial, with fleshy kidney-shaped leaves; white-striped pink flowers intermediate in size between Field and Great Bindweeds (666–667); and at their base broad bracts rather shorter than the calyx. *Habitat:* Widespread, local on sand-dunes, much more rarely on shingle. June–Aug.

669. ***COMMON DODDER**   *Cuscuta epithymum* (L.) (L.)   Pl. 102.   *CTW, p. 850*
A slender leafless, usually annual parasite especially on Gorse (273) and Ling (590), and on many small plants, twining anti-clockwise, with an often dense, network of thin, flaccid thread-like reddish stems. Flowers in unstalked globular heads, tiny, bell-shaped, translucent waxy white, tinged pink, the stamens and styles very slightly protruding; calyx often reddish with pointed teeth.   *Habitat:* Locally frequent, especially on heaths and downs, mainly in England and Wales. July–September. (Incl. *C. trifolii* Babington).

669a. ****Greater Dodder,** *C. europaea* L., is much larger and robuster and grows mostly on large herbaceous plants, especially Stinging Nettle (554). Flowers much larger and rounder, with stamens and styles not protruding; calyx-teeth blunt. Very local and decreasing, in shadier places by rivers, especially the Thames, Wey and Bristol Avon; not in Ireland.

NIGHTSHADE FAMILY Solanaceae

670. ***DUKE OF ARGYLL'S TEA-TREE**   *Lycium halimifolium* Miller
(incl. *L. chinense* Miller)   Plate 8.   *CTW, p. 851*
A bushy, somewhat spiny shrub, up to 8 ft. high, with flexuous, arching stems, often rooting at the tip; leaves alternate, stalked, broad or narrow lanceolate, untoothed, and at their base flowers with a column of yellow anthers and 5 purple petal-like corolla-lobes. Fruit a small, scarlet egg-shaped berry. *Habitat:* Locally frequent in hedges, especially near the sea. June–September.

671. ***DEADLY NIGHTSHADE**   *Atropa bella-donna* L.   Pl. 35.   *CTW, p. 852* ♃
A tall stout, often downy bushy perennial, 2–6 ft. high, with broad, pointed oval stalked leaves, and at their base solitary large drooping bell-shaped, dull purple flowers. Fruit a glossy black berry, the size of a small cherry, surrounded by the broad calyx-lobes. Often confounded with the smaller Woody Nightshade (673).   *Habitat:* Local in bushy places, quarries and among ruins in the S; rare elsewhere; very rarely off chalk or limestone. May–August.

672. ***HENBANE**   *Hyoscyamus niger* L.   Plate 58.   *CTW, p. 853* ♃
A stout evil-looking, evil-smelling biennial, 1–4 ft. high, clammy with sticky white hairs, the broad lower leaves usually with a few large teeth; upper leaves

more toothed, rather narrower and unstalked. Flowers nearly an inch across, lurid creamy buff, purple at the base, normally with a network of purple veins, in a leafy 1-sided spike; calyx green, with 5 broad stiff teeth, the tube swelling in fruit. *Habitat:* Widespread but local in bare or disturbed ground, chiefly in the S and near the sea. June–August.

673. BITTERSWEET *Solanum dulcamara* L.   Plate 8.   *CTW, p. 853*   ℙ
Woody Nightshade
A clambering or prostrate, often downy, occasionally almost velvety perennial, 2–5 ft. long, woody below, and in Darwin's words, 'one of the feeblest and poorest of twiners', twining 'indifferently to the right or left'. Leaves stalked, pointed oval, often with 2 narrow lobes at the base. Flowers distinctive for their bright purple petal-like corolla-lobes, eventually turned back, with a conspicuous close central column of yellow anthers, like those of the Potato (*S. tuberosum* L.); calyx and flower-stalks often purple. Fruit an egg-shaped berry, green then yellow and finally red. *Habitat:* Widespread and frequent in both wet and bushy places, and on coastal shingle. June–September.

674. *BLACK NIGHTSHADE   *S. nigrum* L.   Plate 102.   *CTW, p. 854*   ℙ
A bushy variable annual, 2–12 in. high, with stems often blackish, and pointed oval, toothed, often hairless, alternate purple-edged leaves. Flowers with anthers like the last species, but smaller and with white corolla-lobes. Berry green, finally black (rarely green, yellow or red), much exceeding the calyx. *Habitat:* A locally common weed of cultivated and waste ground in England; rarer elsewhere. July–September. (Incl. *S. miniatum* Willdenow.)
674a. **Green Nightshade**, *S. sarrachoides* Sendtner, is also variable, but is pale green and shaggier, with less stiff, never blackish stems, and a prominent green calyx with large lobes, which enlarges and exceeds the always green berry. An increasing casual. *S. chenopodioides* Lamarck.

675. **THORN-APPLE   *Datura stramonium* L.   Plate 102.   *CTW, p. 854*   ℙ
A distinctive stout hairless annual, 1–3 ft. high, with an unpleasant smell; jaggedly toothed, pointed oval leaves; solitary large 2–3 in. white or purple trumpet-shaped flowers, and a monstrous, spiny, chestnut-like fruit. *Habitat:* An occasional weed or casual in cultivated and waste ground. July till the frosts.

FIGWORT FAMILY   Scrophulariaceae
MULLEINS   *Verbascum*

OUR MULLEINS are all biennials, with leaves in a rosette and alternate up the little- or unbranched stem. Flowers usually yellow, rather large, in spikes; corolla flat with a short tube and 5 petal-like lobes; calyx 5-lobed; stamens 5. Fruits globular or egg-shaped. All the species may hybridise, and several garden species may escape.

676. COMMON MULLEIN   *Verbascum thapsus* L.   Plate 62.   *CTW, p. 858*
A stout, usually unbranched biennial, 2–4 ft. high, covered with thick white wool; leaves flannelly, broad lanceolate, their base running down as wings on to the round stem. Flowers in a dense spike, hardly stalked, nearly an inch across, not quite flat, yellow; stamens, three covered in woolly hairs, two almost or quite hairless; anthers orange; stigma club-shaped. Fruits egg-shaped, hardly exceeding

the calyx. *Habitat:* Widespread and locally frequent on dry grassy banks and similar places. June–August.

676*a*. **Orange Mullein, *V. phlomoides* L., is downy but much less white, with leaves not or hardly running down the stem; and larger, sometimes almost orange, flowers, with shorter stamens and more oblong stigma. An increasing casual.

677. **WHITE MULLEIN *V. lychnitis* L. Plate 101. *CTW, p. 858*

Smaller and thinner than Common Mullein (676), erect-branched like a small candelabrum, with thin greyish down both on the stems, which are angled at the top, and beneath the dark grey-green leaves, which are almost hairless above; leaf-bases not running down the stem. Flowers smaller, white, very rarely yellow, with woolly linear calyx-teeth and whitish hairs on all the stamens; stigma broader than long. Fruits longer than calyx. *Habitat:* Local in dry grassy places, chiefly on chalk and limestone in the SE. July–August.

678. ***HOARY MULLEIN *V. pulverulentum* Villars Plate 62. *CTW, p. 859*

Somewhat taller than the last species, and densely covered all over, including both sides of the leaves, with loose white mealy down; with round stems, often numerous stouter, less ascending branches, broader leaves, rather larger yellow flowers, and a narrow stigma. *Habitat:* Very local in rough grassy places in E. Anglia; casual elsewhere. July–August.

679. *DARK MULLEIN *V. nigrum* L. Plate 62. *CTW, p. 859*

A hairy biennial, 6–18 in. high, with a stiff, ridged usually unbranched, often purple stem; and soft, dark green stalked leaves, not running down on to the stem, the lower with more or less heart-shaped bases, all paler and downier beneath. Flowers rich yellow with orange anthers and purple wool on the stamens. Fruits egg-shaped. *Habitat:* Not uncommon locally in dry grassy places on chalk or sand in the S, thinning out northwards; not in Ireland. June onwards.

680. **LARGE-FLOWERED MULLEIN *V. virgatum* Stokes Pl. 62. *CTW, 860*

Taller, slenderer and greener than Dark Mullein (679), almost hairless below and stickily hairy above, with shining leaves and larger flowers, one or more at the base of a leaf-like bract on stalks shorter than the calyx, yellow, often pale reddish on the back; stamens unequal; anthers orange; fruits globular. *Habitat:* Very infrequent in waste places, mainly in the S. June onwards.

680*a*. **Moth Mullein, *V. blattaria* L., is often perennial and generally has looser spikes of rather smaller flowers, more often pale pink or white, always solitary, with stalks twice as long as the calyx.

681. *LESSER SNAPDRAGON *Misopates orontium* (L.) Rafinesque
Antirrhinum orontium L. Plate 29. *CTW, p. 861*

A usually downy, little branched annual, 6–18 in. high, with linear leaves, and leafy spikes of small pink snapdragon-like flowers with a pouch but no spur behind, shorter than the long narrow unequal calyx-teeth. Fruits globular. *Habitat:* Uncommon in arable in England, Wales and S Ireland. July onwards.

682. *COMMON SNAPDRAGON *Antirrhinum majus* L. Pl. 29. *CTW, 862*

Familiar in many colours in gardens, but usually some shade of red when wild; a stocky, bushy perennial, 6–15 in. high, with narrow lanceolate leaves. Flowers of the well known snapdragon shape, with an upper and lower lip opening when squeezed at the sides to form a mouth, and a pouch behind. *Habitat:* Well naturalised on walls and railway cuttings, mainly in the S. July–September.

683. ***PURPLE TOADFLAX** *Linaria purpurea* (L.) Miller Pl. 7. *CTW, p. 863*
A greyish hairless perennial, 9 in. to 2 ft. high, with numerous linear leaves up the stiffly erect, often unbranched stems. Flowers in spikes, small, bright violet, very rarely pink, snapdragon-like but with a curved spur behind, half as long as the rest of the corolla; calyx-teeth narrow, shorter than the fruit. *Habitat:* Not infrequently naturalised on walls, bombed sites and other waste ground, mainly in the S. June onwards.
683*a*. *****Jersey Toadflax**, *L. pelisseriana* (L.) Miller, is a smaller annual, 4–9 in. high, whose fewer flowers have a white lip and a slender straight spur nearly as long as the rest of the corolla; calyx-teeth longer than the fruit. Extremely rare and uncertain in shaley places in SW Jersey. May–July.

684. ****PALE TOADFLAX** *L. repens* (L.) Miller Plate 7. *CTW, p. 863*
A greyish hairless slender perennial, the stem creeping shortly at the base then erect, with numerous linear leaves up the stems, 1–2 ft. high. Flowers in short spikes, very pale lilac veined with violet, with an orange spot on the lower lip; snapdragon-like but with a short straight spur, later curving. *Habitat:* Scarce in dry grassy and waste places, chiefly in the S; sometimes out of hand in gardens. June–September.

685. **COMMON TOADFLAX** *L. vulgaris* Miller Plate 61. *CTW, p. 864*
Much the commonest yellow snapdragon-like flower, a greyish hairless perennial, 9 in. to 2 ft. high, with usually linear leaves all up the stem. Flowers in spikes, spurred, yellow, with orange on the lower lip; calyx lanceolate, pointed, one-third the length of the fruit. *Habitat:* Widespread and common on grassy banks and in waste places, thinning out northwards and in Ireland. July onwards.

686. *****PROSTRATE TOADFLAX** *L. supina* (L.) Chazelles Pl. 61. *CTW, 864*
An annual, more or less prostrate, much smaller than the last species, with narrower leaves and fewer, smaller flowers, and narrower blunt calyx-teeth nearly equalling the fruit. *Habitat:* Rare in sandy and waste places, mostly in the SW. June–September.

687. *****FRENCH TOADFLAX** *L. arenaria* DC. Plate 61. *CTW, p. 864*
The only yellow Toadflax with sticky hairs all over it; a low bushy annual, 3–6 in. high, with small linear leaves and short spikes of tiny short-spurred yellow snapdragon-like flowers, the spur sometimes pale violet. *Habitat:* Sown on dunes at Braunton Burrows about 1890, now well established. May–September.

688. ***SMALL TOADFLAX** *Chaenorhinum minus* (L.) Lange Pl. 7. *CTW, 865*
A slender, usually downy little annual, 3–6 in. high, with small solitary short-spurred, pale purple snapdragon-like flowers, their mouths closed, on long stalks at the base of the alternate grey-green linear leaves. *Habitat:* Fairly frequent in cornfields and on railway tracks, mainly in the S and especially on chalk and limestone. May onwards. *Linaria minor* (L.) Desfontaines.

689. ***ROUND-LEAVED FLUELLEN** *Kickxia spuria* (L.) Dumortier
Male Fluellen. *Linaria spuria* (L.) Miller Plate 61. *CTW, p. 866*
A low, often prostrate and rather thick-looking, softly hairy annual, with leaves all oval or roundish. Flowers small, solitary, on slender downy stalks at the base

of the leaves, snapdragon-like, the lower lip yellow, the upper lip maroon and the spur usually curved; calyx with broad lanceolate teeth. *Habitat:* Local in cornfields on light, especially chalky soils in the S. July onwards.

690. *SHARP-LEAVED FLUELLEN   K. elatine (L.) Dumortier
Linaria elatine (L.) Miller   Plate 61.   *CTW, p. 866*
Slenderer than the last species, with smaller halberd-shaped less hairy leaves, and smaller flowers with a paler upper lip, a usually straighter spur, almost hairless stalks and rather narrower calyx-teeth. *Habitat:* Often grows with the last species, but extends further N and occurs rarely in S Ireland. July onwards.

691. IVY-LEAVED TOADFLAX *Cymbalaria muralis* Gaertner, Meyer & Scherbius
Mother of Thousands   Plate 7.   *CTW, p. 866*
A trailing hairless perennial, often tinged purplish, with small solitary lilac short-spurred snapdragon-like flowers, with a yellow honey-guide on the lower lip, on long stalks at the base of the roundish, mostly alternate, roughly ivy-shaped long-stalked leaves. Fruits curving downwards into crannies. *Habitat:* Widespread, common on walls. April onwards. *Linaria cymbalaria* (L.) Miller.

692. COMMON FIGWORT   *Scrophularia nodosa* L.   Plate 37.   *CTW, p. 868*
An almost hairless foetid perennial, 2–3 ft. high, with solid stems, square but not winged; and well toothed, pointed oval leaves. Flowers in a leafy open branched cluster, small, globular, helmeted, with a 3-lobed open mouth, the scale on the junction of the two red-brown upper lips broader than long. Fruits oval, sharply pointed at the top. *Habitat:* Widespread and common in woods and dampish shady places. June–August.

692a. **Balm-leaved Figwort, *S. scorodonia* L., is larger, more branched, and downy all over, with very wrinkled soft blunter leaves; the flower-spike leafy; the scale on the upper lips of the flower roundish; and a broad whitish border to the calyx-lobes. Very local in dry bushy places, and on walls, in the SW.

693. WATER FIGWORT   *S. aquatica* L.   Plate 37.   *CTW, p. 868*
Taller and stouter than Common Figwort (692), with a less unpleasant smell, strongly winged leaf-stalks and square winged stems, hollow below; also has blunter leaves, often with a leaflet on either side at the base; and flowers in a narrower, interrupted spike, darker red-brown, with the scale on the upper lips roundish, and a noticeable whitish border to the calyx-lobes. Fruits globular, pointed. *Habitat:* Widespread and common in wet places, especially by rivers and ponds, but thinning out northwards. June–September.

693a. **Western Figwort, *S. umbrosa* Dumortier, is more branched, with the leaves brighter green, tapering at the base and running down to on the even more broadly winged stem, and pointed like those of Common Figwort (692). Flowers olive-brown, in a leafy spike, the scale on the upper lips 2-lobed. Fruits blunter. Very scarce in damp, shady places, mainly in the W.

694. **YELLOW FIGWORT   *S. vernalis* L.   Plate 61.   *CTW, p. 869*
A softly hairy perennial, 1–2 ft. high, with wrinkled pointed oval toothed, yellow-green leaves. Flowers short-stalked in small stalked heads at the base of the upper leaves, yellow, globular, with no scale on the upper lips, stamens protruding, and blunt calyx-lobes. *Habitat:* Very local on walls and in shady places, mainly in the S. April–June.

695. *MONKEY FLOWER   *Mimulus guttatus* DC.   Plate 59.   *CTW, p. 870*
An attractive creeping perennial, 9–18 in. high, downy above, with broad, toothed opposite leaves, the upper unstalked, clasping. Flowers large, stalked, in leafy spikes, showy, normally yellow, 2-lipped (the upper lip 2-lobed, the lower 3-lobed), usually with small red spots inside, the throat nearly closed. *Habitat:* Widespread and locally frequent in wet places, especially by shallow streams. June–September.

695a. **Blood-drop Emlets, *M. luteus* L., is usually smaller, less erect and hairless all over, with fewer flowers on longer stalks, usually with garish red blotches on the lips and the throat more open. Much scarcer, and mainly in the N.

695b. **Musk, *M. moschatus* Lindley, is smaller, half-prostrate and stickily hairy all over, and has paler green leaves all very shortly stalked, no red spots on the much smaller flowers, which grow all up the stem. Has lost the musky smell which gave it its name. Naturalised, chiefly near gardens, in a few places in England and E Ireland.

696. **COMMON MUDWORT   *Limosella aquatica* L.   Plate 66.   *CTW, p. 872*
A small prostrate, dark green hairless aquatic annual, often gregarious, with creeping runners, and tiny white or pinkish flowers, open only in the sun, at the base of the rosette of long-stalked root-leaves, which are narrow elliptical when mature. Calyx-teeth pointed, longer than the short uncoloured corolla-tube, with 5 petal-like lobes; style short. Fruits usually oval, on down-curving stalks. *Habitat:* Widespread, but easily overlooked and nowhere common, on mud. June onwards.

697. ***WELSH MUDWORT   *L. subulata* Ives   Plate 66.   *CTW, p. 872*
Fresher green than the last species, and occasionally perennial, the leaves all very narrowly linear and pointed. Flowers larger, white with blunt calyx-teeth shorter than the longer orange corolla-tube, more prominent also since they do not close in dull weather and last longer; style long. Fruits nearly round, on stalks which arch and force them into the mud. *Habitat:* Rare on mud not far from the sea in S and W Wales. May onwards.

698. **CORNISH MONEYWORT   *Sibthorpia europaea* L.   Pl. 105.   *CTW, p. 873*
A delicate hairy mat-forming prostrate perennial, rooting as it creeps, with thread-like stems; rounded kidney-shaped notched, soft green leaves; and at their base minute solitary long-stalked pinkish flowers with 5 petal-like corolla-lobes. *Habitat:* Local on moist shady woods and stream sides in SW England, S. Wales, Co. Kerry and E Sussex rare elsewhere. June onwards.

699. ***FAIRY FOXGLOVE   *Erinus alpinus* L.   Plate 28.   *CTW, p. 873*
A low tufted unbranched hairy perennial, 2–6 in. high, with small toothed leaves, broadest at the tip, mostly in rosettes, and short leafy spikes of small-stalked purple flowers, with 5 spreading notched petal-like corolla-lobes, and narrow calyx-teeth. *Habitat:* Sometimes grown in rockeries, and occasionally naturalised, usually on walls. May–August.

700. FOXGLOVE   *Digitalis purpurea* L.   Plate 21.   *CTW, p. 874*   𝕻
A stately unbranched downy biennial, 2–5 ft. high familiar in gardens, with large, broad lanceolate soft wrinkled leaves, and handsome, long tapering spikes of large drooping, bright pinkish-purple flowers, 2 in. long, shaped rather like

the finger of a glove and paler and often spotted crimson within. *Habitat:* Widespread and common in woods and on heaths and banks on acid soils; often abundant in clearings. June–September.

SPEEDWELLS *Veronica*

SMALL NON-WOODY plants with opposite leaves. Flowers in spikes or at the base of the leaves up the stem; usually blue, sometimes pink or white, the corolla with a short tube and 4 petal-like lobes, the calyx with usually 4 sepal-like lobes; stamens 2. Fruits flattened, notched.

KEY TO SPEEDWELLS (Nos. 701–721)

PLANT *hairless* 701, 702, 703, 712.

FLOWERS *solitary on long stalks at base of leaves* 716, 717, 718, 719, 720, 721; *in stalked spikes at base of leaves* 701, 702, 703, 704, 705, 706; *terminal* 707, 708, 709, 710, 711, 712, 713, 714, 716; *deep blue* 701, 706, 707, 708, 709, 711, 713, 714, 715, 716, 718, 719, 721; *pale blue* 702, 705, 710, 720; *lilac* 704, 706, 712, 717; *pink* 701, 702a, 706, 712, 720; *whitish* 703, 710, 712, 720; *purple* 704.

FRUITS *longer than calyx* 703, 704, 705, 708, 709, 715; *equalling calyx* 701, 702, 707, 710, 711, 717, 718, 719, 720; *shorter than calyx* 706, 712, 713, 714, 716, 718.

HABITAT: *garden weeds* 710, 712, 713, 717–721; *mountains only* 708, 709, 711.

701. BROOKLIME *Veronica beccabunga* L. Plate 11. *CTW, p. 877*
A sprawling hairless fleshy perennial, rooting as it creeps, with opposite spikes of small deep blue or very rarely pink flowers up the fat round stem at the base of the toothed stalked oval leaves. Fruits roundish, about equalling the calyx. *Habitat:* Widespread and common in wet places. May–September.

702. WATER SPEEDWELL *V. anagallis-aquatica* L. Plate 11. *CTW, p. 877*
More erect than Brooklime (701), and with the leaves longer, lanceolate, unstalked and slightly clasping; and longer erect denser spikes of smaller, paler blue flowers with tiny narrow pointed leaf-like bracts at their base. Fruits on slender erect stalks, usually slightly longer than broad, very slightly notched and no longer than the pointed calyx-lobes. *Habitat:* Widespread and frequent in wet places. June–August.

702a. **Pink Water Speedwell,** *V. catenata* Pennell, is rather smaller and often tinged purplish, and has shorter, less crowded spreading spikes of smaller pinkish flowers, their bracts slightly broader and blunter. Fruits on horizontal stalks, usually broader than long, rather more notched, usually longer than the blunter calyx-lobes. May grow and hybridise with Water Speedwell.

703. *MARSH SPEEDWELL *V. scutellata* L. Plate 105. *CTW, p. 878*
Much slenderer than the Water Speedwells (702), and occasionally downy, with fewer whitish flowers on longer stalks in alternate open spikes up the stem; leaves shorter and much narrower, only minutely toothed, and often olive-brown. Fruits flat, broader than long, deeply notched, much longer than the calyx. *Habitat:* Widespread, not uncommon in wet places, especially on acid soils. June–Aug.

704. HEATH SPEEDWELL *V. officinalis* L. Plate 2. *CTW, p. 878*
A low hairy perennial, with creeping and rooting stems hairy all round, and veined lilac flowers, sometimes purple in bud, in usually alternate erect spikes at the base of the toothed oval leaves, which are narrowed to their short stalks.

Flower-stalks no longer than the leaf-like bracts at their base. Fruits longer than broad, exceeding the calyx. *Habitat:* Widespread and common in dry grassy and heathy places. May–August.

705. *WOOD SPEEDWELL *V. montana* L. Plate 2. *CTW, p. 879*
Differs from both the last and the next species in its longer leaf- and flower-stalks, the latter twice as long as their bracts with fewer flowers in the spikes. Flowers larger and bluer than 704 and smaller and much paler than Birdseye Speedwell (706), from which it also differs in being paler green and usually prostrate, with stems hairy all round. Fruits disc-like, larger than the small bluntish calyx-lobes. *Habitat:* Widespread but rather local in woods. April–July.

706. BIRDSEYE SPEEDWELL *V. chamaedrys* L. Plate 2. *CTW, p. 879*
A weak hairy perennial, 4–12 in. high, with hairs in two thick opposite lines down the stems, which are prostrate at the base. Flowers brilliant azure blue with a white eye, rarely pink or lilac, in erect spikes at the base of the well toothed, pointed oval leaves, with short or no stalks. Flower-stalks no shorter than the tiny leaf-like bracts at their base. Fruits conspicuously hairy, broadly heart-shaped shorter than the pointed calyx-lobes. *Habitat:* Widespread and common in hedge-banks and grassy places. April–July. Germander Speedwell.

707. **SPIKED SPEEDWELL *V. spicata* L. Plate 9. *CTW, p. 880*
(incl. *V, hybrida* L.)
An unbranched downy perennial, 4–12 in. high, with leaves slightly toothed, the lower oval, stalked and often in a rosette, the upper narrower and unstalked. Flowers small, intense blue, with prominent stamens, short-stalked, in long dense terminal spikes. Fruits hairy, no shorter than the short calyx-lobes. *Habitat:* Very local on limestone rocks in the W and in dry grassland in the Breckland. July onwards.

708. ***ROCK SPEEDWELL *V. fruticans* Jacquin Plate 3. *CTW, p. 881*
A creeping perennial, woody and hairless below, with small, toothed, pointed oval, unstalked leaves, and small loose terminal leafy spikes of rich dark blue flowers with a red eye, very large for the plant. Fruits elliptical, hairy, with a long style, exceeding calyx. *Habitat:* Rare on ledges high on a very few Scottish mountains. July–August.

709. **ALPINE SPEEDWELL *V. alpina* L. Plate 3. *CTW, p. 881*
A bluish-green perennial, 2–6-in. high, downy above, with rather wiry stems; unstalked, scarcely toothed oval leaves, and rather crowded terminal spikes of dull deep blue flowers with no red eye, on stalks shorter than the often bluish calyx. Fruits longer than broad, hairless, slightly notched, with a short style, much longer than the calyx. Often confused with the creeping and rooting Mountain Speedwell (711). *Habitat:* Rare on rocks high on more Scottish mountains than the last species. July–August.

710. THYME SPEEDWELL *V. serpyllifolia* L. Plate 2. *CTW, p. 882*
A low neat, often minutely downy perennial, rooting as it creeps, with small oval shiny untoothed leaves on very short or no stalks. Flowers in erect terminal leafy spikes, very pale blue or white with violet-purple veins, on stalks as long as the calyx but shorter than the small leaf-like bracts at their base. Fruits slightly

broader than long, with a long style, scarcely or not exceeding the oblong calyx-lobes. *Habitat:* Widespread and common in thinly grassy and moister waste places and as a garden weed. April onwards.

711. **MOUNTAIN SPEEDWELL   *V. tenella* Allioni   Pl. 3.   *CTW, p. 882***
Very similar to the last species, but more prostrate, its stems rooting for most of their length instead of just at the joints; leaves thinner and broader. Flowers fewer, larger and much bluer, in shorter spikes. Fruits always downy. *Habitat:* The commonest Speedwell high on mountains, from Wales northwards. June onwards. *V. humifusa* Dickson.

712. **AMERICAN SPEEDWELL   *V. peregrina* L.   Plate 2.   *CTW, p. 882***
An erect hairless annual, with one-veined blunt, narrow elliptical, often un-toothed short-stalked leaves, the topmost much longer than the very short-stalked inconspicuous lilac flowers hidden in the long lanceolate calyx-lobes. Fruits broader than long, very slightly notched, with a minute style, much shorter than the narrow calyx-lobes. *Habitat:* A weed, chiefly in gardens in NW Ireland; rare elsewhere. April–June.

713. WALL SPEEDWELL   *V. arvensis* L.   Plate 2.   *CTW, p. 883*
A low hairy annual, 1–6 in. high, with pointed oval leaves, toothed and short-stalked below, narrow, untoothed and unstalked above, and longer than the small short-stalked blue flowers, which are in congested leafy spikes. Fruits about as long as broad, notched, shorter than the often spreading lanceolate calyx-lobes (Fig.). *Habitat:* Widespread and common in dry, usually bare places. March onwards. Figs. all × 3.

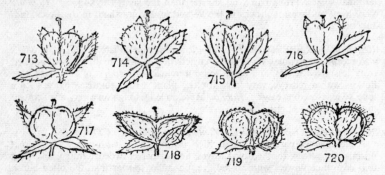

714. ***SPRING SPEEDWELL   *V. verna* L.   Plate 2.   *CTW, p. 883*
Can be very like Wall Speedwell (713), but is smaller, often no more than an inch high, and has much more deeply lobed leaves and a denser fruiting spike, the flower-stalks longer, but shorter than the calyx-lobes. Fruits broader than long (Fig.). *Habitat:* Very rare in sandy fields in the Breckland. April–May.

715. ***BRECK SPEEDWELL   *V. praecox* Allioni   Plate 2.   *CTW, p. 884*
Larger and taller then the last species, and has rounder, less deeply divided leaves, not unlike those of the Grey Field Speedwell (719) and often purple below; flowers darker blue, their stalks longer than both the upper leaves and the

calyx. Fruits longer than broad, hardly notched, longer than the calyx, with a prominent style (Fig.). *Habitat:* Very rare in arable fields in the Breckland. March–June.

716. **FINGERED SPEEDWELL   *V. triphyllos* L.   Plate 2.   *CTW, p. 884*

A low spreading, downy annual, the small dark blue flowers with petal-like corolla-lobes shorter than the calyx, on slender stalks longer than the leaves and the calyx; lower leaves stalked, with 1–7 narrow finger-like lobes. Fruits round, notched, shorter than the calyx-lobes, with style little longer than the notch (Fig.). *Habitat:* Rare in sandy fields in Surrey and the Breckland, perhaps also still in Yorkshire. April–June.

717. IVY SPEEDWELL   *V. hederifolia* L.   Plate 2.   *CTW, p. 884*

A prostrate hairy annual, with small, pale lilac flowers, the petal-like corolla-lobes no longer than the broad-based calyx-lobes, solitary on long stalks along the stem at the base of the roundish shorter-stalked ivy-like leaves, the middle of whose 3–5 lobes is the largest. Fruits fat, hairless, globular, about equalling the enlarged calyx-lobes (Fig.). *Habitat:* A widespread and common weed of disturbed ground. March–August.

718. COMMON FIELD SPEEDWELL   *V. persica* Poiret   Pl. 2.   *CTW, p. 885*

A low sprawling hairy, pale green annual, with more or less oval toothed stalked leaves, usually much shorter than the long stalks of the solitary flowers at their base. Flowers large, the size of Birdseye Speedwell (706), a clear sky blue with darker veins, lower petal-like corolla-lobe usually white. Calyx enlarging in fruit, the lobes broad lanceolate, rather longer and even more diverging than the flattened keeled lobes of the fruit, which is much broader than long; style long (Fig.). *Habitat:* Widespread and now abundant in disturbed ground, especially in gardens. Throughout the year. Buxbaum's Speedwell.

719. GREY FIELD SPEEDWELL   *V. polita* Fries   Plate 2.   *CTW, p. 885*

Generally much smaller and neater than the last species, and with a slightly greyish look; leaves often longer than the flower-stalks and more crowded on the stem. Flowers half the size and usually a uniform darker blue; calyx-lobes shorter and broader. Fruits as broad as long, with smaller, rounded, keelless lobes, and a shorter style (Fig.). *Habitat:* Similar, but a good deal less common. March onwards.

720. *GREEN FIELD SPEEDWELL   *V. agrestis* L.   Plate 2.   *CTW, p. 885*

Very like the last species, but greener and with blunter calyx-lobes and flowers pale blue, at least the lowest corolla-lobe usually white; occasionally all pink or white. Fruits with style still shorter, hardly or not longer than the notch (Fig.). *Habitat:* A widespread weed, but much misrecorded and probably generally scarce. March onwards.

721. **SLENDER SPEEDWELL   *V. filiformis* Smith   Plate 2.   *CTW, p. 886*

A prostrate downy mat-forming perennial, with rather large mauvish-blue flowers solitary on long thread-like stalks at the base of the small short-stalked, bluntly toothed kidney-shaped rounded leaves. Fruit rare. *Habitat:* A fast-spreading escape, especially on lawns and by stream-banks. April–June.

722. LOUSEWORT   *Pedicularis sylvatica* L.   Plate 28.   *CTW, p. 887*

A low, spreading, generally hairless semi-parasitic perennial, with many unbranched stems and toothed, pinnate leaves. Flowers in leafy spikes, bright pink, 2-lipped, the upper lip longer, 2-toothed; calyx usually hairless, with jagged green lobes, soon inflated, no shorter than the fruits. *Habitat:* Widespread and frequent on moors and in damp heathy and boggy places. April–July.

722a. *Red Rattle, *P. palustris* L., is a taller erect annual, often bushy and bronzy, with a single, often purplish branched stem, darker flowers, the upper lip equalling the lower, and a downy calyx shorter than the fruit. Less common and prefers wet grassy, often less acid, places. May–September.

723. YELLOW RATTLE   *Rhinanthus crista-galli* L.[1]   Plate 61.   *CTW, p. 889*

A very variable, normally almost hairless annual semi-parasite, 3 in. to 2 ft. high, with oblong, lanceolate or linear, toothed unstalked opposite leaves; and stiff 4-angled stems often with dark purple streaks. Flowers in loose spikes, mixed with large green toothed triangular leaf-like bracts, canary-yellow or golden-syrup colour, narrow, 2-lipped, somewhat open-mouthed, with a straight corolla-tube and 2 short, often violet teeth, not longer than broad, at the tip of the hooded upper lip; calyx sometimes hairy on mountains, flat, inflated, narrow at the tip with 4 teeth, the flat winged seeds rattling inside when ripe, the style occasionally protruding, curving as the flowers age. *Habitat:* Widespread and frequent in grassy places. May–July. *R. minor* Ehrhart.

723a. ***Greater Yellow Rattle, *R. major* Ehrhart, is generally larger and bushier, with the bracts yellow-green and more deeply toothed, and the flowers larger in more crowded spikes, often closed at the mouth, with the tube slightly curved and the larger teeth on the upper lip distinctly longer than broad, and therefore much more prominent; style always protruding and remaining straight. Extremely scarce. June–September.

724. **CRESTED COW-WHEAT   *Melampyrum cristatum* L.   Pl. 60.   *CTW, 892*

A slightly downy annual semi-parasite, 9–12 in. high, with wide branches and unstalked untoothed, narrow lanceolate leaves. Flowers in a short angular 4-sided spike, yellow variegated with purple, 2-lipped, the mouth almost closed; mixed with bracts, the lowest long, purple and stiffly toothed at the base, green and pointed at the spreading tip. Fruits flat, longer than the unequal calyxteeth; seeds usually 4. *Habitat:* Very local at edges of woods in E England. June–Sept.

725. ***FIELD COW-WHEAT   *M. arvense* L.   Plate 60.   *CTW, p. 893*

Has magenta bracts, broader and more toothed than the last species, the flower-spike much longer and not 4-sided, and the flowers yellow and pink; branches more erect. Fruits much shorter than the long narrow magenta calyxteeth; seeds usually 2, wheat-like. *Habitat:* Now very rare in rough grass and cornfields in S and E England. June–September.

726. COMMON COW-WHEAT   *M. pratense* L.   Plate 60.   *CTW, p. 893*

A very variable weak annual semi-parasite, usually 6–12 in. high, often with wide slender branches; lower leaves lanceolate, untoothed, scarcely stalked.

---

[1] Incl. *R. stenophyllus* (Schur) Druce, *R. spadiceus* Wilmott, *R. calcareus* Wilm., *R. borealis* (Sterneck) Druce, *R. lintoni* Wilm. and *R. lochabrensis* Wilm.

Flowers in pairs all facing much the same way, at the base of often toothed leaf-like bracts at the top of the stem; usually yellow, varying from very deep to very pallid, or on moors sometimes pinkish-mauve; 2-lipped, usually closed at the mouth, the lower lip straight, the corolla-tube much longer than the rather appressed calyx. Fruits usually 4-seeded. *Habitat:* Widespread and locally frequent in woods and on moors. May–September.

727. **SMALL COW-WHEAT *M. sylvaticum* L. Plate 60. *CTW, p. 894*

Often confounded with a deep yellow variety of the last species, but is slenderer, and has the bracts less toothed; the flowers smaller, further apart, always deep yellow; the lower lip turned down, so opening the mouth; carolla-tube equalling the often spreading calyx; and usually 2-seeded fruits. *Habitat:* Scarce in woods in hill districts in the N and N Ireland. June–August.

728. EYEBRIGHT *Euphrasia officinalis* L.[1] Plate 90. *CTW, p. 895*

A low hairy, dark or often bronzy green semi-parasitic annual, 1–10 in. high, with small stiff, deeply toothed, more or less oval leaves. Flowers in leafy spikes, 2-lipped and open-mouthed, the lower lip with 3 spreading lobes, usually white but often tinged violet or red and having purple veins and a yellow spot on the lower lip. Very variable, especially in size, branching and hairiness. *Habitat:* Widespread and frequent in grassy places, high and low. June onwards.

729. RED BARTSIA *Odontites verna* (Bellardi) Dumortier

Bartsia odontites (L.) Hudson Plate 28. *CTW, p. 911*

A downy, rather bushy, often purple-stalked annual semi-parasite, 4–12 in. high, with toothed, narrow lanceolate leaves. Flowers in leafy 1-sided spikes, pink, 2-lipped, the lower lip 3-lobed. Fruits about equalling the calyx. *Habitat:* Widespread and common in cornfields and rough grassy places. June–September.

730. **YELLOW BARTSIA *Parentucellia viscosa* (L.) Caruel

Bartsia viscosa L. Plate 61. *CTW, p. 912*

A stickily hairy, usually unbranched, semi-parasitic annual, 6–15 in. high, with short unstalked toothed lanceolate leaves and long leafy spikes of open-mouthed yellow flowers, the long lower lip 3-lobed. Fruits shorter than the ribbed calyx. *Habitat:* Locally plentiful in wet grassland and dune slacks, chiefly near the coast in the S and W of England and SW Ireland. June onwards.

731. ***ALPINE BARTSIA *Bartsia alpina* L. Plate 3. *CTW, p. 913*

A low downy unbranched semi-parasitic perennial, with a leafy stem 3–6 in. high; unstalked toothed oval leaves, the uppermost purple; and a short spike of 2-lipped open mouthed hairy, rich dark purple flowers. Fruits longer than the purple calyx. *Habitat:* Very rare in damp hill meadows on limestone in N England and on mountain ledges in the Highlands. July–August.

---

[1] Includes the following 24 microspecies: *E. micrantha* Reichenbach, *E. scotica* Wettstein, *E. rhumica* Pugsley, *E. frigida* P., *E. foulaensis* Wettstein, *E. eurycarpa* P., *E. campbellae* P., *E. rotundifolia* P., *E. marshallii* P., *E. curta* (Fries) Wettstein, *E. cambrica* P., *E. occidentalis* Wettstein, *E. nemorosa* (Persoon) Martius, *E. heslop-harrisonii* P., *E. confusa* P., *E. pseudokerneri* P., *E. borealis* Townsend, *E. brevipila* Burnat & Gremli, *E. rostkoviana* Hayne, *E. montana* Jordan, *E. rivularis* P., *E. anglica* P., *E. hirtella* Jordan, and *E. salisburgensis* Hoppe. (P. = Pugsley.)

BROOMRAPE FAMILY   Orobanchaceae

732. *TOOTHWORT   *Lathraea squamaria* L.   Plate 36.   *CTW, p. 914*

A low unbranched, slightly hairy cream or pink perennial, 3–9 in. high, with no leaves but broad scales up the stem; growing usually in clumps as a parasite on the roots of shrubs and trees, especially Hazel (562).   Flowers short-stalked, 2-lipped, open-mouthed, pink, drooping in a 1-sided spike; calyx-teeth hairy, bluntish. Fruits egg-shaped.   *Habitat:* Widespread and locally frequent in woods and hedges. April–May.

BROOMRAPES   *Orobanche*

UNBRANCHED DOWNY parasites on the roots of other plants, and so devoid of green colouring matter, varying widely both in size, from 3 in. to 3 ft., and in colour—yellowish, brownish, reddish, mauve or bluish; persisting rigid and dark brown when dead. They have no proper leaves, but fleshy pointed scales up the stems which are usually swollen at the base, and usually a single similar scale (bract) under each flower, not always readily distinguishable from the deeply divided calyx. Flowers in a spike, the same colour as the plant, relatively large, the corolla 2-lipped, with 4 stamens and 1 style curved down at the tip into 2 stigma-lobes. Fruits egg-shaped, enclosed in the dead flower; seeds dust-like.

Most Broomrapes grow virtually on only one species (occasionally genus or family) of plant, but Common Broomrape (737) grows freely on many different hosts. All the other species are uncommon or rare, and seldom found off Broom (274), Gorse (273), Wild Thyme (753), White Bedstraw (813), Greater Knapweed (917), Thistles (903–913) or Yarrow (888). Thus in practice the readiest method of identifying a Broomrape is to name the host first and then confirm the particular characters of the parasite. It is not, however, always easy to be sure which plant is being parasitised.

733. **GREAT BROOMRAPE   *Orobanche rapum-genistae* Thuillier
   '*O. major*'   Plate 36.   *CTW, p. 917*

Generally our tallest and stoutest Broomrape, capable of attaining 3 ft., honey-brown with many scales near the base and a single bract at the base of and exceeding each flower.   Flowers with the upper lip hooded, the lower unequally 3-lobed; stamens hairless below, separate at the base of the corolla; stigma-lobes pale yellow when fresh; calyx 4-lobed.   *Habitat:* Widespread but extremely local on acid soils, usually on Broom (274), less often on Gorse (273), very rarely on other shrubby peaflowers. June–July.

734. **THYME BROOMRAPE   *O. alba* Willdenow   Plate 36.   *CTW, p. 918*

Differs from Common Broomrape (737) in being usually not more than 6 in. high and deep purplish-red throughout (very rarely with paler flowers); also in having flowers often more erect, with the corolla-tube less narrowed below, longer than the bract at its base and about equalling the calyx; stamens slightly hairy below, separate nearer the bottom of the tube; stigma-lobes always reddish. *Habitat:* Widely scattered but rare on Wild Thyme (753), usually near the sea. June–July. *O. rubra* Smith.

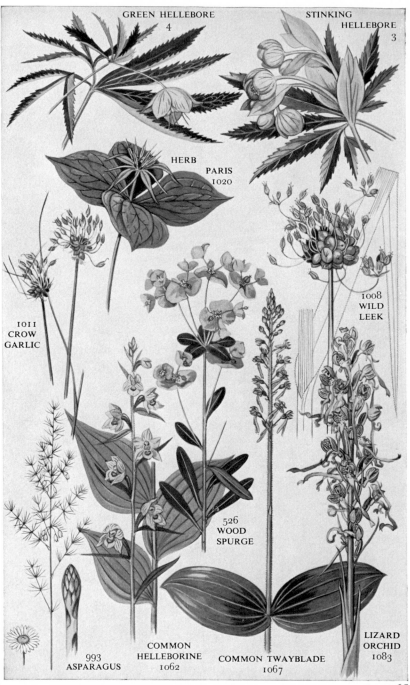

GREEN HELLEBORE
4

STINKING
HELLEBORE
3

HERB
PARIS
1020

1008
WILD
LEEK

1011
CROW
GARLIC

526
WOOD
SPURGE

993
ASPARAGUS

COMMON
HELLEBORINE
1062

COMMON TWAYBLADE
1067

LIZARD
ORCHID
1083

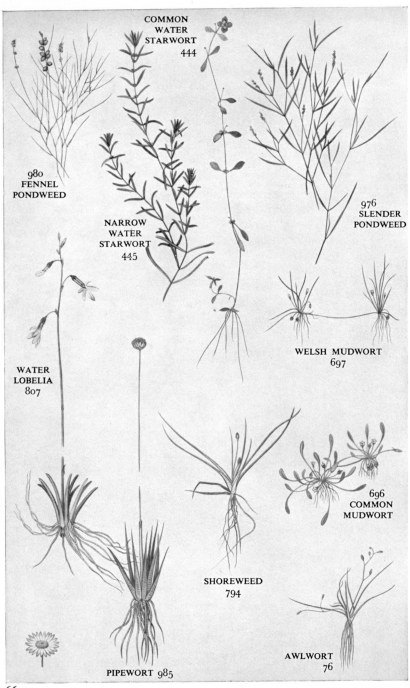

COMMON
WATER
STARWORT
444

980
FENNEL
PONDWEED

NARROW
WATER
STARWORT
445

976
SLENDER
PONDWEED

WATER
LOBELIA
807

WELSH MUDWORT
697

696
COMMON
MUDWORT

SHOREWEED
794

PIPEWORT 985

AWLWORT
76

66

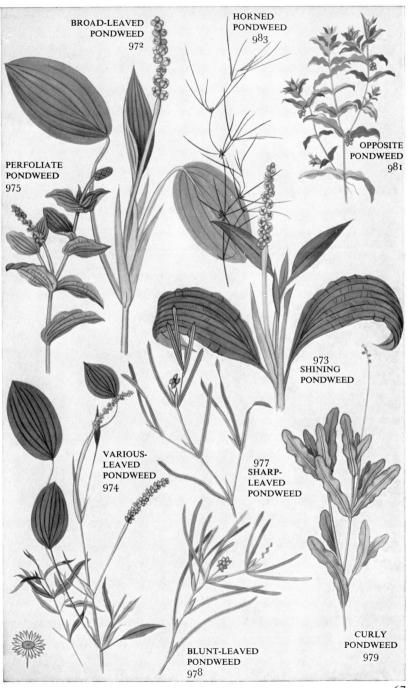

BROAD-LEAVED
PONDWEED
972

HORNED
PONDWEED
983

OPPOSITE
PONDWEED
981

PERFOLIATE
PONDWEED
975

973
SHINING
PONDWEED

VARIOUS-
LEAVED
PONDWEED
974

977
SHARP-
LEAVED
PONDWEED

CURLY
PONDWEED
979

BLUNT-LEAVED
PONDWEED
978

ESTHWAITE
WATER-
WEED
967

TASSEL
PONDWEED
982

SPIKED
WATER-
MILFOIL
44²

COMMON EEL-GRASS
97¹

SLENDER
NAIAD
984

WHORLED
WATER-
MILFOIL
44¹

TAPEGRASS
968

966
CANADIAN
WATERWEED

34
HORNWORT

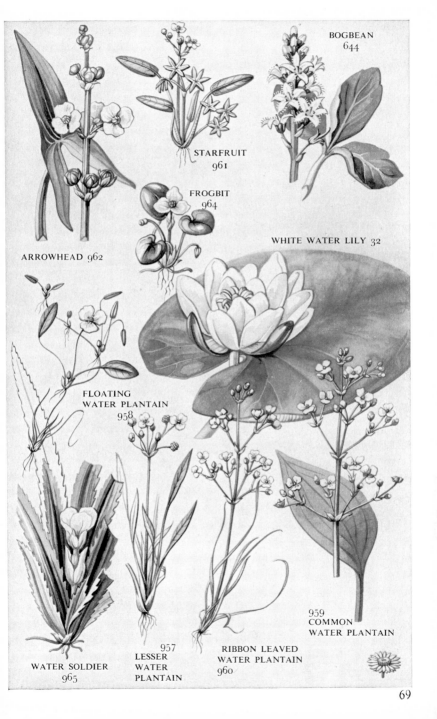

BOGBEAN
644

STARFRUIT
961

FROGBIT
964

WHITE WATER LILY 32

ARROWHEAD 962

FLOATING
WATER PLANTAIN
958

959
COMMON
WATER PLANTAIN

WATER SOLDIER
965

957
LESSER
WATER
PLANTAIN

RIBBON LEAVED
WATER PLANTAIN
960

69

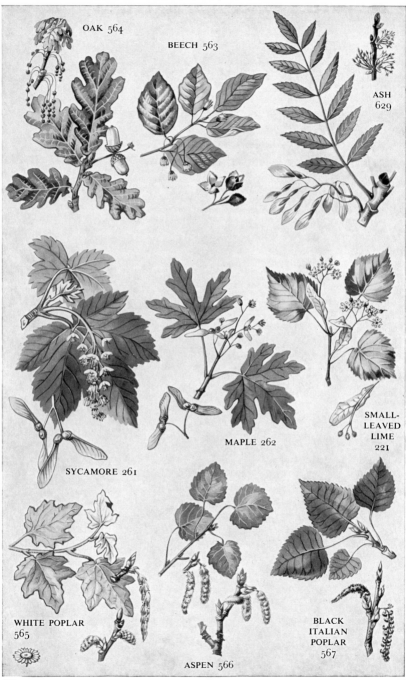

OAK 564

BEECH 563

ASH 629

SYCAMORE 261

MAPLE 262

SMALL-
LEAVED
LIME
221

WHITE POPLAR
565

ASPEN 566

BLACK
ITALIAN
POPLAR
567

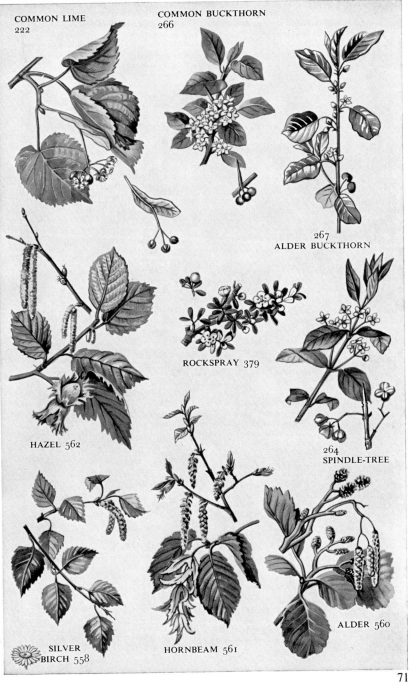

COMMON LIME
222

COMMON BUCKTHORN
266

267
ALDER BUCKTHORN

ROCKSPRAY 379

HAZEL 562

264
SPINDLE-TREE

SILVER
BIRCH 558

HORNBEAM 561

ALDER 560

71

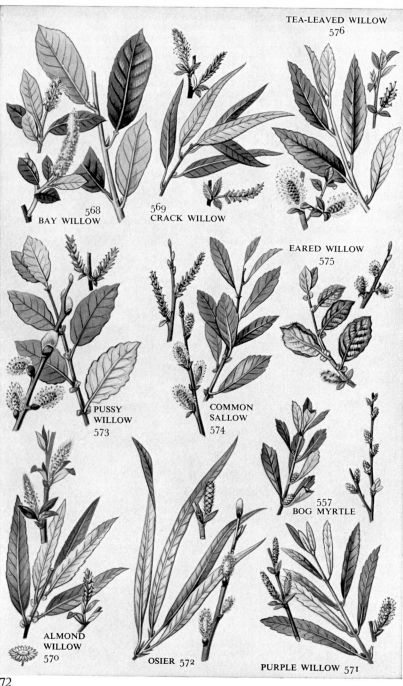

TEA-LEAVED WILLOW
576

568
BAY WILLOW

569
CRACK WILLOW

EARED WILLOW
575

PUSSY
WILLOW
573

COMMON
SALLOW
574

557
BOG MYRTLE

ALMOND
WILLOW
570

OSIER 572

PURPLE WILLOW 571

SEA BUCKTHORN
423

BOX 265

MISTLETOE 446

SPURGE
LAUREL
422

CREEPING WILLOW
577

WHORTLE-
LEAVED WILLOW 579

LEAST
WILLOW 580

DOWNY
WILLOW
578

NETTED WILLOW
581

DWARF BIRCH
559

73

GUELDER ROSE 822

JUNE BERRY 382

WAYFARING TREE 821

WHITE BEAM 384

ROWAN 383

WILD SERVICE TREE 385

DOGWOOD 448

ELDER 820

PRIVET 630

FIELD ROSE 370

BURNET ROSE 371

BLACKTHORN 374

WILD
CHERRY
376

BIRD
CHERRY
377

CHERRY
PLUM
375

PEAR
386

HAWTHORN 380

MEDLAR 381

75

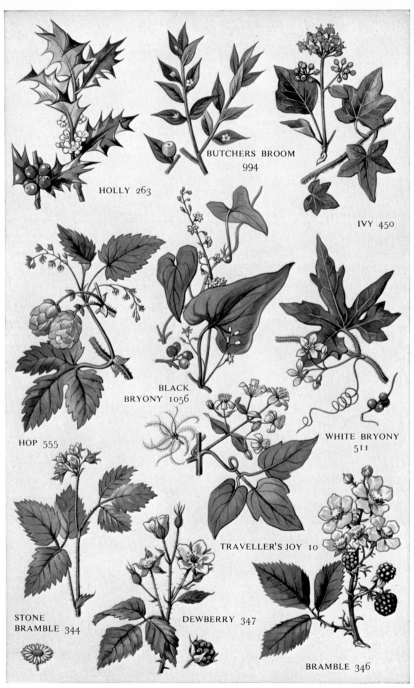

HOLLY 263

BUTCHERS BROOM
994

IVY 450

HOP 555

BLACK
BRYONY 1056

WHITE BRYONY
511

STONE
BRAMBLE 344

DEWBERRY 347

TRAVELLER'S JOY 10

BRAMBLE 346

BEARBERRY 588

605
CROWBERRY

BLACK BEARBERRY
589

587
STRAWBERRY TREE

BILBERRY 597

COWBERRY 596

598
NORTHERN BILBERRY

LABRADOR
TEA 582

DIAPENSIA
603

MOUNTAIN AVENS
362

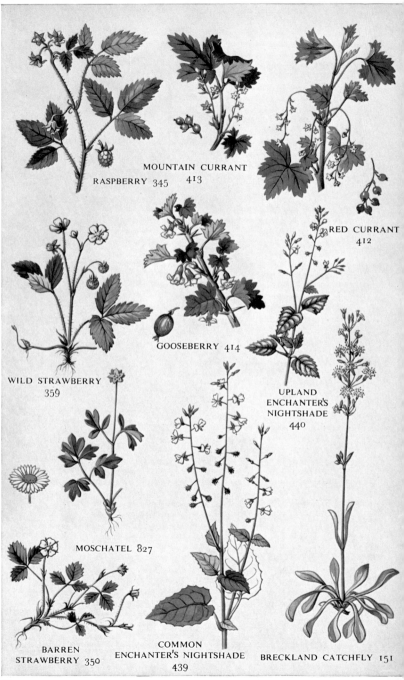

RASPBERRY 345

MOUNTAIN CURRANT 413

RED CURRANT 412

GOOSEBERRY 414

WILD STRAWBERRY 359

UPLAND ENCHANTER'S NIGHTSHADE 440

MOSCHATEL 827

BARREN STRAWBERRY 350

COMMON ENCHANTER'S NIGHTSHADE 439

BRECKLAND CATCHFLY 151

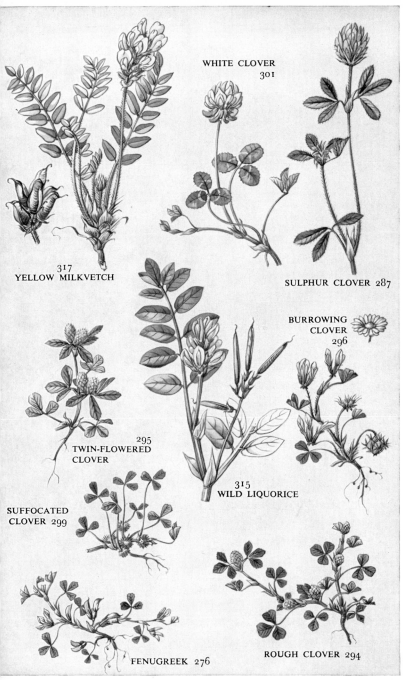

WHITE CLOVER
301

YELLOW MILKVETCH
317

SULPHUR CLOVER 287

BURROWING
CLOVER
296

TWIN-FLOWERED
CLOVER
295

WILD LIQUORICE
315

SUFFOCATED
CLOVER 299

FENUGREEK 276

ROUGH CLOVER 294

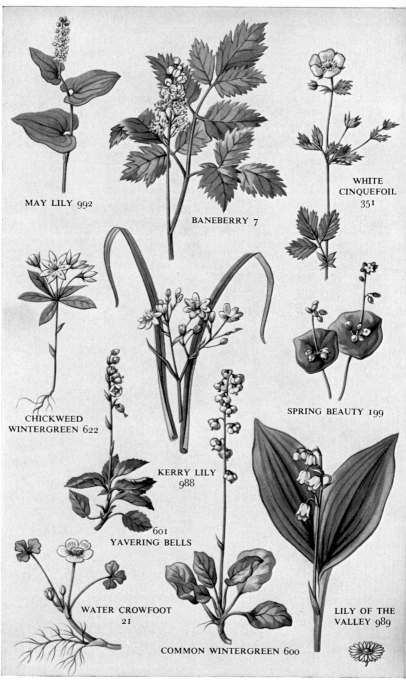

MAY LILY 992

BANEBERRY 7

WHITE CINQUEFOIL 351

CHICKWEED WINTERGREEN 622

SPRING BEAUTY 199

KERRY LILY 988

601 YAVERING BELLS

WATER CROWFOOT 21

COMMON WINTERGREEN 600

LILY OF THE VALLEY 989

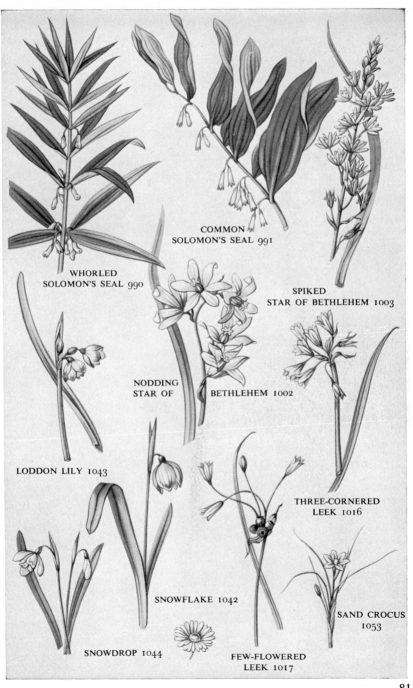

COMMON
SOLOMON'S SEAL 991

WHORLED
SOLOMON'S SEAL 990

SPIKED
STAR OF BETHLEHEM 1003

NODDING
STAR OF   BETHLEHEM 1002

LODDON LILY 1043

THREE-CORNERED
LEEK 1016

SNOWFLAKE 1042

SAND CROCUS
1053

SNOWDROP 1044

FEW-FLOWERED
LEEK 1017

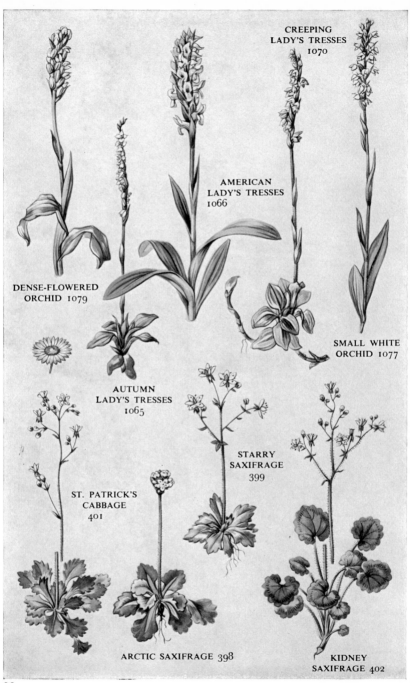

CREEPING
LADY'S TRESSES
1070

AMERICAN
LADY'S TRESSES
1066

DENSE-FLOWERED
ORCHID 1079

SMALL WHITE
ORCHID 1077

AUTUMN
LADY'S TRESSES
1065

STARRY
SAXIFRAGE
399

ST. PATRICK'S
CABBAGE
401

ARCTIC SAXIFRAGE 398

KIDNEY
SAXIFRAGE 402

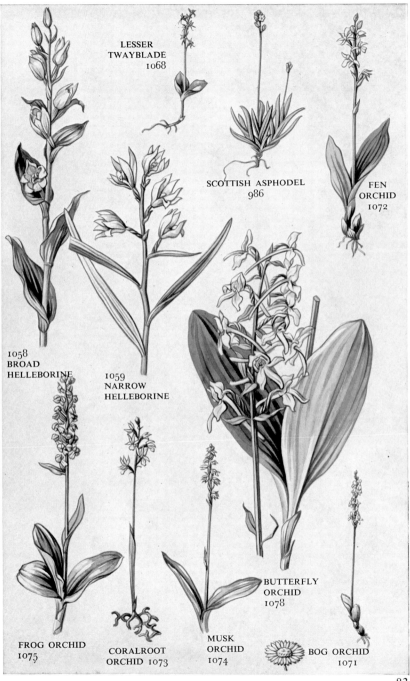

LESSER
TWAYBLADE
1068

SCOTTISH ASPHODEL
986

FEN
ORCHID
1072

1058
BROAD
HELLEBORINE

1059
NARROW
HELLEBORINE

FROG ORCHID
1075

CORALROOT
ORCHID 1073

MUSK
ORCHID
1074

BUTTERFLY
ORCHID
1078

BOG ORCHID
1071

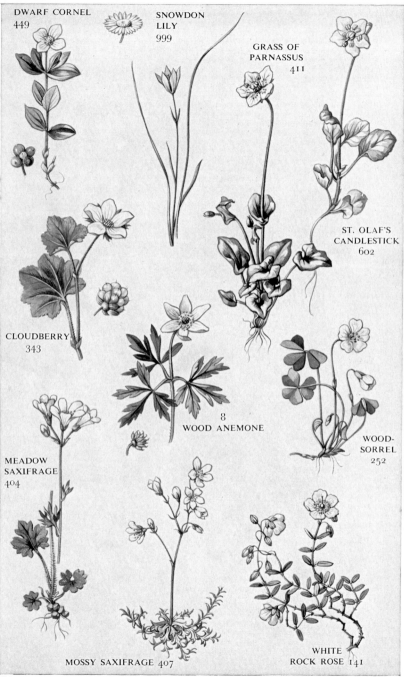

DWARF CORNEL
449

SNOWDON
LILY
999

GRASS OF
PARNASSUS
411

ST. OLAF'S
CANDLESTICK
602

CLOUDBERRY
343

8
WOOD ANEMONE

WOOD-
SORREL
252

MEADOW
SAXIFRAGE
404

MOSSY SAXIFRAGE 407

WHITE
ROCK ROSE 141

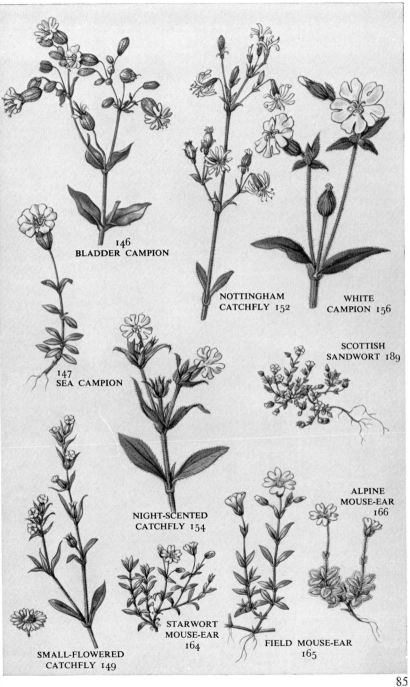

146
BLADDER CAMPION

147
SEA CAMPION

NOTTINGHAM
CATCHFLY 152

WHITE
CAMPION 156

SCOTTISH
SANDWORT 189

NIGHT-SCENTED
CATCHFLY 154

ALPINE
MOUSE-EAR
166

SMALL-FLOWERED
CATCHFLY 149

STARWORT
MOUSE-EAR
164

FIELD MOUSE-EAR
165

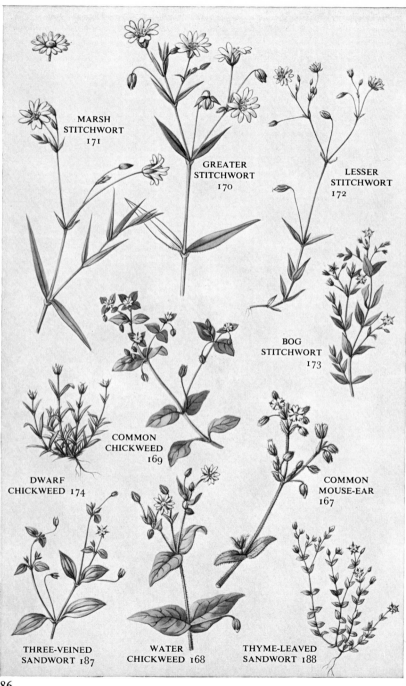

MARSH
STITCHWORT
171

GREATER
STITCHWORT
170

LESSER
STITCHWORT
172

BOG
STITCHWORT
173

COMMON
CHICKWEED
169

DWARF
CHICKWEED 174

COMMON
MOUSE-EAR
167

THREE-VEINED
SANDWORT 187

WATER
CHICKWEED 168

THYME-LEAVED
SANDWORT 188

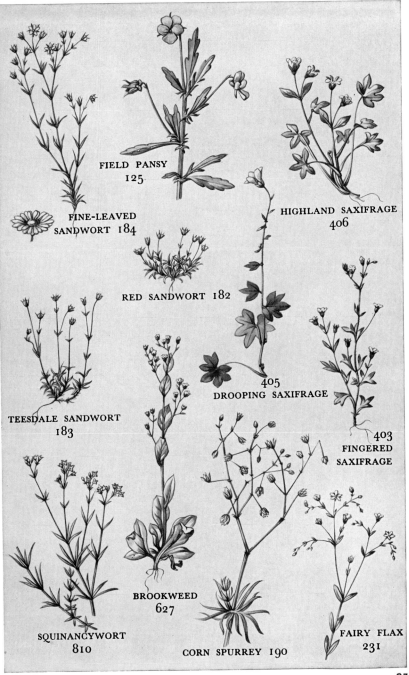

FIELD PANSY
125

FINE-LEAVED
SANDWORT 184

HIGHLAND SAXIFRAGE
406

RED SANDWORT 182

TEESDALE SANDWORT
183

405
DROOPING SAXIFRAGE

403
FINGERED
SAXIFRAGE

BROOKWEED
627

SQUINANCYWORT
810

CORN SPURREY 190

FAIRY FLAX
231

87

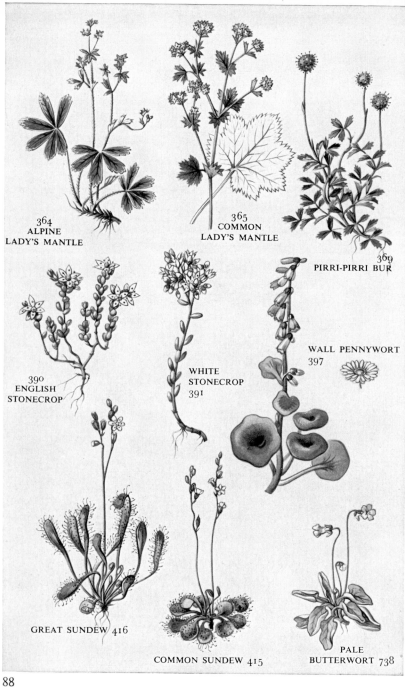

364
ALPINE
LADY'S MANTLE

365
COMMON
LADY'S MANTLE

369
PIRRI-PIRRI BUR

390
ENGLISH
STONECROP

WHITE
STONECROP
391

WALL PENNYWORT
397

GREAT SUNDEW 416

COMMON SUNDEW 415

PALE
BUTTERWORT 738

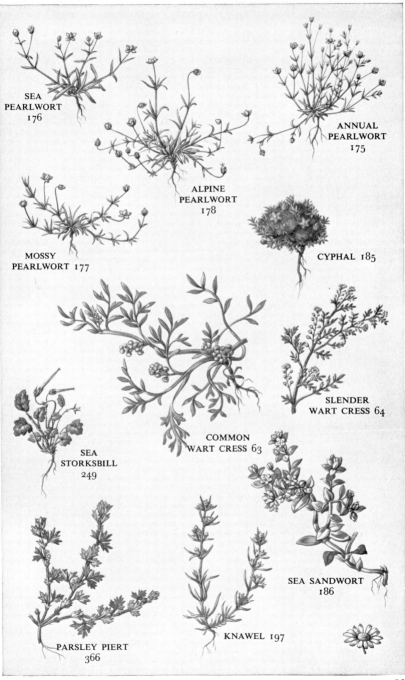

SEA
PEARLWORT
176

ANNUAL
PEARLWORT
175

ALPINE
PEARLWORT
178

MOSSY
PEARLWORT 177

CYPHAL 185

SLENDER
WART CRESS 64

SEA
STORKSBILL
249

COMMON
WART CRESS 63

PARSLEY PIERT
366

KNAWEL 197

SEA SANDWORT
186

89

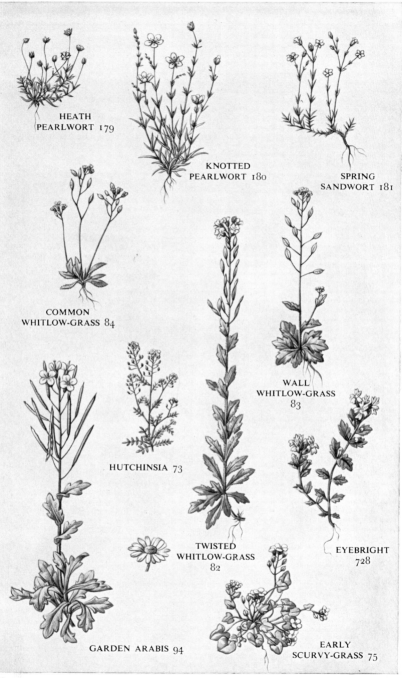

HEATH
PEARLWORT 179

KNOTTED
PEARLWORT 180

SPRING
SANDWORT 181

COMMON
WHITLOW-GRASS 84

WALL
WHITLOW-GRASS
83

HUTCHINSIA 73

TWISTED
WHITLOW-GRASS
82

EYEBRIGHT
728

GARDEN ARABIS 94

EARLY
SCURVY-GRASS 75

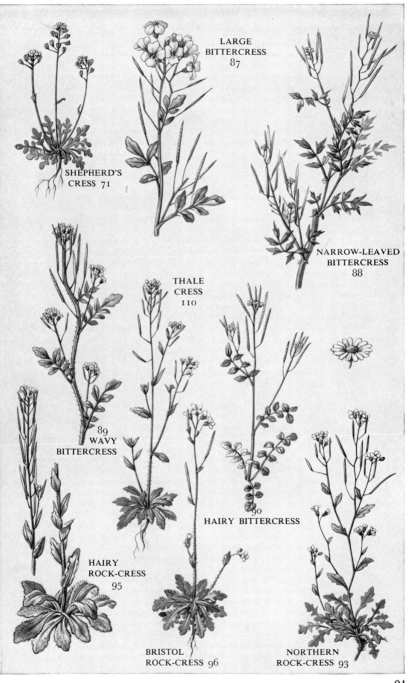

LARGE
BITTERCRESS
87

SHEPHERD'S
CRESS 71

NARROW-LEAVED
BITTERCRESS
88

THALE
CRESS
110

89
WAVY
BITTERCRESS

HAIRY BITTERCRESS
90

HAIRY
ROCK-CRESS
95

BRISTOL
ROCK-CRESS 96

NORTHERN
ROCK-CRESS 93

91

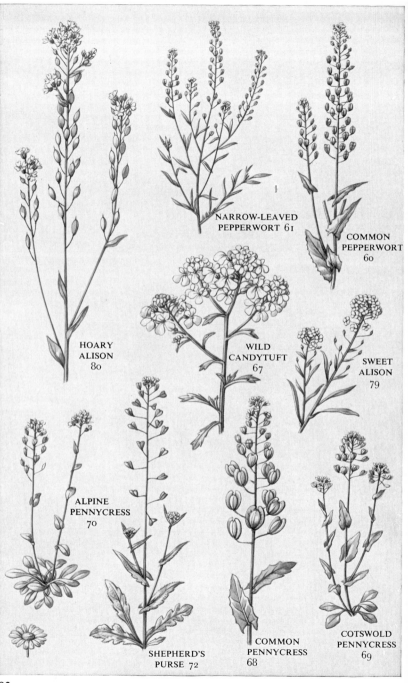

NARROW-LEAVED
PEPPERWORT 61

COMMON
PEPPERWORT
60

HOARY
ALISON
80

WILD
CANDYTUFT
67

SWEET
ALISON
79

ALPINE
PENNYCRESS
70

COMMON
PENNYCRESS
68

COTSWOLD
PENNYCRESS
69

SHEPHERD'S
PURSE 72

DITTANDER
62

SEA ROCKET
59

DAME'S
VIOLET
103

GARLIC
MUSTARD
106

SEA KALE 57

SEA STOCK
102

COMMON
SCURVY-GRASS
74

HORSERADISH
85

WATERCRESS
98

93

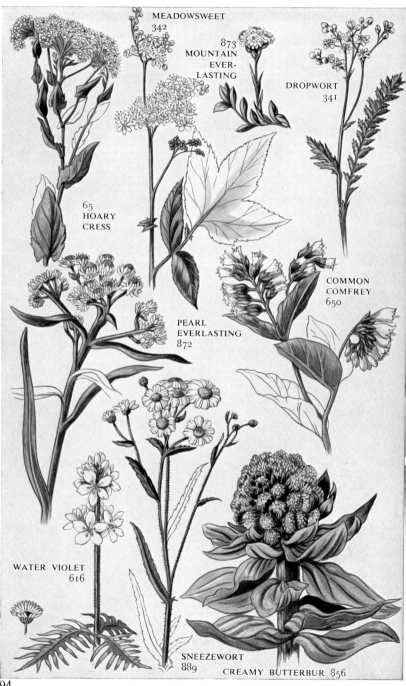

MEADOWSWEET
342

873
MOUNTAIN
EVER-
LASTING

DROPWORT
341

65
HOARY
CRESS

COMMON
COMFREY
650

PEARL
EVERLASTING
872

WATER VIOLET
616

SNEEZEWORT
889

CREAMY BUTTERBUR 856

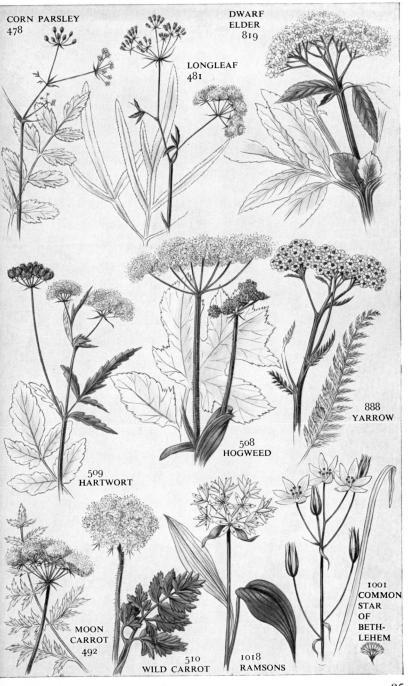

CORN PARSLEY
478

DWARF
ELDER
819

LONGLEAF
481

509
HARTWORT

508
HOGWEED

888
YARROW

MOON
CARROT
492

510
WILD CARROT

1018
RAMSONS

1001
COMMON
STAR
OF
BETH-
LEHEM

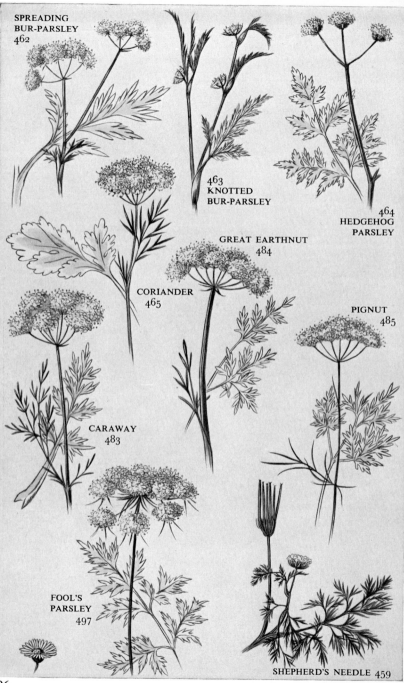

SPREADING
BUR-PARSLEY
462

463
KNOTTED
BUR-PARSLEY

464
HEDGEHOG
PARSLEY

GREAT EARTHNUT
484

CORIANDER
465

PIGNUT
485

CARAWAY
483

FOOL'S
PARSLEY
497

SHEPHERD'S NEEDLE 459

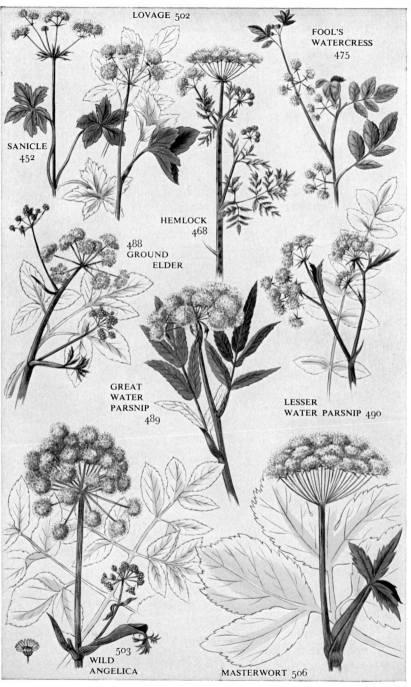

LOVAGE 502

FOOL'S
WATERCRESS
475

SANICLE
452

HEMLOCK
468

488
GROUND
ELDER

GREAT
WATER
PARSNIP
489

LESSER
WATER PARSNIP 490

503
WILD
ANGELICA

MASTERWORT 506

97

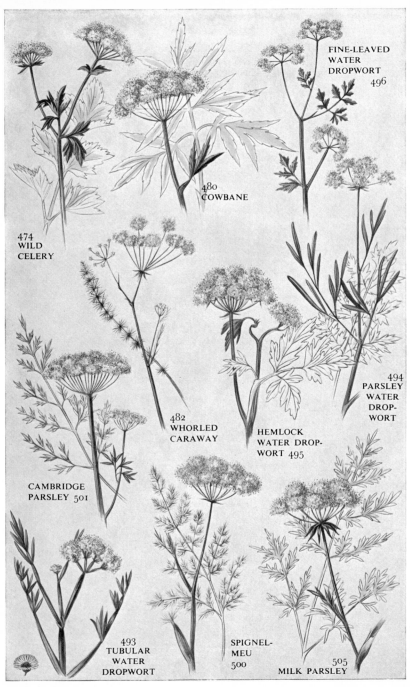

FINE-LEAVED
WATER
DROPWORT
496

480
COWBANE

474
WILD
CELERY

482
WHORLED
CARAWAY

HEMLOCK
WATER DROP-
WORT 495

494
PARSLEY
WATER
DROP-
WORT

CAMBRIDGE
PARSLEY 501

493
TUBULAR
WATER
DROPWORT

SPIGNEL-
MEU
500

505
MILK PARSLEY

98

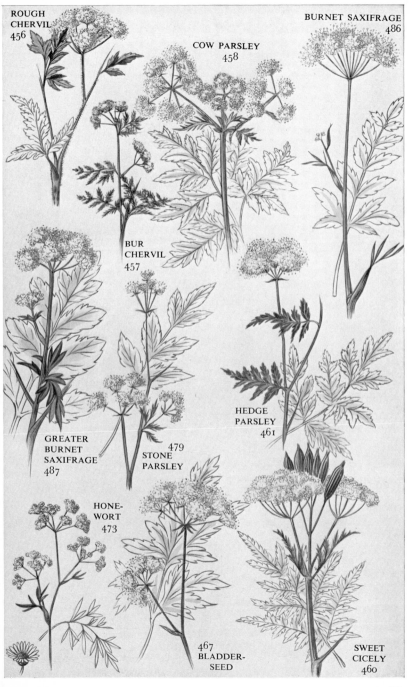

ROUGH
CHERVIL
456

COW PARSLEY
458

BURNET SAXIFRAGE
486

BUR
CHERVIL
457

GREATER
BURNET
SAXIFRAGE
487

479
STONE
PARSLEY

HEDGE
PARSLEY
461

HONE-
WORT
473

467
BLADDER-
SEED

SWEET
CICELY
460

99

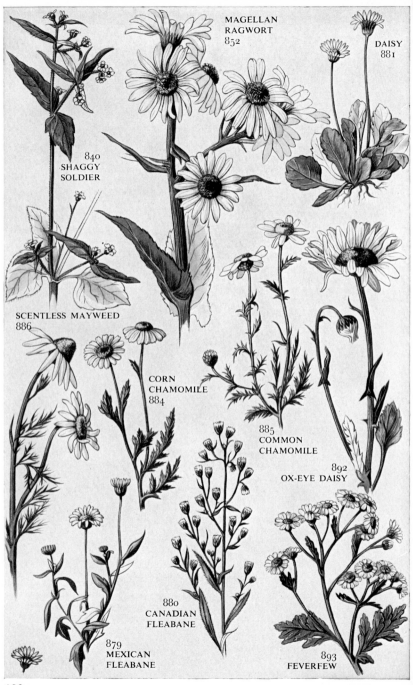

MAGELLAN
RAGWORT
852

DAISY
881

840
SHAGGY
SOLDIER

SCENTLESS MAYWEED
886

CORN
CHAMOMILE
884

885
COMMON
CHAMOMILE

892
OX-EYE DAISY

880
CANADIAN
FLEABANE

879
MEXICAN
FLEABANE

893
FEVERFEW

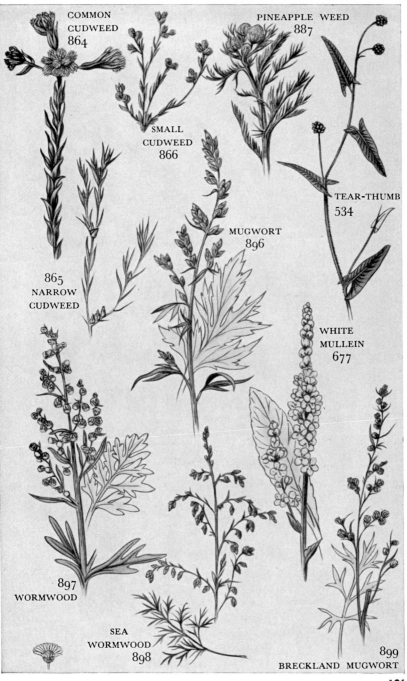

COMMON
CUDWEED
864

PINEAPPLE WEED
887

SMALL
CUDWEED
866

MUGWORT
896

TEAR-THUMB
534

865
NARROW
CUDWEED

WHITE
MULLEIN
677

897
WORMWOOD

SEA
WORMWOOD
898

899
BRECKLAND MUGWORT

101

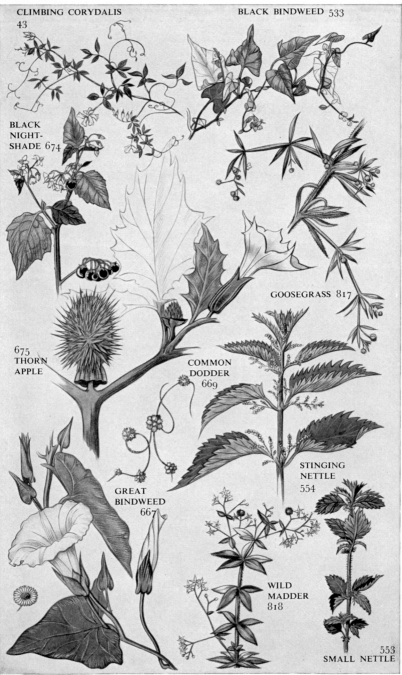

CLIMBING CORYDALIS
43

BLACK BINDWEED 533

BLACK
NIGHT-
SHADE 674

GOOSEGRASS 817

675
THORN
APPLE

COMMON
DODDER
669

STINGING
NETTLE
554

GREAT
BINDWEED
667

WILD
MADDER
818

553
SMALL NETTLE

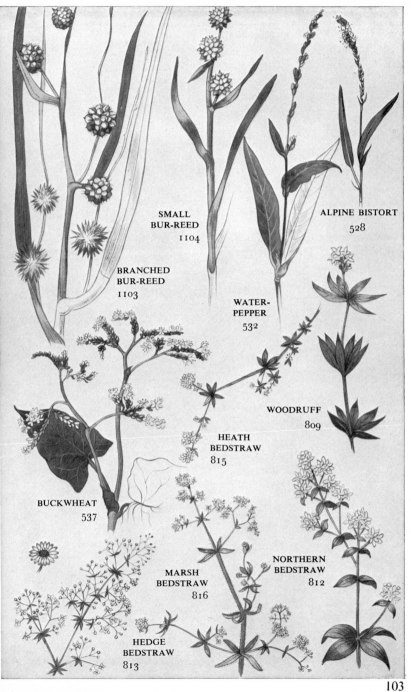

SMALL
BUR-REED
1104

ALPINE BISTORT
528

BRANCHED
BUR-REED
1103

WATER-
PEPPER
532

WOODRUFF
809

HEATH
BEDSTRAW
815

BUCKWHEAT
537

NORTHERN
BEDSTRAW
812

MARSH
BEDSTRAW
816

HEDGE
BEDSTRAW
813

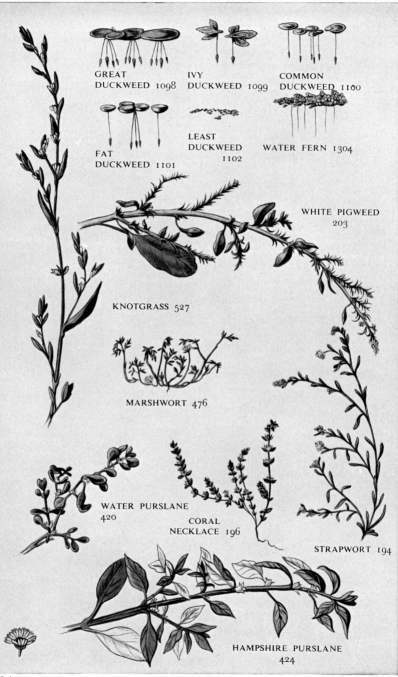

GREAT
DUCKWEED 1098

IVY
DUCKWEED 1099

COMMON
DUCKWEED 1100

FAT
DUCKWEED 1101

LEAST
DUCKWEED
1102

WATER FERN 1304

WHITE PIGWEED
203

KNOTGRASS 527

MARSHWORT 476

WATER PURSLANE
420

CORAL
NECKLACE 196

STRAPWORT 194

HAMPSHIRE PURSLANE
424

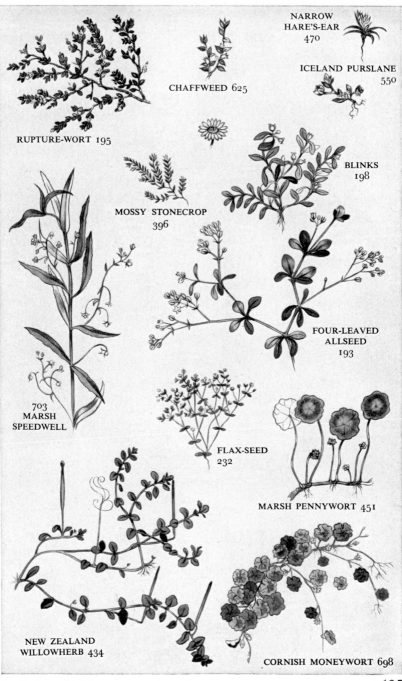

NARROW
HARE'S-EAR
470

CHAFFWEED 625

ICELAND PURSLANE
550

RUPTURE-WORT 195

BLINKS
198

MOSSY STONECROP
396

FOUR-LEAVED
ALLSEED
193

703
MARSH
SPEEDWELL

FLAX-SEED
232

MARSH PENNYWORT 451

NEW ZEALAND
WILLOWHERB 434

CORNISH MONEYWORT 698

105

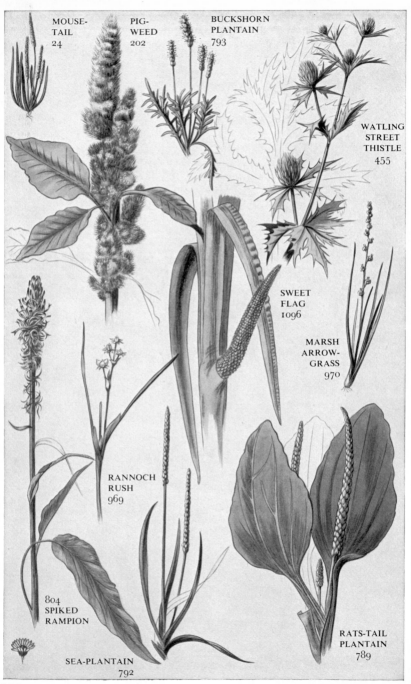

MOUSE-TAIL
24

PIG-WEED
202

BUCKSHORN
PLANTAIN
793

WATLING
STREET
THISTLE
455

SWEET
FLAG
1096

MARSH
ARROW-
GRASS
970

RANNOCH
RUSH
969

804
SPIKED
RAMPION

SEA-PLANTAIN
792

RATS-TAIL
PLANTAIN
789

106

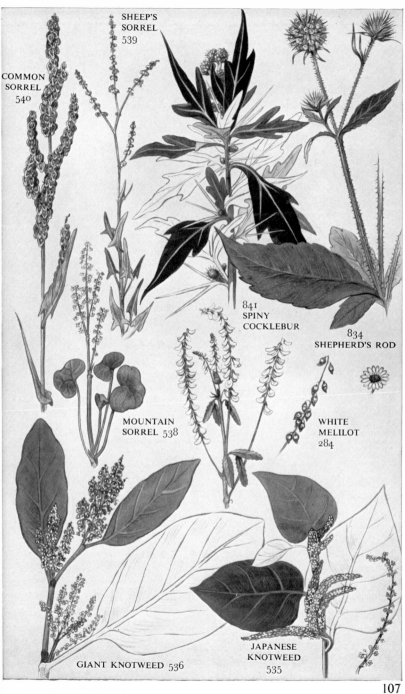

COMMON
SORREL
540

SHEEP'S
SORREL
539

841
SPINY
COCKLEBUR

834
SHEPHERD'S ROD

MOUNTAIN
SORREL 538

WHITE
MELILOT
284

GIANT KNOTWEED 536

JAPANESE
KNOTWEED
535

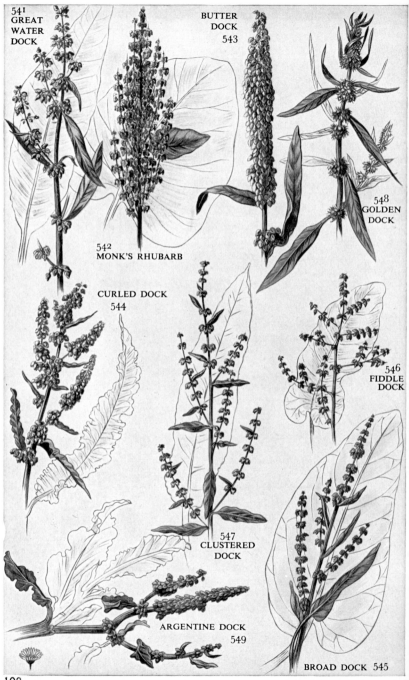

541
GREAT
WATER
DOCK

BUTTER
DOCK
543

548
GOLDEN
DOCK

542
MONK'S RHUBARB

CURLED DOCK
544

546
FIDDLE
DOCK

547
CLUSTERED
DOCK

ARGENTINE DOCK
549

BROAD DOCK 545

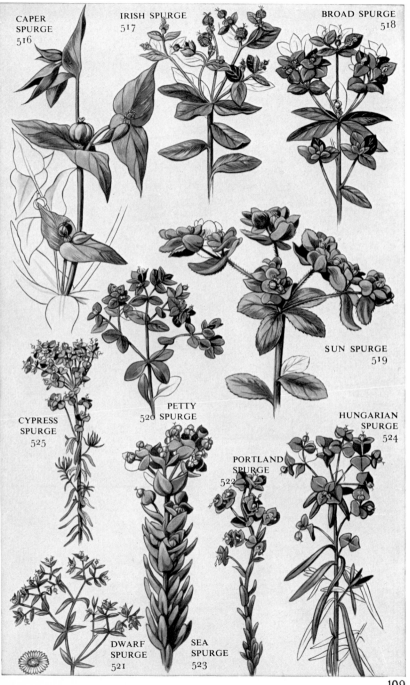

CAPER
SPURGE
516

IRISH SPURGE
517

BROAD SPURGE
518

SUN SPURGE
519

CYPRESS
SPURGE
525

PETTY
520 SPURGE

HUNGARIAN
SPURGE
524

PORTLAND
SPURGE
522

DWARF
SPURGE
521

SEA
SPURGE
523

109

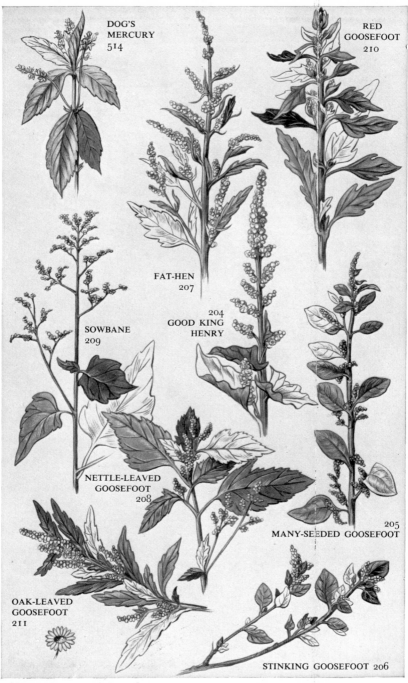

DOG'S MERCURY 514

RED GOOSEFOOT 210

FAT-HEN 207

GOOD KING HENRY 204

SOWBANE 209

NETTLE-LEAVED GOOSEFOOT 208

MANY-SEEDED GOOSEFOOT 205

OAK-LEAVED GOOSEFOOT 211

STINKING GOOSEFOOT 206

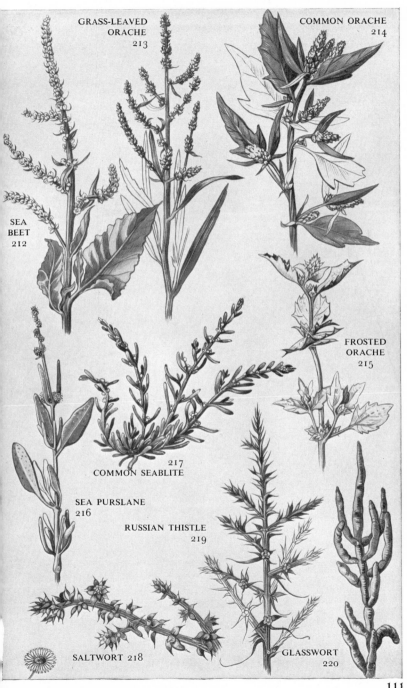

GRASS-LEAVED
ORACHE
213

COMMON ORACHE
214

SEA
BEET
212

FROSTED
ORACHE
215

217
COMMON SEABLITE

SEA PURSLANE
216

RUSSIAN THISTLE
219

SALTWORT 218

GLASSWORT
220

111

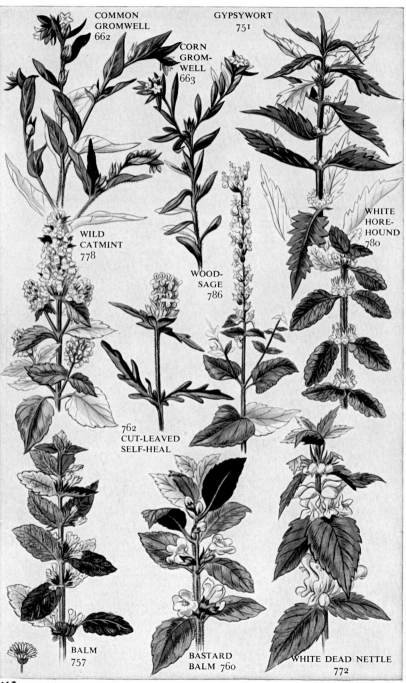

COMMON GROMWELL 662

GYPSYWORT 751

CORN GROMWELL 663

WILD CATMINT 778

WOOD-SAGE 786

WHITE HOREHOUND 780

762 CUT-LEAVED SELF-HEAL

BALM 757

BASTARD BALM 760

WHITE DEAD NETTLE 772

735. *****CLOVE-SCENTED BROOMRAPE** *O. caryophyllacea* Smith
Plate 36.   *CTW, p. 918*
   May be either stubby (on dunes) or taller (in hedges), and has flowers pink
or creamy, with a distinct clove scent, ¾-in. wide, larger than our other species.
Stamens hairy, joined near the base of the corolla-tube, which is longer than
the calyx; stigma-lobes dark purple.   *Habitat:* Rare on White Bedstraw (813),
near the coast in SE Kent. June–July.

736. ****KNAPWEED BROOMRAPE** *O. elatior* Sutton   Pl. 36.   *CTW, p. 919*
   Stout and usually 1–2 ft. high, but never as huge as most Great Broomrapes
(733); flowers with the upper lip often 2-lobed, the stamens hairy at the base and
separate well above the base of the corolla-tube, and the stigma-lobes darker
yellow.   *Habitat:* Very locally plentiful on Knapweeds, nearly always Greater
Knapweed (917), on chalk and limestone. June–July. (Incl. *O. reticulata* Wallroth, restricted to Thistles in Yorks.)

737. ***COMMON BROOMRAPE** *O. minor* Smith   Plate 36.   *CTW, p. 920*
   Much the commonest Broomrape and very variable, 4–15 in. high, most often
with purple stems and mauvish flowers, which equal or are shorter than their
bract. Corolla-tube curved and narrowed at the base, the stamens, usually almost
hairless, separate rather above the base; stigma-lobes purple or yellow.   *Habitat:*
Locally frequent in grassy places and a pest among clover crops, mainly in the
S and E. It grows on many different hosts, including garden plants; one microspecies (*O. hederae* Duby) is not infrequent on Ivy (450) in the W; rare ones are
restricted to Ox-tongues (933–934) & Hawksbeards (950–955) (*O. picridis* Koch);
and Wild Carrot (510) and Sea Holly (454) (*O. maritima* Pugsley). June–Sept.
   737a. *****Yarrow Broomrape,** *O. purpurea* Jacquin (*CTW, p. 916*), is blue-
purplish, and our only Broomrape with 3 unequal bracts under each flower, but
usually shorter than the 4–5-toothed calyx. Corolla-tube narrowed in the middle;
stigma-lobes creamy. Very rare on Composites, usually Yarrow (888), and
recently seen only in N Norfolk, E Kent and the Channel Is. June–August.

BUTTERWORT FAMILY   Lentibulariaceae

738. ****PALE BUTTERWORT** *Pinguicula lusitanica* L.   Pl. 88.   *CTW, p. 923*
   Flowers later than the next species, and has much smaller, pale lilac flowers,
with a pale yellow throat and a blunt-tipped down-turned spur; and an overwintering rosette.   *Habitat:* Local in bogs and on wet heaths in the W, from
Cornwall and Hants to Orkney; more general in Ireland. July onwards.

739. **COMMON BUTTERWORT** *P. vulgaris* L.   Plate 1.   *CTW, p. 923*
   A low, stickily hairy perennial, with a basal rosette, not unlike a greasy green
starfish, of broad oblong untoothed yellow-green leaves, whose margins roll
inwards to trap and digest insects. Flowers solitary, on 2–4-in. leafless stems,
rather the size and colour of a Violet, with a broad white patch at the mouth, the
lobes of the lower lip diverging, and a pointed spur.   *Habitat:* Widespread and
frequent in bogs and on wet heaths and moors, but very scarce in the S. May–June.
   739a. ****Giant Butterwort,** *P. grandiflora* Lamarck, is longer in all its parts and
flaunts magnificent flowers, nearly an inch across, the lobes of the lower lip with
wavy edges and usually overlapping. Very locally plentiful in SW Ireland; very
rarely naturalised in the SW May–June.

F

740. *GREATER BLADDERWORT *Utricularia vulgaris* L. Pl. 59. *CTW, p. 925*
A floating rootless aquatic perennial, whose feathery bushy, much divided
submerged leaves have toothed and bristled segments and all bear numerous
small bladders, which can entrap insects and eventually in autumn fill with water
and sink the plant to the bottom. Flowers in leafless spikes, projecting 6 in. or so
above the water, rich yellow, 2-lipped with a blunt spur; a shy flowerer, especially
in the N. Fruits recurved. *Habitat:* Widespread but uncommon in fairly deep
still fresh water. June–August. (Incl. *U. neglecta* Lehmann ('*U. major*').)

740a. **Irish Bladderwort, *U. intermedia* Hayne (incl. '*U. ochroleuca*'), is
smaller than the last species but larger than the next, and has both feathery green
leaves with toothed and bristled segments and usually no bladders, and colourless
ones (often sunk in the mud) that have bladders only. Flowers smaller, with spur
pointed. Fruits erect. Rare in shallower bog pools, least scarce in Ireland.

741. *SMALL BLADDERWORT *U. minor* L. Plate 59. *CTW, p. 926*
Slenderer than Greater Bladderwort (740), and has its leaves of two kinds,
either with feathery untoothed segments and air-bladders, or with air-bladders
alone. Flowers much smaller, pale yellow, with a very short blunt spur. Fruits
recurved. *Habitat:* Local in shallower water of bog pools. June–September.

VERBENA FAMILY Verbenaceae

742. *VERVAIN *Verbena officinalis* L. Plate 10. *CTW, p. 928*
A rough hairy scentless perennial, with stiff square stems 1–2 ft. high; pinnately lobed toothed opposite leaves, the upper lanceolate, unstalked; and long
slender spikes of small lilac more or less 2-lipped flowers. *Habitat:* Widespread
but somewhat local in dry grassy places, especially on chalk and limestone, thinning out northwards. June–September.

THYME FAMILY Labiatae

NON-WOODY, often aromatic plants with normally 2-lipped flowers, often in
whorled heads or spikes on square leafy stems; the upper lip often undivided or
occasionally missing, the lower usually 3-lobed, or the corolla may have 4–5
more or less equal lobes. Calyx-teeth similarly arranged in two lips; stamens
usually 4, often protruding from the flower. Fruits of 4 nutlets, well covered by
the calyx. Leaves in opposite pairs, undivided.

KEY TO TWO-LIPPED FLOWERS

THIS KEY covers all the Labiates (except the not obviously 2-lipped Mints), as
well as the 2-lipped members of the Figwort Family, and several allied families,
i.e. species Nos. 681–788, except for the Speedwells and Mints. Other 2-lipped
flowers include the Violets (115–122) and the Orchids (1057–1095).

I. Blue Flowers
PLANT *hairless* 781; *creeping* 781, 788.
LEAVES *broad* 758, 788; *toothed* 758, 781; *untoothed* 788.
FLOWERS *with very short upper lip* 788; *with stamens projecting* 758.

II. Purple, Violet or Lilac Flowers
PLANT *aromatic* 752, 753, 754, 756, 759, 766, 767, 768, 770, 771, 773, 779;
    hairless 683, 684, 691, 782; *prostrate* 689, 690, 691, 753, 755, 761; *stickily hairy*
    728, 738, 739; *woolly* 765.

LEAVES *arrow- or halberd-shaped* 690; *pinnate* 742, 785; *with purple sheen* 728, 731,; *clasping stem* 770.

FLOWERS *partly yellow* 689, 690, 691, 724, 728, 738; *partly white* 683a, 728, 739, 755, 773; *with no upper lip* 783, 784, 785; *with stamens projecting* 752, 753, 754, 755, 756, 759; *spurred* 683, 684, 688, 689, 690, 691, 738, 739; *with prickly calyx-teeth* 773, 776, 777.

III. Pink or Red Flowers

PLANT *hairless* 692, 693, 722, 726; *aromatic* 779; *foetid* 692, 693, 767; *not green* 732, 734, 735, 737; *with stem winged* 693.

LEAVES *narrow* 681, 682, 725, 726, 729, 774; *pinnate* 722; *untoothed* 681, 682, 725, 726; *none* 732, 734, 735, 737.

FLOWERS *pouched behind* 681, 682; *with stamens projecting* 779; *fragrant* 735; *partly yellow* 724, 725; *with calyx inflated* 722.

IV. Yellow Flowers

PLANT *aromatic* 769, 787; *creeping* 769; *not green* 733, 736, 737; *hairless* 685, 686, 695, 723, 726, 740, 741; *stickily hairy* 687, 695b, 730; *floating* 740, 741; *prostrate* 686, 689, 690, 695b, 787.

LEAVES *roundish* 689; *pinnate* 740, 741; *lobed* 787; *arrow-shaped* 690; *toothed* 695, 723, 730, 769, 775, 776; *none* 733, 736, 737.

FLOWERS *partly orange* 685; *partly red* 695, 787; *partly purple* 689, 690, 724, 733, 737, 776; *with no upper lip* 786, 787; *spurred* 685, 686, 687, 689, 690, 740, 741; *with stamens projecting* 694; *with calyx inflated* 723.

V. White Flowers

PLANT *aromatic* 757, 760, 772, 778, 780; *woolly* 780.

LEAVES *roundish* 728, 780; *pinnate* 762.

FLOWERS *with pink marks* 760, 778; *with yellow spot* 728; *over 1 in. long* 760; *with stamens projecting* 760.

MINTS *Mentha*

PERENNIALS, varying from prostrate to 3 ft. high, with an aromatic smell, usually of the well known minty savour, but distinctive in several species. Flowers small, usually some shade of lilac, bell-shaped with 4 or more or less equal petal-like corolla-lobes, in close whorls; calyx 5-toothed; stamens 4, often projecting. Mints are very variable, and hybrids, varieties and sports readily perpetuate themselves by runners. The hybrids often occur in the absence of their parents.

KEY TO MINTS (Nos. 743–751)

PLANT *prostrate* 743; *hairless* 743, 748; *not aromatic* 751.

LEAVES *round* 743, 750; *oval* 744, 745, 746, 747, 750; *lanceolate* 748, 749, 751; *untoothed* 743; *unstalked* 748, 749, 751; *shiny* 748.

FLOWERS *along stems* 743, 744, 745, 746, 747, 751; *in spikes* 748, 749, 750; *in heads* 747; *with stamens not protruding* 746, 747a, 748a, 750; *with hairless calyx* 748; *with hairless stalks* 743, 745, 746ab, 747a, 748.

743. ***CORSICAN MINT *Mentha requienii* Bentham Pl. 11. *CTW, p. 933*
A prostrate, often slightly hairy mat-forming perennial, with a minty smell of its own; thread-like creeping and rooting stems; tiny pale green roundish un-toothed, well stalked opposite leaves, and very small lilac flowers, 2 or more together. *Habitat:* Naturalised in a few damp woodland rides. June–September.

744. **PENNYROYAL *M. pulegium* L. Plate 11. *CTW, p. 934*

A downy Mint, with stems 3–9 in. high, prostrate at the base, and small, slightly bluntly toothed stalked oval, often drooping leaves. Flowers in prominent whorls, small, lilac, the calyx hairy and markedly ribbed, the 2 lower teeth narrower than the 3 upper; stamens protruding. *Habitat:* Widespread but now very uncommon on damp heaths, chiefly in the S and W. August onwards.

745. CORN MINT *M. arvensis* L. Plate 10. *CTW, p. 934*

Generally the commonest Mint away from water; hairy, with rather weak leafy stems 3–18 in. high, and stalked toothed, pointed oval leaves, much longer than the whorls of small lilac flowers on sometimes hairy stalks at their base; the uppermost leaves almost always flowerless. Calyx hairy, short, with short, often broadly triangular teeth (Fig.); styles and stamens usually protruding prominently; scent acrid. *Habitat:* Widespread and frequent in arable fields and damp places. June onwards. Figs. × 4.

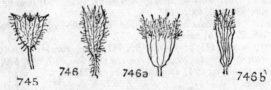

745   746   746a   746b

746. *WHORLED MINT *M. × verticillata* L. Plate 11. *CTW, p. 934*

The hybrid between our two commonest Mints, resembling Corn Mint (745) in its whorls of flowers up the stem, but Water Mint (747) in its nearly always hairy flower-stalks and long calyx, hairy all over and with teeth twice as long as broad (Fig.); stamens normally not protruding. *Habitat:* Widespread and rather frequent in damp places. July onwards.

746a. **Bushy Mint, *M. gentilis* L. (incl. *M. × cardiaca* (Gray) Baker), is less hairy and has stems often red, fresh green leaves and the short calyx hairy only on the teeth (Fig.). Local, often as a garden outcast.

746b. **Tall Mint, *M. smithiana* Graham (*M. rubra* Smith), is often larger, taller, with leaves scarcely hairy, much rounder (especially the upper), all stalked and often with prominent reddish veins. Flowers redder; calyx long, almost hairless, short-toothed (Fig.); stamens protruding. Very local.

747. WATER MINT *M. aquatica* L. Plate 11. *CTW, p. 936*

Our commonest waterside Mint; variable, hairy, often purplish, with stiff stems 9 in. to 2 ft. high, pointed oval toothed stalked leaves, and lilac or reddish flowers in a round terminal head often with a few whorls at the base of the topmost leaves, the calyx long and hairy; stamens and style usually protruding. *Habitat:* Widespread and common in wet places. July–September.

747a. ***Eau-de-Cologne Mint, *M. citrata* Ehrhart, with a lemon instead of a peppermint scent, is much less hairy, and has rounder leaves and stamens not protruding. Very rare, in the S.

748. **SPEAR-MINT *M. spicata* L. Plate 11. *CTW, p. 937*

The usual garden Mint, to go with roast lamb; more or less hairless, with slightly toothed lanceolate, virtually unstalked, shining green leaves, and terminal spikes of lilac flowers; stamens protruding. *Habitat:* Widespread, but nowhere common, and usually as a blatant escape. August–September.

748*a*. ****Peppermint,** *M. piperita* L., with the typical peppermint smell, is often larger, and has a purple stem and all its darker leaves clearly stalked, often purplish, and sometimes hairy beneath; fatter, more interrupted flower-spikes; and stamens not protruding. A rare form is densely hairy. Chiefly in the S and W.

749. *HORSE-MINT *M. longifolia* (L.) Hudson Plate 11. *CTW, p. 938*

Larger, coarser and greyer-green than Spear-mint (748), and more or less hairy all over, especially under the leaves, with a different, less pungent smell; calyx and flower-stalks hairy. *Habitat:* Widespread, but very local by streams and on banks. August–September.

750. **APPLE MINT *M. rotundifolia* (L.) Hudson Plate 11. *CTW, p. 939*

Differs from the last species in its apple scent and in being more thickly covered with whitish hairs, especially beneath the smaller thicker, deeply wrinkled oval leaves. Flower-spike much shorter, with denser whorls of smaller, pinker or almost white flowers. *Habitat:* Ditches and roadsides; fairly frequent in the SW, otherwise rare. August–September. Round-leaved Mint.

750*a*. ***Large Apple Mint,** *M. alopecuroides* Hull, is robuster, taller and darker green, with larger, less wrinkled and more sharply toothed leaves; and larger darker flowers, often in longer thicker spikes. Widespread but local, especially near gardens.

751. GIPSYWORT *Lycopus europaeus* L. Plate 112. *CTW, p. 939*

Rather like a slightly hairy scentless white Mint, 1–3 ft. high, with deeply toothed lanceolate leaves right up the stem, and small bell-shaped purple-dotted white flowers in close whorls at the base of the upper ones. *Habitat:* Widespread and common by fresh water, thinning out northwards. June–September.

752. MARJORAM *Origanum vulgare* L. Plate 26. *CTW, p. 940*

A tufted downy aromatic perennial, 1–2 ft. high, with slender stems branching only above; stalked oval, often slightly toothed leaves; and loose heads of numerous small dark purple buds turning to paler purple 2-lipped flowers with usually purple bracts at their base. *Habitat:* Widespread, locally common in grassy places, usually on chalk or limestone, decreasing northwards. July–Sept.

753. WILD THYME *Thymus drucei* Ronniger Plate 28. *CTW, p. 942*

A prostrate mat-forming faintly aromatic perennial, with extensively creeping and rooting thin woody runners; flowering stems short, squarish, with the hairs dense on two faces and sparse or none on the other two. Leaves opposite, very small, short-stalked, leathery, more or less oval, varying from almost hairless to quite woolly, often twisted so as to lie flat. Flowers reddish-purple, small, in showy, roundish terminal heads; calyx dark. *Habitat:* Widespread and often abundant in dry grassy and heathy places and on dunes; rare in the SE, and there only on chalk downs. June–August.

753*a*. ***Large Wild Thyme,** *T. pulegioides* L. (*T. ovatus* Miller), is generally more upright in growth, except where closely grazed, and has no long creeping runners. Flowering stems taller, square, with hairs in rows down the four corners, short hairs on the two narrow faces and none on the two broad faces. Leaves larger, oval, stalked, usually thin, strongly and distinctively aromatic, hairless. Flower-heads elongated, often with one or more separate whorls at the base.

Habitat: Common on chalk downs, more rarely on heaths, in S and E England; rare elsewhere. July onwards.

753*b*. ***Breckland Wild Thyme**, *T. serpyllum* L., is much shorter than most forms of the common Wild Thyme, and has small upright leaves broadest towards the tip, and flowering stems more or less round and evenly hairy. Confined to the brecks of E Anglia. July–August.

754. *COMMON CALAMINT *Calamintha ascendens* Jordan Pl. 29. *CTW, 944*
A little branched mint-scented tufted hairy perennial, 12–18 in. high, with open, rather 1-sided spikes of pale violet pink flowers spotted darker, in shortly stalked opposite clusters at the base of the rather small stalked, slightly toothed oval dark green leaves. Flower-stalk at an angle off the often purple calyx, which has teeth fringed with long hairs, and short hairs not protruding from its throat after flowering. *Habitat:* Local on dry grassy banks, especially on chalk and limestone, in England, Wales and S Ireland. July–September. '*C. officinalis*'.

754*a*. **Lesser Calamint**, *C. nepeta* (L.) Savi (incl. '*C. baetica*'), is more branched, with much smaller downier grey, less toothed leaves and denser clusters of paler lilac, less spotted flowers on stalks in a straight line with the calyx which has shorter hairs fringing its teeth and other hairs plainly visible at its mouth after flowering. More local, in drier grassland, mostly in E Anglia; not in Ireland.

754*b*. ***Wood Calamint**, *C. sylvatica* Bromfield ('*C. intermedia*'), has larger leaves and a dark corolla up to $\frac{3}{4}$ in., more than twice as long as the calyx. On a single shady bank on chalk in the Isle of Wight. August onwards.

755. *BASIL THYME *Acinos arvensis* (Lamarck) Dandy Pl. 10. *CTW, p. 946*
A low, often prostrate hairy annual, not aromatic, with small stalked, slightly toothed oval leaves, the veins prominent, and at the base of all but the lowest ones small whorls of violet flowers, the corolla with a white patch on the lower lip and longer than the waisted calyx. *Habitat:* Widespread but local in bare dry places, especially on chalk and limestone; very local in Scotland and Ireland. May onwards. *Calamintha acinos* (L.) Clairville.

756. WILD BASIL *Clinopodium vulgare* L. Plate 29. *CTW, p. 946*
A downy, faintly aromatic, generally unbranched perennial, 9–18 in. high, with whorls of largish pinkish-purple flowers at the base of the topmost stalked, slightly toothed, pointed oval leaves; the whorls look woolly since the calyx, which is often maroon, and the numerous bristle-like bracts are white with hairs. *Habitat:* Widespread and frequent in dry and bushy grassy places, especially on chalk and limestone, thinning out northwards; very rare in Ireland. July onwards. *Calamintha vulgaris* (L.) Druce.

757. **BALM *Melissa officinalis* L. Plate 112. *CTW, p. 947*
A hairy yellow-green lemon-scented perennial, 1–2 ft. high, with stalked toothed wrinkled, pointed oval leaves, the lowest heart-shaped at the base. Flowers small, narrow, white, with the corolla-tube bent slightly upwards, in clusters at the base of the upper leaves. *Habitat:* A bee-plant occasionally escaped in the S. July–September.

758. **MEADOW SAGE *Salvia pratensis* L. Plate 10. *CTW, p. 949*
A showy rarity, with prominent whorled spikes of fine bright violet-blue open-mouthed flowers, for which the next species is often wishfully mistaken.

A hairy, very slightly aromatic perennial, 1–2 ft. high, with long narrow, bluntly toothed wrinkled leaves, chiefly at the base. Calyx downy but with no white hairs, much shorter than the ¾-in. corolla, the centre of the three top teeth being tiny; lower lip of corolla often paler; stamens 2. *Habitat:* Very local in grassy places on chalk or limestone in the S. June–July.

759. *CLARY *S. horminoides* Pourret ('*S. verbenaca*') Plate 10. *CTW, p. 949*
Smaller, greyer and much less showy than the last species, with a leafier stem, more jaggedly toothed leaves, and paler, mauver, compacter flowers, their mouth more closed, the calyx with white hairs. *Habitat:* Widespread and locally frequent in dry grassy places, especially in the S and E. June–September.

760. **BASTARD BALM *Melittis melissophyllum* L. Plate 112. *CTW, p. 950*
Our largest-flowered Labiate, a hairy, strong-smelling perennial, 9 in. to 2 ft. high with white and pink flowers 1–1½ in. long at the base of the toothed pointed oval leaves. *Habitat:* Very local in shady places in Wales and SW England; very rare further E. May–July.

761. SELF-HEAL *Prunella vulgaris* L. Plate 10. *CTW, p. 951*
A short creeping downy perennial, prostrate or up to 8 in. high, not aromatic, with pointed oval leaves not or only slightly toothed, the lower stalked. Flowers violet, occasionally pink or white, in oblong or squarish terminal heads; calyx large, purple. *Habitat:* Widespread and abundant in grassy places. June onwards.

762. **CUT-LEAVED SELF-HEAL *P. laciniata* (L.) L. Plate 112. *CTW, p. 951*
Differs from the last species in its heads of somewhat larger and creamy white flowers, and hairier leaves, the upper more or less pinnate. Hybridises with the last species. *Habitat:* Very local in dry grassy places in S England, usually on chalk or limestone. June–August.

763. BETONY *Betonica officinalis* L. Plate 29. *CTW, p. 953*
A slightly hairy, usually unbranched perennial, a foot or so high, with stalked, slightly toothed oblong, blunt leaves, wide apart on the stems, but the topmost unstalked beneath the oblong spike of brilliant reddish-purple flowers. *Habitat:* Widespread and locally frequent in heathy and bushy places; local in Scotland and Ireland. June onwards. *Stachys officinalis* (L.) Treviranus.

764. *FIELD WOUNDWORT *Stachys arvensis* (L.) L. Plate 10. *CTW, p. 954*
A hairy annual, 4–12 in. long, usually half-prostrate, with stalked, bluntly toothed oval leaves, the topmost unstalked, and whorls of small dull purple flowers, much pinker than Basil Thyme (755), in a long leafy spike; corolla little longer than the calyx, which has 5 rather long equal teeth. *Habitat:* A local weed of arable land, commoner in the W and preferring acid soils. April onwards.

765. ***DOWNY WOUNDWORT *S. germanica* L. Plate 29. *CTW, p. 954*
An unbranched, somewhat mullein-like perennial, 1–3 ft. high, with a thick covering of long white silky hairs; leaves pointed oval, toothed, with prominent veins, sometimes greenish beneath, the upper with very short or no stalks, the lowest broad at the base. Flowers pale pinkish-purple in close whorls in a leafy spike; the bristle-like bracts at their base nearly as long as the calyx. Often confused with the shorter, somewhat foetid Lambsear (*S. lanata* Jacquin), an

occasional garden outcast, which grows in a mat, and is whiter and even more densely felted, so that the calyx is quite buried in the wool, which also hides the veins on the upper side of the scarcely toothed leaves, narrower at the base. *Habitat:* Now only in a very few hedge-banks in mid-Oxfordshire. July onwards.

766. MARSH WOUNDWORT   *S. palustris* L.   Plate 29.   *CTW, p. 955*

A stout hairy creeping perennial, sometimes faintly aromatic, with hollow, usually unbranched stems 2–3 ft. high, and toothed lanceolate leaves on very short or no stalks. Flowers pale rose-purple in whorled spikes; calyx often maroon, with teeth at least half as long as the tube. Hybridises with the next species. *Habitat:* Widespread and locally common by fresh water, especially in ditches, and as an arable weed. July onwards.

767. HEDGE WOUNDWORT   *S. sylvatica* L.   Plate 29.   *CTW, p. 955*

A roughly hairy, dark green creeping perennial, 1–3 ft. high, with a pungent smell, solid stems, and its leaves all stalked, toothed and heart-shaped. Flowers narrow-looking, dark beetroot-purple with whitish blotches, in whorled spikes; calyx-teeth at least half as long as the tube; a minute bristle-like bract at the base of and about equalling each flower-stalk. *Habitat:* Widespread and common in hedge-banks and shady waste places. June onwards.

767*a.* ***Limestone Woundwort, *S. alpina* L., is velvety and has no smell or creeping rootstock, and softer, blunter, more widely heart-shaped leaves. Flowers dull pinky-red blotched cream, in thick whorls in leafy spikes; calyx-teeth unequal, much less than half as long as their tube; and broader bracts nearly as long as the calyx. Very rare by woods and in hedges on limestone in the Cotswolds and Denbighshire.

768. BLACK HOREHOUND   *Ballota nigra* L.   Plate 29.   *CTW, p. 956*

A rather bushy untidy weedy hairy perennial, 1–2 ft. high, with a pungent smell; leaves stalked, toothed, pointed oval. Flowers purplish-pink, in clusters up the leafy stem; calyx funnel-shaped, ribbed. *Habitat:* Frequent on roadsides and waste ground in England and Wales; local elsewhere. June onwards.

769. YELLOW ARCHANGEL   *Galeobdolon luteum* Hudson   Pl. 60.   *CTW, 957*

Less hairy than White Dead-nettle (772), with numerous leafy runners, narrower and darker green leaves, and yellow flowers with reddish-brown honey-guides. *Habitat:* Widespread and locally common in woods; rare in S Scotland and SE Ireland. May–June. *Lamium galeobdolon* (L.) L.

770. HENBIT   *Lamium amplexicaule* L.   Plate 28.   *CTW, p. 958*
(incl. *L. molucellifolium* Fries)

Differs from Red Dead-nettle (771) in its more deeply and bluntly toothed leaves being always rounded, the topmost ones unstalked and often half-clasping the stem. Flowers gayer, in whorls at wider intervals up the stem, rich peony-purple in bud, with an erecter, usually long slender corolla-tube, and a densely hairy hooded upper lip; calyx silky white, with teeth erect or converging. *Habitat:* A widespread but local weed of cultivated ground. April–August.

771. RED DEAD-NETTLE   *L. purpureum* L.   Plate 28.   *CTW, p. 959*

A sprawling downy annual, 3–9 in. high, often tinged purplish, pungent when crushed, and with square stems often leafless below the leafy flower-spike. Leaves all stalked, oval, often pointed at the tip and heart-shaped at the base, wrinkled, bluntly toothed. Flowers pale or dark pinkish-purple, the corolla with a small hooded upper lip, the lower lip 2-lobed and toothed at the base, and more than twice as long as the calyx. *Habitat:* A widespread and abundant weed of cultivated ground. Throughout the year.

771*a*. *Cut-leaved Dead-nettle, *L. hybridum* Villars, has more triangular and jaggedly toothed leaves (Fig. × ½), and corolla-tube hardly longer than calyx. Much more local.

771*b*. **Spotted Dead-nettle, *L. maculatum* L., is a much larger perennial, and has a more evenly leafy stem, usually with a large pale blotch on the rather more deeply toothed leaves. Flowers of a rather richer purple, with a tall erect upper lip like the next species. An occasional garden escape. May onwards.

771a

772. WHITE DEAD-NETTLE *L. album* L.   Plate 112.   *CTW, p. 959*

A hairy, faintly aromatic creeping perennial, 6–12 in. high, with stout square stems. Leaves more or less heart-shaped, toothed, slightly resembling Stinging Nettle (554), but with no stinging hairs, and at their base whorls of rather large white flowers with a wide open mouth; calyx-teeth 5, long, almost bristle-like. *Habitat:* Widespread and common in hedge-banks and waste places; local in Scotland and Ireland. March onwards.

773. **MOTHERWORT   *Leonurus cardiaca* L.   Plate 29.   *CTW, p. 960*

A tall unbranched, slightly downy, dark green perennial, 2–4 ft. high, with a pungent smell and whorls of furry pinkish-purple flowers up the leafy stems; fruiting calyx with 5 exceedingly stiff prickly teeth. Leaves often held horizontally, long-stalked, tapering to the base with 3–5 deep pointed lobes. *Habitat:* A rare herb, usually near buildings. July–September.

774. RED HEMP-NETTLE   *Galeopsis angustifolia* Hoffmann   Pl. 28.   *CTW, 961*

Never so large as Common Hemp-nettle (776), with stems softly downy or almost hairless and hardly swollen at the joints, smaller narrower leaves, and large flowers of a fine deep pink, flecked with white on the lip, the corolla-tube much longer than the green calyx. *Habitat:* Local on arable land and shingle in England and Wales; scarce elsewhere. July onwards. (Incl. *G. ladanum* L.)

775. ***DOWNY HEMP-NETTLE   *G. dubia* Leers   Plate 60.   *CTW, p. 962*

A very softly downy annual, 1–2 ft. high, with stems not swollen at the joints, unlike Large Hemp-Nettle (777); toothed lanceolate leaves; and pale yellow flowers an inch or so long, rather few in the whorl, the corolla-tube much longer than the calyx and much larger than Common Hemp-Nettle (776). *Habitat:* Now only seen, and not every year, on arable land in one small area of N Wales. July onwards.

776. COMMON HEMP-NETTLE   *G. tetrahit* L.   Plate 28.   *CTW, p. 962*

A variable, stiffly hairy annual, 4 in. to 2 ft. high, with stems swollen at the joints, and broad lanceolate, toothed stalked leaves. Flowers in whorls on the leafy stem, usually pale pinkish-purple but sometimes white or pale yellow, the corolla-tube usually scarcely longer than the often dark brown calyx, which has long prickly bristle-like teeth. Hemp-nettles are our only Labiates with 2 small bumps at the angle between the 2 outer and the centre lobes of the lower lip.

Habitat: Widespread and fairly frequent on arable land, also in woods and fens. July–August. (Incl. *G. bifida* Boenninghausen.)

777. *LARGE HEMP-NETTLE *G. speciosa* Miller Plate 60 *CTW, p. 963*
Showier, stouter and often more broadly branched than the last species, with pale yellow flowers nearly twice the size, the lower lip darker and the central lobe normally purple; corolla-tube much longer than the green calyx. *Habitat:* A local weed of arable land, chiefly in the N. July–September.

778. **WILD CATMINT *Nepeta cataria* L. Plate 112. *CTW, p. 964*
A stiff grey downy perennial, 6 in. to 2 ft. high, with a minty smell relished by cats; leaves heart-shaped, toothed, stalked. Flowers in broad whorls, the upper ones rather crowded, on a leafy, branched spike, white with dark pink spots; calyx 5-toothed. The very different more sprawling Garden Catmint (*N. × faasenii*), with bright violet flowers, sometimes escapes and is recorded as the wild plant. *Habitat:* Local and never plentiful on dry hedge-banks and roadsides, chiefly in England and Wales. July–September.

779. GROUND IVY *Glechoma hederacea* L. Plate 10. *CTW, p. 965*
A low, usually soft hairy, often purplish, pungently aromatic perennial, with long rooting runners, and long-stalked kidney-shaped leaves with blunt teeth. Flowers conspicuous in loose whorls at the base of the leaves, blue-violet, rarely larger and pink. *Habitat:* Widespread and common in woods and hedge-banks, sometimes on bare ground. March–June. *Nepeta hederacea* (L.) Treviranus.

780. *WHITE HOREHOUND *Marrubium vulgare* L. Pl. 112. *CTW, p. 965*
A stiff perennial, 12–18 in. high, with a thymy aromatic smell, hoary with white down; leaves roundish, bluntly toothed, stalked, grey-green and wrinkled above, paler beneath. Flowers all white, in dense whorls up the leafy stem; calyx with 10 narrow hooked teeth. *Habitat:* Widespread but local in rather bare dry places on chalk downs and by waysides, also in fields manured with shoddy; Scotland and Ireland, only in the S. June onwards.

781. COMMON SKULLCAP *Scutellaria galericulata* L. Pl. 11. *CTW, p. 966*
An often downy creeping perennial, 6–12 in. high, with short-stalked, bluntly toothed lanceolate leaves. Flowers in pairs up the leafy stem, ½-in. long, bright blue, with a slightly curved corolla-tube much longer than the blunt calyx. *Habitat:* Widespread, frequent by fresh water and in wet grassy places. June–Sept.

782. *LESSER SKULLCAP *S. minor* Hudson Plate 28. *CTW, p. 967*
Bushier, much smaller and less downy than Common Skullcap (781), rarely above 6 in. high, and with shorter and less toothed leaves, the topmost ones untoothed, and flowers pale pinkish-purple spotted darker. Hybridises with 781. *Habitat:* Widespread but local in damp heathy places. July onwards.

783. ***WALL GERMANDER *Teucrium chamaedrys* L. Pl. 28. *CTW, p. 968*
A tufted, scarcely branched hairy perennial, about a foot high, with short-stalked, pointed oval, toothed, shiny, dark green leaves. Flowers crimson-purple, lacking an upper lip, in short leafy whorled spikes. *Habitat:* Rare on old walls and dry banks, mainly in the S. July–September.

784. ***WATER GERMANDER *T. scordium* L. Plate 10. *CTW, p. 968*
A sprawling grey downy perennial, 3–12 in. high, with unstalked, toothed, oblong leaves. Flowers in whorls up the leafy stems, pale purple, with no upper lip. *Habitat:* Frequent in dune slacks at Braunton Burrows and along the lakes of the R. Shannon; now very rare by fresh water in E. Anglia and elsewhere in Ireland. July onwards.

785. ***CUT-LEAVED GERMANDER *T. botrys* L. Plate 28. *CTW, p. 969*
A low downy annual, 3–12 in. high, one of the few Labiates with small, deeply cut triangular leaves, the lower almost 2-pinnate. Flowers rich pink, with no upper lip, in small clusters along the leafy stems; calyx waisted, pouched behind. *Habitat:* Rare in open and arable ground on chalk or limestone from Kent to the Cotswolds. July–September.

786. WOOD-SAGE *T. scorodonia* L. Plate 112. *CTW, p. 969*
Our only Labiate with greenish-yellow flowers and no upper lip; a downy perennial, about a foot high, with stalked, bluntly toothed wrinkled, pointed oval leaves. Flowers in pairs in branched 1-sided leafless spikes, with prominent maroon stamens. *Habitat:* Widespread and locally abundant in dry shady and heathy places, also on old dunes and scree, preferring acid soils. July–September.

787. **GROUND-PINE *Ajuga chamaepitys* (L.) Schreber Pl. 61. *CTW, p. 970*
A bushy hairy grey-green annual, prostrate or to 6 in. high, with a faint smell of pine resin, the leaves with 3 very narrow linear lobes; generally looking somewhat like a bushy pine seedling. Flowers 1–2 together up the leafy, often purple stem, yellow with tiny red spots in the throat and a very short upper lip. *Habitat:* Very local on open and arable ground on chalk in SE England. May–September.

788. BUGLE *A. reptans* L. Plate 10. *CTW, p. 970*
An unbranched perennial, 6 in. or so high, with stems hairy on two opposite sides, and rooting runners; leaves oblong, hairless, hardly toothed, sometimes bronzy-purple, long-stalked below and in opposite almost unstalked pairs up the stiff stem, the topmost often purplish, especially underneath. Flowers rich powder-blue, veined, occasionally pink, cream or white, with a very short upper lip, in a dense leafy spike. *Habitat:* Widespread and common in dampish woods and shady grassy places. April–June.
788a. *****Limestone Bugle**, *A. pyramidalis* L., is greyer, with no runners, stems hairy all round, root-leaves hairy and purer blue flowers shorter than the topmost leaves; a shy flowerer. Very local and elusive on limestone rocks in N Scotland and around Galway Bay. April–May.

PLANTAIN FAMILY Plantaginaceae

OUR NATIVE Plantains are rather dull perennials (Buckshorn Plantain (793) may be annual), very variable in size, with ribbed or veined leaves in rosettes at the base of unbranched leafless stems topped by dense spikes of minute flowers, which have their corolla-lobes, sepals and stamens in fours, and long prominent stamens. Mousetail (24), Arrow-grasses (970) and Adderstongue (1306) could all be mistaken for Plantains.

789. RATSTAIL PLANTAIN *Plantago major* L. Plate 106. *CTW, p. 973*

Our stoutest coarsest Plantain, usually hairless and 3–18 in. high, the stalked, sometimes toothed, often wavy, broad oval leaves with prominent unbranched veins below. Flowers in greenish spikes up to 6 in. long on unfurrowed stalks, tiny, very pale yellow, with conspicuous anthers, purple when young. *Habitat:* Widespread and common in bare waste or well-trodden places such as waysides, farmyards and lawns. June onwards.

790. HOARY PLANTAIN *P. media* L. Plate 26. *CTW, p. 973*

A downy, rather grey plant, 4–12 in. high, with a flat rosette of broad or narrow elliptical leaves gradually narrowing to the very short winged stalk, with prominent ribs. Flower-spikes 1–3 in., on unfurrowed stalks, grey-green, looking pale pinkish-purple from its stamens. *Habitat:* Widespread and locally frequent in lawns and other grassy places, especially on chalk and limestone, but thinning out northwards; not native in Ireland. May–August.

791. RIBWORT PLANTAIN *P. lanceolata* L. Plate 37. *CTW, p. 973*

A familiar plant, used for the game of 'soldiers', often hairy, 6 in. to 2 ft. high, the long, slightly toothed stalked lanceolate leaves with 3–5 prominent unbranched ribs below. Flowers in dense stubby spikes $\frac{1}{2}$–1 in. long, on furrowed stalks, blackish-brown or greenish before flowering but pale brown afterwards, with prominent pale yellow or purple anthers. *Habitat:* Widespread and abundant in grassy and waste places; too often on lawns. April onwards.

792. SEA PLANTAIN *P. maritima* L. Plate 106. *CTW, p. 974*

A low, normally hairless plant, 4–9 in. high, the thick fleshy, sometimes slightly toothed linear leaves with 3–5 obscure veins, flatter and broader than Sea Arrowgrass (970*a*). Flowers in a dense 1–3-in. greenish spike on an unfurrowed stem, with minute brownish flowers and pale yellow anthers on long slender stamens. Fruits 2-seeded. *Habitat:* Widespread and common on sea-shores, especially in salt-marshes; also on mountains. June–August.

793. BUCKSHORN PLANTAIN *P. coronopus* L. Plate 106. *CTW, p. 974*

A low, usually downy biennial, sometimes extremely small and quite prostrate, the narrow leaves being in a rosette and normally pinnately lobed but occasionally linear and hardly toothed, but even then they are shorter and more prostrate than Sea Plantain (792) and have only a single vein. Flower-spikes also shorter than the last species. Fruits 3–4 seeded. *Habitat:* Widespread and locally common on bare ground near the sea; less frequently inland in dry sandy places in the S. May–July.

794. *SHORE-WEED *Littorella uniflora* (L.) Ascherson Pl. 66. *CTW, p. 975*

A low hairless aquatic perennial, often with rooting runners, sometimes forming swards, with tufts of half-cylindrical leaves 1–6 in. long, usually flat on one side but rounded on the other, sheathing at the base. Flowers greenish, shyly produced under water; male solitary on leafless stalks with long, prominent, slender stamens; female unstalked, at the base of the same plant. Under water the plant is normally flowerless with much longer leaves. Can be confused with Awlwort (76), Water Lobelia (807) and Quillwort (1266) leaves. *Habitat:* Widespread and locally frequent in and by lakes and pools with acid water, mainly in the N, June–August.

BELLFLOWER FAMILY Campanulaceae

PERENNIALS WITH alternate undivided leaves, distinctive for their stalked bell-shaped flowers, the corolla usually blue, with 5 short lobes; persisting above the globular fruits; stamens 5; style 1; seeds numerous.

795. **IVY-LEAVED BELLFLOWER *Wahlenbergia hederacea* (L.)
Campanula hederacea L.   Reichenbach Plate 7. *CTW, p. 977*
An extremely delicate hairless low creeping, pale green perennial, with small, pale blue bell-shaped flowers, on hairlike stalks longer than the stalked, somewhat ivy-shaped leaves. *Habitat:* Local in damp places on moors and heaths, and in woodland rides, chiefly in the W and SE, and SW Ireland. July–August.

796. *GIANT BELLFLOWER *Campanula latifolia* L. Plate 4. *CTW, p. 979*
A handsome, softly hairy perennial, with bluntly angled, unbranched stems 3–5 ft. high, and toothed lanceolate leaves, the lower with a winged stalk, the upper narrower and unstalked. Flowers 2 in. long, purplish-blue, singly in a long leafy spike, the lower ones opening first; calyx-teeth narrow, hairless, often spreading. *Habitat:* Widespread and locally frequent in woods and hedge-banks mainly in the N, thinning out southwards to the Midlands; not in Ireland or S. England. July–September.

796a. *Nettle-leaved Bellflower, *C. trachelium* L., is not so tall and more roughly hairy, with more sharply angled stems; irregularly and coarsely toothed triangular long pointed leaves; the upper ones sometimes short-stalked and the lower ones broader; and smaller shorter-stalked, darker blue flowers, 1–3 together in a shorter spike, the top ones opening first, and with shorter broader hairy calyx-teeth. Locally frequent in the S, especially on chalk and limestone, thinning out northwards to the Scottish Lowlands; also in SE Ireland.

797. *CREEPING BELLFLOWER *C. rapunculoides* L. Pl. 4. *CTW, p. 980*
Small and slenderer than Nettle-leaved Bellflower (796a), and much less hairy, with underground creeping runners; the stem hardly angled; narrower, more evenly toothed leaves; an often longer tapering spike of narrower drooping flowers opening mostly from the bottom; and calyx slightly hairy at the base, the teeth spreading or down-turned. *Habitat:* Widespread but local in hedge-banks and waste places, usually in or near gardens. July–September.

798. *CLUSTERED BELLFLOWER *C. glomerata* L. Plate 4. *CTW, p. 980*
A stiff hairy perennial, 2–12 in. high, with the upper leaves narrow and half-clasping, the lower broader and stalked. Flowers mostly in heads, unstalked, a handsome violet. Occasional tiny, dwarfed plants with solitary flowers have been mistaken for gentians, which however have opposite leaves. *Habitat:* Locally frequent in chalk or limestone grassland in Great Britain. June onwards.

799. HAREBELL *C. rotundifolia* L. Plate 4. *CTW, p. 981*
A slender hairless creeping perennial, 6–18 in. high, with hairlike stems, small roundish root-leaves that usually wither early, and linear stem-leaves, the upper unstalked. Flowers blue, nodding, in a loose truss. *Habitat:* Widespread and frequent in dry grassland. July onwards. Bluebell (in the N.)

800. ***SPREADING BELLFLOWER*** *C. patula* L.   Plate 4.   *CTW, p. 981*
A graceful, almost hairless perennial, 1–3 ft. high, with angled stems, lower leaves oblong and gradually narrowed to the stalk, and stem-leaves narrower and unstalked. Flowers similar to Creeping Bellflower (797), but smaller, redder and more deeply lobed, on many spreading few-flowered branches; calyx with linear teeth, broad at the base. *Habitat:* Extremely scarce on banks and in shady places, chiefly in W England and Wales. June–July.

800*a*. ***Rampion Bellflower**, *C. rapunculus* L., is stiff and unbranched, and has a thick fleshy root and milky juice. Flowers smaller, shorter-stalked, violet, less open, in longer, usually unbranched spikes, and calyx-teeth narrow at the base. More widespread, but rarer, and usually near houses.

801. ***CANTERBURY BELL*** *C. medium* L.   Plate 4.   *CTW, p. 982*
A favourite garden plant; a roughly hairy biennial, 9–18 in. high, with un-stalked lanceolate leaves. Flowers twice as large as any of our other Bellflowers, usually purple in the wild, but sometimes mauve, pink or white, with large down-turned appendages between the calyx-lobes. *Habitat:* Well established on a few chalky railway cuttings and old walls in S England. June.

802. *VENUS'S LOOKING-GLASS   *Legousia hybrida* (L.) Delarbre
   Specularia hybrida (L.) DC., *Campanula hybrida* L.   Plate 7.   *CTW, p. 982*
A curious little hairy annual, 2–8 in. high, with unstalked oblong wavy leaves. Flowers small, dark or pale purple, the petal-like corolla-lobes flat and only half as long as the calyx-teeth, closing in dull weather to reveal their paler undersides. Fruits grooved, triangular, very long and narrow. *Habitat:* Widespread and locally frequent in arable fields, especially on chalk and limestone; chiefly in the S and E. May–August.

803. **ROUND-HEADED RAMPION *Phyteuma tenerum* Schulz Pl. 8. *CTW, 983*
A usually hairless unbranched perennial, 2–18 in. high, with broad long-stalked root-leaves and narrow unstalked stem-leaves, all bluntly toothed. Flowers narrow, dark blue, long and curved in bud, in globular heads, differing from Sheepsbit (805) in the petal-like corolla-lobes being at first joined at the top around the long slender style, making a 'bird-cage' round the 5 stamens. *Habitat:* Locally frequent on chalk downs S of the Thames. July–August. '*P. orbiculare*'.

804. ***SPIKED RAMPION*** *P. spicatum* L.   Plate 106.   *CTW, p. 983*
A hairless perennial, 1–2 ft. high, with long-stalked toothed heart-shaped root-leaves, becoming narrower lanceolate and less stalked up the stem. Flowers similar to the last species, but pale yellowish-white with withered brown ones persisting below, and in a stout spike. *Habitat:* Confined to woods and copses in one small area in E Sussex. June–July.

805. *SHEEPSBIT   *Jasione montana* L.   Plate 8.   *CTW, p. 984*
A slightly hairy, somewhat scabious-like biennial, with narrow oblong, some-times wavy untoothed leaves, the lower short-stalked, the upper unstalked. Flowers in a rounded head, soft blue, with prominent petal-like corolla-lobes, 5, narrow. On poor open soil it has thread-like stems and grows low and often bushily, with small flower-heads; on cliffs it has a stout, stiffly erect, less branched stem up to a foot high, with stout heads. *Habitat:* Widespread but local on acid soils, in grassland, and on heaths, cliffs and shingle. May onwards.

LOBELIA FAMILY   Lobeliaceae

806. ***HEATH LOBELIA   *Lobelia urens* L.   Plate 7.   *CTW, p. 985*
A more or less hairless perennial, 6–18 in. high, with acrid milky juice and alternate, irregularly toothed oblong leaves. Flowers in leafy spikes, purplish-blue, 2-lipped, like the next species.   *Habitat:* Rare in damp heathy places in Sussex, Hants and Devon. August–September.

807. **WATER LOBELIA   *L. dortmanna* L.   Plate 66.   *CTW, p. 985*
A hairless, aquatic perennial, with a slender, hollow, leafless stem, milky juice, and submerged rosettes of small untoothed linear leaves, hollow with 2 tubes. Flowers in open spikes 6 in. or so above the water, drooping, very pale lilac, 2-lipped, the upper lip 2-lobed, the lower 3-lobed, the lobes pointed; the same shape as the dwarf blue garden bedding Lobelia (*L. erinus* L.).   *Habitat:* Locally frequent in quiet lakes and pools with acid water from Wales northwards and in Ireland, often with the similar-leaved Quillwort (1266). July–August.

BEDSTRAW FAMILY   Rubiaceae

NON-WOODY PLANTS with weak, often scrambling, 4-angled stems; small unstalked lanceolate leaves and similar leaf-like stipules in whorls of 4–12; and clusters of small flowers, the corolla with normally 4 petal-like lobes. Only Field Madder (808) has a calyx. Fruits 2-lobed nutlets, a berry in 818.

KEY TO BEDSTRAW FAMILY   (Nos. 808–818)
STEM *with prickles* 813b, 816, 817, 818.
LEAVES *4 only* 810, 811, 812, 816, 818; *3-veined* 811, 812; *with forward-pointing prickles* 808, 809, 813, 815–6; *with backward-pointing prickles* 815a, 816–8.
FLOWERS *pink* 808, 810; *yellow* 811, 814; *white* 809–10, 812–3, 815–7; *green* 817b, 818.
FRUITS *rough* 808, 809, 810, 812, 813, 815, 816, 817; *a berry* 818.

808. FIELD MADDER   *Sherardia arvensis* L.   Plate 26.   *CTW, p. 987*
A prostrate hairy annual, with square stems and whorls of 4–6 small stiff leaves. Flowers in small heads, surrounded by leaf-like bracts, tiny, pale purple, with a long slender corolla-tube; calyx-teeth enlarging to crown the round fruit. *Habitat:* Widespread and frequent in arable fields and other bare places, especially on chalk and limestone.   May onwards.

809. WOODRUFF   *Galium odoratum* (L.) Scopoli   Plate 103.   *CTW, p. 987*
An almost hairless erect carpeting perennial, 6–12 in. high, with slightly shiny leaves, edged with minute forward-pointing prickles, in whorls of 6–9 up the unbranched stem. Flowers small, white, in loose heads, the corolla lobes as long as the tube. Fruits with hooked bristles.   *Habitat:* Widespread, locally frequent in woods, mainly on chalk and limestone. April–June. *Asperula odorata* L.

810. *SQUINANCYWORT   *Asperula cynanchica* L.   Plate 87.   *CTW, p. 988*
A low, usually prostrate hairless slender perennial, with whorls of 4, sometimes unequal, linear leaves. Flowers in terminal clusters, small, veined, pinkish-white, the corolla-lobes pointed and as long as their tube.   *Habitat:* Locally frequent in open chalk and limestone turf, and on dunes, mainly in the S; in Ireland only in the S and W. June–September.

811. CROSSWORT   *Galium cruciata* (L.) Scopoli   Plate 50.   *CTW, p. 990*
A tufted, softly hairy perennial, 9–15 in. high, branched only at the base, with whorls of small yellow fragrant flowers at the base of the 4 elliptical 3-veined yellowish-green leaves.   *Habitat:* Widespread and locally frequent in grassy and bushy places, especially on chalk or limestone; Ireland, only at Downpatrick. April–June.

812. **NORTHERN BEDSTRAW   *G. boreale* L.   Plate 103.   *CTW, p. 991*
Our only white Bedstraw with 3-veined leaves; an erect perennial, 6–15 in. high, with whorls of 4 dark green rough-edged leaves, terminal leafy clusters of white flowers, and fruits covered with hooked bristles.   *Habitat:* Locally frequent in bare and rocky places from Wales northwards and in Ireland. July–August.

813. HEDGE BEDSTRAW   *G. mollugo* L.   Plate 103.   *CTW, p. 991*
A floppy scrambling perennial, with smooth square, often downy stems, 1–3 ft. high, and markedly swollen under the whorls of 6–8 one-veined leaves, edged with minute forward-pointing prickles and ending in a point. Flowers small, white, in much branched spreading terminal clusters, the petal-like corolla-lobes ending in a fine point. Fruits hairless, tiny, wrinkled. Hybridises with Lady's Bedstraw (814).   *Habitat:* Widespread and common in dry bushy grassland, especially hedge-banks, thinning out northwards. July–August.
813a. ***Upright Hedge Bedstraw,** *G. erectum* Hudson, is smaller, stiffer, neater, more delicate and narrower, since the stems, branches and flower clusters are more erect; leaves narrower, flowers and fruits larger, and stems little swollen under the whorls. Much more local, on dry grassy slopes, especially on chalk and limestone. June–September.
813b. ****Wall Bedstraw,** *G. parisiense* L. (incl. *G. anglicum* Hudson) (*CTW, p. 998*), is a smaller slenderer annual, 6–12 in. long, with prickles on the angles of the stem and flowers less than half the size. Very local on old walls, more rarely in sandy ground, in S and E England. June–July.

814. LADY'S BEDSTRAW   *G. verum* L.   Plate 50.   *CTW, p. 992*
The common yellow Bedstraw with 1-veined leaves; a more or less sprawling, usually hairless perennial, 6 in. to 2 ft. high, smelling of new-mown hay, with whorls of 8–12 linear leaves, the margins slightly inrolled below. Flowers small, bright golden-yellow, in heads towards the top of the stem.   *Habitat:* Widespread and common in dry grassy places. July onwards.

815. HEATH BEDSTRAW   *G. saxatile* L.   Plate 103.   *CTW, p. 993*
A low slender weak, often prostrate and mat-forming hairless perennial, with whorls of 4–6 short elliptical, abruptly and sharply pointed leaves, with a very few minute forward-pointing marginal prickles. Flowers small, white, with a sickly fragrance, in opposite clusters along the stem on stalks shorter than the lengths of stem between each cluster. Fruits hairless, rough.   *Habitat:* Widespread and often abundant in grassy and heathy places on acid soils. June–August. *G. harcynicum* Weigel.
815a. ****Slender Bedstraw,** *G. pumilum* Murray, is variable but slenderer and bushier, the longer narrower leaves with usually backward-pointing prickles, and the erect longer, more pyramidal flower-clusters on stalks longer than the lengths of stem between each; fruits smoother. Not infrequent on limestone in the N and W; rare in Ireland and on chalk in the S. June–July.

816. **MARSH BEDSTRAW** *G. palustre* L. Plate 103. *CTW, p. 994*

A variable hairless perennial, 2–3 ft. high, with stems weak and roughish at the angles, and whorls of 4–5 blunt lanceolate leaves, edged with minute prickles. Flowers small, white, in loose spreading stalked clusters. *Habitat:* Widespread and frequent in wet places. June–August.

816a. ***Slender Marsh Bedstraw,** *G. debile* Desvaux, is much smaller, slenderer and weaker, and has less spreading branches, shorter linear, less blunt and rough leaves, and pinkish flowers. Very rare at the edges of ponds in England.

816b. *Fen Bedstraw,** *G. uliginosum* L., is somewhat smaller and has rougher stems with down-turned prickles on the angles, and narrower leaves, 6–8 in a whorl, with a minute point at the tip and smaller flower-clusters. Widespread and frequent in fens.

817. **GOOSEGRASS** *G. aparine* L. Plate 102. *CTW, p. 997*

A far-straggling weedy annual, 1–4 ft. long, readily clinging to clothing by the tiny down-turned prickles on its fruits, stems and leaves; leaves in whorls of 6–8, narrow, broader at the tip and ending in a minute bristle. Flowers inconspicuous, white, in small, stalked clusters longer than the leaves at their base. Fruits covered with small white swollen-based hooked bristles, on straight spreading stalks. *Habitat:* Widespread and abundant in hedge-banks and fens, and on disturbed and waste ground and coastal shingle. May onwards.

817a. **Small Goosegrass,** *G. tricorne* Stokes, is smaller, with fewer creamier flowers in each cluster on stalks shorter than the narrower leaves; fruits rough, not bristly; on shorter thicker down-curved stalks. Very local and elusive in cornfields and waste places, especially on chalk and limestone, in the S and E.

818. *WILD MADDER** *Rubia peregrina* L. Plate 102. *CTW, p. 999*

Rather like a large long straggling perennial Bedstraw, with fat, sharply 4-angled stems up to 10 ft. long, rough on the angles with down-turned prickles; and whorls of 4–6 dark green shining leathery evergreen lanceolate leaves, with prickles on the edges and on midrib beneath. Flowers small, yellowish-green, with 5-petal-like corolla-lobes, in small stalked clusters at the base of the leaves. Fruit a black berry the size of a pea. *Habitat:* Locally frequent on cliffs and in other bushy places, on the S and W coasts of England, Wales and Ireland; very rare inland. June–August.

HONEYSUCKLE FAMILY Caprifoliaceae

819. **DWARF ELDER** *Sambucus ebulus* L. Plate 95. *CTW, p. 1000*

A hairless, somewhat foetid unbranched creeping perennial, 3–5 ft. high, often confused with small or cut-down Elder (820) bushes, but its leaves have more numerous and narrower leaflets and leafy stipules at their base, and the white, often pink-tipped flowers have violet anthers; also is not woody, and dies down in winter. *Habitat:* Widespread, but not common and mainly in the S, usually by roadsides. July–August.

820. **ELDER** *S. nigra* L. Plate 74. *CTW, p. 1001*

A foetid deciduous shrub or small tree, our only native shrub with opposite pinnate leaves; also with fissured corky bark, white pith, and young twigs with numerous scales; the large, dark green leaves with usually 5 broad lanceolate toothed, rarely pinnate leaflets, and no or tiny stipules at their base. Flowers in large flat-topped umbel-like clusters, small, fragrant, creamy-white, with 5 very pale yellow anthers. Fruit a juicy berry, ripening black or very rarely green or whitish. American Elder (*S. canadensis* L.), seen in gardens and on railway banks, is always bushy, and has fewer scales on the twigs, usually 7 large bright green or yellowish leaflets, larger hummocky flower-clusters appearing a month or more later, and purplish berries. *Habitat:* Widespread and common in woods, hedgerows and bushy and waste places, often on chalk downs and near rabbit warrens. June–July.

821. *WAYFARING TREE   *Viburnum lantana* L.   Plate 74.   *CTW, p. 1002*

A downy deciduous shrub, 6–12 ft. high, with scurfy twigs, and opposite minutely toothed wrinkled oval leaves, ribbed beneath and with no protective scales in bud. Flowers all alike, in close, rather flat-topped umbel-like clusters, creamy white, with a sickly fragrance. Fruit a red berry, turning black. *Habitat:* Widespread in bushy places, especially on chalk or limestone; locally frequent in S England, thinning out northwards and westwards; not in Ireland. April–May.

822. GUELDER ROSE   *V. opulus* L.   Plate 74.   *CTW, p. 1002*

A large deciduous shrub or small tree, 6–12 ft. high, with small pimples on the hairless twigs, and 3–5-lobed, toothed leaves, downy only on the veins below, maple-like but with short hair-like stipules at their base; turning a flaming red in autumn. Flowers white, slightly fragrant, in flattish umbels, the outer ones sterile, with 5 showy petal-like corolla-lobes, much larger than the inner ones. Fruit a shiny red berry. *Habitat:* Widespread and frequent in woods, fens and dampish bushy places. June–July.

823. *SNOWBERRY   *Symphoricarpos rivularis* Suksdorf   Pl. 17.   *CTW, p. 1003*

A usually hairless, little branched deciduous shrub, 3–6 ft. high, often planted and suckering freely to form thickets; leaves thin, opposite, oval, stalked, untoothed but sometimes deeply lobed. Flowers small, pink, bell-shaped, towards the end of the branches. Fruit a white berry. *Habitat:* Fairly frequently naturalised in hedges, by streams, etc. June–September.

824. **TWINFLOWER   *Linnaea borealis* L.   Plate 23.   *CTW, p. 1003*

A charming delicate creeping downy little evergreen perennial, woody below, with small stalked toothed oval leaves and pink, funnel-shaped drooping fragrant flowers, in pairs on 4–5-in. slender leafless stalks. *Habitat:* Very local in pinewoods in E Scotland. June–August.

825. ***FLY HONEYSUCKLE   *Lonicera xylosteum* L.   Pl. 64.   *CTW, p. 1004*

An upright downy deciduous shrub, with unstalked, unscented, 2-lipped yellowish flowers, sometimes tinged reddish, in pairs at the base of the opposite short-stalked oval leaves. Fruit a red berry. *Habitat:* Very rare outside shrubberies, but long known in Sussex. May–June.

826. HONEYSUCKLE   *L. periclymenum* L.   Plate 64.   *CTW, p. 1005*

A deciduous woody climber, twining clockwise and often somewhat downy, with opposite untoothed oval leaves, paler beneath, short- or unstalked but never united at the base, appearing in December or January. Flowers 2 in. long, in close heads, with small bracts at their base, 2-lipped with a long slender tube, 5 protruding stamens and one style; cream, deepening to orange-buff after

VALERIAN FAMILY 167

pollination, tinged crimson outside, very sweet-scented. Fruit a red berry. *Habitat:* Widespread, common in woods, hedges and bushy places. June–Sept.

826a. ***Perfoliate Honeysuckle, L. caprifolium** L., is hairless with broader leaves, the topmost and the larger bracts united at the base into a shallow cup; and more orange berries. Very rarely naturalised in the S; not in Ireland. May–June.

MOSCHATEL FAMILY Adoxaceae

827. MOSCHATEL *Adoxa moschatellina* L. Plate 78. *CTW, p. 1006*
A weak hairless perennial, 2–4 in. high, with long-stalked 2-trifoliate lobed root-leaves, not unreminiscent of a small Wood Anemone (8), but fleshier. Flowers small, greenish, in heads of 5, at right angles to each other, at the top of unbranched stems bearing only one pair of trifoliate leaves. *Habitat:* Widespread and locally frequent in woods and hedge-banks, also on mountains. In Ireland only near Belfast. April–May.

VALERIAN FAMILY Valerianaceae

828. CORNSALAD *Valerianella locusta* (L.) Betcke Plate 7. *CTW, p. 1009*
A low, much forked, almost hairless annual, 2–12 in. high, with unstalked opposite oblong leaves, excellent as a winter salad. Flowers tiny, pale lilac, in small heads, also often solitary in the fork of the branches, these fruits ripening first. Fruits flattened hairless, with inconspicuous calyx-teeth (Fig.). *Habitat:* Widespread and not uncommon in arable and open ground and on walls. April–July. Lamb's Lettuce. Figs. all × 4.

828   828a   828b   828c   828d

828a. **Keeled Cornsalad, *V. carinata*** Loiseleur, has fruits narrower oblong and more or less 4-sided, with a deep groove on one side and slightly keeled on the other (Fig.). Very local and mainly in the S.

828b. *Smooth-fruited Cornsalad, *V. dentata*** (L.) Pollich, looks less leafy, with thinner stiffer stems, leaves often with a tooth at the base, less leafy flower-heads, pinkish-white flowers, and small, occasionally hairy fruits flat on one face and rounded on the other, crowned by the short calyx-teeth (Fig.). Local, and chiefly on chalk and limestone.

828c. **Broad-fruited Cornsalad, *V. rimosa*** Bastard, differs from Smooth-fruited Cornsalad in its larger fatter pointed, always hairless fruits, with a broad shallow groove down one side (Fig.). Extremely scarce, and mainly in the S and E.

828d. ***Italian Cornsalad, *V. eriocarpa*** Desvaux, differs from Smooth-fruited Cornsalad in its much larger prominently toothed calyx-teeth above the always hairy fruits (Fig.). Rare, occasionally as a relic, and mainly in the S.

829. COMMON VALERIAN *Valeriana officinalis* L. Plate 21. *CTW, p. 1010*
A variable, usually unbranched perennial, 6 in. to 4 ft. high, hairy chiefly below, with pinnate leaves, the lower stalked, the leaflets toothed. Flowers small,

very pale pink, darker in bud, numerous, in close terminal umbel-like clusters; the corolla pouched at the base; stamens 3; the calyx forming a pappus in fruit. *Habitat:* Widespread and frequent in woods and rough grassy places, both damp and dry. June–August.

830. ****GIANT VALERIAN**   *V. pyrenaica* L.   Plate 21.   *CTW, p. 1011*
Taller and stouter than the last species, sometimes up to 6 ft., with broader, deeply toothed undivided heart-shaped downy leaves. *Habitat:* Naturalised in plantations, mainly in the N and W. June–July.

831. ***MARSH VALERIAN**   *V. dioica* L.   Plate 21.   *CTW, p. 1011*
Usually very much smaller than Common Valerian (829), 4–12 in. high, with longer runners; root-leaves small, oval, undivided, untoothed, on often long stalks; stem-leaves not always pinnate; and large male and smaller female flowers on different plants, the corolla-tube shorter. *Habitat:* Widespread but local in marshy fields and fens; not in Ireland. May–June.

832. **RED VALERIAN**   *Centranthus ruber* (L.) DC.   Plate 21.   *CTW, p. 1011*
A hairless, greyish perennial, 2–3 ft. high, growing in large tufts, with undivided, pointed oval leaves, the lowest stalked. Flowers in close terminal clusters, generally resembling Common Valerian (829), but with the corolla narrow, twice as long, and spurred at the base, red, rose or white; 1 stamen. *Habitat:* Widespread and locally frequent on cliffs, quarries, walls and chalky banks, mainly in the S and W. May onwards.

TEASEL FAMILY   Dipsacaceae

NON-WOODY PLANTS in many ways resembling the Daisy Family (p. 169), especially for their well-stalked dense compound flower-heads, but distinguishable by the 4 stamens projecting from the individual white or mauvish flowers, the anthers not joined in a tube round the style, corolla 4–5-lobed. The true calyx is very narrow, with 4–5 segments, sometimes bristle-like and sits in a small green cup; what appear to be the calyx-teeth of the compound flower-head are actually a series of bracts. Leaves all opposite. Fruits small, seeded.

833. **WILD TEASEL**   *Dipsacus fullonum* L.   Plate 9.   *CTW, p. 1013*
Easily recognised by its bluntly conical, prickly flower-heads 2–3 in. high, which persist on the dead stems throughout the winter; a gaunt hairless biennial, 2–6 ft. high, prickly on stems and leaves, with a rosette of oblong 'goose-fleshy' root-leaves withering before flowering, and narrower stem leaves, often cupped at the base and liable to fill with water. Flowers pale purple, a belt of those in the middle opening first, surrounded by spines; larger spines under each flower-head. *Habitat:* Widespread and locally frequent in rough grassy and bushy places. July–August. *D. sylvestris* (Hudson).

834. ****SHEPHERD'S ROD**   *D. pilosus* L.   Plate 107.   *CTW, p. 1014*
A tall biennial, 3–6 ft. high, hairy at the top of the stems, with short stiff prickles on the stems and the midrib under the leaves; the lower leaves oblong, the upper narrower, all often with a pair of leaflets at the base. Flowers white with violet anthers, in small globular heads, under an inch high, looking more like a Scabious than a Teasel; sepal-like spines as long as the flowers, woolly, with

dark purple spiny points. *Habitat:* Uncommon in woods and hedge-banks in England and Wales. July–September. Small Teasel.

835. FIELD SCABIOUS *Knautia arvensis* (L.) Coulter Pl. 8. *CTW, p. 1015*
A hairy perennial, 1–3 ft. high, with leaves mostly pinnately lobed, but some undivided. Flowers small, in flattish pincushion heads, $1\frac{1}{2}$ in. across, with two rows of unequal lanceolate sepal-like bracts; most commonly bluish-lilac, with pink anthers, the 4 corolla-lobes unequal, especially on the larger outer flowers; calyx-teeth 8, not persisting very hairy. *Habitat:* Widespread and common in dry grassy places and cornfields, thinning out northwards. June onwards.

836. SMALL SCABIOUS *S. columbaria* L. Plate 8. *CTW, p. 1016*
Smaller and slenderer than Field Scabious (835), and with stems less hairy and leaves finely cut; can readily be told by the calyx-teeth ending in a long fine, dark purple bristle. Flowers rather paler, the corolla 5-lobed, the head elongating in fruit; sepal-like bracts in one row only. *Habitat:* Locally frequent in chalk and limestone grassland, and on dunes, in England, Wales and S Scotland. July onwards.

837. DEVILSBIT SCABIOUS *Succisa pratensis* Moench Pl. 8. *CTW, p. 1017*
A sometimes hairy perennial, 1–3 ft. high, with a very short rootstock (once believed to have been bitten off by the Devil), and stalked, elliptical leaves, often blotched purplish, the stem ones few, narrower, sometimes toothed. Flowers all the same size, in $\frac{1}{2}$-in. rounded heads, dark bluish-purple or pink, with pink or purple anthers. *Habitat:* Widespread and frequent in dampish grassy places and woods, and in fens. June onwards. *Scabiosa succisa* L.

DAISY FAMILY Compositae

THE LARGEST family of flowering plants, distinguished by having its tiny individual flowers all packed closely into a compound head, which often looks like a single large flower, surrounded by apparent sepals, which are actually bracts. The tiny flowers are unstalked, with the ovary below the 5 petals, which are joined into a corolla and are of two types: (1) with a symmetrical tubular corolla (disk-florets), and (2) with an asymmetrical strap-shaped corolla (ray-florets). The compound flower-heads are consequently of three types: (a) 'unrayed', with usually blue or purple disk-florets only, like the Thistles; (b) 'rayed', with yellow disk-florets in the centre and white or yellow ray-florets round the edge, like the Daisy; and (c) those with ray-florets only, like the Dandelion.

Each tiny flower has 5 stamens joined into a tube, and a 2-lobed stigma. The place of their true sepals is often taken either by chaffy scales on top of the ovary, or by undivided or feathered hairs (the pappus), which, when enlarged as thistle-down or dandelion-clocks float away in the wind, bearing suspended from the parachute the fruit, a small narrow nut.

838. NODDING BUR-MARIGOLD *Bidens cernua* L. Pl. 58. *CTW, p. 1034*
Differs from the next species in having rather thicker hairy stems; unstalked, undivided leaves; nodding flower-heads, usually larger and broader and very rarely rayed; and narrower fruits with 3–4 barbed bristles. *Habitat:* Similar but rather less common. July onwards.

839. TRIFID BUR-MARIGOLD   *B. tripartita* L.   Plate 58.   *CTW, p. 1034*

Our Bur-marigolds are unscented and have stout round-topped heads of yellow disk-florets which normally have no ray-florets. This is an almost hairless annual, 6–18 in. high, with stems often purplish, and opposite leaves, mostly with 3 lanceolate lobes, the middle lobe much the longest, on winged stalks. Flowerheads unrayed, nearly erect, like yellow round-topped buttons; sepal-like bracts blackish, the outer slightly longer and broader than the inner. Fruits smooth, flattened, oblong, with a barbed bristle projecting from each of the top corners so that they stick tenaciously to clothing.   *Habitat:* Widespread and frequent by fresh water, and on the dried beds of ponds. July onwards.

839a. ***Beggar-Ticks**, *B. frondosa* L. (*CTW*†), has thinner, stiffer and purpler stems, and is usually taller, with longer-stalked leaves, more distinctly lobed and usually pinnate; and smaller flower-heads with the outer sepal-like bracts shorter than the inner. Spreading from waste, usually dry, places in the W.

840. **SHAGGY SOLDIER   *Galinsoga ciliata* (Rafinesque) Blake
Plate 100.   *CTW, p. 1035*

A hairy, often dark green annual, 6–18 in. high, its stems white with spreading hairs; leaves stalked, opposite, pointed oval, toothed, narrowing up the stem. Flower-heads in open clusters, often one or more longer-stalked in the fork of each branch; small, stalked, yellow, with 4–5 flat white rays; scales among the disk-florets narrow lanceolate, not toothed. Fruits with numerous long hairs. *Habitat:* An increasing casual of waste places in England and Wales. June onwards.

840a. **Gallant Soldier**, *G. parviflora* Cavanilles, is often yellower-green, with usually almost hairless stems; less toothed leaves; flower-stalks with very short hairs; shorter, much narrower, grooved and so less prominent rays; and scales broader, with a small tooth on each side. Fruits with a few short hairs. Commoner in London.

841. **SPINY COCKLEBUR   *Xanthium spinosum* L.   Pl. 107.   *CTW, p. 1037*

A stiff annual, 6 in. to 2 ft. high, with short-stalked diamond-shaped 3–5-lobed leaves, dark shiny green above, downy white beneath, with one or two sharp, 3-forked orange spines at the base. Flower-heads small, unrayed, covered with hooked spines; male and female flowers in separate heads, the globular male above the egg-shaped female.   *Habitat:* A widespread casual, especially on fields manured with shoddy. September onwards.

KEY TO DAISY-TYPE FLOWERS

I. Flower-heads Purple-rayed

PLANT *hairless and fleshy* 875.   HABITAT: *maritime* 875; *mountains* 878.

II. Flower-heads Wholly Yellow

PLANT *fleshy* 861; *hairless* 842, 861, 891; *silvery* 851; *tall* 849, 858; *woody* 851.

LEAVES *broad* 853; *pinnate* 842, 843, 844, 845, 851, 883; *untoothed* 859, 861, 862; *grey beneath* 883.

FLOWERS *solitary* 859, 891; *larger than a Daisy* 853, 858, 859, 861, 883, 891; *equalling a Daisy* 842, 843, 844, 845, 849, 850, 851, 862.

HABITAT: *maritime* 861; *wet places* 843, 849.

III. Flower-heads White-rayed

PLANT *hairless* 886; *aromatic* 884, 885, 886ab, 893.

LEAVES *broad* 852, 881, 892; *narrow* 875a, 879, 892; *pinnate* 884, 885, 886, 893; *toothed* 879, 881, 892; *untoothed* 875a, 879; *shiny* 852; *downy beneath* 884; *yellowish* 893.

FLOWERS *solitary* 879, 881, 886, 892; *larger than a Daisy* 852, 886, 892; *with red-tipped rays* 881.

HABITAT: *wet places* 852, 875a; *walls* 879, 893.

842. COMMON RAGWORT *Senecio jacobaea* L. Plate 57. *CTW, p. 1039*

An often hairless biennial, 1–4 ft. high, branched only at the top, with deeply pinnately lobed leaves, the lobes toothed and the end one small and blunt. Flower-heads in large dense flat-topped terminal clusters, yellow, nearly always rayed, and daisy-like, the rays also yellow, minutely toothed at the tip; outermost sepal-like bracts few, much shorter than the dark-tipped inner. Fruits of the disk-florets downy, of the ray-florets hairless. *Habitat:* Widespread and often abundant in dry sandy or chalky grassland and on dunes. June onwards.

843. MARSH RAGWORT *S. aquaticus* Hill Plate 57. *CTW, p. 1040*

Shorter, more widely branched and less stiff than the last species, the glossier leaves mostly with a large end lobe and much smaller forward-pointing side-lobes; root-leaves oval, often undivided. Flower-heads much larger, an inch or more across, in broader, looser clusters; all fruits hairless. Autumnal shoots from mutilated plants of Common Ragwort can, however, look very similar, except for the downy fruits of the disk-florets. *Habitat:* Widespread and locally frequent in wet meadows. June onwards. (Incl. '*S. erraticus*'.)

844. *HOARY RAGWORT *S. erucifolius* L. Plate 57. *CTW, p. 1040*

Usually narrower, less bushy, more erectly branched and greyer with sparse cottony down than Common Ragwort (842), with very short creeping runners; smaller, more deeply and narrowly lobed leaves, the end lobe narrow and pointed; smaller, paler yellow, flower-heads; the outer row of sepal-like bracts about half as long as the rest; and the fruits all downy. *Habitat:* Widespread but local in grassy places in the lowlands, mostly on clay or chalk. In Ireland only round Dublin. July onwards, at its best when most Common Ragwort is over.

845. *OXFORD RAGWORT *S. squalidus* L. Plate 57. *CTW, p. 1041*

A branched, straggling annual or perennial, about a foot or so high, more like a short Marsh Ragwort (843) than Common Ragwort (842), and virtually hairless, with glossy leaves varying from deeply pinnately lobed to undivided, only the lower ones stalked. Flower-heads large, yellow, the rays minutely notched but not toothed; sepal-like bracts tipped blackish, the outer row much shorter. Fruits normally all downy. *Habitat:* An increasing invader of walls, waysides, railway banks, waste and cultivated ground, though still far from everywhere and very local in the N and Ireland. April onwards.

846. HEATH GROUNDSEL *S. sylvaticus* L. Plate 57. *CTW, p. 1041*

Rather like a large downy branched grey-green, somewhat foetid Groundsel (848), with more deeply and irregularly cut leaves; many narrow conical stalked flower-heads; very short rays rolled back; sepal-like bracts purple-tipped, the outer minute, the inner very long; and downy fruits. Taller, less stickily hairy and less branched than Sticky Groundsel (847). *Habitat:* Widespread and locally frequent in sandy, gravelly and heathy places. July onwards.

847. *STICKY GROUNDSEL　*S. viscosus* L.　Plate 57.　*CTW, p. 1042*

An often rather bushy, dark grey-green annual, somewhat like the last species but with sticky hairs all over. Flower-heads larger, more widely conical, pale yellow, with short rays soon rolled back; outer sepal-like bracts half the length of the inner; none black-tipped. Fruits hairless. *Habitat:* Widespread and increasing, but still local, in bare and waste places, especially by the sea, and in fens. July onwards.

848. GROUNDSEL　*S. vulgaris* L.　Plate 57.　*CTW, p. 1042*

A ubiquitous, variable annual weed, 3–9 in. high, sometimes downy or even shaggy below, with narrow, pinnately lobed leaves, hairless above. Flower-heads small, yellow, usually rayless, cylindrical not conical, on stalks short at first, in terminal, sometimes nodding, clusters; sepal-like bracts narrow, not greyish, with pointed black tips, the outer very short. Fruits very hairy. *Habitat:* A widespread and abundant weed of disturbed ground, often in gardens. Throughout the year.

849. **SARACEN'S WOUNDWORT　*S. fluviatilis* Wallroth　Pl. 59.　*CTW, 1043*

A tall stout perennial, 3–5 ft. high, with long runners, the unstalked hairless, elliptical, pointed leaves with erect teeth. Flower-heads in terminal clusters, yellow, like Common Ragwort (842) but with fewer rays. *Habitat:* Widespread but rare in wet, sometimes shady places. August–September. '*S. sarracenicus*'.

850. *FIELD FLEAWORT　*S. integrifolius* (L.) Clairville　Pl. 56.　*CTW, 1044*
S. campestris (Retzius) DC.; (incl. *S. spathulifolius* Turczinow)

A neat unbranched perennial, 3–12 in. high, often covered with whitish down, with a grooved stem; a basal rosette of stalked oval leaves, flat on the ground, wrinkled and hairless above, cottony beneath; and a few unstalked, narrower stem-leaves. Flower-heads in a loose umbel, long-rayed like Ragwort (842), yellow, with the centre often darker. Fruits hairy. *Habitat:* Local in short turf on the chalk downs of the S; a taller robuster form occurs on cliffs near Holyhead and on Mickle Fell. May–June.

851. **SILVER RAGWORT　*S. cineraria* DC.　Plate 57.　*CTW, p. 1045*

A woody bushy silvery perennial, 1–2 ft. high, with a dense white felt covering the stems and undersides of its toothed or pinnately lobed leaves, which are downy but green above. Flower-heads in clusters, yellow, rayed, ragwort-like; stalks and sepal-like bracts whitely woolly. *Habitat:* Well naturalised on sea-cliffs and shingle beaches in S and SW England, S Wales and E Ireland. June–August.

852. ***MAGELLAN RAGWORT　*S. smithii* DC.　Plate 100.　*CTW, p. 1046*

A stout perennial, 2–3 ft. high, with large shiny, dark green leaves, the basal broadly oblong, and heads of large white-rayed yellow-centred daisy-like flowers. *Habitat:* Moist places in the extreme N of Scotland. July–August.

853. **LEOPARDSBANE　*Doronicum pardalianches* L.　Pl. 56.　*CTW, p. 1046*

A softly hairy yellow-green perennial, 1–2 ft. high, with stalked toothed, broad heart-shaped leaves, the middle ones broadening below the winged stalk to clasp the stem, the topmost unstalked. Flower-heads usually several on one stem, 1½–2 in. across, stalked, rayed, like large yellow Daisies. *Habitat:* Widespread but not common in woods and copses. May–June.

854. COLTSFOOT *Tussilago farfara* L. Plate 55. *CTW, p. 1047*

A low perennial, with leafless, whitely woolly, purplish stems bearing many overlapping fleshy, purplish scales right up to the flower-heads, which taper into the stalk and do not open very widely, but differ from Dandelion (956), in having both disk- and ray-florets, the latter striped orange outside. The heads droop after flowering, but rise again in fruit, when much white pappus is formed. Leaves large, finely black-toothed, broadly heart-shaped, polygonal, covered at first with whitish down, but becoming green above. *Habitat:* Widespread and common on all kinds of bare and sparsely vegetated ground, especially on clay; also in mountains. February–April, well before the leaves.

855. *BUTTERBUR *Petasites hybridus* (L.) Gaertner, Meyer & Scherbius
Tussilago petasites L. Plate 21. *CTW, p. 1049*

A creeping patch-forming perennial, whose very stout hollow 6–12 in. stems bear numerous green strap-shaped bracts and spikes of short-stalked, pale lilac-pink unrayed unscented flower-heads, with white anthers; male and female flowers on separate plants. Leaves immense (up to 3 ft. across—the one on Plate 21 is small), usually long-stalked, toothed, heart-shaped, rhubarb-like, green above when mature, greyish downy beneath. *Habitat:* Widespread and fairly frequent on wet ground by streams and ditches, roadsides and damp copses; female plants rare outside N England. March–May, before the leaves.

856. **CREAMY BUTTERBUR *P. japonicus* (Siebold & Zuccarini) Schmidt
Plate 94. *CTW, p. 1050*

A low creeping perennial, with dense broad branched clusters of short-stalked, fragrant, unrayed, creamy white flower-heads, framed by broad, spreading leaf-like bracts overlapping up the leafless stem, the whole looking not unlike a small cauliflower. Florets divided to under halfway; sepal-like bracts pale yellow-green, broad lanceolate, not divided quite to the base. Leaves like Winter Heliotrope (857), but larger, more deeply toothed and fresher green. *Habitat:* Naturalised in a few moist spots in the S. March–April, before the leaves.

856a. **White Butterbur, *P. albus* (L.) Gaertner, has looser sweet-scented long-stalked white flowers, the florets more deeply divided, with leaf-like stem-bracts fewer, much narrower and inrolled, and sepal-like bracts bright green, hairless, narrow lanceolate, and divided to the base. Leaves on shaggy stalks, whitely downy beneath, with prominent and uneven teeth. Local in plantations and by roadsides, chiefly in the N.

857. WINTER HELIOTROPE *P. fragrans* (Villars) Presl Pl. 21. *CTW, p. 1050*

Another creeping perennial, with coltsfoot-sized leaves, much smaller and rounder than Butterbur (855), evenly toothed, green on both sides, paler and downier below. Flower-heads lilac, heliotrope- or vanilla-scented, fewer and in a looser head, appearing much earlier and with the leaves, which succumb in severe winters. *Habitat:* Now a widespread and locally frequent garden escape, chiefly on roadsides. November–March.

858. **ELECAMPANE *Inula helenium* L. Plate 56. *CTW, p. 1052*

A tall stout hairy perennial, with stalked, elliptical root-leaves a foot or more long, broader unstalked leaves clasping the stem, all toothed and downy beneath. Flower-heads in small terminal clusters, 2–3 in. across, yellow, daisy-like, with numerous very narrow spreading rays. *Habitat:* Widespread but uncommon on grassy roadsides and in copses. July–August.

859. ***IRISH FLEABANE*** *I. salicina* L.   Plate 56.   *CTW, p. 1052*

A leafy perennial, 1–2 ft. high, with rather stiff oblong, sometimes slightly toothed leaves, arched back, the upper unstalked and half-clasping the stem. Flowers solitary or in small terminal clusters bright yellow, rayed, daisy-like, an inch across; a shy flowerer. Sepal-like bracts broad, hairless. Pappus a single row of hairs. *Habitat:* Confined to the marshy limestone shores of L. Derg in the R. Shannon. July–August.

860. *PLOUGHMAN'S SPIKENARD* *I. conyza* DC.   Plate 52.   *CTW, p. 1053*

A downy perennial, branched chiefly above, with stiff purplish stems 6 in. to 4 ft. high, and slightly toothed, lanceolate foxglove-like leaves, the lower soon withering, the upper unstalked. Flower-heads rather small and numerous, in an irregular umbel, dull yellow, with no or very small rays; the inner sepal-like bracts narrow, purplish-brown, prominent in bud; the outer ones green, curved back. *Habitat:* Locally frequent in open woods and rough grassland in England and Wales, especially on chalk or limestone. July onwards.

861. **GOLDEN SAMPHIRE** *I. crithmoides* L.   Plate 56.   *CTW, p. 1054*

Our only yellow-rayed daisy-like flower with fleshy leaves; stout tufted hairless perennial, 12–18 in. high, with fleshy linear leaves up the stem, sometimes 3-toothed at the tip. Flower-heads in irregular umbel-like terminal clusters, an inch across, golden-yellow, rayed; sepal-like bracts narrow, appressed. Fruits with white pappus. *Habitat:* Local on sea-cliffs and drier salt-marshes in the SE, S and W, and in S and E Ireland. July–August.

862. **COMMON FLEABANE**   *Pulicaria dysenterica* (L.) Bernhardi
 Inula dysenterica L.   Plate 56.   *CTW, p. 1055*

A downy or shaggy perennial, 8 in. to 2 ft. high, with lanceolate, often slightly toothed leaves, the upper wrinkled, heart-shaped at the base and half-clasping the stem. Flower-heads in loose flat-topped terminal clusters, long-rayed, daisy-like, golden yellow, about ¾-in. across. Sepal-like bracts linear. Pappus with an inner row of hairs and an outer row of small scales. *Habitat:* Widespread and common in ditches, damp roadsides and wet meadows, but not in the Highlands. July–September.

863. **SMALL FLEABANE**   *P. vulgaris* Gaertner   Plate 52.   *CTW. p, 1055*

A much branched downy annual, 4–12 in. high, with narrow oblong, wavy-edged, sometimes toothed leaves, the upper scarcely clasping the stem. Flower-heads numerous, only about half the size of the last species, dull yellow, with the rays erect and very short, not exceeding the sepal-like bracts. *Habitat:* Decreasing and now very scarce in moist places in the S, especially near ponds on commons. August–September. *Inula pulicaria* L.

CUDWEEDS   *Filago* and *Gnaphalium*

A GROUP OF rather small plants, mostly annuals, all more or less covered with white wool or down, with numerous small linear leaves arranged spirally on the stems, and clusters or loose spikes of small unrayed white, yellow or brown flower-heads. The *Filagos* differ from the *Gnaphaliums* in having chaffy scales between the florets, which are nearly concealed by the sepal-like bracts.

864. COMMON CUDWEED *Filago germanica* (L.) L. Pl. 101. *CTW, p. 1057*
A silvery-grey woolly annual, 4–8 in. high, with tough wiry branches arising at a wide angle, sometimes from the base and always from below the flower clusters; leaves narrow oblong, widest below, blunt or pointed, and wavy-edged. Flowers yellow, inconspicuous, 20–40 together in narrow unrayed heads, closely grouped into conspicuous globular terminal woolly clusters ½-in. across, over-topped by side branches but not by the upper leaves. Sepal-like bracts linear, erect, with straw-yellow bristle-tips. *Habitat:* Widespread and frequent in sand and gravel-pits and dry sandy fields, and on heaths, thinning out northwards. July–August.

864a. ****Red-tipped Cudweed,** *F. apiculata* Smith, is slenderer and erecter, with leaves yellowish-woolly, sharp-pointed and not wavy; flower-heads fewer in the clusters, which are more conical and woollier; and the sepal-like bracts conspicuously tipped crimson. Rare in sandy fields in the S. June–August.

864b. ****Broad-leaved Cudweed,** *F. spathulata* Presl, is less erect and more branched below, the lower branches half-prostrate, the upper horizontal; with less wavy leaves, not wider below, all sharp-pointed; flower-heads in sharply 5-angled globular, less woolly clusters, well overtopped by 3–5 large upper leaves; and the outer sepal-like bracts with down-curved yellowish points. Scarce in sandy and chalky fields in the S half of England.

865. ***NARROW CUDWEED *F. gallica* L. Plate 101. *CTW, p. 1058*
Differs from the next species in having much longer, spreading green-edged leaves, the topmost longer than the flower-clusters, and the outer fruits being enclosed by some of the swollen-based inner bracts. Larger specimens are also more widely branched. *Habitat:* Perhaps now only in dry fields in one area of Essex. June–September.

866. *SMALL CUDWEED *F. minima* (Smith) Persoon Pl. 101. *CTW, p. 1058*
A very slender inconspicuous annual, grey with silky down, the tiny linear appressed topmost leaves shorter than the very small, narrow conical flower-clusters, which contain only 3–6 yellowish flower-heads; sepal-like bracts tipped yellowish, the outer 5 sharply angled and spreading star-like in fruit. *Habitat:* Widespread and locally frequent in bare dry gravelly and sandy places. June–September.

867. *HEATH CUDWEED *Gnaphalium sylvaticum* L. Pl. 37. *CTW, p. 1060*
A greyish woolly perennial with prostrate leafy shoots from the base and an unbranched erect flowering-stem, 4 in. to 2 ft. high; leaves linear, 1-veined, pointed, green and hairless above, white-felted beneath, larger and stalked in the basal rosette, becoming smaller up the stem. Flower-heads small, narrow oblong, pale yellow, with close-set sepal-like bracts, grey-green with a dark brown tip and shiny brown margins, woolly below; solitary or in clusters in a long leafy spike. Fruits cylindrical with a reddish-brown pappus. *Habitat:* Widespread and locally common in dry open heathy woods and fields. July–September.

867a. *****Highland Cudweed,** *G. norvegicum* Gunnerus, is half as tall, woollier and with no barren basal shoots, and has much broader 3-veined leaves, downy on both sides, only shorter among the flowers; and a much shorter compacter flower-spike, with shorter darker sepal-like bracts. Rare, usually on granite rocks high in the Highlands. August.

868. **DWARF CUDWEED   *G. supinum* L.   Plate 37.   *CTW, p. 1060*
A small tufted perennial, about 2 in. high, with narrow leaves downy on both sides and small brown flower-heads in small compact terminal clusters or spikes, not exceeded by the leaves; sepal-like bracts broad, woolly and olive-green, with a broad dark brown margin.   *Habitat:* Locally frequent on bare mountain tops in the Highlands. June–July.

869. WAYSIDE CUDWEED   *G. uliginosum* L.   Plate 37.   *CTW, p. 1061*
A low weak, often bushily tufted annual, 1–6 in. high, with narrow leaves tapering to the base and cottony on both sides, the topmost overtopping the crowded clusters of small yellowish-brown, unstalked flower-heads; sepal-like bracts brownish.   *Habitat:* Widespread and frequent in bare damp sandy fields and on moist paths in heathy woods. July–August.

870. ***JERSEY CUDWEED   *G. luteoalbum* L.   Plate 52.   *CTW, p. 1061*
A densely woolly, grey odourless annual, 6–12 in. high, with erect unbranched stems spreading from the base, and leaves grey on both sides, inrolled at the margins, the root ones broader and blunt, the upper very narrow, pointed, erect, wavy and half-clasping. Flower-heads egg-shaped, pale yellow, with bright red stigmas, with shiny chaffy straw-coloured sepal-like bracts, in dense terminal umbels. Often confused with the next two species.   *Habitat:* Very rare in sandy fields and dunes in E Anglia and the Channel Is. July–September.

871. ***CAPE CUDWEED   *G. undulatum* L.   Plate 52.   *CTW, p. 1062*
Taller and much more branched and bushy than the last species, also foetid and with flower-heads half the size and broader spreading leaves, apple green above, running down a short way on to the stem at the base, and with a minute bristle at the tip.   *Habitat:* Walls and in bare places in the Channel Is. July–September.

872. **PEARL EVERLASTING   *Anaphalis margaritacea* (L.) Bentham
   Antennaria margaritacea (L.) Gray   Plate 94.   *CTW, p. 1062*
A stout leafy bushy 'everlasting' perennial, 1–2 ft. high, white with woolly hairs, with narrow pointed leaves. Flower-heads numerous, yellow, unrayed, in broad terminal clusters, looking white from the broad pearly tips of the prominent sepal-like bracts. Male and female often on different plants.   *Habitat:* Well established in waste and grassy places, especially in the S Welsh valleys. August.

873. *MOUNTAIN EVERLASTING   *Antennaria dioica* (L.) Gaertner
                                          Plate 94.   *CTW, p. 1063*
A short neat perennial, with creeping rooting runners and an erect flowering stem 3–8 in. high; leaves narrow spoon-shaped, 1–2 in. long in the basal rosette, narrow lanceolate, and appressed on the stem; all white-woolly beneath and normally green above. Flower-heads, male and female on separate plants, 2–8 in close terminal umbels, with the sepal-like bracts chaffy above, woolly below, white and spreading on male heads and pink and erect on female heads.   *Habitat:* Widespread on heaths, mountain slopes and dry pastures; common in hill districts, very rare in the S. June–July.

874. GOLDEN-ROD   *Solidago virgaurea* L.   Plate 57.   *CTW, p. 1063*
A variable, little branched, often slightly downy perennial, 3 in. to 2 ft. high, with leaves sometimes slightly toothed, stalked and oblong at the base, narrower

lanceolate and unstalked up the stem. Flower-heads in branched spikes, small, bright yellow, shortly rayed, the sepal-like bracts narrow, greenish-yellow. *Habitat:* Widespread and locally frequent in dry woods, heaths and hedge-banks, and on rocks. July–September.

874*a*. **Garden Golden-rod,** *S. altissima* L. ('*S. canadensis*'), is always much taller, with a creeping root stock, downy stems, longer leaves, Flower-heads many, in dense, often spreading, 1-sided spikes in widely triangular branched terminal heads, usually darker yellow, much smaller and neater, with short rays. A familiar garden plant, often well established in waste places. August onwards.

874*b*. ***Early Golden-rod,** *S. gigantea* Aiton (*S. serotina* Aiton), is stockier and usually shorter than Garden Golden-rod, almost or entirely hairless and often greyish, with broader deeper-toothed leaves, and larger well-rayed, rich yellow flower-heads. Much less common. July–August.

875. SEA ASTER *Aster tripolium* L. Plate 9. *CTW, p. 1065*

A stout hairless fleshy perennial, 6 in. to 3 ft. high, often much branched above, the dark green lanceolate leaves with a prominent midrib. Flower-heads very like garden Michaelmas Daisies, with yellow disk-florets and usually also pale purple or whitish ray-florets, in loose irregular umbels; sepal-like bracts rather few, lanceolate. *Habitat:* Widespread and locally abundant by the sea, especially in salt-marshes; very rare inland. July onwards.

875*a*. *Michaelmas Daisy,** *A. novi-belgii* L., is the commonest of a very variable and confusing group of escaped garden plants, which includes *A. novae-angliae* L., *A. puniceus* L., *A. longifolius* Lamarck, *A. laevis* L., *A. lanceolatus* Willdenow and *A. salignus* Willdenow. They are generally taller than the Sea Aster with leaves never fleshy, but flowers varying widely in size and in the colour of the rays, being purple, mauve, pink or white. Widely naturalised, in dry and damp places. August onwards.

876. ***GOLDILOCKS *Linosyris vulgaris* DC. Plate 52. *CTW, p. 1067*

A graceful unbranched hairless perennial, 6–12 in. high with many 1-veined, pale green linear leaves. Flower-heads bright golden-yellow, unrayed, egg-shaped, with prominent yellow styles and stigmas, in a loose erect terminal umbel. Differs from Golden Samphire (861) in its many narrower, not fleshy leaves, unrayed flower-heads and leaf-like bracts very narrow, the outer spreading. *Habitat:* Very rare, on five dry limestone cliffs along the W coast of England and Wales. September–October. *Aster linosyris* (L.) Bernhardi.

877. *BLUE FLEABANE *Erigeron acer* L. Plate 8. *CTW, p. 1068*

A roughly hairy annual or biennial, 4–18 in. high, with stiff, often purple stems, and small short lanceolate untoothed leaves, the stem ones narrower and half-clasping. Flower-heads rather small, cylindrical, with erect dingy purple ray-florets not much longer than the yellow disk-florets, solitary or in loose spikes; sepal-like bracts narrow, dull purple. Fruits hairy with a long reddish-white pappus. *Habitat:* Locally frequent in dry grassy places and on dunes in England and Wales; more local in Ireland, rare in Scotland. July onwards.

878. ***HIGHLAND FLEABANE *E. borealis* (Vierhapper) Simmons
'*E. alpinus*' Plate 23. *CTW, p. 1069*

A hairy unbranched perennial, 3–6 in. high, with a basal rosette of stalked, narrow spoon-shaped leaves, and a few very narrow stem-leaves. Flower-heads

solitary, ½-in. across, larger than the last species, with the more spreading pinky-
purple ray-florets much longer than the yellow disk-florets. *Habitat:* Rare on
mountain rock-ledges in the E Highlands and on and near Ben Lawers. July–Aug.

878a. ***Purple Coltsfoot, *Homogyne alpina* (L.) Cassini (*CTW†*), has shiny,
leathery kidney-shaped root-leaves, an inch or so across, hairy chiefly on their
long stalks; a few very narrow lanceolate stem-leaves, and solitary purplish
flower-heads, tapering below, with a single row of ray-florets, at the top of the
purplish, sparsely woolly 4–6-in. stem. Known only from one rock-ledge in the
parish of Cortachy and Clova, Angus. May–July.

879. **MEXICAN FLEABANE   *E. mucronatus* DC.   Plate 100.   *CTW, p. 1069*
A pretty, slightly downy perennial, up to a foot high, with slender branches
and lanceolate leaves up the stem, the lower often with a broad tooth at each side.
Flower-heads remarkably like a Daisy (881), solitary, on long slender stalks, with
yellow disk-florets and ray-florets white, fading to pink; sepal-like bracts
narrower. Fruits with a pappus. *Habitat:* Common on walls in the Channel Is.;
occasional in SW England and SW Ireland. May onwards.

880. *CANADIAN FLEABANE   *Conyza canadensis* (L.) Cronquist
   Erigeron canadensis L.   Plate 100.   *CTW, p. 1069*
A slightly hairy, pale green weedy annual, with numerous narrow lanceolate
leaves up the stem, and loose branched spikes of small oblong flower-heads, with
short dirty white rays and yellow disk-florets. *Habitat:* A frequent and increasing
weed of disturbed and waste ground, locally abundant in SE England, thinning
out northwards and westwards; not yet in Ireland. June onwards.

881. DAISY   *Bellis perennis* L.   Plate 100.   *CTW, p. 1070*
Perhaps the most familiar flower of all, 'wee, modest, crimson-tipped'; a
downy perennial, 2–4 in. high, with a basal rosette of broad, spoon-shaped,
slightly toothed leaves. Flower-heads solitary, on leafless stalks, the disk-florets
yellow, the rays white, often tipped crimson. Fruits with no pappus, on a conical
base. *Habitat:* Widespread and often abundant on lawns and in short grassland.
Throughout the year.

882. HEMP AGRIMONY   *Eupatorium cannabinum* L.   Pl. 21.   *CTW, p. 1071*
A tall downy perennial, not looking like a Composite, 2–4 ft. high, with the
stem often reddish and usually branched above; leaves palmate, the segments
lanceolate, toothed, the branch ones undivided, lanceolate, very short-stalked.
Flower-heads small, in large dense terminal trusses, somewhat recalling Common
Valerian (829), each with only 5–6 loose whitish-pink disk-florets; styles long,
white; sepal-like bracts long, purple-tipped. *Habitat:* Widespread and frequent
by fresh water and in fens and wet woods; also rarely in woods on the chalk.
July–September.

CHAMOMILES and MAYWEEDS   *Anthemis, Matricaria, etc.*

A GROUP of not very tall, branched plants with daisy-like flowers, usually with
white rays, and pinnately divided leaves with very narrow, more or less cylindrical
segments; often aromatic or strongly scented. The Chamomiles differ from the
Mayweeds in having chaffy scales among the disk-florets.

883. ***YELLOW CHAMOMILE *Anthemis tinctoria* L. Pl. 56. *CTW, p. 1072*
A stiff perennial, 9–18 in. high, with yellow flower-heads like Corn Marigold
(891), but smaller and sometimes unrayed; the stems and undersides of the leaves
are grey with woolly down; leaves smaller, crisper and very deeply pinnately
divided. *Habitat:* Rare in hot dry waste places. July–August.

884. *CORN CHAMOMILE *A. arvensis* L. Plate 100. *CTW, p. 1073*
A scarcely scented annual, differing from Scentless Mayweed (886) in having
grey downy stems, somewhat broader leaf-segments, hairy or whitely downy
beneath, and flowers fragrant, the heads solid and conical from the first, with
pointed lanceolate scales between the yellow disk-florets; the white rays with
styles; and sepal-like bracts all green. *Habitat:* Widespread but local in arable
and waste ground. May–July.

885. *COMMON CHAMOMILE *Chamaemelum nobile* (L.) Allioni
Anthemis nobilis L. Plate 100 *CTW, p. 1074*
Shorter and more spreading than the last species, but is perennial, turf-forming
and strongly and pleasantly aromatic, with no down beneath the leaves. *Habitat:*
Rather local in grassy and heathy places, especially on sandy soils; now rarely
used for lawns. June–August.

886. SCENTLESS MAYWEED *Tripleurospermum maritimum* (L.) Koch
Matricaria maritima L. (incl. *M. inodora* L.) Plate 100. *CTW, p. 1078*
A often half-prostrate scentless hairless annual (rarely perennial by the sea),
6–18 in. high, the bushy 2–3-pinnate leaves with long fine hair-like segments.
Flower-heads rather large, an inch or so across, daisy-like with no chaffy scales
between the yellow disk-florets, and the white ray-florets usually with a style;
flat at first, but forming a solid cone in fruit; sepal-like bracts bordered brown.
Fruits with 3 corky ribs on the inner face and 2 small points near the top. *Habitat:*
Widespread and common on bare and disturbed ground. June onwards.

886a. ***Scented Mayweed,** *M. recutita* L. ('*M. chamomilla*'), is pungently
aromatic, slenderer and more upright, with leaves not quite so thread-like, and
smaller flowers, the heads hollow and sooner conical, the rays turning down soon
after flowering; sepal-like bracts bordered whitish; and fruits much smaller, with
5 small white ribs on their inner face. Only locally common, mainly in the S.

886b. ***Stinking Chamomile,** *Anthemis cotula* L. (*CTW, p. 1073*), differs from
Scented Mayweed in having a sickly sweet smell, slightly hairy stems, shorter and
broader leaf-segments, flowers between the last two in size, rays usually without a
style, solid heads with scales between the disk-florets, and sepal-like bracts
whitish with a narrow green midrib. A locally common weed, mainly in the S.

887. PINEAPPLE WEED *M. matricarioides* (Lessing) Porter
M. suaveolens (Pursh) Buchenau Plate 101. *CTW, p. 1080*
A dark green, hairless, bushy, strongly apple-scented annual, 2–10 in. high,
with 2–3-pinnate leaves, the segments thread-like. Flower-heads unrayed, with
4-toothed yellowish-green disk-florets; conical, hollow, with blunt whitish tips
and chaffy margins to the sepal-like bracts. *Habitat:* Now widespread and
common in waste, especially trodden, places. June onwards.

888. YARROW *Achillea millefolium* L. Plate 95. *CTW, p. 1075*
A downy, little branched, aromatic, dark green perennial, 6–18 in. high, with
creeping runners; tough downy stems; and long narrow, rather bushy, 2–3-pinnate

leaves with tiny linear leaflets. Flower-heads small, numerous, in flattish terminal umbels with usually 5 short broad blunt 3-toothed white or pink ray-florets, and creamy disk-florets with dark styles; sepal-like bracts overlapping, grey-green with brown margins. *Habitat:* Widespread and common in grassy places, including lawns. June onwards.

889. *SNEEZEWORT *A. ptarmica* L. Plate 94. *CTW, p. 1076*
A greyish perennial, 1–2 ft. high, with stiff angular stems hairy above and dark green, half-clasping, pointed, finely saw-toothed linear leaves. Flower-heads creamy white, rather Yarrow-like but larger and fewer in a looser umbel. *Habitat:* Widespread but local in damp grassland, fens and scrub on heavy or acid soils. July–August.

890. ***COTTONWEED *Otanthus maritimus* (L.) Hoffmannsegg & Link
Diotis maritima (L.) Hooker   Plate 52. *CTW, p. 1077*
A stout creeping perennial, about a foot high, covered all over with a thick white silvery down; leaves small, oblong, toothed. Flower-heads small, fat, unrayed, yellow, in small terminal clusters. *Habitat:* Now confined to the sandy shingle beach at Lady's Island Lake, Co. Wexford. August onwards.

891. *CORN MARIGOLD *Chrysanthemum segetum* L. Pl. 56. *CTW, p. 1081*
A greyish hairless annual, 6–18 in. high, with rather fleshy pointed, jaggedly toothed wedge-shaped leaves, clasping above. Flower-heads about 2 in. across, solitary on stalks thickened at the top, bright yellow, conspicuously yellow-rayed and daisy-like. *Habitat:* Widespread as a conspicuous gregarious arable weed, but only locally frequent, usually on sandy soils. June onwards.

892. OX-EYE DAISY *C. leucanthemum* L. Plate 100. *CTW, p. 1082*
A familiar large Daisy, a slightly hairy, unbranched perennial, 1–2 ft. high, with small dark glossy green, well toothed leaves, the upper narrow lanceolate and slightly clasping, the lower very long-stalked and spoon-shaped, sometimes deeply lobed on mountains. Flower-heads solitary, about 1–2 in. across, with yellow disk-florets and conspicuous white rays, sepal-like bracts green, neatly edged brown and straw-colour. *Habitat:* Widespread and often abundant in grassy places. May onwards. Moon Daisy, Dog Daisy, Marguerite.

893. *FEVERFEW *C. parthenium* (L.) Bernhardi Plate 100. *CTW, p. 1082*
A somewhat downy perennial, 6–18 in. high, readily known by its pungently aromatic yellowish foliage; leaves 1–2-pinnate. Flowers in loose terminal umbel-like clusters, daisy-like, yellow with short broad white rays. *Habitat:* Widespread and frequent, especially near gardens and on walls. July onwards.

894. TANSY *C. vulgare* (L.) Bernhardi Plate 52. *CTW, p. 1083*
A stiff stout, dark green aromatic perennial, 1–3 ft. high, with pinnate leaves, the numerous leaflets narrow and deeply toothed. Flower-heads small, hard, flat-topped, button-like, golden-yellow, with apparently no ray-florets, in large umbel-like clusters. *Habitat:* Widespread and fairly frequent on grassy verges, river banks and waste places. July onwards. *Tanacetum vulgare* L.

895. ***BUTTONWEED *Cotula coronopifolia* L. Plate 52. *CTW, p. 1084*
A short hairless yellow-green fleshy annual, 6–12 in. high, with alternate leaves, sheathing the stem, and varying, even on the same stem, from deeply pinnate to broad linear and untoothed. Flower-heads yellow, apparently unrayed, small,

flat, tansy-like, aromatic, solitary on long stalks. *Habitat:* Well established in marshy ground near the sea in the Wirral. July onwards.

896. MUGWORT *Artemisia vulgaris* L. Plate 101. *CTW, p. 1085*
A slightly aromatic perennial, 2–4 ft. high, with ribbed downy, often purplish stems, much branched above and 1–2-pinnate leaves, only the lower ones stalked, the leaflets toothed and pointed, dark green and nearly hairless above, silvery downy beneath. Flower-heads small, egg-shaped, with a few yellow or purplish-brown disk-florets; numerous in dense, much-branched spikes; sepal-like bracts cottony. *Habitat:* Widespread and common on roadsides and in waste places. August-September.

896*a*. ****Chinese Mugwort,** *A. verlotorum* Lamotte, is not quite so tall and forms patches. It is much more aromatic, with longer, darker green leaflets, less white and downy beneath; and its elliptical flowers do not appear till November, when the whole plant is still fresh-looking. Increasing in S and E England, especially around London.

897. *WORMWOOD *A. absinthium* L. Plate 101. *CTW, p. 1086*
A not unbeautiful plant with its grey foliage and branched spikes of numerous small yellow buttony flower-heads, but less tall and much more strongly aromatic than Mugwort (896), with stems and both sides of leaves covered with white silky down; leaf-segments broader, blunt. Flower-heads larger, globular, drooping yellow. *Habitat:* Widespread but scattered on roadsides and waste ground. July-August.

898. SEA WORMWOOD *A. maritima* L. Plate 101. *CTW, p. 1087*
A pungently but pleasantly aromatic perennial, about a foot high, with stems and both sides of leaves silvery grey with down; leaves mostly 2-pinnate with linear leaflets. Flower-heads like Mugwort (896), but smaller; and brighter yellow or orange, sometimes drooping. *Habitat:* Widespread and locally frequent in drier salt-marshes and on sea-walls, thinning out northwards; rare in Ireland. July-September.

899. ***BRECKLAND MUGWORT *A. campestris* L. Pl. 101. *CTW, p. 1087*
An unscented perennial, 1–2 ft. high, with stems almost hairless, and 2–3-pinnate leaves with narrow pointed segments, silky on both sides at first but becoming hairless. Flower-heads similar to Mugwort (896), but rounder and yellower, in a less branched spike. *Habitat:* Confined to the Breckland grasslands; a very rare casual elsewhere. August-September.

900. ***SCOTTISH WORMWOOD *A. norvegica* Fries Plate 37. *CTW†*
A tufted perennial, 2–4 in. high, greyish with silky hairs, with deeply pinnately cut leaves and ½–¾-in. unrayed yellow button-like nodding flower-heads up to ½-in. across, usually solitary, but sometimes 2–5 together on stalks 2–3 in. long; sepal-like bracts with wide dark brown margins. *Habitat:* Discovered in 1952 on bare ground on a mountain in W Ross. June–September.

KEY TO THISTLE-LIKE FLOWERS (Nos. 901–923)
(Not including the somewhat thistle-like Sea-holly (454), Watling-street Thistle (455) and Teasels (833–834).
1. Purple Flowers
PLANT *creeping* 909, 912, 916; *with prickly or spiny stems* 903–5, 907–8, 915.

G

LEAVES *broad* 902; *pinnate* 906, 907, 908, 919, 920, 921, 923; *not prickly* 902, 908, 919, 920, 921, 923; *with white lines* 914.

FLOWER-HEADS *large* 904, 906, 907, 914, 915; *solitary* 904, 910, 911, 912, 913, 914, 915, 919, 920, 921; *fragrant* 909, 916.

SEPAL-LIKE BRACTS *brown* 919; *hooked* 902; *not spiny* 902, 909, 916, 919, 923.

PAPPUS *feathery* 906, 907, 908, 909, 911, 912, 913, 916.

II. **Yellow Flowers**

PLANT *whitely downy* 922. LEAVES *pinnate* 922; *prickly* 901.

901. *CARLINE THISTLE *Carlina vulgaris* L. Plate 52. *CTW, p. 1089*

A stiff spiny biennial, 4–12 in. high, with prickly thistle-like leaves, the lower cottony. Flower-heads 1½ in., terminal, usually 2–5 together, yellow-brown, unrayed, with spiny cottony leaf-like outer bracts and conspicuous purple-based narrow straw-yellow sepal-like inner bracts, which look like rays and fold over in wet weather. Yellowish dead plants, looking much the same as in flower, often survive the winter. *Habitat:* Widespread and locally frequent in grassland and scrub, mainly on chalk and limestone. July onwards.

902. BURDOCK *Arctium minus* (Hill) Bernhardi Plate 31. *CTW, p. 1091*

A stiff stout downy biennial, 2–3 ft. high, with many arching stems, and alternate leaves broad pointed oval or roughly heart-shaped, the upper narrower, the lower sometimes a foot or more long, on unfurrowed, usually hollow stalks up to a foot long. Flower-heads egg-shaped in bud, thistle-like, up to ¾-in. across, short-stalked, in open terminal spikes, unrayed, the purple florets longer than the purple-tipped sepal-like bracts, which are all hooked, and closed up at the top when in fruit, forming the oval burs which adhere so readily to clothing. *Habitat:* Widespread and common in drier woods, and on roadsides and waste ground. July–September.

902a. **Great Burdock,** *A. lappa* L. (*A. majus* Bernhardi), is stouter, the longer, rather butterbur-like but rough leaves with rounded tips; solid lower stalks with a furrow on the upper surface; flower-heads few in flat-topped clusters, much larger, 1–1½ in. across, globular, long-stalked, with equally spreading cottony or green sepal-like bracts whose tips about equal the florets and are wide open in fruit. Less common and usually on heavier soils.

902b. **Wood Burdock,** *A. nemorosum* Lejeune & Courtois ('*A. vulgare*'), is variable, and somewhat intermediate between the other two Burdocks, having the hollow lower leaf-stalks of the common species, but furrowed above, looser spikes of short-stalked globular flower-heads an inch across, the florets about equalling the maroon-tipped sepal-like bracts, which are nearly as open in fruit as Great Burdock. In many districts the commonest Burdock.

THISTLES *Carduus* and *Cirsium*

THISTLES ARE notoriously spiny, sometimes woundingly so, always on the more or less wavy leaves, usually also on the sepal-like bracts. Flower-heads unrayed, brush-like, with all florets tubular and deeply divided, of some shade of purple, occasionally white. The difference between Thistles of the genera *Carduus* (903–905) and *Cirsium* (906–913) is that the former has its thistledown (pappus) composed of rough unbranched hairs, the latter a pappus of branched feathery hairs. Nearly all the species rather rarely hybridise with each other.

903. *SEASIDE THISTLE *Carduus tenuiflorus* Curtis Pl. 31. *CTW, p. 1092*
A rather slender, whitish-grey downy annual or biennial, 6 in. to 4 ft. high, with stems usually well winged, and small, narrow oblong, pale pink flower-heads which fall when the fruits are ripe. Leaves cottony below; sepal-like bracts with spreading spines. *Habitat:* Widespread and locally frequent in grassy and waste places near the sea; scarce inland and in the N. June–Aug. '*C. pycnocephalus*'.

904. MUSK THISTLE *C. nutans* L. Plate 30. *CTW, p. 1093*
One of our handsomest Thistles, with its large, often solitary, drooping reddish-purple, fragrant flower-heads on spine-free upper stalks; sepal-like bracts very large, conspicuous, spreading, purple, spine-tipped. A grey cottony downy biennial, 1–3 ft. high, with very spiny leaves running down on to the stems as spiny wings. *Habitat:* Widespread and locally frequent in open grassland and quarries, mainly on chalk or limestone, thinning out northwards. June onwards.

905. WELTED THISTLE *C. crispus* L. Plate 31. *CTW, p. 1093*
Has been confused with Marsh Thistle (908), but is greener, laxer and much more branched, with stems spiny-winged below, but usually not immediately under the flower-heads, which are usually clustered, broader, egg-shaped and redder, with long narrow half-spreading woolly green sepal-like bracts; hairs of thistle-down not feathery. *Habitat:* Widespread, frequent in hedge-banks and grassy places, thinning out northwards. June onwards. (Incl. *C. acanthoides* L.)

906. **WOOLLY THISTLE *Cirsium eriophorum* (L.) Scopoli Pl. 30. *CTW, 1095*
A superb stately biennial Thistle, 2–4 ft. high, with a stiff grey woolly unwinged stem, and very large pinnately cut basal leaves, up to 18 in. long, the prickly-hairy segments 2-lobed, one lobe pointing upwards, the other down, dark green above, cottony beneath, ending in long spines; stem-leaves smaller and arched. Flower-heads several, long-stalked, huge, up to $2\frac{1}{2}$ in. across, globular, with a stout brush of rich red-purple disk-florets; sepal-like bracts numerous, narrow, spreading, spiny, thickly spider-webbed with white wool below. *Habitat:* Local in grassland, scrub and old pits on chalk and limestone in England and Wales. July–September. *Carduus eriophorus* L.

907. SPEAR THISTLE *C. vulgare* (Savi) Tenore Plate 30. *CTW, p. 1096*
Our commonest large-flowered Thistle, a stout downy biennial, 1–5 ft. high, with pinnately lobed leaves, spiny above and running down on to the stem to form long spiny wings. Flower-heads solitary or 2–3 together, reddish-purple, over an inch across and 1–2 in. high, the narrow sepal-like bracts with yellow-tipped spines, less cottony than the last species. *Habitat:* Widespread and common in grassy and waste places. July onwards. *Carduus lanceolatus* L.

908. MARSH THISTLE *C. palustre* (L.) Scopoli Plate 31. *CTW, p. 1096*
A tall, little branched, hairy biennial, 2–6 ft. high, with numerous leafy prickles on the dark green winged stem and narrow pinnately lobed leaves, the spines often purple-tipped. Flower-heads numerous, $\frac{3}{4}$-in., egg-shaped, reddish-purple; sepal-like bracts cottony-grey, tipped purple, short and appressed, and the thistle-down feathery; the bracts and down affording important distinctions from Welted Thistle (905). *Habitat:* Widespread and common in grassy places and woods, often in wet ground. June onwards.

909. **CREEPING THISTLE**   *C. arvense* (L.) Scopoli   Plate 31.   *CTW, p. 1097*
Carduus arvensis (L.) Hill
Our only Thistle with smallish fragrant pale lilac flower-heads, in terminal clusters; male and female usually on different plants. A usually hairless, little branched creeping perennial, 1–5 ft. high, with leaves shortly running down on to the spineless stems, sometimes cottony beneath; and sepal-like bracts purplish-green, broad, appressed, pointed but scarcely spiny.   *Habitat:* A widespread and common pest of fields, roadsides and waste places. June onwards.

910. **DWARF THISTLE**   *C. acaulon* (L.) Scopoli   Plate 30.   *CTW, p. 1098*
A low perennial, 2–6 in. high, with a basal rosette of shiny spiny, wavily pinnately cut leaves, from which rises a solitary short- or unstalked flower-head, the numerous hairless purplish sepal-like bracts mostly lightly appressed into a long conical head, surmounted by a wide crown of deep-cleft red-purple disk-florets.   *Habitat:* Locally frequent in short turf on chalk and limestone in the S; rare elsewhere. July onwards. *Carduus acaulos* L.

911. *****MELANCHOLY THISTLE**   *C. heterophyllum* (L.) Hill
Carduus heterophyllus L.   Plate 30.   *CTW, p. 1099*
Much taller and robuster than the next species, with stout grooved cottony stems and larger undivided oblong leaves, toothed, only softly and shortly spined, with a thicker white felt beneath; stem-leaves with broader bases, half-clasping. Flower-heads half as large again.   *Habitat:* Locally frequent in moist places in hill districts in the N; rare in N Ireland. July–August.

912. *****MEADOW THISTLE**   *C. dissectum* (L.) Hill   Plate 31.   *CTW, p. 1100*
Carduus pratensis Hudson
A scarcely spiny, usually unbranched creeping perennial, 1–2 ft. high, cottony all over, with lanceolate, often wavy-edged gently spiny leaves, whiter beneath, the lower deeply lobed, the upper half-clasping the round unwinged stem. Flower-heads usually solitary, reddish-purple, with lanceolate sepal-like bracts, the outer ones spiny, green and contrasting with the grey foliage.   *Habitat:* Local in wet peaty meadows, less acid bogs and fens in the S. June–August.

913. ******TUBEROUS THISTLE**   *C. tuberosum* (L.) Allioni   Pl. 30.   *CTW, 1100*
Usually taller than the last species, and has spindle-shaped tuberous roots, no runners, and leaves pinnately lobed and green on both sides. Hybridises with Dwarf Thistle (910).   *Habitat:* Rare in chalk and limestone turf in Cambridge-shire, Wiltshire and S. Wales. June–August. *Carduus tuberosus* L.

914. ****MILK THISTLE**   *Silybum marianum* (L.) Gaertner   Pl. 30.   *CTW, p. 1101*
Our only Thistle which normally has conspicuous white veins on its leaves; a stout annual or biennial, 1–3 ft. high, with unwinged downy stems and hairless leaves wavy-edged, sharply spiny and shining dark green above. Flower-heads solitary on the branches, purple, unrayed; sepal-like bracts long, the lower lanceolate, spreading, and ending in very sharp stout yellow spines. Fruits large, shiny, wrinkled, dark brown, with a long toothed pale brown pappus.   *Habitat:* Widespread but only locally common in waste places, or in scrub on limestone, chiefly near the sea.   June–August. *Carduus marianus* L.

915. ****SCOTCH THISTLE**   *Onopordum acanthium* L.   Plate 30.   *CTW, p. 1102*
A tall stout, often broad biennial, 2–4 ft. high, white with cottony down, the stems very strongly winged with triangular spines, and the oblong leaves also

spiny. Flower-heads globular, solitary, unrayed, pale purple, with cotton-based sepal-like bracts ending in conspicuous spreading yellow spines. *Habitat:* Widespread but uncommon on roadsides and waste ground; very rare in Scotland, despite its name; not in Ireland. July–September.

916. **PURPLE HAWKWEED *Saussurea alpina* (L.) DC. Pl. 3. *CTW, p. 1103*
A stout stocky stiff unbranched perennial, with shaggy stems up to a foot high, and more or less toothed lanceolate leaves, dark green above and shaggy beneath. Flower-heads in a compact terminal cluster, unrayed, purple, fragrant, with appressed oval sepal-like bracts, the inner very hairy. *Habitat:* Local on mountain ledges in the N; very rare in Ireland. August–September.

917. GREATER KNAPWEED *Centaurea scabiosa* L. Pl. 31. *CTW, p. 1105*
A handsome perennial, 1–2 ft. high, with stiff downy grooved stems swollen at the top, and irregularly pinnately lobed, sparsely bristly leaves. Flower-heads large, terminal, solitary, globular below, purple, with the outer disk-florets enlarged, sterile, spreading in a crown, bearing 4–5 prominent narrow pointed petals, and simulating ray-florets; sepal-like bracts oval-based, grey-green, with black-brown horseshoe-shaped, tightly appressed fringed appendages. It is usually larger and robuster than the rayed form of 919, and can at once be told by its green sepal-like bracts and pinnately lobed upper leaves. *Habitat:* Widespread and common in grassy places, especially on chalk or limestone, thinning out northwards. July onwards.

918. **CORNFLOWER *C. cyanus* L. Plate 9. *CTW, p. 1105*
Well known in gardens in various colour forms, a rather grey downy annual, 1–2 ft. high, with stiff thin grooved stems slightly swollen under the 1-in. flower-heads, and narrow leaves, the upper unstalked and lanceolate, the lower stalked and pinnately lobed. Flower-heads similar in form to the last species, but smaller, narrow below, with shorter enlarged outer florets which are bright blue; sepal-like bracts narrower, with silvery-edged appendages. *Habitat:* Now very scarce in cornfields and more often seen as a garden escape. June–August.

919. HARDHEAD *C. nigra* L. Plate 31. *CTW, p. 1107*
Black Knapweed, Lesser Knapweed; *C. obscura* Jordan
A downy perennial, 6 in. to 2 ft. high, with stiff ribbed stems, often swollen under the hard-based flower-heads; and lanceolate leaves, only the lower toothed. Buds hard, globular, developing into solitary, usually unrayed purple flower-heads, with numerous overlapping flat sepal-like bracts, their top part broader, dull brown or blackish, and feathered with long fine teeth. Fruits with no pappus. Freely hybridises with the two other Hardheads. *Habitat:* Widespread and common in grassy places. June onwards.
919a. **Slender Hardhead,** *C. nemoralis* Jordan, has slender branches; leaves narrower and less toothed; stems not swollen under the rather smaller flower-heads, which are more often rayed; a short pappus; and sepal-like bracts usually pale brown. Thinning out northwards. July onwards.
919b. ****French Hardhead,** *C. jacea* L., differs from Slender Hardhead in its purpler, always rayed flowers, with shiny concave sepal-like bracts, not or only shallowly toothed, and edged paler. Fruits with no pappus. Widespread but scarce; sometimes a casual.

920. ***ROUGH STAR THISTLE *C. aspera* L.   Plate 31. *CTW, p. 1108*

Rather like a prostrate unrayed Hardhead, but with the upper leaves sometimes pinnately lobed, and the yellowish sepal-like bracts with 3–5 spreading or down-turned reddish spines. *Habitat:* Locally plentiful in grassy and waste places in the Channel Is.; casual elsewhere. June onwards.

921. **STAR THISTLE *C. calcitrapa* L.   Plate 31. *CTW, p. 1108*

A bushy biennial, a foot or so high, with many stiff hairless branches spreading from the base; and sparsely hairy leaves, the lower deeply pinnately lobed, spine-pointed, grey-green, withering early; the upper unstalked and narrower. Flower-heads narrow, solitary, apparently at the base of the branches; disk-florets pale purple-red, unrayed, with many stout rigid spreading yellow-green sepal-like bracts, ending in stiff yellow spines about ½-in. long, with smaller spines below. *Habitat:* Scarce in bare places on chalk in SE England; a rare casual elsewhere. July–September.

922. ***ST BARNABY'S THISTLE *C. solstitialis* L.   Plate 56. *CTW, p. 1109*

A hoary grey downy annual, 1–2 ft. high, with broad wings on the stems, and lower leaves pinnately lobed, the upper narrow, running down the stem. Flower-heads solitary, unrayed, yellow, the rather cottony sepal-like bracts ending in a spreading yellow spine, with some smaller ones at the base. *Habitat:* A scarce casual, usually in fields of Lucerne (278). July–September. Yellow Star Thistle.

923. *SAWWORT *Serratula tinctoria* L.   Plate 31. *CTW, p. 1110*

A slender hairless perennial, 1–2 ft. high, with stiff stems and pinnately lobed or almost undivided, finely saw-toothed leaves. Flower-heads narrowly conical below, thistle-like, in a loose, branched terminal cluster, unrayed, purple; sepal-like bracts closely appressed, shiny, purplish-green. Fruits with pappus hairs not feathery. *Habitat:* Local in grassland, scrub, open woods and heathy places on both chalky and acid soils N to SW Scotland. July–September.

KEY TO DANDELION-TYPE FLOWERS   (Nos. 924–956)

The principal groups of yellow dandelion-like flowers can be quickly told apart on the following characters; stems leafy unless stated otherwise.

NIPPLEWORT (925): Slender much branched annual, no milky juice or pappus.

CATSEARS (927–929): Stems leafless and hairless; narrow chaffy scales between the florets; at least the inner fruits beaked; pappus feathery.

HAWKBITS (930–932): Stems leafless; inner pappus feathery, outer unbranched.

OX-TONGUES (933–934): Covered with bristly, often hooked hairs; inner pappus of feathery hairs.

GOATSBEARD (935): Hairless, with grass-like leaves; fruits beaked, the feathery pappus with woody rigid rays; milky juice.

LETTUCES (938–940): Milky, flowers small; fruits flattened, beaked, with un-branched white pappus.

SOW-THISTLES (941–944): Hairless; very milky; fruits flattened; pappus un-branched.

HAWKWEEDS (946–948): Pappus brownish, unbranched; fruits neither beaked nor narrowed at the top.

HAWKSBEARDS (950–955): Outer sepal-like bracts turned down, the inner erect; pappus hairs white, not feathery; fruits beaked or narrowed at the top.

DANDELIONS (956): Hollow, very milky unbranched leafless stems; pappus not feathery; fruits flattened, beaked.

I. Blue or Purple Flowers

PLANT *with milky juice* 936, 945; *with stems swollen under flower-heads* 936.

LEAVES *grass-like* 936; *lobed* 924, 945.

SEPAL-LIKE BRACTS *longer than rays* 936; *shorter than rays* 924, 945.

II. Orange Flowers: 949.

III. Yellow Flowers

PLANT *bristly* 933, 934; *with pale bristled pimples* 933; *prickly* 938; *with milky juice* 935, 937, 938, 939, 940, 941, 942, 943, 944, 956.

STEMS *with neither bracts nor leaves* 926, 932, 948, 956; *with bracts only* 927, 928, 929, 930, 931; *abruptly swollen under flower-heads* 927, 928, 929, 931, 935; *gradually tapered under flower-heads* 930, 932.

LEAVES *arrow-shaped* 938, 939, 941, 943, 954, 955; *clasping stem* 933, 934, 938, 939, 940, 941, 942, 943, 944, 950, 951, 952, 953, 954, 955; *grass-like* 935, 937; *hairless* 926, 928, 930, 935, 937, 939, 940, 943, 944, 954, 956; *with long white hairs* 948; *spiny* 938, 941, 942; *spotted darker* 929, 947; *wrinkled* 944.

FLOWER-HEADS *solitary* 926, 927, 928, 929, 931, 932, 935, 937, 948, 956; *small* 925, 926, 928, 938, 939; *with chaffy scales* 927, 928, 929.

SEPAL-LIKE BRACTS *broad* 935, 956; *longer than rays* 928, 935; *outer row tiny* 925; *with yellowish hairs* 942.

PAPPUS *none* 925, 926; *brownish* 932, 946, 947, 948, 954; *pure white* 933, 952; *with feathery hairs* 927, 928, 929, 930, 931, 932, 933, 934, 935, 937; *with fruits beaked, producing a 'dandelion-clock'* 927–9, 932–5, 937–40, 943–4, 950–1, 956.

924. *CHICORY *Cichorium intybus* L.   Plate 9.   *CTW, p. 1112*

A stiff perennial, 1–3 ft. high, with tough stems, a few often long branches, unstalked lanceolate upper, and pinnately lobed lower leaves. Flower-heads in twos and threes at the base of the leaves up the stem, an inch or more across, unstalked, with ray-florets only, like bright blue Dandelions (956). *Habitat:* Widespread but local in grassy and waste places, especially on chalk or limestone. June onwards. Succory.

925. NIPPLEWORT *Lapsana communis* L.   Plate 53.   *CTW, p. 1113*

An annual, 9 in. to 2 ft. high, with stiff, leafy stems, often shaggy especially below, the leaves pointed oval, toothed, often with small narrow pinnate lobes at the base, and a winged stalk. Flower-heads in open branched clusters, on long slender stalks, yellow like tiny Dandelions (956). No pappus on the fruit; no chaffy scales between the florets; outer row of sepal-like bracts tiny. *Habitat:* Widespread and common in shady places, also a garden weed. June onwards.

926. **SWINE'S SUCCORY *Arnoseris minima* (L.) Schweigger & Koerte
   Lamb's Succory   Plate 58.   *CTW, p. 1114*

A hairless annual, 3–12 in. high, with leaves all basal, lanceolate, toothed and shortly stalked. Flowers like tiny yellow Dandelions (956) with very short rays, solitary at the end of sometimes branched stems, which are prominently swollen under the flower-heads and even more so under the fruiting heads. No pappus, but a membranous crown on the fruits; no chaffy scales among the florets. *Habitat:* Rare in sandy fields in E England and E Scotland. June–August.

CATSEARS and HAWKBITS *Hypochoeris* and *Leontodon*

YELLOW DANDELION-LIKE flowers, with no white juice, leaves all basal, often in a rosette, and leafless stems, often thicker under the flower-head; pappus feathery. Catsears differ from Hawkbits in the chaffy scales among their ray-florets.

927. **COMMON CATSEAR**   *Hypochoeris radicata* L.   Plate 54.   *CTW, p. 1115*
An erect tufted perennial, a foot or so high, with narrow oblong leaves, broadly toothed or pinnately lobed, usually roughly hairy with unforked hairs, and short scale-like bracts scattered up the otherwise leafless greyish, very sparingly branched stems, which swell slightly but abruptly underneath the solitary flower-heads. Flowers yellow, dandelion-like, an inch or more across, the ray-florets about four times as long as broad, the outer ones greenish or greyish beneath, and much exceeding the often partly bristly sepal-like bracts. Fruits mostly beaked, the outer pappus hairs unbranched, the inner feathery. *Habitat:* Widespread and common in grassy places, including lawns. June onwards.

928. ****SMOOTH CATSEAR**   *H. glabra* L.   Plate 55.   *CTW, p. 1115*
An inconspicuous, less erect annual, differing from the last species in its very shiny, almost hairless leaves; fewer scale-like bracts on the flower-stems, which are less swollen at the top; and flower-heads half the size, not opening widely except in full sun, with ray-florets only about twice as long as broad and no longer than the sepal-like bracts. *Habitat:* Widespread but local in grassy places on sandy soils; rare in Ireland. June onwards.

929. ****SPOTTED CATSEAR**   *H. maculata* L.   Plate 55.   *CTW, p. 1116*
A stout, roughly hairy perennial, 1–2 ft. high, with leaves broad oblong, strongly toothed and often spotted with purplish-black; stems with a few tiny leaves or scale-like bracts, sometimes once branched, swollen under the distinctly waisted solitary flower-heads, which are large, to 2 in., pale yellow, with shaggy sepal-like bracts. Fruits with pappus hairs all feathery. *Habitat:* Rare in chalk or limestone turf in E England and on sea-cliffs in W England, N Wales and Jersey. June–August.

930. **AUTUMN HAWKBIT**   *Leontodon autumnalis* L.   Plate 55.   *CTW, p. 1117*
A variable perennial, less than half the size of Common Catsear (930) and much slenderer and broader, with leaves shiny, usually much more deeply lobed and more often hairless, the scale-like bracts concentrated on the more tapering swollen part of the branched stems just below the flower-heads. Flowers yellow, dandelion-like, with no chaffy scales between the florets, the outer of which are usually reddish beneath. Fruits not beaked; pappus all feathery. *Habitat:* Widespread and common in grassy places. July onwards.

931. **GREATER HAWKBIT**   *L. hispidus* L.   Plate 55.   *CTW, p. 1118*
A common dandelion-like, roughly hairy perennial, usually 6–18 in. high, with oblong, more or less erect, lobed or toothed leaves, rough with forked hairs, and unbranched stems often densely hairy, slightly swollen under the flower-head, leafless and with no, 1 or 2 tiny scale-like bracts. Flower-heads solitary, terminal, over an inch across, yellow, the outer florets often reddish or orange beneath, with shaggy sepal-like bracts. Pappuses making a 'clock'. *Habitat:* Widespread and common in grassy places, especially on chalk and limestone. June onwards.

932. **LESSER HAWKBIT**   *L. taraxacoides* (Villars) Mérat
   L. leysseri (Wallroth) Beck, '*L. hirtus*'   Plate 55.   *CTW, p. 1119*
A low tufted perennial, smaller and less roughly hairy than the last species, with only sparse hairs on the prostrate leaves, and no scale-like bracts, but often a few hairs, on the stems, which are slenderer and hardly swollen below the

flower-heads, which are only half the size, the outer florets grey beneath; sepal-like bracts brown-edged, much less hairy or even hairless; buds drooping. Outer fruits with scales instead of pappus. *Habitat:* Widespread and common in dry grassy places, especially dunes, thinning out northwards. June onwards.

933. BRISTLY OX-TONGUE *Picris echioides* L. Plate 53. *CTW, p. 1120*
One of the most distinctive of the yellow dandelion-like flowers, a leafy annual or biennial, 1–2 ft. high, extremely bristly and almost prickly all over, with its stems and oblong leaves pimply with large pale swollen-based bristles, the upper leaves clasping. Flower-heads in branched clusters, rather pale yellow, with broad triangular half-spreading sepal-like outer bracts. Fruit with a very long slender beak, easily broken off. *Habitat:* Widespread and locally frequent in hedge-banks and rough grassy places, especially on clay soils and near the sea, chiefly in England and Wales. June onwards. *Helmintia echioides* (L.) Gaertner.

934. *HAWKWEED OX-TONGUE *P. hieracioides* L. Pl. 54. *CTW. p. 1121*
Sometimes taken for a Hawkweed (946), but is very stiffly erect, often reddish on the stem below and usually with several long branches at right angles, all covered with rough bristles, especially below; lanceolate wavy leaves; outer sepal-like bracts bristly, narrow, spreading in a ruff, the inner erect, appressed; and a feathery pappus and virtually unbeaked fruit. *Habitat:* Locally frequent in grassy and waste places, especially on chalk or limestone, in England and Wales; uncommon in Ireland and S Scotland. July onwards.

935. GOATSBEARD *Tragopogon pratensis* L. Plate 58. *CTW, p. 1122*
Jack-go-to-bed-at-noon; (incl. *T. minor* Miller)
A greyish hairless milky, little branched perennial, 1–2 ft. high, distinctive among yellow dandelion-like flowers for its narrow fleshy, grass-like leaves, sheathing the stem, which is very slightly swollen under the flower-heads, which only open out in the morning. Sepal-like bracts narrow, pointed, often blackish round the bottom, usually much exceeding the yellow florets. Pappuses feathered, the main rays very stiff and woody, forming a large round dandelion-like clock. *Habitat:* Widespread and common in grassy places. June onwards.

936. **SALSIFY *T. porrifolius* L. Plate 9. *CTW, p. 1123*
An unfortunately outmoded root-vegetable, very like the last species, but with stems swollen under the much larger flower-heads, which have dull purple florets. *Habitat:* Very occasional, chiefly by the sea or in waste places. June–August.

937. ***VIPER'S GRASS *Scorzonera humilis* L. Plate 58. *CTW, p. 1124*
An almost hairless, pale green perennial, up to about a foot high, rather like a smaller, paler Goatsbeard (935), and containing milky juice. Leaves lanceolate, untoothed, becoming very small and narrow up the stem, and simulating the scale-like bracts of the Catsears. Stems sometimes forked, not swollen beneath flower-heads, which have pale green sepal-like bracts shorter than the lemony yellow florets. Fruits unbeaked; pappus with several rows of hairs. *Habitat:* Very rare in marshy fields in Dorset and Warwickshire. May–July.

938. *PRICKLY LETTUCE *Lactuca serriola* L. Plate 53. *CTW, p. 1125*
An unattractive weedy hairless foetid yellow-green biennial, 2–4 ft. high, with milky juice in the stiff brown leafy stems, which may be prickly below; and oblong,

sometimes irregularly lobed, greyish alternate leaves, weakly spiny on the margins, more sharply so on the midrib beneath, clasping the stem with arrow-shaped points; in the sun the upper leaves are twisted so that their margins are held in the vertical plane. Flower-heads numerous, like small narrow pale yellow Dandelions (956), in large untidy branched spikes; sepal-like bracts overlapping, unequal, often purplish. Fruits pale brown, flat, elliptical, ribbed, equalling their long slender pale beak; pappus unbranched. *Habitat:* Fairly frequent and increasing on waste ground in the S. July–September.

938*a.* *Greater Prickly Lettuce *L. virosa* L., is usually taller, stouter, darker green and more widely branched below, with stems often purple below; larger, often purplish, less divided, less prickly, more horizontal leaves; slightly smaller flowers; and rather larger fruits of a beautiful maroon with a white beak. Prefers chalky soils, often near the sea.

939. **LEAST LETTUCE *L. saligna* L.   Plate 53.   *CTW, p. 1127*

Much smaller and slenderer than the Prickly Lettuces (938), and usually prostrate at the base, with no spines or prickles on the leaves and the upper ones narrow, untoothed and held almost vertical, clasping the stem with arrow-shaped points. Flower-spike also very much slenderer, with green-tipped sepal-like bracts. Fruits half as long as their beak. *Habitat:* Very local in short grass or on shingle near the sea in the S. July–August.

940. *WALL LETTUCE *Mycelis muralis* (L.) Reichenbach   Pl. 53.   *CTW, 1128*

A hairless, slender and often quite graceful, sometimes purplish perennial, 1–2 ft. high, with milky juice and thin, narrowly and irregularly pinnately lobed leaves, the end lobe large and triangular, the upper clasping the stem with blunt lobes. Flower-heads small, narrow cylindrical below, with usually 5 rather broad yellow ray-florets, toothed at the tip, in a loose terminal candelabra-like cluster; inner sepal-like bracts long and narrow; outer very short. *Habitat:* Widespread but rather local on walls, rocks and shady banks, and at the edge of woods, especially on chalk. July–September. *Lactuca muralis* (L.) Gaertner.

941. ***MARSH SOW-THISTLE *Sonchus palustris* L.   Pl. 53.   *CTW, p. 1129*

Very much taller and stouter than the next species, growing in great tufts 3–10 ft. high, with no creeping runners; leaves greyish, narrow, with straighter, more parallel sides and more pointed lobes, clasping the hollow stem with narrow lobes. Flower-heads relatively much smaller, paler yellow, in a denser umbel-like cluster, with sticky olive hairs on the stalks and sepal-like bracts. Fruits straw-colour. *Habitat:* Rare in reed-beds, usually by tidal water, in the Broads district, and by the R. Medway. July–September.

942. CORN SOW-THISTLE *S. arvensis* L.   Plate 53.   *CTW, p. 1129*

A showy perennial, 2–4 ft. high, with creeping underground runners, milky juice, and lanceolate, pinnately lobed leaves, edged with softly spiny teeth, clasping the stem with broad lobes, shiny dark green above, greyish beneath. Flower-heads 2 in. or so across, few, in open terminal clusters, dandelion-like, rich yellow, the appressed dull olive-green sepal-like bracts and stalks usually covered with sticky yellow hairs. Fruits ribbed, flattened oblong, unbeaked, reddish or dark brown. *Habitat:* Widespread and common in wet and cultivated ground. July onwards.

943. SMOOTH SOW-THISTLE   *S. oleraceus* L.   Plate 53.   *CTW, p. 1130*

A greyish hairless annual, 6 in. to 3 ft. high, with milky juice and dull, more or less pinnately lobed leaves, the terminal lobe much the largest, paler beneath, with scarcely spiny teeth, rather loosely clasping the stem with arrow-shaped points. Flower-heads in terminal clusters, like small, very pale yellow Dandelions (956). Fruits wrinkled, yellow then dark brown, their pappuses forming a dandelion clock.   *Habitat:* A widespread and abundant weed of waste and disturbed ground, dunes, walls, etc. June onwards.

944. PRICKLY SOW-THISTLE   *S. asper* (L.) Hill   Plate 53.   *CTW, p. 1130*

Has very similar flowers to the last species, but its leaves are less or not pinnate, crisped, very wavy-edged, spine-toothed, and closely clasping the stem with rounded lobes. Fruits either pale yellow then brown, or pale fawn, white or olive.   *Habitat:* An equally common weed. June onwards.

945. **BLUE SOW-THISTLE   *Cicerbita macrophylla* (Willdenow) Wallroth
Plate 9.   *CTW, p. 1131*

A pale green, hairy creeping perennial, 2–5 ft. high, with stems branched at the top; milky juice; lower leaves slightly toothed with hairy edges, on long winged stalks, and with a large, more or less rounded terminal lobe which is heart-shaped at the base, and usually a much smaller lobe on either side; and upper leaves more toothed, waisted, clasping. Flower-heads 2 in. across, in broad loose terminal clusters, like pale blue-violet Chicory (924); sepal-like bracts pale violet-green; leaf-like bracts much shorter than flower-stalks. Fruits elliptical, hairless, unbeaked, slightly winged, ¼-in. long.   *Habitat:* Widespread and increasing by roadsides and near gardens. July–September.

945a.   ***Alpine Sow-thistle, *C. alpina* (L.) Wallroth (*Lactuca alpina* (L.) Gray), is rather smaller and tufted, with unbranched stems; more numerous side-lobes and a triangular end-lobe on the hairless leaves, which clasp the stem with pointed toothed lobes; flower-heads bluer, much smaller, in dense erect spikes; and leaf-like bracts linear, sleekly hairy, exceeding the lowest flowers. Very rare in damp places and on ledges out of reach of the deer on mountains in the E Highlands.

HAWKWEEDS   *Hieracium*

HAIRY PERENNIALS with dandelion-like flowers, nearly always yellow but rarely orange-red, with alternate leaves, milky juice, no chaffy scales between the florets, the hairs of the pappus not feathery and generally pale tawny, and the fruits neither beaked nor narrowed at the top. The leaves are very variable, from linear to nearly round, not or deeply toothed, and sometimes purple-spotted.

Owing to their seeds normally ripening without fertilisation (a phenomenon known as apomixis and found in other difficult genera, such as Dandelions), the Hawkweeds are immensely variable, and small local chance variations come true from seed and are readily perpetuated. These variations have been divided in Britain into some 260 microspecies. For most people, however, it will be enough to know a Hawkweed from the other dandelion-like flowers. We have therefore adopted the Gordian solution, of 'lumping' these all into four groups, two normally with creeping roots, and two tufted, of which one has leafy stems and the other nearly leafless ones. These last two, however, are very arbitrary, and almost every intermediate gradation may be found.

946. LEAFY HAWKWEED Group *Aphyllopoda* Koch Pl. 54. *CTW, 1136–45*
The common Hawkweed group of late summer, taller than the next group, and including forms with no rosette and stems up to 4 ft. with often numerous leaves. Flower-heads usually plentiful in well branched clusters. *Habitat:* Widespread and common, especially in sandy and heathy places and on riversides. July onwards. (Incl. '*H. sabaudum*', *H. umbellatum* L., & *H. prenanthoides* Villars.)

947. FEW-LEAVED HAWKWEED Groups *Phyllopoda* Koch and *Transitoria* Pugsley Plate 54. *CTW, pp. 1145–62*
Includes those forms with an often flat rosette, and stems 6–15 in. high, usually unbranched and with few or no stem-leaves, not usually more than 4 and 7 at the most. Flower-heads yellow, rarely pale greenish-yellow, 1–10 in a cluster. *Habitat:* Widespread and common on walls, dry banks, mountain ledges, etc. May–July. (Incl. '*H. murorum*', '*H. cerinthoides*', and *H. alpinum* L.)

948. MOUSE-EAR HAWKWEED *Hieracium pilosella* L.
(incl. *H. peleteranum* Mérat) Plate 55. *CTW, p. 1164*
A very variable, hairy, often shaggy, perennial, 2–15 in. high, with a basal rosette of untoothed elliptical leaves, pale green and covered with long white hairs above and whitish beneath, and long creeping leafy runners. Flower-heads solitary, on long, usually leafless stalks, lemon-yellow, the outer florets often reddish beneath. *Habitat:* Widespread and common in short turf. May onwards.

949. **FOX AND CUBS *H. aurantiacum* L. Plate 58. *CTW, p. 1165*
A densely hairy perennial, 6–12 in. high, with long leafy rampant runners, and rosettes of lanceolate leaves with a few up the stems, which are clothed with blackish hairs. Flower-heads in close terminal clusters, brownish or reddish-orange, sometimes paler in the centre, the sepal-like bracts covered with blackish hairs. *Habitat:* An occasional garden escape, especially on railway banks. June–September. Grim the Collier; (incl. *H. brunneocroceum* Pugsley).

HAWKSBEARDS *Crepis*

YELLOW DANDELION-LIKE Composites, differing from other similar flowers in having leafy branched stems; one conspicuous row of erect sepal-like bracts, with another much smaller, often half-spreading, ruff-like row at the base of the flower-head; and a white pappus with unbranched hairs. Leaves, except in Northern Hawksbeard (952), are irregularly lobed or toothed like a Dandelion (956), with a large terminal lobe; mostly basal, but the stem ones half-clasping it. Flower-heads in loose branched terminal sprays.
Hawksbeards differ from Catsears (927–929) and Hawkbits (930–932) in their leafy stems and non-feathery pappus; from Catsears also in having no scales between the florets; from Ox-tongues (933–934) in their unbranched pappus and no coarse bristles on the leaves; from the Hawkweeds (946–949) in their white pappus (except Marsh Hawksbeard (955)), and fruits beaked or narrowed above; and from Dandelions (956) in their solid leafy stems with no milky juice.

950. ***SOUTHERN HAWKSBEARD *Crepis foetida* L. Pl. 54. *CTW, p. 1167*
A rather short annual or biennial, smelling strongly of bitter almonds when bruised, branching widely from the base of the erect stem; leaves narrow densely and closely hairy, the basal in a rosette, narrowly pinnately lobed with a large terminal diamond-shaped tooth, the upper small, lanceolate, toothed and clasping.

Flower-heads few, drooping in bud, the florets golden-yellow within; inner sepal-like bracts very narrow, erect. Outer fruits short-beaked, the inner long-beaked; pappus very white. *Habitat:* Very rare on shingle in SE England. June–Aug.

951. BEAKED HAWKSBEARD *C. vesicaria* L. Plate 54. *CTW, p. 1167*

A stout, stiffly erect downy perennial, 9 in. to 2 ft. high; stem red below and pinnately lobed leaves half-clasping it with short lobes. Flower-heads about ¾-in. across, erect in bud, the outermost florets usually orange beneath; outer row of sepal-like bracts more or less equal, spreading, about ¼ the length of the inner row. All fruits equally long-beaked. *Habitat:* Widespread and common in grassy and waste places, still spreading northwards in Scotland. May–June. *C. taraxacifolia* Thuillier.

952. **NORTHERN HAWKSBEARD *C. mollis* (Jacquin) Ascherson
Plate 54. *CTW, p. 1168*

A hairy perennial, about a foot high much like a Hawkweed, with leaves not or only slightly toothed, the upper clasping the stem with rounded bases, and flowers larger than the last species, the florets almost twice as long as the sepal-like bracts. Fruits yellow, not beaked. *Habitat:* Rare by streams and in shady places in hill districts in the N. July–August.

953. *ROUGH HAWKSBEARD *C. biennis* L. Plate 54. *CTW, p. 1169*

Robuster, hairier, more branched above and usually much taller (3–4 ft. high) than Beaked Hawksbeard (951), which is often taken for it, and with the stem less red at the base; flower-heads usually fewer, almost twice as large; outer florets all yellow, outer row of sepal-like bracts unequal and about half as long as the inner row; and fruits not beaked. *Habitat:* Locally frequent in rough grassland and roadsides, preferring chalk or limestone; rare in the N. June–July.

954. SMOOTH HAWKSBEARD *C. capillaris* (L.) Wallroth Pl. 55. *CTW, 1169*

A variable, mostly hairless, rather slender annual, 6–15 in. high, with shiny leaves, variously toothed or lobed, the lower often numerous, rather dandelion-like with a winged stalk, the upper fewer, narrower, clasping the stem with arrow-shaped points. Flower-heads usually ½-in., on slenderer stalks than the other Hawksbeards, the outer florets often reddish beneath; fruits not beaked. Pappus not feathery. *Habitat:* Widespread and common in grassy and waste places. June onwards.

955. *MARSH HAWKSBEARD *C. paludosa* (L.) Moench Pl. 54. *CTW, 1171*

Closely resembles an almost hairless Leafy Hawkweed (946), but with flower-heads of a distinctive hard dull orange-yellow, contrasting with the single row of sepal-like bracts. Leaves pointed, usually shiny, unstalked, yellow-green, shortly toothed, clasping the stem with downward-pointed bases. Fruits slightly narrowed above, not beaked, the pappus dirty white. *Habitat:* Locally frequent in damp and wet places in Ireland and the N. July–September.

956. DANDELION *Taraxacum officinale* Weber[1] Plate 55. *CTW, p. 1172*

Dandelions are very variable perennials, 2–12 in. high, well known as tiresome lawn weeds, a golden blaze in the May meadows and banks. All have milky

---

[1] Incl. *T. paludosum* (Scopoli) Schlechtendahl (*T. palustre* (Lyons) DC.), *T. spectabile* Dahlstedt, *T. laevigatum* (Willdenow) DC. and *T. erythrospermum* Besser.

juice and basal rosettes of leaves, sometimes downy, occasionally purple-spotted, deeply lobed or toothed (*dent de lion*), with the teeth usually pointing backwards and a large, rather blunt terminal lobe. The fine large flowers are composed entirely of numerous bright yellow ray-florets, and are always solitary on hollow fleshy rubbery leafless stalks, narrower at the top. The fruits have a beak, surmounted by a non-feathery spreading pappus, which together make the well-known 'dandelion clocks'. *Habitat:* Widespread and abundant in grassy and waste places. Throughout the year, but in greatest profusion in April–May.

WATER-PLANTAIN FAMILY   Alismataceae

957. *LESSER WATER-PLANTAIN   *Baldellia ranunculoides* (L.) Parlatore
Alisma ranunculoides L.   Plate 69.   *CTW, p. 1176*
   A hairless perennial, 4–9 in. high, tufted or creeping and rooting at the joints, the narrow lanceolate root-leaves with long stout stalks. Flowers pale pink, 3-petalled, rather under ½-in. across, very long-stalked, in terminal umbels on leafless stalks, often also in a whorl lower down the stem. The fruits consist of globular heads (not close rings), ¼-in. across, of green nutlets, rather like those of a Buttercup but smaller. *Habitat:* Widespread but local and decreasing in peaty fresh water, and dykes and ponds in fen districts, thinning out northwards. May–August.

958. **FLOATING WATER-PLANTAIN   *Luronium natans* (L.) Rafinesque
Alisma natans L.   Plate 69.   *CTW, p. 1176*
   A slender aquatic perennial, with floating, rooting stems, the submerged leaves narrow and tapering, the floating ones small, neat, elliptical, shiny, long-stalked. Flowers stalked, ½–¾–in. across, the 3 white petals each with a yellow spot at the base, normally solitary. *Habitat:* Rare in tarns, canals and quiet water, mostly in Wales. July–August.

959. COMMON WATER-PLANTAIN   *Alisma plantago-aquatica* L.
                                                        Plate 69.   *CTW, p. 1177*
   A stout hairless perennial, 1–2 ft. high, with a tuft of long-stalked, broad lanceolate root-leaves, more or less rounded or heart-shaped at the base, on long

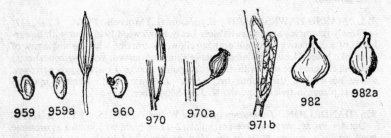

959   **959a**   **960**   **970**   **970a**   **971b**   **982**   **982a**

stalks stout and spongy below; and leafless stems bearing pyramidal, repeatedly whorl-branched spikes of numerous small lilac-white 3-petalled flowers. Fruiting heads with the nutlets in one close ring, the long beak arising at or below the middle of the nutlets (Fig.), which are shorter than the stamens. *Habitat:* Widespread and frequent by fresh water, thinning out northwards. June–August.

959a. *Narrow Water-Plantain, *A. lanceolatum* Withering, is somewhat smaller, with narrower, more pointed lanceolate leaves tapering into the stalk (Fig.); pinker flowers; and a short beak arising near the top of the nutlet (Fig.). More local, and mainly in the S; very local in Ireland.

960. ***RIBBON-LEAVED WATER-PLANTAIN   *A. gramineum* Gmelin
Plate 69.   *CTW, p. 1178*
A hairless, often submerged aquatic perennial 6–9 in. high, with a tuft of narrow ribbon-like leaves, broader towards their tips and hardly distinguishable from their stalks; and pale lilac flowers, in one or more whorls, smaller than Lesser Water-Plantain (958), the petals soon falling. Fruits in a close ring, about equalling the stamens; beak coiled at the side of and about half as long as the nutlet (Fig.).   *Habitat:* Confined to one pond near Droitwich. June.

961. **STAR-FRUIT   *Damasonium alisma* Miller   Plate 69.   *CTW, p. 1178*
Rather like a very small Water-Plantain (959), but with leaves floating or submerged, blunt, oblong and heart-shaped at the base; smaller white flowers; and only a few much larger fruiting heads, with 6 long-beaked nutlets, spreading like a 6-pointed star.   *Habitat:* Rare and decreasing in, or more often on the mud by, ponds on commons in SE England. June–July.

962. *ARROW-HEAD   *Sagittaria sagittifolia* L.   Plate 69.   *CTW, p. 1179*
A striking hairless aquatic perennial, 2–3 ft. high, with large, long-stalked, conspicuously arrow-shaped leaves, 6 in. or more above the water; and taller leafless stems bearing whorled spikes of flowers, nearly an inch across, with a purple patch at the base of each of their 3 white petals. Male and female flowers separate. Fruiting heads globular, ½-in. across, of many nutlets. In faster water there are also translucent linear submerged leaves and oval or lanceolate floating ones.   *Habitat:* Widespread and locally frequent in fresh water, thinning out northwards. July–August.

FLOWERING-RUSH FAMILY   Butomaceae

963. *FLOWERING RUSH   *Butomus umbellatus* L.   Plate 21.   *CTW, p. 1180*
One of our handsomest aquatics, with its large umbels of inch-wide rose-pink flowers, with 6 similar petals and sepals at the top of leafless stems. A tall perennial 3–4 ft. high, with a tuft of long stout grass-like leaves, and heads of purple fruits.   *Habitat:* Widespread but local in and by fresh water, especially in the S; rare in Wales and Scotland. July–September.

FROG-BIT FAMILY   Hydrocharitaceae

964. *FROG-BIT   *Hydrocharis morsus-ranae* L.   Plate 69.   *CTW, p. 1181*
A floating aquatic perennial, not rooting on the bottom, with thick spongy stalked kidney-shaped bronzy-green floating leaves, about 1 in. across. Flowers above the water, nearly an inch across, the 3 white petals each with a yellow spot near the base; male and female separate.   *Habitat:* Local in ponds, ditches and canals in the S, and in Ireland. July–August.

965. **WATER SOLDIER *Stratiotes aloides* L.   Plate 69.   *CTW, p. 1182*
A most distinctive dark brownish-green aquatic perennial, usually completely submerged either on the bottom or suspended in the water, but appearing partly above the surface at flowering time and producing runners. Leaves numerous, stiff, lanceolate, with spiny teeth along the margins, in a basal tuft. Flowers white, 3-petalled, 1½ in. across; male and female on separate plants, but the stalked, male flowers, 1–3 together, are very much rarer than the very short-stalked solitary female ones. Fruits never produced. *Habitat:* Very local in broads, dykes and other quiet water, mainly in E England. June–August.

966. CANADIAN WATERWEED *Elodea canadensis* Michaux Pl. 68. *CTW, 1182*
A submerged waterweed, with brittle stems, and many close overlapping whorls, usually of three neat, narrow oblong, ⅓-in. bluntish translucent un-stalked olive-green leaves. A shy flowerer, the female flowers small, very pale pink floating on thread-like, often 6-in.-long stalks, and looking like loose petals; male flowers, on different plants, extremely rare. *Habitat:* Widespread and locally plentiful in fresh water. May onwards. Water-thyme.

967. ***ESTHWAITE WATERWEED *E. nuttallii*   Pl. 68. *CTW, 1183*
Slenderer, and less bushy than Canadian Waterweed (966), with thinner stems and longer, pointed much narrower, flaccid, paler green leaves, ½–¾-in. long, in whorls of 3–4. Flowers not yet observed in Britain. *Habitat :* Only in Esthwaite Water and near Renvyle (Connemara). ' *H. lithuanica* '.

968. ***TAPE-GRASS *Vallisneria spiralis* L.   Plate 68.   *CTW, p. 1184*
A submerged aquarist's waterweed, with tufts of narrow, ribbon-like root-leaves, about 2 ft. long, blunt and slightly toothed at the tip, smooth on both sides, with 3–5 parallel veins. Flowers small, pinkish-white, on long, thread-like stalks; males breaking off and floating, females with stalks twisting spirally after flowering. Fruits rare. *Habitat:* Naturalised in canals, especially near mills, in Yorks, Lancs. and Glos. June and September.

RANNOCH-RUSH FAMILY Scheuchzeriaceae

969. ***RANNOCH RUSH *Scheuchzeria palustris* L.   Pl. 106.   *CTW, p. 1184*
A low hairless, rather rush-like perennial, 6–12 in. high, the long narrow leaves with alternate inflated sheathing bases and a curious terminal pore, over-topping the spike of insignificant stalked 6-petalled yellow-green flowers. Nutlets large, inflated, spreading, beaked, usually in groups of 3. *Habitat :* Now known only in bog-pools on Rannoch Moor and in C Ireland. May–June.

ARROW-GRASS FAMILY Juncaginaceae

970. MARSH ARROW-GRASS *Triglochin palustris* L.   Pl. 106.   *CTW, p. 1185*
A slender, rather inconspicuous hairless perennial, 6–12 in. high, with a few long grasslike fleshy leaves, and numerous short-stalked small greenish flowers in a long narrow interrupted spike at the top of the leafless stem, the style forming a short white tuft. Fruits long, thin, narrowed at base, erect (Fig., p.'194, × 2), with 3 segments attached at the top, spreading below, opening arrow-fashion when ripe. *Habitat:* Widespread but somewhat local in fenny meadows. May–August.

970*a*. **Sea Arrow-grass,** *T. maritima* L., is stouter, with thicker fleshier leaves, but narrower than in Sea Plantain (792); fatter, more plantain-like flower-spikes, shorter flower-stalks, and much fatter, narrowly egg-shaped fruits with 6 segments Fig. p. 194, not arrow-shaped when ripe. Widespread and frequent in salt-marshes.

EEL-GRASS FAMILY Zosteraceae

EEL-GRASSES or GRASS-WRACKS *Zostera*

THE ONLY flowering plants that grow completely submerged in the sea, looking at low tide like patches of grass or green seaweed. Unlike seaweeds, however, they have roots. They are all perennials, with alternate, long, narrow, grass-like leaves. Their inconspicuous flowers are petalless, and reduced to 1 anther or 1 style with 2 stigmas, alternate in 2 flat rows, partly enclosed in sheaths, towards the bottom of some of the lower leaf-like branches. Male and female flowers are separate on the same plant.

971. ***COMMON EEL-GRASS** *Zostera marina* L. Plate 68. *CTW, p. 1187*
Has stems branched, with leaves about ¼-in. wide, often only 6 in. but sometimes over 3 ft. long, blunt or pointed at tip and with 3 or more parallel veins. Seeds egg-shaped, ribbed. *Habitat:* Widespread but now very local in the sea near and below low-water mark of spring tides. June onwards.

971*a*. ****Narrow-leaved Eel-grass,** *Z. hornemanniana* Tutin, is very similar but has much narrower and usually shorter leaves, 1–3-veined and notched at the tip when mature. More local, higher up the shore and usually in muddier places.

971*b*. ****Dwarf Eel-grass,** *Z. nana* Roth, has shorter, still narrower, almost thread-like leaves, notched at the tip and usually 1-veined, flower-sheaths inflated, a small marginal appendage across base of each male flower (Fig., p. 194), and seeds smooth and rounder. Still more local, also higher up shore and oftener on mud.

PONDWEED FAMILY Potamogetonaceae

PONDWEEDS *Potamogeton & Groenlandia*

PERENNIAL WATERWEEDS, usually growing in large clumps of stems 3–6 or more feet long, with submerged and sometimes floating leaves, which decay as the plant ripens. In most of our species each leaf has its at base a stipule, which may be erect and leaf-like or else sheath-like and enfolding the stem either completely or with the margins overlapping. Pondweeds are extremely variable, the size and shape of the leaves varying according to the composition, depth and speed of the water, and the age of the plant. Moreover they hybridise readily, some hybrids being not infrequent and persisting in the absence of one or both parents.

Their small greenish 4-sepalled petalless flowers are in stalked spikes at the base of the leaves, often projecting above the water but sinking again in fruit; anthers 4; stigmas 4. The fruits have 4 nutlets.

Pondweeds grow in many kinds of fresh and brackish water, still and moving, such as lakes, ponds, rivers, canals, streams and ditches. They may grow almost or quite uncovered, with stems a few inches long or rooting at the leaf-junctions.

972. **BROAD-LEAVED PONDWEED** *Potamogeton natans* L. Pl. 67. *CTW, 1192*
Floating leaves broad oval, long-stalked, apparently jointed at the base of the rather thick and leathery, brownish-green blade. Submerged leaves reduced to

narrow stalks at flowering-time. Stipules long, narrow, closely sheathing at base. Flower-spikes stout, long-stalked. Fruits large, roundish, with a short beak. *Habitat:* Widespread and frequent in still or sluggish water, often completely covering ponds. May–September.

972*a*. **Bog Pondweed,** *P. polygonifolius* Pourret, is much shorter, always brighter green and sometimes a reddish-brown, with narrower floating leaves not jointed to the stalk; submerged leaves stalked with a lanceolate blade, which is often absent in shallow water; stipules short and blunt; and fruits smaller and scarcely beaked. Widespread and frequent in peaty pools on bogs and moors on acid soils. May onwards.

972*b*. *Plantain-leaved Pondweed,** *P. coloratus* Hornemann, is rather like Bog Pondweed, but has the submerged leaves broad like the floating ones and all short-stalked, translucent, red-brown and net-veined; narrow blunt stipules; and small fruits with a short curved beak. Local in shallow ponds, pools and ditches on fen peat and chalky soils. May–July.

972*c*. **Loddon Pondweed,** *P. nodosus* Poiret (*P. drucei* Fryer), is like the last, but has all leaves more leathery, longer, narrower and long-stalked, but only the submerged ones net-veined; stipules broader, longer, pointed. Fruits scarce, large, with a prominent ridge. Confined to a few rivers in S England. August–September.

973. SHINING PONDWEED *P. lucens* L. Plate 67. *CTW, p. 1195*

A large Pondweed with only submerged leaves, up to 6 in. long, scarcely stalked, translucent, thin, wavy, shiny, pointed, oblong lanceolate, often yellowish-green; stipules blunt. Flower-stalks thickening upwards. Fruits medium-sized, with a small beak. *Habitat:* Widespread and frequent, preferring deepish water. June–September.

973*a*. *Reddish Pondweed,** *P. alpinus* Balbis (*CTW, p. 1198*), may have floating leaves, which are like the submerged ones in being somewhat broadened, very short-stalked, narrowed to each end, often reddish-brown, and hooded at tip when young; stipules broad, blunt. Flower-stalks not thickened; fruits similar, with a prominent ridge and a longer beak. Commoner in the N.

973*b*. *Long-stalked Pondweed,** *P. praelongus* Wulfen (*CTW, p. 1198*), has no floating leaves, and submerged ones bright translucent green, long, narrowest at the hooded tip, broadest at the roundish base, which clasps the round stems; stipules blunt. Flower-stalks very long, not thickening upwards; fruits larger. Widespread, but local and mainly in deep water in the N. May–August.

974. **VARIOUS-LEAVED PONDWEED *P. gramineus* L.

P. heterophyllus Schreber   Plate 67. *CTW, p. 1196*

Very variable, much branched at the base, sometimes with floating leaves like Bog Pondweed (972*a*), but much smaller, blunter and less leathery, and sub-merged leaves narrow lanceolate, unstalked, wavy, 2–3 in. long; stipules ribbed, pointed. Stems rounded; flower-stalks thickened towards the top. Fruits medium with a short beak. *Habitat:* Widespread but scarce. June–August.

974*a*. ***American Pondweed,** *P. epihydrus* Rafinesque (*CTW, p. 1200*), has slender flattened stems; submerged leaves long and linear, up to 5 in., their midribs bordered by air-spaces; stipules broad and blunt; and flower-stalks not thickened upwards. Only known from S Uist, and canals in SW Yorks.

975. PERFOLIATE PONDWEED *P. perfoliatus* L. Plate 67. *CTW, p. 1199*

A distinctive Pondweed with its long stems, very dark green, bluntly oval leaves, which clasp the stems and are opposite at the junctions; no floating leaves;

stipules soon falling. Flower-spikes short, with few flowers. *Habitat:* Widespread and locally frequent, often in deepish water. June–September.

976. **SLENDER PONDWEED** *P. berchtoldii* Fieber Plate 66. *CTW, p. 1203*
Slender, much branched, with slightly flattened stems, and all leaves submerged, narrow, grass-like, always 3–veined, flat, mostly rather rounded at the tip, with air-spaces along the midrib; stipules longish, open, blunt. Flower-spikes short, on short stalks. Nutlets small, smooth, usually 4 to each flower. *Habitat:* Widespread and frequent. June–September.

976a. ****Lesser Pondweed,** *P. pusillus* L., has closed tubular stipules and in no air-spaces in its stiffer, paler, more pointed leaves. Less common.

976b. ***Hairlike Pondweed,** *P. trichoides* Chamisso & Schlechtendahl, has narrower 1-veined leaves, pointed stipules and longer flower-stalks; nutlets warty, only 1 to each flower. Frequent in the S, thinning out northwards; not in Ireland.

977. ****SHARP-LEAVED PONDWEED** *P. acutifolius* Link Pl. 67. *CTW, 1205*
Rather slender, always submerged, with flattened zigzag stems; dark green gradually pointed grass-like leaves with three main and many smaller veins; and stipules pointed, finely ribbed. Flower-spikes small, short-stalked; a shy flowerer. Fruits fairly large, slightly flattened, often wavy, with a curved beak. *Habitat:* Very local, mainly in the S, often in canals. June–July.

978. ***BLUNT-LEAVED PONDWEED** *P. obtusifolius* Mertens & Koch
Plate 67. *CTW, p. 1202*
A rather slender bushy grass-leaved Pondweed, with stems slightly flattened; leaves all submerged, bright green, thin, narrow, rounded at the tip, with a very small point and usually three main veins and no intermediate ones; and stipules broad, blunt. Flower-spikes short, short-stalked. Fruits fairly large with a short straight beak. *Habitat:* Rather local, in ponds and canals. June–September.

978a. ***Flat-stalked Pondweed,** *P. friesii* Ruprecht (*CTW, p. 1200*), has shorter narrower leaves with usually 5 unequally spaced veins, stipules tubular below at first, longer flower-stalks slightly thicker at the top, and smaller fruits. Locally frequent in lowland districts. June–Aug. (Incl. *P. rutilus* Wolfgang.)

978b. ****Wrack-like Pondweed,** *P. compressus* L. (*P. zosteraefolius* Schumacher) (*CTW, p. 1205*), has the leaf-tips and blunt stipules of Blunt-leaved Pondweed but the broader leaves and flatter stems and veining of Sharp-leaved Pondweed (977). Very local and mainly in the S half of England.

979. **CURLY PONDWEED** *P. crispus* L. Plate 67. *CTW, p. 1206*
Readily told by its short, very curly crimped alternate translucent, slightly toothed leaves, all submerged; stems 4-angled. Flower-spikes small; fruits medium with long curved beak. *Habitat:* Widespread and frequent. May onwards. Frog's Lettuce.

980. **FENNEL PONDWEED** *P. pectinatus* L. Plate 66. *CTW, p. 1208*
A slender bushy, well branched, very dark green Pondweed, the very thin leaves like a leather boot-lace with air-filled spaces round the midrib, enlarged into a long sheath with a whitish edge. Flower-spikes short, with a few well spaced whorls, often submerged. Fruits rather large. *Habitat:* Widespread and frequent, often in brackish water. June–Sept. (Incl. *P. interruptus* Kitaibel.)

980a. **Slender-leaved Pondweed,** *P. filiformis* Persoon (*CTW, p. 1207*), has flattened, much less branched stems; sheaths tubular below at first; long-stalked flower-spikes with very distant whorls and much longer than the leaves; and smaller fruits with a shorter beak. Local in Anglesey, Scotland and N Ireland. May–August.

981. **OPPOSITE PONDWEED** *Groenlandia densa* (L.) Fourreau Pl. 67. *CTW, 1209*
Sparingly branched, with many small unstalked broad pointed submerged leaves in pairs up the stem, which they half-clasp; no floating leaves or stipules. Flower-spikes submerged, with few flowers, shorter than the leaves, turning down in fruit. Fruits medium, with a very small beak. *Habitat:* Widespread and quite frequent, often in rapid water. May–September. *Potamogeton densus* L.

TASSEL-PONDWEED FAMILY   Ruppiaceae

982. ***TASSEL PONDWEED**   *Ruppia maritima* L.   Plate 68.   *CTW, p. 1210*
A slender limp submerged perennial waterweed, a foot or more long, the very narrow leaves, with a sheathed base like Fennel Pondweed (980), but with 2 greenish 2-anthered flowers rising to the surface on long stalks from the base of the leaves, the individual stalks at first about equalling the common one, but lengthening in fruit to 4–6 in. Fruits swollen at base, asymmetrical, with a straight beak (Fig., p. 194, × 5). *Habitat:* Widespread but local in brackish pools and ditches. July–September. *R. rostellata* Koch.

982a. **Coiled Pondweed,** *R. spiralis* Dumortier, has broader leaves and sheaths and the individual flower-stalks very much shorter than the common one, which later often coils to submerge the roundish fruits with a blunt beak (Fig., p. 194, × 5). Less frequent. Often flowering later.

HORNED-PONDWEED FAMILY   Zannichelliaceae

983. **HORNED PONDWEED**   *Zannichellia palustris* L.   Plate 67.
(incl. *Z. gibberosa* Reichenbach, *Z. pedunculata* Rchb.)   *CTW, p. 1211*
A very slender, rather short, somewhat variable, submerged perennial water-weed, about 2 ft. long, with very narrow, normally opposite leaves and clusters of minute unstalked greenish flowers at their base, thus differing from all true Pondweeds (972–981). Fruits with a very long slender beak or horn. *Habitat:* Widespread and not uncommon in fresh water. May–August.

NAIAD FAMILY   Najadaceae

984. **SLENDER NAIAD**   *Najas flexilis* (Willdenow) Rostkovius & Schmidt
Plate 68.   *CTW, p. 1212*
A slender grassy submerged annual, 4–10 in. long, the fine-toothed translucent linear leaves tapering to a point, opposite or in whorls of 3, with a sheathed base. Flowers solitary, small, green, unstalked at base of leaves, male and female separate. Fruits narrow, egg-shaped. *Habitat:* Extremely local in quiet bays in lakes in the Lake District, Scotland and W Ireland. August–September.

984a. ***Holly-leaved Naiad,** *N. marina* L., has longer stems often toothed near the top and leaves sharply toothed. Possibly only female plants occur in Britain. Confined to 3–4 Norfolk Broads. July–August.

PIPEWORT FAMILY   Eriocaulaceae

985. **PIPEWORT *Eriocaulon septangulare* Withering   Pl. 66.   *CTW, p. 1213*
A hairless aquatic perennial, with a dense basal tuft of short stiff narrow tapering pointed translucent leaves, not unlike Water Lobelia (807). Flowers tiny, white, in flat button-heads on unbranched leafless stems, 4–18 in. high, projecting a few inches above the surface of the water. *Habitat:* Very locally frequent in quiet fresh water in W Ireland and on Skye and Coll. July–September.

LILY FAMILY   Liliaceae

986. **SCOTTISH ASPHODEL *Tofieldia pusilla* (Michaux) Persoon
T. borealis (Wahlenberg) Wahlenberg   Plate 83.   *CTW, p. 1216*
A short hairless perennial, 3–6 in. high, like a miniature whitish Bog Asphodel (987), with a basal tuft of a few stiff, flat, sword-shaped leaves, and a longer, flat stem bearing a very short spike of small greenish-yellow flowers, each with 3 blunt incurved petals, 3 sepals and 3 styles. *Habitat:* Very local in open marshy places on hills in the N. June–August.

987. *BOG ASPHODEL *Narthecium ossifragum* (L.) Hudson   Pl. 63.   *CTW, 1216*
A hairless creeping perennial, 6 in. or so high, with basal tufts of small flattened sword-shaped, often orange-green iris-like leaves, and longer stems bearing spikes of bright yellow star-like flowers, ¾-in. across, with tufts of white hairs on the six orange anthers, turning a conspicuous deep orange in fruit. *Habitat:* Widespread in bogs and on wet heaths, locally abundant in the N and W, much more local and decreasing in the S and E. July–August.

988. ***KERRY LILY *Simethis planifolia* (L.) Grenier & Godron Pl. 80. *CTW, 1217*
A hairless perennial, 4–12 in. high, with a basal tuft of narrow grass-like, often curled grey leaves, and a leafless stem bearing a loose head of a few white star-like flowers, tinged purplish outside and nearly an inch across. *Habitat:* Now known only from dry heathy ground near Derrynane (Kerry). June–July.

989. **LILY OF THE VALLEY *Convallaria majalis* L.   Pl. 80.   *CTW, p. 1218*
A much beloved, richly fragrant garden flower; a hairless, creeping perennial, 6–9 in. high, with a pair of erect, broad, elliptical root-leaves, and 1-sided spikes of a few small, drooping, round bell-like white flowers, followed by red berries. *Habitat:* Local, but often carpeting dry woods on limestone or sand; rare in Ireland. May–June.

990. ***WHORLED SOLOMON'S SEAL   *Polygonatum verticillatum* (L.)
Allioni   Plate 81.   *CTW, p. 1219*
A hairless perennial, 1–3 ft. high, with a stout tuberous creeping rootstock, and narrow lanceolate leaves in numerous whorls of 4–5 up the angled stem, usually not easily detected in the herbage. Flowers small, white, tipped green, bell-shaped, unscented, stalked, 1–3 together at each whorl. Fruit a small red berry. *Habitat:* Very rare in shady places in the N, perhaps now only in Perthshire. June–July.

991. *COMMON SOLOMON'S SEAL   *P. multiflorum* (L.) Allioni
Plate 81.   *CTW, p. 1220*
A hairless creeping perennial, 1–2 ft. high, similar to the usual Solomon's Seal of gardens (991 × 991a), with round, arching stems; broad erect elliptical

alternate leaves; and at their base small hanging clusters of 1–3 unscented greenish-white bell-like flowers, waisted in the middle. Fruit a blue-black berry. *Habitat:* Local in woods in England and Wales. May–June.

991a. **Angular Solomon's Seal**, *P. odoratum* (Miller) Druce (*P. anceps* Moench), is often shorter, with angled stems and larger fragrant flowers only 1–2 together and not waisted in the middle. More local, and mainly on limestone in the W and NW. June–July.

992. ***MAY LILY** *Maianthemum bifolium* (L.) Schmidt Pl. 80. *CTW, p. 1221*
A slender creeping perennial, 3–6 in. high, with two shiny heart-shaped leaves on the stem, the lower long-stalked, and a spike of small white flowers with prominent stamens. Fruit a red berry, rare. *Habitat:* Very rare in one or two woods in N England; occasionally planted elsewhere. May–June.

993. *ASPARAGUS** *Asparagus officinalis* L. Plate 65. *CTW, p. 1221*
A tall, much branched hairless perennial, whose young shoots are familiar as a vegetable, with numerous tufts of weak short needle-like leaves, which are actually reduced stems. Flowers, male and female on separate plants, small, stalked, greenish-white, bell-like, 1–2 together at the base of the branches. Fruit a small red berry. *Habitat:* Occasional on dunes and waste places. June–Aug.

993a. ***Sea Asparagus**, *A. prostratus* Dumortier, is prostrate, and has stiffer, fleshier, blue-grey leaves. Rare on sea-cliffs in the SW and in SE Ireland.

994. *BUTCHER'S BROOM** *Ruscus aculeatus* L. Plate 76. *CTW, p. 1222*
A curious stiff evergreen bush, usually a foot or two high, with the true leaves minute and the stem-branches flattened to resemble oval leaves with branched veins, ending in a sharp spine and bearing on their upper surface one or more tiny whitish flowers; male and female flowers on different plants. Fruit a red berry, but scarce. *Habitat:* Local in dry woods in the S; occasionally naturalised elsewhere. March–April.

995. **TURKSCAP LILY** *Lilium martagon* L. Plate 32. *CTW, p. 1223*
A well known garden Lily; a bulbous perennial, 3–4 ft. high, with distant whorls of dark glossy green spreading elliptical leaves up the stem, and drooping flowers, their dull pink petals spotted dark purple and turned back to make the fanciful Turk's cap. *Habitat:* Rare in scattered woods in the S. June–July.

996. ***PYRENEAN LILY** *L. pyrenaicum* Gouan Plate 63. *CTW, p. 1223*
Has larger flowers shaped like Turkscap Lily (995), but yellow, with numerous small dark spots, and is also much less tall, 1–2 ft. high, and has narrower, erect and more numerous alternate leaves. *Habitat:* Established in hedge-banks near South Molton (N Devon); very rarely elsewhere. June–July.

997. **FRITILLARY** *Fritillaria meleagris* L. Plate 34. *CTW, p. 1224*
One of our most distinctive and attractive wild flowers, with solitary nodding tulip-like blooms, varying from dark dull purple to creamy white, chequered with darker blotches. A hairless greyish, highly gregarious perennial, up to a foot high, with grass-like leaves up the stem. *Habitat:* Locally abundant in damp meadows in the S, chiefly in the Thames valley and Suffolk. April–May.

998. ***WILD TULIP** *Tulipa sylvestris* L. Plate 63. *CTW, p. 1224*
Much slenderer and shorter, 6–12 in. high, than the garden Border Tulips, the narrower grass-like leaves hooded at the tip and with no prominent veins.

Flowers yellow, greenish outside, nodding, fragrant, with long pointed petals, usually extremely shyly produced. *Habitat:* Very local in woods and fields in England and S Scotland. April–May.

999. ***SNOWDON LILY *Lloydia serotina* (L.) Reichenbach Pl. 84. *CTW, 1225*
A low, slender hairless perennial, 3–4 in. high, with very narrow, grass-like leaves and solitary white purple-veined flowers, ½-in. across. *Habitat:* Very rare on high rock-ledges in Snowdonia. May–June.

1000. **YELLOW STAR OF BETHLEHEM *Gagea lutea* (L.) Ker-Gawler
Plate 63. *CTW, p. 1225*
A charming little spring flower, recalling to some people a dainty pale, umbelled Lesser Celandine (22), with its umbel-like cluster of yellowish-green flowers, often sparingly produced. A low, almost hairless perennial, 3–9 in. high, with leaves much like Bluebell (1006), but yellower-green, usually much more hooded at the tip and with three prominent ridged veins on the back instead of one; and two large leaf-like bracts at the base of the flower-cluster. Fruits 3-sided. *Habitat:* Very local in damp woods chiefly in mid and N England; not in Ireland. March–May.

1001. **COMMON STAR OF BETHLEHEM *Ornithogalum umbellatum* L.
Plate 95. *CTW, p. 1226*
A hairless unbranched perennial, 6–12 in. high, often seen in gardens, with a nearly round stem and narrow, dark green limp crocus-like root-leaves, grooved and with a central white stripe. Flowers in large open umbel-like head, white, with a green stripe on the back of each of the 6 petals, opening star-like in the sun. Fruits with 6 rounded ribs. *Habitat:* Widespread but very local in grassy places, mainly in E Anglia; elsewhere usually an escape. May–June.

1002. ***NODDING STAR OF BETHLEHEM *O. nutans* L. Pl. 81. *CTW, 1227*
Stouter than the last with broader leaves and a spike of fewer larger bell-shaped flowers on shorter stalks, erect in bud, spreading in flower and finally nodding. *Habitat:* Rare outside gardens, on grassy banks. April–May.

1003. ***SPIKED STAR OF BETHLEHEM *O. pyrenaicum* L.
Plate. 81. *CTW, 1227*
An unbranched hairless perennial, 2–3 ft. high, with a close spike of greenish-white narrow-petalled flowers, the narrow leaves all basal and soon withering. *Habitat:* Very local in woods and hedge-banks in S England, not infrequent in parts of N Wessex and N Bedfordshire. June. Bath Asparagus.

1004. *SPRING SQUILL *Scilla verna* Hudson Plate 6. *CTW, p. 1228*
A charming little spring flower; a hairless perennial, 2–8 in. high, often gregarious, with very narrow root-leaves and leafless stalks bearing short spikes of star-like blue flowers, mixed with bluish bracts. *Habitat:* Locally common in grassy places near the sea in SW England, on either side of the Irish Sea, and in Scotland and Northumberland. April–June.

1005. **AUTUMN SQUILL *S. autumnalis* L. Plate 6. *CTW, p. 1228*
Differs from the last species mainly in its autumn flowering, but also in its longer spike of purplish flowers with no bracts. *Habitat:* Very local in dry grassy places, usually near the sea, in the S. July–September.

1006. BLUEBELL　*Hyacinthoides non-scripta* (L.) Rothmaler　Pl. 6.　*CTW, 1229*
　Endymion non-scriptus (L.) Garcke ; *Scilla non-scripta* (L.) Hoffmansegg & Link
　A favourite spring flower, often carpeting woods; a hairless bulbous perennial, with a fleshy leafless stem about a foot high, the keeled linear leaves with a hooded tip. Flowers fragrant, blue-violet, occasionally white, in a usually 1-sided spike, drooping at the tip; anthers creamy. Fruits egg-shaped; seeds black. The garden Bluebell *E. hispanicus* (Miller) Chouard, which has broader leaves, a larger, less 1-sided erect spike of paler flowers, and blue anthers, is occasionally naturalised. *Habitat:* Widespread and often abundant in woods and hedge-banks, also on sea-cliffs and mountains. April–June. Wild Hyacinth.

1007. **GRAPE HYACINTH　*Muscari atlanticum* Boissier & Reuter
　'*M. racemosum*'　　　　　　　　　　　　　　Plate 6.　*CTW, p. 1230*
　A hairless perennial, 5–9 in. high, rather like several garden species, with long narrow grooved semi-cylindrical limp root-leaves. Flowers small, egg-shaped, in a dense spike on a leafless, often purple-tinged stem, the upper ones deep blue, the lower darker and duller, looking fancifully like a bunch of grapes.　*Habitat:* Very local in dry grassland, chiefly in the Breckland and Cotswolds. April–May.

GARLICS　*Allium*

HAIRLESS UNBRANCHED bulbous perennials, characterised by their pungent smell of garlic or onion and their flowers, which are often partly or wholly replaced by the bulbils, being in either a tight head or a more open umbel, and enclosed by one or more papery bracts. Leaves all long, though often sheathing for some distance up the stem, and either cylindrical, or linear, flat and keeled, except in Ramsons (1018). The cultivated onion, leek, shallot and garlic belong to this genus, and are occasionally found as garden outcasts on rubbish heaps, etc.

1008. ***WILD LEEK　*Allium ampeloprasum* L.　Plate 65.　*CTW, p. 1233*
　(incl. *A. babingtonii* Borrer)
　Rather like a garden Leek (*A. porrum* L.), but with purple-lilac instead of white flowers and yellow not reddish anthers; stout, 3–4 ft. high, with finely toothed, broadly linear greyish leaves, and loose or compact umbels, 2–3 in. across, of a few flowers with protruding stamens, numerous large bulbils and sometimes long stalks bearing secondary heads.　*Habitat:* Rare in hedge- and other banks near the sea in the SW, W Wales and W Ireland. July–August.

1009. **SAND LEEK　*A. scorodoprasum* L.　Plate 32.　*CTW, p. 1233*
　A rather inconspicuous plant, except for the vivid purple of its heads, 1½ in. across, with a few flowers and bulbils; stamens not projecting. Stems stiff, 2–3 ft. high; leaves flat, very finely toothed.　*Habitat:* Very local in hedge-banks and rough herbage in the N half of England, the S half of Scotland and S Ireland. May–August.

1010. ***ROUND-HEADED LEEK　*A. sphaerocephalon* L.　Pl. 32.　*CTW, 1233*
　A rarity with stiff stems about a foot high; hollow, almost cylindrical leaves; short papery bracts; small globular heads an inch across of numerous pinky-purplish flowers; protruding stamens and no bulbils.　*Habitat:* Now probably only on St Vincent's Rocks, Bristol, where Keeled (1013) and Rosy Garlics (1015) are frequently taken for it. August.

1011. CROW GARLIC *A. vineale* L. Plate 65. *CTW, p. 1234*
Has a stiff stem a foot or so high; hollow cylindrical leaves; papery bracts shorter than the flowers; and heads or umbels of greenish or pinkish flowers, the stamens protruding, usually mixed with bulbils and often tight with bulbils only. *Habitat:* Widespread but local in farmland and dry grassy dunes and commons; locally sometimes a pest in the S, thinning out northwards. June–July.

1012. **FIELD GARLIC *A. oleraceum* L. Plate 35. *CTW, p. 1234*
About as tall as the last species, with leaves usually roundish, rarely flat; papery bracts with long points often much exceeding the flowers; and loose umbels of a few pinkish-brown flowers, the stamens not protruding, or rarely with bulbils only. *Habitat:* Widespread but much more local in dry grassland. July–Aug.

1013. ***KEELED GARLIC *A. carinatum* L. Plate 32. *CTW, p. 1235*
A distinctive foot-high Garlic with its very long, 3–4-in. pointed, papery bract; vivid pink stalked blunt-petalled flowers mixed with unstalked bulbils; protruding stamens; and leaves flat, linear, grooved above and keeled below. *Habitat:* Naturalised on rocks and in a few waste places, chiefly in the N. July–August.

1014. **CHIVES *A. schoenoprasum* L. Plate 32. *CTW, p. 1235*
A herb used for flavouring, 6–9 in. high, tufted, with greyish cylindrical hollow rush-like leaves, and a dense roundish head of long spreading rich purple-pink flowers, with a short papery bract, stamens not protruding, and no bulbils. *Habitat:* Widespread but very local, usually on limestone cliffs or on ledges by lakes and rivers. June–September. (Incl. *A. sibiricum* L.)

1015. ***ROSY GARLIC *A. roseum* L. Plate 32. *CTW, p. 1237*
Taller than Keeled Garlic (1013), the attractive large long-stalked pink flowers, often mixed with bulbils; stamens not protruding. Leaves, few channelled; papery bracts short. *Habitat:* Rare on rocks and in grassy places in the S. May–June.

1016. **THREE-CORNERED LEEK *A. triquetrum* L. Pl. 81. *CTW, p. 1237*
Locally known as White Bluebell, and from a distance not unlike one, but readily distinguished by its garlic smell; has winged 3-angled stem, 6–15 in. high; long narrow, sharply keeled leaves, curled at the top; and heads of several drooping white flowers with a narrow bright green line down the centre of each petal. *Habitat:* Locally abundant on moist banks and roadsides, usually not far from the sea in Devon, Cornwall and the Channel Is., much less so in S Wales and S Ireland; very rare elsewhere. April–June.

1017. ***FEW-FLOWERED LEEK *A. paradoxum* (Bieberstein) Don
Plate 81. *CTW, p. 1237*
An often gregarious perennial, with a slender, leafless, 3-sided stem about 18 in. high, usually a single, very narrow, strongly keeled root-leaf, and a few all-white or creamy flowers, some very unequally stalked, mixed with several bulbils, which are mostly in a compact head. *Habitat:* Naturalised in a few plantations, mainly in the N. April.

1018. RAMSONS *A. ursinum* L. Plate 95. *CTW, p. 1238*
Our only broad-leaved Garlic, growing in masses, the broad leaves reminding some people of Lily of the Valley (989), but brighter green and easily known by

their smell; is also our only plant with the leaf-stalk twisted through 180°. Flower-stalks 3-sided, up to a foot high, bearing a broad umbel of long-stalked white flowers with narrow, pointed petals longer than the stamens; no bulbils. *Habitat:* Widespread and locally frequent in damp woods, and in the N sometimes in more open situations. April–June.

1019. **MEADOW SAFFRON *Colchicum autumnale* L. Pl. 34. *CTW, p. 1239* ⚘
A hairless perennial, producing in autumn, after the leaves have died, long weak whitish 'stalks' bearing rosy mauve, crocus-like flowers, differing from Autumn Crocus (1051) in their orange anthers and 6 stamens. The tufts of broad lanceolate, bright green leaves and long-stalked egg-shaped fruits an inch or more long appear in spring. *Habitat:* Local in damp meadows in W England, E Anglia and Yorkshire, and in woods, especially in the Cotswolds and Wiltshire; rare elsewhere. August–September. Naked Ladies.

HERB-PARIS FAMILY Trilliaceae

1020. **HERB PARIS *Paris quadrifolia* L. Plate 65. *CTW, p. 1239*
A distinctive, hairless perennial, up to a foot high, with an unbranched stem, leafless except at the top, where are normally 4 large unstalked, pointed oval leaves with branched veins below the curious flower, whose 4 very narrow yellow-green petals are slightly shorter than the 4 lanceolate green sepals and a little longer than the 8 erect green stamens with yellow anthers. All these are surmounted by the purplish-black berry, which is crowned by the 4 purple styles. *Habitat:* Local in dampish woods on soils rich in lime; not in Ireland. May–June.

RUSH FAMILY Juncaceae

RUSHES *Juncus*

HAIRLESS GRASS-LIKE or sedge-like plants, mostly perennials, usually erect and tufted, growing in badly drained places. Stems sometimes filled with white pith. Leaves sheathing, very narrow, often rigid, sometimes hollow with cross-partitions inside. Flowers small, green, brown or pale yellow; usually in tufted clusters on one side of or at the tip of the stem, often with 2 leaf-like bracts at their base. Fruit a small 3-valved capsule. Rushes differ from both Grasses and Sedges in having regularly formed flowers, with sepals and petals similar, 6 in all (petals not described unless they differ from sepals), and 6 stamens.

KEY TO RUSHES (Nos. 1021–1035; '10' omitted)

PLANT *over 4 ft. high* 29a; *creeping* 23, 24, 26, 32, 33.

STEMS *leafless* 21, 26, 27, 28, 30, 34, 35; *leafy only at base* 29; *grooved* 34; *ridged* 26, 28; *thread-like* 25; *flat* 23; *jointed* 31a; *triangular* 23; *sharply pointed* 29; *greyish* 26; *glossy* 27.

LEAVES *none* 26, 27, 28; *flat* 29, 31; *grooved* 21, 25, 33; *rounded* 21, 22; *jointed* 31, 32; *sharp-pointed* 29; *thread-like* 24, 30, 33, 34; *hollow* 31, 32; *in a rosette* 21.

FLOWER-HEADS *lateral* 26, 27, 28, 29; *terminal, with leaf-like bract longer* 22, 23a, 24, 25a, 30, 34; *terminal, with leaf-like bract shorter* 21, 23, 25, 32, 34; *widely branched* 23, 31.

FLOWER-HEADS *whitish-yellow* 25, 29, 31a; *blackish* 23, 31.

1021. *HEATH RUSH *Juncus squarrosus* L. Plate 114. *CTW, p. 1243*

A tough rigid perennial, 6–18 in. high, with a thick tuft of numerous wiry, grooved, curved leaves, bent sharply back with a rosette and very stiff, leafless stems bearing terminal clusters of pale silvery brown flowers much overtopping the leaf-like bract at their base; sepals rather pointed, chestnut brown with silvery edges. Fruits larger than in most Rushes, egg-shaped, blunt in outline but with a small point at the top, shorter than the sepals (Fig.). *Habitat:* Widespread and locally abundant on heaths and moors. June–July.

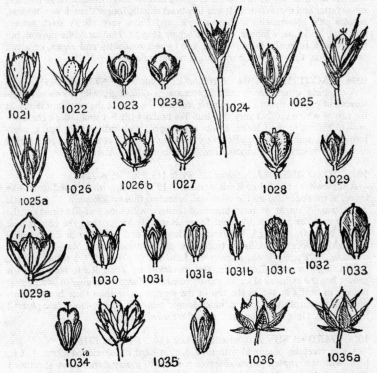

Fruits of Rushes and Woodrushes ×3, except 1035 with 3 fruits (×2)

1022. **SLENDER RUSH *J. tenuis* Willdenow Plate 114. *CTW, p. 1243*
(incl. *J. dudleyi* Wiegand)

A slender perennial, 6–15 in. high, with flat, grooved leaves mostly in a basal tuft. Flowers in a loose terminal cluster, much overtopped by the two narrow leaf-like bracts at its base; sepals greenish at first, later straw-coloured, narrowly lanceolate, very pointed. Fruits small, pale, shortly oval, blunt, not or hardly beaked (Fig.). *Habitat:* Widespread, locally common and increasing on damp road- and path-sides and track ruts, especially on acid soils. June–September.

1023. *SALTMARSH RUSH J. gerardii Loiseleur Plate 114. CTW, p. 1244
    A slender foot-high creeping perennial, growing in large patches, with dark
green leaves, mostly from the lower part of the stem, which is 3-sided towards the
top. Flowers very dark brown, in a loose cluster, usually overtopping the leaf-like
bract at its base. Fruits egg-shaped, glossy, chestnut-brown, beaked, about
equalling the very dark brown blunt sepals (Fig.). Habitat: Widespread and
locally common in brackish marshes. June–July.
    1023a. *Round-fruited Rush, J. compressus Jacquin, is very similar, often
shorter, not salt-loving, nor so far-creeping and so never in such large patches;
stems fatter and more flattened; leaf-like bract usually longer than flower-clusters,
flowers pale brown with a shorter style, and fruits very glossy dark brown,
globular, and much longer than the sepals (Fig.). Habitat: Widespread but
rather local, normally inland in fens and by wet roadsides and rivers, on chalk
or limestone, thinning out northwards; not in Ireland.

1024. **SCOTTISH RUSH J. trifidus L. Plate 114. CTW, p. 1245
    A creeping, often densely tufted perennial, 3–6 in. high, with no proper root-
leaves but papery sheaths and shining scales at the base of the very thin stems, at
the top of which are 2–3 very thin leaf-like bracts with 1–3 small, dark chestnut-
brown flowers in their forks. Fruits egg-shaped, with rather long beaks, overtopping the pointed oval sepals (Fig.). Habitat: Locally common on rock ledges
and stony moors on high mountains in Scotland. June–August.

1025. TOAD RUSH J. bufonius L. Plate 113. CTW, p. 1245
    A somewhat unrush-like Rush, annual, 2–12 in. high, with grooved, grass-like
leaves at the roots and up the often well branched thin hollow stem. Flowers pale
green, usually single, in much branched clusters, with long leaf-like bracts at the
base of each, and pointed lanceolate sepals usually longer than the oblong pale
brown blunt fruits (Fig.). Habitat: Widespread and common in damp sandy
or muddy places, especially by tracks and paths round ponds. May–September.
    1025a. ***Pygmy Rush, J. mutabilis Lamarck (CTW, 1252), a tufted annual,
1–3 in. high, often suffused pink and mimicked by Toad Rush, with which it
grows, has the cylindrical leaves mostly basal, their sheaths ending in two points;
flowers in heads of 1–5 at the top of the stem, shorter than their bract; sepals
greenish or purplish, narrower, much longer than the oblong-lanceolate pointed
fruits (Fig.). Only on damp heaths on the Lizard. June.

1026. HARD RUSH J. inflexus L. Plate 114. CTW, p. 1246
    A stiff creeping perennial with tufts of thin hard bluish ridged stems, 1–2 ft.
high, with interrupted pith and leaves reduced to glossy dark brown sheaths at
their base. Flowers brownish, in tufts of lax branches on one side and towards
the top of the stem; sepals narrow lanceolate, finely pointed, equalling the dark
brown narrow pointed fruits (Fig.). Habitat: Widespread and common in
dampish grassy places, preferring heavy or chalky and avoiding very acid soils;
thinning out northwards and westwards. June–August. J. glaucus Sibthorp.
    1026a. **Lakeside Rush, J. filiformis L., is less than half as high, with the
small dense, greenish or straw-coloured fewer-flowered clusters halfway or lower
down the slender, scarcely ridged stems with pith not interrupted, and the round
fruits only minutely pointed. Rare in turf on stony lake-shores in the Lake
District and C Scotland.
    1026b. **Baltic Rush, J. balticus Willdenow, is shorter and has stouter shoots

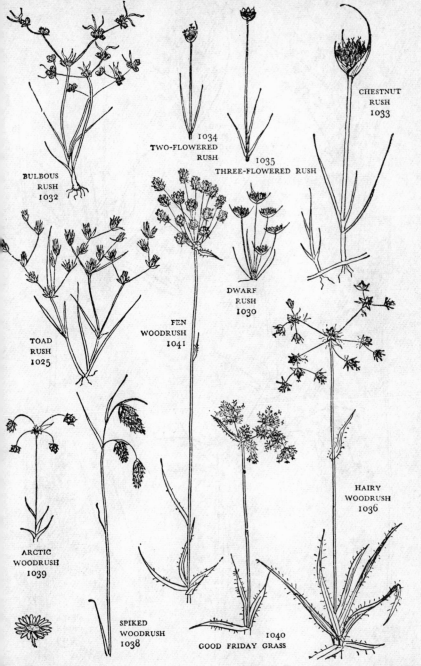

BULBOUS
RUSH
1032

1034
TWO-FLOWERED
RUSH

1035
THREE-FLOWERED RUSH

CHESTNUT
RUSH
1033

TOAD
RUSH
1025

FEN
WOODRUSH
1041

DWARF
RUSH
1030

HAIRY
WOODRUSH
1036

ARCTIC
WOODRUSH
1039

SPIKED
WOODRUSH
1038

1040
GOOD FRIDAY GRASS

113

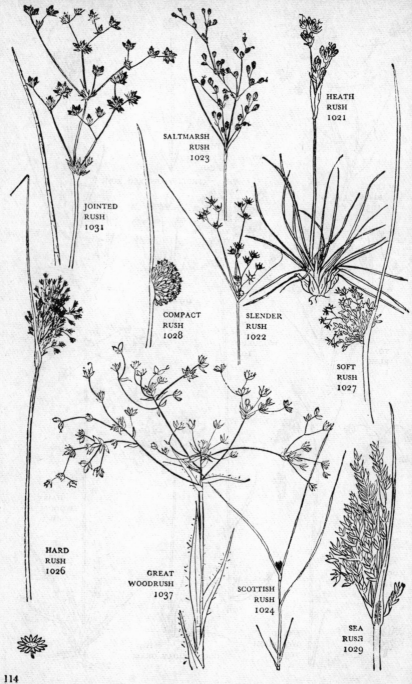

SALTMARSH
RUSH
1023

HEATH
RUSH
1021

JOINTED
RUSH
1031

COMPACT
RUSH
1028

SLENDER
RUSH
1022

SOFT
RUSH
1027

HARD
RUSH
1026

GREAT
WOODRUSH
1037

SCOTTISH
RUSH
1024

SEA
RUSH
1029

114

arising from the creeping rootstock in straight lines like a palisade, and the clusters of broader, darker brown flowers nearly at the top of the stems, which are smooth and have continuous pith. Fruits broader and shorter (Fig.). Very local in dune slacks and moist places in Lancashire and E and N Scotland.

1027. SOFT RUSH *J. effusus* L. (*J. communis* Meyer) Plate 114. *CTW, p. 1246*
Probably our commonest Rush, a perennial 1–4 ft. high, with large tufts of soft, yellowish-green glossy stems, stouter than Hard Rush (1026), smooth to the touch when fresh and with the pith continuous; sheaths at their base dull brownish; no proper leaves. Flowers brown, numerous, in either tight or loose heads near the top of the stems; sepals lanceolate, pointed. Fruits yellowish to chestnut brown, egg-shaped, slightly indented at the top (Fig.). *Habitat:* Widespread and abundant in damp grassy and marshy places. June–August.

1028. COMPACT RUSH *J. conglomeratus* L. Plate 114. *CTW, p. 1247*
Often confused with the tight-headed form of the last species, but is darker green and less stout and has stems not glossy, markedly ridged and roughish to the touch, especially just below the flower-head. Fruits darker brown, with the remains of the style in the deeper notch at the top (Fig.). *Habitat:* Locally nearly as common in damp grassy and marshy places, but rare in chalk and limestone districts. May–July, starting appreciably earlier.

1029. SEA RUSH *J. maritimus* Lamarck Plate 114. *CTW, p. 1248*
A stiff perennial, 1–2 ft. high, forming clumps of tough, pale grey-green stems, smooth when fresh, with continuous pith and ending in a very sharp point; leaves all basal, flat, sharply pointed. Flowers pale yellow, in a rather large loose cluster with ascending branches near the top of the stem. Fruits bluntly 3-sided, abruptly pointed, about equalling the lanceolate sepals (Fig.). *Habitat:* Widespread and frequent in drier salt-marshes and among rocks near the sea; thinning out northwards. July–August.

1029a. **Sharp Rush,** *J. acutus* L., is a magnificent plant, much taller, 3–5 ft. high, and robuster, flowering much earlier and growing in large tufts, with stems and leaves tapering to a stout spine which has the sharpest point of any British plant; fewer, very large leaves; larger and compacter clusters of browner flowers, the broader sepals only half as long as the very large bay-brown egg-shaped fruits (Fig.). Very locally abundant in dune-slacks in the SW and in SE Ireland; very rare in SE England. June.

1030. ***DWARF RUSH *J. capitatus* Weigel Plate 113. *CTW, p. 1249*
A low neat stiff annual, 1–2 in. high, with a tuft of bristle-like root-leaves, soon withering and with no points to their sheaths; and leafless stems bearing a single terminal cluster of flowers, greenish at first, later brownish, overtopped by one of the two leaf-like bracts at its base. Fruits egg-shaped, shorter than the curved, broad lanceolate sepals, whose fine points are curved outwards (Fig.). *Habitat:* Very local on damp heaths and ledges in Anglesey, Cornwall and the Channel Is. May–June.

1031. JOINTED RUSH *J. articulatus* L. Plate 114. *CTW, p. 1250*
An often half-prostrate perennial, 1–2 ft. high or long, with curved flattened hollow, transversely jointed leaves up the unjointed stems. Flowers greenish to

very dark brown, in long open, broadly branched terminal clusters; sepals lanceolate, pointed. Fruits dark glossy brown, egg-shaped, abruptly contracted to a broadly conical point (Fig.). *Habitat:* Widespread and locally common in marshes, fens and wet meadows, often on chalk or limestone. June–August.

1031*a*. *Fen Rush, *J. subnodulosus* Schrank (*J. obtusiflorus* Hoffmann), is paler, weaker, more upright, up to 4 ft., and less tufted, with stems jointed and leaves with both horizontal and vertical partitions, but not flattened or curved. Flowers pale buff-brown, becoming red-brown, in densely branched clusters, many branches bent back at an obtuse angle giving a twiggy appearance. Fruits pale brown, 3-sided, rather blunt with a minute point, slightly longer than the pale blunt incurved sepals (Fig.). Locally common in fens, and in dune hollows near the sea, always on limy peat, and in E England, thinning out W and N to S Scotland. July–September.

1031*b*. Sharp-flowered Rush, *J. acutiflorus* Hoffmann (*J. sylvaticus* Reichenbach), is usually taller, to 3 ft., and has jointed upright stems; straight, less flattened leaves; the branches of the flower-head diverging at an acute angle from the main stem; sepals tapering to minute bristle-like points, the outer curved outwards, and much narrower smaller fruits gradually narrowed to a sharper point (Fig.). Almost as common as Jointed Rush, with which it hybridises, but typical of acid marshes and bogs. July–September, starting later.

1031*c*. ***Alpine Rush, *J. alpinoarticulatus* Chaix (*J. alpinus* Villars), is like a small erect Jointed Rush, but has leaves scarcely flattened, fewer slenderer erecter branches in the cluster of dark flowers, blunter sepals and fruits, blunt, (Fig.). Rare in meadows and wet stony places in hill districts in Teesdale and Scotland. July–September.

1032. BULBOUS RUSH   *J. bulbosus* L.   Plate 113.   *CTW, p. 1252*

A low grass-like perennial, most commonly 2–4 in. high, very variable indeed, being either tufted and erect, creeping and rooting, or floating, with weak, slender stems slightly swollen at the base. Leaves hollow, bristle-like or grass-like, obscurely jointed, both basal and up the stems. Flowers few, reddish-brown, in branched terminal heads; sepals pointed. Fruits pale brown, oblong, blunt (Fig.), often replaced by sprouting leafy buds. *Habitat:* Widespread and locally common in wet heathy places, and rides and cart ruts in woods, mainly on acid soils. June–September. (Incl. *J. kochii* Schultz.)

1033. ***CHESTNUT RUSH   *J. castaneus* Smith.   Plate 113.   *CTW, p. 1253*

A stocky perennial, 3–6 in. high, spreading by runners, with soft, bristle-like, grooved leaves up the smooth, rounded stems; sheaths not pointed. Flowers rather large, dark chestnut brown, in small dense terminal heads, overtopped by a leaf-like bract. Fruits oblong, large, glossy brown, abruptly pointed, much longer than the narrow lanceolate, pointed sepals (Fig.). *Habitat:* Rare in very wet places on high mountains in the Highlands. July.

1034. ***TWO-FLOWERED RUSH   *J. biglumis* L.   Plate 113.   *CTW, p. 1253*

Usually shorter than the next species, with stems grooved, sheaths with shorter points, darker flowers in terminal pairs, one above the other, usually overtopped by the leaf-like bract, and much darker brown fruits broadest at the middle, notched at the top, much longer than the oblong sepals (Fig.). *Habitat:* Rare in wet bare places on lime-rich mountains in the Highlands. June–July.

1035. **THREE-FLOWERED RUSH *J. triglumis* L. Pl. 113. *CTW, p. 1253*

A tufted perennial, 2–6 in. high, with a leafless stem, sheaths with two long points, and curved, bristle-like leaves. Flowers pale purplish-brown, in a head of 2–5, usually all more or less horizontal, not overtopped by the leaf-like bract at their base. Fruits large, red-brown, egg-shaped, abruptly pointed, slightly longer than the broad lanceolate, blunt sepals (Fig.). *Habitat:* Local in bogs and wet places on hills and mountains in the N; not in Ireland. June–July.

WOODRUSHES *Luzula*

Tufted perennials, with limp flat grass-like leaves fringed with long white cottony hairs, rather leafy stems bearing terminal clusters of rush-like flowers, and fruits containing only 3 seeds. They grow in drier places.

1036. HAIRY WOODRUSH *Luzula pilosa* (L.) Willdenow Pl. 113. *CTW, 1255*

Tufted, 4–12 in. high, with glossy, often yellowish-green leaves. Flowers brown, with conspicuous yellow-green styles, 1–3 each on long slender stalks, which radiate in all directions from the top of the stem, beginning to turn downwards as soon as they open and remaining so in fruit. Fruits egg-shaped, abruptly narrowed above the middle to a broad blunt top (Fig.), longer than the transparent-bordered sepals. *Habitat:* Widespread and locally frequent in woods and hedge-banks. April–June.

1036a. *Narrow-leaved Woodrush, *L. forsteri* (Smith) DC., is smaller and less stiff, with narrower leaves, and the flower-stalks, which usually each bear several flowers, not radiating in all directions, but forming a V-shaped head, nearly erect or slightly inclined to one side, remaining so in fruit. Fruits hardly longer than the sepals gradually narrowed towards the top, ending in a long fine point (Fig.). Hybridises with the last species. Only in dry woods in the S.

1037. GREAT WOODRUSH *L. sylvatica* (Hudson) Gaudin Pl. 114. *CTW, 1255*

A stout, densely tufted plant, 1–2 ft. high, superficially like the stouter Wood Club-rush (1114), from which it can always be told by its glossy, hairy leaves; much larger than the last two species and with more, broader ($\frac{1}{4}$–4 in. wide) and paler green leaves. Flowers chestnut-brown, in groups of 3 in the broad, richly and loosely branched cluster; anthers yellow, conspicuous. Fruits egg-shaped, beaked, about equalling the sepals. *Habitat:* Widespread and locally frequent in woods on acid soils and among mountain rocks, chiefly in the W. June–July.

1038. **SPIKED WOODRUSH *L. spicata* (L.) DC. Plate 113. *CTW, p. 1256*

A low tufted dingy brown plant, with curved, somewhat grooved, only slightly hairy leaves, and chestnut-brown flowers in a branched oval head drooping to one side, the sepals with bristle-like points, about equalling the egg-shaped fruits. *Habitat:* Locally frequent on bare ground and rock-ledges on mountains in the N. June–July.

1039. ***ARCTIC WOODRUSH *L. arcuata* Swartz Plate 113. *CTW, p. 1257*

Smaller and neater than the last species, with leaves more deeply grooved and almost hairless, branches of the flower-heads long but drooping on both sides and each bearing clusters of flowers, and sepals less finely pointed and a good deal longer than the oblong fruits. *Habitat:* Locally common above 4000 ft. on a very few mountains in the Highlands, chiefly in the Cairngorms. July.

1040. GOOD FRIDAY GRASS *L. campestris* (L.) DC. Plate 113. *CTW, p. 1257*
A short, creeping plant, 3–8 in. high, with rather short leaves and dark chest-nut-brown flowers drooping in a cluster of close short-stalked heads; anthers yellow, conspicuous, much longer than their stalks. Fruits egg-shaped. *Habitat:* Widespread and common in dry, sunny turf. April–May. Sweep's Brush.

1040a. Heath Woodrush, *L. multiflora* (Retzius) Lejeune, is rather taller, 6–15 in. high, and more rush-like, with few or no runners, flower-heads paler brown, either long-stalked or more usually almost unstalked; anthers about as long as their stalks, and fruits globular. Locally frequent on heaths and moors and in woods, especially on acid soils. May–June.

1041. ***FEN WOODRUSH *L. pallescens* Swartz Plate 113. *CTW, p. 1258*
Rather like Heath Woodrush (1040a), but is only 6–12 in. high, and has leaves smaller, paler and less hairy; many more branches to the flower-head; flowers smaller, more numerous in each cluster, very pale yellow-brown; and fruits egg-shaped. *Habitat:* Very rare in rather dry fens in Huntingdonshire. June.

DAFFODIL FAMILY Amaryllidaceae

1042. ***SNOWFLAKE *Leucojum vernum* L. Plate 81. *CTW, p. 1259*
Fatter than Snowdrop (1044), with 1-in. petals broader, pointed, tipped green and all of equal size; flowers usually solitary or in pairs; orange anthers; broader brighter yellow-green leaves; and fruits fig-shaped. *Habitat:* Very rare in moist shady places in SW England. February–March.

1043. **LODDON LILY *L. aestivum* L. Plate 81. *CTW, p. 1260*
Much taller than Snowflake (1043), and in large tufts, with smaller flowers on unequal stalks in clusters of 3–6. *Habitat:* Very local in wet meadows by the Rivers Thames, Loddon and Shannon; an occasional garden escape in drier places elsewhere. April–May. Summer Snowflake.

1044. **SNOWDROP *Galanthus nivalis* L. Plate 81. *CTW, p. 1260*
A universally known hairless perennial, 4–8 in. high, with long, linear, grooved and keeled, grey-green leaves. Flowers solitary, drooping, surmounted by a greenish leaf-like hood, with 3 large white outer petals and 3 rather bell-like inner ones, green outside, white with a green tip inside; anthers green. Fruits egg-shaped. *Habitat:* Widespread but local in damp woods and shady river banks, usually a garden escape; not in Ireland. February–March.

1045. *WILD DAFFODIL *Narcissus pseudonarcissus* L. Pl. 63. *CTW, p. 1261*
Too well known to need detailed description, but the usual wild plant has nodding flowers smaller than most garden forms with the trumpet-like tube of inner petals as long as but darker yellow than the more spreading outer ones; leaves long, linear, greyish. Many other species, varieties and hybrids of *Narcissus* may become naturalised. The most frequent of these are Pheasant's Eye (*N. majalis* Curtis), whose richly scented flowers with a short red-tipped yellow trumpet and flatter white outer petals appear in May, and Primrose Peerless (*N.* × *biflorus* Curtis), with smaller primrose-coloured flowers, 2 on each stalk. *Habitat:* Widespread but rather local in damp woods and meadows, commonest in the SW. March–April.

1045a. ***Tenby Daffodil, *N. obvallaris* Salisbury, has flowers uniformly deep yellow and less nodding, the trumpet longer than the outer petals. Long known in a few grass fields near Tenby.

IRIS FAMILY   Iridaceae

1046. **BLUE-EYED GRASS *Sisyrinchium angustifolium* Miller Pl. 6. *CTW, 1265*
A variable, hairless perennial, 6–10 in. high, with a tuft of linear leaves, and
blue flowers, with very pointed petals, closed in dull weather and so often hard
to detect among herbage, in a small terminal cluster on a stiff winged leaf-like
stem. Fruits globular. *Habitat:* Local in damp grassy places in W Ireland;
elsewhere a very occasional escape. July.

1047. ***YELLOW-EYED GRASS *S. californicum* (Ker-Gawler) Aiton
Plate 63. *CTW, p. 1266*
Rather stouter than the last species, with larger 1-in. orange-yellow flowers,
broader leaves and more broadly winged stem. *Habitat:* Known only in one
marshy meadow near Wexford Harbour. June–July.

IRISES   *Iris*

STOUT HAIRLESS perennials, with narrow, sword-shaped, flat leaves. The conspicuous flowers have 3 spreading outer petals (falls), 3 more or less erect and
twisted inner ones (standards), all with narrow basal portions (Fig.), and 3 large
and rather petal-like stigmas. In many garden Irises the falls are bearded, but our
wild species are beardless. The branched tips of the styles are the crests.

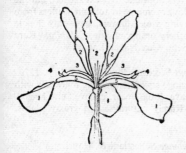

Typical Iris Flower
1. Falls.   2. Standards.   3. Style arms.
4. Crests.   5. Hafts

1048. ***BUTTERFLY IRIS *Iris spuria* L.   Plate 6.   *CTW, p. 1267*
Not unlike the Spanish or Dutch Irises (*I. xiphium* L.), which are bulbous and
occur as garden relics, especially in the extreme SW; 1–2 ft. high, sparingly or
not branched, with rather narrow leaves, the blue-violet flowers with the roundish
blade of the falls half as long as the haft, standards slightly shorter and narrower,
and crests violet, 2-toothed and somewhat shorter still. Fruits 6-sided, with a
very long beak; seeds smooth, brown, with a dark papery covering. *Habitat:*
Moist meadows near the sea in Lincolnshire and Dorset. June–July.
   1048a. ***Purple Water Flag, *I. versicolor* L., a taller branched blue-purple
Iris, in some respects like Yellow Flag (1050), but with solid stems; flowers much
like the garden *I. sibirica* L.; and broader leaves with no markedly raised midrib.
Falls broadly oval and horizontal, but drooping at the tip, the blade about as
long as the haft; standards much shorter and narrower, inclining outwards; crests

nearly white, slightly longer. Fruits small, oblong, 3-sided; seeds dark brown, hard, smooth, pitted, D-shaped, with a thin covering. *Habitat:* Naturalised in wet spots at Epping Forest, Ullswater and L. Tay.

1049. *ROAST-BEEF PLANT   *I. foetidissima* L.   Plate 6.   *CTW, p. 1267*
Grows in thick tufts, with dark evergreen leaves, 1–2 ft. high, acrid and sweetly foetid when crushed, not every tuft producing the rather shorter flattened inconspicuous flower-stems. Flowers look small and neat, and are short-lived, of a remarkable slaty grey-purple with darker veins, very rarely pale yellow; falls oval, as long as the limb; standards narrower and shorter, about equalling the small, triangular, yellower crests. Fruits bright green, oblong, blunt, 3-sided, 2 in. long, splitting open in winter to show the rows of round fleshy bright orange-scarlet seeds inside. *Habitat:* Rather local in woods and scrub in the S especially on chalk or limestone, and on bushy cliffs near or by the sea; rare in Scotland and Ireland. June.

1050. YELLOW FLAG   *I. pseudacorus* L.   Plate 59.   *CTW, p. 1268*
Much the commonest wild Iris, with stiff broad leaves having a raised midrib, and conspicuous stout, well branched flower-stems, 3–6 ft. high. Flowers rich yellow. Fruits 3-sided, oblong; seeds pale brown, flattened. *Habitat:* Widespread and common by fresh water, often in quantity. June–August.

1051. ***AUTUMN CROCUS   *Crocus nudiflorus* Smith   Pl. 34.   *CTW, p. 1270*
A hairless perennial, with leaves and flowers both like the next species, but the leaves appear in spring and die before the flowers emerge in autumn. Differs from the earlier Meadow Saffron (1019) in having violet flowers, and only 3 pale yellow stamens, much shorter than the feathery orange stigma. *Habitat:* Rare in grassy places, mainly in NW England. Sept.–Oct. Naked Ladies.

1052. ***SPRING CROCUS   *C. purpureus* Weston   Plate 6.   *CTW, p. 1270*
Resembles many garden Crocuses, the orange styles contrasting markedly with the dark to pale purple or white petals. Leaves long, linear, grooved and keeled, with the midrib white above. *Habitat:* Rarely naturalised in grassy places. March. '*C. vernus*'.

1053. ***SAND CROCUS   *Romulea columnae* Sebastiani & Mauri
                           Plate 81.   *CTW, p. 1271*
Like a tiny garden Crocus, 1–2 in. high, with flowers greenish outside, but opening fully in the sun to ½-in. across; petals narrow, pointed, pale purple, yellow at the base, with purple veins; anthers bright yellow. Leaves like green wires, scarcely distinguishable from the grass in which they grow except by their curly appearance. *Habitat:* Now only in short sandy turf by the sea on Dawlish Warren and in the Channel Is. April.

1054. **MONTBRETIA   *Crocosmia × crocosmiflora* (Lemoine) Brown
                           Plate 63.   *CTW, p. 1271*
A hairless man-made hybrid perennial, familiar in gardens, 1–2 ft. high, with flat iris-like leaves, and a 1-sided spike of reddish-orange flowers. *Habitat:* Now well established on cliffs and banks and by fresh water, especially near the sea and in the S. July–August.

1055. ***GLADIOLUS *Gladiolus illyricus* Koch Plate 34. *CTW, p. 1272*

Has narrower iris-like leaves and 1-sided flower-spikes similar to garden Gladioli, but is smaller in all its parts, a foot or so high, with flowers up to an inch long, always reddish-purple with pointed petals; anthers shorter than their stalks and diverging at their base. *Habitat:* Very rare among Bracken in heathy places, now probably only in the New Forest. July.

YAM FAMILY Dioscoreaceae

1056. *BLACK BRYONY *Tamus communis* L. Plate 76. *CTW, p. 1273* 🝋

A hairless perennial climber, twining clockwise, and readily told from White Bryony (511) by its shiny, broad heart-shaped leaves and lack of tendrils. Flowers tiny, yellowish-green, 6-petalled, in long loose interrupted, sometimes branched spikes; male and female on separate plants. Fruit a scarlet berry. *Habitat:* Frequent in hedgerows and thickets in the S, thinning out northwards; not in Scotland; in Ireland only around L. Gill. May onwards.

ORCHID FAMILY Orchidaceae

PERENNIALS, WITH either a creeping fleshy rootstock or a pair of root-tubers, and leaves always undivided and untoothed, often long, narrow, keeled and somewhat fleshy. Flowers often but by no means always showy, in unbranched terminal spikes, very various but always with 3 sepals which are usually the same colour as the 2 upper petals; lowest petal extremely variable, usually much larger than the others and in the form of a lip, often remarkably shaped and spurred behind. The flowers are in fact usually upside down; if not, the lip is uppermost. Each flower has a small leaf-like bract at its base, and the stamen and stigmas joined in a single column in the centre. The fruits are egg-shaped or cylindrical, with immensely numerous seeds like grains of dust.

1057. ***LADY'S SLIPPER *Cypripedium calceolus* L. Pl. 63. *CTW, p. 1279*

A very rare and very distinctive Orchid, up to a foot high, with broad lanceolate, strongly ribbed, pale green leaves, and a solitary flower, more than twice as large as any of our other Orchids, with long maroon-coloured sepals and a huge yellow lip, hollowed into the fancied shape of a slipper and spotted red inside; our only Orchid with 2 stamens. *Habitat:* A great rarity, still in one or two woods on limestone in N England. May–June, not flowering every year.

1058. *BROAD HELLEBORINE *Cephalanthera damasonium* (Miller) Druce
  C. latifolia Janchen   Plate 83. *CTW, p. 1280*

An attractive white-flowered Orchid, with a ridged hairless stem 12–18 in. high, and broad lanceolate, slightly bluish-green, erect leaves becoming narrower right up it. Flowers rarely fully open, unstalked, scentless, fattish, creamy white, the base of the unspurred lip orange-yellow inside (hence the name of Poached-egg Plant), with 3 ridges; all but the topmost shorter than the conspicuous leaf-like bracts at their base; sepals and petals blunt; ovary, short and hairless. *Habitat:* Locally common in beechwoods in the S. May–July.

1059. **NARROW HELLEBORINE *C. longifolia* Fritsch Pl. 83. *CTW, 1281*

Slenderer and more graceful than the last species, with stem rather less ridged, and much longer and narrower, parallel-sided, darker green leaves, spreading but markedly drooping at the tip. Flowers smaller, more spreading and widely open, pure white, with more pointed sepals and a much smaller orange spot on the lip, which has 4–5 slenderer white ridges; in an apparently leafless spike, the bracts, all but sometimes the lowest, being tiny and much shorter than the flowers; ovary slender. *Habitat:* Widespread, but very local and apparently decreasing, in beech and other woods, mainly on chalk or limestone. May–June, beginning earlier.

1060. ***RED HELLEBORINE *C. rubra* (L.) Richard Pl. 34. *CTW, p. 1281*
A rarity a foot high, with the stem slightly hairy above, a few sharply pointed, narrow lanceolate leaves, not drooping, and brilliant purple-pink flowers, rather long and narrow, unscented, and mostly longer than the leaf-like bracts at their base; sepals pointed, spreading and hairy on the back, and petals broader and bending inwards, with an unspurred whitish lip; ovary downy. *Habitat:* Confined to a few beechwoods on the Cotswolds, where it only flowers irregularly, when the degree of half-shade it needs is exactly right. June–July.

1061. *MARSH HELLEBORINE *Epipactis palustris* (L.) Crantz
Plate 35. *CTW, p. 1283*
Our only Orchid with purplish-brown and white flowers, 4–18 in. high, with stem downy above and often purplish below, and narrow lanceolate, keeled and folded leaves. Flowers in a loose spike, mostly turned to one side, longer than the leaf-like bracts at their base; sepals purplish-brown outside, purple inside; petals white outside and crimson and white within, with a long 2-jointed lip whose outer half is white and frilly like a cravat, with a yellow spot at the top, the cup-shaped inner half being crimson-streaked within. Fruiting ovary downy, olive-green, long pear-shaped, hanging. *Habitat:* Uncommon but locally plentiful in fens marshes and dune-slacks in England, Wales and S Scotland. July–August.

1062. *COMMON HELLEBORINE *E. helleborine* (L.) Crantz Pl. 65. *CTW, 1284*
A variable Orchid, 1–2 ft. high, with solitary stems downy above, often purplish below; and broad, pointed oval, dull green, sometimes purplish leaves, half-clasping and alternating spirally up the stem. Flowers in an often dense 1-sided spike, equalling the leaf-like bracts at their base, unscented, greenish-yellow or purplish, with pointed sepals and the heart-shaped tip of the unspurred lip finally curved under (Fig.); ovary hairless. *Habitat:* Widespread but local in woods and shady places. July–September.

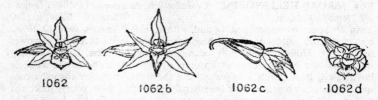

1062   1062 b   1062 c   1062 d

1062a. **Violet Helleborine, *E. purpurata* Smith (*E. sessilifolia* Peterman), has stout, tufted, pale purple stems, downy above, and narrow parallel-sided leaves, greyish above and heavily tinged with purple below. Flowers crowded, pale greenish-white inside, purplish-green outside, shorter than the leaf-like bracts at their base. Local in dark woods, especially beechwoods, mainly in the S half of England. August onwards.

1062*b*. **Narrow-lipped Helleborine**, *E. leptochila* (Godfery) Godfery, is pale yellow-green, never reddish or purple-tinged, and has narrower elliptical, never oval leaves, and yellowish-green flowers, equalling or shorter than the leaf-like bracts and with longer, spreading and more pointed petals and sepals, the lip being whitish and considerably longer than broad with the pointed tip not curved underneath (Fig.). Very local in woods, especially of beech on chalk, in the S. July.

1062*c*. **Green-flowered Helleborine**, *E. phyllanthes* Smith (incl. *E. vectensis* (Stephenson) Brooke & Rose, *E. pendula* Thomas, and *E. cambrensis* Thomas), has weakly veined, grass-green, leaves, and the lowest leaf-like bracts longer than the apple-green flowers, which are very variable in lip-shape, usually only partially opening, and hang downwards more markedly than any of the other Helleborines (Fig.). Very local, usually in shady places, mostly on chalk and limestone, and on sand-dunes, In England, Wales and SE Ireland. July–August.

1062*d*. ***Dune Helleborine**, *E. dunensis* (Stephenson) Godfery (incl. *E. cleistogama* Thomas), differs from the last species in its dingy yellowish- or pinkish-green flowers never opening widely, the tip of the narrow lip being usually a darker pink and curved under (Fig.). Very local on sand-dunes in NW England and N Wales. June–July.

1063. **DARK RED HELLEBORINE**   *E. atrorubens* (Hoffmann) Schultes
E. atropurpurea Rafinesque   Plate 34.   *CTW, p. 1288*
Smaller than Common Helleborine (1062), with shortly oval purplish-green leaves and the slightly fragrant flowers always a unique shade of dark red, the sepals and petals short and blunt with rough bosses on the broadly heart-shaped lip. (Fig., p. 222). Stem and ovary very downy. *Habitat:* Very local on open limestone rocks and in ash woods in the N and W, and in W Ireland. June–July.

1064. ***GHOST ORCHID**   *Epipogium aphyllum* Swartz Pl. 36.   *CTW, p. 1289*
A remarkable Orchid, rarely appearing above ground and recorded only in nine years in the past hundred. It is leafless and its straw-coloured stems, mauver above and much thicker at the base, have only 1–2 tiny pale brown bracts and never grow over 5 in. high. Flowers hanging, 1–3 together, palest yellow with a very pale mauve lip bent back almost to touch the fat white spur, which points upwards; ovary biscuit-coloured, streaked pale mauve. *Habitat:* Very easily overlooked, since its pallid and varied colours camouflage it among the shady leaf-litter in beech- or oak-woods; recently seen only in the Chilterns, but formerly on the Welsh Border. May–September. *E. gmelini* Richard.

1065. *AUTUMN LADY'S TRESSES*   *Spiranthes spiralis* (L.) Chevallier
                                 Plate 82.   *CTW, p. 1291*
One of our smaller conspicuous Orchids, usually only 3–6 in. high, differing from all except American (1066) and Creeping Lady's Tresses (1070) in its white flowers being arranged in an obvious spiral up the stem. Leaves bluish-green, pointed oval, unstalked, in a basal rosette which withers before producing a grey-downy flowering stem with a few meagre scale-like leaves. Flowers small, fragrant, not spurred, with downy sepals and petals, green-centred within; ovary egg-shaped, downy. *Habitat:* Local in dry grassy places in the S and in S Ireland; rare elsewhere. August–September.

1066. ***AMERICAN LADY'S TRESSES*** *S. romanzoffiana* Chamisso
Plate 82. *CTW, p. 1292*
Taller than the last species, with all its leaves lanceolate and growing up the stem. Flowers twice as large, in 3 spiral rows on the much broader spike, fragrant, white, greenish at the fatter base; leaf-like bracts prominent. *Habitat:* Very rare in wet grassy places in SW and N Ireland, and W Scotland. August–September.

1067. **COMMON TWAYBLADE** *Listera ovata* (L.) Brown Pl. 65. *CTW, 1293*
An unobtrusive Orchid, a foot or two high, with a distinctive single pair of broad oval, opposite unstalked dull green leaves low down on the stem, and a long spike of small yellowish-green flowers, with a long narrow forked, often down-turned and horizontal unspurred lip. *Habitat:* Widespread and not uncommon in woods and open grassy places. May–July.

1068. **LESSER TWAYBLADE** *L. cordata* (L.) Brown Pl. 83. *CTW, 1294*
A slender inconspicuous little Orchid, usually only 2–4 in. high, like a miniature Common Twayblade (1067) but with leaves smaller, glossy green and heart-shaped and fewer pinkish flowers with a more deeply lobed lip and two small side-lobes near the base. *Habitat:* Widespread but nowhere common, growing in moss on moors and in bogs and woods, especially pinewoods, quite often hidden under the heather; least infrequent in Scotland and Ireland; not in the Midlands and SE. June–August.

1069. *BIRDSNEST ORCHID** *Neottia nidus-avis* (L.) Richard Pl. 36. *CTW, 1295*
A singular plant, about a foot high, honey-coloured all over, feeding on rotting vegetation with the aid of a fungus partner; leaves very short, pale; taking its name from the fancied likeness of its cluster of roots. Flowers with a rancid sickly fragrance, not spurred, the lowest often widely spaced down the stem. Differs from the shorter and yellower Birdsnest (604), which grows in similar places, in its erect flower-spike and large hanging 2-lobed lower lip. The somewhat similar Broomrapes (733–737) have short 3-lobed lower lips and grow in the open in the roots of green plants. *Habitat:* Widespread but local in deep shade in woods, especially beechwoods, mainly in the S. June–July.

1070. *CREEPING LADY'S TRESSES** *Goodyera repens* (L.) Brown
Plate 82. *CTW, p. 1296*
A creeping Orchid, 4–9 in. high, rather like Autumn Ladies' Tresses (1065) with its spiral spike of rather unpleasant-smelling unspurred white flowers, which are shorter and fatter and have blunt sepals and petals. Leaves stalked, pointed oval, net-veined, sometimes marbled, in overwintering rosettes with a pair at the base and much smaller ones up the stems. *Habitat:* Locally frequent in pinewoods in Scotland and the Lake District, especially in the Highlands; also near Holt, Norfolk. July–August.

1071. **BOG ORCHID** *Hammarbya paludosa* (L.) Kuntze
Malaxis paludosa (L.) Swartz   Plate 83. *CTW, p. 1297*
Our smallest native Orchid, inconspicuous and usually 2–5 in. high, with two bulbous swellings at the base of the stem and neat bluntly rounded leaves, sometimes with minute bulbils on the margins. Flowers tiny, yellowish-green, with the unspurred lip twisted round to the back or top of the flower. *Habitat:* Widespread but generally rare and local in very wet moss or shallow pools in bogs and on heaths and moors; least infrequent in Scotland and the New Forest. July–Sept.

1072. **FEN ORCHID *Liparis loeselii* (L.) Richard Plate 83. *CTW, p. 1298***

Resembles the last species in having bulb-like swellings at the base of the stem, but is robuster and taller, 3–9 in. high, with an opposite pair of large broad lanceolate, rather greasily shiny yellowish-green leaves at the base of the stem, and larger yellower flowers, the sepals and petals longer and narrower, with the broad, upright lip at the top. *Habitat:* Rare in mossy fens in E Anglia, and very locally plentiful as a dwarfer plant in dune-slacks in S Wales. June–July.

1073. ****CORALROOT ORCHID *Corallorhiza trifida* Chatelin Pl. 83. *CTW, 1299***

A yellowish-green creeping leafless Orchid, 4–9 in. high, greener than our two other Orchids which feed on decayed vegetation, the Ghost (1064) and Birdsnest Orchids (1069). Flowers whitish- or greenish-yellow, the unspurred lip slightly 3-lobed and marked with red. *Habitat:* Very local in moist pinewoods and bushy dune-slacks in Scotland and extreme N England. June–July.

1074. **MUSK ORCHID *Herminium monorchis* (L.) Brown Pl. 83. *CTW, 1300***

A slender inconspicuous Orchid, usually 3–6 in. high, misleadingly named as it smells strongly of honey rather than musk. Leaves broad, blunt, yellowish-green, 2–3 close together at the base of the stem. Flowers in a dense spike, tiny, yellowish-green, the very shortly spurred lip shaped like a broad arrow. *Habitat:* Scattered but very local in chalk or limestone turf from Kent to the Cotswolds. June–July.

1075. *FROG ORCHID *Coeloglossum viride* (L.) Hartman Pl. 83. *CTW, 1301***

A rather inconspicuous Orchid, 2–10 in. high, with lanceolate leaves, broad at the base, narrower up the stem. Flowers in a short spike, yellow-green or reddish-brown, with the sepals hooded, and the very short-spurred yellow or red-brown lip strap-shaped and forked near the tip with a small tooth in the middle; lowest leaf-like bract sometimes longer than the flower. *Habitat:* Widespread but very local in chalk and limestone turf in the S, and in meadows and on mountain rock-ledges in the N and in Ireland. June–August. *Habenaria viridis* (L.) Brown.

1076. SCENTED ORCHID *Gymnadenia conopsea* (L.) Brown Pl. 32. *CTW, 1302***

An attractive Orchid about a foot high, whose very long slender spur separates it from all our other pinkish Orchids except the Pyramidal (1095). Leaves long, rather narrow, strongly keeled, unspotted, in 2 ranks up the stem. Flowers in a rather long dense spike, typically with a rather rancid-sweet fragrance, usually pale purplish-pink, with a short more or less equally 3-lobed lip. *Habitat:* Widespread and locally frequent in grassy places, especially on chalk or limestone. June–July. Fragrant Orchid; *Habenaria conopsea* (L.) Bentham.

*1076a. **Larger Scented Orchid, *G. densiflora* Wahlenberg, is usually much taller and robuster, with broader leaves and denser spikes of darker, richly clove-scented flowers, with a longer lip and unequal lobes, and blunter, usually square-tipped sepals. The robust form is local in fens, and a smaller form in damp hill pastures in the N. July–August.

1077. **SMALL WHITE ORCHID *Leucorchis albida* (L.) Schur***
Habenaria albida (L.) Brown Plate 82. *CTW, p. 1303*

A slender Orchid, 6–12 in. high, with narrow leaves up the stem and a dense spike of small fragrant hooded cream-coloured flowers, their lip short-spurred and deeply 3-lobed. *Habitat:* Local in hill pastures and on damp rock-ledges in mountain districts in the N and W; very rare elsewhere. May–June.

1078. *BUTTERFLY ORCHID   *Platanthera chlorantha* (Custer) Reichenbach
Habenaria virescens Druce   Plate 83.   *CTW, p. 1304*
One of our most graceful and attractive Orchids, usually with a single pair of
elliptical, shining, unspotted root-leaves, and much smaller, unstalked, lanceolate
stem-leaves. Flowers vanilla-scented, in a broad loose, rather pyramidal spike,
greenish-white, with an inch-long, down-curved spur, rather broader at the tip,
and an undivided strap-shaped lip (Fig.); pollen-masses diverging below (Fig.);
sepals lanceolate, nearly at right angles.   *Habitat:* Widespread but local, chiefly
in woods and pastures in the S, often on chalk or limestone. June–July.

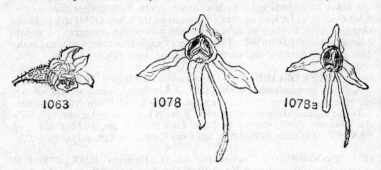

1063   1078   1078a

1078a. *Lesser Butterfly Orchid, *P. bifolia* (L.) Richard (*H. bifolia* (L.) Brown),
is usually smaller in all its parts, and has a narrower denser, more cylindrical spike of flowers with the spur slenderer and proportionately, longer; root
leaves narrower. Can always be separated from Butterfly Orchid by the closely
parallel pollen-masses (Fig.). There are two forms, a larger white-flowered one
in similar places to Butterfly Orchid, and a smaller one with shortly oval leaves
and greenish flowers on moors and in bogs. Commonest in the N.

1079. ***DENSE-FLOWERED ORCHID   *Neotinea intacta* (Link) Reichenbach
Habenaria intacta (Link) Bentham   Plate 82.   *CTW, p. 1304*
A smallish Orchid, up to a foot high, with leafy stems and short dense spikes
of flowers, which are usually greenish-white with unspotted leaves, but rarely
pinkish with spots on the leaves. Flowers have hooded sepals, a short blunt spur
and a 3-lobed lip, and soon give way to the prominent seed-capsules.   *Habitat:*
Local in rocky and sandy limestone grasslands in the Burren, rare in Cos. Mayo
and Galway. May.

1080. *BEE ORCHID   *Ophrys apifera* Hudson   Plate 34.   *CTW, p. 1306*
A most attractive Orchid, 6–12 in. high, whose swollen, unspurred flower-lip
bears a remarkable resemblance to the rear of a small bumble-bee apparently
visiting the flower; narrow oval leaves up the stem. Flowers few on a spike, with
pointed bright pink sepals, narrow square-tipped green petals, and a brown furry
lip, having a pale U surrounding a square honey-coloured patch, and an appendage which is normally tucked right under and out of sight (Fig.); pollen-masses
long-stalked. In the form known as the Wasp Orchid (*O. trollii* Hegetschwer),
found chiefly in Glos., this appendage projects straight downwards, the lip is
yellow with a broken pattern of honey-brown spots, with no U-shaped loop.

and the sepals darker. *Habitat:* Widespread but local, sometimes plentiful, in turf, mainly on chalk and limestone, thinning out northwards. June–July.

1080*a*. ***Late Spider Orchid, *O. fuciflora* (Crantz) Reichenbach, has a much larger, furrier lip, with a more elaborate pattern, turning up at the end to form a heart-shaped appendage (Fig.); petals triangular, pink, downy; pollen-masses short-stalked. Very rare in chalk turf in E Kent. June.

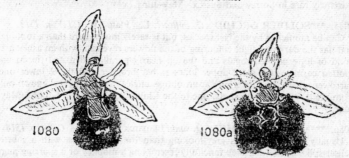

1081. **SPIDER ORCHID   *O. sphegodes* Miller   Plate 34.   *CTW, p. 1308*
Like an early flowering Bee Orchid (1080) with yellow-green sepals and petals. and no appendage at the tip of the dark brown lip, which is marked in the form of a very glossy bluish Greek pi (π). *Habitat:* Now very local in turf on chalk in Kent and Sussex and on limestone in Purbeck. March–May.

1082. *FLY ORCHID   *O. insectifera* L.   Plate 34.   *CTW, p. 1308*
Taller and much slenderer than Bee Orchid (1080), with shiny not waxy leaves, green sepals, very narrow antenna-like dark brown petals, and a blue patch across the middle of the much narrower chocolate-brown lip, which is 3-lobed, the middle lobe being forked, and not at all recurved beneath. *Habitat:* Local in scrub at the edges of woods, where it can be hard to spot in the dappled shade, on chalk and limestone in England and Wales, thinning out northwards; rare in fens in C Ireland. May–June. *O. muscifera* Hudson.

1083. ***LIZARD ORCHID   *Himantoglossum hircinum* (L.) Sprengel
Orchis hircina (L.) Crantz   Plate 65.   *CTW, p. 1309*
A singular rarity, rather stout and grey-green, 1–2 ft. high, its raggle-taggle spike of fancifully lizard-like flowers often merging into the surrounding herbage; smelling of billy goat, especially in a confined space. It has a few stem-leaves, which soon wither, and a stout spike of short-spurred, purplish grey-green flowers, with hooded sepals. The 3-lobed lip is 2 in. long, spirally coiled back in bud, white with purple spots above, grey on the twisted strap-like middle lobe. *Habitat:* Increasing but still rare in turf on chalk or limestone, and on dunes, mainly in the S half of England. June–July.

1084. **LADY ORCHID   *Orchis purpurea* Hudson   Plate 33.   *CTW, p. 1313*
A stately Orchid, 1–2½ ft. high, its individual flowers capturing the grace of a lady in a Regency flowered chintz crinoline and a purple poke-bonnet. Leaves few, thin, very large, oblong, shining green, unspotted, mostly in a rosette at the base of the stout stems. Flowers in a broad spike, each with a tiny bract, with a delicate sugary fragrance, the oval sepals blotched with deep purple-brown or

paler purple, on a green ground, and hooded over the shortly spurred lip, which is pale pink or white with tufts of crimson hairs and has normally two narrow lobes at the top broadening gradually at the base into 2 broader squarish lobes, with usually a tiny tooth in the acute angle between. In E Kent plants are usually taller with a larger looser spike. *Habitat :* Widespread and locally frequent in small colonies in sheltered scrub and woods on chalk in Kent; extremely rare in Surrey and Sussex. May–June.

1085. ***SOLDIER ORCHID *O. militaris* L. Plate 33. *CTW, p. 1313*

Can be mimicked by the last species, but is rarely much more than a foot high and has the dark and light colouring of the flowers reversed, with an ashen grey hood of long pointed sepals and the lip nearly parallel-sided and tipped and spotted carmine-red, the 2 upper lobes rather broader and the 2 lower ones narrower, oblong and diverging at an obtuse angle. *Habitat:* Now known only from chalk scrub in two spots, one in the Chilterns, and one in Suffolk. May–June.

1086. ***MONKEY ORCHID *O. simia* Lamarck Plate 33. *CTW, p. 1314*

Usually smaller and less grey-looking than the last species, with a shorter denser spike of flowers, each fancifully resembling a monkey or a sparring pugilist. Hood white, faintly streaked outside with rose or pale violet, the deeply divided, long, narrow, parallel-sided white lip forming the 'body' with raised crimson dots on the 'chest', with the very narrow 'arms' and 'legs' curled inwards, and, like the tip of the very short 'tail', crimson; spur white, sometimes pouched at the end. The only Orchid whose spike opens from the top downwards. Sometimes the plant is more pink or purple. *Habitat:* Now extremely rare in chalk turf and recently seen only in two localities in Kent and one in the Chilterns. June.

1087. **BURNT-TIP ORCHID *O. ustulata* L. Plate 33. *CTW, p. 1314*

A tiny neat replica of the Lady Orchid (1084), rarely 6 in. high, with the hoods dark maroon at first, giving the tip of the flower-spike the characteristic burnt appearance, but gradually becoming paler; leaves few, small, up the stem and near the base. Flowers heliotrope-scented, very short-spurred, the lip 4-lobed, white with a few pink dots, and no tooth in the acute angle between the broad lower lobes. *Habitat:* Local, varying greatly in quantity, in short turf on chalk or limestone, very rarely in damp meadows, in England, chiefly in the SE. May–June.

1088. *GREEN-WINGED ORCHID *O. morio* L. Plate 33. *CTW, p. 1315*

Somewhat smaller than Early Purple Orchid (1090), and distinguishable by the very dark parallel greenish veins on the purple sepals, which form a hood instead of spreading; leaves never spotted. Flowers scented, spurred, ranging in colour from deep purple through salmon-pink to white; lip widening below, with 3 short teeth and the edges turned down, but rather variable. *Habitat:* Widespread and locally frequent, sometimes abundant in rich meadows, and dry pastures and on downs, thinning out northwards and not in Scotland. May–June.

1089. ***LOOSE-FLOWERED ORCHID *O. laxiflora* Lamarck
Plate 33. *CTW, p. 1315*

Differs from the next species in having a looser spike of darker purple flowers, with a short spur and the central lobe of the lip either very small or none. Leaves unspotted; leaf-like bracts at base of flowers with 3 or more veins. *Habitat:* Moist grassy places in Jersey and Guernsey. May–June.

1090. EARLY PURPLE ORCHID *O. mascula* L. Plate 33. *CTW, p. 1316*

A frequent Orchid, a foot or so high, with long leaves, mostly at or near the base of the stem, where they are broader, usually blotched with purplish-black. Flowers in a loose spike, rather large, normally of some shade of purple but occasionally pink or white; 1 sepal and 2 petals forming a hood, the other 2 sepals erect and backing against each other; lip broad, wavy, shallowly lobed, with a small longer central lobe; spur long, usually curving upwards, as long as the ovary. Leaf-like bracts at base of flowers 1–3-veined. *Habitat:* Widespread and locally frequent in woods, often with Bluebells; less often in meadows. April–June.

1091. HEATH SPOTTED ORCHID *Dactylorchis maculata* (L.) Vermeulen
Orchis ericetorum (Linton) Marshall; *O. maculata* L. Pl. 33. *CTW, p. 1318*

A frequent, very variable Orchid, 6–12 in. high, with narrow keeled and folded leaves up the solid stem and usually spotted purplish-black. Flowers in a short broad cylindrical spike, pale pink, pale purple or white with small or coarse crimson dots or blotches; sepals spreading sideways like an alighting bird's wings; lip very broad, widened below, with a wavy edge and a narrow, very short central tooth (Fig.); spur long, slender, about equalling the ovary. Leaf-like bracts about equalling the flowers. *Habitat:* Widespread and often abundant on damp acid heaths and moors and in bogs, especially in the N, W and SE; rare in the Midlands. May–July.

1091a. Common Spotted Orchid, *D. fuchsii* (Druce) Vermeulen (*O. fuchsii* Druce) (incl. *O. okellyi* Druce), is also very variable, but usually taller and robuster, with broader basal leaves and a longer, denser, more pointed spike of sometimes darker pink flowers, the lip less wavy-edged, marked with crimson lines rather than dots, and with 3 well separated lobes, the middle one pointed and about equalling the blunter, divergent outer ones (Fig.). Frequently hybridises with the last and next species. Equally widespread, but commonest in the S and E, in a wide variety of wooded and grassy places from dry downland to marshes and fens, avoiding acid soils. June–August.

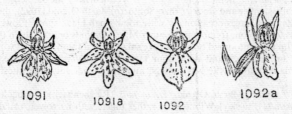

1091   1091a   1092   1092a

1092. *SOUTHERN MARSH ORCHID *D. praetermissa* (Druce) Vermeulen
Orchis praetermissa Druce (incl. *O. pardalina* Pugsley) Pl. 33. *CTW, p. 1320*

Marsh Orchids are very variable even in one small area and form fertile hybrids readily; any one specimen therefore may well be aberrant. They differ from the Spotted Orchids (1091) in having mostly hollow stems, and rather fatter flower-spikes with their leaf-like bracts broader and often purplish and longer than the flowers, whose shorter spur is usually shorter than the ovary. They also prefer much wetter places.

Southern Marsh Orchid is often suffused purple at the top of the robust 6–18-in. stem and among the bracts; leaves erect, dark green, normally unspotted, hardly hooded at the tip. Its flowers are in thick spikes, usually dark rose-purple, with sepals spread outwards and forwards like a bird's wings; lip with darker spots and streaks, broad, normally with a small central tooth, concave with the edges curled up at first, later turned down; spur stout, curved, with a blunt tip (Fig.). *Habitat:* Locally plentiful in fens, marshes, swamps, wet meadows and dune slacks in the S, very rarely in drier spots. June–July.

1092*a*. ***Early Marsh Orchid,** *D. incarnata* (L.) Vermeulen (*Orchis incarnata* L., *Orchis strictifolia* Opiz, '*Orchis latifolia*'), is slightly shorter and slimmer, with a very hollow stout green stem, and fewer erecter yellower-green unspotted leaves, keeled, markedly hooded and narrowing from the base. Flowers smaller, waxy, extremely variable in colour, most often flesh-coloured, but also of many shades of pink, rose, brick-red, mauve, purple and straw-yellow; lip with neat double loops, with a very small central tooth and looking very narrow since the sides are soon folded right back; spur straight, more tapering (Fig.). The most widespread Marsh Orchid, but local, in peaty or valley marshes and fens, and in dune slacks. May–July.

1092*b*. ***Connaught Marsh Orchid,** *D. cruenta* (Müller) Vermeulen (*O. cruenta* Müller), mostly has the leaf-like bracts, more pointed leaves (which are broadest well above the base), and sometimes the stem too, streaked or stained on both sides with dark reddish-purple. Flowers rose-purple, with a scarcely lobed, sometimes down-turned lip. At present known only from limestone marshes in Galway and Mayo.

1092*c*. ***Pugsley's Marsh Orchid,** *D. traunsteineri* (Sauter) Vermeulen, is rather slender, with a less hollow stem; fewer long, very narrow blunt, usually spotted leaves; and somewhat looser, very few-flowered spikes, the larger flowers with a less broad-based lip, slightly folded back at the sides, 3-lobed with a larger central lobe, and large, intensely dark purple markings. Widespread but rare in rich fens. May–June. *O. traunsteinerioides* (Pugsley) Pugsley.

1093. **NORTHERN MARSH ORCHID *D. purpurella* (Stephenson)

Orchis purpurella Stephenson   Vermeulen Plate 33. *CTW, p. 1320*

Generally smaller and stockier than Southern Marsh Orchid (1092), the darker green, less erect leaves occasionally with a few small black spots. Flowers more vinaceous, of a colour found among other Marsh Orchids only rarely in the Early (1092*a*); lip flat, untoothed or with a very small central tooth, marked with heavy irregular broken lines and dots; spur tapering. *Habitat:* Locally frequent in wet and damp grass in the NW and N, and in Ireland. July, the latest Marsh Orchid.

1093*a*. ***Irish Marsh Orchid,** *D. majalis* (Reichenbach) Vermeulen (incl. *O. occidentalis* (Pugsley) Wilmott), is rather taller, with narrower, usually well-spotted leaves and larger paler flowers with a broad, more 3-lobed lip and a curved cylindrical spur. Frequent in W Ireland, occasional in W Scotland. May–June.

1094. **MAN ORCHID *Aceras anthropophorum* (L.) Smith Pl. 58. *CTW, 1323*

The only Orchid with a marionette-like lip which has yellow or brown-lipped flowers; stems up to a foot or so high, with a few small leaves, the rest at the base, unspotted. Flowers in a long, rather narrow spike, yellow-green or brownish-red, not spurred, with the sometimes chocolate-edged lip deeply lobed to make the straight 'arms' of varying length, the straight 'legs' and the 'body' of the flat-helmeted 'man'. *Habitat:* Very local in pastures, scrub and old quarries, on chalk or limestone in the S; locally plentiful in Kent and Surrey. June.

1095. *PYRAMIDAL ORCHID *Anacamptis pyramidalis* (L.) Richard
Orchis pyramidalis L.   Plate 32. *CTW, p. 1324*

A 6–12-in. high Orchid with a few narrow unspotted leaves up the stem and a dense pyramidal or dome-shaped spike of often foxy-smelling, deep pink flowers, with hooding sepals, an equally deeply 3-lobed lip with 2 ridges at the base, and a very long slender curved spur that separates it from all our pinkish Orchids except Scented Orchid (1076). *Habitat:* Widespread and locally frequent in dry pastures and sand-dunes, preferring chalk or limestone, thinning out northwards. July–August, later than the Scented Orchid.

ARUM FAMILY Araceae

1096. **SWEET FLAG *Acorus calamus* L.   Plate 106. *CTW, p. 1326*

A fairly stout hairless aquatic perennial, 2–3 ft. high, smelling of tangerines when crushed, with long, flat, sword-like leaves, somewhat resembling Yellow Flag (1050), but with the thicker midrib often not central and one or both edges crinkled. (Beware occasional leaves of Great Water Grass (1172) similarly crinkled towards the tip.) Flowers tiny, green, densely packed in a stout spike projecting upwards three-quarters of the way up the stem; a shy flowerer. *Habitat:* Widespread but local by fresh water, and mainly in the S. June–July.

1097. LORDS AND LADIES *Arum maculatum* L.   Plate 35.   *CTW, p. 1327*

A low hairless perennial, with large stalked, dark green, bluntly arrow-shaped glossy net-veined root-leaves, often spotted with purplish black, appearing in January. Flowers tiny, the male above the female, in dense whorls around the base of a cylindrical club-shaped organ, the spadix, of which the naked upper part is usually purple, and backed by a broad, pointed, pale green hood, whose lower part encloses and conceals the flowers. The hood withers before the appearance of the conspicuous spike of poisonous orange-red berries. *Habitat:* Widespread and common in hedgerows and copses, thinning out northwards. April–May. Cuckoo Pint.

1097a. ****Large Cuckoo Pint,** *A. neglectum* (Townsend) Ridley ('*A. italicum* '), has much larger, more triangular leaves, which are well developed long before Christmas, with rather creamy veins. Spadix always yellow, tip of larger hood sometimes drooping. Very local in lighter shade, nearly always near the sea, from W Sussex to Glamorgan and the Isle of Man; most frequent in the extreme SW. May–June, a month later than Lords and Ladies.

DUCKWEED FAMILY Lemnaceae

TINY OR MINUTE floating aquatics, slightly submerged or on the surface, with roots hanging from the fronds (except for Least Duckweed (1102)), no stems or apparent leaves, and minute greenish flowers, which are very rarely observed in Britain, 2 male and 1 female separate flowers together in a sheath. They grow in still or stagnant water, often making an uninterrupted sheet of green on the surface, which is relished by ducks; two or more species often grow together.

1098. *GREAT DUCKWEED *Lemna polyrhiza* L.   Plate 104.   *CTW, p. 1328*
Floats on the surface, and has roundish 5–11-veined fronds up to ¼-in. across, often purplish beneath, with a tuft of several roots up to an inch long. *Habitat:* Widespread but local, and thinning out northwards. July.

1099. *IVY DUCKWEED *L. trisulca* L.   Plate 104.   *CTW, p. 1329*
A distinctive Duckweed which often floats just under the surface of the water, with translucent lanceolate fronds up to ½-in. long, each with one short root, narrowed to a stalk, several at right angles to each other, apparently forming one branched plant. *Habitat:* Widespread, local, thinning out northwards. May–July.

1100. COMMON DUCKWEED *L. minor* L.   Plate 104.   *CTW, p. 1329*
Much the commonest Duckweed, with tiny rounded 1–5-veined fronds, up to ⅛-in. across, flat on both sides and floating on the surface; 1 root, about ⅛-in. long, from each leaf. *Habitat:* Widespread and frequent. June–July.

1101. *FAT DUCKWEED *L. gibba* L.   Plate 104.   *CTW, p. 1329*
Larger than the last species, and has the fronds markedly swollen, convex and spongy beneath, with one root on each. *Habitat:* Widespread but much more local, especially in Scotland and Ireland. June–July.

1102. **LEAST DUCKWEED *Wolffia arrhiza* (L.) Wimmer Pl. 104.   *CTW, 1330*
Our smallest 'flowering' plant, with tiny, rootless egg-shaped fronds the size of this 'o', which feel like lumps of grit when rolled between the fingers, and appear like minute dots among the fronds of other Duckweeds. Flowers never recorded in Britain. *Habitat:* Very local in the S. *Lemna arrhiza* L.

BUR-REED FAMILY Sparganiaceae

1103. BRANCHED BUR-REED *Sparganium erectum* L.
S. ramosum Hudson; (incl. *S. neglectum* Beeby)   Plate 103.   *CTW, p. 1331*
A hairless aquatic perennial with stiff solid stems 1–2 ft. high, and long stiff erect iris-like leaves, 3-sided especially towards the sheathing base, the long veins translucent with no dark border, the cross-veins indistinct; floating leaves rare. Flowers small, greenish in unstalked round heads, arranged in leafy branched spikes, the many male, yellow with soon-fading anthers, above the fewer female, which swell into bur-like heads of conspicuously beaked fruits. *Habitat:* Widespread and common by fresh water. June–August.

1104. *SMALL BUR-REED *S. simplex* Withering Plate 103.   *CTW, p. 1331*
Rather smaller than 1103, with generally narrower, sometimes floating leaves keeled below, whose translucent long veins have a dark green border, and conspicuous cross-veins. Flower-heads fewer in an unbranched spike, the lower female flowers usually stalked. Fruits slenderer, short-stalked with a longer beak. *Habitat:* Widespread and fairly frequent in and by fresh water. June–August.

1104a. **Floating Bur-reed, *S. angustifolium* Michaux (*S. affine* Schnizlein), is normally floating, with all stems long, weak and flexible; narrower grass-like leaves, flat or rounded on the back at the base, with inflated sheaths; and fewer flower-heads. Mainly in peaty pools in N and W hill districts, and in Ireland.

1104b. **Least Bur-reed, *S. minimum* Walbroth, is distinctly smaller and yellower-green than Floating Bur-reed, with flat, very narrow thinner, often floating leaves, the sheaths not inflated; and very few flower-heads, only one usually male. Fruits unstalked, egg-shaped, with a shorter beak. Widespread but uncommon in and by still peaty water.

REEDMACE FAMILY Typhaceae

1105. FALSE BULRUSH *Typha latifolia* L. Plate 35. *CTW, p. 1333*

A familiar tall aquatic perennial, which ever since Alma-Tadema painted it surrounding the infant Moses in his basket has usurped the name of Bulrush from *Scirpus lacustris* (1117). Leaves long, 1–1½-in wide, stiff, greyish, fleshy, overtopping the dense, sausage-shaped chocolate-brown spike, 4–6 in. long, of small close-set female flowers, immediately below the fluffy golden male ones, which soon wither with their stalk. Fruits cotton-tufted. *Habitat:* Widespread and common in swamps and by fresh water, often filling up small ponds; thinning out northwards. June–August. Great Reedmace.

1106. *LESSER BULRUSH *T. angustifolia* L. Plate 35. *CTW, p. 1333*

Has much narrower, paler green leaves, ½–¾-in. wide, than the last species, and a slenderer, paler brown milk-chocolate female flower-spike, separated from the male flowers by a gap. *Habitat:* Widespread but local, in similar places, especially near the sea. June–August. Lesser Reedmace.

SEDGE FAMILY Cyperaceae

UNBRANCHED GRASS-LIKE or rush-like perennials, very rarely annuals, with unstalked leaves usually linear but sometimes reduced to sheaths. Flowers minute, generally grouped in spikelets, with the petals and sepals reduced to bristles, and often with a scale-like bract (glume) at their base. Several spikelets may form a flower-head. The anthers often hang out as tufts of bright yellow. Fruit a nutlet. Members of the Sedge Family differ from Rushes and Woodrushes in having no petals or sepals in their flowers, which are often separately male and female. From Grasses they can be told by the stems being often 3-sided and never hollow; the leaves not being jointed at their junction on the stem (where there are therefore no knots) with their sheaths, which are usually closed.

KEY TO RUSH-LIKE SEDGES (Nos. 1107–1126; '11' omitted)

PLANT *creeping* 07, 10, 12, 13, 14, 16, 17, 30, 24, 25; *tufted* 08, 09, 11, 15, 18, 26; *floating* 19; *with small white tubes* 10a; *over 6 ft. high* 17, 25; *under 6 in. high* 10, 18, 19, 21, 26.

STEMS *3-sided* 07a, 14, 20, 21, 24, 25; *sharply 3-angled* 13, 17ab; *4-angled* 10.

LEAVES *apparently none* 09, 10, 11, 12, 15, 17, 22; *saw-edged* 25.

FLOWER-HEADS *large* 13, 14, 15, 20, 25; *roundish* 13, 15; *with solitary spikelets* 08, 09, 10, 11, 12, 16, 18, 19, 22, 24, 26; *shorter than leaf-like bract* 13, 14, 15, 17ab, 18, 20, 21, 22, 23, 24, 25; *equalling leaf-like bract* 07, 16; *longer than leaf-like bract* 07, 14, 17, 19; *with no leaf-like bract* 08, 10, 11, 12, 19, 26.

FRUITS *cottony* 07, 08.

HABITAT *in water* 07, 12, 13, 17, 19, 20; *in drier places* 08, 09, 15.

1107. COMMON COTTON-GRASS *Eriophorum angustifolium* Honckeny
Bog Cotton; *E. polystachion* L. Plate 115. *CTW, p. 1336*

A low, often gregarious perennial, 6–18 in. high, dark or often purplish-green, with young stems round, and grooved grass-like linear leaves narrowed to a long 3-sided point, the topmost with a short ligule. Flowers small, brownish green with yellow anthers, in a terminal cluster of several nodding egg-shaped heads, which later look totally different when they develop the very conspicuous long white cottony threads on the fruits; spikelet-stalks smooth, almost hairless. *Habitat:* Widespread and common in swamps and bogs; mostly on acid soils, often whitening the ground; more local in the S. April–May.

1107*a*. ***Slender Cotton-grass**, *E. gracile* Roth, is much slenderer and has narrower leaves 3-sided throughout; downy spikelet-stalks; and always very short 'cotton'. Very rare in very wet bogs in S England.

1107*b*. **Broad-leaved Cotton-grass**, *E. latifolium* Hoppe, is tufted, with stems 3-sided above; shorter broader flat, pale green leaves, the uppermost with no ligule; and rough stalks to the spikelets, which have shorter 'cotton' in fruit. More local, in fens and marshes on chalk or limestone, never in acid bogs.

1108. HARESTAIL   *E. vaginatum* L.   Plate 115.   *CTW, p. 1338*

Differs from Common Cotton-grass (1107) in being tussocky, and having much narrower root-leaves and a flower-spike of only a single egg-shaped erect head, making a pale yellow tuft in flower and a white one in fruit. The stem-leaves are short, broad and pale and form inflated sheaths to the stem. *Habitat:* Widespread and locally abundant on wet heaths and moors and in bogs, but now very local and scarce in the S. April–May.

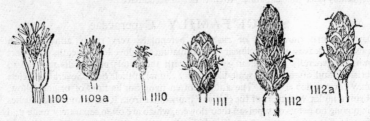

1109   1109a   1110   1111   1112   1112a

1109. DEER-GRASS   *Scirpus cespitosus* L.   Plate 116.   *CTW, p. 1339*

A densely tufted, sometimes gregarious perennial, with faintly ridged round wiry stems up to a foot high, somewhat resembling the shorter, more chocolate Few-flowered Spike-rush, but always distinguishable by the short blade of the topmost of the several pointed sheaths at the base of the stem, which are all that remains of the leaves. Flowers in a very small narrow, pale brown terminal head, with the lowest pointed ribbed green glume as long as the rest of the head (Fig.). *Habitat:* Widespread and often abundant over vast areas of peaty bog and moorland in the N and W and in Ireland, thinning out on wet heaths in the S and E. May–June. *Trichophorum cespitosum* (L.) Hartman. Figs. × 2.

1109*a*. **Few-flowered Spike-rush**, *Eleocharis quinqueflora* (Hartmann) Schwartz (*Scirpus pauciflorus* Lightfoot), is smaller and less tufted, and has the topmost sheath almost square with no blade and all the pale brown glumes pointed, the lowest fertile, long-pointed and nearly as long as the spikelet, which it encircles at the base (Fig.). Widespread but local mainly in the N, in open marshes and fens. June–July. *Eleocharis pauciflora* (Lightfoot) Link.

1110. **NEEDLE SPIKE-RUSH   *Eleocharis acicularis* (L.) Roemer & Schultes
Scirpus acicularis L.   Plate 116.   *CTW, p. 1341*

A very slender, creeping, often lawn-forming, bright green perennial, 2–4 in. high but taller in water, with thread-like 4-angled stems; sheaths brown, the top one pointed; and the glumes blunt and brownish, the lowest at least half as long

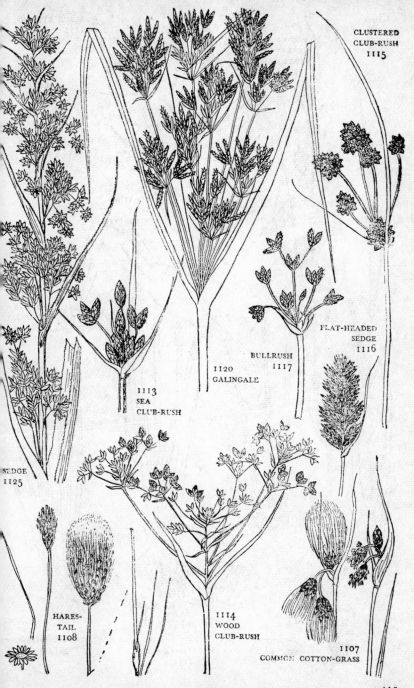

CLUSTERED
CLUB-RUSH
1115

FLAT-HEADED
SEDGE
1116

BULLRUSH
1117

1120
GALINGALE

1113
SEA
CLUB-RUSH

SEDGE
1125

HARES-
TAIL
1108

1114
WOOD
CLUB-RUSH

1107
COMMON COTTON-GRASS

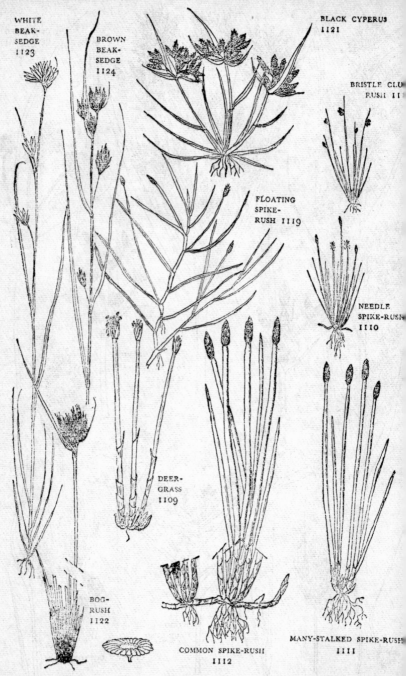

WHITE
BEAK-
SEDGE
1123

BROWN
BEAK-
SEDGE
1124

BLACK CYPERUS
1121

BRISTLE CLU
RUSH 11

FLOATING
SPIKE-
RUSH 1119

NEEDLE
SPIKE-RUSH
1110

DEER-
GRASS
1109

BOG-
RUSH
1122

COMMON SPIKE-RUSH
1112

MANY-STALKED SPIKE-RUSH
1111

116

as the whole brown spikelet (Fig., p. 230). *Habitat:* Widespread but local in and by ponds. August onwards.

1110*a*. ***Estuarine Spike-rush,** *E. parvula* (R. & S.), Bluff, Nees & Schauer, is smaller, with fatter fleshier, darker green round stems; tiny white tubers on the whitish runners; very narrow leaves, the uppermost sheath leafless and greenish glumes. Very rare in muddy places near the sea, mostly estuaries, in SW England, N Wales, and SE and W Ireland. *S. parvulus* R. & S.

1111. *MANY-STALKED SPIKE-RUSH   *E. multicaulis* (Smith) Smith
Scirpus multicaulis Smith   Plate 116.   *CTW, p. 1342*
Thinner and never so large as Common Spike-Rush (1112), and always tufted and without a creeping rootstock, with the topmost sheath obliquely pointed and all the glumes blunt, a short empty one at the base of the spikelet; stigmas 3. (Fig., p. 230). *Habitat:* Widespread but local in pools of wet acid bogs, mainly in the S and W. July–August.

1112. COMMON SPIKE-RUSH   *E. palustris* (L.) Roemer & Schultes
Scirpus palustris L.   Plate 116.   *CTW, p. 1342*
Much the most frequent Spike-rush, a hairless perennial, usually 6–18 in. high, with a creeping rootstock: leaves reduced to sheaths at the base of the soft, rather swollen rush-like stems, the topmost sheath blunt, not ending obliquely. Flowers in small terminal spikelets, with all glumes blunt, the two empty ones at the base being short and not more than half encircling the bottom of the spikelet; stigmas 2 (Fig., p. 230). *Habitat:* Widespread and frequent in fresh-water wet places. May–July.

1112*a*. **Slender Spike-rush,** *E. uniglumis* (Link) Schultes, is slenderer and has only 1 empty glume at the base of and more or less encircling the spikelet (Fig.). Local in brackish or fenny meadows, mainly near the sea in the S.

1113. SEA CLUB-RUSH   *Scirpus maritimus* L.   Plate 115.   *CTW, p. 1343*
A stout hairless, bulrush-like perennial, 2–3 ft. high, with sharply 3-angled stems roughish towards the top, and flat keeled coarse grasslike leaves rough on the edges. Flower-spikelets dark brown, narrow egg-shaped, $\frac{1}{2}$–1 in. long, in a terminal, sometimes stalked cluster, overtopped by the long narrow leaf-like bracts. *Habitat:* Widespread, locally common in ditches near sea. July–Aug.

1114. *WOOD CLUB-RUSH   *S. sylvaticus* L.   Plate 115.   *CTW, p. 1344*
A stout hairless rush-like perennial, 1–3 ft. high, with creeping roots, sometimes mistaken for the hairy Great Wood-rush (1037) or the rare, reddish Galingale (1120). Stems 3-sided, smooth; leaves long, flat, grass-like, not keeled, roughish on the edges and midrib when rubbed downwards. Flower-head very large and somewhat rush-like, much branched, with numerous long-stalked clusters of olive-brown flower-spikelets, scarcely overtopped by the narrow leaf-like bracts. *Habitat:* Widespread but local in marshy woods and shady ditches. June–July.

1115. ***CLUSTERED CLUB-RUSH   *S. holoschoenus* L.
Holoschoenus vulgaris Link   Plate 115.   *CTW, p. 1344*
A stout densely tufted, hairless, rush-like perennial, with rigid smooth rounded stems 3–4 ft. high, continuing as a thin bract overtopping the cluster of stalked, globular, pale brown flower-heads. Leaves few, small, channelled, near the base of the stem, often reduced to sheaths only. *Habitat:* Plentiful in dune-slacks on Braunton Burrows; very rare in Somerset; also at Barry Docks. Aug.–Sept.

1116. *FLAT-HEADED SEDGE   *Blysmus compressus* (L.) Link
                                         Plate 115.   *CTW, p. 1345*
  A hairless perennial, 6–10 in. high, with smooth, rounded, leafy stems longer
than the flat keeled rough-edged grass-like leaves. Flower-spikelets bright
reddish-brown, in two opposite rows in a flat spike, with a leaf-like bract. *Habitat:*
Local in lime-rich fens and wet meadows in England, N Wales and S Scotland.
June–July.
  *1116a. *Chestnut Sedge, B. rufus* (Hudson) Link, has rush-like leaves with
inrolled edges, and dark brown flowers in a much smaller spike as long as the
bract. Widespread but local in grassy salt-marshes in Scotland; rare further S.

1117. BULRUSH   *Scirpus lacustris* L.   Plate 115.   *CTW, p. 1347*
  A tall stout hairless perennial, 3–8 ft. high, with soft rounded green rush-like
stems up to ¾-in. across that are still used for basket-making; usually leafless but
sometimes with strap-shaped floating or submerged leaves. Flower-spikelets
reddish-brown, egg-shaped, unequally stalked, in terminal clusters usually overtopping the leaf-like bract; stigmas normally 3, anthers bearded, scale-like glume
at base of each flower broad, blunt, smooth. *Habitat:* Widespread and often
common in rivers and round lakes. June–July. *Schoenoplectus lacustris* (L.) Palla.
  *1117a. ***Triangular Bulrush, S. triquetrus* L. (*Sch. triquetrus* (L.) Palla), is
shorter and has strongly triangular greyer stems, a short leaf-blade on the topmost sheath at the base of the stem, and the bract much longer than the flower-
cluster; stigmas 2. In muddy estuaries of the Tamar and Shannon. Aug.–Sept.
  *1117a × 1117c. ***S. × arunensis* Druce is in the Rivers Medway, Arun and
Tamar, persisting in the two former despite the extinction of one parent.
  *1117b. ***Sharp Bulrush, S. americanus* Persoon (*Sch. americanus* (Pers.)
Volkart), is smaller than Triangular Bulrush and has 2–3 narrow leaves, flower-
heads of a very few unstalked spikelets, and glumes with pointed lobes. Only in
dune-slacks in Lancashire and by St. Ouen's Pond in Jersey. June–July.
  *1117c. *Greyish Bulrush, Sch. tabernaemontani* Gmelin (*S. tabernaemontani*
(Gm.) Palla), is shorter and slenderer than Bulrush and has greyish stems, leaves
never floating, flower-heads usually compacter, stigmas usually 2, anthers not
bearded, and glumes covered with raised dots. Widespread and quite frequent in
ditches and by rivers near the sea; rare inland.

1118. *BRISTLE CLUB-RUSH   *S. setaceus* L.   Plate 116.   *CTW, p. 1348*
  A low, very slender tufted plant, 1–4 in. high, with very fine wiry stems continuing as a bract overtopping the 1–3 small, egg-shaped, brown and green
flower-spikelets, which thus appear to be on the side of the stem. Leaves few,
thread-like, grooved. Nutlets ribbed, shiny. *Habitat:* Widespread but local in
open moist places. May–July. *Isolepis setacea* (L.) Brown.
  *1118a. **Small Bristle Club-rush, S. cernuus* Vahl (*I. cernua* (Vahl) Roemer &
Schultes), is still slenderer, with the terminal bract hardly overtopping the
usually solitary spikelet and the nutlets smooth and matt. More local, mainly in
sandy or peaty places, especially near the sea in the S and W.

1119. *FLOATING SPIKE-RUSH   *S. fluitans* L.   Plate 116.   *CTW, p. 1349*
  A fresh green aquatic perennial, often floating in mats, with flattened branched
leafy stems and short narrow spreading, very pale green grass-like leaves, which
might be taken for those of a miniature Pondweed. Flower-spikelets solitary,
terminal, brown, somewhat resembling Common Spike-rush (1112), projecting

above the water. *Habitat:* Widespread but local in still waters and slow streams, on acid soils. May–July. *Eleogiton fluitans* (L.) Link.

1120. °*GALINGALE *Cyperus longus* L. Plate 115. *CTW, p. 1350*
A gregarious hairless perennial, 3–4 ft. high, with smooth 3-sided leafy stems and rough-edged glossy arching grass-like leaves ½-in. broad. Flower-spikelets red-brown, flat, the flowers arranged in two opposite ranks, in large forked clusters which form a loose and graceful spray, well overtopped by the long leaf-like bracts. Sometimes confused with Wood Club-rush (1114) which has olive-brown glumes arranged spirally in cylindrical spikelets. *Habitat:* Rare in moist places in the S, chiefly in the SW; frequent in the Channel Is. September.

1121. **BLACK CYPERUS *C. fuscus* L. Plate 116. *CTW, p. 1350*
A low hairless annual, varying in size and lushness, with smooth 3-sided stems longer than the narrow grass-like leaves. Flower-spikelets dark brown, the flowers arranged in two opposite ranks, in a closely fingered terminal head, overtopped by the leaf-like bracts. *Habitat:* Very rare by a few muddy ponds in S England, much increasing there in dry seasons. July–September.

1122. *BOG-RUSH *Schoenus nigricans* L. Plate 116. *CTW, p. 1351*
A hairless, densely tufted sedge-like perennial, 1–2 ft. high, with rigid smooth rounded stems, overtopping the wiry half-cylindrical leaves with inrolled margins and glossy black sheathing bases. Flower-spikelets blackish-brown, in a V-shaped head, shorter than the dark broad-based rigid pointed leaf-like bracts at the side, which partially enclose their base. *Habitat:* Widespread but local in fens on chalk or limestone, and in less acid bogs. May–July.

1123. *WHITE BEAK-SEDGE *Rhynchospora alba* (L.) Vahl Pl. 116. *CTW, 1352*
A slender hairless sedge-like perennial, up to a foot high, with thin rounded stems sometimes 3-sided at the top and longer than the narrow, grooved rough-edged, pale green leaves. Flower-spikelets small, paper-white, later pale red-brown, in a small flat-topped terminal V-shaped cluster as long as or longer than the leaf-like bract. *Habitat:* Widespread, local in and by bog pools. June–Sept.

1124. **BROWN BEAK-SEDGE *R. fusca* (L.) Aiton Pl. 116. *CTW, p. 1352*
Rather stockier than the last species, and with a shortly creeping rootstock, shorter leaves, and larger longer chestnut-brown flower-heads much overtopped by the long bracts. *Habitat:* Very local on wet heaths and in bog pools, mainly in the SW; widespread and commoner in W Ireland. May–July.

1125. *SEDGE *Cladium mariscus* (L.) Pohl Plate 115. *CTW, p. 1353*
A fine stout perennial, 6 ft. or so tall, still cut for litter in E Anglia, with hollow leafy stems, and long thick greyish evergreen leaves nearly an inch across at the base, keeled, very sharply saw-edged and ending in a sharp triangular spine. Flower-spikelets glossy reddish-brown, in richly branched clusters at the base of the long leaf-like bracts, and in an open terminal spray. *Habitat:* Locally abundant and forming dense beds in fens in E Anglia and W Ireland; widespread but rare elsewhere. July–August.

1126. ***FALSE SEDGE *Kobresia simpliciuscula* (Wahlenberg) Mackenzie
   K. caricina Willdenow   Plate 117. *CTW, p. 1354*
A low hairless sedge-like perennial, 3–4 in. high, with stiff, 3-sided stems longer than the tuft of narrow leaves. Flower-spikelets dark brown in a short terminal

spindle-shaped head, the male flowers above the female, which (unlike all *Carex*) have their nuts only partly enveloped by one of the two scale-like glumes at their base. *Habitat:* Rare on damp limestone mountain moors in N England and the C Highlands. June–July.

SEDGES *Carex*

UNBRANCHED, USUALLY HAIRLESS perennials, with solid, usually leafy stems and grass-like leaves, usually keeled beneath and channelled above; differing from Grasses in having the flowers arranged all round their stalk instead of in opposite rows, and the male and female flowers always distinct and often in separate spikes but always on the same plant, except in Separate-headed Sedge (1166). Most have 3 stigmas; in flower the yellow anthers are conspicuous; bracts at the base of and usually exceeding each flower-spike may be leaf-like or bristle-like. The fruits, whose nutlets are wholly encased in a little sac, are essential for identification in many species. Those from the middle of spikes are most typical.

N.B. 'Spike' in *Carex* = 'Spikelet' in other Cyperaceae.

Sedges can be divided into three main groups:

1. Those with male and female flowers in separate dissimilar stalked or unstalked spikes on the same stem (1127–51), the male at the top.
2. Those with male and female flowers together in the same spike, several such usually grouped in a single head; male usually at the top (1152–1162).
3. Those with a solitary terminal spike, usually containing both male and female flowers (1163–1166).

Beware, however, plants with the male or female spikes missing, or with an odd flower or two of the wrong sex at the top or bottom of a spike.

KEY TO TRUE SEDGES

(Nos. 1127–1166; see also Key to Rush-like Sedges, p. 229) ('11' omitted)

I. **Male and Female Flowers** usually wholly *on Separate Dissimilar Spikes* on the same stem, one or more terminal spikes usually wholly male (1127–1151).

PLANT *prostrate* 28, 29, 38, 44, 47; *6 in. or under* 28, 29, 31, 34, 37, 38, 39, 40, 41, 42, 44, 45, 46, 47, 48, 49, 50, 51*d*; *3 ft. or over* 32, 35, 36, 51; *tussocky* 51*a*.

STEMS *short and curved* 28, 29, 39*a*, 44, 48; *long and arching* 27, 30, 32, 36; *shorter than leaves* 28*c*, 28*d*, 32, 33, 35, 45, 46, 47, 51; *sharply triangular* 32, 33*a*, 33*b*, 35, 36, 51; *rough at least at top* 27*a*, 27*b*, 27*c*, 27*d*, 28, 32, 33, 34, 35, 37, 38, 40, 42, 43, 44, 45, 46, 47, 48, 49, 50, 51; *smooth* 27, 28, 29, 30, 31, 33, 36, 39, 41, 42, 43, 45, 47, 48, 49.

LEAVES *hairy or downy* 37, 42, 46, 48; *broad* 27*a*, 31*a*, 32, 35, 36; *very narrow* 38, 40, 43.

LOWEST BRACT *leaf-like, shorter than top spike* 27, 30, 31, 33*b*, 34, 36, 38, 39, 40, 41, 42, 44, 45, 51; *bristle-like* 45, 46, 49*ab*; *sheath-like* 47, 48; *chaffy or none* 45*a*, 46, 47, 48, 49*b*.

FLOWER-SPIKES *female all stalked* 27, 28, 29, 30, 31, 32, 33, 34, 35, 37, 38, 39, 40, 41, 42, 43, 45, 47, 48, 49, 50, 51; *female all unstalked* 28, 29, 35, 36, 43, 44, 45, 46, 51; *lower nodding* 27, 30, 31, 32, 33, 35, 36, 40, 41, 49, 51*a*; *all clustered at the top of stem* 28, 29, 31, 32, 37, 44, 45, 46, 48, 49, 50, 51; *male inconspicuous, overtopped by females* 31, 37, 48, 49*b* (cf. 40*a*); *top one male at base only* 49, 50 (cf. 31, 37, 38; *beware others with male spike missing*); *solitary female near base of stem* 27, 28, 31, 34, 39, 42; *2 or more male* 27*a*, 33, 34, 35, 41, 42, 43, 51; *females long and thin* 27, 30, 36; *females long and fat* 32, 33, 35, 41, 42, 43; *stigmas two…*33*b*, 34, 35, 49*b*, 51.

FRUITS *downy* 38, 42, 43, 44, 45, 46, 47, 48, 50; *long-beaked* 27, 28, **30**, **31**, 32, 33, 35, 42; *virtually unbeaked* 28e, 37, 38, 39, 40, 41, 44, 45, 46, 47, 48, 49a, 51.
HABITAT *mountains only* 33b, 34, 39a, 40, 49, 50, 51d.

II. Male and Female Flowers more or less *Mixed in Similar*, usually *Close-clustered Spikes* (all with 2 stigmas and hairless beaked fruits). (1152–1162 (cf. 08, 16, 22, 24, 49, 50)).

PLANT *far creeping* 54, 55; *prostrate* 54, 55, 59, 60, 61, 62; *6 in. or under* 54, 59, 62; *3 ft. or over and tussocky* 52.
STEMS *curved* 54, 55, 62; *shorter than leaves* 54, 55; *sharply triangular* 52, 53, 54; *round* 55; *rough at least at top* 52–54, 56–62; *smooth* 55, 59.
LEAVES *smooth* 55; *broader* 52, 53; *very narrow* 52a, 52b, 54, 58.
LOWEST BRACT *leaf-like* 54ab, 60; *bristle-like, no shorter than whole spike* 53, 54b, 56, 62; *bristle-like, shorter than whole spike* 52, 53, 54, 55, 56, 57, 59; *none or chaffy* 52, 55, 58, 61, 62.
FLOWER-SPIKES *in close heads* 52, 53, 54, 55, 57, 58, 59, 62; *in branched heads* 52, 53, 54, 56, 57, 58; *in very small head* 55a; *markedly spaced down stem* 56, 60; *male at base* 58, 59, 60, 61, 62 (cf. 49, 50); *male in middle* 54a; *male at top* 52, 53, 54, 55, 56, 57.

III. Small Plants with Solitary Spikelets (leaves all narrow, fruits all hairless) (1163–1166; cf. 09, 10, 11, 12, 16, 18, 19, 22, 24, 54, 55).
STEMS *rough at top*; *smooth* 65, 66.   LEAVES *all smooth* 66; *curled* 63.
FLOWER-SPIKES *male above, female below* 63, 64, 65; *male and female on different plants* 66; *slender and compact* 63, 64, 66; *broader and open* 64, 65; *stigmas two* 65, 66; *stigmas three* 63, 64.   FRUITS *unbeaked* 63; *spreading* 64, 65.

1127. MOOR SEDGE *Carex binervis* Smith   Plate 120.   *CTW, p. 1370*
A slender tufted Sedge, 1–2 ft. high, with brownish-green leaves shorter than the smooth 3-sided stems, and a very short blunt ligule. Flower-spikes stalked, long and thin, the top one male and silvery-black with 2–3 spindle-shaped, scarcely drooping female ones spaced out below it and shorter than their leaf-like bracts; female glume blunt with a sharp projecting point, dark purplish-brown with a bright green midrib. Fruits pear-shaped, flattened, long-beaked, brownish-green, with 2 prominent dark green ribs (Fig.). *Habitat:* Widespread and locally common on heaths, moors and rough grassy places on acid soils. June.

1127a. **Smooth Sedge, *C. laevigata* Smith (*C. helodes* Link) (*CTW, p. 1368*), is taller and tufted, with stems rough at the top; softer broader, pale green leaves; a longer, more pointed ligule; 1–2 yellow-brown male and 2–4 longer drooping yellow-green female spikes; and female glumes sharply taper-pointed. Fruits green, spindle-shaped, with a long beak (Fig.). Local in marshes and boggy woods, usually on acid soils.

1127b. *Distant Sedge, *C. distans* L.   (*CTW, p. 1369*), is tufted and has almost flat shiny greyish-green leaves with a triangular ligule; female glumes dark reddish-brown or greenish-brown with a pale green midrib, tapering to a projecting nerve; and fruits many-ribbed with a tapering beak (Fig.). Local in fens and brackish marshes, mainly near the coast.

1127c. **Dotted Sedge, *C. punctata* Gaudin, is rather smaller and paler than Distant Sedge, with leaves nearly all basal; a short, very blunt ligule; the lowest bract sometimes overtopping the top spike; female glumes shorter, very pale yellow-brown; and fruits more spreading, pale green, shining, more minutely

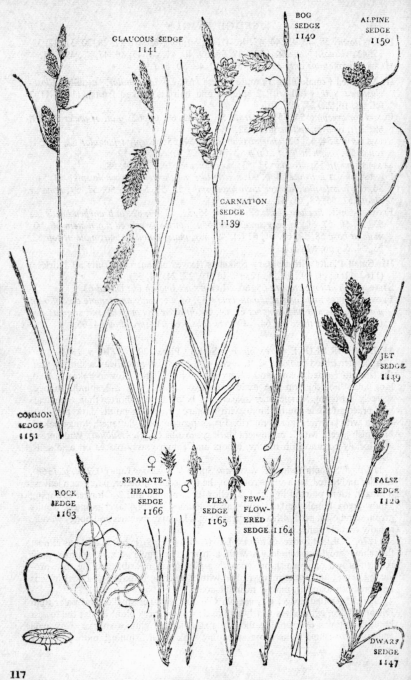

GLAUCOUS SEDGE
1141

BOG
SEDGE
1140

ALPINE
SEDGE
1150

CARNATION
SEDGE
1139

COMMON
SEDGE
1151

JET
SEDGE
1149

ROCK
SEDGE
1163

♀

SEPARATE-
HEADED
SEDGE
1166

♂

FLEA
SEDGE
1165

FEW-
FLOW-
ERED
SEDGE 1164

FALSE
SEDGE
1128

DWARF
SEDGE
1147

117

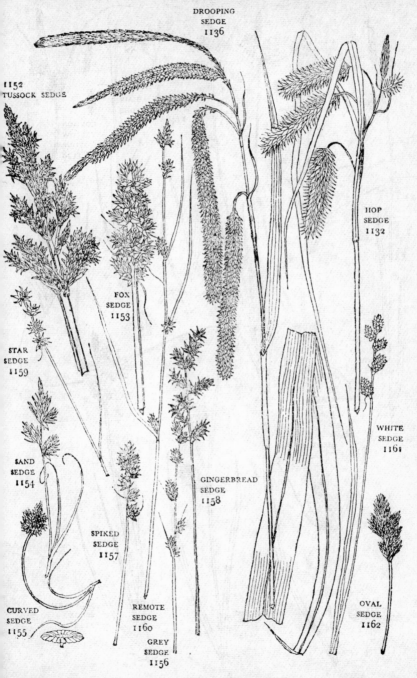

DROOPING
SEDGE
1136

1152
TUSSOCK SEDGE

HOP
SEDGE
1132

FOX
SEDGE
1153

STAR
SEDGE
1159

SAND
SEDGE
1154

GINGERBREAD
SEDGE
1158

WHITE
SEDGE
1161

SPIKED
SEDGE
1157

CURVED
SEDGE
1155

REMOTE
SEDGE
1160

GREY
SEDGE
1156

OVAL
SEDGE
1162

118

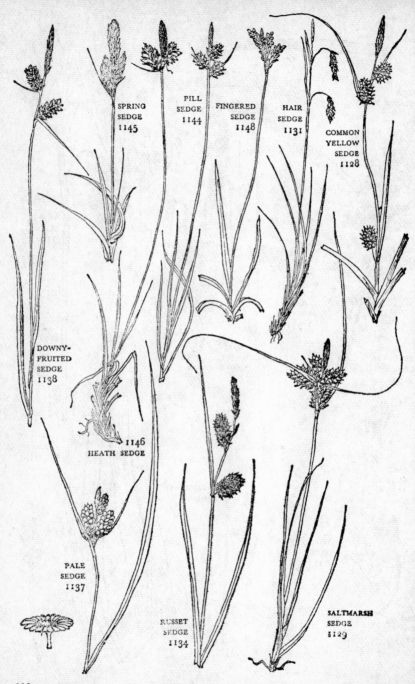

SPRING
SEDGE
1145

PILL
SEDGE
1144

FINGERED
SEDGE
1148

HAIR
SEDGE
1131

COMMON
YELLOW
SEDGE
1128

DOWNY-
FRUITED
SEDGE
1138

1146
HEATH SEDGE

PALE
SEDGE
1137

RUSSET
SEDGE
1134

SALTMARSH
SEDGE
1129

119

MOOR
SEDGE
1127

POND
SEDGE
1135

BOTTLE
SEDGE
1133

WOOD
SEDGE
1130

HAIRY
SEDGE
1142

BLADDER
SEDGE
1133a

SLENDER-LEAVED
SEDGE
1143

120

dotted, inflated, not ribbed, abruptly beaked (Fig.). Very local in wet places near the sea, mainly in the W.

1127d. **Tawny Sedge**, *C. hostiana* DC., is also creeping, but differs mainly in having the more spreading female glumes pointed, with no projecting nerve, dark brown with a broad pale margin and midrib; and yellow-green egg-shaped, more inflated fruits with a longer beak and numerous ribs (Fig.). Widespread and locally frequent in open fens.

1127e. *****Large-fruited Sedge**, *C. depauperata* Withering (*CTW, p. 1376*), is distinctive for its very short, widely separated flower-spikes on long stalks with very long leaf-like bracts at their base; rough leaves; and large, long-beaked fruits (Fig.). Very rare on dry hedge-banks on chalk or limestone and now certainly only in Somerset and Surrey. May.

1128. COMMON YELLOW SEDGE   *C. demissa* Hornemann
'*C. flava*'   Plate 119.   *CTW, p. 1373*
A tufted perennial, with stems 3–8 in. high, sometimes curved or prostrate, and flat narrow smooth yellow-green leaves about three-quarter their length; a single thin stalked terminal pale brown all-male spikelet and 2–4 globular female spikelets not or shortly stalked, the lowest not infrequently a long distance below the others and on a long stalk, all with long leaf-like bracts. Fruits tapering fairly rapidly to the beak, the lowermost sometimes very slightly curved when ripe, the nut only loosely enclosed (Fig.). *Habitat:* The commonest Yellow Sedge, widespread on damp acid soils. June–July.

1128a. *****Large Yellow Sedge**, *C. flava* L., is usually larger, even up to 3 ft., with much longer and broader leaves than any other Yellow Sedge and often exceeding the straight erect stems. Terminal spikelet shorter, unstalked and occasionally female in the middle; female spikelets 3–4, the upper unstalked and crowded, the lower sometimes shortly stalked and much lower down. Fruits over twice as large with a long much more tapering beak, curved down when ripe (Fig.). Rare, on wet limy peat at Malham (Yorks) and Roudsea (N Lancs).

1128b. ***Long-stalked Yellow Sedge**, *C. lepidocarpa* Tausch, is slenderer and much shorter than 1128a, rarely over 1 ft., with narrower leaves only half the length of the stems; the terminal spikelet longer and all-male on a longer stalk which often sticks out at a sharp angle from the main stem, or may be missing. Female spikelets 1–3 not normally very close together, the lower usually stalked but with none very much lower down. Fruits two-thirds the size of 1128a (Fig.). Widespread and locally frequent, always in lime-rich fens, or on mountains.

1128c. ***Dwarf Yellow Sedge**, *C. serotina* Mérat ('*C. oederi*'), is typically much more dwarf, neat and compact than Common Yellow Sedge but may rarely reach 10 in. It has narrower inrolled leaves often longer than the straight stiff stems, the terminal spikelet unstalked, occasionally female at the base and occasionally missing, with 3–5 females unstalked and closely clustered, the lowest occasionally distant and stalked. Fruits small two-thirds the size, straight, very shortly and abruptly beaked (Fig.). Local in wet open sandy and gravelly situations.

1128d. ****Northern Yellow Sedge** *C. scandinavica* Davies is never so tall as the last and flowers a month earlier. It is always compact and darker green, the leaves rather narrower and nearly always shorter than the stems; the terminal spikelet longer, all-male and never missing and usually short-stalked; females 2–3 remoter and darker. Fruits uninflated never so large, greyer with a still shorter beak, tightly enclosing nut (Fig.). Replaces 1128c in NW Scotland. May–June.

1129. *SALTMARSH SEDGE *C. extensa* Goodenough Pl. 119. *CTW, 1374*

A rather stiff Sedge, with egg-shaped or globular flower-spikes mimicking a Yellow Sedge (1128), up to a foot high; with smooth 3-sided, almost leafless stems; narrow grooved greyish leaves; short bluntly-pointed ligules; and unstalked flower-spikes, 1 male at the top, 2–3 short fat females immediately **below**, or the lowest a little distant, with very long spreading grass-like bracts at their base, the lowest much exceeding the male spike. Female glumes minutely pointed, pale brown. Fruits grey-green (Fig.). *Habitat:* Widespread but local in sandy salt-marshes. June–August.

1130. WOOD SEDGE *C. sylvatica* Hudson Plate 120. *CTW, p. 1374*

A graceful tufted Sedge, a foot or so high, with smooth slender 3-sided stems; short, rather broad shiny flaccid leaves; a short, bluntly pointed ligule; rather slender loose-flowered drooping flower-spikes, 1 short-stalked male at the top, 3–4 long thin long-stalked female spaced out below, the lowest leaf-like bract not overtopping the male spike; and the female glume very pale brown with a green midrib and pale margins. Fruits roundly 3-sided, long-beaked, green (Fig.). *Habitat:* Widespread and locally common in woods. May–June.

1130a. ****Thin-spiked Wood Sedge,** *C. strigosa* Hudson (*CTW, p. 1381*), is less tufted, with shorter broader greyer leaves; a longer more pointed ligule; female spikes shorter-stalked but longer, thinner, erecter and often more numerous and scattered rather distantly up the stem, the short smooth stalks almost hidden in the sheaths of the long bracts; and female glumes green. Fruits smaller, more angled, narrowed at both ends, with no real beak (Fig.). Generally scarce in wetter parts of woods, often on chalk or limestone; not in Scotland.

1131. **HAIR SEDGE *C. capillaris* L. Plate 119. *CTW, p. 1375*

A low Sedge, 4–8 in. high, with stiff smooth 3-sided, almost leafless stems, and tufts of fresh green leaves, whose upper surface is rough when stroked downwards; ligule short and blunt. Flower-spikes very slender and short, normally drooping, 1 tiny inconspicuous male and 2–3 short fat silvery female, which are loose, often rather close together and drooping on long thread-like stalks; lowest leaf-like bract sheathing the stem and often longer than the male spike; female glumes translucent, silvery. Fruits beaked, pale brown (Fig.). *Habitat:* Very local on wet ledges and in lime-rich flushes on mountains in the N. July.

1132. *HOP SEDGE *C. pseudocyperus* L. Plate 118. *CTW, p. 1376*

An attractive, bright yellow-green tufted Sedge, 2–3 ft. high, with sharply 3-sided stems rough on the angles and shorter than the broadish rough-edged leaves with a long, pointed ligule. Flower-spikes stalked, drooping, sausage-shaped, up to 2 in. long, 1 male above 3–5 long fat female, the upper very close together, like a cluster of drooping spruce-cones, the lowest distant; leaf-like bracts mostly longer than the male spike; and female glumes long, very narrow, pale. Fruits egg-shaped, beaked, ribbed, shining, green (Fig.). *Habitat:* Widespread but local by still and slow-moving fresh water; rare in Scotland. May–June.

1133. BOTTLE SEDGE *C. rostrata* Stokes Plate 120. *CTW, p. 1377*

A greyish Sedge, 1–2 ft. high, with stems 3-sided above and rough when rubbed downwards, more rounded below, shorter than the inrolled leaves, which are also roughish on the edges and midrib when rubbed downwards, and have a short blunt ligule. Flower-spikes stalked, erect, sausage-shaped, 2–4 male above

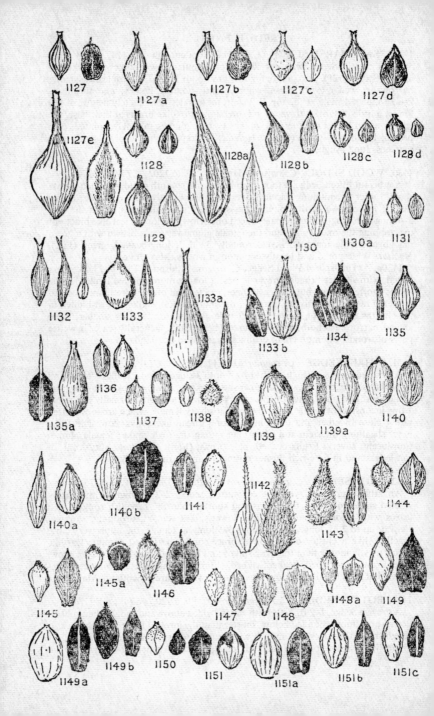

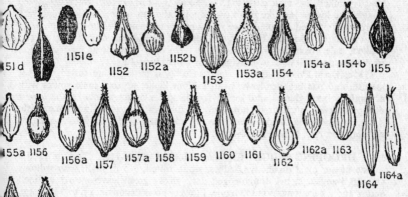

Fruits of Sedges, all × 4, with female glumes of 1127–1151.

2–4 shortish fat female at intervals down the stem, the lowest of the leaf-like bracts equalling or overtopping the top spike and sheathing the stem. Fruits yellow-green, shiny, swollen, shaped like crême-de-menthe bottles, suddenly narrowed to the long beak (Fig.). *Habitat:* Widespread and locally frequent in all kinds of wet peaty swamps. June–July.

1133*a.* **Bladder Sedge,** *C. vesicaria* L., is dark green, not greyish, and normally taller, with stems sharply 3-angled throughout; leaves flatter and broader with a longer, pointed ligule; shorter flower-spikes; the lowest bract always overtopping the top spike; and the fruits larger, shiny, and much more gradually narrowed to the long beak (Fig.). More local, in marshy places and by fresh water.

1133*b.* *****Mountain Bladder Sedge,** *C. grahami* Boott, is rather smaller and darker than Bladder Sedge, with fewer male spikes, the lowest bract not over-topping the top spike nor sheathing the stem, and ribbed, pale brown fruits in more cylindrical spikes (Fig.). Very rare on a few mountains in the C Highlands.

1134. ****RUSSET SEDGE** *C. saxatilis* L. Plate 119. *CTW, p. 1378*
A low Sedge, with 3-sided stems 4–8 in. high, and narrow leaves with a very short blunt ligule. Flower-spikes long egg-shaped, 1 male and 1–2 female fairly close together, the lower stalked with its leaf-like bract not quite exceeding the male spike nor sheathing the stem. Fruits smooth, shiny, rich dark brown, tapered to a beak (Fig.). *Habitat:* Very local in mountain bogs on limestone in Scotland. July.

1135. **POND SEDGE** *C. acutiformis* Ehrhart Plate 120. *CTW, p. 1379*
A slender greyish Sedge, 3–4 ft. high, rough in all its parts when rubbed down-wards, with sharply 3-angled stems shorter than some of the rather broad keeled leaves, which have a long, pointed ligule. Flower-spikes long but fattish, not or

shortly stalked, 2–3 male close together above 3–4 rather more widely separated female, the lowest leaf-like bract overtopping the top spike; female glume very narrow and pointed, purple-brown with a paler brown midrib, the male one being blunt or scarcely pointed. Fruits much flattened, greyish egg-shaped, very shortly beaked, pale green, with 3 styles (Fig.). *Habitat:* Widespread and common in swamps and still or slow-moving fresh water. June–July.

1135*a*. **Great Pond Sedge,** *C. riparia* Curtis, is larger, more tufted and not greyish, and has broader leaves with a blunt ligule, up to 6 male spikes with abruptly pointed glumes, and longer female spikes on longer stalks, the lowest drooping; fruits much larger, not compressed but cylindrical, yellow, not greyish, shiny, many-nerved, and tapered to the cleft top (Fig.). Equally common, especially on river banks. April–June.

1136. DROOPING SEDGE *C. pendula* Hudson Plate 118. *CTW, p. 1380*

One of our most distinctive Sedges, stout, tufted, 3–5 ft. high, with willowy smooth 3-angled stems, rough-edged dark glossy green leaves nearly an inch across and a very long, pointed ligule. Flower-spikes drooping, up to 5 in. long, unstalked, 1 male above 4–5 long thin female scattered up the stem; female glumes egg-shaped, pale brown with a green midrib; the lowest leaf-like bract sheathing the stem and about equalling the male spike. Fruits short, flattened, greyish, very shortly beaked (Fig.). *Habitat:* Widespread and locally frequent in damp clayey woods. May–June.

1137. *PALE SEDGE *C. pallescens* L. Plate 119. *CTW, p. 1381*

A tufted, slightly hairy, very pale green Sedge, a foot or so high, with sharply 3-angled stems, narrow leaves and a short blunt ligule. Flower-spikes short, very short-stalked, pallid, 1 male more or less hidden among the cluster of 2–3 short fat female, the lowest of which is sometimes a little down the stem; lowest leaf-like bract often overtopping the top spike. Fruits oval, bright yellow-green, shiny, almost beakless (Fig.). *Habitat:* Widespread but rather local in wet meadows and woods. May–June.

1138. **DOWNY-FRUITED SEDGE *C. filiformis* L. Pl. 119. *CTW, p. 1382*

A tufted Sedge, 9–18 in. high, hairless except for its fruits, with flat narrow roughish leaves shorter than the stiff roughish 3-angled stems; ligule short, blunt. Flower-spikes short, fattish, short-stalked, 1 male at the top, 1–2 egg-shaped female down the stem, their leaf-like bracts equalling or exceeding the male spike. Fruits pear-shaped, downy, rather abruptly short-beaked (Fig.). *Habitat:* Very local in dry or damp grassland in the S, mainly on chalk or limestone and in the Thames Valley. May–June. '*C. tomentosa*'.

1139. CARNATION SEDGE *C. panicea* L. Plate 117. *CTW, p. 1382*

A greyish Sedge about a foot high, differing from Glaucous Sedge (1141) in having only a single male flower-spike, which droops when the plant is in fruit, and in its stiffer shorter fewer-flowered, more widely spaced female spikes, with broader fawn scale-like glumes; fruits larger, beakless, swollen, pale greyish-green or pinkish-brown (Fig.). *Habitat:* Widespread and frequent in fens and wet meadows, not on very acid soils. May–June.

1139*a*. **Sheathing Sedge,** *C. vaginata* Tausch, is apple-green and has smaller narrower flower-spikes with very loose sheaths to the leaf-like bracts at their base. Very local on Scottish mountain-ledges. July.

1140. *BOG SEDGE *C. limosa* L. Plate 117. *CTW, p. 1383*

A short creeping Sedge, up to a foot high, with stiff rough 3-angled stems longer than the narrow grey grooved leaves with minutely toothed edges; ligule short, pointed. Flower-spikes stalked, 1 erect male above 1–2 spaced-out loose few-flowered short fat nodding female, whose bracts are shorter than the male spike, and whose glumes are egg-shaped, milk-chocolate colour, ending in a tiny point. Fruits ribbed, swollen, grey, beakless (Fig.). *Habitat:* Widespread and frequent in bog-pools in the N; rare and local in the S. June.

1140a. **Tall Bog Sedge,** *C. paupercula* Michaux (*C. magellanica* Lamarck), is taller and has smooth stems; broader ungrooved leaves less toothed on the edges; smaller female spikes whose bracts overtop the male one, with longer, very pointed glumes; and broader, less ribbed fruits (Fig.). Rare, and only in the N; Ireland, only in Co. Antrim.

1140b. ***Mountain Bog Sedge,** *C. rariflora* (Wahlenberg) Smith, is like a small dark Bog Sedge, with smooth, less angled stems; leaves not grooved and less toothed; very short lower bracts; female glumes blunt, almost black; and fruits narrower and blunter at the top (Fig.). Very rare in high bogs in the Highlands.

1141. GLAUCOUS SEDGE *C. flacca* Schreber Plate 117. *CTW, p. 1385*

One of our commonest Sedges, often confused with Carnation Sedge (1139), 4–12 in. high, with a creeping rootstock; smooth, bluntly 3-sided stems usually longer than the roughish keeled greyish leaves; and short blunt ligules. Flower-spikes 1–3 thin erect male, 2 long-stalked fattish drooping female, rather close together at the top of the stem, with brown glumes; and leaf-like bracts usually shorter than the top spike. Fruits elliptical, flattened, grey-green, minutely downy, with no real beak (Fig.). *Habitat:* Widespread and common in chalk or limestone grassland and fens, less often in sandy grassland and damp woods. April–June. Carnation-grass.

1142. HAIRY SEDGE *C. hirta* L. Plate 120. *CTW, p. 1385*

A common Sedge, 6–18 in. high, immediately recognisable by the numerous long white hairs on its leaf-sheaths and its 2–3 long fattish female spikes spaced well down the stem, often almost to the bottom; with long, pointed scale-like glumes at their base and very long leaf-like bracts. Stems hairless, shiny, 3-angled, longer than the slightly hairy, grooved leaves; ligule short, blunt. Male spikes 2–3, rather slender and inconspicuous, the topmost stalked and about equalling the topmost female leaf-like bract; their glumes hairy and their bracts bristle-like. Fruits beaked, ribbed, thickly downy, green, rather fat (Fig.). *Habitat:* Widespread and frequent in damp grassy and shady places and by ponds; also on dry banks. April–June. Hammer Sedge.

1143. *SLENDER-LEAVED SEDGE *C. lasiocarpa* Ehrhart Pl. 120. *CTW, 1386*

A 2–3 ft. Sedge with very narrow long arching grooved grey-green leaves, no shorter than the stiff 3-sided stems; ligule short, blunt, dark-tipped. Flower-spikes with no or very short stalks, 1–3 male above 1–3 slender cylindrical female with narrow brown glumes; spaced out at the top of the stem; the leaf-like bracts sometimes overtopping the top spike. A shy flowerer. Fruits heavily downy grey (Fig.). *Habitat:* Widespread but local in very wet bogs and fens. June–July.

1144. PILL SEDGE *C. pilulifera* L. Plate 119. *CTW, p. 1386*

A tufted Sedge, 4–12 in. high or long, with narrow, rather pale green leaves much shorter than the often prostrate slender flaccid 3-angled stems; ligule very short, blunt. Flower-spikes short, unstalked, 1 compact small thin male, 2–4 globular female close together at the top of the stem, the lowest leaf-like bract short, narrow, not sheathing the stem nor usually overtopping the top spike; glumes brown with a green midrib. Fruits roundish, ribbed, downy, green (Fig.) on much elongated stems. *Habitat:* Widespread and locally common in dry grassy and heathy places on acid soils. May–June.

1145. SPRING SEDGE *C. caryophyllea* Latourette Pl. 119. *CTW, p. 1388*
   Darker green than the last species, with a much shorter stiffer stouter erect stem 3–4 in. high; shorter leaves twice as broad; a rather less compact cluster of flower-spikes, the male much longer and fatter with pointed milk-chocolate glumes, the female long egg-shaped, unstalked, with pointed glumes and a green midrib; and the almost bristle-like bracts sheathing the stem with a broad base. Fruits olive-green, downy (Fig.). *Habitat:* Widespread and common in dry grassy places, especially on chalk or limestone. April–May.
   1145a. **Breckland Spring Sedge,** *C. ericetorum* Pollich, has broader leaves; narrower male spike with black silvery-edged blunt glumes; female glumes blunt with a pale midrib; tiny bristle-like bracts; and very small downy greenish-brown fruits (Fig.). Very local in short turf on chalk in the Breckland and Lincolnshire, and on limestone in N England.

1146. **HEATH SEDGE *C. montana* L. Plate 119. *CTW, p. 1388*
   Often mistaken for Pill Sedge (1144), but has bright green leaves, very slightly downy when young, arising from a shaggy rootstock, and short pointed ligules. Flower-spikes, blackish when young, 1 cylindrical dark brown male, 1–3 globular black unstalked female, bunched in a terminal cluster. Fruits larger, elliptical, more downy, yellow-green, with black glumes (Fig.). *Habitat:* Rare in heathy grassland in the S half of England. April–May.

1147. **DWARF SEDGE *C. humilis* Leysser Plate 117. *CTW, p. 1389*
   Much smaller and less erect than Spring Sedge (1145), with leaves longer than the 1–3-in. stems, flower-spikes stalked, the female ones greyish, spaced out and enclosed by a brownish sheath-like bract. Fruits egg-shaped, downy (Fig.). *Habitat:* Locally plentiful in short turf on chalk in Wessex, also on limestone in W England. March–April.

1148. **FINGERED SEDGE *C. digitata* L. Plate 119. *CTW, p. 1389*
   A distinctive Sedge, 4–6 in. high with slender, bluntly 3-sided stems about equalling the smooth yellowish-green leaves, wihch are sometimes slightly downy beneath, and have a short ligule. Flower-spikes rather thin, 1–3 short-stalked finger-like female ones clustering round and overtopping the single male; glumes chocolate brown; bracts bristle-like. Fruits roundish, milk-chocolate, downy (Fig.). *Habitat:* Very local in limestone woods in W and N England. May.
   1148a. **Small Fingered Sedge,** *C. ornithopoda* Willdenow, is smaller and greyer, with the flower-spikes more spreading, and has the smaller much paler female glumes pointed instead of notched, and shorter than the smaller fruits (Fig.), not enfolding them. Very local in limestone turf in the N half of England.

1149. **JET SEDGE *C. atrata* L. Plate 117. *CTW, p. 1391*
   A fine Sedge, 6–9 in. high, with smooth, greyish leaves shorter than the stiff 3-angled stems; ligule short, blunt. Flower-spikes fat, black, stalked, nodding, 3–5 close together at the top of the stem, top one male at base only, the rest

female; glumes black; lowest bract leaf-like and overtopping the top spike. Fruits egg-shaped, pale green, minutely dotted (Fig.). *Habitat:* Very local on mountain ledges in the N. June–July.

1149*a*. ***Arisaig Sedge, *C. buxbaumii* Wahlenberg (*C. polygama* Schkuhr), has taller stems slightly rough at the top, erect less or unstalked flower-spikes, and female glumes narrow, pale. Fruits larger, grey-green, virtually unbeaked (Fig.). Now only by one loch near Arisaig (W Inverness).

1149*b*. ***Small Jet Sedge, *C. atrofusca* Schkuhr, is much smaller, with the terminal spike all male, or sometimes female at the base, and short bracts all bristle-like. Fruits narrower, black (Fig.). Very rare in bogs, Perthshire and Rhum.

1150. ***ALPINE SEDGE *C. norvegica* Retzius Plate 117. *CTW, p. 1391*

Differs from Jet Sedge (1149) in having stems rough above; flower-spikes much smaller, egg-shaped, erect, hardly or not stalked, and usually in a group of 3 side by side, rather like the Ace of Clubs; lowest bract leaf-like and shorter than the top spike. Fruits much smaller, pale green, minutely downy (Fig.). *Habitat:* Very rare on damp rock-ledges on high mountains in the C and E Highlands and on N Uist. June–July. *C. alpina* Liljeblad.

1151. COMMON SEDGE *C. nigra* (L.) Reichard Plate 117. *CTW, p. 1395*

A very variable Sedge, 1–3 ft. high, with 3-angled stems rough above, narrow greyish leaves and a short ligule. Flower-spikes with very short or no stalks, 1–2 black male (the lower usually much smaller) above 2–3 rather short sausage-shaped female, on short stalks, either close together or spaced out; glumes black; lowest leaf-like bract sometimes overtopping top spike. Fruits compressed, shortly egg-shaped, grey-green, later brown, longer than the short black blunt glumes (Fig.); stigmas 2. *Habitat:* Widespread and frequent in all kinds of wet peaty places. May–July. '*C. caespitosa*', *C. goodenowii* Gay.

1151*a*. *Tufted Sedge, *C. elata* Allioni (*C. hudsonii* Bennett) (*CTW, p. 1392*), is tussocky and much taller, reaching 3 ft., with roughish, sharply 3-angled stems, the leaf-sheaths later becoming torn with long fibres hanging from them; ligule long, pointed. Flower-spikes with no or very short stalks, 1–2 male above 2–3 female, spaced out, the female glumes large, egg-shaped, intense black with a green midrib, the lowest bract rather short and bristle-like. Fruits larger (Fig.). Widespread but local in fens and on peat by fresh water.

1151*b*. *Graceful Sedge, *C. acuta* L. (*CTW, p. 1393*), is like Tufted Sedge, but has broader leaf-like bracts, the lowest often equalling or exceeding the top spike; female spikes nodding; a shorter ligule; sheaths not fibrous; female glumes narrower than fruits, sharply pointed; and fruits somewhat flattened (Fig.). Widespread but local in wet places, especially river banks. May–June.

1151*c*. *Straight-leaved Sedge, *C. aquatilis* Wahlenberg (*CTW, p. 1393*), has bluntly 3-sided stems and leaves pale above but dark below, with a long, pointed, ligule. Flower-spikes 2–4 male above 3–4 female, which are long in proportion to width, well spaced out down the stem, only the lower stalked, the lowest bract usually exceeding the top spike, and the second lowest equalling it. Egg-shaped fruits (Fig.) and glumes very small, but coloured as in Graceful Sedge. Local by fresh water in the N, and in Wales and Ireland. July.

1151*d*. ***Wick Sedge, *C. recta* Boott ('*C. salina*'), differs from Straight-leaved Sedge chiefly in its long-stalked flower-spikes, long-pointed female glume and fatter ribbed fruits (Fig.). Hybridises freely with Straight-leaved Sedge. Known only by the Wick River in Caithness, and there rare.

1151e. *Stiff Sedge, *C. bigelowii* Schweinitz (*C. rigida* Goodenough), is like a dwarf Common Sedge, but has stouter sharply angled stems; broader rigid curved leaves with inrolled margins; only 1 male flower-spike; narrower glumes and less rounded fruits (Fig.). Frequent on mountain tops in the N and in Ireland. June–July.

1152. TUSSOCK SEDGE   *C. paniculata* L.   Plate 118.   *CTW, p. 1396*

Distinctive for its often huge tussocks, recalling Pampas grass (*Cortaderia selloana*) reaching as much as 4 ft. high and 3 ft. wide, with stiff 3–5-foot stems and long leaves, both extremely rough with upward-directed prickles; ligule short, blunt. Flower-spikes numerous, stalked or not, with male and female flowers mixed, in a close or loose compound spike; bracts bristle-like, short, or none. Fruits small, 3-sided, with a winged beak (Fig.). *Habitat:* Widespread but local in marshes and wet woods on peaty soils. May–June.

1152a. **Lesser Tussock Sedge, *C. appropinquata* Schumacher (*C. paradoxa* Willdenow), is smaller with flat-faced stems, narrower yellow-green leaves and the beak of the fruit not winged (Fig.). Very locally frequent in fens in E England; rare elsewhere.

1152b. * Lesser Fox Sedge, *C. diandra* Schrank (*C. teretiuscula* Goodenough), is slenderer and not tussocky, with convex faces to the narrow stems; narrow grey-green leaves with minutely toothed tips; a close cylindrical spike of dark brown flower-spikes; and narrower fruits (Fig.). Local in open fens on chalk or limestone.

1153. FOX SEDGE   *C. otrubae* Podpera ('*C. vulpina*')   Plate 118.   *CTW, p. 1398*

A common stout, tufted Sedge, 2–3 ft. high, with stems rather soft, sharply 3-angled but not winged. the faces nearly flat, very rough when rubbed downwards; leaves broad, rather weak, similarly rough on the edges and midrib, with a long, pointed diagonal ligule, and loose sheaths. Flower-spikes unstalked, with male and female flowers mixed, in a close compound spike, yellow-green or pale brown, with the bracts of varying length. Fruits smooth, ribbed, tapering to a beak (Fig.). *Habitat:* Widespread, common in damp grassy places. June–July.

1153a. **Greater Fox Sedge, *C. vulpina* L., flowers earlier, and is stouter, with very sharply angled, almost winged stems with concave faces; leaves up to ¾-in. broad; fibrous leaf-sheaths; shorter transverse broader ligules; very short inconspicuous bristle-like bracts clasping the stem with dark arms; reddish-brown flowers; and narrower, less ribbed fruits (Fig.). Scarce or overlooked by rivers and in ditches and osier-beds in the S half of England. May–June.

1154. SAND SEDGE   *C. arenaria* L.   Plate 118.   *CTW, p. 1399*

A short Sedge, 3–9 in. high, with far-creeping underground stems and 3-angled rough, often rather curved erect stems; ligule short, pointed. Flower-spikes 5–12, unstalked, short, the upper male, the lower female, in a close, compound spike, with short bristle-like bracts. Fruits rather large, beaked, pale yellow-brown, with toothed wings (Fig.). *Habitat:* Widespread on sand-dunes, common by the sea, local on open sandy ground inland in England. June–July.

1154a. *Brown Sedge, *C. disticha* Hudson, has straight stems and blunt ligules; flower-spikes warm brown, in two opposite rows like Flat-headed Sedge (1116), but not flattened and with a terminal spike, the middle ones male, with female above and below them; bracts sometimes leaf-like, the lowest longer than the whole head; fruits narrowly winged (Fig.). Local in fens and damp grassy meadows.

1154*b*. *Divided Sedge, *C. divisa* Hudson, has leaves sometimes longer than the slenderer, straight 9–18-in. stems; the two-ranked flower-spikes smaller than Brown Sedge, dark glossy brown, the lower sometimes spaced out a little; bracts leaf-like or bristle-like, the lowest sometimes overtopping the whole spike; and fruits not winged, with a shorter beak (Fig.). Locally common in meadows, usually near the sea, in England and Wales; rare in Ireland. May–June.

1155. **CURVED SEDGE   *C. maritima* Gunnerus   Plate 118.   *CTW, p. 1401*

A small, partly buried prostrate Sedge, with a far-creeping rootstock, and narrow curved leaves, their margins inrolled, equalling or exceeding the smooth rounded, markedly curved stems; ligule short, blunt. Flower-spikes all very close together in an egg-shaped head, sometimes likened to spiky rabbit droppings; male flowers almost hidden; no bracts. Fruits very dark brown or blackish, with a projecting beak (Fig.). *Habitat:* Very local in sand in Scotland and Holy Is. (Northumberland). June. *C. incurva* Lightfoot.

1155*a*. ***Altnaharra Sedge, *C. chordorrhiza* L., is taller and slenderer and rather between the last and the next species, with straight leaves shorter than the straight 3-sided stems, the flower-heads looking like starved specimens of Curved Sedge, but with chaffy bracts and shorter fatter fruits (Fig.). Known only from bogs at Altnaharra, Sutherland.

1156. *GREY SEDGE   *C. divulsa* Stokes   Plate 118.   *CTW, p. 1402*

A greyish-green tufted Sedge, 1–2 ft. high, with slender roughish 3-angled stems longer than the narrow roughish leaves; ligules very short, bluntly pointed. Flower-spikes green, unstalked, spaced down the stem, the lowest sometimes branched, with male and female flowers mixed; bristle-like bracts at base of lower spikes, rarely shorter. Fruits pale green, short, egg-shaped, rather abruptly beaked (Fig.). *Habitat:* Widespread and locally frequent in dry, often sandy hedge-banks and rough grassy places; not in Scotland. June–July.

1156*a*. **Tall Spiked Sedge, *C. polyphylla* Karelin & Kirilov, has broader leaves, ligules rounded, the flower-spikes fatter, less spaced, sometimes longer than the bracts, and the fruits half as long again, gradually tapered and spreading when ripe (Fig.). Locally frequent in chalk or limestone hedge-banks. May–June.

1157. SPIKED SEDGE   *C. spicata* Hudson   Plate 118.   *CTW, p. 1402*
C. contigua Hoppe

Differs from Grey Sedge (1156) in having longer leaves, the bases of the older ones usually tinged purplish-red; a longer blunter ligule; and the flower-spikes, except sometimes the lowest, close together in a short cylindrical head, with bristle-like bracts. Fruits like Grey Sedge (1156), but with a fairly long beak, and almost stalked at the base (Fig.). *Habitat:* Widespread and locally frequent on grassy roadsides and by ditches on chalk or clay, thinning out northwards. June.

1157*a*. *Lesser Spiked Sedge, *C. pairaei* Schultz, is very similar, but has narrower leaves, even closer flower-heads, the ligule shorter and pointed, no purplish-red tinge and smaller shorter, more abruptly beaked fruits (Fig.). Local in dry sandy ground and by roads, mainly in the S; rare in Ireland.

1158. **GINGERBREAD SEDGE   *C. elongata* L.   Plate 118.   *CTW, p. 1403*

A slender Sedge, 1–2 ft. high, growing in large tufts, with thin rough 3-angled arching stems usually slightly exceeding the long narrow leaves; ligule short, pointed. Flower-spikes male at base, female at tip, in a fairly close but branched, prickly looking head, dark reddish-brown, with short chaffy bracts at their base. Fruits stiff, ribbed, rather long-beaked (Fig.). *Habitat:* Very local in marshy osier woods and by fresh water in England, S Scotland and N Ireland. May–June.

1159. STAR SEDGE   *C. echinata* Murray   Plate 118.   *CTW, p. 1404*

A shortish Sedge, 6–10 in. high, with slender smooth 3-sided stems longer than the channelled leaves, very short blunt ligules. Flower-spikes unstalked, close together in a grey-green cylindrical head, with both male and female flowers; small chaffy bracts at their base. Fruits beaked, grey-green or yellow, spreading starwise (Fig.). *Habitat:* Widespread and frequent in bogs and marshes on mildly acid soils, commonest in the N and W. June–July.

1160. REMOTE SEDGE   *C. remota* L.   Plate 118.   *CTW, p. 1404*

A slender, tufted Sedge, 9–18 in. high, with small unstalked, pale green flower-spikes, containing both male and female flowers, well spaced out down the stem, and with the leaf-like bracts at the base of the lower ones exceeding the whole head. Stems weak, 3-sided, slightly rough at the top when rubbed downwards; leaves very narrow, pale green, channelled, similarly roughish at the edges; ligule short; bracts of upper flower-spikes tiny, chaffy. Fruits compressed, egg-shaped, shiny green with a short beak (Fig.). *Habitat:* Widespread and frequent in wet or damp shady places. June–August.

1161. *WHITE SEDGE   *C. curta* Goodenough   Plate 118.   *CTW, p. 1405*

A tufted Sedge, 1–2 ft. high, sometimes confused with Grey Sedge (1156), with stems 3-angled, rough at the top, no shorter than the pale grey-green leaves; ligule short, pointed. Flower-spikes whitish-grey, unstalked, spaced out a little down the stem, with both male and female flowers; bracts bristle-like. Fruits grey-green, ribbed, shortly beaked (Fig.). *Habitat:* Widespread but local on wet peat on acid soils, often in light shade. May–June. '*C. canescens*'.

1162. OVAL SEDGE   *C. ovalis* Goodenough   Plate 118.   *CTW, p. 1406*

A coarse tufted Sedge, 1–2 ft. high, with stiff 3-sided stems, roughish at the top, longer than the rough-edged leaves; ligule short, bluntly pointed. Flower-spikes unstalked, rather large, closely clustered in a rather pointed egg-shaped head, with both male and female flowers, their glumes pale brown, the bracts bristle-like, the lowest sometimes overtopping the head. Fruits beaked, brownish-green (Fig.). *Habitat:* Widespread and frequent in rough grassy, heathy and marshy places on acid soils. June.

1162a. ***Mountain Oval Sedge,** *C. lachenalii* Schkuhr, is much smaller, with leaves as long as the stems, blunter ligules, darker glumes, the lower bracts shorter and chaffy, and smaller, pale green fruits (Fig.). Very rare in wet places high on mountains in the Highlands. June–July.

1163. ***ROCK SEDGE   *C. rupestris* Allioni   Plate 117.   *CTW, p. 1406*

A low tufted Sedge, 2–3 in. high, with 3-angled stems equalling the thin leaves, which are strongly curled like a pig's tail; ligules short, blunt. Flower-spikes solitary, very slender, male at top, female below, the bracts chaffy, the glumes at the base of the female flowers persisting in fruit, mimicking young Flea Sedge (1165), with which it often grows. Fruits flask-shaped, erect, yellow (Fig.); stigmas 3. Often a shy flowerer. *Habitat:* Very local on dry rock ledges in Scotland. June–July.

1164. *FEW-FLOWERED SEDGE *C. pauciflora* Lightfoot Pl. 117. *CTW, 1407*
Paler than Flea Sedge (1165), with 3-sided stems, 3 stigmas and 2–4 narrowly lanceolate, horizontal, not flattened, straw-coloured fruits (Fig.). *Habitat:* Local on very wet moors and bogs in the N, and N Ireland. May–June.

1164a. ***Breadalbane Sedge, *C. microglochin* Wahlenberg, has more flowers in the spike and the fruits rather more turned down, longer, with a stout bristle at the base protruding with the stigmas from the top (Fig.). Known only from one boggy col near Ben Lawers. July–August.

1165. FLEA SEDGE *C. pulicaris* L. Plate 117. *CTW, p. 1408*
The commonest of the four Sedges with only a solitary flower-spike, male at the top and female below; 4–9 in. high, with stiff thin smooth, rounded stems, slightly longer than the very narrow channelled leaves; ligule very short, blunt. Fruits spindle-shaped, $\frac{1}{4}$-in. long, shiny, dark brown, erect at first, turned down when ripe (Fig.); female glumes falling off in fruit; stigmas 2. *Habitat:* Widespread but local in fens and damp places, commonest in the N and W. June–July.

1166. *SEPARATE-HEADED SEDGE *C. dioica* L. Plate 117. *CTW, p. 1408*
Our only Sedge that normally has male and female flowers on separate plants; 3–4 in. high, with thin stiff rounded leafless stems longer than the channelled leaves; ligule very short, blunt. Flower-spikes solitary, the narrow, pale brown male (♂) ones soon going over, the female (♀) shortly egg-shaped. Fruits egg-shaped, beaked (Fig.). *Habitat:* Widespread but local in bogs, not on very acid soils, commonest in the N and W. May.

GRASS FAMILY Gramineae

GRASSES DIFFER from Sedges in having their usually round and never 3-angled stems almost always hollow, except at the swollen leaf-junctions, and their flowers arranged in opposite rows in spikelets, each flower with two small bracts. Their leaves are alternate in two rows, usually long, narrow, untoothed, keeled or flat, with parallel veins and sheathing the stem, the lower sheaths usually split on the side opposite the leaf. At the leaf-junction is very often a tiny colourless flap- or strap-like ligule, a useful diagnostic character best seen by pulling the leaf away from the stem.

The actual flowers are minute, usually with 3 stamens and 2 feathery styles, but not petals or sepals; each flower is enclosed within 2 scale-like bracts (pales) arranged one or more together in a spikelet, at the base of which are 2 more scale-like bracts (glumes). The spikelets (stalked or not) often bear bristles (awns) and are arranged in terminal flower-heads, which vary from small dense cylinders to widely branched sprays. The branched heads may look very different when their branches are spreading in flower, and when they are closed and cylindrical in bud or in fruit. The fruits, not important for identification, are small dry nutlets.

KEY TO GRASSES
I. Flower-heads Branched
PLANT *floating* 1171; *prostrate* 1243; *tussocky* 1169, 1173a, 1222, 1228, 1246a; *hairy* 1198, 1202, 1203, 1204, 1216, 1217, 1221, 1245, 1253; *greyish* 1189a, 1190, 1219, 1226, 1227; *with swollen stem-base* 1191a, 1220.
STEMS *flattened* 1190.
LEAF-SHEATHS *keeled* 1171ab, 1172, 1187, 1190, 1192, 1193, 1219; *inflated* 1243; *rough* 1167a, 1172, 1174, 1191b, 1192, 1193, 1222, 1224, 1226, 1243, 1244.

LIGULE *pointed* 1171, 1172, 1188, 1191, 1192, 1198, 1219, **1222**, 1226, 1227, 1231, 1232, 1243, 1244, 1245*a*; *long* 1171, 1192, 1193, 1196*a*, 1218, 1222, 1227, 1228, 1230, 1242, 1245; *absent* 1252; *a ring of hairs* 1168, 1169, 1170, 1250, 1251.

LEAVES *bristle-like* 1175, 1176, 1177, 1180, 1181, 1182, 1216, 1222, 1223, 1224, 1225, 1226, 1230*a*; *rough-edged* 1167, 1172, 1173, 1174, 1222, 1228, 1229, 1242, 1244, 1252, 1253.

FLOWER-HEADS *one-sided* 1173, 1180, 1181, 1184, 1185, 1186, 1193, 1199, 1203*c*, 1251; *narrow and spike-like* 1169, 1170, 1175*b*, 1176, 1180, 1181, 1186, 1199, 1216, 1219, 1223, 1224, 1226, 1227, 1228, 1230, 1232, 1243, 1245, 1246; *nodding* 1168, 1173, 1174, 1175*a*, 1181, 1188, 1189, 1191, 1192, 1197, 1198, 1199, 1201, 1202, 1203, 1204, 1218, 1219*a*, 1220, 1222, 1242; *with a cluster of spikes* 1250, 1251, 1253.

SPIKELETS *rounded* 1196, 1197, 1244; *1-flowered* 1167, 1169, 1189, 1192*b*, 1198, 1227, 1228, 1229, 1230, 1231, 1232, 1242, 1243, 1246, 1250, 1251, 1253; *with straight awns* 1174, 1175, 1176, 1180, 1181, 1193, 1201, 1202, 1203, 1204, 1221, 1222, 1226, 1228, 1229, 1230, 1231, 1232, 1252; *with bent awns* 1217, **1218**, 1219, 1220, 1221*a*, 1224, 1225, 1230*b*, 1245; *viviparous* 1177, 1188, 1122*a*.

II. Flower-heads Unbranched (or apparently so)

PLANT *floating* 1241; *prostrate* 1247*b*; *hairy* 1205, 1206, 1215, 1235; *greyish* 1208, 1209, 1210, 1211, 1237; *with swollen stem base* 1136, 1141*b*.

LEAF-SHEATHS *keeled* 1200, 1204; *inflated* 1195, 1233, 1235, 1236*c*, 1238, 1239, 1240, 1241, 1247; *rough* 1279, 1233, 1247.

LIGULE *pointed* 1233, 1236*b*, 1238; *long* 1195, 1233, 1238, 1247; *a ring of hairs* 1254, 1255.

LEAVES *bristle-like* 1234, 1249; *rough-edged* 1200, 1215, 1241*b*.

FLOWER-HEADS *one-sided* 1186, 1194, 1195, 1199, 1234, 1249; *rounded* 1195, 1235, 1247; *nodding* 1199, 1205, 1207, 1235.

SPIKELETS *1-flowered* 1195, 1212, 1213, 1214, 1233, 1234, 1235, 1236, 1237, 1238, 1239, 1240, 1241, 1247, 1248, 1249, 1254, 1255; *awned* 1179, 1194, 1195, 1200, 1205, 1206, 1207, 1212, 1213, 1214, 1215, 1233, 1235, 1236, 1237, 1239, 1240, 1241, 1249, 1254, 1255; *stalked* 1186, 1194, 1195, 1200, 1205, 1213, 1214, 1233, 1236*a*, 1237, 1238, 1239, 1240, 1241, 1247, 1254, 1255; *unstalked* 1178, 1179, 1186, 1194, 1207, 1208, 1209, 1210, 1211, 1212, 1213, 1214, 1215, 1234, 1235, 1236, 1249.

1167. ****RICE-GRASS** *Leersia oryzoides* (L.) Swartz Plate 131. *CTW, p. 1416*
A slightly hairy, loosely tufted, pale green perennial, 1–4 ft. high, with stiff, hooked bristles (which may be rough up or down in different parts, unlike any other Grass) on the leaf-sheaths; very short ligule; flat rough-edged leaves; and in favourable seasons an open spreading branched flower-head, the 1-flowered spikelets having minute glumes and hairy pales. Except in hot summers the flower-head remains unexpanded in the swollen sheath. *Habitat:* Rare by fresh water from Dorset to Sussex. August onwards. Cut-grass.

1168. **REED** *Phragmites communis* Trinius Plate 134. *CTW, p. 1417*
Our tallest Grass, a stout, almost hairless perennial, 5–8 ft. high, often forming extensive beds with its creeping rootstock, the very stiff stout stems persisting as hard canes in winter. Leaves deciduous, flat, smooth, ¾-in. or more broad, greyish below; a ring of hairs replacing the ligule. Flower-heads large, 5–10 in. long, rather dense, 1-sided, branched, spreading, with numerous 2–6-flowered purplish spikelets, fading to pale brown, often drooping, with no awns but long

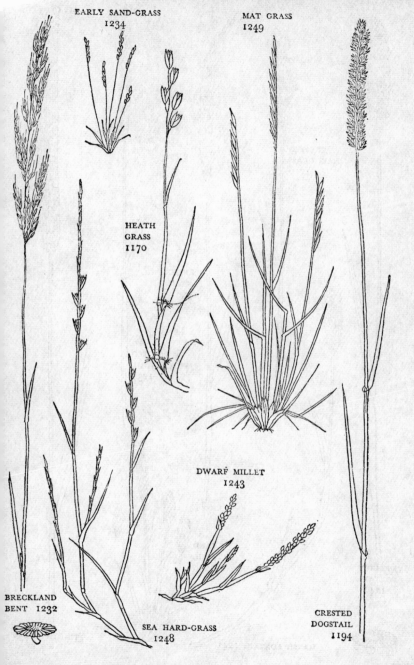

EARLY SAND-GRASS
1234

MAT GRASS
1249

HEATH
GRASS
1170

DWARF MILLET
1243

BRECKLAND
BENT 1232

SEA HARD-GRASS
1248

CRESTED
DOGSTAIL
1194

121

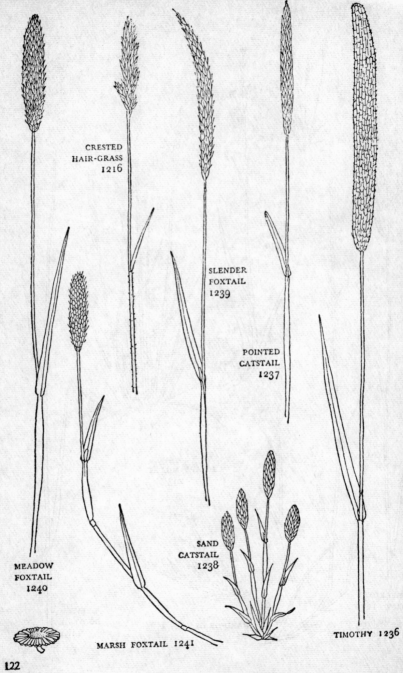

CRESTED
HAIR-GRASS
1216

SLENDER
FOXTAIL
1239

POINTED
CATSTAIL
1237

SAND
CATSTAIL
1238

MEADOW
FOXTAIL
1240

MARSH FOXTAIL 1241

TIMOTHY 1236

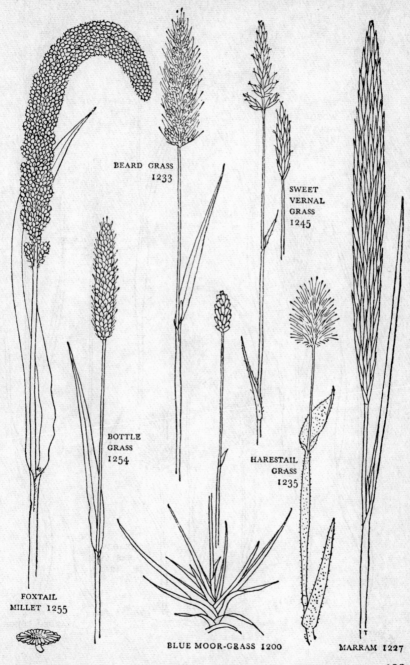

BEARD GRASS
1233

SWEET
VERNAL
GRASS
1245

BOTTLE
GRASS
1254

HARESTAIL
GRASS
1235

FOXTAIL
MILLET 1255

BLUE MOOR-GRASS 1200

MARRAM 1227

123

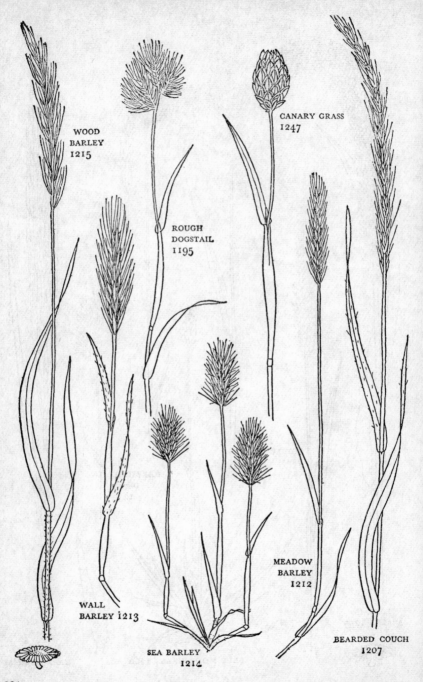

WOOD
BARLEY
1215

ROUGH
DOGSTAIL
1195

CANARY GRASS
1247

WALL
BARLEY 1213

SEA BARLEY
1214

MEADOW
BARLEY
1212

BEARDED COUCH
1207

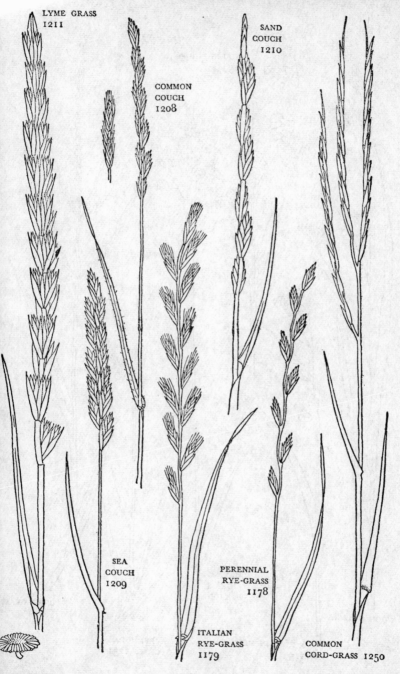

LYME GRASS
1211

COMMON
COUCH
1208

SAND
COUCH
1210

SEA
COUCH
1209

PERENNIAL
RYE-GRASS
1178

ITALIAN
RYE-GRASS
1179

COMMON
CORD-GRASS 1250

125

GIANT
QUAKING-GRASS
1197

QUAKING
GRASS
1196

WOOD MELICK
1198

MOUNTAIN MELICK
1199

BERMUDA
GRASS 1251

CRAB GRASS
1253

126

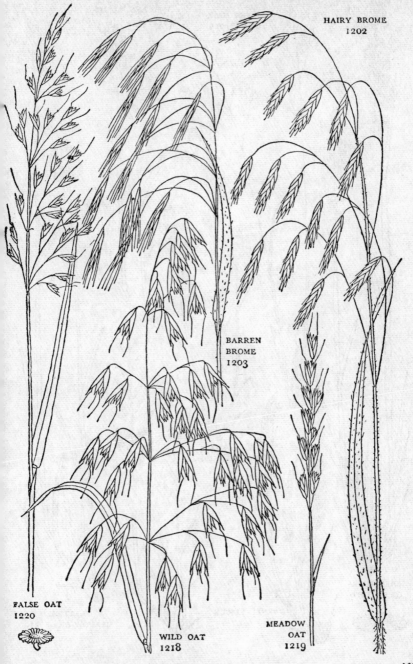

HAIRY BROME
1202

BARREN
BROME
1203

FALSE OAT
1220

WILD OAT
1218

MEADOW
OAT
1219

127

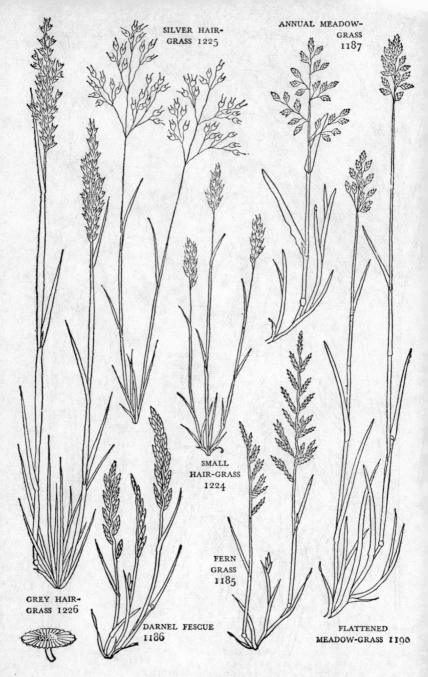

SILVER HAIR-
GRASS 1225

ANNUAL MEADOW-
GRASS
1187

SMALL
HAIR-GRASS
1224

GREY HAIR-
GRASS 1226

DARNEL FESCUE
1186

FERN
GRASS
1185

FLATTENED
MEADOW-GRASS 1190

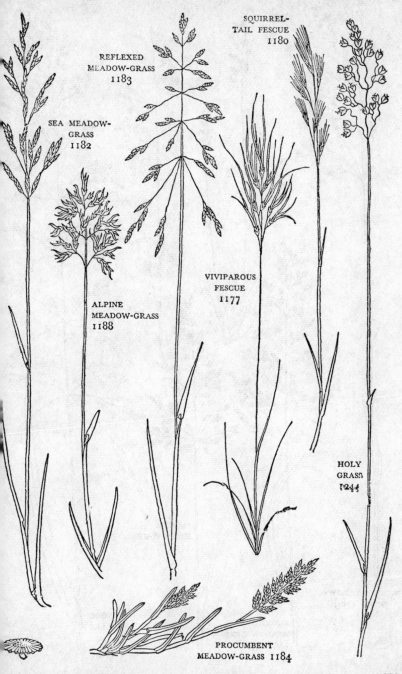

SQUIRREL-
TAIL FESCUE
1180

REFLEXED
MEADOW-GRASS
1183

SEA MEADOW-
GRASS
1182

ALPINE
MEADOW-GRASS
1188

VIVIPAROUS
FESCUE
1177

HOLY
GRASS
1244

PROCUMBENT
MEADOW-GRASS 1184

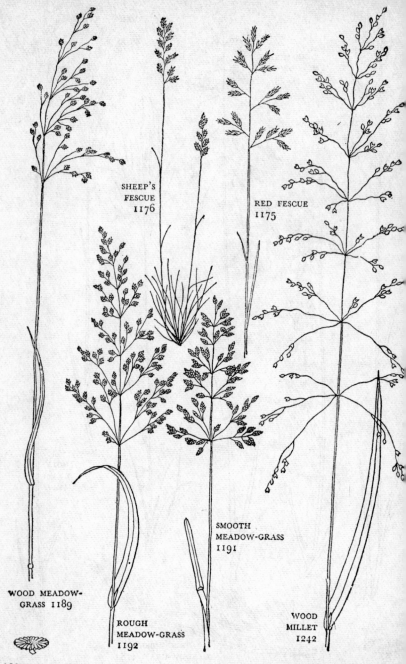

SHEEP'S
FESCUE
1176

RED FESCUE
1175

WOOD MEADOW-
GRASS 1189

ROUGH
MEADOW-GRASS
1192

SMOOTH
MEADOW-GRASS
1191

WOOD
MILLET
1242

130

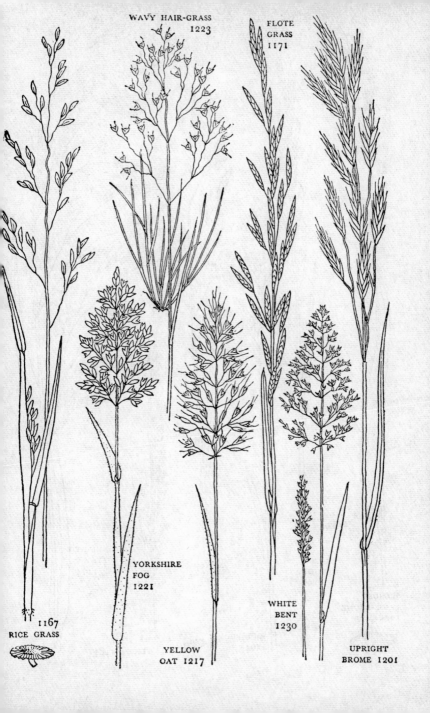

WAVY HAIR-GRASS 1223

FLOTE GRASS 1171

1167 RICE GRASS

YORKSHIRE FOG 1221

YELLOW OAT 1217

WHITE BENT 1230

UPRIGHT BROME 1201

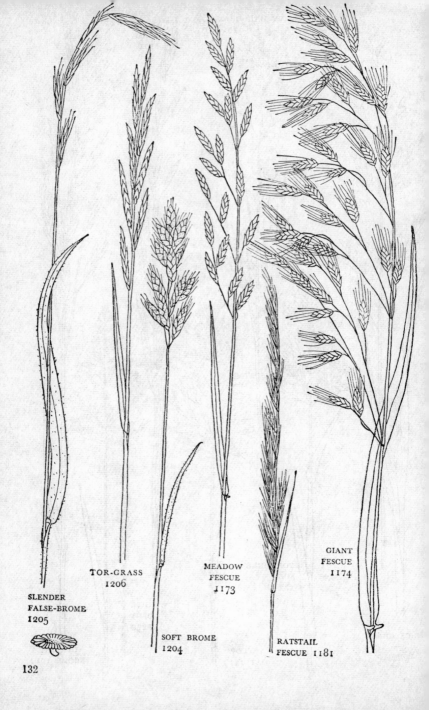

SLENDER
FALSE-BROME
1205

TOR-GRASS
1206

SOFT BROME
1204

MEADOW
FESCUE
1173

RATSTAIL
FESCUE 1181

GIANT
FESCUE
1174

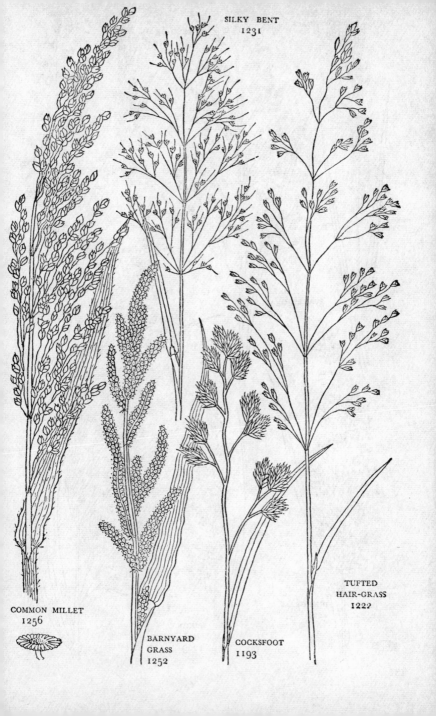

SILKY BENT
1231

COMMON MILLET
1256

BARNYARD
GRASS
1252

COCKSFOOT
1193

TUFTED
HAIR-GRASS
1222

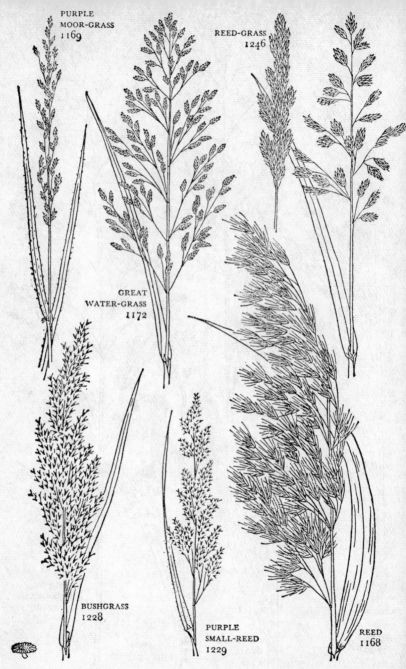

PURPLE
MOOR-GRASS
1169

REED-GRASS
1246

GREAT
WATER-GRASS
1172

BUSHGRASS
1228

PURPLE
SMALL-REED
1229

REED
1168

silky hairs on the stalks, which are especially conspicuous in fruit; lower pales long pointed. *Habitat:* Widespread and locally abundant in swamps and shallow fresh or brackish water; also on cliffs. August onwards. *Arundo phragmites* L.

1169. PURPLE MOOR-GRASS *Molinia caerulea* (L.) Moench
Plate 134. *CTW, p. 1418*

A coarse, variable, slightly hairy perennial, usually forming dense tussocks, with wiry stems 1–3 ft. high, stiff flat greyish leaves, a ring of hairs replacing the ligule; purplish leaf-sheaths; and a long, branched flower-head, either rather tenuous and spreading or narrowly spike-like, the very small often purple spikelets having 1–4 flowers. *Habitat:* Widespread and locally abundant in marshes, fens and on wet heaths and moors. July–September.

1170. HEATH GRASS *Sieglingia decumbens* (L.) Bernhardi Pl. 121. *CTW, 1418*
A slightly hairy perennial, 6–18 in. high, growing in often flattened tufts, with stiff fattish stems; short flat or rolled pale green leaves, a conspicuous ring of hairs replacing the ligule; flattened sheaths; and short narrow spike-like, very shortly branched flower-heads, with usually 3–6 swollen egg-shaped 4–6-flowered very shiny, green or purple spikelets; lower pales minutely 3-toothed at the top. *Habitat:* Widespread and locally common in dampish heathy places on acid soils. July–August. *Triodia decumbens* (L.) Beauvois

1171. FLOTE-GRASS *Glyceria fluitans* (L.) Brown Plate 131. *CTW, p. 1420*
A sprawling hairless aquatic perennial, 2–3 ft. long, the weak stems and roughish, pale green leaves often floating on the surface of the water, with smooth rounded sheaths and a long, pointed ligule. Flower-heads little-branched, spreading in flower but narrowly spike-like in fruit, with many-flowered green or purplish spikelets solitary or in groups of 2 or 3; lower pale fairly sharply pointed; glumes long. Hybridises with the next species. *Habitat:* Widespread, common in and by still and slow water. June–Aug. *Poa fluitans* (L.) Scopoli.

1171*a.* **Sweet-grass**, *G. plicata* Fries, differs in its broader, darker green leaves; roughish keeled leaf-sheaths; shorter rounded ligules; shorter, more branched flower-heads, spreading in fruit; shorter spikelets; bluntly pointed lower pale, and shorter anthers. Also widespread but rather less common, mainly in England.

1171*b.* *****Small Flote-grass**, *G. declinata* Brébisson, is smaller and neater than the last two, with parallel-sided, abruptly pointed leaves; leaf-sheaths keeled and usually smooth; stems and flower-heads less erect, much more curved and little branched, the lower pale bluntly pointed and obviously 3-toothed at the tip, the upper 2-toothed. More local and usually in muddier places.

1172. GREAT WATER GRASS *G. maxima* (Hartman) Holmberg Plate 134
A stout hairless reed-like perennial, 3–8 ft. tall and quite unlike the last three species, creeping and forming large patches but rarely so extensive as the Reed (1168), from which it can be told by its broader greener leaves with a short blunt, sometimes abruptly pointed, ligule and a brownish band where the sheath joins the leaf; leaves sometimes mimicking Sweet Flag (1096), being crinkled towards the tip. Flower-spikes also quite different, pale green, much branched, more stiffly spreading, not often tinged purple, with no silky hairs on the stalks of the several-flowered spikelets. *Habitat:* Widespread and common at the margins of fresh and brackish water; thinning out northwards. June–Aug. *Poa aquatica* L.

1173. MEADOW FESCUE *Festuca pratensis* Hudson Pl. 132. *CTW, p. 1423*

A stout hairless perennial, 1–3 ft. high, the base of the stems usually covered with decaying remnants of the dark brown sheaths; leaves rather narrow, rough-edged, tapering evenly, clasping the stem; ligule short, blunt. Flower-heads somewhat nodding, 1-sided, branched, the branches often in unequal pairs, the shorter one bearing only a single spikelet; spikelets rather large, loose, narrow lanceolate, many-flowered, glossy sometimes purplish. Hybridises with 1178. *Habitat:* Widespread and common in damp meadows. June–August. *'F. elatior.'*

1173a. **Tall Fescue,** *F. arundinacea* Schreber, is larger, more graceful, up to 5 ft. high, and often in coarse tussocks, with the decaying leaf-sheaths whitish; stiffer leaves twice as broad, only tapering above; and numerous broader compact egg-shaped spikelets on both branches of a pair. In rougher meadows, roadsides and dry clayey places near the sea.

1174. GIANT FESCUE *F. gigantea* (L.) Villars Plate 132. *CTW, p. 1424*

A stout hairless, loosely tufted perennial, 2–4 ft. high, with long broad shining rough-edged leaves, clasping the stem with short arms and reddish-purple at their junction with the roughish sheaths; ligule short, blunt. Flower-heads large, branched, spreading, drooping, the spikelets 3–7-flowered, each flower with a long awn. The somewhat similar Hairy Brome (1202), has green leaf-junctions, conspicuously hairy sheaths, and the spikelets and their stalks longer. *Habitat:* Widespread and locally frequent in woods and on shady banks. July–August, starting a month later than Hairy Brome. *Bromus giganteus* L.

1174a. ****Wood Fescue,** *F. altissima* Allioni (*F. silvatica* Villars), has the leaves almost as wide, but not shining or clasping the stem, leaf-junctions green ligules long, and less drooping, unawned spikelets. Local in rocky woods, usually near water, in the N and W, and in Sussex and Ireland. June–July.

1175. RED FESCUE *F. rubra* L. Plate 130. *CTW, p. 1425*

A very common, very variable, slightly hairy perennial, 6–15 in. high, usually shortly creeping but sometimes tufted, with the leaves of the flowering stems flat and bluntish, and those of the non-flowering stems inrolled, wire-like and pointed; sheaths split only at the top when young; ligule very short and blunt. The form growing on dunes has bluish-green leaves. Flower-heads branched, spreading, the spikelets sometimes reddish or purplish but usually green, many-flowered, each flower with a short awn. Varieties are grown in lawns as Chewings Fescue or Cumberland Sea-washed Turf. *Habitat:* Widespread and often abundant in all kinds of grassy places, including sand-dunes and salt-marshes. May–June. (Incl. *F. commutata* Gaudin, *F. arenaria* Retzius.)

1175a. ****Grandmother's Hair,** *F. heterophylla* Lamarck, is much taller, 2–4 ft. high, always tufted and not creeping, and has the lower leaves even more thread-like, the upper broad, and the flower-heads slightly nodding and green. Uncommon in plantations in the S, nearly always with 1191b. June–July.

1175b. *****Rush-leaved Fescue,** *F. juncifolia* St. Amans, is always bluish-green and far-creeping, and has very narrow stiff thicker, sharply hard-pointed leaves on the flowering stems. Flower-heads less spreading, with spikelets larger and usually greenish. Rare on dunes, on the E coast of England. June–July.

1176. SHEEP'S FESCUE *F. ovina* L.[1] Plate 130. *CTW, 2. 1426*

A very common, very variable, usually hairless perennial, 3–12 in. high, much

---

[1] Including *F. tenuifolia* Sibthorp (no awns, common on acid soils), *F. longifolia* Thuillier (*F. trachyphylla* (Hackel) Krajina), and *F. glauca* Lamarck.

tufted and not creeping, with all leaves short, very narrow, inrolled, usually almost hairlike and sometimes waxy-green, their sheaths split more than halfway to the base even when young; ligules very short, blunt. Flower-heads branched, spreading or fairly compact, the small greenish or purplish spikelets many-flowered, each flower with a short awn larger than in Red Fescue (1175), which also differs in its flat upper leaves and creeping runners, *Habitat:* Widespread and often abundant in drier grassland, especially on chalk and limestone. May–July.

1177. *VIVIPAROUS FESCUE *F. vivipara* (L.) Smith Pl. 129. *CTW, p. 1427*
Like a Sheep's Fescue (1176) in which the spikelets are never awned and the flowers are replaced by leafy green bulbils, so that small green blades sprout from the fruiting spikelets. Other species of Grass occasionally behave in this way, but none so commonly. *Habitat:* Widespread and common, mostly on mountains in the N and W. June–August.

1178. PERENNIAL RYE-GRASS *Lolium perenne* L. Plate 125. *CTW, p. 1428*
A common variable hairless perennial, with wiry stems 6–18 in. high, and smooth narrow shiny deep green leaves, somewhat folded when young. Flower-heads unbranched, spike-like, flat, with unstalked, many-flowered, sometimes purplish spikelets on either side of the stem and edgeways on to it; no awns; the only glume 5-nerved, shorter than the spikelet. Hybridises with 1173. *Habitat:* Widespread and common in grassy places; often cultivated. June–August.

1179. ITALIAN RYE-GRASS *L. multiflorum* Lamarck Pl. 125. *CTW, p. 1428*
Larger, stiffer, lusher and more distinctly tufted than the last species, and is annual or biennial with roughish stems and sheaths, broader leaves which are rolled when young, and a conspicuous awn on each flower in the longer spikelet, which has more (10–20) flowers. *Habitat:* Commonly cultivated and frequently persisting, especially on roadsides and the margins of fields, and in farmyards. May onwards. (Incl. *L. italicum* Braun.)

1179a. ***Darnel, *L. temulentum* L. (incl. *L. remotum* Schrank) ⚥, another annual, may or may not be awned, but always has the 3-nerved outer glume no shorter than the fatter 4–5-flowered spikelet. Now a rare casual. July onwards.

1180. SQUIRREL-TAIL FESCUE *Vulpia bromoides* (L.) Gray
Festuca bromoides L.   Plate 129. *CTW, p. 1430*
A very slender, almost hairless annual, 3–18 in. high, with thin stems and thread-like leaves, the margins inrolled. Flower-heads branched, often spreading,

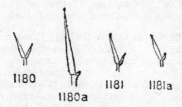

usually erect, 1-sided, distant from the topmost leaf-sheath; spikelets many-flowered, each flower with a long awn; lower pales obscurely 5-veined; lower glumes at least half as long as the upper, which are 3-veined (Fig.). *Habitat:* Widespread and frequent in dry bare places. May–July. Figs. × 2.

1180a. **Dune Fescue, *V. membranacea* (L.) Dumortier (*F. membranacea* (L.) Druce), superficially like a slender Wall Barley (1213), has larger spikelets than Squirrel-tail Fescue in a compact, stiffly erect, bright orange-brown 1-sided spike; longer awns; the lower pale prominently 1-veined; the lower glume minute, less than $\frac{1}{12}$ as long as the upper (Fig.); and the upper leaf-sheath inflated. Local on sand-dunes in the S, and in E Ireland.

1181. *RATSTAIL FESCUE   *V. myuros* (L.) Gmelin   Plate 132.   *CTW, p. 1431*
Usually taller than Squirrel-tail Fescue (1180), with the top leaf-sheath reaching the base of the flower-spike, which is longer, compacter, sometimes rather curved, and straw-coloured in fruit; lower glume $\frac{1}{4}$–$\frac{1}{3}$ as long as the 1-veined upper (Fig., p. 271). *Habitat:* Widespread and locally frequent in dry, bare places, mainly in the S. June–July. *Festuca myuros* L.

1181a. **Purple Fescue, *V. ambigua* (Le Gall) More (*F. ambigua* Le Gall), turns conspicuously reddish as it goes over, and is shorter, with stems almost smooth; leaf-sheaths often purplish; shorter, slenderer, less stiffly erect flower-spikes; and larger red-brown spikelets, the lower glume only $\frac{1}{6}$ as long as the upper (Fig.). Very local on walls and dunes on the S coast of England; rare inland.

1182. SEA MEADOW-GRASS   *Puccinellia maritima* (Hudson)
Poa maritima Hudson   Parlatore Pl. 129.   *CTW, p. 1432*
A hairless sward-forming perennial, often prostrate, a foot or so long, with runners and the margins of the short, very narrow, often greyish leaves usually inrolled; stem-leaves stiffly spreading; and ligule short, blunt. Flower-heads branched, usually more or less spreading, but the fruiting spikelets erect; spikelets usually purplish, many-flowered. *Habitat:* Widespread and locally abundant in salt-marshes. July–August.

1183. REFLEXED MEADOW-GRASS   *P. distans* (L.) Parlatore
                                    Plate 129.   *CTW, p. 1432*
Differs from the last species in being tufted and erect, not forming a sward, and having no runners; leaves often flat and greyer; and the branches of the flower-head long, devoid of spikelets in their lower half, erect before flowering, spreading in flower and turned down in fruit.   *Habitat:* Widespread and frequent on mud in dykes, brackish marshes and elsewhere near the sea; very rare inland. July–August. *Poa distans* L; (incl. *Puc. pseudodistans* (Crépin) Janssen & Wachter).

1183a. **Borrer's Saltmarsh Grass, *P. fasciculata* (Torrey) Bicknell, is shorter and has the branches of the flower-head covered with more numerous clustered spikelets to the base, and not turned down in fruit; often a solitary spikelet in the fork of the branches. Local on mud near the sea in the S, and in SE Ireland.

1184. **PROCUMBENT MEADOW-GRASS   *P. rupestris* (Withering)
Poa rupestris With.   Fernald & Weatherby   Plate 129.   *CTW, p. 1433*
Much shorter and stouter than Reflexed Saltmarsh Grass (1183), annual, often prostrate, and usually 4–6 in. long; with flat roughish leaves; the upper sheaths inflated; and compacter 1-sided, less spreading flower-heads, the branches short, very narrow, flattened, stiff and spreading, rather like Fern Grass (1185) in habit. *Habitat:* Local in barer places near the sea in the S. June–September.

1185. *FERN GRASS   *Catapodium rigidum* (L.) Hubbard   Pl. 128.   *CTW, 1434*
A distinctive, very stiff hairless annual, 2–9 in. high, long persisting when dead, with narrow, often purplish leaves; ligule short, blunt. Flower-heads rigid, often

1-sided, with stiff narrow ascending branches, the small, often purplish, many-flowered spikelets on stalks shorter than themselves. *Habitat:* Widespread and locally frequent on walls, rocks and other dry bare places, especially in the S. May–September. *Poa rigida* L., *Desmazeria rigida* (L.) Tutin.

1186. **DARNEL FESCUE *C. marinum* (L.) Hubbard Pl. 128. *CTW, 1453*
Greener and fleshier than the last species, with a narrower unbranched flower-head, the broader spikelets usually not stalked, but the lower ones sometimes on very short stalks; leaves somewhat broader. *Habitat:* Local in bare sandy or stony places by the sea. May–July. *P. loliacea* Hudson, *D. marina* (L.) Druce.

1187. ANNUAL MEADOW-GRASS *Poa annua* L. Plate 128. *CTW, p. 1436*
A ubiquitous, pale green, more or less tufted, variable hairless annual 2–10 in. high, with flat leaves hooded at the tip, and often transversely wrinkled when young; ligule longish, blunt. Flower-heads more or less triangular in outline, branched, the branches often in pairs, spreading, often turned down in fruit; spikelets many-flowered, pale whitish-green, occasionally purplish. *Habitat:* Widespread and abundant in all kinds of waste, bare and cultivated places. Throughout the year.

1188. **ALPINE MEADOW-GRASS *P. alpina* L. Plate 129. *CTW, p. 1438*
A stiff bluish-green hairless perennial, 4–9 in. high, the rootstock covered with the remains of old leaf-sheaths; leaves ending abruptly in a blunt point; ligule blunt or pointed. Flower-heads branched, rather dense, the branches usually in pairs, spreading, the large, often purplish, 2–5-flowered spikelets often replaced by sprouting bulbils like Viviparous Fescue (1177). *Habitat:* Uncommon on mountain ledges in the N; rare in W Ireland. June–August.
1188*a.* *****Wavy Meadow-grass**, *P. flexuosa* Smith ('*P. laxa*'), is smaller, slenderer, diffuser, and never viviparous, with narrower leaves, tapering gradually to a fine point, and compacter, more oblong flower-heads with slightly wavy branches. Very rare on scree on Ben Nevis and Lochnagar.

1189. WOOD MEADOW-GRASS *P. nemoralis* L. Plate 130. *CTW, p. 1439*
A variable weak graceful, dark green hairless tufted perennial, 9 in. to 2 ft. high, with delicate narrow leaves spreading more or less at right angles to the flowering stems; ligule blunt, very short, Flower-heads branched, spreading, sometimes rather nodding, the tiny, very slender, 1–5-flowered, usually whitish spikelets on long, hair-like stalks. *Habitat:* Widespread and frequent in dry woods and on shady banks, also on mountains, where it looks rather different; rare in Ireland. June onwards.
1189*a.* ****Bluish Mountain Meadow-grass**, *P. glauca* Vahl, is much shorter, 4–8 in. high, and more tufted, with stiffer waxy-bluish leaves, a longer ligule, and smaller stiffer erecter flower-heads, the spikelets on shorter, thicker stalks. Very local on high mountains in the N. July–August.
1189*b.* ****Mountain Meadow-grass**, *P. balfourii* Parnell, is somewhat intermediate between the Bluish and Wood Meadow-grasses, and readily taken for the latter from which it differs in its longer upper ligules, and from the former mainly in its greener, less waxy and weaker leaves and more spreading flower-heads. Rare on mountains in the N. July–August.

1190. FLATTENED MEADOW-GRASS *P. compressa* L. Pl. 128. *CTW, 1440*
A rather stiff, often tufted perennial, 6–15 in. high, with flattened flowering stems and rather greyish leaves, the topmost longer than its sheath; ligule short, blunt. Flower-heads small, branched, only slightly spreading, rather 1-sided, with many-flowered spikelets, which extend to the base of the branches. *Habitat:* Widespread and locally frequent in dry, rather bare places, less often on walls than the next species; rare in Ireland. June–August.

1191. SMOOTH MEADOW-GRASS *P. pratensis* L.
(incl. *P. angustifolia* L., *P. subcaerulea* Smith)   Plate 130. *CTW, p. 1440*
A very variable, usually hairless, often tufted, rather stiff stocky creeping perennial, 2 in. to 2 ft. high, with green or slightly bluish or greyish leaves hooded and blunt or abruptly pointed at the tip; sheaths smooth to the touch, keeled below; ligule short, blunt. Flower-heads branched, spreading, often narrowly triangular in outline, with 2–5-flowered, often purplish spikelets. *Habitat:* Widespread and abundant in drier grassy places. May–June.

1191*a*. ****Bulbous Meadow-grass**, *P. bulbosa* L., is smaller, 4–9 in. high, earlier flowering and not creeping, with the stems swollen and more or less bulbous at the base, the bulbs and narrower lower leaves pinkish-brown; a longer, pointed ligule; and a smaller more compact flower-head. Very locally plentiful on dunes in S England; very rare on limestone inland. March–April.

1191*b*. ****Broad-leaved Meadow-grass**, *P. chaixii* Villars, is very much larger, to 4 ft., and conspicuously tufted, with flattened, slightly rough, sharply keeled sheaths, short leaves ¼-in. or more wide, and flower-heads 4–10 in. long. Naturalised in a few plantations, usually with Grandmother's Hair (1175*a*). May–July.

1192. ROUGH MEADOW-GRASS *P. trivialis* L. Plate 130. *CTW, p. 1442*
Paler than Common Meadow-grass (1191), with short runners above instead of below ground; stems often slenderer; leaf-sheaths rough to the touch; more acutely pointed flatter weaker leaves; long jagged pointed ligules; and rather smaller spikelets; lower pales keeled, 5-nerved, pointed. *Habitat:* Widespread and common in moister and often shadier grassy places. June–July.

1192*a*. ****Narrow-leaved Meadow grass**, *P. palustris* L., is taller near water, but elsewhere somewhat like Wood Meadow-grass (1189); with no creeping runners, smooth sheaths, narrow tapering leaves, shorter blunter ligules and smaller spikelets. Very local, near fresh water and on waste ground.

1192*b*. ***Water Whorl-grass**, *Catabrosa aquatica* (L.) Beauvois, is rarely over a foot high, with roots at the joints of its far-creeping runners, and soft sweet-tasting stems and leaves; leaves pale green, weak, blunt-tipped, broader, and smooth sheaths. Flower-heads distinctly branched, with half-whorls alternating up the stem, the very short blunt purple glumes and protruding green pales giving a two-coloured appearance to the 1–3-flowered spikelets; lower pales rounded on the back, 3-nerved, blunt at top. Widespread but scarce and decreasing in or by shallow fresh water. June–August.

1193. COCKSFOOT *Dactylis glomerata* L. Plate 133. *CTW, p. 1444*
One of our commonest and most distinctive Grasses, with its branched, 1-sided flower-head of egg-shaped clusters of green or purplish spikelets, the lowest often on a long stalk more or less at right angles to the stem. A stout, coarsely tufted, usually hairless perennial, 6 in. to 3 ft. high, with flat keeled, slightly rough-edged leaves; rough, shortly keeled sheaths; and long blunt,

slightly torn ligules, Spikelets 2–5-flowered, each flower with a short awn, their glumes with a bristly keel. *Habitat:* Widespread and abundant in grassy and waste places. May onwards. (Incl. *D. polygama* Horvats.)

1194. CRESTED DOGSTAIL *Cynosurus cristatus* L. Pl. 121. *CTW, p. 1444*
Another distinctive Grass, with its dense narrow 1-sided, flower-spike, 1–2 in. long, fancifully likened to the tail of a dog. A wiry tufted hairless perennial, 6–15 in. high, with short narrow leaves and very short, blunt ligules. Spikelets close-set, flattened, sometimes purplish, some 2–5-flowered, the rest sterile and persisting on very short or no stalks, each flower usually with a very short awn. *Habitat:* Widespread and common in meadows and pastures. June–August.

1195. **ROUGH DOGSTAIL *C. echinatus* L. Plate 124. *CTW, p. 1445*
A hairless annual, 6–8 in. high, with broad leaves, the upper sheaths slightly inflated, and long, bluntly pointed ligules. Flower-heads egg-shaped, prickly, one-sided, the sometimes purplish spikelets fertile and 1–5-flowered or sterile and persistent, each flower with a conspicuous awn. *Habitat:* Uncommon in waste and sandy places, especially by the sea, mainly in the S. June–July.

1196. QUAKING-GRASS *Briza media* L. Plate 126. *CTW, p. 1445*
A distinctive Grass, with its glossy, very shortly oval or triangular, green or purplish spikelets hanging on long slender stalks and shaking in the wind; a hairless, loosely tufted perennial, 9–18 in. high, with very short, blunt ligules, and open branched flower-heads, the spikelets sometimes green, many-flowered, the pales closely overlapping. *Habitat:* Widespread and common on downs and in dry or moist grassland. June–August.
1196*a*. *****Lesser Quaking-grass**, *B. minor* L., is annual and usually larger and taller, with longer ligules; broader and more finely pointed leaves; broader flower-heads; and numerous triangular, pale green spikelets. Frequent on arable or waste ground in the Channel Is.; scarce elsewhere. June–September.

1197. ***GIANT QUAKING-GRASS *B. maxima* L. Plate 126. *CTW, p. 1446*
A distinctive hairless annual, 6–12 in. high, with long blunt ligules, and a branched nodding flower-head with few, long, egg-shaped, many-flowered silvery green spikelets, 4 times as large as Common Quaking-grass (1196). *Habitat:* Dry bare places in the Channel and Scilly Is.; rare elsewhere. May–July.

1198. WOOD MELICK *Melica uniflora* Retzius Plate 126. *CTW, p. 1447*
A graceful pale green perennial, 12–18 in. high, with the tubular often hairy leaf-sheaths ending in a fine bristle opposite the limp flat leaves, which are downy above and roughish beneath; ligules short, abruptly pointed. Flower-heads open, with a few spreading branches, often nodding, with a very few purplish-brown, roundly egg-shaped long-stalked 1-flowered spikelets. Fruits large, swollen, green. *Habitat:* Widespread, locally frequent in woods and hedge-banks. April–July.

1199. **MOUNTAIN MELICK *M. nutans* L. Plate 126. *CTW, p. 1447*
Differs from the last species especially in its narrow 1-sided unbranched flower-spike, also in its leaves being smooth beneath, the sheaths not downy and with no bristle, and the ligules very short and blunt. The larger 2–3-flowered spikelets droop in a neat row from the stem. *Habitat:* Local in woods and shady places on limestone in the N; very rare further S; not in Ireland. May–July.

1200. *BLUE MOOR-GRASS *Sesleria caerulea* (L.) Arduino Pl. 123.*CTW,1448*

A stiff hairless perennial, 6–12 in. high, with leaves and sheaths both keeled, and leaves greyish, blunt with a minute point at the tip, roughish on edges downwards; ligules very short, blunt. Flower-heads unbranched, egg-shaped, very compact with unstalked 2–3-flowered violet-blue spikelets, the stalks lengthening in fruit, each flower with a minute awn. *Habitat:* Locally frequent in open and grassy places on limestone in N England and W Ireland; rare on mountains in the Highlands. April–May. Blue Mountain-Grass.

1201. *UPRIGHT BROME *Bromus erectus* Hudson Plate 131. *CTW, p. 1449*
Zerna erecta (Hudson) Gray.

A stiff stout sometimes slightly hairy perennial, 2–4 ft. high, with the upper leaves flat and broader than the inrolled lower ones; ligules short, blunt. Flower-heads branched, usually erect, with very long-stalked, usually purplish-green compressed, many-flowered spikelets, each flower with a long bristle; anthers orange. *Habitat:* The typical tall grass of dry chalk and limestone grassland, locally abundant in the S, thinning out northwards; local in Ireland. May–July.

1202. HAIRY BROME *B. ramosus* Hudson Plate 127. *CTW, p. 1449*

A very large stout graceful hairy, loosely tufted perennial, 3–5 ft. high, with dark green, rather broad drooping leaves, sheaths covered with long downturned hairs and blunt ligules. Flower-heads open, often very large, on long arching stems, conspicuously drooping, branched, with many-flowered, often purplish spikelets an inch or more long, each flower with a long awn. Sometimes confused with Giant Fescue (1174), which is hairless and less drooping, with reddish leaf-junctions. *Habitat:* Widespread and common in woods and hedgebanks. June–August, earlier than 1174. *Zerna ramosa* (Hudson) Lindman.

1203. BARREN BROME *B. sterilis* L. Plate 127. *CTW, p. 1451*

A rather floppy weedy downy annual, 6–18 in. high, often turning purplish-red; ligules short, bluntly pointed. Flower-heads loose, long, branched, markedly drooping, with 1–2 large wedge-shaped spikelets, many flowered, 2 in. long, narrow, much shorter than their stalks, the individual flowers each with an awn up to an inch long. *Habitat:* Widespread and common in waste places and by waysides. May–July. *Anisantha sterilis* (L.) Nevski.

1203a. **Compact Brome, *B. madritensis* L. (*A. madritensis* (L.) Nevski), is usually shorter, with more jagged ligules and erect, scarcely branched dense bushy flower-heads, the spikelets much longer than their stalks. Rare in dry bare places in the S, and in S Ireland.

1203b. **Great Brome, *B. diandrus* Roth (*A. gussonii* (Parlatore) Nevski; '*B. maximus*') (incl. *B. rigidus* Roth (*A. rigida* (Roth) Hylander)), is often stouter and has the stems hairy below the less lax flower-heads, and the spikelets about 3 in. long, including the 1–2-in. long awns. Established in waste places, not infrequent in the Channel Is., rare elsewhere in S England.

SOFT BROMES *Bromus mollis*

A VARIABLE group of slender greyish, softly downy annuals or biennials, with flat leaves rolled in bud, a short blunt ligule and tubular sheaths soon splitting, the lower usually hairy. Flower-heads varying from small, erect and compact to large, open and drooping; spikelets fat-looking, oblong, narrowed at the top, rather flattened, usually hairless and breaking up when ripe; lower glume broad and swollen, generally distinctly veined; pales overlapping, the lower with a slender, hardly spreading awn; anthers normally short, on short stalks.

1204. SOFT BROME *B. mollis* L. Plate 132. *CTW, p. 1454*

Has a short oval flower-head, normally both erect and compound, with many short-stalked, usually very downy egg-shaped spikelets; pales long, rounded, very tightly overlapping. Especially by the sea in the S it may be only 2 in. high, with spreading awns. *Habitat:* Widespread and very common in fields and waste places. June–August, the earliest of the group to flower. (Incl. *B. ferronii* Mabille; *B. thominii* Hardouin (*B. hordeaceus* L.); *B. interruptus* (Hackel) Druce.)

1204a. *Slender Brome, *B. lepidus* Holmberg, has a neater, shorter flower-head, with shorter smaller, usually hairless, narrow elliptical spikelets, more spreading in fruit; glumes with broad transparent margins; pales also smaller, short, with an angled shoulder. Less common.

1204b. *Smooth Brome, *B. racemosus* L., is slenderer and much less hairy, with a longer looser, usually unbranched flower-head; spikelets few, long-stalked, rather large, tapering, usually hairless, often pinkish, shining; glumes with weaker veins. In richer meadows.

1204c. *Meadow Brome, *B. commutatus* Schrader is stouter than Smooth Brome, with a broader elongated branched flower-head rather drooping to one side; many broad green spikelets; and larger pales.

1204d. **Rye Brome, *B. secalinus* L., has a long flower-head more or less branched and finally markedly drooping to one side; many long-stalked spikelets, with spreading awns, not readily breaking up; pales very loosely overlapping. Rather rare in cornfields.

1205. SLENDER FALSE-BROME *Brachypodium sylvaticum* (Hudson) Beauvois
Plate 132. *CTW, p. 1459*

A tufted perennial, sparsely to softly hairy, 1–2 ft. high, with rather broad flaccid soft green leaves and short blunt ligules. Flower-spikes unbranched, usually nodding, the spikelets long, short-stalked, many-flowered, each flower with a long awn. *Habitat:* Widespread and frequent in woods and hedge-banks. July–August.

1206. *TOR-GRASS *B. pinnatum* (L.) Beauvois Plate 132. *CTW, p. 1459*

Stiffer and much less downy than the last species, creeping and often forming conspicuous yellowish patches, with stems and sheaths usually hairless; leaves green or orange-green, either flat or stiffer, narrower, inrolled and stiffly hairy on the margins. Flower spikes erect, the flowers with shorter awns. *Habitat:* Locally common and increasing in open chalk and limestone grassland in S England; rather rare elsewhere. June–August. Heath False-Brome.

1207. BEARDED COUCH *Agropyron caninum* (L.) Beauv. Pl. 124. *CTW, 1460*

Shorter, slenderer, softer, paler green and more flaccid than Common Couch (1208), tufted and with no creeping runners; stem joints usually downy; wider softer leaves; flower-heads compact but longer and drooping, the individual flowers always with a long straight awn. *Habitat:* Widespread and locally frequent in and by damp woods, on hedge-banks and by streams. June–August.

1207a. ***Don's Twitch, *A. donianum* Buchanan-White, is stiffer, never in large tufts, and has much smaller awns and no bearded joints on the stem. Very rare on rock-ledges in the Highlands. July–September.

1208. COMMON COUCH *A. repens* (L.) Beauvois Plate 125. *CTW, p. 1461*

A far-creeping, coarse, tenacious perennial weed, occasionally bluish-green, with hairless stems 1–3 ft. high, the lower sheaths sometimes slightly hairy; ligules very short, blunt. Flower-spikes unbranched, stiffly erect, rather short and open, the unstalked, many-flowered spikelets arranged singly and alternately in two rows up opposite sides of the stem and broadside on to it; lower pale rounded on the back, untoothed, sometimes ending in a very short awn. *Habitat:* Widespread and common in cultivated and waste ground. June–Sept. Twitch.

1208a. Bread Wheat, *Triticum aestivum* L. (*CTW, 1463*), is stouter, annual and not creeping, with thicker hollow stems, fatter spikelets and the lower pales keeled in the upper half. A frequent relic of cultivation. Rivet Wheat (*T. turgidum* L.), less often cultivated, has solid stems and lower pales keeled throughout.

1209. *SEA COUCH *A. pungens* (Persoon) Roemer & Schultes
Plate 125. *CTW, p. 1461*

Differs from Common Couch (1208) in being always hairless and with a bluish or greyish tinge; the margins of the broader, sharply pointed, much stiffer leaves often inrolled; larger spikelets, overlapping those on the other side of the stem; and the lower pales only rarely and shortly awned; non-flowering shoots erect. *Habitat:* Widespread and locally common on sea-walls and banks near the sea and in drier salt-marshes; not in Scotland and N Ireland. July–September.

1210. SAND COUCH *A. junceiforme* (Löve) Löve Plate 125. *CTW, p. 1462*

Much greyer than Sea Couch (1209), with fatter, brittle flowering stems, prostrate non-flowering shoots, leaves with downy ribs, and fatter flower-heads with larger spikelets, widely spaced and hardly overlapping those on the opposite side of the stem. Hybridises with Common Couch (1208) and Sea Couch (1209). *Habitat:* Widespread and common on sandy shores, often forming small dunes in front of the main Marram (1227) dunes. June–August. '*A. junceum*'

1211. *LYME GRASS *Elymus arenarius* L. Plate 125. *CTW, p. 1463*

A stout creeping, intensely grey perennial, 2–4 ft. high, with stiff, broad, sharply pointed, sometimes inrolled leaves; ligule short, blunt. Flower-heads very large, unbranched, spike-like, with pairs of downy unstalked many-flowered spikelets broadside on as in Common Couch (1208), alternating up either side of the stem. Sometimes confused with the far smaller Sand Couch (1210), whose spikelets are not in pairs, but is more like Marram (1227) in size and build. *Habitat:* Widespread but local on dunes by the sea, often among Marram, commonest in the N and E. June–August.

1212. *MEADOW BARLEY *Hordeum secalinum* Schreber Pl. 124. *CTW, 1464*

A perennial, up to 18 in. high, taller and slenderer than the next species, also less leafy and not tufted, with the upper leaf-sheaths not inflated, and shorter, softer, less stout grey-green flower-heads. *Habitat:* Widespread and locally frequent, especially in meadows and pastures on clay, thinning out northwards; rare in Scotland and Ireland. June–July. '*H. nodosum*'

1213. WALL BARLEY *H. murinum* L. Plate 124. *CTW, p. 1464*

A coarse, pale green tufted annual, 6–12 in. high, with the flowering stems prostrate at the base; lower sheaths usually hairy, the upper slightly inflated; leaves sometimes slightly hairy; and ligules short and blunt. Flower-heads unbranched, spike-like, grass-green, with 1-flowered spikelets arranged in alternating groups of 3 broadside up the stem, the middle of each trio larger and unstalked; each spikelet furnished with 3 rough stiff awns up to an inch long. *Habitat:* Widespread and common by waysides and in waste places, especially near the sea. June–July.

1213*a*. **Barley,** *H. vulgare* L., has the spikelets in 6 rows, all 3 spikelets in each trio producing a grain, unlike Two-rowed Barley (*H. distichon* L.), which is less often cultivated, and has the spikelets in 2 rows, the middle spikelet only in each trio being fertile. A frequent relic of cultivation.

1213*b*. ***Rye,** *Secale cereale* L., has 2 flowers in each spikelet, and the spikelets solitary instead of in threes. Not often cultivated, so uncommon as a relic.

1214. *SEA BARLEY *H. marinum* Hudson Plate 124. *CTW, p. 1465*
Shorter, stiffer and bluer-green than Wall Barley (1213), with flowering stems more prostrate at the base before bending upwards; and bushier flower-spikes only half as long, with more spreading awns, the lowest almost at right angles to the stem. *Habitat:* Widespread but very local near the sea; not in Ireland or N Scotland. June–July. Squirrel-tail Grass.

1215. **WOOD BARLEY *Hordelymus europaeus* (L.) Harz Pl. 124. *CTW, 1465*
A downy perennial, 1–3 ft. high, somewhat like a tall Meadow Barley (1212), but paler green with the joints of the stem, sheaths and longer broader leaves all downy; flower-heads longer, looser and narrower. *Habitat:* Widespread and scarce, but locally common in woods and hedge-banks, especially on chalk or limestone. June–July. *Hordeum europaeum* (L.) Allioni.

1216. CRESTED HAIR-GRASS *Koeleria gracilis* Persoon
'*K. cristata*'; (incl. *K. albescens* DC.) Plate 122. *CTW, p. 1467*
A rather stiff, minutely downy, greyish-green tufted perennial, 4–12 in. high, with leaves either narrow and inrolled or flat and well ribbed. Flower-heads very shortly branched but narrow, interrupted and spike-like, with shining silvery purplish, greenish or whitish, very short-stalked, 2–3-flowered spikelets, the glumes with translucent silvery margins. *Habitat:* Widespread and locally frequent in dry turf, especially on dunes and on chalk or limestone. June–July.

1216*a*. *****Somerset Hair-grass,** *K. vallesiana* (Honckeny) Bertoloni, is markedly tufted, with the stems somewhat woody, conspicuously swollen at the base, and thickly covered with a network of dead leaf-sheaths, and the flower-heads never interrupted. Confined to a few limestone hills near Weston-super-Mare.

1217. YELLOW OAT *Trisetum flavescens* (L.) Beauvois
Avena flavescens L. Plate 131. *CTW, p. 1468*
A pale, slender often softly hairy perennial, 6–18 in. high, with narrow, flat leaves and short blunt ligules. Flower-heads dainty, branched, spreading, with pale shining yellow, almost erect, oat-like (but much smaller than in the other Oats), 2–4-flowered spikelets, each flower with a bent awn. *Habitat:* Widespread and frequent in grassy places, especially on chalk or limestone. June–July.

1218. WILD OAT *Avena fatua* L. Plate 127. *CTW, p. 1469*
A stout loosely tufted annual, 1–4 ft. high, with the lower leaf-sheaths usually somewhat hairy, broad, roughish leaves, and long blunt ligules. Flower-heads large, branched, spreading, nodding, with characteristically oat-like

spikelets, green, 2–3-flowered, each flower with a long, often bent awn and a tuft of tawny hairs, its lower pale toothed at the tip. *Habitat*: Widespread and abundant as a pest of arable fields. June–August. (Incl. *A. ludoviciana* Durieu.)

1218*a*. *Black Oat, *A. strigosa* Schreber, has no tuft of tawny hairs in the flowers, and its lower pale has a pair of terminal awns up to ½-in. long. The cultivated oat of Ireland and parts of the N and W, where it is a frequent relic; elsewhere an uncommon casual.

1218*b*. Oat, *A. sativa* L., has neither the tuft of tawny hairs nor the terminal awns on the lower pale. A common relic of cultivation.

1219. MEADOW OAT   *Helictotrichon pratense* (L.) Pilger
Avena pratensis L.   Plate 127.   *CTW, p. 1470*

A hairless perennial, 1–2 ft. high, with stiff, grooved, bluish-green, blunt-tipped leaves, narrower than in Wild Oat (1218), and pointed ligules. Flower-heads not branched or spreading, with shining, green or purplish, 3–6-flowered, short-stalked silvery oat-like spikelets, much smaller than in Wild Oat, each flower with a bent awn. *Habitat:* Widespread and locally frequent in established grassland, especially on chalk or limestone; not in Ireland. June–July.

1219*a*. Downy Oat, *H. pubescens* (Hudson) Pilger (*A. pubescens* Hudson), is greyer, softly hairy on the lower leaf-sheaths and has softer flat green leaves, the flower-heads more branched and spreading, and the 2–4-flowered spikelets more numerous. In rougher grass and on dunes; local in Ireland. May–July.

1220. FALSE OAT   *Arrhenatherum elatius* (L.) Presl   Plate 127.   *CTW, p. 1471*

A coarse, usually hairless perennial, 2–4 ft. high, with finely pointed, roughish leaves and short blunt ligules; rootstock often bulbous. Flower-heads branched, spreading, often nodding, with shining green or purplish, 2-flowered spikelets shorter than in Meadow Oat (1219), oat-like but with the awn straight; usually 1 flower male and awned, the other male and female and usually unawned. *Habitat:* Widespread and abundant in waste places and by roads. June onwards.

1221. YORKSHIRE FOG   *Holcus lanatus* L.   Plate 131.   *CTW, p. 1472*

A grey, softly downy tufted perennial, 1–2 ft. high, with downy leaves and sheaths, and short blunt ligules. Flower-heads downy, thick, branched, more or less spreading, with pinkish or whitish, 2-flowered spikelets, each flower with a very short awn, which does not protrude. *Habitat:* Widespread and abundant in all kinds of grassy places. May onwards.

1221*a*. Creeping Soft-grass, *H. mollis* L., is slenderer and greener, with far-creeping rootstock, stem-joints conspicuously bearded, the leaf-sheaths and stems usually hairless, and a prominent bent awn protruding from each flower. Common, in open woods and on heaths, preferring acid soils. July–August.

1222. TUFTED HAIR-GRASS   *Deschampsia cespitosa* (L.) Beauvois
Aira cespitosa L.   Plate 133.   *CTW, p. 1473*

A stout coarse hairless perennial, 1–4 ft. high, growing in tussocks, with broad flat rough-edged, deeply grooved leaves and very long, pointed ligules. Flower-heads branched, much taller than the leaves, spreading, with 2-flowered, often silvery or purplish spikelets, each flower with a very short awn arising at the base of the upper pale. *Habitat:* Widespread and common in neglected ill-drained grass fields and woods; also on moors and mountains. June–August.

1222a. ***Alpine Hair-grass, *D. alpina* (L.) Roemer & Schultes, is much smaller, with rather stiff leaves, the awn arising above the middle of the pale, and much more often has the flowers replaced by leafy bulbils, as in Viviparous Fescue (1177). Rare on bare ground on mountains in the N, and in W Ireland. July–August.

1223. WAVY HAIR-GRASS *D. flexuosa* (L.) Trinius Plate 131. *CTW, p. 1474*
Aira flexuosa L.
A graceful, hairless perennial, 9–18 in. high, growing in tufts, with rather short, dark green bristle-like leaves, their sheaths usually roughish, and short, very broad blunt ligules. Flower-heads branched, usually spreading, with shining silvery or purplish, 2-flowered spikelets on hair-like stalks, the glumes transparent, each flower with an awn. *Habitat:* Widespread and locally common on dry heaths and in heathy woods, moors and mountains, on acid soils. June–July.

1223a. ***Bog Hair-grass, *D. setacea* (Hudson) Hackel (*A. setacea* Hudson), is rather taller, with leaf-sheaths always smooth; and long narrow pointed ligules; and the second flower of each spikelet stalked and projecting. Rare in very wet bogs and damp dune-slacks. July–August.

1224. SMALL HAIR-GRASS *Aira praecox* L. Plate 128. *CTW, p. 1475*
A small pale hairless annual, 2–6 in. high, with smooth leaf-sheaths, inrolled, bristle-like leaves, and long pointed ligules. Flower-heads shortly branched, compact, egg-shaped, spike-like, with silvery, 2-flowered spikelets, each flower with a bent awn; very distinctive in their silvery sheaths. *Habitat:* Widespread and frequent in dry bare places on acid soils; occasionally in turf in the far N. April–June.

1225. SILVER HAIR-GRASS *A. caryophyllea* L. Plate 128. *CTW, p. 1475*
Larger and more silvery-looking than the last species, and with the leaf-sheaths roughish, and widely spreading, longer-branched flower-heads. *Habitat:* Widespread, frequent in dry bare places on sandy and gravelly soils. May–July.

1226. **GREY HAIR-GRASS *Corynephorus canescens* (L.) Beauvois
Aira canescens L. Plate 128. *CTW, p. 1476*
A greyish-blue, hairless tufted perennial, 6–15 in. high, with flower-stems only a little longer than the stiff, sharply pointed bristle-like leaves; purplish-pink roughish leaf-sheaths; and short, pointed ligules. Flower-heads branched, spreading in flower but compact in fruit, with 2-flowered, purplish spikelets, each flower with a club-shaped awn, the tip of which is thickened like the antenna of a butterfly, unlike the awns of our other Grasses. *Habitat:* Very local on dunes by the sea in E Anglia, Channel Is., and Morayshire; occasional elsewhere. June–July.

1227. MARRAM *Ammophila arenaria* (L.) Link Plate 123. *CTW, p. 1477*
Psamma arenaria (L.) Roemer & Schultes
A stout far-creeping perennial, 1–4 ft. high, with broad, stiff, sharp-pointed leaves, the margins inrolled, shiny outside, greyish-green inside; ligule pointed, up to an inch long. Flower-heads long, thick and spike-like, shaped like a fox's brush, with densely crowded short-stalked 1-flowered spikelets, whitish from the long silky hairs of the flowers. *Habitat:* Widespread and locally abundant on dunes by the sea, where it is also often planted to bind the sand. July–August.

1228. *BUSH GRASS *Calamagrostis epigejos* (L.) Roth Pl. 134. *CTW, 1478*
A stout coarse reed-like hairless perennial, often in patches, 3–5 ft. high, with
flat, roughish leaves and long blunt ligules. Flower-heads branched, thick, fat,
half-spreading, with usually purplish-brown, 1-flowered spikelets, each flower
with a short but prominent awn and numerous silky hairs twice as long as the
pales. *Habitat:* Widespread but local on clay soils in damp woods and fens,
and on roadsides; chiefly in the S. July–August.

1229. **PURPLE SMALL-REED   *C. canescens* (Weber) Roth
Plate 134. *CTW, p. 1478*
Slenderer than the last species, with the leaves slightly downy above; ligules
shorter, blunter; shorter looser, more spreading, redder purple flower-heads;
virtually no awn, and hairs on the flowers. *Habitat:* Locally frequent in fens
and damp shady places in England and Wales; rare in Scotland. June–July.

1229a. **Narrow Small-reed**, *C. stricta* (Timm) Koeler ('*C. neglecta*') (incl.
C. scotica (Druce) Druce), is slenderer still, with leaves roughish only on the
edges and often with inrolled margins; ligules still shorter and blunter; and a
less spreading, almost spike-like flower-head, with smaller spikelets and the hairs
on each flower shorter than the pales. Very scarce and local in fens and marshes
in Scotland, N and E England, and around L. Neagh. June–August.

1230. WHITE BENT   *Agrostis stolonifera* L.   Plate 131. *CTW, p. 1482*
A variable, often creeping, more or less tufted, hairless perennial, with runners,
6–18 in. high, with flat, roughish leaves, and longish, bluntly pointed ligules.
Flower-heads whorl-branched, spreading in flower but contracted in fruit, with
numerous, very small, straw-coloured 1-flowered spikelets, the flowers normally
with no awn, if so from above the middle; pales more or less equal. *Habitat:*
Widespread and abundant in established grassland and wet ground, and as a
weed of bare places. July–August. Creeping Bent; *A. palustris* Hudson.

1230a. *Bristle Bent*, *A. setacea* Curtis, is not creeping, and has tufts of stiff
bristle-like leaves, rather like Wavy Hair-grass (1223) but grey-green; narrow
pointed ligules; yellow-green flower-heads always contracted and spike-like;
and an obvious awn on each flower. Locally frequent on heaths and moors from
W Surrey to Cornwall and Glamorgan. June–July.

1230b. Brown Bent, *A. canina* L., has creeping runners which sometimes root;
narrow but flattened leaves; pointed ligules; smallish flower-heads either spreading or contracted, not obviously whorl-branched, more delicate than Fine Bent;
and usually a bent awn from below the middle, short but obvious in each purple-
brown flower; upper pale minute. Widespread and common in both damp and
dry grassland, on heaths and in heathy woods, preferring acid soils. June–August.

1230c. Fine Bent, *A. tenuis* Sibthorp, is usually less creeping, and has flat
leaves; short blunt ligules; flower-heads always spreading, rather loose, and
obviously whorl-branched; and nearly always no awn in the purple flowers.
Widespread and locally abundant mainly on acid soils.

1230d. *Black Bent*, *A. gigantea* Roth, is often taller, to 3 ft., than the other
Bents, and has a creeping rootstock; wider flat, roughish leaves; long blunt, often
toothed ligules; much larger spreading flower-heads, and flowers usually with no
awn. Widespread and frequent in grassy places and damp woods, also as a weed
on light soils.

1230e. ***Water Bent*, *A. semiverticillata* (Forskal) Christensen (*Polypogon
semi-verticillatus* (Forsk.) Hylander), has creeping runners, flat, roughish leaves,

blunt ligules, rather small contracted flower-heads with densely crowded spikelets, and flowers with no awn. Established in waste places, especially at the foot of walls in Guernsey. June–August.

1231. *SILKY BENT   *Apera spica-venti* (L.) Beauvois   Plate 133.   *CTW, p. 1483*
An attractive graceful hairless, often tufted annual, 1–2 ft. high, with flat, roughish leaves and longish, bluntly pointed ligules. Flower-heads rather large, branched, spreading, delicate and feathery-looking, with 1-flowered spikelets, each flower with a conspicuous long, straight awn up to 4 times as long as the spikelet. *Habitat:* Uncommon in waste places on light soils, mainly in S and E England. June–July. *Agrostis spica-venti* L.

1232. **BRECKLAND BENT   *A. interrupta* (L.) Beauvois
Plate 121.   *CTW, p.1483*
A hairless annual, 4 in. to 2 ft. high, with roughish flat leaves, and short, pointed ligules. Flower-heads very shortly branched, scarcely spreading, with distinct gaps on the stem between the lower branches; spikelets like the last species. *Habitat:* Local in dry bare, sandy or chalky fields in the Breckland; casual elsewhere. June–July.

1233. **BEARD GRASS   *Polypogon monspeliensis* (L.) Desfontaines
Plate 123.   *CTW, p. 1483*
A hairless, often tufted annual, 6–18 in. high, with leaf-sheaths slightly inflated and sometimes roughish; leaves broad, flat and roughish; and ligules long, pointed. Flower-heads spike-like, stout and extremely silky, rather like a Meadow Foxtail (1240) in shape, but far stouter and silkier, with closely packed very short-stalked 1-flowered spikelets, each with one long and sometimes also one short awn. *Habitat:* Very local in muddy ditches and brackish marshes near the sea in the S; casual elsewhere. June–August.
1233a. ***Nitgrass, *Gastridium ventricosum* (Gouan) Schinz & Thellung (*G. lendigerum* (L). Gaudin) (*CTW, p. 1485*), is often shorter, with more tapering flower-spikes, the spikelets shortly stalked, bright yellow-green, very glistening, and swollen and fancifully nitlike below. Rare in the S, usually in waste places and near the sea.

1234. ***EARLY SAND-GRASS   *Mibora minima* (L.) Desvaux
Plate 121.   *CTW, p. 1485*
A diminutive delicate hairless annual, 1–4 in. high, with tufts of short, very narrow, greyish-green leaves and short, blunt ligules. Flower-heads spike-like, 1-sided, with the spikelets unstalked, 1-flowered, usually purplish. *Habitat:* Very locally plentiful on dunes in Anglesey and the Channel Is.; also in nursery-gardens in Dorset and Suffolk. January–May.

1235. ***HARESTAIL GRASS   *Lagurus ovatus* L.   Plate 123.   *CTW, p. 1486*
A distinctive downy tufted annual, usually 2–8 in. high, with inflated leaf-sheaths, short flat broad leaves, and short blunt ligules. Flower-heads egg-shaped, unbranched, dense, soft, woolly and whitish like a rabbit's scut, the 1-flowered spikelets having long feathery glumes and a long, bent awn in each flower. *Habitat:* Local on dunes in the Channel Is. and at Dawlish Warren; very rare elsewhere. June–August.

1236. TIMOTHY *Phleum pratense* L.   Plate 122. *CTW, p. 1487*

A stout, hairless perennial, 9 in. to 4 ft. high, with broad, roughish leaves and blunt ligules. Flower-heads unbranched, narrowly cylindrical, 2 to 6 in. long, differing from the earlier flowering Meadow Foxtail (1240) in being rough to the touch and having glumes not tapering but cut off straight, except for the awn point; spikelets unstalked, 1-flowered, shaped like the end of a stretcher, each glume with a short stout awn. *Habitat:* Widespread and common in grassy places; often cultivated. June–August.

1236a. Catstail, *P. nodosum* L., is smaller, slenderer and greyer, with swollen bulbous stem-bases, narrower leaves, more pointed ligules, and flower-heads only half as long, $\frac{1}{2}$–2 in. Widespread and common in drier grassland.

1236b. ***Alpine Catstail, *P. commutatum* Gaudin ('*P. alpinum*'), is 6–12 in. high, with smooth leaves; upper leaf-sheaths inflated; ligules short and blunt; flower-heads fat, roundish and usually purplish; and awns longer than in any of our other Catstails or Timothies. *Habitat:* Very local in wet grassy places high on mountains in the N. July–August.

1237. **POINTED CATSTAIL *P. phleoides* (L.) Karsten Pl. 122. *CTW, 1488*

Smaller and slenderer than Timothy (1236), with less erect stems; short narrow blunt-tipped greyish leaves; short blunt ligules; and much narrower, more pointed greyish flower-heads, the glumes a little tapered above into points rather than awns. *Habitat:* Very local in dry chalky grassland from near Hitchin to King's Lynn, chiefly in the Breckland. June–August.

1238. *SAND CATSTAIL *P. arenarium* L.   Plate 122. *CTW, p. 1488*

Our only annual Catstail, 2–8 in. high, usually tufted, with short, smooth, pale green leaves, their upper sheaths inflated, and longish, bluntly pointed ligules. Flower-heads unbranched, dense, egg-shaped, tapering below, up to 2 in. long, the spikelets pale greyish-green, 1-flowered, the glumes tapered throughout to a point, as in Meadow Foxtail (1240) but with no awns on the pales. *Habitat:* Widespread and locally frequent on dunes, mainly in the S; and on sandy heaths in the Breckland. May–July.

1239. SLENDER FOXTAIL *Alopecurus myosuroides* Hudson Pl. 122. *CTW, 1498*

Slenderer than the next species, and annual, with stems often prostrate at the base, and narrower tapering, sharply pointed, green, white or reddish-brown flower-heads with glumes joined $\frac{1}{3}$–$\frac{1}{2}$-way up and rather shorter awns. *Habitat:* A widespread weed of cultivated ground, frequent in the S, thinning out northwards, and rare in Ireland. May onwards.

1240. MEADOW FOXTAIL *A. pratensis* L.   Plate 122. *CTW, p. 1490*

A hairless, more or less tufted perennial, 1–4 ft. high, often confused with Timothy (1236), with roughish leaves, their upper sheaths inflated, and blunt ligules. Flower-heads unbranched, 1–2 in. long, cylindrical, greyish or purplish, smooth and silky to the touch, with 1-flowered spikelets, the glumes tapering to a point, each flower with a long awn on the lower pale. *Habitat:* Widespread and usually abundant in meadows and on roadsides. April–July.

1240a. ***Alpine Foxtail, *A. alpinus* Smith, is smaller, with grey, very silky, shorter, less cylindrical flower-heads, the flowers with a short or no awn. Very rare in wet grassy places on high mountains in the Highlands and Teesdale. July–August.

1241. MARSH FOXTAIL *A. geniculatus* L. Plate 122. *CTW, p. 1490*

Greyer-green and much smaller than Meadow Foxtail (1240), with the rooting stems markedly bent at the base and often at each joint; leaves smooth beneath, flower-heads much shorter and purplish, the glumes blunt, transparent-tipped, not pointed, pale, long-awned; anthers yellow or rusty-coloured, becoming violet-yellow. *Habitat:* Widespread and frequent in wet meadows and in or by fresh or brackish water. June–September.

1241*a*. ****Orange Foxtail,** *A. aequalis* Sobolewski (*A. fulvus* Smith), may be only annual, and has a narrower flower-head with the awns shorter and much less conspicuous, and the glumes more translucent, so giving it a smoother appearance; anthers shorter, white at first, becoming orange. Much more local; not in Scotland or Ireland.

1241*b*. ****Bulbous Foxtail,** *A. bulbosus* Gouan, has stems markedly swollen at the base, smooth leaves and pointed glumes. Local in damp brackish meadows in England and Wales; very rare in Scotland. May–August.

1242. *WOOD MILLET *Milium effusum* L. Plate 130. *CTW, p. 1492*

A slender graceful hairless tufted perennial, 2–5 ft. high, with broad flat pale leaves; ligules long, bluntly pointed; and flower-heads pagoda-like, branched, spreading, nodding at the tip, shining, pale green, with egg-shaped 1-flowered spikelets. *Habitat:* Widespread and locally frequent in dry woods, thinning out northwards. May–July.

1243. ***DWARF MILLET *M. scabrum* Richard Plate 121. *CTW, p. 1492*

A usually prostrate roughish little annual, 1½–4 in. long, with inflated ridged leaf-sheaths, short flat leaves and long pointed ligules. Flower-heads small, purplish branched but contracted, with 1-flowered egg-shaped spikelets. *Habitat:* Confined to short sandy turf in Guernsey. March–May.

1244. ***HOLY GRASS *Hierochloë odorata* (L.) Beauvois Pl. 129. *CTW, 1493*

A fresh green, almost hairless creeping perennial, 1–2 ft. high, with flat rough-edged leaves and short pointed ligules. Flower-heads reminiscent of Common Meadow-grass (1191), branched, spreading, the lower branches drooping, with shining, rounded, 3-flowered spikelets. *Habitat:* Very rare, on river banks in N and W Scotland, and by L Neagh. April–May.

1245. SWEET VERNAL GRASS *Anthoxanthum odoratum* L. Pl. 123. *CTW, 1494*

A variable slender unbranched, often slightly hairy perennial, 1–2 ft. high, aromatic when dried and giving its characteristic smell to new-mown hay; leaves flat; ligules blunt; flower-heads 1–1½ in. long, slightly branched, long egg-shaped, somewhat spike-like, with 3-flowered, often purplish short-stalked elongated chaffy-looking spikelets, each flower with 1 straight and 1 bent awn. *Habitat:* Widespread and common in all kinds of grassland and in open woods. April–July.

1246. REED-GRASS *Phalaris arundinacea* L. Plate 134. *CTW, p. 1495*
Digraphis arundinacea (L.) Trinius.

A stout hairless tufted reed-like perennial, 3–6 ft. high, with flat smooth broad keeled pointed rough-edged leaves, and short, blunt ligules, the dead leaves persisting throughout the winter, unlike the Reed (1168), from which it also differs in its paler, much smaller and compacter, less spreading branched flower-head, appearing lobed, the 1-flowered spikelets silky but without silky hairs inside.

Habitat: Widespread and frequent in wet places, especially on river and pond banks, and in ditches, rarely forming extensive reed-beds. June–August.

1247. *CANARY GRASS *P. canariensis* L. Plate 124. *CTW, p. 1496*

A tufted hairless annual, 9 in. to 3 ft. high, with flat, often roughish, rather' broad leaves, the upper sheaths inflated and well below the tightly globular or egg-shaped flower-head of greyish, scarcely stalked 1-flowered spikelets, the glumes whitish-green, keeled and broadly winged. *Habitat:* Widespread and locally frequent in waste places, and near fowl-runs, mainly in the S. June–Sept.

1247a. **Lesser Canary Grass,** *P. minor* Retzius, is rather slenderer, with shorter narrower leaves, narrower, more elongated flower-heads and smaller, shortly stalked spikelets, the glumes with a narrower wing, scarcely ever untoothed, extending not more than half way down the keel. Frequent in the Channel Is.; chiefly on rubbish dumps elsewhere.

1248. *SEA HARD-GRASS *Parapholis strigosa* (Dumortier) Hubbard
Plate 121. *CTW, p. 1497*

A curious slender hairless annual, 6–10 in. high, prostrate below, with short, narrow leaves, the upper sheaths not inflated and well down the stem of the mature plant; ligules short, blunt. Flower spikes unbranched, forming a very narrow cylinder with the flowers and appearing like a continuation of the stem; straight, with unstalked, shining, 1-flowered spikelets closely appressed to the stem, not overlapping. *Habitat:* Widespread but rather local in short salt-marsh turf and on bare muddy ground by the sea; rare N of the Forth. July–August.

1248a. **Curved Hard-grass,** *P. incurva* (L.) Hubbard (*Lepturus incurvatus* Trinius), is smaller, with often purple, usually strongly curving stems and flower-spikes, the upper leaf-sheaths inflated and just below or actually enfolding the base of the flower-spikes; anthers less than half as long. In drier and more stony and sandy places near the sea in S England.

1249. MAT-GRASS *Nardus stricta* L. Plate 121. *CTW, p. 1498*

A wiry, almost hairless perennial, 4–9 in. high, with very dense tufts of hard grey-green bristle-like leaves, with broad sheaths. Flower-spikes unbranched, very slender, spike-like, 1-sided, with unstalked purplish-black 1-flowered spikelets, each with a short awn; style 1. *Habitat:* Widespread and locally abundant on moors and peaty mountain grassland in the N and W; less common on damp peaty heaths in the S and E; the hall-mark of a poor soil. June–August.

1250. *COMMON CORD-GRASS *Spartina townsendii* Groves
Rice-grass Plate 125. *CTW, p. 1500*

A coarse stout, almost hairless creeping yellowish gregarious perennial, 2–4 ft. high; leaves thick, broad, stiff, flat or inrolled, much grooved above, tapering to a long slender point; ligule a ring of hairs. Flower-heads in a bunch of 4–5 unbranched spikes, up to 9 in. long, with unstalked, 1-flowered, downy, yellow-brown spikelets ½–¾-in. long, closely pressed to the slightly wavy stem, which projects well beyond the tip of the end spikelet; stigmas feathery and conspicuous. *Habitat:* Locally common on maritime mud in the S, and still spreading in England and Ireland where it is much planted to bind the mud. July onwards.

1250a. **Lesser Cord-grass,** *S. maritima* (Curtis) Fernald (*S. stricta* (Aiton) Roth), is shorter, and has narrower leaves, tapering to a stouter point, with downier, less yellow flower-spikes not more than 6 in. long and usually only 2–3 in the bunch, the terminal stem-point being much shorter and not overtopping the spike; spikelets only ½-in. long. Local in established salt-marshes in S England and S Wales. July–September.

1251. **BERMUDA GRASS** *Cynodon dactylon* (L.) Persoon Pl. 126. *CTW, 1501*
A creeping, often hairless perennial, 4–15 in. high, with rooting runners; stiff roughish, sometimes slightly downy leaves; and a ring of hairs for a ligule. Our only Grass with flower-heads in a fan of 4–5 finger-like unbranched 1-sided spikes, with unstalked purplish spreading 1-flowered spikelets. *Habitat:* Uncommon in sandy and waste places, usually near the sea in S England. August–September.

1252. **BARNYARD GRASS** *Echinochloa crusgalli* (L.) Beauvois
Cockspur; *Panicum crusgalli* L. Plate 133. *CTW, p. 1502*
A variable hairless tufted annual, 1–4 ft. high, with broad soft rough-edged leaves and no ligules. Flower-heads often quite large, branched, spreading, the branches densely covered on one side with short-stalked, shining, usually purple 1-flowered spikelets; each flower with a short, usually not very obvious awn. *Habitat:* A casual of cultivated ground and rubbish dumps in the S. August–September.

1253. ***CRAB-GRASS** *Digitaria sanguinalis* (L.) Scopoli Pl. 126. *CTW, 1503*
A weak annual, somewhat hairy at least below, 6–15 in. high, with broad, flat, rough-edged leaves and short, blunt ligules. Flower-heads in four or more unbranched finger-like spikes, with very short-stalked, purplish-brown, 1-flowered lanceolate spikelets closely pressed along one side of the stem. *Habitat:* Very scarce on dry waste and disturbed ground, especially at the foot of walls and on lighter soils, in the S. August onwards. *Panicum sanguinale* L.

1254. **BOTTLE-GRASS** *Setaria viridis* (L.) Beauvois Pl. 123. *CTW, 1504*
A loosely tufted annual, 3–12 in. high, with slightly hairy sheaths, flat, roughish leaves, and a ring of hairs for the ligule. Flower-heads unbranched, dense, cylindrical, 1–2 in. long, very bristly, the short-stalked, often purplish, 1-flowered spikelets each having 1–3 long, toothed awns with teeth pointing forwards; lower pale smooth. *Habitat:* An uncommon casual of dry waste and cultivated places in the S. August onwards. *Panicum viride* L.

1255. **FOXTAIL MILLET** *S. italica* (L.) Beauvois Plate 123. *CTW†*
A variable annual, 1–2 ft. high, merging into stout forms of Bottle-grass (1254); its 4–8 in. spikes, an inch or so thick, often curving down at the tip and somewhat interrupted, are commonly sold intact for hanging upside down in bird-cages. Leaves broad, ½–¾-in. across. The ripe fruit falls separately from and not with the rest of the spikelet. *Habitat:* Frequent on rubbish dumps. August onwards.

1256. **COMMON MILLET** *Panicum miliaceum* L. Plate 133. *CTW†*
A stout, coarse annual, 2–3 ft. high, with roughish broad leaves and large dense nodding flower-heads with rather erect branches. Seeds large. *Habitat:* A regular constituent of bird-seed mixtures often to be found on rubbish-tips and waste places. August–September.

PINE FAMILY Pinaceae

1257. *SCOTS PINE *Pinus sylvestris* L. Plate 64. *CTW, p. 61*

Our only native Pine, a tall evergreen tree, flat- or dome-topped when mature, with rufous bark flaking off in large scales. Buds cylindrical, sticky, resin-smelling; leaves in pairs, needle-like, twisted and somewhat flattened, greyish-green, 1½–3 in. long. Male flowers orange-yellow, in clusters at base of young shoots; female solitary, terminal, pinkish-green when young. Fruit a woody cone 2–3 in. long. *Habitat:* Widespread and frequent in woods and on heaths, especially in Scotland and on sandy soils in the S; often planted. May–June.

1257a. ***Austrian Pine, *P. nigra* Arnold, is of broader pyramidal outline, with rougher dark blackish-grey bark; and longer, straighter, darker green needles, less twisted, sharply pointed and 3–5 in. long. Commonly planted and may appear naturalised, e.g. in the New Forest.

1257b. ***Maritime Pine, *P. pinaster* Aiton, has a rounded outline when mature; trunk rugged; branches stouter; buds not resinous, their scales turned back at the tip; needles 4–8 in long, stout, stiff, curved, finely toothed, dark green; and larger bright brown broad cones, 3–6 in. long, often clustered, long-lasting. Well naturalised on sandy soils in E Dorset, occasionally elsewhere.

1257c. ***Douglas Fir, *Pseudotsuga menziesii* (Mirbel) Franco (*CTW, p. 57*), is a tall, very pointed pyramidal tree, with greyish corky bark; non-resinous shiny brown, rather beech-like buds; downy young shoots; shorter, rather soft needles 1–1½ in. long, bluish-green, crowded and arranged spirally or in two loose ranks on the main stems, leaving a disc-like scar when they fall; and cones 2–4 in. long, hanging downwards. Often planted, but rarely naturalised, e.g. in the New Forest. *P. taxifolia* (Poiret) Britton.

1257d. ***Norway Spruce, *Picea abies* (L.) Karsten (*CTW, p. 57*), familiar when young as the Christmas tree, has rather smooth brown bark; branches whorled up the trunk; short stiff solitary 4-sided, deep glossy grass-green needles thickly spirally ranked up the stems, on prominent peg-like bases which persist after they have fallen; and long hanging cylindrical shiny pale brown cones, 4–6 in. long. Often planted and occasionally appearing naturalised.

1257e. **European Larch, *Larix decidua* Miller (*CTW, p. 59*), occasionally naturalised, has tufts of pale green deciduous needles and small egg-shaped cones.

CYPRESS FAMILY Cupressaceae

1258. *JUNIPER *Juniperus communis* L. Plate 64. *CTW, p. 66*
(incl. *J. sibirica* Burgsdorf (*J. nana* Willdenow))

A graceful grey-green evergreen shrub, 4–12 ft. high, either spreading and bushy or narrowly conical, with whorls of 3 short spine-tipped awl-like leaves. Flowers small, yellow, at the base of the leaves, male and female usually on separate plants. Fruit a green berry-like cone, turning a sloe-like blue-black in its second year. A prostrate northern hill form has the leaves shorter, greyer, broader, overlapping and scarcely prickly. *Habitat:* Widespread but local and decreasing on chalk downs, limestone hills, heaths and moors, and in pine- and birch-woods, chiefly in parts of SE England and the Highlands. May–June.

YEW FAMILY Taxaceae

1259. *YEW *Taxus baccata* L. Plate 64. *CTW, p. 68*

A stout broad-topped evergreen tree, with spreading branches and one or more substantial trunks; bark reddish-brown, scaling; leaves dark glossy green, linear, pointed, pinnately arranged. Flowers small, greenish, at the base of the leaves, male and female on separate trees, male with many yellow stamens, female egg-shaped. Fruit a coral-pink fleshy cup surrounding the seed. *Habitat:* Widespread but local in dry woods and scrub, rarely forming pure woods on chalk in the S. March–April.

FERNS AND THEIR ALLIES   Pteridophyta

A VERY ancient order of flowerless plants, comprising the Ferns, Horsetails, Clubmosses and Quillworts, all perennial except for the rare Jersey Fern (1279). They have no seed, but reproduce themselves by minute dust-like spores. These are produced in tiny capsules (sporangia), and give rise without any sexual process to tiny short-lived plants called prothalli, which bear male and female organs and carry out the reproductive process in the presence of moisture and not by insect or wind fertilisation, leading to the formation of a new fern plant. This process is called alternation of generations. In the Ferns the prothalli are usually small green heart-shaped scale-like plants, $\frac{1}{4}$–$\frac{1}{2}$ in. across, which may often be found in damp shady spots near fern colonies, sometimes with tiny fern plants growing from them.

The Mosses, Liverworts, Stoneworts (*Chara* and *Nitella* species), Algae, Seaweeds and other more primitive flowerless plants have only cellular and not fibrous or vascular tissue, and lack true roots and usually stems as well, but are sometimes very hard to distinguish except by a knowledge of their reproductive habits.

CLUBMOSS FAMILIES Lycopodiaceae & Selaginellaceae

A DISTINCTIVE GROUP of low, often prostrate, perennials, robuster than true mosses, with small pointed leaves, about $\frac{1}{4}$ in. long, overlapping along the stems. Spore-capsules carried at the base of the scales in erect cylindrical cones, or in Fir Club-moss (1260) grouped round the stem at the base of the ordinary foliage leaves.

1260. *FIR CLUBMOSS *Urostachys selago* (L.) Herter Plate 135. *CTW, p. 2*
A stout bushy tufted plant with erect stems forking 2–3 times, 2–4 in. high, with untoothed leaves. Spore-capsules in several zones, at the base of the leaves, alternating with zones of leaves without capsules; vegetative buds often near top of stem. *Habitat:* Locally frequent on hills and mountains, and in mountain bogs, now only in the N and W and in Ireland· extinct in the lowlands of the S and E. June–August. *Lycopodium selago* L.

1261. **MARSH CLUBMOSS *Lycopodium inundatum* L. Plate 135. *CTW, p. 2*
Stems prostrate and little branched, dying back to leave only the terminal bud in winter; leaves untoothed. Cones solitary, at the top of erect leafy stalks, their scales green and like the foliage leaves but larger and toothed below. Differs from the paler slenderer Lesser Clubmoss (1265) basically in having its spores all alike. *Habitat:* Widespread but local on wet heaths in the lowlands, usually on bare moist peat. June–September.

1262. **INTERRUPTED CLUBMOSS *L. annotinum* L. Pl. 135. *CTW, p. 3*
Rather tufted, with 4–6 in. main stems, creeping and rooting, with stiff pointed green leaves all round, bearing erect branches, which appear constricted at

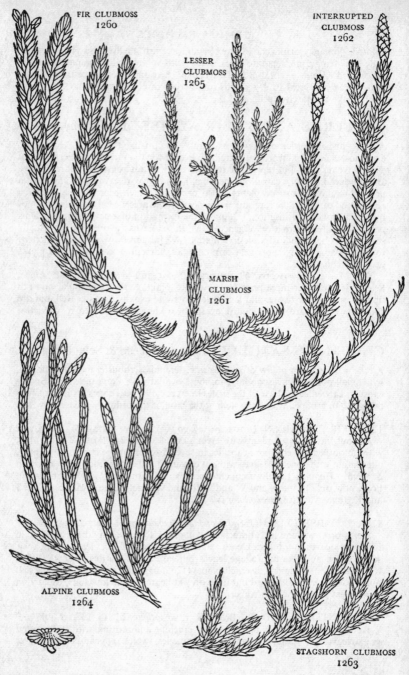

FIR CLUBMOSS
1260

INTERRUPTED
CLUBMOSS
1262

LESSER
CLUBMOSS
1265

MARSH
CLUBMOSS
1261

ALPINE CLUBMOSS
1264

STAGSHORN CLUBMOSS
1263

135

DUTCH RUSH
1268

PILLWORT
1303

COMMON QUILLWORT
1266

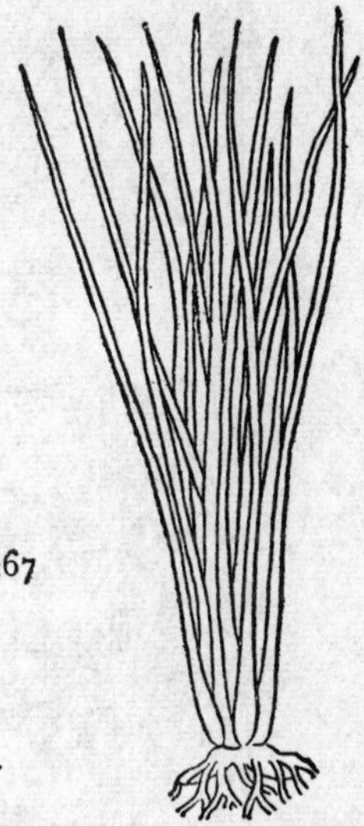

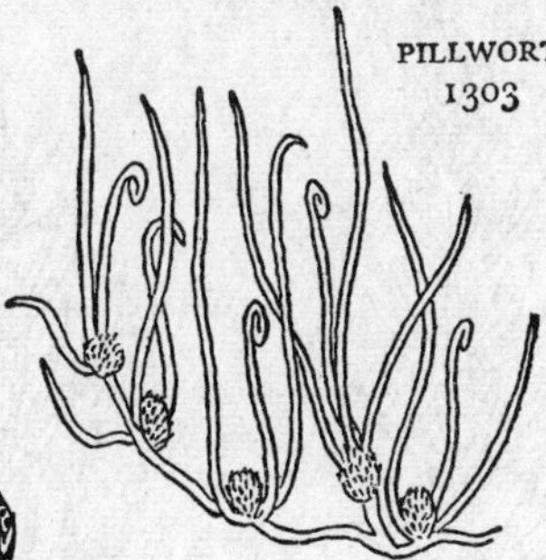

SAND QUILLWORT 1267

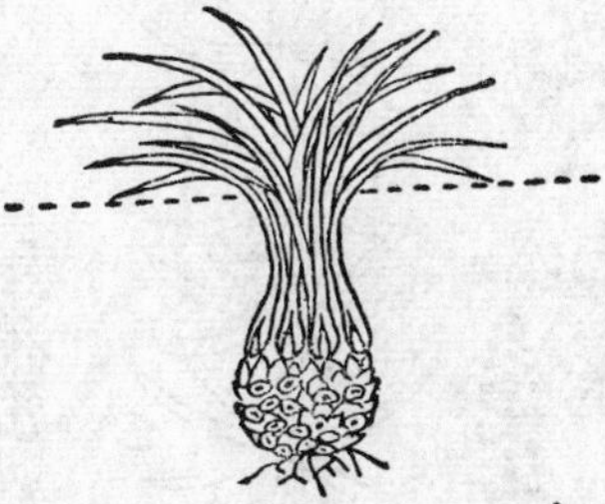

MOONWORT
1305

ADDER'S
TONGUE
1306

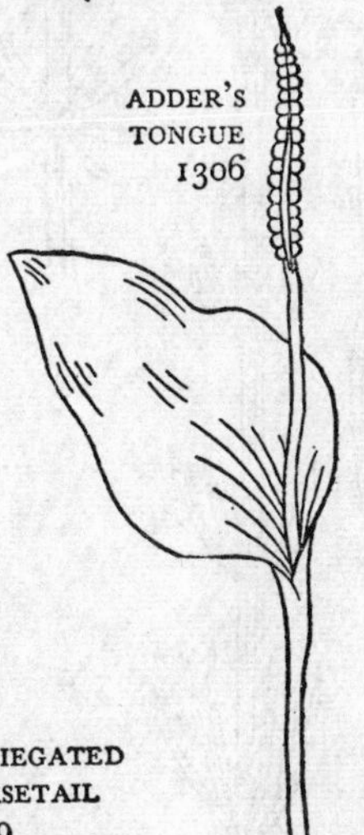

VARIEGATED
HORSETAIL
1269

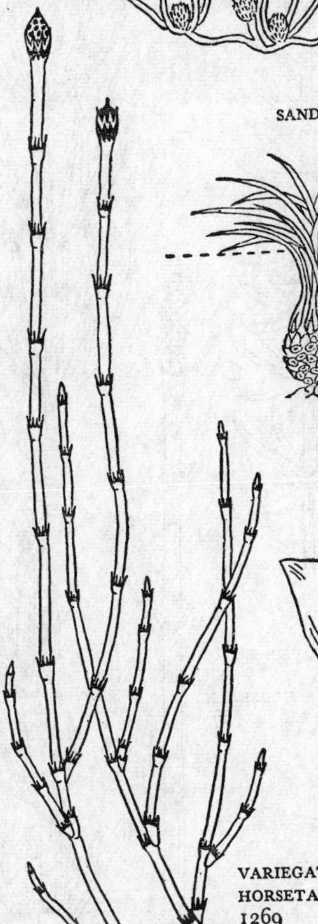

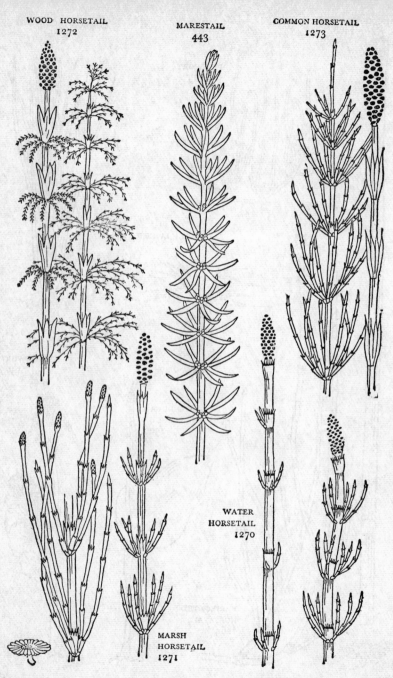

WOOD HORSETAIL
1272

MARESTAIL
443

COMMON HORSETAIL
1273

WATER
HORSETAIL
1270

MARSH
HORSETAIL
1271

intervals. Cones solitary, terminal, on leafy branches; cone-scales yellow and very unlike the foliage leaves, toothed and broad-based. *Habitat:* Uncommon on high moors in Scotland; very rare in N England. June–August.

1263. *STAGSHORN CLUBMOSS *L. clavatum* L.   Plate 135.   *CTW, p. 3*

Has the main stem creeping and rooting, as in Interrupted Clubmoss (1262), but longer than the other Clubmosses and sometimes extending for yards, with closely set green leaves, toothed, with white bristle points, and not spreading. Cones solitary or in pairs on long stalks, which bear scattered yellow scales, not green leaves; cone-scales yellow, toothed. *Habitat:* Widespread and locally frequent among heather on moors and mountain sides, mainly in the N and W and in Ireland; very local in heathy woods and old quarries in the S and E. June–September.

1264. *ALPINE CLUBMOSS *L. alpinum* L.   Plate 135.   *CTW, p. 3*

Has main stems prostrate, bearing tufts of more or less erect branches, with blunt untoothed greyish fleshy-looking closely appressed leaves. Cones solitary, on leafy stalks, their scales grey-green, even greyer than the foliage leaves. *Habitat:* Locally frequent on hills, moors and mountains in the N and W; very rare in the S. June–August.

1265. *LESSER CLUBMOSS *Selaginella selaginoides*(L.)Link Pl. 135.   *CTW, 4*

Like a weaker version of Bog Clubmoss (1261), merging in the grass, with often prostrate but sometimes erect stems, thickly clothed with small lanceolate, toothed leaves. Cones solitary, terminal, on erect leafy stalks, their scales green and more conspicuously toothed. *Habitat:* Locally frequent in damp grass or moss in hill districts, and in dune slacks in the N and W and in Ireland. June–Sept.

QUILLWORT FAMILY   Isoetaceae

SMALL TUFTED perennials with rather hollow, quill-like leaves, in whose broad flattened bases are either larger female or minute male spores.

1266. **COMMON QUILLWORT *Isoetes lacustris* L. Plate 136.   *CTW, p. 6*

An evergreen submerged aquatic, with a stiff tuft, often curved back, of translucent dark green cylindrical pointed leaves 3–6 in. long, with capsules containing warty yellowish female spores at the swollen base of the outer leaves and minute male spores in capsules at the swollen base of the inner ones. Confusable with leaves of Awlwort (76), Shoreweed (794), Water Lobelia (807) and Pipewort (985). *Habitat:* Local in lakes and tarns, on acid soils in mountain districts, not often on peat, in the N and Ireland. May–July.

1266a. ***Small Quillwort,* I. echinospora* Durieu, is smaller and has rather weak, paler green leaves, never over 4 in. long, with the female spores spiny and more often white. Rare in peaty pools or lakes in the W, N and W Ireland.

1267. ***SAND QUILLWORT *I. histrix* Durieu   Plate 136.   *CTW, p. 7*

An inconspicuous terrestrial with a fat white tufted base, with very narrow leaves, 2–3 in. long, which normally curl back to be flat on the ground. In most years they wither in early summer, but rarely survive till August, growing erectly in the grass.. *Habitat:* Very rare in moist or cliff-top turf near the sea in the Lizard peninsula and the Channel Is. April–May.

HORSETAIL FAMILY   Equisetaceae

A DISTINCTIVE family of leafless and flowerless creeping perennials, with tubular jointed, furrowed, usually erect stems; joints crowned by toothed sheaths, which replace the leaves. At the joints of some species there are more or less regular whorls of ribbed and jointed linear green branches. Spores are borne 4–6 together on the underside of hexagonal scales, which fit closely together to form a pavement-like surface to the long egg-shaped terminal cones, which in our rarer species end in a very fine point. In some common species the cones are borne on separate, earlier, fatter, pale brown unbranched stems, which appear and wither early in the year, and are followed by the taller thinner greener barren stems, which last till autumn. The foetid submerged Stoneworts (*Chara* and *Nitella*) might be taken for Horsetails or Marestail (443), but have no true roots and orange fructifications on their branches. *Charas* are brittle and lime-encrusted; *Nitellas* are smooth and translucent.

KEY TO HORSETAILS (Nos. 1268–1273; '12' omitted)

STEMS *white* 73a; *rough* 68; *smooth* 70, 71, 72, 73a; *prostrate* 69, 72; *unbranched* 68, 70; *forked at base* 69; *with whorls of branches* 70, 71, 72, 73.

BRANCHES *branched* 72, 73; *drooping* 71a, 72.

SHEATHS *whitish* 68; yellowish 71a.

SHEATH-TEETH *black* 69a, 70, 71, 73a; *black-tipped* 73; *with blackish midrib* 69, 71a; *brown* 71a, 72, 73; *green* 73; *whitish* 69; *fine-pointed* 69a; *as many as furrows* 68, 69, 70, 73; *fewer than furrows* 72, 73.

FERTILE AND BARREN STEMS *similar* 68, 69, 70, 71; *distinct, same colour and appearing at same time* 71a, 72; *distinct, different colours, fertile first* 73.

HABITAT: *fresh water* 70; *shady places* 68, 72, 73a; *dunes* 69, 73; *dry places* 68, 73.

1268. ***DUTCH RUSH *Equisetum hyemale* L. Plate 136. *CTW, p. 9*

A simple Horsetail, consisting merely of a very stiff rough, dark green evergreen stem 2 ft. or so high, somewhat inflated between the joints, the central hollow at least two-thirds the width of the stem. Sheaths about as long as broad, black with a green central band, the small teeth soon falling. Some stems usually bear pointed cones. *Habitat:* Widespread but rare on marshy banks, usually in woods, mostly in the N. July–August.

1268 × 1269. ***E. × trachyodon* Braun, grows away from either parent, sparsely in Ireland, and very rarely in E Scotland.

1268a. ***E. × moorei* Newman, is known only on dunes and rocky and clayey banks near the sea between Wexford Harbour and Ardmore Point in SE Ireland.

1269. **VARIEGATED HORSETAIL   *E. variegatum* Weber & Mohr

Plate 136. *CTW, p. 10*

A variable evergreen Horsetail, 6 in. to 2 ft. long, sometimes half-prostrate or creeping, with stems often forked at the base, the central hollow only one-third the width of the stem, which is slenderer and more furrowed than the last species, the ridges rough, 4–10. Sheaths rather loose, black with a green band round the base; teeth triangular, whitish with a black midrib, as many as the furrows. Some stems usually bear rather sharply pointed cones. *Habitat:* Uncommon on dunes and dune slacks and in moist places, mostly in mountain districts, chiefly in the N and Ireland. July–August.

1269a. ***Boston Horsetail, *E. ramosissimum* Desfontaines, has the central hollow less than two-thirds of the width; ridges 8–20; sheaths green, turning brown with a black band below; teeth black with white edges and a very fine point. Known only from a grassy river bank near Boston. August–September.

1270. WATER HORSETAIL *E. limosum* L. Plate 137. *CTW, p. 11*

A smooth, pale green Horsetail with stems 2–5 ft. long, the central hollow at least four-fifths of the width; furrows 10–30, very shallow, Perhaps most often the stems have no branches, or at most a few coming irregularly and chiefly from the lower half; but sometimes there are regular whorls of branches. Sheaths green, with as many black teeth as the furrows; cones black, unpointed, at tip of most stems. *Habitat:* Widespread and frequent in marshes and well out into the water, often in abundance. June–July. *E. fluviatile* L.

1270 × 1273. ***E.* × *litorale* Kühlewein, is widespread but scarce and may occur in the absence of both parents.

1271. MARSH HORSETAIL *E. palustre* L. Plate 137. *CTW, p. 12*

A dark green Horsetail, 1–2 ft. high, the stems with a small central hollow, 4–8 deep furrows, and whorls of slender branches, whose lowest jointed section is much shorter than the green, rather loose stem-sheaths, with 4–8 black teeth. Cones not pointed at tip of stems, and rarely of branches too. *Habitat:* Widespread and frequent in marshy meadows and fens. May–July.

1271a. ***Shady Horsetail, *E. pratense* Ehrhart, has distinct fertile and barren stems, appearing at the same time in spring. Barren stems end abruptly with the top whorl of branches, and have the central hollow occupying about half their width, 8–20 furrows, sheath-teeth brown with a blackish midrib, and the branches often somewhat drooping, their lowest jointed section usually longer than the stem-sheath. Fertile stems end in a cone and have yellowish sheaths, their teeth paler and dark-ribbed. Rare on grassy stream-banks in the N, and in N Ireland. April.

1272. *WOOD HORSETAIL *E. sylvaticum* L. Plate 137. *CTW, p. 12*

Our most graceful Horsetail, and the only one that normally has branched branches which may droop at the tip; separate barren and fertile stems, 6–12 in. high, appearing at the same time, are smooth and light or yellowish green, with 10–18 grooves, the central hollow occupying half the width; sheaths green, with 3–6 broad, pale brown, lobed and ribbed teeth; branches in whorls at the joints. Fertile stems are similar, but only shortly branched. *Habitat:* Fairly frequent in damp woods and on moors and railway banks in the N and Ireland; rare in boggy woods in the S. April–May.

1273. COMMON HORSETAIL *E. arvense* L. Plates 36, 137. *CTW, p. 13*

Our commonest Horsetail, especially in dry places, 4–12 in. high, with erect fertile stems appearing before the sometimes prostrate barren ones. Fertile stems pale brown, unbranched, with 4–6 loose sheaths and 6–12 dark brown teeth; cones milk-chocolate colour, 1 in. long, ¼ in. wide. Barren stems green, roughish, continuing beyond the last whorl of branches; furrows 6–19, deep; central hollow less than half the width; sheaths green with black-tipped green teeth as many as the furrows; the lowest jointed section on the branches longer than the stem-sheath. *Habitat:* Widespread and common in rough bare and cultivated places, especially railway embankments, and on dunes. April.

1273a. *Giant Horsetail, E. telmateia* Ehrhart, is paler and much larger and robuster, often over 3 ft., with the barren stems fat, smooth and ivory-white, their teeth blackish, central hollow at least two-thirds of the width, and lowest jointed section of branches shorter than stem-sheath. Fertile stems fat, pale brown, with numerous sheaths and 20–30 dark teeth, cones to 2 in. long and ½-in. wide. Locally frequent in damp places, usually indicating a springline; chiefly in the S.

THE TRUE FERN FAMILIES

Osmundaceae, Hymenophyllaceae and Polypodiaceae

OUR FERNS are non-woody perennials, except for the rare Jersey Fern (1279), with an obvious family resemblance, their leaves (fronds) folded crozier-like in bud and arising from a creeping or an often well-tufted rootstock that may be covered with a brown shaggy mass of decayed leaves. Only Hartstongue (1282) has completely undivided leaves, the rest being either deeply lobed (Rusty-back 1289) or 1–3 pinnate. The spores are contained in minute cases, which are grouped into raised brown heaps (sori), covered by an indusium, on the back or edges of the leaves, except in Royal Fern (1274). Many species are very variable, and young plants, especially sterile ones, are extremely hard, if not impossible, to identify. They all affect damp or shady places, and so are plentiful in the W.

KEY TO FERNS
(Royal Fern, Filmy Fern and Polypody Families only, Nos. 1274–1302)
('12' and '13' omitted)

PLANT *over 3 ft.* 74, 77, 94–5; *1–3 ft.* 74, 90, 94–6, 98–9; *3 in. to 1 ft.* 75, 78, 80–9, 90*b*, 91, 94*bc*, 95*c*, 96–7, 00–2; *under 3 in.* 76, 79, 86–9, 93; *under 1 in.* 76, 87, 93; *prostrate* 75–6; 80, 85–6, 89, 90*b*, 92, 00–02; *creeping* 75–8, 80, 92, 99, 01–02; *tufted* 74, 78–9, 81–91, 93–8; *tussocky* 74, 90, 94–5; *moss-like* 76; *with fertile and barren stems different* 74, 78–9, 81, 99.

LEAVES *translucent* 75–6; *scented* 94*c*, 98; *triangular* 77, 80, 83, 92, 94*c*, 95, 00–01; *lanceolate* 74, 81, 84, 90–1, 93–4, 96–9, 02; *parallel-sided* 82, 86, 92; *undivided* 82; *pinnately lobed* 89; *forked* 88; *1-pinnate* 76, 81, 85–6, 93–4, 97–00; *2-pinnate* 74–5, 77–80, 83–4, 87, 90–1, 93–6, 98–01; *3-pinnate* 75, 77–80, 83, 87, 90–2, 95, 01; *hairy* 77, 93, 02; *scaly beneath* 82, 87, 89, 93–7; *wintergreen* 75–6, 80–3, 85–9, 94*a*, 95–7.

LEAF-STALKS *brown* 74–6, 79–86; *dark brown below, green above* 77, 82, 84, 86*a*, 87–9, 91–2, 99–01; *green* 74, 77–8, 82, 86*a*, 89–90, 94, 00–02; *markedly winged* 75–6, 85; *scaleless* 74–80, 83–8, 90, 93*a*, 99–02; *few-scaled* 78, 80–4, 90–3, 96–01; *shaggy at least below* 74, 82, 89, 90, 94–8.

LEAFLETS *concave* 94*b*, 95*b*; *hair-pointed* 94–7; *linear* 88; *with margins inrolled* 77–8, 80–1, 99; *end ones untoothed* 74, 76–7, 81–2, 89, 94, 98–00, 02.

SPORE-HEAPS *roundish* 74–6, 90*a*–02; *kidney-shaped* 90, 94–5; *oblong elliptical* 78, 84, 90; *linear* 77, 79–83, 85–90; *on both sides of leaf* 74, 82; *in a spike* 74; *felting whole underside* 89; *marginal* 74–80, 93, 00; *with no cover* 74, 78–80, 89, 90*a*, 00–02; *hairy* 93.

HABITAT *mountains only* 86*c*, 90*ab*, 92–3, 94*b*, 97; *in wetter places* 74–6, 92, 94*d*, 95, 99.

ROYAL FERN FAMILY Osmundaceae

1274. **ROYAL FERN *Osmunda regalis* L. Plate 138. *CTW, p. 14*
A MAGNIFICENT plant when fully grown, with a fine large tuft of erect pale green
2-pinnate leaves reaching to over 6 ft. in favourable spots. The narrow upper
branches of some of the central leaves are thickly covered on both sides with rich
brown spore-cases giving the superficial appearance of spikes of brown flowers.
This is our only fern whose spores are green with chlorophyll when ripe. *Habitat:*
Very local in boggy or marshy woods and in fens, now mainly in the SW and
Ireland. June–August.

FILMY FERN FAMILY Hymenophyllaceae

OUR THREE Ferns in this small family differ from the Polypody Family in having
their leaves thin and translucent, somewhat resembling seaweed, and their spore-
cases in pouches arising from the ends of the side veins of the leaflets.

1275. ***KILLARNEY FERN *Trichomanes speciosum* Willdenow
‘*T. radicans*’ Plate 139. *CTW, p. 16*
A smallish Fern, with blackish hairs on the far-creeping rootstock and a winged
stalk to the sharply pointed 2–3-pinnate 3–9 in. long leaves. Spore-cases attached
to a spike, which projects from a tubular pouch on the upper margin of the
leaflets. *Habitat:* Rare on shady usually moist rocks in N and W Ireland,
N Wales, and W Scotland. July–September.

1276. *TUNBRIDGE FILMY FERN *Hymenophyllum tunbrigense* (L.) Smith
Plate 140. *CTW, p. 16*
A tiny, moss-like Fern, with a shiny black wire-like creeping rootstock, and
on it pinnate leaves, translucent like oiled silk, on delicate hairless stalks, the
leaflets with flat parallel-sided lobes, their veins not reaching the tip. Spore-cases
in clusters in 2-valved pouches with toothed edges. *Habitat:* Local on rocks or
tree trunks in moist sheltered shady places in acid soils in the W and N and
Ireland; very local on sand-rocks in the Weald. June–July.

1276a. *Scottish Filmy Fern, *H. wilsonii* Hooker (‘ *H. unilaterale* ’), has longer
narrower leaves, the lobes always longer on the upper side and curved slightly
backwards, their veins reaching the tip, and pouches with the edges not toothed
and projecting from the margin of the leaf. May grow with the last and in open
turf; rather commoner in many parts of the W, especially over 1000 ft.; not in
the SE.

POLYPODY FAMILY Polypodiaceae

THE GREAT majority of our Ferns belong to this family, all but the Hartstongue
(1282) having divided leaves, and all having opaque leaves.

1277. BRACKEN *Pteridium aquilinum* (L.) Kuhn Plate 138. *CTW, p. 20*
A very familiar stout tall gregarious Fern, sometimes reaching over 6 ft.
Leaves 3-pinnate, or 2-pinnate with the long narrow leaflets pinnately lobed, on
a stout, tough stalk arising direct from the far-creeping, usually underground,
rootstock; appearing in May and dying down in autumn, but persisting as a
copper-brown carpet. Spore-cases all round the margins of the leaflets, which are

BRACKEN 1277

ROYAL FERN 1274

COMMON BUCKLER FERN 1295

MALE FERN 1294

MARSH FERN 1299

LADY FERN 1290

LANCEOLATE SPLEENWORT 1284

LEMON-SCENTED FERN 1298

HARD SHIELD FERN 1296

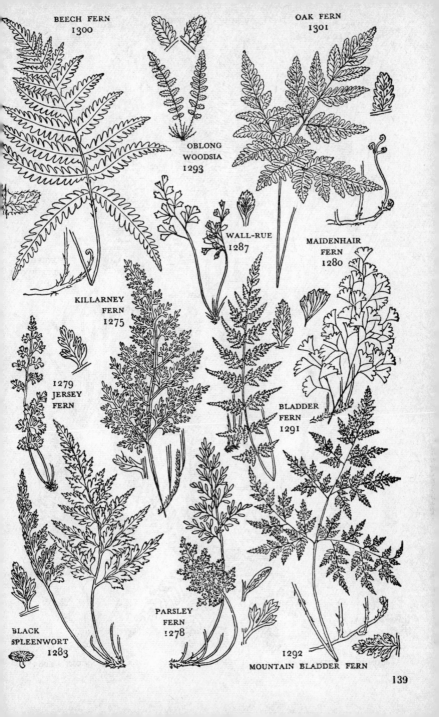

BEECH FERN
1300

OAK FERN
1301

OBLONG
WOODSIA
1293

WALL-RUE
1287

MAIDENHAIR
FERN
1280

KILLARNEY
FERN
1275

1279
JERSEY
FERN

BLADDER
FERN
1291

BLACK
SPLEENWORT
1283

PARSLEY
FERN
1278

1292
MOUNTAIN BLADDER FERN

139

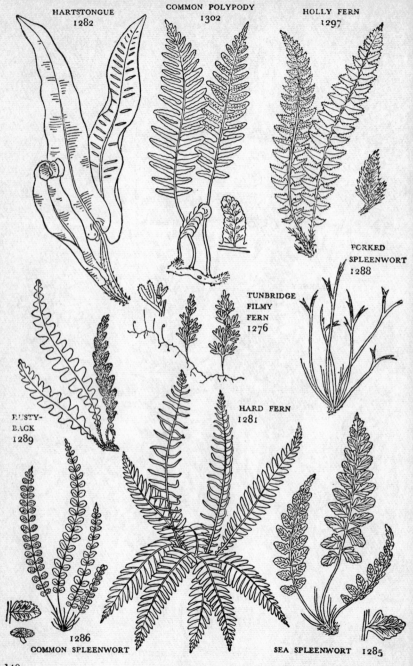

HARTSTONGUE
1282

COMMON POLYPODY
1302

HOLLY FERN
1297

FORKED
SPLEENWORT
1288

TUNBRIDGE
FILMY
FERN
1276

RUSTY-
BACK
1289

HARD FERN
1281

1286
COMMON SPLEENWORT

SEA SPLEENWORT 1285

turned back to cover them. *Habitat:* Widespread, locally abundant in woods and on heaths and hills, preferring light dry acid soils. July–Aug. *Pteris aquilina* L.

1278. **PARSLEY FERN *Cryptogramma crispa* (L.) Hooker
Allosorus crispus (L.) Bernhardi Plate 139. *CTW, p. 21*
A bright green tufted Fern, 4–10 in. high, with 3-pinnate leaves, their stalks bare except for a few brownish scales at the base. Outer leaves barren and shorter than the fertile inner ones, which have numerous narrow leaflets with their margins inrolled, at first almost hiding the spore-cases, which eventually form an almost continuous ribbon along the outer edge of the leaflets. *Habitat:* Locally frequent on rocks and screes on acid, especially slaty, soils in hill districts from N Wales northwards; very rare in Ireland. June–August.

1279. ***JERSEY FERN *Anogramma leptophylla* (L.) Link
Gymnogramma leptophylla (L.) Desvaux Plate 139. *CTW, p. 21*
Our only annual Fern, scarcely reaching 3 in. high, with small delicate 2-pinnate leaves, only the inner ones fertile, and bearing linear spore-cases running along the veins of the roundish leaflets and almost filling their undersides; leaf-margins flat. *Habitat:* Confined to banks in the Channel Is. March–May.

1280. **MAIDENHAIR FERN *Adiantum capillus-veneris* L. Pl. 139. *CTW, 22*
Our native Maidenhair is rather smaller and not quite so showy as the two species most often seen in greenhouses, where it is rarely to be seen itself. Leaves up to about 6 in. long, 2–3-pinnate, the leaflets fan-shaped; stalk wiry and blackish. Spore-cases under semicircular inrolled portions of the margins of the leaflets. *Habitat:* Very local in moist sheltered cracks in rocks and cliffs by the sea in SW and NW England, S Wales, and W Ireland; rarely established elsewhere. May–September.

1281. HARD FERN *Blechnum spicant* (L.) Roth Plate 140. *CTW, p. 23*
A distinctive tufted fern, with tough, lanceolate leaves, 4–15 in. long, dark green when mature, once pinnate only, the leaflets short and narrow, extending almost to the base of the leaf, longest in the middle; stalk dark brown. Outer leaves barren and spreading; inner ones not always present, fertile, taller and more upright, with narrow inrolled leaflets, the spore-cases forming a continuous line down either side of the midrib of each leaflet. *Habitat:* Widespread and locally common in woods, on heaths and moors and among rocks, mainly on acid soils: common in the W and N, thinning out towards the SE. June–August.

1282. HARTSTONGUE *Phyllitis scolopendrium* (L.) Newman Pl. 140. *CTW, 24*
Our only true Fern with undivided leaves, which are in tufts and pointed strap-shaped, and may be anything from a few inches to 2 ft. long, 2 inches across, with rounded base and short green or dark brown stalks. Spore-cases in diagonal rows on the underside of the leaves. *Habitat:* Widespread on rocks, walls and hedge-banks; locally abundant in the W, thinning out and mainly on walls in the E. July–August. *Scolopendrium vulgare* Smith

1283. BLACK SPLEENWORT *Asplenium adiantum-nigrum* L. Pl. 139. *CTW, 25*
A small tufted Fern, with shiny triangular 2–3-pinnate leaves, 3–8 in. long, the leaflets toothed and pointed; stalk blackish, midrib green. Spore-heaps narrow-oblong, in the centre rather than at the edges of the leaflets. *Habitat:* Widespread

and locally frequent on rocks and walls and in hedgebanks, commonest in the W. June onwards.

1284. **LANCEOLATE SPLEENWORT *A. obovatum* Viviani Pl. 138. *CTW, 26*
Differs from the last species in having the lowest pair of primary leaflets shorter than those above, giving a lanceolate shape to the leaf; also in having the spore-cases in heaps near the edges of the leaflets rather than in the centre. *Habitat:* Very local on rocks, walls and hedge-banks, usually near the sea and with a curious predilection for old mine-shafts; in SW England, Wales, SW Scotland and S Ireland. June–September. '*A. lanceolatum*'.

1285. *SEA SPLEENWORT *A. marinum* L. Plate 140. *CTW, p. 27*
A smallish Fern, with a tuft of narrow, rather leathery 1-pinnate shiny bright green leaves, 4–12 in. long; leaflets oblong, bluntly toothed, longest in the middle of the leaf; stalk brown, midrib green. Spore-cases in linear heaps on the side-veins of the leaflets. *Habitat:* Widespread and locally frequent in cracks in sea-cliffs in the N and W; inland at Killarney. June–September.

1286. COMMON SPLEENWORT *A. trichomanes* L. Plate 140. *CTW, p. 27*
A small tufted Fern whose long narrow 1-pinnate 2–8-in. long leaves have oval or oblong leaflets, often slightly toothed and both stalk and midrib blackish. Spore-cases in lines. *Habitat:* Widespread and locally frequent on rocks and walls. May onwards.
1286*a*. **Green Spleenwort, *A. viride* Hudson, is usually smaller with the leaf-stalk and midrib distinctively bright green (blackish only at the base of the stalk), and the edges of the leaflets more indented. Local on limestone hill rocks in the W and N and in S and W Ireland. June–September.

1287. WALL-RUE *A. ruta-muraria* L. Plate 139. *CTW, p. 28*
A small tufted Fern, whose 2-pinnate leaves, 1–3 in. long, are broadest across the middle and have a few more or less toothed, rounded secondary leaflets; stalk green, often greyish, with a blackish base. Spore-cases arranged in lines, finally running into each other and covering the whole centre of the leaf. *Habitat:* Widespread and frequent on walls and rocks. June onwards.

1288. ***FORKED SPLEENWORT *A. septentrionale* (L.) Hoffmann
Plate 140. *CTW, p. 29*
A distinctive little, dark green tufted fern, with its 2–4-in. leaflets very narrow and hardly distinguishable from their stalks; they usually fork twice with one major and one subsidiary fork, the leaflets toothed at the tip; stalks green, blackish at the base. Lines of spore-cases narrow, covering almost the whole underside of the leaflets. *Habitat:* Rare in cracks in rocks, and occasionally on walls, chiefly in the N. June onwards.

1289. *RUSTY-BACK *Ceterach officinarum* DC. Plate 140. *CTW, p. 30*
A very distinctive little tufted fern, whose narrow, wavily pinnately lobed, dark green leaves, 2–6 in. long, are encrusted beneath with rust-coloured scales, which partly hide the lines of spore-cases. *Habitat:* Locally frequent on lime-stone and mortared walls in W England, Wales and Ireland; local elsewhere. April onwards.

1290. LADY FERN *Athyrium filix-femina* (L.) Roth   Plate 138.   *CTW, p. 31*
Asplenium filix-femina (L.) Bernhardi

More graceful and delicate than Male Fern (1294), and its leaves have their narrow primary leaflets pinnately divided into secondary leaflets, which are pinnately lobed instead of being just toothed. Leaf-stalks green or purplish, with lanceolate brown scales towards the base. Spore-heaps and their toothed cover incurved or straight, much more elongated lines. A highly variable Fern, ranging from less than 1 to 4–5 ft. in height.   *Habitat:* Widespread and locally frequent in damp woods and on damp rocks, hedge banks and hillsides, mainly on acid soils; very local in E Anglia and the Midlands. July–August.

1290*a*. ****Alpine Lady Fern**, *A. alpestre* (Hoppe) Rylands (*Polypodium alpestre* Hoppe), can only certainly be told by spore-heaps being rounded, their cover withering early, so that they appear naked. A very rare and very marked variety (*A. flexile* (Newman) Druce) has smaller, narrower leaves, which are bent sharply backwards near the base, and spore-cases mainly on the lower part of the leaf. Local on rocks and screes high in the Highlands.

1291. *BLADDER FERN *Cystopteris fragilis* (L.) Bernhardi   Pl. 139.   *CTW, 32*

A very graceful variable small fern, with its tuft of 2–3-pinnate, lanceolate leaves, usually not more than a foot long, broadest in the middle; stalks blackish at base and with very few scales. Covers over the spore-heaps are whitish inflated, and egg-shaped with a sharp point, on either side of the midrib of the leaflets. *Habitat:* Widespread on rocks and walls, especially on limestone; locally frequent in the N and W, but very local in the S and E of both England and Ireland. July–August.

1292. ***MOUNTAIN BLADDER FERN *C. montana* (Lamarck) Desvaux
Plate 139.   *CTW, p. 33*

Looks quite different from the last species, growing in patches with its leaves rising individually from a creeping rootstock, the lowest primary leaflets on each side being 2-pinnate and much longer, giving the whole leaf a broadly triangular 3-lobed outline. Spore-heap covers less sharply pointed. Not unlike a small neat Oak Fern (1301).   *Habitat:* Rare on mountain rocks in Scotland. July–August.

1293. ***OBLONG WOODSIA *Woodsia ilvensis* (L.) Brown   Pl. 139.   *CTW, 34*

A very small tufted Fern, with oblong pinnate leaves, rarely more than 2 in. and often only ½-in. long, the leaflets more or less pinnate, rather widely spaced; stalks pale red-brown, with lanceolate brown scales near the base, and numerous hair-like scales and zigzag hairs higher up and on the undersides of the leaves. Spore-cases near the margins of the leaflets, with tufts of hairs at the base of each cluster, and on the leaves even when very young; these alone distinguish the two Woodsias from immature forms of other Ferns.   *Habitat:* Very rare on mountain rocks in N Wales, N England, and the Highlands. July–August.

1293*a*. *****Alpine Woodsia**, *W. alpina* (Bolton) Gray, is usually even smaller with shorter broader stubbier triangular leaflets, and fewer paler scales or hairs on their stalks or undersides. Still rarer, in N Wales, S Highlands and Inner Hebrides.

1294. MALE FERN *Dryopteris filix-mas* (L.) Schott   Plate 138.   *CTW, p. 37*

After Bracken (1277) perhaps our most familiar Fern; stout, 2–4 ft. high, with a tuft of lanceolate pinnate leaves, broadest in the middle, arising directly from the rootstock, the numerous primary leaflets close together, deeply pinnately lobed into secondary leaflets, which are themselves toothed and rather bluntly pointed; leaf-stalk covered with uniformly coloured pale brown scales. Covers over the spore-heaps kidney-shaped, on either side of the midrib of the leaflet-lobes. *Habitat:* Widespread and common in woods and hedge-banks, also among rocks and on scree. July–August. *Aspidium filix-mas* (L.) Swartz

1294a. *Golden-scaled Male Fern, *D. borreri* Newman, is very similar, but the leaves are more leathery and persist longer, lobes of the secondary leaflets being less toothed and broader based, with their ends usually cut off abruptly instead of rounded, and a short-lived black patch at their base; the scales are redder brown and far more numerous, making the leaf-stalk shaggy. Commonest in the W, usually in damper and shadier places on more or less acid soils.

1294b. ***Small Male Fern, *D. abbreviata* (DC.) Newman, is smaller, with the leaflets and their lobes rather curved upwards, giving a crinkly appearance. Rare on mountain slopes and screes.

1294c. **Rigid Buckler Fern, *D. villarsii* (Bellardi) Woynar (*Aspidium rigidum* Swartz), has rather fleshy and downy thick leaves of a characteristic dull blue-green, smelling of balsam and definitely 2-pinnate, with the secondary leaflets bearing pointed, but not needle-like teeth; the primary leaflets are equal in size for some distance above the base. Very local among limestone rocks in NW England and N Wales.

1294d. ***Crested Buckler Fern, *D. cristata* (L.) Gray (*Aspidium cristatum* (L.) Swartz, has the parallel-sided leaves arising in crowns, 2-pinnate with the second-ary leaflets joined at their bases, very broadly triangular, larger at the base of the primary leaflets, bluntly lobed and bearing very sharply pointed teeth which are sometimes bent inwards. Rare in fens and wooded sphagnum bogs in a few places N to the Clyde.

1295. COMMON BUCKLER FERN *D. dilatata* (Hoffmann) Gray
'*D. austriaca*,'   Plate 138. *CTW, p. 41*

A stout tufted, rather variable Fern, with triangular leaves up to about 4 ft. long, 3-pinnate, the primary leaflets spaced out up the midrib, the lowest pair rather larger than the others; tertiary leaflets usually convex above, with obvious, finely pointed incurved teeth. Leaf-stalk dark brown at the base, with characteris-tic sharply pointed scales, dark brown in the centre, paler at the edges, though some local mountain forms have uniformly pale scales. Covers over the spore-heaps roundish, kidney-shaped, usually fringed with dots, on either side of the midrib of the tertiary leaflets. *Habitat:* Widespread and common in woods and hedge-banks, also on heaths and mountain-sides. July–September.

1295a. *Narrow Buckler Fern, *D. spinulosa* (Müller) Watt (*A. spinulosum* (Müller) Swartz, has parallel-sided leaves with equal primary leaflets; the scales on the stalks blunt and uniformly pale brown; and the covers over the spore-cases usually not fringed with dots. Local, usually confined to marshy woods and bogs.

1295b. **Hay-scented Buckler Fern, *D. aemula* (Aiton) Kuntze (*A. aemulum* (Aiton) Swartz), is smaller, with more broadly triangular bright green 3-pinnate leaves not more than about 2 ft. long; the lowest pair of primary leaflets notably larger than the others; the tertiary leaflets concave above and so having a crisped appearance; and the leaf-stalk dark brown with long pointed, often jagged uniformly pale brown scales. The hay-like fragrance of the dried leaf is not usually obvious. Locally frequent on sheltered banks or rocks, and in woods, in the W and Ireland; very local in the SE.

1296. *HARD SHIELD FERN *Polystichum aculeatum* (L.) Roth Plate 138.

P. lobatum (Hudson) Presl, *Aspidium aculeatum* (L.) Swartz. *CTW, p. 44*

Rather like a small, narrow-leaved Male Fern (1294), but with stiff, somewhat leathery, usually dark green 2-pinnate leaves; the primary leaflets curved towards the tip of the leaf; the lower secondary leaflets with spiny points, and sharply angled bases (Fig.) but the junction with the side-rib broad; the secondary leaflet on the upper side at the base of each primary leaflet noticeably longer than the others. Scales on leaf-stalks brown. Spore-heaps in rows, with roundish covers, situated on veins which run beyond them to the margin. *Habitat:* Widespread but local in woods and hedge-banks and among rocks; commonest in the W and N, especially in mountainous districts. July–August. Figs. × 3.

1296 1296a

1296a. *Soft Shield Fern, *P. setiferum* (Forskal) Woynar (*P. angulare* (Willdenow) Presl, is often larger and brighter green, with often less evergreen soft leaves, with the primary leaflets straight, the lower secondary leaflets with blunt-angled bases (Fig.), but sharply turned in to a narrower junction with the side-rib; the secondary leaflet on the upper side at the base of each primary leaflet not noticeably longer than the others; and the veins terminating at the spore-heaps. Frequent in the W, especially in the hedgerows and wooded valleys, not so high or so far north.

1297. **HOLLY FERN *P. lonchitis* (L.) Roth Plate 140. *CTW, p. 44*

Aspidium lonchitis (L.) Swartz

A tufted Fern, with notably leathery, lanceolate, 1-pinnate leaves, 4–12 in. long, the leaflets well toothed with spiny teeth. Covers of spore-cases roundish, in rows down either side of the midrib of the leaflets. *Habitat:* Local in rock crevices in mountain districts in the N, and in W Ireland. June–August.

1298. *LEMON-SCENTED FERN *Thelypteris oreopteris* (Ehrhart) Slosson

Aspidium oreopteris (Ehrhart) Swartz Plate 138. *CTW, p. 46*

A fairly stout tufted Fern, with an erect rootstock, lemon-scented when crushed; leaves 2-pinnate, lanceolate, yellow-green, 1–2 ft. long; lower primary leaflets much shorter than those in the middle, giving a narrowly tapered appearance to the leaf-outline; midribs of leaflets slightly hairy; secondary leaflets unstalked, untoothed and convex above. Spore-cases in round clusters near margins of leaflets, their covers small, irregular and disappearing early. *Habitat:* Widespread and locally frequent in woods and on heaths and mountains, especially beside mountain streams on acid soils in the N and W; local in sheltered places in the SE. July–August.

1299. *MARSH FERN *T. palustris* Schott Plate 138. *CTW, p. 47*

A delicate Fern, with a black far-creeping, usually underground rootstock, from which arise at intervals lanceolate, pale green 2-pinnate leaves, 1–3 ft. high, the secondary leaflets unstalked and untoothed; leaf-stalks usually without scales. There are separate sterile and fertile leaves, the fertile ones appearing later and being taller and stiffer, with their margins turned back partly over the heaps of spore-cases, which have kidney-shaped covers. *Habitat:*

Very local in fens and marshy woods, chiefly in England and Ireland. July–August.
Aspidium thelypteris (L.) Swartz

1300. **BEECH FERN   *T. phegopteris* (L.) Slosson   Plate 139.   *CTW, p. 47*
Polypodium phegopteris L.
A graceful Fern with a creeping rootstock; solitary hairy, broadly triangular
2-pinnate leaves, 4–8 in. long, with the secondary leaflets unstalked and untoothed; and lower primary ones markedly longer, pointing forwards and downwards. Spore-cases in round heaps near the margins of the leaflets, but with no
cover. *Habitat:* Widespread but local in damp woods and on moist rocks;
common in the N and W; very rare in the SE. June–August.

1301. **OAK FERN   *T. dryopteris* (L.) Slosson   Plate 139.   *CTW, p. 48*
Polypodium dryopteris L.
An even more graceful Fern with a creeping rootstock, and solitary triangular
3-pinnate very fragile, hairless, yellowish- or emerald-green leaves, 4–6 in. long;
the two lowest primary leaflets each nearly as large as the rest of the leaf, which
thus appears 3-lobed; the young leaves first emerge like three tiny balls on thin
black wires which slowly uncoil. Spore-cases as in Beech Fern (1300). *Habitat:*
Widespread but uncommon in damp woods and on rocks and mountain screes,
on acid soils in the N and W; rare in Ireland. July–August.
1301*a*. ****Limestone Polypody,** *T. robertiana* (Hoffmann) Slosson (*Phegopteris
robertiana* (H.) Braun, *Polypodium robertianum* H.), is the lime-loving counterpart of the Oak Fern, with tougher, dull green, mealy-looking, less extremely
3-lobed leaves. Local on rocks and screes on limestone in England; rare elsewhere.

1302. COMMON POLYPODY   *Polypodium vulgare* L.   Plate 140.   *CTW, p. 50*
Our most widespread Fern whose pinnate leaves have blunt leaflets that are not
either lobed or toothed, though sometimes with rather wavy edges. Leaves evergreen, variable in shape, 2–12 in. long, arising individually from a thick creeping
rootstock covered with brown scales, broader and longer-stalked than Hard Fern
(1281). Spore-cases in round orange heaps in rows on either side of the midrib of
the leaflets, with no cover. *Habitat:* Widespread and common in woods, especially
in the W, where it often grows on trees; also on rocks and walls. June–September.

PILLWORT FAMILY   Marsileaceae

1303. **PILLWORT   *Pilularia globulifera* L.   Plate 136.   *CTW, p. 51*
A slender grass-like, flowerless creeping aquatic perennial, with very narrow
cylindrical leaves 1–2 in. long and differing from grass in being coiled like
croziers when young. Spore-cases like small round hard hairy pills, $\frac{1}{8}$-in. across,
one at the base of each leaf, each containing numerous small partitions. *Habitat:*
Widespread but scarce by, in or even floating on fresh water, on acid soils. June–
September.

WATER FERN FAMILY   Azollaceae

1304. **WATER FERN   *Azolla filiculoides* Lamarck   Plate 104.   *CTW, p. 52*
A very pretty flat moss-like hairy little floating aquatic perennial, with solitary
thread-like roots, growing in dense masses $\frac{1}{2}$–$\frac{3}{4}$-in. across, with minute 2-lobed

leaves overlapping along the branched stems, bluish-green or silvery, turning red in autumn. Spore-heaps in pairs under the leaves. *Habitat:* Locally naturalised in still fresh water, mainly in the S. June–September.

ADDER'S TONGUE FAMILY Ophioglossaceae

1305. *MOONWORT *Botrychium lunaria* (L.) Swartz Plate 136. *CTW, p. 53*
A curious little Fern, 2–8 in. high, long-stalked, and forked into a 'leaf', pinnate with toothed and moon- or fan-shaped leaflets, and a fertile portion, 2-pinnate, bearing the clusters of yellow spore-cases in a usually longer, superficially flower-like spike. *Habitat:* Widespread but uncommon in drier grassy places and dunes, and on rock-ledges. June–August.

1306. *ADDER'S TONGUE *Ophioglossum vulgatum* L. Pl. 136. *CTW, p. 54*
Is stalked and forked into two as in the last species, but the sterile 'leaf' is oval and undivided, the network of veins having numerous free endings Fertile portion a longer slender plantain-like unbranched spike, bearing the spore-cases, but often absent. *Habitat:* Widespread but local in grassy places, probably often overlooked as it easily merges into the herbage; thinning out northwards. May–August.

1306a. ***Early Adder's Tongue, *O. lusitanicum* L., is much smaller, a bare inch or so high, and slenderer, with lanceolate 'leaves', the simpler network of veins with no free endings. Very rare, on bare ground on or near exposed cliffs in the Scilly and Channel Is. January–April.

386a. ***Plymouth Pear, *P. cordata* Desvaux, is a tall Crab-like shrub, thorny at least below, sometimes suckering, with smaller flowers, often pink on the back, and densely woolly sepals. Leaves small, hairless except when very young, rounded at the base. Fruits much smaller and roundish, long-stalked, not capped by the sepals. Very rare, perhaps only in a few hedges around Plymouth. May.

THE GENERAL KEYS

THE GENERAL KEYS are composed of four main parts. The first three divide all the plants in the book into three main categories, *Woody Plants* (Trees and Shrubs), *Non-woody Land Plants*, and *Waterweeds*, which are plants which actually grow in the water. The keys to Trees and Shrubs and Waterweeds are intended to be reasonably comprehensive; that to the Non-woody Land Plants, the great bulk of the plants in the book, is of necessity briefer, and intended to give pointers to certain more conspicuous and unusual characters. See p. xii for a note on how to use the keys.

The remaining part of the General Keys is the Flower Colour Key, indicating flowers which do not fall into their appropriate colour section of the plates.

WOODY PLANTS (*Trees and Shrubs*)

Larger Trees

Small-lvd Lime 221, Com Lime 222, Sycamore and Plane 261, Maple 262, Wild Cherry 376, Rowan 383, White Beam 384, Wild Service Tree 385, Pear 386, Elms 556, Birches 558, Alder 560, Hornbeam 561, Beech 563, Oaks and Chestnuts 564, White Poplar 565, Aspen 566, Black Poplars 567, Crack and White Willows 569, Ash 629, Pines etc. 1257, Yew 1259.

BARK *scaling or peeling* 261, 376, 558, 1257; *black and white* 558; *red-brown* 376, 1257, 1259.

SUCKERING FREELY 556, 565–567; *often pollarded*, 561, 569, 629.

TWIGS *corky* 262, 556; *with sticky buds* 564c, 566, 567, 1257.

LEAVES *evergreen* 1257, 1259; *pinnate* 383, 629; *lobed*, 261–2, 384–5, 564–6; *needle-like* 1257, 1259; *wrinkled* 384, 556, 561; *downy beneath* 221a, 376, 384, 560a, 565, 566, 569a; *silvery beneath* 384, 565; *silvery on both sides* 569a; *with fleshy warts on stalks* 376.

FLOWERS *catkins* 261, 558, 560, 561, 563–567, 569; *pink or purple* 556, 629, 1257e; *white* 376, 383–386, 564d; *greenish* (not catkins) 221, 222, 262, 629; *fragrant* 221, 222; *foetid* 383, 564c; *appearing before leaves* 556, 560, 565–567, 629; *yellow* (not catkins) 1257, 1259.

FRUITS *fleshy* 376, 383–6, 1259; *red or orange* 376, 383–4, 1259; *cones* 560, 1257; *discs or keys* 261, 262, 556, 558, 629; *nuts* 561, 563, 564; *spiny* 563, 564c; *with woolly seeds* 565–567, 569.

Smaller Trees and Larger Shrubs

Barberry 30, Tamarisk 143, Holly 263, Spindle 264, Box 265, Com Buckthorn 266, Alder Buckthorn 267, Bladder Senna 312, Willow Spiraea 340, Field Rose 370, Dog Rose 372, Downy Rose 373, Blackthorn 374, Cherry-plum 375, Sour Cherry 376a, Bird Cherry 377, Khasia Berry 378, Hawthorn 380, Medlar 381, June Berry 382, Plymouth Pear 386a, Crab Apple 387, Sea-buckthorn 423, Fuchsia 438, Dogwood 448, Hazel 562, Willows 568, 570–572, Osier 572, Sallows 573–576, Strawberry-tree 587, Irish Heath 594, Buddleia 628, Privets 630, Elder 820, Wayfaring Tree 821, Guelder Rose 822, Juniper 1258. (See also Maple, Rowan, White Beam, Birches and Aspen and other Larger Trees.)

CLAMBERERS, 370, 372, 373.

SUCKERING FREELY 340, 370–3, 376a, 386, 562.

TWIGS *prickly or thorny* 30, 266, 370, 372–374, 380, 381, 386, 387, 423; *pithy* 820; *with sticky buds* 568.

LEAVES *evergreen* 143, 263, 265, 587, 594, 1258; *half-evergreen* 378, 630; *prickly* 263; *spiny* 1258; *pinnate* 312, 370, 372, 373, 820; *ivy-like* 822; *needle-like* 594, 1258; *feathery* 143; *downy only beneath* 312, 340, 372, 373, 380, 573, 574; *silvery only beneath* 423, 572, 628; *silvery on both sides* 340, 575; *wrinkled* 562, 573. 575, 821; *turning red or yellow in autumn* 264, 374, 375, 380–382, 448, 562, 820, 822; *aromatic* 373a; *foetid* 820; *with fleshy warts on stalks* 376a, 822.

FLOWERS *catkins* 562, 568, 570–576; *peaflowers* 312; *red, pink or purple* 143, 340, 372, 373, 378, 380, 386a, 387, 438, 562, 594, 628; *yellow* (not catkins) 30, 312, 1258; *white* 143, 263, 370, 372, 374–5, 376a, 377, 380–2, 386a, 448, 587, 630, 820–822, *green* (not catkins) 264, 265–267, 423; *fragrant* 370, 372, 373, 380, 628, 820, 822; *foetid* 821; *appearing before leaves* 374, 423, 562, 571–575.

FRUITS *fleshy: black* 266–7, 374, 377, 382, 438, 448, 630, 820–1, 1258; *brown* 381, 386a; *red, orange or pink* 30, 263, 264, 267 (unripe), 370, 372, 373, 375, 376a, 378, 380, 387, 423, 587, 821 (unripe), 822; *yellow* 375, 630, 822; *green* 387, 820; *nuts* 562; *inflated pods* 312; *warty* 587; *with woolly seeds* 568, 570–576.

Smaller Shrubs and Bushes

Shrubby Seablite 217a, Tree Lupin 269, Gorses 273, Broom 274, Raspberry 345, Bramble 346, Shrubby Cinquefoil 348, Burnet Rose 371, Gt. Orme Berry 378a, Currants 412, Mountain Currant 413, Gooseberry 414, Bog-myrtle 557, Creeping Willow 577, Labrador Tea 582, Tea-tree 670, Snowberry 823, Fly Honeysuckle 825, Butchers Broom 994. (See also Eared Sallow, etc., under Larger Shrubs, and Dewberry, etc., under Undershrubs; Tree Mallow 226 appears shrub-like but is biennial.)

CLAMBERERS, 346, 670.

SUCKERING FREELY 345, 371, 557, 670, 823; *rooting at the tip* 346, 670. TWIGS *prickly or thorny,* 345–7, 371, 414, 670, 994.

LEAVES *evergreen* 217a, 273, 582, 994; *half-evergreen* 269, 346; *prickly or spiny* 273, 346, 994; *pinnate* 371, 823; *5-foliate* 345–6, 348; *trefoil* 274, 345–6; *palmate* 269; *needle-like or very narrow* 217a, 273, 274; *wrinkled* 345, 346, 414, 582; *fleshy* 217a; *untoothed* 670, 994; *reddish beneath* 582; *downy beneath only* 269, 412, 577; *silvery on both sides* 577; *aromatic* 412a, 557.

FLOWERS *catkins* 557, 577; *peaflowers* 269, 273, 274; *pink or purple* 346, 371, 378a, 670, 823; *yellow* (not catkins) 269, 273, 274, 348, 825; *white* 345, 346, 371, 582, 823, 994; *greenish* (not catkins) 217a, 412–414; *appearing before leaves* 557, 577; *fragrant* 273.

FRUITS *fleshy: black* 346, 371, 412a; *red* 345, 346 (unripe), 371 (unripe), 412, 413–4, 670, 825, 994; *yellow* 345, 414; *white* 412, 823; *green* 217a, 414; *pods* 269, 273, 274; *with woolly seeds* 577.

Undershrubs or Woody Perennials

Oregon Grape 31, Tutsan 130, Rose of Sharon 131, Rock-roses 140–142, Sea-heath 144, Rupture-wort 195, Sea-purslane 216, Dyer's Greenweed 270, Petty Whin 271, Hairy Greenweed 272, Dwarf Gorse 273b, Rest-harrows 275, Dewberry 347, Mountain Avens 362, Pirri-pirri Bur 369, Rockspray 379, Mezereon 421, Spurge-laurel 422, Mistletoe 446, Dwarf Birch 559, Alpine Willows 578–581, Wild Azalea 583, Menziesia 584, St Dabeoc's Heath 585, Bog Rosemary 586, Bearberry 588, Black Bearberry 589, Ling 590, Cross-lvd Heath 591, Dorset

L

Heath 592, Bell Heather 593, Cornish Heath 595, Cowberry 596, Bilberry 597, Northern Bilberry 598, Cranberry 599, Diapensia 603, Crowberry 605, Peri-winkles 631, Bittersweet 673, Thymes 753, Wall Germander 783, Twinflower 824, Silver Ragwort 851. (Overlapping with previous headings where shrubs such as Alder-buckthorn, Broom, Burnet Rose, Creeping Willow and Juniper may be quite prostrate.)

CLAMBERER 673.

SUCKERING FREELY 31, 275, 586; *rooting at tip* 631.

STEMS *spiny* 271, 275, 347; *with milky juice* 631.

LEAVES *half-evergreen* 130, 272, 347; *deciduous* 421, 597, 598; *spiny or prickly* 273*b*, 347; *pinnate* 31, 369; *trefoil* 275, 347; *roundish* 559, 580; *wrinkled* 581; *silvery on both sides* 142, 276, 578, 851; *needle-like* 144, 584, 585, 590–593, 595, 605; *turning red or yellow in autumn*, 31, 144, 347, 379*a*, 589.

FLOWERS *catkins* 559, 578–581; *peaflowers* 270–272, 273*b*, 275; *daisy-type* 851; *blue or purple* 631, 673; *pink or red* 144, 275, 379, 421, 583–586, 590–3, 595–6, 597, 599, 605, 753, 783, 824, 826; *yellow* (not catkins) 31, 130, 131, 140, 142, 216, 270–271, 273*b*, 851; *white* 141, 347, 362, 369, 379*a*, 588, 589, 603; *greenish* 195, 216, 369, 422, 446, 588, 589, 597, 598, 605; *appearing before leaves* 421, 578; *fragrant* 273*b*, 421, 824.

FRUITS *fleshy: black or dark bluish* 31, 130, 347, 422, 589, 596, 597, 598, 605; *red* 130 (unripe), 347 (unripe), 379, 421, 588, 599, 673; *yellow* 673 (unripe); *white* 446; *greenish* 131; *feathery* 362; *bur-like* 369; *pods* 270–272, 273*a*, 275; *with woolly seeds* 578–581.

Woody Climbers and Clamberers

Travellers' Joy 10, Bramble 346, Roses 370, 372–3, Ivy 450, Russian Vine 533*b*, Tea-tree 670, Bittersweet 673, Honeysuckle 826.

CLIMBERS *twining clockwise* 533*b*, 826; *with twisting leaf-stalks* 10; *by suckers* 450; *leaves* evergreen 450, pinnate 10, ivy-like 450, undivided 533*b*, 826; *flowers* yellowish 826, white 533*b*, greenish 10, 450, fragrant 826; *fruits* red 826, black 450, feathery 10.

CLAMBERERS 346, 370, 372–3, 670, 673 (see under Shrub headings).

NON-WOODY LAND PLANTS

(*Generally excluding Sedges, Grasses and Ferns*)

CLIMBERS *twining clockwise* Black Bindweed 533, Hop 555, Black Bryony 1056; *twining anticlockwise* Bindweeds 666–667, Dodders 669; *with tendrils* Climbing Corydalis 43, Vetches 323–324, 326–330, Peas and Vetchlings 331–337, White Bryony 511.

NON-GREEN PLANTS: Yellow Birdsnest 604, Dodders 669, Toothwort 732, Broomrapes 733–737, Ghost orchid 1064, Birdsnest Orchid 1073, Coral-root 1073, Com Horsetail 1273. N.B. Many green plants later turn red or purple.

PLANTS WITH STICKY HAIRS: Catchflies 148–149, 151–154, Mouse-ears 167, Spurreys 190–192, Com Storksbill 251, Rest-harrows 275, Fingered Saxifrage 403, Sundews 415–416, Henbane 672, Yellow Bartsia 730, Butterworts 738–739, Heath and Sticky Groundsels 846–847.

PLANTS GREY *with meal* Goosefoots 205–207, 209, 211, Oraches 214–215, Sea Purslane 216, Hoary Mullein 678; *with silky hairs* Small Alison 78, Silverweed 352, Ling 590, Hoary Ragwort 851, Cudweeds 864–871, Everlastings 872–873,

Cotton-weed 890, Wormwoods 897–898; *with velvety hairs* Marsh Mallow 227, Mulleins 676–678, Downy Woundwort 765, Com Fleabane 862.

GRASS-LIKE PLANTS: Mousetail 24, Awlwort 76, Maiden Pink 161, Grass Vetchling 332, Shoreweed 794, Blue- and Yellow-eyed Grasses 1046–1047, Quillworts 1266–7, Dutch Rush 1268, Pillwort 1303; cf. also Rush and Sedge Families and Waterweeds.

MOSS-LIKE PLANTS: Moss Campion 150, Mossy Pearlwort 177, Heath Pearlwort 179, Cyphal 185, Mossy Saxifrage 407, Bog Clubmoss 1261, Lesser Clubmoss 1265, Filmy-ferns 1276.

ERECT PLANTS RARELY OR NEVER OVER 2 IN. HIGH: Arctic Pearlwort 178c, Flax-seed 232, Mossy Stonecrop 396, Iceland Purslane 550, Chaffweed 625, Slender Cicendia 632, Guernsey Centaury 633.

OTHER ERECT PLANTS WHICH MAY BE UNDER 1 IN. HIGH: Com Whitlow-grass 84, Hairy Bittercress 90, Mouse-ears 167, Dwarf Chickweed 174, Pearlworts 175–176, 179, Blinks 198, Red Goosefoot 210, Dovesfoot Cranesbill 244, Storksbills 251, Parsley Piert 366, Fingered Saxifrage 403, Narrow Haresear 470, Dwarf Spurge 521, Scots Primrose 611, Slender Centaury 634, Felwort 643, Early Forget-me-not 660, Speedwells 713–714, Eyebright 728, Clustered Bellflower 798, Com Groundsel 848, Dwarf Cudweed 868, Bog Orchid 1071.

PLANTS OFTEN OVER 6 FT.: Tree Mallow 226, Himalayan Balsam 260, Gt Willow-herb 425, Rose-bay 435, Hemlock, 468, Hogweeds 508, Knotweeds 535–536, Gt Water Dock 541, Patience Dock 544b, Hemp Agrimony 882, Marsh Thistle 908, Scotch Thistle 915, Marsh Sow-thistle 941, Reed-maces 1105–1106, Bracken 1277, and many others.

JUICE *white*: Poppies 35–39, Milk Parsley 505, Spurges 515–526, Rampion Bell-flower 800a, Heath Lobelia 806, Goatsbeard 935, Lettuces 938–940, Sow-thistles 941–945, Hawkweeds 946–947, Dandelions 956; *yellow or orange* Poppies 35–36, Welsh Poppy 40, Yellow Horned Poppy 41, Gt Celandine 42.

Scent Features

AROMATIC (PLEASANTLY, WHOLE PLANT, WHEN FRESH): Italian Cranesbill 240, Storksbills 250–251, Agrimonies 363, Sweet Cicely 460, Spignel 500, Mints 743–750, Marjoram 752, Thymes 753, Calamints 754, Balm 757, Clary 759, Catmint 778, White Horehound 780, Lady's Bedstraw 814, Ploughman's Spikenard 860, Chamomiles 884–885, 886a, Pineapple-weed 887, Yarrow 888, Feverfew 893, Tansy 894, Buttonweed 895, Mugworts and Wormwoods 896–898, Sweet Flag 1096.

CUCUMBER-SCENTED: Salad Burnet 368, Borage 651.

PARSLEY-SCENTED: Wild Celery 474, Parsley 477, Corn Parsley 478, Fennel 498, Pepper Saxifrage 499, Cambridge Parsley 501, Lovage 502.

STRONG-SMELLING: Herb Robert 247, Wild Basil 756, Bastard Balm 760, Woundworts 766–767, Black Horehound 768, Yellow Archangel 769, Dead-nettles 771–772, Ground-Ivy 779.

FOETID: Stinking Hellebore 3, Stinkweed 54, Wall Rocket 55, Stinking Goosefoot 206, Coriander 465, Hemlock 468, Stone Parsley 479, Houndstongue 647, Henbane 672, Thorn-apple 675, Com Figwort 692, Danewort 819, Heath and Sticky Groundsels 846–847, Cape Cudweed 871, Stinking Mayweed 886b, Roast-beef Plant 1049.

GARLICKY: Garlic Mustard 106, Garlics 1008–1018.

FLOWERS STRONGLY FRAGRANT: Sweet Alison 78, Stocks 102, Dame's Violet 103, Wallflower 105, Sweet Violet 115, Cheddar Pink 160, Meadowsweet 342, Evening

Primroses 436–437, Cowslip 612, Clove-scented Broomrape 735, Twinflower 824, Winter Heliotrope 857, Musk Thistle 904, Creeping Thistle 909, Lily of the Valley 989, Wild Tulip 998, Lady's Tresses Orchids 1065–6, Musk Orchid 1074, Scented Orchid 1076, Butterfly Orchids 1078.

FLOWERS WITH AN UNPLEASANT SMELL: Pink Masterwort 453, Hogweed 508, Heath Bedstraw 815, Lizard Orchid 1083, Pyramidal Orchid 1095.

Stem Features

SPINES OR PRICKLES: Spiny Rest-harrow 275a, Tear-thumb 534, Goosegrass 817, Wild Madder 818, Teasels 833–834, Spiny Cocklebur 841, Thistles 903–905, 907–908, 915, Prickly Lettuce 938.

RED OR PURPLE SPOTS: Evening Primrose 436, Rough Chervil 456, Hemlock 468. Giant Hogweed 508a, Hawkweeds 947.

WHITE: Dittander 62, White Pigweed 203.

ZIGZAG: Lesser Meadow-rue 28, Wavy Bittercress 89, Zigzag Clover 288, Milk-vetch 315, Fingered Saxifrage 403, Honewort 473, Sharp Dock 547a, Matted Sea-lavender 608, Rannoch Rush 969.

BULBILS AT BASE OF LEAF-STALKS: Lesser Celandine 22, Lady's Smock 86, Coral-wort 91, Knotted Pearlwort 180, Saxifrages 404–405.

MARKEDLY SWOLLEN AT BASE OF LEAF-STALKS: Pink Family 146–197, Balsams 257–260, Chervils 456–457, Cow Parsley 458, Redlegs 531, Hemp-nettles 774–777, Hedge Bedstraw 813; Grass Family 1167–1256.

CONSPICUOUS LONG RUNNERS: Marsh Marigold 1, Creeping Buttercup 12, Lesser Spearwort 19, Sweet Violet 115, Mossy Pearlwort 177, Sleeping Beauty 253, Silverweed 352, Cinquefoils 357, Strawberries 359, Sheep's Sorrel 539, Yellow Archangel 769, Ground-ivy 779, Bugle 788, Hawkweeds 948–949, Water-plantains 957–958; and some Grasses.

Leaf Features

PRICKLY OR SPINY: Saltwort 218, Russian Thistle 219, Sea-holly 454, Watling St. Thistle 455, Tear-thumb 534, Teasels 833–834, Thistles 901, 903–915, Prickly Lettuce 938, Prickly Sow-thistle 944, Sea Rush 1029.

BRISTLY OR VERY ROUGH: Hartwort 509, Wild Carrot 510, Madwort 649, Comfreys 650, Borage 651, Small Bugloss 654, Viper's Bugloss 655, Ox-tongues 933–934.

ARROW-SHAPED, STALKED: Black Bindweed 533, Tear-thumb 534, Buckwheat 537, Sorrels 539–540, Bindweeds 666–667, Sharp-lvd Fluellen 690, Arrowhead 962, Lords and Ladies 1097.

CIRCULAR (MORE OR LESS): Wall Pennywort 397, Kidney Saxifrage 402, Golden Saxifrages 410, N.Z. Willow-herb 434, Marsh Pennywort 451, Mountain Sorrel 538, Creeping Jenny 619, Cornish Moneywort 698, Corsican Mint 743, Harebell 799.

BLOTCHED OR SPOTTED *darker*: Ivy-lvd Crowfoot 21a, Lesser Celandine 22, Com Mallow 224, Dusky Cranesbill 238, Bermuda Buttercup 255, Spotted Medick 282, Redlegs 531, Loosestrifes 620–621, Spotted Catsear 929, Hawkweeds 947, Dandelions 956, Dense-fld Orchid 1079, Early Purple Orchid 1090, Spotted Orchids 1091, Marsh Orchids 1092a, 1093, Lords and Ladies 1097; *paler* C & B Buttercups, 12, 13, Lesser Celandine 22, Red Clover 286, Zigzag Clover 288, White Clover 301, Sweet Cicely 460, Sowbread 617, Lungworts 655, Spotted Dead-nettle 771b, Ground-ivy 779, Bristly ox-tongue 933. (N.B. Other species may have their leaves streaked or spotted paler by virus diseases.)

VEINED PALER: Milk Thistle 914, Large Cuckoo-pint 1097a, Stars of Bethlehem 1001–2, Crocuses 1051–1052.

REDDISH BENEATH: Arctic Saxifrage 398, Speedwells 705, 706, 715, Eyebright 728, Bugle 788.

CONSPICUOUSLY WHITE OR GREY BENEATH: Silverweed 352, Hoary Cinquefoil 353, Mountain Avens 362, Alpine Lady's Mantle 364, Bog Rosemary 586, Spiny Cocklebur 841, Coltsfoot 854, Butterburs 855–856, Win. Heliotrope 857.

PINNATE, WITH MIXED LARGE AND SMALL LEAFLETS: Gt Celandine 42, Meadowsweet 342, Silverweed 352, Water Avens 361, Agrimonies 363.

PERFOLIATE (with the stalk appearing to pass through the leaf): Spring Beauty 199, Thorow-wax 469, Yellow-wort 638, Henbit 770.

Flower Features

SPURRED: Mousetail 24, Columbine 25, Corydalises 43–44, Fumitory 45, Violets 115–122, Pansies 123–125, Balsams 257–260, Toadflaxes 683–691, Red Valerian 832, Orchids 1064, 1074–1079, 1084–1093, 1095.

CALYX CONSPICUOUSLY INFLATED: Campions 146–149, 154–156, Corn-cockle 158, Mallows 223, Red and Yellow Rattles 722–723.

CALYX OR SEPAL-LIKE BRACTS PRICKLY OR SPINY: Sea-holly 454, Watling St. Thistle 455, Motherwort 773, Com Hemp-nettle 776, Teasels 833–834, Thistles 901, 903–910, 912, 914–915, Star-thistles 920–922.

APPEARING BEFORE LEAVES: *Spring* Winter Aconite 5, Abraham, Isaac and Jacob 652, Coltsfoot 854, Butterburs 855–856; *autumn* Sowbread 617, Autumn Squill 1005, Meadow Saffron 1019, Autumn Crocus 1051.

Fruit Features

BERRIES *black or dark bluish*: Baneberry 7, Deadly Nightshade 671, Black Nightshade 674, Wild Madder 818, Danewort 819, Solomon's Seal 991, Herb Paris 1020; *red or orange ripe* Cloudberry 343, Stone Bramble 344, Strawberries 359, Dwarf Cornel 449, White Bryony 511, Bittersweet 673, Black Nightshade 674, Lily of the Valley 989, Whorled Solomon's Seal 990, May-lily 992, Asparagus 993, Roast-beef Plant 1049, Black Bryony 1056, Lords and Ladies 1097; *yellow unripe* White Bryony 511, Bittersweet 673, Black Bryony 1056; *green ripe* Caper Spurge 516, Nightshades 674, Moschatel 827.

BUR-LIKE *with hooked spines, often adhering to clothing* Herb Bennet 360, Water Avens 361, Agrimonies 363, Pirri-pirri Bur 369, Enchanter's Nightshades 439–440, Sanicle 452, Sea-holly 454, Houndstongue 647, Forget-me-nots 657–660, Woodruff 809, Goosegrass 817, Bur-marigolds 838–839, Burdocks 902, Barleys 1212–1214; *with straight spines or very stiff bristles* Buttercups 14, 20a, Poppies 37, 38, Bur Chervil 457, Bur Parsleys 462–464, Thorn-apple 675, Bur-reeds 1103–1104.

FEATHERY: Pasque flower 9, Mountain Avens 362, Valerians 830–832, many Composites 838–956, Reed-maces 1105–1106, Cotton-grasses 1107–1108; *with feathery seeds* Willow-herbs 425–435.

WATERWEEDS (*Plants Growing in the Water.*)

Small Submerged Tufted Plants

Awlwort 76, Waterworts 145, Shoreweed 794, Water Lobelia 807, Pipewort 985, Com Quillwort 1266, Pillwort 1303.

PLANT *creeping* 145, 794, 1303.

LEAVES *opposite* 145; *grass-like*, 76, 794, 807, 985, 1266, 1303.

FLOWERS OR SPORE-BEARING ORGANS *above water* 807, 985; *normally submerged* 76, 145, 794, 1266, 1303; *at base of leaves* 794, 1266, 1303; *pinkish* 145; *whitish* conspicuous 807, 985, inconspicuous 76; *greenish* 794, 1266, 1303.

Other Plants with Submerged Leaves Only

Water Crowfoot 21, Hornworts 34, Water-milfoils 441–442, Marestail 443, Narrow Water-starwort 445, Bladderworts 740–741, Canadian Waterweed 966, Esthwaite Waterweed 967, Tape-grass 968, Eel-grasses 971; Pondweeds: Shining 973, Perfoliate 975, Slender 976, Sharp-lvd 977, Blunt-lvd 978, Curly 979, Fennel 980, Opposite 981, Tassel 982, Horned 983; Slender Naiad 984, Bulbous Rush 1032, Ivy Duckweed 1099.

PLANT *free-floating* (or apparently so) 34, 740–741, 1099.

LEAVES *opposite* 445, 975, 981, 983, 984; *alternate* 21, 740–741, 971, 973, 975–980, 982, 1032; *whorled* 34, 441–443, 966–967, 984; *curly* 979; *feathery* 21, 34, 441–443, 740–741; *lanceolate* 965, 973, 979, 981; *forked* 34; *roundish* 966–967, 975, 1099; *bearing bladders* 740–741; *grass-like* long 968, 971, 976–980, 982–983, 1032; *short* 984–985, 1032.

FLOWERS *above water* 21, 441, 740–741, 966, 973, 975–976, 979; *normally submerged* 34, 76, 441, 445, 794, 971, 977–978, 980–981; *at base of leaves* 34, 443, 445, 971, 982–984, 1099; *floating* 21, 966, 968; *spurred* 740–741; *in close spikes* 441–442, 973, 975–981; *pinkish* 442–443, 966; *yellow* 740–741; *whitish* 21; *greenish* 34, 441–442, 445, 971, 973, 975–984, 1032, 1099.

FRUITS *spiny* 34; *horned* 983.

HABITAT *only in sea* 971.

Plants well away from Shore or Bank, Usually Partly Floating

Water Crowfoot 21, White Water-lily 32, Yellow Water-lilies 33, Marsh St John's Wort 138, Marestail 443, Com Water-starwort 444, River Water-dropwort 496a, Bogbean 644, Fringed Water-lily 645, Floating Water-plantain 958, Grass-lvd Water-Plantain 960, Arrowhead 962, Frogbit 964, Water-soldier 965; Pondweeds: Broad-lvd 972, Reddish 973a, Various-lvd 974; Duckweeds: Gt. 1098, Com. 1100, Fat 1101, Least 1102; Bulrush 1117, Floating Spike-rush 1119, Bottle and Bladder Sedges 1133, Reed 1168, Flote-grasses 1171, Water Horsetail 1270, Water Fern 1304.

PLANT *minute* 1098, 1100–1102, 1304; *free-floating* (or apparently so) 645, 958, 964–965, 1098, 1100–1102, 1304; *very tall* 1117, 1168.

LEAVES *floating only* 21, 32, 645, 958, 964, 972, 1098, 1100–1102, 1304; *opposite* 444; *alternate* 21, 496a, 972, 973a, 974; *whorled* 443, 1270; *in floating rosettes* 444; *roundish or oval* 32, 33, 138, 444, 645, 958, 964, 972–974, 1098, 1100–1102, 1304; *lanceolate* 962, 965, 972–974; *arrow-shaped* 962; *more or less grass-like* 960, 962, 974, 1117, 1119, 1133, 1168, 1171; *feathery* 21, 496a; *lobed* 21; *trifoliate* 644; *soft* 138; *none* 1270; *blotched darker* 964; *red beneath* 964, 1098.

FLOWERS *minute*, normally none 1098, 1100–1101; *at base of leaves* 443–444; *in close spikes* 972–974, 1119, 1133; *in cones* 1270; *in umbels* 496a; *3-petalled* 958, 960, 962, 964–965; *purplish or brownish* 1117, 1119, 1133, 1168, 1171; *pinkish* 443; *yellow* 33, 138, 645; *whitish* 21, 32, 496a, 644, 958, 960, 962, 964–965; *greenish* 443–444, 972–974; *with a yellow spot* 958, 964; *with a purple spot* 962.

Plants Spreading from Shore or Bank, Often Partly Floating

Lesser Spearwort 19, Watercress 98, Gt. Yellow Cress 101, Water Chickweed 168, Bog Stitchwort 173, Blinks 198, Marsh Cinquefoil 349, Water Purslane 420,

Fool's Watercress 475, Marshwort 476, Cowbane 480, Lesser Water-parsnip 490, Tubular Water-dropwort 493, Fine-lvd Water-dropwort 496, Amphibious Bistort 530, Gt Water-dock 541, Tufted Loosestrife 621, Water Forget-me-not 656, Brooklime 701, Com Water-plantain 959, Starfruit 961, Flowering Rush 963, Yellow Flag 1050, Sweet Flag 1096, Branched Bur-reed 1103, Simple Bur-reed 1104, False Bulrush 1105, Lesser Bulrush 1106. See also Nos. 1031–1032 in the Rush Key (p. 206), Nos. 1110, 1112–1113, 1117, 1119 and 1125 in the Rush-like Sedge Key (p. 229), Nos. 1132–1133, 1135 and 1151 in the Sedge Key (p. 236), and Nos. 1168, 1171–1172, 1191a, and 1250 in the Grass Key (p. 253). There is inevitably some overlapping between this and the preceding section of the Key, and no account is taken of plants which may become temporary waterweeds during floods.

PLANT *tufted* 168, 541, 959, 961; *very tall* 541 963, 1050, 1105–1106; *unbranched* 963, 1050, 1096, 1105–1106; *aromatic* 1096.

LEAVES *opposite* 168, 173, 198, 349, 420, 701; *alternate* 19, 98, 101, 349, 475–476, 480 490, 493, 496, 530, 541, 656; *some floating* 19, 530, 959, 1103, 1104; *pinnate* 98, 475–476, 480, 490, 493, 496; *palmate* 349; *lanceolate* 19, 101, 168, 173, 198, 420, 530, 541, 621, 656; *sword-like* 963, 1050, 1096, 1103–1106; *toothed* 101, 349, 701.

FLOWERS *submerged at base of leaves* 198, 420; *in umbels* 745–476, 480, 490, 493, 496; *in round heads* 1103–1104; *in close spikes* 530, 621, 656, 701, 1096, 1105–1106; *3-petalled* 959, 961; *blue* 656, 701; *pink* 349, 530, 963; *brown* 1105–1106; *yellow* 19, 621, 1050; *whitish* 98, 168, 173, 198, 475–476, 480, 490, 493, 496, 959; *greenish* 420, 541, 1096, 1103–1104.

FRUITS *long-beaked* 961, 1103–1104; *pods* 98, 101, 1050; *woolly* 1105–1106.

FLOWER COLOUR

Flowers which may have more than one colour, e.g. Milkworts, are grouped on the plates only under the colour occurring most frequently. A few 'abc' flowers are of different colour from their main numbered species. The following lists indicate the flowers in these categories, and the plates on which they are to be found. Flowers which are of such a pale pink, lilac or yellow as to appear white are not included in the lists, and will be found on the White and Green Plates, Nos. 65–112.

Flowers that Change Colour

Lesser Celandine 22 (yellow to white, Pl. 38); Small Alison 78 (yellow to white, Pl. 44); Peas 337–339 (pinkish-purple to blue, Pl. 18); Hawthorn 380 (white to pink, Pl. 75); Fragrant Evening Primrose 437 (yellow to red, Pl. 62); Ash 629 (purple to green, Pl. 70); Comfreys 650 (pink to blue, Pl. 94); Lungworts 655 (pink to purple, Pl. 13); Changing Forget-me-not 659 (yellow to blue, Pl. 61); Purple Gromwell 661 (purple to blue, Pl. 13); Oysterplant 664 (pink to blue, Pl. 13); Viper's Bugloss 665 (pink to blue, Pl. 13); Burnt-tip Orchid 1087 (purple to white, Pl. 33).

Flowers that may have Different Colours

1. BLUE, VIOLET, LILAC AND BLUISH-PURPLE FLOWERS

(a) *On Red, Pink and Pinkish-Purple Plates*: Pl. 18, Spring Vetch 329b; Pl. 26, Scarlet Pimpernel 624; Pl. 31, Creeping Thistle 909. (b) *on Yellow Plates*: Pl. 42,

Mountain Pansy 123; Pl. 45, Wild Radish 56; Pl. 49, Yellow Vetch 328; Pl. 52, Carline Thistle 901. (c) *on White and Green Plates*: Pl. 65, Com. Helleborine 1062; Pl. 90, Early Scurvy-grass 75, Eyebright 728; Pl. 91, Large Bittercress 87; Pl. 93, Sea Rocket 59, Sea Stocks 102, Dame's Violet 103; Pl. 94, Comfreys 650; Pl. 102, Thorn-apple 678. N.B. Many Grasses 1167–1256 are purple-tinged.

2. RED, PINK AND PINKISH-PURPLE FLOWERS

(a) *On Blue, Violet and Bluish-Purple Plates*: Pl. 1, Violets, esp. Sweet Violet 115; Pl. 2, Speedwells, esp. Green Field S. 720; Pl. 4, Canterbury Bell 801; Pl. 5, Com. Milkwort 126, Yorks Milkwort 129a; Pl. 7, Com. Forget-me-not 658, Purple Toadflax 683; Pl. 8, Sweet Scabious 835a, Devilsbit 837; Pl. 9 Michaelmas Daisy 875a; Pl. 10, Self-heal 761, Ground-ivy 779, Bugle 788; Pl. 11, Water Forget-me-not 656, Brooklime 701, Water Speedwells 702; Pl. 12, Columbine 25, (b) the *Brown Plates* include several dark red flowers. (c) *on Yellow Plates*: Pl. 40. Primrose 615; Pl. 41, Wallflower 105; Pl. 49, Kidney Vetch 306, Com. Birdsfoot Trefoil 307; Pl. 60, Com. Cow-wheat 726; Pl. 62, Moth Mullein 680a; Pl. 64, Larch 1257e. (d) *on White and Green Plates*: Pl. 68, Spiked Water-milfoil 442; Pl. 69, Bogbean 644; Pl. 71, Wallspray 379a, Alder 560, Hazel 562, Poplars 565–567; Pl. 72, Bog-Myrtle 557, Purple Willow 571; Pl. 73, Whortle Willow 579; Pl. 75, Burnet Rose 371; Pl. 76, Bramble 346; Pl. 77, Cowberry 596, Bilberry 597, Crowberry 605; Pl. 79, Fenugreek 276, White Clover 301; Pl. 84, Wood Sorrel 252; Pl. 85, Bladder Campion 146, Small-fld. Catchfly 149, Night-scented Catch-fly 154; Pl. 87, Squinancy-Wort 807; Pl. 94, Dropwort 341, Comfreys 650, Mountain Everlasting 873; Pl. 95, Knotgrass 527, Yarrow 888; Pl. 95–99, see Umbellifer Key, p. 91; Pl. 102, Gt. Bindweeds 667, Pl. 103, Upland Bistort 528, Water-peppers 532ab, Buckwheat 537; Pl. 107, Sorrels 538–540; Pl. 108, Docks 541–549; Pl. 112, Bastard Balm 760.

3. BROWN FLOWERS

(a) *On Yellow Plates*: Pl. 58, Man Orchid 1094. (b) *on White and Green Plates*: Pl. 83, Frog Orchid 1083; Pl. 101, Mugwort 896; p. 106, Sea and Buckshorn Plantains 792–793; Pls. 114–115, Rushes 1021–1035, Wood-rushes 1036–1041.

4. YELLOW FLOWERS

(a) *On Blue, Violet and Bluish-Purple Plates*: Pl. 1, Sweet and Fen Violets 115 and 121, Heartsease 124; Pl. 5, Bush Vetch 327. (b) *on Red, Pink and Pinkish-Purple Plates*; Pl. 15, Kaffir Fig 201; Pl. 29, Snapdragon 682; Pl. 28, Com. Hemp-Nettle 776; Pl. 33, Early Marsh Orchid 1092a. (c) *on Brown Plates*: Pl. 36, Yellow Birdsnest 604, Birdsnest Orchid 1069; Pl. 37, Scottish Wormwood 900. (d) *on White and Green Plates*: several very pale yellow and bright yellow-green flowers, and all yellow catkins. Note that many Wood-rushes 1036–1041, Sedges 1107–1166 and Grasses 1167–1256 look yellow from their conspicuous anthers.

5. WHITE AND GREEN FLOWERS (excluding casual albinos)

(a) *On Blue, Violet and Bluish-Purple Plates*: Pl. 1, Sweet Violet 115; Pl. 2, Thyme Speedwell 710; Pl. 9, Michaelmas Daisy 875a; Pl. 11, Apple Mint 750. (b) *on Red, Pink and Pinkish-Purple Plates* Pl. 17, Dog Rose 372; Pl. 19, Crimson Clover 291, Haresfoot Clover 292, Alsike Clover 300; Pl. 20, Pale Willowherb 428; Pl. 22, Com. Storksbill 251; Pl. 23, Pink Purslane 200; Pl. 25, Lady's Smock 86; Pl. 26, Fumitory 45, Pale Persicaria 531a; Pl. 27, Field Bindweed 666; Pl. 33, Spotted Orchids 1091, Early Marsh Orchid 1092a. (c) *on Brown Plates*: Pl. 35, Salad Burnet 368, Marsh Helleborine 1061. (d) *on Yellow Plates*: Pl. 45, Wild Radish 56; Pl. 50, Mignonettes 114ab; Pl. 62, Moth Mullein 680a.

GLOSSARY

The definitions given here are not necessarily the same as in more technical botanical works.

Acid: of soils, lacking chalk or lime.

Alkaline: of soils, containing chalk or lime.

Alternate: not opposite or whorled.

Annual: a plant completing its life-cycle in 12 months.

Anther: the case on top of the stamen, containing the pollen grains.

Appressed: flat against a surface.

Awn: bristle attached to the glume or pale of a grass-flower.

Beaded: of seed-pods where the outline of the seeds appears through the pod like a string of beads.

Beak: the tip of a seed-pod, short and stout or long and slender.

Berry: a rounded fleshy fruit.

Biennial: a plant taking more than 12 but usually less than 24 months to complete its life-cycle.

Bog: a wet, marshy area on acid peat, usually dominated by bog-mosses (*Sphagnum*).

Bract: a modified leaf, usually small and green, either at the base of a flower-stalk, looking more or less leaf-like, or at the base of a flower-head, looking more or less sepal-like.

Bulbil: a tiny bulb-like growth at the base of a leaf-stalk, in a flower-head, or underground.

Bur: a fruit with hooked spines, often adhering to clothing.

Bush: small shrub, usually less than 5 ft.

Calyx: the sepals joined at the base, often into a tube.

Casual: a plant that appears one year but often not the next.

Catkin: a limp hanging crowded spike of tiny flowers of one sex.

Clamberer: a plant that scrambles over other plants without tendrils and without twining round them.

Claw: the narrow lower part of a petal.

Climber: a plant that climbs either by twining or with the aid of tendrils.

Cluster: a loose head of flowers.

Corolla: the petals joined at the base, often into a tube.

Deciduous: with leaves falling annually in autumn.

Drift line: the line reached by the highest tides, where scraps of sea-weed and other refuse collect.

Dunes: the irregular hillocks into which sand blows above high-tide mark and occasionally inland; the damp or wet hollows between them are the "dune-slacks."

Egg-shaped: the shape of a hen's egg.

Elliptical: oblong, with bluntly pointed ends.

Evergreen: keeping its leaves in winter.

Family: a group of related genera.

Female: a flower with only fruiting organs, viz. the style and ovary.

Fen: a wet marshy area, dominated mainly by sedges, rushes and grasses, on alkaline, neutral or slightly acid peat.

Filament: the lower, stalk-like part of the stamen.

Flush: a wet patch on a hillside or moor, where the water flows out from springs.

Fruit: the case holding the seeds.

Genus: a group of closely related species.

Glume: small empty chaff-like bract at base of grass or sedge spikelet.

Halberd: a medieval weapon whose shape is still used to describe leaf-shape, i.e. arrow-shaped with lobes at right angles.

Half-evergreen: keeping some of its leaves in winter.

Heart-shaped: shaped like a heart at cards.

Hoary: with greyish down.

Honey-guide: a mark on the petal of a flower which guides bees to honey.

Keel: ridge like the bottom of a boat; also the lower petal of a Peaflower.

Key: a fruit with a long narrow wing.

Lanceolate: shaped like the head of a lance, longer than broad and broadest two-thirds of the way up.

Leaflet: a portion of a divided leaf with its own stalk; or a very small leaf or leaf-like bract.

Ligule: see p. 253.

Linear: long and very narrow with parallel sides.

Lip: one of two more or less lip-like divisions of a calyx or corolla.

Lobe: a division of a leaf, calyx, corolla or other organ, larger than a tooth but without a separate stalk.

Male: a flower with only pollen-producing organs, i.e. the stamens.

Marsh: a wet area on a clay or silty subsoil rather than on peat.

Microspecies: a distinct group of plants within a species, having minute but constant differences from all others.

Midrib: the central raised vein of a leaf.

Netted: with a network of veins.

Neutral: of soils, intermediate between acid and alkaline.

Oblong: parallel-sided with equally blunt rounded ends.

Opposite: of leaves, in opposite pairs.

Oval: the two-dimensional shape of a hen's egg.

Ovary: the young seed-vessel below the style.

Pale: see p. 253.

Palmate: lobed or divided like the fingers of a hand.

Pappus: a usually feathery or hairy appendage of a seed, becoming the parachute of thistle-down.

Perennial: a plant that lives for over 2 years.

Petals: the most conspicuous part of most flowers, usually brightly coloured.

Pinnate: of a leaf, divided into leaflets on opposite sides of a central stalk; *2-pinnate* where the leaves are in turn pinnate.

Pinnately lobed: a pinnate leaf which has lobes instead of distinct leaflets.

Pollen: small grains which contain the male reproductive cells of the flower.

Ray: one of the stalks of an umbel.

Rootstock: an often creeping underground stem.

Rosette: leaves arranged rose-like around the stem, normally at its base and often flat on the ground.

Runner: a prostrate rooting shoot.

Salt-marsh: a marsh by the sea, which is either flooded regularly by the tide or wet with brackish water.

Scale: a small, mostly dry and colourless leaf or bract.

Scree: a mass of rocks and stones on a slope.

Seed: the embryo with its immediate coat, enclosed in the fruit.

Sepals: the outer casing of a flower-bud, which remains when the flower opens as a usually green outer row, divided to the base into two or more segments; sometimes coloured and then often looking like petals.

Shrub: a woody perennial with branches low down and no obvious trunk, larger than a bush.

Shy flowerer: a plant which may not flower every year.

Spike: an elongated unbranched head of flowers at the top of the stem.

Spikelet: See Grasses (p. 253) and Sedges (p. 229).

Spore: the minute fruiting body of the Ferns and their allies.

Spreading: standing outwards or horizontally.

Spur: a hollow, more or less cylindrical projection at the back of some petals.

Stalk: the immediate stem of a flower or leaf.

Stamen: the whole male or pollen-bearing organ, consisting of the filament and anther.

Standard: the broad upper petal of a Peaflower.

Stem: used only of the main stem or branches of a plant, not of flower- or leaf-stalks.

Stigma: the top of the style, sometimes split into two or more parts.

Stipules: a pair of usually small or leaf-like appendages at the base of a leaf-stalk.

Style : the stalk connecting the stigma and the ovary in the female flower, usually thicker than the filaments.

Sucker: a shoot arising directly from the roots of a tree or shrub, often at a distance.

Tendril: a slender twining outgrowth, usually at the end of a leaf.

Tree: a woody perennial with a distinct trunk.

Trefoil, Trifoliate: a leaf composed of 3 leaflets; *2-trifoliate* where the leaflets are in turn trifoliate.

Umbel: a compound flower head, whose rays arise from the same point, like the spokes of an umbrella.

Undershrub: a woody perennial smaller than a bush, rarely as much as 3 ft. high and often prostrate.

Wings: a thin flat lateral extension of a stalk or fruit; or the side petals of a Peaflower.

Whorl: 3 or more flowers or leaves together round a stem.

For abbreviations, see p. x.

A NOTE ON THE ILLUSTRATIONS

THE ILLUSTRATIONS are in three continuously numbered series, Nos. 1–64 in colour, Nos. 65–112 in black and white, and Nos. 113–140 in line drawings. Roughly speaking plants with coloured flowers will be found in the colour plates, plants with white or green flowers in the black-and-whites, and Grasses, Sedges, Rushes, Ferns and their allies in the line drawings. As a general rule flowers of similar colour, and to some extent also of similar shape, size, habitat or other character, are grouped on the same plate. An indication of size is provided by the Daisy head on each plate.

The grouping of flowers by colour inevitably gave rise to difficulties, such as how to treat those, like Comfrey and Milkwort, which regularly have flowers of different colours, those, like Viper's Bugloss, which change colour in the course of development, and those, like Field Cow-wheat, which have prominent bracts, stems or leaves coloured differently from their flowers, but not green, especially when, as with Mossy Stonecrop, the whole plant turns bright red and the flowers are insignificant and greenish. The lists on pp. 315–6 of the General Keys have been drawn up to meet some of these difficulties.

Again, it is often hard to decide what colour a flower really looks; the dividing line between white and yellow in, say, Breckland Catchfly or Wild Mignonette, or between white and pink in Water-plantain and many umbellifers, is particularly misty. As a rule, however, pallid flowers have been grouped with the whites and greens, together with the often red-tinged Docks and Sorrels and the catkin-bearing plants, whose catkins are often red or yellow for a time.

The broad colour grouping of the great bulk of plants is, however, clear enough. Where there is any doubt, however, it should not take long to glance at similar flowers of other colours and then consult the list on p. 315 of the General Keys, already mentioned. Almost every red, purple or blue flower may occasionally be paler or white, though nearly always there will be normal-coloured flowers nearby.

Except for the two totally distinct phases of the Common Horsetail, there was no space to illustrate any plant more than once. Plants which vary widely in form, and which might well have had several pictures each to show their variations, have been covered so far as possible by careful descriptions in the text. Nor can one do more than mention that plants often grow untypically in the autumn, especially in the aftermath by roadsides and in stubbles, when the leading shoots have been cut off and sideshoots develop and may flower long after the normal time. As W. H. Fitch, the original illustrator of Bentham and Hooker, put it: 'as no two flowers are exactly alike, it is hardly to be expected that a drawing should keep pace with their variations in size and colour'.

No plant should ever be named solely by reference to the plates. It is essential to refer to the text as well, and it is for this purpose that the number of each plant is given on the plate. This is particularly important, not only because the best picture can be inadequate, but because the choice of plants for illustration was made largely for their general distinctiveness from others, and 400 somewhat similar species—the '*a b c*' plants, see p. ix above—are described in the text with reference to the picture of the plant most like them.

The figures in the text are natural size (xi) except where otherwise stated.

INDEX TO ENGLISH NAMES

Figures in bold type indicate plate numbers

INDEX TO LATIN NAMES

† signifies that the name is to be found only in a synonym (see p. vii)

INDEX TO KEYS